The American Voter Revisited

The American Voter REVISITED

Michael S. Lewis-Beck, William G. Jacoby,
Helmut Norpoth, and Herbert F. Weisberg

With a Foreword by Philip E. Converse

THE UNIVERSITY OF MICHIGAN PRESS
ANN ARBOR

To Angus, Phil, Warren, and Don

Copyright © by the University of Michigan 2008
All rights reserved
Published in the United States of America by
The University of Michigan Press
Manufactured in the United States of America
∞ Printed on acid-free paper

2011   2010   2009   2008   4   3   2

A CIP catalog record for this book is available from the British Library.

Library of Congress Cataloging-in-Publication Data

The American voter revisited / Michael S. Lewis-Beck . . . [et al.] ;
   with a foreword by Philip E. Converse.
      p.   cm.
   Includes bibliographical references and index.
   ISBN-13: 978-0-472-07040-4 (cloth : alk. paper)
   ISBN-10: 0-472-07040-1 (cloth : alk. paper)
   ISBN-13: 978-0-472-05040-6 (pbk. : alk. paper)
   ISBN-10: 0-472-05040-0 (pbk. : alk. paper)
      1. Elections—United States.   2. Voting—United States.   3. Party
   affiliation—United States.   4. Political participation—United
   States.   5. Political parties—United States.   I. Lewis-Beck,
   Michael S.

   JK1967.A834   2008
   324.60973—dc22   2008002876

Foreword

When I was first informed that a quartet of political scientists was laying out plans for a detailed replication of our 1960 volume entitled *The American Voter*, I was willing to lend a blessing to the enterprise not only on my own behalf, but for my three coauthors, now departed. I was willing to do so chiefly because of the known quality of the new foursome as scholars, although, frankly, I was less than clear just how the operation would be carried out. One colleague, mindful of the substantial number of new books over the past 45 years that have woven the phrase "the American voter" into their titles, was of the mischievous opinion that the new authors might be hard pressed to find a suitably descriptive title not already in use.

With the final manuscript in hand, I find that our authors here have cleared this hurdle and many more serious ones very handsomely. Of course, the core idea of an exact replication of our data tabulations for the 1952 and 1956 national presidential election surveys at the University of Michigan, using the parallel surveys for the 2000 and 2004 elections, has an obvious scientific merit of its own, addressing questions that have lingered for nearly half a century as to how many and which of the 1950s findings were shaped by oddities of the immediate political period, as opposed to being reliable reflections of more lasting features of electoral politics in the United States. But the authors' handling of this replication has artfully achieved much more "value added" as well. For example, the text in which the comparative tabulations are embedded, while mirroring the original in high degree, manages to modernize the language while most often saying the same thing in fewer words. More importantly, each substantive chapter ends with a section entitled "Commentary and Controversy," devoted to a review of the intervening decades of debate over diverse issues of methods and findings. These are invaluable source materials in and of themselves, and combined with the comparisons of raw findings, produce a sort of double prism in the time dimension that is at the very least novel, and to me thoroughly intriguing. I think that students of electoral behavior will find this volume both stimulating and useful.

Philip E. Converse
Ann Arbor, Michigan
July 22, 2007

Contents

Preface   ix

How to Read This Book   xiii

Section I ▪ *Introductory*

  1. Setting   3

  2. Theoretical Orientation   19

Section II ▪ *Political Attitudes and the Vote*

  3. Perceptions of the Parties and Candidates   31

  4. Partisan Choice   60

  5. Voting Turnout   82

Section III ▪ *The Political Context*

  6. The Impact of Party Identification   111

  7. The Development of Party Identification   138

  8. Public Policy and Political Preference   161

  9. Attitude Structure and the Problem of Ideology   201

 10. The Formation of Issue Concepts and Partisan Change   254

Section IV ▪ *The Social and Economic Context*

 11. Membership in Social Groupings   305

 12. Class and Other Social Characteristics   334

 13. Economic Antecedents of Political Behavior   365

Section V ■ *The Electoral Decision and the Political System*

14. The Electoral Decision   393

15. Electoral Behavior and the Political System   415

Afterword: The American Voter Then and Now   424

Appendix A: Counterpart Tables and Figures   429

Appendix B: Replication of *The American Voter*   435

References   441

Index   481

Preface

The American Voter, by Angus Campbell, Philip E. Converse, Warren E. Miller, and Donald E. Stokes, was published in 1960 as a report on the 1952 and especially the 1956 U.S. presidential elections. Researchers at the University of Michigan's Institute for Social Research had published an earlier book on the 1952 election, a report on the 1954 congressional election, and a few journal articles, but *The American Voter* was the definitive work, establishing a paradigm for scholarly research on voting. It was followed by a collection entitled *Elections and the Political Order* plus further journal articles and then several studies of elections in other countries collaboratively with scholars from those countries, but the only book-length treatment of American elections that any of them subsequently produced was Warren Miller and Merrill Shanks's *The New American Voter*, which employed a very different analysis strategy than the original book.

The surveys that *The American Voter* analyzed have become the gold standard in the field. They have been conducted virtually every two years since 1952, leading to an invaluable time series. They are now known as the National Election Studies and are sponsored by the National Science Foundation. While there are differences in detail, their basic design is the same as in the 1950s, with preelection and postelection face-to-face interviews with the same respondents. There are now other major election surveys that take telephone interviews throughout the election year, and those surveys are more suitable for examining the development of attitudes and changes in vote intention. However, the original study design used in *The American Voter* remains powerful for analyzing the correlates of individual voting decisions.

Revisiting *The American Voter* is valuable for several reasons. One is to see what it actually said. Within a few years of publication a stereotype developed according to which the authors viewed voting as based on immutable party identification and superficial characteristics of the candidates, because voters were too unsophisticated to consider ideology and the issues. That is a more apt characterization of the abridged version (1964) than of the original, which was much more subtle than the conventional view credits. The effect of issues on changes in people's party identification is emphasized in many chapters, as is the possibility that different results might be obtained in different elections. Contrary to V. O. Key's (1966) implication, *The American Voter* did not suggest that voters are fools, though its view of voters is compatible with the "cognitive miser" notion that social psychologists were to develop later. Second, revisiting *The American Voter* leaves one with an admiration of the authors' methodological skill despite a primitive computing technology, a recognition of the complexity of some of their statistical analyses, and a respect for their ability to present results with simple cross-tabulations. Third, reencountering *The American Voter* may spur research on voting behavior, as we see which topics could benefit from more modern social-psychological perspectives or more modern techniques of analysis.

In revisiting *The American Voter,* we have stayed fairly close to its approach. Our chapters follow the original in theme and style of analysis. Thousands of journal articles and conference papers have been published and presented on the subject of voting behavior in the decades since 1960, pieces that have reconsidered the original work of Campbell, Converse, Miller, and Stokes with more modern statistical analysis techniques. Yet the original work remains elegant in its very simplicity. Indeed, it is humbling to realize that the authors produced their classic book without the use of computers as we know them today. At the same time, it is important to move to more advanced analysis of topics and to take notice of controversies in the field, so we have added sections at the end of each chapter updating the topic both methodologically and substantively. We have dropped some topics, either because the needed questions have not been included in recent election studies or because the topic has lost its urgency over the years (such as their treatment of agrarian political behavior). We have expanded a few topics, such as the voting behavior of blacks and of women, which have increased in importance in ways that the original authors could not have foreseen. We have, however, resisted the temptation to switch to new theoretical approaches (either modern political psychology or formal theory) or to expand greatly the set of topics (such as the primary season, the media, or the campaign), since other books cover them so ably.

The chapters of *The American Voter Revisited* correspond to those of the original as follows:

CHAPTER TITLE	The American Voter Revisited	The American Voter
	CHAPTER NUMBER	
Setting	1	1
Theoretical Orientation	2	2
Perceptions of the Parties and Candidates	3	3
Partisan Choice	4	4
Voting Turnout	5	5
The Impact of Party Identification	6	6
The Development of Party Identification	7	7
Public Policy and Political Preference	8	8
Attitude Structure and the Problem of Ideology	9	9
The Formation of Issue Concepts and Partisan Change	10	10
Membership in Social Groupings	11	12
Class and Other Social Characteristics	12	13 & 17
Economic Antecedents of Political Behavior	13	14
The Electoral Decision	14	19
Electoral Behavior and the Political System	15	20

We have retained the original authors' focus on major party voting, leaving out the "little details" that were important aspects of the 2000 and 2004 elections, including minor party candidacies, legal skirmishes about recounts, the mathematics of the Electoral College, and the role of the Supreme Court in deciding an outcome. We understand that these decisions will be controversial, just as so many chapters of *The American Voter* have proved controversial. We have tried to provide a report on the 2000 and especially the 2004 U.S. presidential elections that is close to what the original "four horsemen" would have produced if they were describing voting in these elections; we leave it to the reader to judge the relative value of the model in *The American Voter* and of subsequent efforts to understand voting behavior. In any case, we hope that drawing attention back to *The American Voter* will help revitalize the study of electoral behavior, now that more than half a century of NES surveys have been conducted.

We want to acknowledge our debts to several people. Discussants at the Midwest, American, and Southern Political Science Association annual meetings, as well as colleagues on other occasions, gave us helpful suggestions, particularly Paul Abramson, John Aldrich, Paul Beck, Jack Citrin, Aage Clausen, Russ Dalton, Bob Erikson, James Garand, John Geer, Mark Hetherington, Sunshine Hillygus, Patricia Hurley, M. Kent Jennings, Mike Kagay, Rick Lau, Milt Lodge, Diana Mutz, Andrew Perrin, David Sears, J. Merrill Shanks, Paul Sniderman, Jim Stimson, and Laura Stoker, as did students in our classes at the Ohio State University and Stony Brook University. We received excellent research assistance from Erin McAdams, Dino Christenson, Jeremy Duff, Robert Moore, Kurt Pyle, Hoon Lee, Nadia Khatib, Mary-Kate Lizotte, Andrew Sidman, and Sung-jin Yoo. Like all researchers on voting behavior, we are deeply indebted to the National Election Studies for their continuing series of election surveys and to the National Science Foundation for its support of these surveys. We thank the people with the University of Michigan Press for their excellent work on this volume, including our anonymous reviewers. A special appreciation goes to the director, Phil Pochoda, for encouragement of this project. And, we thank the University of Chicago Press for permitting us to base this volume on the original *American Voter*. Appropriately, our greatest debt is to Angus Campbell, Philip E. Converse, Warren E. Miller, and Donald E. Stokes for their intellectual contributions, for how much they taught us directly and indirectly, and for their friendships, and we also thank their families for their kind words about our work on this project.

How to Read This Book

Most books in political science can be read in linear fashion, the chapters in their given sequence developing the theme announced by the title. *The American Voter Revisited* can certainly be read that way, but it goes better with a twist. The twist involves knowing the context. Each chapter parallels a chapter from the original *The American Voter*, published in 1960. (For more on this, flip back to the Preface). The titles, order, and topics evoke the earlier work. (Of course, the data sets analyzed are entirely different.) We have attempted to preserve the theory, methods, and—most importantly—the spirit of Campbell, Converse, Miller, and Stokes. While we cannot hope to do these pioneers full justice, we have tried. Any errors or missteps, of course, remain entirely our own.

Although much can be said within this adopted framework, not everything can be. Hence, we devote the closing portion of each chapter to discussion of contemporary issues and controversies. These "Commentary and Controversy" (C&C) sections complement the findings that begin each chapter, enabling the reader to see where American voter studies have traveled, and where they might go in the future. We have eschewed adding our own "new" angle on the material, but we have not been shy about referring to our own contributions in the C&C sections. What makes *The American Voter Revisited* original, we believe, is that it offers a replication of *The American Voter,* demonstrating that this classic still, after 50 years, provides a sound lens through which to study U.S. political behavior.

SECTION I

Introductory

CHAPTER 1

Setting

Voting has become a virtually universal means by which individuals make collective decisions. It is used by legislatures and reading groups, by panels of judges, church conclaves, and the United Nations, and, most importantly, it has become the way that nations represent their mass public in determining governmental actions. The importance of voting in modern society is seen in the rapidity with which free elections were adopted by the new nations that emerged with the end of the Cold War.

The scholarly literature on voting has exploded in the last several years, as regards voting in the United States but even more so voting in other nations. In addition to coverage of the field in the general political science journals, there are now the specialty publications *Political Behavior, Electoral Studies,* and *Journal of Elections, Public Opinion, and Parties.* Furthermore, voting continues to receive attention in a wide variety of disciplines. Political sociologists, political psychologists, and public choice economists have found voting a fertile topic for their research, applying their own theoretical perspectives to this fascinating democratic behavior.

If we are to add to the research on voting, we must locate our work in broad perspective in three important ways, which will be discussed in this chapter. First, voting occurs within a larger political system. Research on voting behavior is valuable to the extent that it contributes to the literature on political systems more broadly. Second, any election occurs within a particular historical setting. We focus in this book on two elections that occurred four years apart, and the particular period in which they were held affects the results that we obtain. Therefore, it is essential to consider how the historical context of these elections affects our conclusions. Third, our study is part of a lengthy series of studies on voting. The substantive topics we examine and the methodology we use to examine them flow from these earlier studies.

VOTING AND THE POLITICAL SYSTEM

While voting is of great interest to a variety of social sciences, it is important not to lose track of its political import. Researchers may study voting because of what it reveals about attitude formation and change, social group identification, the effects of social status, the role of personality factors, the role of the media, the economic rationality of voting, and its geographical structure. Those interpretations of voting data are worthwhile, and some will be covered in chapters in this book. Still, voting behavior is of interest primarily because of its effects on the political system. Voting is so important because of its import at the collective level. However much we focus on the determinants of individuals' votes, it is their impact on the political system that matters in the end.

Elections are fundamental to democracy. Governments allocate resources within their jurisdictions, and elections are the main means by which the governed control and consent to this process. Furthermore, if these elections are to be meaningful, they must be free and competitive, with some candidates being elected to power and others being denied election, through a peaceful process of leadership selection and transfer of authority. Direct democracy may seem an attractive alternative to representative democracy, but the latter is more realistic given the size of modern nations and the complexity of issues that they face.

Elections are one form of decision making in democracies; decisions are also made in legislatures, the executive, and the courts. Each of these forums has a constitutional basis, amplified by laws, with actors deciding according to specified rules and with various influences affecting the decisions. Of course, these are intertwined processes in a democracy, not independent ones. For example, the legislative process is inherently a matter of representation affected by elections, and the actions of legislators and other elected officials are always influenced by possible electoral consequences.

Our focus in this volume will be on elections for the U.S. presidency. The determination of who will be the executive head is important in every country, but it is the key choice in the United States. When it was instituted in the United States, choice of the president by the electorate was very rare. In parliamentary systems the electorate does affect the determination of the executive, though even more indirectly than in the United States, in which the Electoral College elects the president. But whether the electorate chooses the executive directly by popular vote or indirectly through an Electoral College or parliamentary system, such systems are more democratic than ones in which the electorate is manipulated, controlled, or permitted no real choice. Most totalitarian countries profess to have elections, but the electorate has no genuine choice. As democratic theorists have long emphasized, popular consent through elections is meaningful only when voters are given genuine alternatives.

We and other scholars are interested in the governmental process more generally, and not just how voters choose between presidential candidates. The presidential vote, however, provides a useful focus for the current inquiry, illuminating decision making in elections that receive considerable public attention and thereby providing a standard for comparison with elections that receive less public attention.

Another important topic is the effects of elections on the governmental process. In voting for president, the public considers actions taken by the president, the executive more broadly, the legislative branch, the judicial branch, and other parts of the federal government. In turn, the election results affect subsequent government action by the president, by the executive, the legislative branch, the judicial branch, and other parts of the federal government, sometimes directly and sometimes through their interpretations of the significance of the election result.

This book focuses on the United States. However, our interest in voting transcends national boundaries, and many of the ideas in this book are applicable to other nations as well. There are major differences between the political systems of different nations, particularly between presidential and parliamentary systems and between two-party and multiparty systems, that suggest caution is in order when one draws generalizations. But still we contend that the framework provided here offers a useful beginning point for studying voting in other nations, with due allowance for differences between the systems.

In focusing on the presidential election, we do not intend to slight the significance of other elections. The vote for Congress is important, and the comparison between presidential and midterm elections is important. Indeed, some of our results hold for nonpresidential elections.

But there are also real differences between presidential and nonpresidential elections, so generalizations from our results to nonpresidential elections should be made with care. The presidential choice by itself provides enough material for this book, though it should be seen as part of the broader study of voting behavior.

In short, voting is important, free elections are vital to democracy, and U.S. presidential elections are among the most significant elections in the world. There are associated topics researchers do study, including the effects of presidential elections on the government, voting in other nations, and voting in nonpresidential elections. However, the study of voting in U.S. presidential elections is itself a sufficient topic for this book.

THE HISTORICAL CONTEXT

Our goal is to develop an explanation of voting that is not bound to any single time period. However, the specific elections and period studied inevitably affect the conclusions drawn, so it is necessary to begin with a description of the historical context of the elections considered in this book. Indeed, many of the results reported in this book describe these elections, though our goal is to provide a theoretical understanding of individual voting. A theory can be seen as positing the relationships among variables, indicating which independent variables affect the dependent behaviors of interest. Descriptive studies at any single historical point indicate the values of the variables at that point. The theory helps determine which variables should be examined, thereby guiding the descriptive historical analysis.

Some examples help show how theory can guide description. First, consider the effects of social class on voting. These effects vary over time. Rather than show only that class and voting are related, we are interested in showing how they vary, using that variance to test hypotheses and to describe how presidential politics has changed over the years. Second, our social-psychological theory of voting emphasizes the role of particular partisan attitudes in determining voting decisions. We use our measurements of those attitudes both to test our theoretical hypotheses and to describe systematically the factors that lead to particular election outcomes. Third, our theory is that people's psychological identification with a party affects these partisan attitudes but can also be affected by them. This possibility of partisan attitudes leading to changes in partisan identification leads to a fivefold classification of presidential elections: maintaining, deviating, reinstating, realigning, and balancing. At the same time, it is necessary to admit that the historical period being studied inherently limits our theories. We observe elections in a particular period, and all we can do is to use those elections to develop and test our theories. Experiments can be useful in examining how manipulation of key variables affects dependent variables, but it is difficult to conduct experiments on elections. Researchers in studies of voting behavior cannot manipulate many of the essential variables. It is also difficult to control several variables simultaneously, especially since key variables are often too highly correlated to separate their effects fully. Another difficulty is the limited amount of variation in these key variables, particularly in a particular historical period. Since some variables may not vary during the period studied, researchers may not understand their importance, may not think of including them in their theories, and may not be able to estimate their true importance even when they are studied.

In this book, we examine voting in two presidential elections, using interviews with probability samples of the national electorate. We focus on the 2000 and 2004 presidential elections, using surveys taken by the National Election Studies.[1] Where appropriate, we also use surveys taken in earlier years.

The 2000 presidential election followed two decades of increased partisan division. Ronald Reagan brought the presidency back into Republican hands in 1980 and moved public policy in a more conservative direction, but always facing a Democratic House of Representatives. George H. W. Bush succeeded Reagan in 1988 and continued most of his policies, while facing unified Democratic control of Congress. Divided government led to the defeat of Reagan's nomination of Robert Bork to the Supreme Court and Bush's nomination of John Tower to be secretary of defense, resulting in more heated fights between the political parties in Congress. The Bush administration was marked by the collapse of the Soviet Union, the U.S. invasion of Panama, and by the Gulf War to undo Iraq's seizure of Kuwait.

Bill Clinton defeated Bush in 1992, in a campaign that focused on the weak economy. While he received nearly 6 percent more of the vote than

---

1. The National Science Foundation sponsored these surveys. They are primarily face-to-face surveys taken in respondents' homes, though half of the 2000 interviews were instead conducted on the telephone. The methodology is discussed in more detail at the end of this chapter.

Bush, Clinton won only 43 percent of the popular vote, with H. Ross Perot's independent candidacy obtaining 19 percent. The Democratic president worked with the Democratic Congress in 1993–94 to pass several important new laws, including the Family and Medical Leave Act, the Brady Bill, which imposed limits on handgun purchases, and higher taxes in the Omnibus Budget Reconciliation Act of 1993, along with ratification of the North American Free Trade Agreement. However, Congress forced Clinton to compromise on allowing openly gay people in the military, and Congress shelved his plans for health care reform. The Republicans used dissatisfaction with several of these Clinton initiatives, a scandal in the House of Representatives, and their Contract with America to return the country to divided government in the 1994 midterm election, with Republicans winning control of the Senate and the House together for the first time in 40 years. The major legislative accomplishments in 1995–96 were the passage of welfare reform and the Defense of Marriage Act, which allowed states to refuse recognition of same-sex marriages.

Clinton handily defeated Bob Dole in the 1996 presidential election (49 percent to 41 percent, with Perot obtaining 8 percent), though Clinton still faced a Republican Congress. He forced Congress to pass his budget in 1996 after initial defeat of that bill led to a shutdown of many government services. While this was not a period of major legislative accomplishment, the economy soared during the Clinton years. A major scandal erupted in 1998 over allegations that Bill Clinton had an affair with White House intern Monica Lewinsky. Clinton retained his popularity with the public, and Democrats gained seats in the 1998 congressional elections, but the Republicans continued to control an increasingly polarized Congress. After the midterm election, Clinton became the second president in U.S. history to be impeached. The Republican House of Representatives impeached him in 1999 because of alleged perjury and obstruction of justice in court testimony about his relationship with Lewinsky; the Senate failed to convict him on these charges, so he was able to finish his term in office. On the foreign front, U.S. troops led a NATO force in a successful bombing campaign against Serbian dominance in Kosovo in spring 1999, and there were attempts to bring peace in Northern Ireland and the Middle East. There were other scandals during the Clinton administration, but the major issues going into the 2000 election were a slowing economy and the aftermath of the Clinton moral scandal and impeachment.

The 2000 presidential election featured Democratic vice president Al

Gore running against George W. Bush, the son of the forty-first president. Gore was not able to separate himself from Clinton's moral problems while still associating himself with the strong economy of the Clinton years. Ralph Nader's Green Party candidacy threatened to take liberal votes from Gore, though in the end Nader won under 3 percent of the vote. Pat Buchanan's Reform Party candidacy took some votes from Bush, but he received less than 0.5 percent of the vote. Gore had a popular vote plurality of more than 500,000 votes over Bush, but the 2000 election became the first in over 100 years when the leader in the popular vote lost the Electoral College. The election was so close that the result finally depended on Florida, which ultimately gave George W. Bush a 537-vote victory when the U.S. Supreme Court called a halt to ballot recounts. Bush began with a Republican Congress, but the party switch of one senator gave control of the Senate to the Democrats in early 2001. Still, Bush was able to get some of his domestic agenda through Congress, especially tax cuts and his "No Child Left Behind" education program.

The al-Qaeda attack on the United States on September 11, 2001, quickly led to foreign and defense policies becoming the main focus of the Bush administration. President Bush declared a war on terrorism; the 2001 war in Afghanistan quickly defeated its Taliban government, and the 2003 war in Iraq removed its president, Saddam Hussein. The original war on terrorism and the Afghan campaign were highly popular, helping the Republicans to win control of both chambers of Congress in the 2002 midterm election. However, the Iraq war became highly controversial by the time of the 2004 election when there proved to be no indication that Iraq had possessed weapons of mass destruction and U.S. casualties mounted in the aftermath of the war.

The 2004 presidential election was a contest between George W. Bush, seeking to win the popular vote as well as the Electoral College, and Senator John Kerry. Kerry sought to portray himself as a leader, pointing to his bravery in the Vietnam War, but negative ads brought his war and postwar activities into question, negating that campaign appeal. Kerry portrayed himself as better able to handle the ongoing war on terrorism and the Iraq situation, but a majority of the country decided to stay with Bush. While Bush won a majority of the popular vote, this time the Electoral College result finally depended on the vote in Ohio, which in the end narrowly went to Bush.

How much political change occurred during the 1996–2004 years? The Democratic vote varied by less than 1 percentage point across these three presidential elections: 49 percent in 1996 and 48 percent in 2000 and 2004. However, there was a 10 percentage point gain in the Republican vote from 1996 to 2004, increasing from Dole's 41 percent in 1996 to Bush's 51 percent in 2004. So we see both stability and change in presidential vote results. Correspondingly, we will find considerable continuity in voting patterns during this period, but with some indications of change. Still, our ability to examine partisan change during this limited period is constrained.

However, one important change during this period was increased partisan polarization. As stated above, polarization began to increase during the 1980s, increasing further during the Clinton years of the 1990s and even more during the George W. Bush terms. This polarization was evident in Congress, where roll call votes became more and more sharply divided along party lines. It was also evident in the information media in 2004, with talk radio, Internet blogs, and political films (like Michael Moore's anti-Bush film *Fahrenheit 9/11* and Carlton Sherwood's anti-Kerry film *Stolen Honor*) being highly partisan. Thus, the conclusions about individual voting to be made in this book reflect a period of heightened partisan conflict, and we could expect some results to be different in a more quiescent period. Some of these differences will be discussed in later chapters.

THE COURSE OF VOTING RESEARCH

Research on voting dates back to the 1920s, when social sciences began to be more empirically oriented (Merriam and Gosnell 1924). Of course there were earlier historical and journalistic accounts of elections and voting, but they were anecdotal rather than systematic. At best some of the earliest work analyzed voting patterns by geographical areas such as regions, states, counties, or precincts. Analysis of these geographical units does provide useful insights when they are highly homogeneous, but can be misleading when the units are heterogeneous. As Robinson (1950) has demonstrated, causal inferences about individual behavior based on aggregate ("ecological") data can be fallacious, though sophisticated statistical methods that attempt to deal with that problem are now available (e.g., King 1997). That problem aside, aggregate election data are not useful for understanding the psychological and attitudinal factors underlying individual voting behavior.

These difficulties led early work on voting to be primarily sociological, as in analyzing voting along racial, ethnic, urbanization, and class lines, using aggregate data in small areas that were homogenous in one of those dimensions in the hope that the results would generalize to other locations. For example, voting in a very heavily Catholic precinct could be examined to see how Catholics voted. The findings could be generalized to how Catholics in general voted, but only if one assumes that Catholics vote the same way in heavily Catholic precincts and in areas that are less Catholic. Even if that assumption was correct—and it is not necessarily so—such analysis was incapable of analyzing the attitudinal bases of the Catholic vote.

Research in voting behavior was revolutionized with the advent of survey research, starting with academic surveys in the 1920s and surveys by commercial polling firms in the 1930s. No longer did the field have to rely on aggregate data. Those early surveys showed that information could be obtained about individual people and their voting behavior. However, the early studies still concentrated on the sociological correlates of voting.

The ability of election surveys to help us gain theoretical understanding of voting was first illustrated in studies by Columbia University researchers of Erie County, Ohio, in 1940 (Lazarsfeld, Berelson, and Gaudet 1948) and Elmira, New York, in 1948 (Berelson, Lazarsfeld, and McPhee 1954). These highly innovative studies demonstrated the capability of the survey method. The 1940 study actually was a "panel" survey in which respondents were reinterviewed throughout the year so researchers could follow attitudes and vote intentions at different stages of the campaign. That study also examined how the cross-pressure of different sociological factors (e.g., a Catholic with higher social class standing) affected voting plans. The 1948 study added further topics, such as the role of interpersonal influence in making voting decisions and the life of political issues during the campaign. These were very influential studies, but they were limited by their focus on a single community.

The first national academic voting survey was taken in 1944 by the National Opinion Research Center (Korchin 1946). The second was a small survey taken by the University of Michigan's Survey Research Center in 1948 (Campbell and Kahn 1952). The Michigan SRC happened to include a question about the election in a nonpolitical survey conducted early that autumn. When Harry Truman confounded commercial pollsters by winning the election, the SRC reinterviewed its respondents and found that a large proportion of people who had been undecided broke for Truman.

That 1948 survey was the immediate precursor to the series of U.S. voting surveys that has become known as the National Election Studies (NES). The Survey Research Center conducted a major preelection face-to-face interview with a national sample of respondents in 1952 and followed up with a large postelection face-to-face interview with the same respondents (Campbell, Gurin, and Miller 1954). The 1956 survey by the SRC followed the same pattern, but with a wider range of questions (Campbell et al. 1960).

These surveys shifted the focus from the collection of sociological variables to the measurement of attitudes. They asked open-ended questions about people's reactions to contemporary politics, permitting analysts to describe the person's cognitive map of the election campaign. Moving past description, analysts could classify these reactions in terms of a set of partisan attitudes. For example, a person might view the experience of the Republican candidate as a plus, moving the person toward a Republican vote. However, that person might have identified with the Democratic Party for many years and favor the Democrats on domestic issues, both of which would push the person toward a Democratic vote. Statistical analysis of these data yields a powerful prediction of the individual's vote.

It is important to recognize in what way this approach improves on the sociological approach. When the sociological approach focused just on socio-demographics such as a person's race, religion, or education, it examined characteristics that are long term in nature. The national vote can vary considerably from one election to the next, but these socio-demographic variables are too stable to explain such change. Attitudes toward political objects, on the other hand, are short term in nature. They can, and do, change between elections enough to account for the large changes that sometimes occur in the vote. Additionally, these attitudinal variables yield a much more political understanding of elections than do socio-demographic variables.

These studies, now called the American National Election Studies (ANES or NES), have been conducted regularly since that time. The two most recent, from 2000 and 2004, provide almost all the raw material for the analysis contained herein.

COMMENTARY AND CONTROVERSY

The National Election Studies

The National Election Studies have flourished over the years. National surveys of the electorate have been conducted in conjunction with each presidential election since 1948. While private foundations funded the original surveys, the National Science Foundation now funds them. The format remains an approximately one-hour preelection face-to-face interview in respondents' homes, with a similarly long postelection interview. (The one exception was in 2000, when half of the interviews were taken by telephone as a prelude to switching to phone interviewing exclusively—a change that was quickly rescinded when the phone interviews proved not to be fully comparable to the face-to-face interviews.)[2] Additionally, the NES has conducted surveys in most midterm election years during this period, usually concentrating on the elections for the House of Representatives.

The hallmark of the NES has been its continuity in questions over the decades. Some old questions are dropped and new questions are added each year to capture changed circumstances, such as when questions about the Cold War were dropped and when questions about the war on terrorism were added. However, many of the questions first asked in 1948, 1952, or 1956 surveys are still asked today, including the basic party identification question and the open-ended questions asking people what they like and dislike about the parties and the presidential nominees. This continuity provides a great advantage in allowing comparisons over the years, though it has restricted innovation in survey content and question wording.

At the same time, there are design differences between the different surveys. For example, the western part of the United States actually had a small population as late as the 1950s, so the early NES surveys double sampled in the West in order to get enough respondents there to generalize about their voting behavior. The researchers were especially interested in the voting behavior of African Americans after the passage of the Civil Rights Act of 1964, so the 1964 NES double sampled blacks. In these instances, by the way, weighting would have to be used when analyzing the

---

2. In order to have enough respondents for reliable analysis, we analyze the face-to-face interviews together with the telephone interviews for 2000. However, see Bowers and Ensley 2003 for discussion of problems in analyzing the two modes together.

whole electorate so as to bring these groups back down to their appropriate proportion.

The NES also has conducted several panel studies, reinterviewing the same respondents in a presidential election year, the following midterm year, and the next presidential year. The first of these was in 1956-58-60, and the design was repeated for 1972-74-76. There was also a panel survey in 2000-02-04, but it contained many fewer respondents, which limits its value for this book. NES conducted an innovative Senate election study during the 1988-1990-1992 Senate election cycle, interviewing for each Senate seat.

The Changed Setting

While there is considerable continuity to questions in the NES surveys, the political setting is very different now than it was during the first national election surveys. When we look back in historical perspective, the 1950s turn out to have been a fairly quiescent political era. Issues such as domestic Communism may have seemed important at the time, but they did not elicit strong reactions from the public (Campbell et al. 1960).

The issues became more heated by the late 1960s, with the civil rights revolution, urban unrest, and the Vietnam War and protests against it. Not surprisingly, researchers found issues to be more important for voting in that era than they had been in the 1950s (Nie, Verba, and Petrocik 1979). As described above, politics became more polarized starting in the 1980s, with partisan conflict reaching new highs in 2000 and 2004. A study published in the late 1970s, *The Changing American Voter* (Nie, Verba, and Petrocik 1979), considered the survey results of the 1950s to be atypical since during that period issues affected voting less than they did during the late 1960s and 1970s. We now realize that the 1960s and 1970s were also atypical, since that period had more heated issues and political protest than later decades. Indeed, the results of *The New American Voter* (Miller and Shanks 1996) for the 1992 election were more similar to those of *The American Voter* than to those of *The Changing American Voter*.

We must also recognize that the 2000–2004 period described in this book may look atypical when historians look back from the vantage of 2020. However, the real point is that no period is fully typical. Some eras are quiescent politically, while others are heated. Partisanship may be muted in some eras, while highly polarized in others. Rather than worry about whether any particular period is typical, we need to have in-depth analysis of elections across a wide range of periods. More fundamentally, every election has elements that are typical as well as atypical, and we can distinguish what is typical only by comparing elections. It is too easy to view the 1950s period as quiescent, the 1960s and 1970s as heated, and the 2000 and 2004 elections as polarized, without recognizing that voting shares many commonalities across these disparate election settings.

Comparative Election Studies

This book focuses on voting in American elections, a case that cannot be generalized to all voting. The constitutional rules in the United States about elections are very specific and are not common across the world. In particular, the U.S. combination of a federal system with a presidential system with an Electoral College is unique. This makes it important to study other nations as well in order to understand the determinants of voting.

The approach taken by *The American Voter* has by now been generalized to studying voting in many other countries. Indeed, the Michigan authors of *The American Voter* themselves exported their approach to other countries, especially in the Butler and Stokes (1969) study *Political Change in Britain* and the Converse and Pierce (1986) study *Political Representation in France*. The early comparative work tended to apply the American model directly, but later work became more sensitive to the different contexts in other nations.

An important turn in recent years is collecting comparable data in election studies in several nations. The Comparative Study of Electoral Systems (CSES) puts a common set of questions on each participant country's postelection survey. The Comparative National Election Project (CNEP) is now a 23-country effort (Gunther, Montero, and Puhle 2007).

Methodology

Methods for analyzing data have developed considerably over the past half-century. When the Michigan authors were analyzing the 1952 and 1956 election surveys, the data were punched into computer cards. Each card could contain a maximum of 80 pieces of information in separate columns, so each respondent required several cards. Computers were not available for data analysis. Card-sorting machines could sort the cards into piles according to the value punched into a column. It was relatively easy to obtain the frequency distribution of a variable or even a cross-tabulation of two variables, but it was much harder to do a regression analysis or a factor analysis. That the researchers managed to do such analysis is very impressive.

Modern computers now allow data analysis to be performed with much greater ease. The data are available on computer files that can be accessed on the Internet. Sophisticated programs can perform many types of statistical analysis, including some techniques that are more appropriate than those the Michigan researchers were able to use. In particular, they used multiple regression analysis to determine which factors significantly affect how people vote, but regression analysis is, strictly speaking, inappropriate when studying dichotomous variables (such as if a person voted Republican or Democrat). Logit or probit analysis is more appropriate, and now it is easy to perform such analysis on modern computers.

The NES surveys are based on probability samples of the United States. These are samples in which every person has a known nonzero probability of selection, which allows the computation of sampling error on its results. The sampling is multistage areal sampling: first dividing the nation into four regions, then sampling smaller areas within each region, and eventually sampling houses on randomly chosen blocks and then randomly selecting a designated respondent in each of those houses. The sample is entirely residential, omitting institutional sites such as college dorms, hospitals, nursing homes, military bases, and prisons. Interviewers are trained professionals who are instructed to develop rapport with respondents so that the respondents feel comfortable giving honest answers to the questions. The main cost of face-to-face interviews is getting the interviewer to the sampled houses, so NES asks a full hour of questions in both the pre- and postelection surveys since the length of the interview does not materially increase the cost of the interviewing. In addition to sampling error and the frame error caused by omitting institutional residences, error can enter the process because of question wording and because selected respondents may be unwilling to be interviewed.

While face-to-face interviewing was the standard survey approach in the 1950s, telephone surveys became prevalent by the 1970s and Internet surveys by early 2000s. Each of these types of surveys has advantages and disadvantages. These newer survey modes are much less expensive than face-to-face interviewing. However, phone and Internet surveys are much shorter than face-to-face surveys and have much lower response rates. Weisberg (2005) provides further discussion of interviewing modes.

The Survey Design

The basic pre- and postdesign of NES is very useful, but has real limitations. It allows investigators to ask questions about potential causes of the vote before the election, and then find out how the person voted after the election along with considerable auxiliary information about the respondent. Interviewing 1,200–1,800 people in this design, however, does not allow researchers to examine campaign effects in any detail.

The NES pioneered a "continuous monitoring" design in 1984, taking a small number of interviews nightly throughout the election year. Since then, the National Annenberg Election Surveys of 2000 and 2004 have used this continuing monitoring design with samples of over 100,000 people over the course of the campaign, allowing close examination of the effects of campaign events (Johnston, Hagen, and Jamieson 2004). Yet this design does not allow researchers to examine whether those campaign events changed attitudes or vote intentions of specific respondents (see Katz 2001; cf. Weisberg and Wilcox 2004).[3]

Another design issue is the use of national election surveys without taking state variation into account. While citizens vote for president in every state, the conditions vary considerably from state to state. For example, the health of the economy often differs from state to state. More important, one party may have such a strong lead in some states that there is no real contest for their electoral votes, while there is a vigorous contest in competitive states. Campaigns naturally focus on the battleground states, so the media environment that voters face there differs from states that are virtually conceded to one party or the other. The NES approach has been to take a probability sample of voters across the country, stratified to ensure appropriate coverage of each region and clustered to minimize costs of face-to-face interviewing. The logic of that approach is that voters are voters, regardless of where they live. However, an alternative design would be to focus more directly on battleground states, recognizing that voters in those states are the real targets of political campaigns (Shaw 2006).

The NES surveys continue to be important because their continuity permits comparisons over the years that would not be possible with

---

3. The NES in 1980 used a four-wave panel design, interviewing the same people early in the year, again in midspring, again before the election, and then after the election. That design permits one to study change across the election year, but does not provide any extra leverage on the effects of campaign events in the crucial post–Labor Day period.

other designs. Yet many researchers consider it important to continue innovating in study design in order to measure better the influences on voting.

Contextual Data

Researchers who are interested in studying the effects of campaign events are also likely to desire additional types of data beyond straight survey data. One approach is to study the campaign televised ads, along with data on which ads are being employed in which areas. Another version is to study interpersonal communication patterns, asking respondents whom they talk to about elections and then interviewing that person, or asking the original respondents about their perceptions of the attitudes of those conversation partners. Additionally, it has become common to supplement NES survey data with additional "contextual" data about the communities in which the respondents live. For example, variables connected to state voting laws can be added, or variables measuring characteristics of the city or town of residence. Advocates of these types of studies would argue that the basic NES election surveys are too plain. Voting, they would argue, occurs within a context—whether a context of campaign ads, conversation partners, or at least state laws and community characteristics—and looking at individual voting outside of that context misses an essential part of the story.

CHAPTER 2

Theoretical Orientation

Several theoretical approaches can be used to study voting behavior. There are distinct sociological and psychological approaches, which have followed separate paths in the investigation of voting. Their findings are not contradictory, but the two approaches have not addressed one another. Each has advantages, so that a combination of the two is more powerful than the two taken separately. We seek to develop a theoretical approach that builds on the strength of each.

In studying voting behavior, we must address both whether a person will vote and how a person will vote. Both turnout and vote choice are complex behaviors, so we should not expect either to be explained by a simple single-variable cause. We need a framework that encompasses a broad range of potential causes that unite to generate the two aspects of voting behavior.

THE FUNCTIONS OF THEORY

A classic debate is whether science seeks to understand behaviors or predict them. Our interest is in understanding the processes that lead to voting behavior, with only peripheral interest in predicting it. Finding that a particular variable happens to predict voting would be of little theoretical use if it we could not understand how it helped "cause" voting. For example, if we found that left-handed people were more likely to vote Democrat, we could use that knowledge to predict voting, but it would not provide us greater understanding of voting or any theoretical leverage—unless we identified conditions under which this pattern held. For example, if left-handed people were more likely to vote Democrat when the Democratic nominee is left-handed, one could theorize that people are more likely to vote for people like themselves. Furthermore, achieving understanding does not guarantee that we can predict behavior. For example, we might understand that foreign policy crises in the two weeks before a presidential election affect its outcome without being able to predict the occurrence of such crises. Still, we benefit when we discover more and more factors that help us understand voting behavior, even if prediction remains elusive.

We are interested in assessing causation, but the concept of causation is itself controversial. Minimally, it requires a time dimension: a cause must precede its effect, so a cause of voting has to occur before the election rather than afterward. Additionally, there must be a relationship between the cause and effect, without both being the product of a third variable (the "spurious relationship" problem). But when we look at voting we find a multitude of causes. We can highlight the difficulties presented by the question of causality and individual voting by evaluation of the following case study notes (which are hypothetical):

1. Man in Oklahoma. Had been Democrat but wife, a Republican from Atlanta, convinced him to change. Used to work on oil rig, before that dried up. He liked Clinton, not Gore. Felt he was informed about politics. Voted Republican in 2000 and 2004.
2. Meat cutter, Iowa. Recently become a Democrat. Regularly votes. In 2000 thought Bush favored the rich with tax cuts. Liked that Bush wanted minorities to make it on their own. Believes he is better off than most economically. Voted Democratic in 2000, and Republican in 2004.
3. Woman, just moved to Vermont. Came to region because of its liberal politics. Does organic farming and wool-weaving. Old family ties to New England. Although comes from a long line of Republicans, she always votes Democratic, and is especially concerned about the war in Iraq.
4. Radiation therapist, Louisiana. Has been a Republican since the first time she voted, for Reagan. A conservative Christian, concerned about family values and disgusted by Clinton. Feels that Bush is a religious man and can "speak to the people." Voted Republican in 2000 and was going to vote in 2004 but didn't get around to it.

5. Bricklayer, California. Work was good during the recent housing boom, which he attributed to Bush probusiness politics. Feels government should stay out of the free market, and regularly quarrels over politics with other bricklayers at his work site. He is worried about sending his daughter to college. Voted Democratic in 2000, Republican in 2004.

6. Insurance adjuster, Indiana. The insurance industry better off under Bush's attempts to limit liability and regulation. Has doubts about how the war on terrorism is being waged. Wants the kind of leadership her dad says an Eisenhower could provide. Thinks America is its own worst enemy. Voted Republican in 2000 and in 2004.

7. Retired postal carrier, Wyoming. Is a Democrat, like the other mail carriers he knows. Fears that the Republicans want to squeeze moderate-income federal employees like himself. Wished he had been able to wear a Clinton button at work. He and his wife disagree every night at the dinner table over politics. He votes straight Democrat, she straight Republican.

8. Fruit grower, Oregon. Apple crops have been bad. Republicans claim they are for small business, like her orchard, but they are really not. The Farm Bureau, she says, just wants to help the big growers, and always is pushing for subsidies for them. Her son is draft age, and she says they will go to Canada if that happens. Voted Nader in 2000, and Kerry in 2004.

9. Teacher, Texas. The uncontrolled immigration over the border has got to stop. Local people who can't speak Spanish can't get work. Her students don't understand her lessons. It did not help that John Kerry was French. She voted Bush in 2000 and in 2004.

These personal stories provide a window on some obstacles we must overcome in order to explain a current vote in 2004. One beguiling approach would be to identify the critical life event that took place just before the vote. But this straightforward method poses serious intellectual difficulties. For example, we could enumerate different categories of causes that appeared behind these nine votes: (1) political interest; (2) economic issues; (3) fear of war; (4) religious conviction; (5) cost of education; (6) leadership; (7) social pressures; (8) family concerns: (9) ethnicity. For instance, in case 4, religion might be judged most important, whereas in case 6 political leadership stands out.

However, in examining each of the cases fully, one cannot help but see that multiple reasons can be brought forward for each vote choice in 2004. But it makes no sense to develop a special theory for each voter. A scientific theory of electoral behavior has to apply across a number of voters, fitting them as data points into an overall explanatory model of behavior. Economic concerns were raised by several voters. But why by some and not by others? And among those who mentioned economics, how important was it compared to other issues? Finally, did that stimulus generate a reliable political response?

Confronted with such a variety of possible forces affecting the vote, we seek some way of imposing a higher theoretical order on the observations. One possible approach is to limit ourselves to broad conceptual variables. For instance, if we looked at two possibilities, economics and war, we might give at least a partial accounting of the majority of these cases. Another way would be to predict the person's vote in 2004 from his or her vote in 2000, which would work in over half the cases. Still, either approach discards the rest of our knowledge about each case. For example, what about the important characteristics of family and social pressure, that some expressed? These and other variables seem worth incorporating systematically in a fuller theory of the vote. What is required is a framework that encompasses each of these factors and more, allowing for multiple levels of explanation, with each factor having a clear status in the explanatory system. Our goal is to offer such an explanatory system.

A STRUCTURE FOR THEORY: THE FUNNEL OF CAUSALITY

To understand the causal flow that leads to voting behavior, think of the causal chain as constituting a funnel, a funnel of causality. This is, of course, just a metaphorical funnel (see figure 2.1)[1] that provides a useful way to think about the causal process. The main axis of our funnel is the time dimension, with events following one another over time from the mouth of the funnel to its tip. There are a multitude of potential causes at the mouth, and they narrow down to cause vote turnout and vote direction in a particular election at the tip. Thus, if we were trying to explain voting in 2004, then Election Day 2004 would be at the tip of the funnel. If we took a cross-section of the funnel (a plane at a right angle

---

1. The funnel metaphor and the broader theory of this chapter are based on a term paper written by Philip Converse (see Converse 2006, 606).

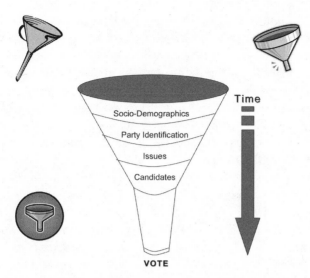

Fig. 2.1. Funnel of causality model

to the time axis), we would have a representation of all the occurrences at the corresponding point in time, such as the images of the candidates and the campaign issues being discussed the day before the first presidential debate in 2004. This metaphor usefully reminds us that the conceptual nature of a variable includes its time status. However, working through to develop a theory of voting behavior requires attention to more than just the time dimension.

First, it is necessary to distinguish between relevant and irrelevant factors. For example, a young mother may plan to vote after her babysitter comes to the house to take charge of her children, but the sitter never shows up, so the mother does not get to the polls. Why the sitter did not show up is beyond our theoretical interests; the causes are best seen as irrelevant to our theory of voting turnout. If, by contrast, the mother lacked sufficient motivation to vote, that would be of theoretical interest to us, but the accidental conditions that threw off her plans need not be incorporated in our theory. This point seems obvious, but it has an important implication: it will diminish our predictive success, since some factors that affect behavior are ruled out of consideration. Our predictions will not be perfect, since we are ignoring some factors.

Second, we distinguish between factors of which the person is aware ("personal conditions") and those of which he or she is not aware ("external conditions"). Consider the funnel for the 2004 election at the point before most voters were aware that John Kerry was going to run for the presidency (and had little idea of who he was). We seek to study the person's perception of the political world, and Kerry was irrelevant to that perception before he became an active candidate. Electoral laws constitute another set of external considerations. For example, registration laws affect whether a person can be a lawful voter on Election Day, but the citizen need only operate within those laws and need not perceive that laws may differ in another state. Why one person was nominated rather than another, and why the electoral laws are what they are, are examples of matters that we need not consider in our analysis of voting behavior in a particular election. Those are both important questions, but extraneous to our focus on the determinants of individual voting behavior. They might be relevant matters if we went back deep into the funnel, but we can put them aside when we analyze the behavior at its tip.

Third, we distinguish between political and nonpolitical conditions, though this is not an easy distinction to make. For example, economic conditions are not inherently political, but campaigns often make them politically relevant. That example points to an important point: the events that are political become a larger proportion of the events as one moves closer to the election and thus the tip of the funnel. By Election Day, there will be greater focus on one set of events that are socially defined as political, with others being cleaved off and therefore having no effect on voting. The events that are left by Election Day will be highly political in nature.

It is important to recognize that external nonpolitical events can become personal and political by the time of the election. External events become personal through a communication process, as when the media made people aware that John Kerry was running for the presidency and as people developed impressions of him through the media. Nonpolitical events become political through a "political translation" process. Thus, the state of the economy becomes a political factor through a political translation process, often aided by the parties politicizing economic news.

STRATEGIES OF EXPLANATION

The framework proposed here, a funnel of causality, is meant to be all-encompassing. We have not excluded any set of factors: the political candidates are relevant and so are the issues, influences from one's current family and from one's family of origin, social demographic factors, con-versations about the election with friends and coworkers, the media, and countless other matters. Investigating all of these creates a large research agenda for those studying voting behavior.

The *Voter Decides* (Campbell, Gurin, and Miller 1954) introduced an attitudinal approach to understanding voting. It focused on predictors near the tip of the funnel that are close to the voting decision: particu-larly a citizen's orientation toward the parties, the issues, and the candi-dates in an election. That approach leads to a parsimonious model, using a small number of variables that have a high degree of explana-tory power since they are proximate to the voting decision. This mode of explanation follows Kurt Lewin's "field theory," in which the field at one point in time is seen as dependent on the field at the previous point in time. According to this approach, the effects of distant events (such as 9/11) on voting in 2004 must be present in some manner immediately prior to the voting. For example, Republicans might be favored on for-eign and defense policy, and 9/11 would have its effect on voting through that preference. Similarly, if a person's vote in 2004 was affected by one's parents' partisanship, the effect would probably operate through a more proximate variable, presumably the voter's own party identifica-tion, which encapsulates all of a person's previous associations with po-litical parties.

The use of attitudes proximate to the vote to explain behavior has considerable explanatory power. For one thing, extraneous factors are minimized if we consider predictors close to the vote. For another, our surveys are conducted fairly close to the election, so that they can mea-sure attitudes that are proximate—though we also measure long-term matters. We prefer to measure current attitudes rather than asking re-spondents about their past opinions, since recall questions are generally less reliable. Finding which proximate variables affect the vote provides direction for further research on the forces closer to the mouth of the funnel that cause those proximate variables.

Proximate attitudes also have disadvantages as explanations of votes. One potential problem is that the variables are so proximate to the vote decision that they are actually caused by the vote decision rather than causing it. For example, those who have decided to vote for the Republican nominee because they prefer his foreign policy may also conclude that he is better on domestic issues, reversing our usual assumption as to causal direction. Second, measuring only attitudes may allow researchers to predict behavior but may not go back deep enough into the funnel to permit good understanding of the causes of behavior. This suggests that we need also to consider variables that are deeper in the funnel in order to obtain a broader understanding of voting behavior.

A sociological approach to voting that focuses on the social demographics of voting does go deeper into the funnel. However, these variables may not have political significance unless a process of translation makes them political. We would expect the predictive power of social demographics to be weaker than that of proximate attitudes because the former are more distant from the dependent voting behavior. Further, social demographics do not change fast enough to account for fluctuations in the vote from election to election. Establishing that a particular social group tends to vote for a particular party has little theoretical significance, because the group's voting pattern may eventually change. It is important to determine the factors that lead that group to vote for a particular party, since they can provide leverage on the conditions under which the group's vote may change.

COMMENTARY AND CONTROVERSY

The Funnel of Causality

It is useful to consider how the basic theoretical model presented in this chapter and proposed alternatives have fared over the years. The concept of a "funnel of causality" is very simple but does effectively organize several factors that together affect the voting decision. Yet the funnel model has not always been treated well in the subsequent literature. An abridged version of The American Voter, published in 1964, omitted this theoretical chapter, depriving the book of its underlying framework.

Later work by the Michigan researchers did not explicitly employ the funnel model but instead differentiated between long-term and short-term factors that affected the vote (Campbell 1964). Social demographic factors such as gender, race, and social class are long term. Two important political predispositions are also considered long term: party identification and political ideology. By contrast, the candidates competing in a campaign and the issues raised in it are considered short-term factors. A citizen's conversations with family and friends about how to vote are also short term. The long-term factors can be seen as providing a baseline from which short-term, campaign-specific factors operate.

Attitudes versus Rational Choice

The focus in *The American Voter* on attitudes, nowadays referred to as a "social-psychological approach," remains important today, but there are several alternatives. One in particular, the rational-choice approach, was developed a few years before *The American Voter* was written. The authors were aware of it and included in their last chapter a discussion of Anthony Downs's (1957) rational-choice perspective, posed there in terms of factors affecting party strategies in choosing positions on a liberal-conservative dimension so as to attract votes. (We discuss this further in chapter 15.)

The general rational-choice approach explains voting in terms of a person's self-interest. Whether or not a person votes depends on that person's cost-benefit analysis of the potential gains from his or her preferred candidate being elected in comparison to the costs they must pay to vote—the time involved in registering and voting, gathering information about the election, and so on. Which party the person votes for is determined in a pure rational-choice model by which party's ideological position is closest to the voter's.

The rational-choice approach has over time become closely identified with the idea of economic voting. Indeed, the approach developed out of economics, and voting for one's economic self-interest is seen as rational. This assumption has led to considerable attention to the macroeconomic state of the economy as the election approaches, as well as to the effect of individual economic situations on decisions—for example, whether the unemployed are more likely to vote, or whether those whose economic status is slipping are more likely to vote against the incumbent party. Economic voting is fully considered in chapter 13.

Alternative Approaches

In addition to rational choice, several additional alternatives to the social-psychological approach may be delineated. A sociological approach focuses on the social group correlates of voting, while a psychological approach focuses on the effect of personality factors, such as whether voters with authoritarian tendencies are more likely to favor a particular party. The pure social and psychological approaches were dormant for a long time, but have received greater attention in recent years. There is also a historical-institutional approach, which emphasizes the effects of historical changes and voting laws; and there is political psychology, which applies insights derived from modern cognitive psychology. If this broad set of approaches does not suffice, communication scholars focus on the effects of the media, while geographers focus on the spatial correlates of voting.

The authors of *The American Voter* would have a clear response to this cacophony of alternatives. Today their funnel of causality is not considered a high-level theory, but they would contend that the model provides an appropriate organizing framework that can encompass all of the factors we have mentioned, from long-term sociological, psychological, historical-institutional, and geographic factors to short-term social-psychological, political-psychological, economic, and communication factors. The funnel model is indeed comprehensive, but *The American Voter* emphasized just a small portion of the funnel: party identification, candidate orientations, and attitudes on issues.

The emphasis on attitudes proximate to the vote has been controversial, as the authors expected, because they are so close to the vote as to be virtually equivalent to the person's voting decision. In particular, if one measures attitudes toward the Democratic and Republican candidates just prior to an election, one would expect respondents to vote for the candidate they like the most. There is no theoretic distance. Indeed, some researchers use the voter's relative rating of the major party nominees, rather than the vote itself, as their dependent variable since the relative rating provides a continuous measure that can be analyzed by standard statistical techniques that would strictly speaking be inappropriate for a dichotomous vote variable.

Of course, arguments can also be made against the other models. As the authors of *The American Voter* argue in chapter 2, a pure sociological model fails in that people's social demographics are stable and cannot explain variations in election outcomes, let alone why groups associate with one party or the other. When the rational-choice model argues that people vote in their self-interest as they define it, the argument borders on the tautological. This is not to say that the attitudinal model in *The American Voter* is the correct one, just that it is no less correct than the alternatives. Thus, we have argued in this chapter for considering the full range of factors that affect the vote; doing so results in a more realistic assessment than does focusing on a single set of causal factors.

SECTION II

Political Attitudes and the Vote

CHAPTER 3

Perceptions of the Parties and Candidates

Voters cast their ballots in secret but not in the dark. To understand a voter's choice, we must come to grips with the way a voter sees the elements that enter into the decision. Foremost among them are the candidates on the ballot, the parties they represent, and the issues on which the parties and candidates may take different positions. Like Plato's cave-dwellers, some voters glimpse only flickering shadows of these objects, especially if they are complicated issues of policy. Regardless of how distorted these perceptions may be, the decision to cast a certain vote—or not to vote at all—makes sense only in terms of the subjective imprint of the political world in the citizen's mind. We believe that electoral choice is guided by a simple premise: Whatever does not register in a voter's mind cannot make a difference in the voter's behavior.

If a voter's electoral choice is guided by a "cognitive map," to use Hyman's famous phrase, this is not an objective drawing of the political world. In fact, it is an affectively colored map. Voters are guided not by accurate perceptions of candidates (accurate in some agreed-on sense), but by *evaluations* of the candidates in positive or negative terms. One citizen's evaluation may sharply differ from another's. What one voter sees as decisiveness in a candidate, another voter sees as rashness. Each of these subjective assessments is real to the person who makes it. Of critical importance for behavior, the positively toned perception is likely to motivate a vote for the candidate so perceived, while the negatively toned perception does so for the opponent. Moreover, a shift of the affective balance of such perceptions over time helps explain the dynamics of electoral change.

THE INFLUENCE OF HISTORICAL REALITY

Despite the subjectivity of assessments, individuals do not have unlimited leeway to construct their own image of the political world. Some facts are difficult to interpret in different ways. Profound historical events such as economic depressions, wars, domestic upheavals, and major scandals are bound to leave similar impressions in the general public. As the salient facts change, therefore, general perceptions move along with them. For this reason, one cannot account for common images of parties and their candidates without recognizing the influence of the flow of historical reality.

This chapter focuses on the impact of changes in the political environment on perceptions of parties and candidates. In doing so we should not lose sight of the distinction between image and reality. The two are not the same. The translation from one to the other is not automatic or identical for all members of the mass public. It is worth reminding ourselves that political reality can influence voters at the polls only by getting into their mind and under their skin. Thus, we have to pay attention to psychological processes of cognition and affect.

Given the importance of perceptions in motivating behavior, it is imperative to learn how changes in the real world of politics alter the voters' cognitive map of that world. This insight will lead us a long way toward an understanding of the changing fortunes of the political parties in national elections. To gauge the images of candidates and parties held by the American electorate, we turn to data that have been collected by asking respondents what they like or dislike about those individuals and institutions.

Before exploring responses to those questions, let us note several limitations of this analysis. Given our focus on the two most recent presidential elections, we are considering only a short time horizon. Observations from two national surveys spanning a four-year interval may make a strong case for the effect of historical reality on images, but will fall short of definitive proof. In particular, historical events may have determined popular images long before the period in which our surveys asked about perceptions. It remains a matter of inference to trace the imprint of past events in the content and tenor of images recorded today. What is more, we capture only the end result of an intricate process that yields an affectively laden perception. Our data do not systematically measure the elements of political reality or the content and tenor of their coverage in the mass media. We do not doubt the importance of mass communication for the formation of popular perceptions; we simply lack the measures to explore this factor.

A CASE STUDY OF PERCEPTIONS

Our study examines the public image of George W. Bush, as a candidate in 2000 and as president in 2004, of his two Democratic opponents, of the Democratic and Republican parties, and of the issues and groups with which the parties and candidates are linked. Comparing these images over the four-year interval yields a rich portrait of popular perceptions of the major objects in American politics and points to important changes of content, tenor, and salience in public images. The instrument to capture popular perceptions was designed, by way of open-ended questions, to elicit unprompted expressions, not ratings on preestablished scales. Individuals were given an opportunity to volunteer how and why they felt the way they did about national politics, specifically what they *liked* and *disliked* about each party and candidate.[1]

The question setup was predicated on the assumption that the public's image of politics has an affective flavor. Individuals do not associate certain attributes to parties and candidates neutrally, but with either favorable or unfavorable feelings. The two-party system has imposed a bipolar structure on this evaluative dimension, where being favorable to one party (or its candidate) means being unfavorable to the opposing party (candidate). Hence, in presenting the responses to questions in tables, we typically lump together pro-Democratic and anti-Republican

---

1. For this purpose, a standard set of eight open-ended questions was used in preelection interviews of 2000 and 2004 (as has been the NES practice since 1952). For each of the parties and for each of the major-party candidates one question sought favorable reactions and one question sought unfavorable reactions. For the parties, the questions read: "Is there anything in particular that you like (dislike) about the Democratic (Republican) Party?" For the candidates, the questions read: "Is there anything in particular about George W. Bush (John Kerry / Al Gore) that might make you vote for (against) him?" Respondents who answered yes to a given question were then queried, "What is that?" and further probed, "Anything else?" until they said no. The answer to each of those questions was coded according to the NES "party-candidate master code" (see appendix of the National Election Studies, 2000 and 2004). For each answer, up to five distinct comments were coded. They are included as separate variables in the data sets of the election studies.

references in one affective category and compare its magnitude with that of pro-Republican and anti-Democratic references grouped in the other category. Now and then, of course, it will be instructive to find out how much of that overall feeling comes from liking one side as opposed to disliking the other. The findings presented in this chapter will not only illuminate the dynamics of attitude change, but also fill in important details for the more abstract statistical analysis of electoral choice provided in subsequent chapters.

Though many of the responses to candidates and parties were stirred by the campaigns that immediately preceded the two elections examined here, the echoes of an earlier past are unmistakable. The two major political parties, after all, have been around for a century and a half. A good part of their public images has been a fixture of political discourse for quite some time. Many notions that emerge in the responses today originated during the Great Depression and the subsequent New Deal. Some voters enjoying retirement in 2000 may well remember the creation of Social Security and the desperation of the breadlines. And only a generation separated their parents from the era of the Civil War and Reconstruction.

At the same time, the images of the presidential candidates are less burdened by the events of the past. Though defined in large measure by the parties whose banners they carry, candidates bring novel and distinctive features into the political arena, including personal characteristics and achievements or failures in office. A change in the public image of the political world is far more likely to originate with actions by political leaders than with anything the parties might be able to do.

WAR AND PEACE

In recent years the historical event that has most dramatically altered the public's image is the terrorist attacks of September 11, 2001. A comparison of responses given to surveys during the two Bush elections establishes three points of impact that can be traced to the 9/11 attacks and their aftermath, in particular, the decisions to invade Afghanistan and then Iraq. One is that "war and peace" turned from a negligible to a dominant concern for the American public. Now candidates and parties would be measured by the demands exacted by this newly salient issue. Two, the partisan tone of the public's responses was quite dissonant. Perhaps surprisingly for such a traumatic experience, neither one of the major parties gained a decisive edge over the other in the broad domain of war and peace. And third, the salience of war and peace put a premium on qualities in the candidates commensurable with the president's role as commander in chief. That proved of great help in the short run to the White House incumbent, George W. Bush, and hurt the prospects of the challenger, John Kerry, his wartime service in Vietnam notwithstanding.

As shown by table 3.1, the concern of the American public with war and peace surged dramatically between 2000 and 2004. With the Cold War over and no comparable confrontation looming, in 2000 this issue hardly mattered in appraisals of the parties and candidates. Whatever opinion registered in the war-and-peace responses that we have examined gave the edge to the Republican side, but in the manner of a fish in a tiny pond. Four years later the pond had grown almost sevenfold. By 2004, the volume of references to parties and candidates in terms of war and peace exceeded that of any other issue domain.

The surge, however, did not extend the Republican edge on war and peace. It was a mixed blessing for them, at best. Indeed, by 2004, the partisan balance on this issue had swung against the Republicans. Most of that had to do with the war in Iraq, as table 3.2 makes clear. Responses to the open-ended questions about parties and candidates were highly unfavorable to the Bush administration in connection with the

TABLE 3.1. References to War and Peace

	2000	2004
Pro-Democratic and anti-Republican	90	1,171
Pro-Republican and anti-Democratic	223	897
Total	313	2,068

Note: In this and subsequent tables the number of responses in 2004 has been increased by the ratio of the size of the 2004 sample to the size of the 2000 sample to make possible a direct comparison of frequencies in the two years. The effect of the adjustment is to equate frequencies whose size relative to the size of their respective samples is the same. In reading these tables it should be kept in mind that one respondent could make more than one reference; hence the number of references may be larger than the number of individuals mentioning a given subject.

TABLE 3.2. References to the Iraq War and Terrorism in 2004

	Iraq War	Terrorism
Pro-Democratic and anti-Republican	727	91
Pro-Republican and anti-Democratic	225	298
Total	952	389

ongoing involvement of the United States in Iraq. Almost half of all war-and-peace references in 2004 concerned the Iraq war, and they ran better than three to one against the Republican side. In contrast, references to terrorism favored Republicans by about that same ratio. The public strongly applauded the Bush administration's war on terrorism in the aftermath of the 9/11 attacks, yet the issue commanded far less attention than did the Iraq war. If we judge by the pattern of these responses, it appears that the claim of President Bush that the Iraq war was an extension of the war on terrorism fell mostly on deaf ears.

The edge on the issue of terrorism nonetheless prevented Republicans from being swamped by negative responses in the war-and-peace domain. It must also be noted that while the responses to Iraq were dominated by negative feelings about Republicans, there was not a great deal of positive comment about the Democrats.[2] Meanwhile, much of the reaction to terrorism was favorable for Republicans rather than unfavorable for Democrats. Hence it seems doubtful that the Democratic Party stands to gain a long-term advantage on the war-and-peace dimension once the Iraq war is settled.

It has been claimed that in American history foreign war has never anchored or realigned public attitudes toward the parties. The war that did have long-lasting consequences for political life in this country was fought on American soil. The politics of the region where the Civil War was fought reverberated for more than a century. While no foreign war compares in impact, it can be argued that U.S. interventions in Korea and especially Vietnam left the public with a sense that Republicans had a better handle on war and peace than the Democrats. What is so striking about the responses to war and peace in 2000 is that eight years of relative peace—in the sense of avoiding long and bloody American involvements abroad—under the Clinton administration failed to give the Democrats an edge in this domain. It took a costly and contentious intervention by the Bush administration in Iraq to do so. Success in the war on terror, however, might help the Republican Party restore its lead in the area of war and peace. In the short run, at least, the prominence of war and peace appears to have left an imprint of another sort that was

---

2. This is in sharp contrast to the pattern of the wartime election of 1952. While the incumbent Democrats drew a strongly negative response over their handling of the war in Korea, war-and-peace references to the Republican Party and to its candidate, Eisenhower, were strongly favorable (Campbell, Gurin, and Miller 1954, 57–61; also Campbell et al. 1960, 49–53).

highly favorable to the Republican incumbent in comparison to his Democratic challenger. That effect has to do with the public's assessment of candidate qualities in the 2004 election, to which we will turn later in this chapter.

DOMESTIC ISSUES

Within the domestic arena, we also see evidence of historical reality intruding on popular views of the parties and candidates. References to the economy, broadly speaking, turned markedly unfavorable for the Republicans between 2000 and 2004, as the U.S. economy went into recession. The salience of the economic domain rose somewhat, judging by the total number of references in table 3.3, and much of the increase reflected misgivings over bad times under the Bush administration as well as revived memories of good times under Democratic administrations. Dating back to the experience of the Great Depression and the recovery under the Roosevelt administration, the Democrats had acquired an image as the party of prosperity, in contrast to the Republicans as the party of bad times. For the most part of history since then, the Democratic Party has enjoyed a marked edge over the Republicans in managing the economy.

One way for Republicans to blunt that edge would be proof of success in avoiding economic downturns when the party was in office. The other way would be for Democrats to squander their advantage by having the economy slip into economic distress on their watch. By 2000, both of these conditions had come true at various times and established a more even playing field for the parties in the economic domain. In the 1980 election, the Democrats lost the White House amid ill feelings about high inflation and recession, aptly captured by Ronald Reagan's question in the debate with Carter, "Are you better off than you were four years ago?" Four years later, economic recovery helped Reagan secure a landslide victory. Prosperity no longer was a Democratic trademark. Moreover, the

TABLE 3.3. References to Economic Conditions and Policies

	2000	2004
Pro-Democratic and anti-Republican	468	714
Pro-Republican and anti-Democratic	453	504
Total	921	1,218

Reagan formula for economic success, in particular tax cuts, had given his party a clear advantage over the Democrats in the way government handled the economy. Hence it may not be surprising that the boom of the 1990s under the Clinton administration failed to restore the Democratic edge in the area of economic management.

While on the specifics of good times versus bad times, the Democrats were highly favored in 2000, those references made up barely one-quarter of the pro-Democratic volume reported in table 3.3. Prosperity in 2000 was helpful for Democrats, but it was not a big deal—a sign perhaps that good times (i.e., good news) matter less than bad times (bad news). We should also recognize that when one considers the other component of the results in table 3.3, economic policy, especially taxes and spending, the Republican Party has the upper hand with the American public, a legacy that dates back at least to the Reagan years.

Social welfare policies are another domestic domain where the Democratic Party gained a commanding lead in popular feelings during the Depression and the New Deal, especially with programs like Social Security. By 2000, however, much of that lead had eroded. As shown in table 3.4, most responses still approve of the Democratic Party for its handling of these issues, but its advantage over the Republican Party is quite modest. Gone are the days when Republicans had to fear for their political life if they proposed tinkering with Social Security or cutting social programs. Instead, as responses in our interviews make clear, the Democratic Party nowadays suffers from a widespread image of being "too liberal." When a sweeping welfare reform was proposed by a Republican Congress after the 1994 election, it was adopted with the support of a Democratic president. At the same time, initiatives of the Bush administration to extend and even expand social welfare policies, most notably in education and prescription drugs, took the partisan sting out of this domain. As a token of appreciation, the public's concern with issues of

TABLE 3.4. References to Social Welfare Policies

	2000	2004
Pro-Democratic and anti-Republican	1,315	904
Pro-Republican and anti-Democratic	1,071	703
Total	2,386	1,607

Note: This tabulation is limited to domestic policies clearly in the area of social welfare. References to economic policies such as taxes, regulation, etc., or matters of civil rights and moral issues are not included.

social welfare, as indicated by the total number of responses, lessened noticeably during the first Bush term.

A domain of public debate where the Republican Party expected to gain ground in the first Bush term was the one concerned with moral issues, or as some see it, the "culture war." The moral deficiencies of Bill Clinton in the White House had personalized these concerns at the highest level of government, raising a cloud over the prospects of the Democratic candidate in the 2000 election. Republican strategists put great hope in the power of moral issues to solidify the party's electoral support for the foreseeable future. Opposition to gay marriage and support for traditional values with a patriotic cast, especially in the aftermath of 9/11, sounded like a winning formula. Yet instead of gaining support relative to the Democrats, Republicans under Bush lost popular approval for their handling of moral issues, as shown in table 3.5. The battles against abortion, gay rights, and stem cell research did not earn the party additional support among those who cared. On the contrary, it cost Republicans in popular approval. What is more, Republicans did not make much headway with their efforts to change the public agenda. While responses to moral issues did increase between 2000 and 2004, the gain was paltry. Even worse for the Republicans, in the 2004 election this issue domain lagged far behind issues like war and peace, social welfare, and economics in the responses examined here. Contrary to the Election Day exit poll, moral concerns were not the dominant issue in the Bush-Kerry contest, according to the results reported here.

SOCIAL GROUPS

Despite efforts over the years to improve the party's record on economic and social policies, the Republican Party has proved spectacularly unsuccessful in changing its group image, which dates back to the Depression era. In overwhelming numbers Americans still look favorably upon the Democratic Party and unfavorably upon the Republican Party because of

TABLE 3.5. References to Moral Issues

	2000	2004
Pro-Democratic and anti-Republican	321	412
Pro-Republican and anti-Democratic	469	477
Total	790	889

the social groups each of them is thought to promote and protect. There is no discernible movement between 2000 and 2004, as table 3.6 shows, and the lopsided ratio in favor of the Democrats is a faithful replica of the pattern in the 1950s, when responses of the kind examined here were first elicited. Given the enormous strides of American society toward affluence in the past half century, that is nothing short of astounding.

The Democratic Party still enjoys a groundswell of good feeling for favoring the "common man," "little people," "working people," the "poor," the "needy," and so on, whereas the Republican Party is chastised for being in bed with "big business," the "rich," the "upper class." Expressions like these sound like echoes of the past, in particular the desperate experience of the Depression and the appeal of FDR's New Deal to the forgotten part of America. Yet images of this sort are hard to sustain without reinforcement. Republican tax policies that "favor the rich" do not mute the stark contrast of group associations in the public mind, while Democratic proposals for "fair" tax cuts remind people of this enduring legacy. It is noteworthy that one of the biggest social changes in the last half of the twentieth century, namely the growth of the middle class, seems to have done nothing to level the images of the parties. References to the "middle class" in our surveys invariably favor the Democratic Party. The Democrats nowadays are approved as the party of the "middle class," as they were the champions of the "working class" in the 1930s. Whatever image right-wing pundits typically conjure up of the "Democrat" Party—beholden to "secular progressives," radical environmentalists, feminists, gay activists, and flag burners—finds scant resonance in the popular image of the Democratic Party. The party with a group image problem remains the Republicans.

MANAGEMENT OF GOVERNMENT

A party in office for a long time is bound to suffer a decline in public esteem for its honesty and efficiency in running the government. There

TABLE 3.6. References to Groups

	2000	2004
Pro-Democratic and anti-Republican	1,506	1,492
Pro-Republican and anti-Democratic	292	238
Total	1,798	1,730

TABLE 3.7. References to Government Management

	2000	2004
Pro-Democratic and anti-Republican	1,189	1,459
Pro-Republican and anti-Democratic	1,322	1,618
Total	2,511	3,077

were signs of that in 2000, after eight years of the Clinton administration, as can be seen in table 3.7. Appraisals of the parties' abilities to manage government were slightly less favorable to the Democrats that year than to Republicans. As with other views of parties and candidates, long-held beliefs undoubtedly echoed in current assessments here. Democrats are not generally known as the party of "businesslike administration" operating at high "efficiency" with "cautious spending." Whatever the record, Republicans are more likely to get a free pass on management than Democrats. They also fared quite well during the first term of the Bush administration. Not losing the party's edge while running the government must be seen as an accomplishment.

What is astonishing, however, is the public's lack of concern with highly publicized scandals of the Clinton administration. Barely a handful of respondents in 2000 brought up Whitewater, White House sleepovers, or campaign finance irregularities, and only a few more mentioned Clinton's sexual affairs. "It's time for a change" was a comment voiced rarely in 2000. Given that Bill Clinton was only the third president to be subjected to impeachment, it may seem shocking how few responses in 2000 referred to such a grave matter of Clinton's tenure.[3]

The response to Clinton administration scandals, or better, the lack of a response, demonstrates an important but often overlooked principle of public opinion. Intense coverage of an issue in the media along with convulsion in the government over it is no guarantee that the general public cares. Whatever the revulsion against Clinton's conduct, most Americans did not approve of him any less for the job he was doing as president (managing the government, in other words), nor did they connect his personal shortcomings with their general image of the Democratic Party. That is not to say views of Clinton were of no consequence for evaluation of the candidates in the 2000 election.

---

3. Technically, Richard Nixon was not impeached, but impeachment proceedings in the House of Representatives led to a committee vote in favor of impeachment.

CANDIDATE ATTRIBUTES

A presidential election is a contest where the electorate awards the grand prize to just one individual. The changing cast of contestants makes a big difference in the balance of partisan strength from one election to the next. A party that can count on only a minority of faithful supporters in the general public is well advised to recruit a candidate with attributes that have wide popular appeal. No candidate, of course, can totally escape association with the foreign and domestic policies, or with the group interests, of his party. But this tie may vary a great deal based on the background of the candidate and the circumstances of a given election. Of great importance is the degree to which a candidate is connected to a previous administration. Someone, for example, who served as vice president in the outgoing administration is likely to reap the benefit or pay the price for the deeds of his senior partner, at least as they are appraised by the public. The same goes for a candidate with a family member who previously served in the same office. For many voters, these connections may be a good enough reason to support (or reject) a current candidate. However, candidates need not be much concerned with associations with group interests (see table 3.8). That is largely a party reserve, and for the most part the candidates are ignored. The group-party images persist as candidates come and go.

TABLE 3.8. References to Groups by Party and Candidate

	2000	2004
Associated with the Republican Party	707	642
Associated with the Democratic Party	680	702
Associated with Bush	193	214
Associated with Gore (2000), Kerry (2004)	217	172
Total	1,797	1,730

TABLE 3.9. References to Domestic Issues by Party and Candidate

	2000	2004
Associated with the Republican Party	1,496	1,263
Associated with the Democratic Party	1,541	1,380
Associated with Bush	1,185	952
Associated with Gore (2000), Kerry (2004)	1,156	784
Total	5,378	4,379

That was not the case, however, for domestic issues in the two Bush elections. Both Bush and Gore were heavily appraised in terms of domestic policies, though somewhat less than were their respective parties (see table 3.9). If that is surprising for nonincumbent candidates, we have to remember that both Bush and Gore had obvious connections to previous administrations. Basing its assessment on those connections, the public may have had little trouble passing judgments about what the two candidates stood for on domestic policies. Although it may seem odd that Bush was more widely appraised on domestic issues in 2000, when he ran as a candidate seeking the office, than he was as an incumbent seeking reelection in 2004, the decline is easily explained. The volume of responses to domestic issues declined for all parties and candidates, as foreign policy, in particular war and peace, eclipsed domestic policy in the aftermath of 9/11.

Between 2000 and 2004, references to George W. Bush in terms of foreign policy rose 15-fold, from a trickle to a flood, which surpassed references to any other candidate in any domain in the two elections in which he ran (see table 3.10). For a wartime president, that goes with the job description. In the 2004 election, foreign policy was *the* battleground for the two candidates, but only for them, not their parties. The latter were bystanders, neither hindering nor helping the candidates in this domain. While the sitting president garnered far more attention on foreign policy than did his challenger, in this case bigger was not better. Much of the response to Bush on foreign policy, as might be expected from table 3.2, referred to the Iraq war, and most of that response was unfavorable. In effect, the battleground over war and peace in 2004 had only one contestant, who was wrestling with this issue rather than his challenger in the election. But that is perhaps to be expected with an incumbent seeking confirmation from the electorate.

The most obvious connection of a candidate is, of course, with his or

TABLE 3.10. References to Foreign Issues by Party and Candidate

	2000	2004
Associated with the Republican Party	147	352
Associated with the Democratic Party	93	178
Associated with Bush	81	1,245
Associated with Gore (2000), Kerry (2004)	57	421
Total	378	2,196

her party. That is how the ballot identifies candidates for office. Nonetheless, few respondents cite a candidate's party as an important reason in their evaluation, even though most voters, as we shall see in a later chapter, hold favorable or unfavorable views of candidates largely on the basis of the voter's own partisan loyalties. What table 3.11 indicates, nonetheless, is that a candidate who has held the office for a term (as Bush had in 2004) is less likely to be evaluated in terms of party than one who is trying to gain it for the first time.

The bulk of references to candidates concerns personal attributes, including record and experience, qualifications and abilities, and personality traits (see table 3.12). While respondents referred more often to Vice President Al Gore's attributes in 2000 than to Texas governor George W. Bush's, Bush surprisingly trailed his Democratic challenger four years later in the volume of personal attributes mentioned by respondents. Whatever the reason for that pattern, bigger was not better for the Democratic candidates. Both Gore and Kerry attracted less favorable attention, on balance, than did George W. Bush. The contrast is especially stark in 2004, where negative comments about John Kerry outnumber positive ones by nearly 50 percent. In our examination of the public's image of parties and candidates we have encountered few broad domains where the Republicans have held the better cards. They

TABLE 3.11. References to Candidates in Terms of Party

	2000	2004
Favorable to Bush	86	9
Unfavorable to Bush	85	9
Favorable to Gore (2000), Kerry (2004)	101	102
Unfavorable to Gore (2000), Kerry (2004)	52	17
Total	324	137

TABLE 3.12. References to Personal Attributes of the Candidates

	2000	2004
Favorable to Bush	968	1,165
Unfavorable to Bush	945	916
Total	1,913	2,081
Favorable to Gore (2000), Kerry (2004)	1,006	957
Unfavorable to Gore (2000), Kerry (2004)	1,125	1,416
Total	2,131	2,373

do so here, and this may have been the factor that contributed most to their win on Election Day. We are especially curious to find out the specific attributes that changed between the two elections and put Bush in a much stronger position vis-à-vis his Democratic challenger.

A detailed breakdown of favorable references to Bush (table 3.13) points to one attribute, in particular, where the public's image of him soared: being decisive. Only a handful of Americans tapped him for this quality in 2000, when he ran as someone untested in national policy-making. Bush was also seen more as a leader and a "uniter," to use his phrase. At the same time, having to make decisions (being "the decider," as he put it) did not dent Bush's image for honesty, the most dominating quality when he ran for president in 2000. Instead references to his honesty and

TABLE 3.13. Favorable References to Bush

	2000	2004
Generally good man, capable, experienced	70	53
Record and experience		
Military service, war record	5	5
Government experience	63	94
Close to former President Bush	48	1
Qualifications and abilities		
A leader, has vision, inspires people	17	50
Unites country	8	49
Strong, decisive	16	191
Independent	14	7
Good people around him	13	16
Intelligent	53	22
I like his ideas, stands (unspecified)	56	35
Good speaker	25	28
Good in debates	9	4
Good campaign	10	6
Lesser evil, I dislike opponent	58	51
Personal qualities		
Honest, has integrity, ideals	182	243
Sense of duty, patriotism, dedicated	17	31
Religious	29	97
Kind, warm	2	2
Likable, nice personality, I like him	61	45
Good family, family man, I like spouse	93	54
Humble	2	2

Note: Since a number of minor categories have been omitted from tables 3.13 through 3.16, the totals in these tables are somewhat smaller than the entries of table 3.12.

religious devotion increased. What seemed to help him in that first run, namely the Bush family name, no longer mattered in 2004. The pattern of responses suggests that in 2004 Bush was honored in large part for his performance as president in office. The finding that so many responses praised him as strong and decisive (someone who "sticks to his guns") seems hard to understand without the "decisions" he made in his first term, in particular the decision to go to war with Iraq in order to remove Saddam Hussein. This was not a character trait many sensed in Bush in 2000. It was the result of watching him in office and approving of the way he handled certain issues. Calling Bush "decisive" must be read as a compliment for the Iraq policy chosen. A voter opposed to a policy is not likely to call a leader decisive for adopting it. The words in that case would be wrongheaded, stubborn, reckless, and all would register with negative affect. Indeed, eight in ten respondents who saw Bush as decisive (or a leader and uniter) voiced approval of his handling of the Iraq war in response to a closed-ended question.

The flaws of the Bush image mostly receded between 2000 and 2004 (table 3.14). Misgivings about Bush being unqualified, about his lack of experience and his dependence on his family nearly vanished. Yet some flaws persisted, such as doubts about his intelligence, with some respondents not afraid to call Bush "dumb," or about his speaking ability. There is only one category where the negatives rose sharply: his honesty. Policy, not just personality, had something to do with the increase. A good portion of Americans accused Bush of having lied about the reasons for getting the country into the Iraq war. Oddly enough, as more Americans worried about honesty in the Bush presidency, more also praised this quality, as we have noted. On balance, however, the popular verdict on honesty favored Bush in 2004, as it had done already in 2000. One of the potential bombshells during the 2004 campaign that might have hurt Bush proved to be a dud. The notorious CBS story about Bush's National Guard service failed to resonate with the general public. Nor did the epithet "divider" stick. Few were troubled by Bush's religious devotion.

The responses to Bush's opponents are harder to summarize because we are dealing with two different candidates. If that sounds obvious, it nonetheless underscores the importance of the changing cast of characters for popular images. For all the similarity of party, ideology, and background, Al Gore and John Kerry evoked sharply different themes in public reactions. Favorable references to Gore emphasized his experience as a vice president in the Clinton administration, his general qualifications, and especially his intelligence (table 3.15). John Kerry, in turn, was applauded for his military record in Vietnam and also for his intelligence, but each of those attributes was dwarfed in public responses by one over which Kerry had little control—the fact that he was not Bush. A diffuse dislike for Bush strongly motivated a favorable view of Kerry.

Unfavorable responses to the Democratic candidates often proved to be mirror images of their favorable responses. Gore's experience in the Clinton administration was seen as a liability by many respondents who disapproved of Bill Clinton ("too close to Bill Clinton"). In Kerry's case, a good number of responses voiced questions about his service in Vietnam raised by the Swift boat campaign, while others were troubled by his actions and statements after coming home from Vietnam. On balance, neither candidate was able to draw much comfort from an attribute that

TABLE 3.14. Unfavorable References to Bush

	2000	2004
Generally not a good man, not qualified	76	35
Record and experience		
Joined the National Guard	4	16
Lacks experience	114	25
Too close to former President Bush	49	5
Qualifications and abilities		
Not a leader, lacks vision, uninspiring	16	11
Divides country	0	5
Weak, indecisive, wishy-washy	26	47
Not independent, run by others	32	27
Bad people around him	0	7
Dumb	87	73
I don't like his ideas, stands (unspecified)	26	33
Poor speaker	66	62
Not good in debates	13	8
Campaign tactics	47	12
Personal qualities		
Dishonest	106	157
Not dedicated	14	28
Too religious	3	20
Cold, aloof	3	7
Too negative	1	0
Not likable, I don't like him	61	68
Family background	34	48
Too cocky	29	22

defined his strength in this domain. Even more important, the biggest liabilities of each Democratic candidate registered in personal attributes where Bush had his strongest assets. In 2000 that was honesty, and in 2004 it was decisiveness. Judging from the responses in table 3.16, nothing hurt Gore more than the belief that he was not honest (if only for claiming undeserved credit for certain accomplishments). For Kerry, it was the perception that he was a "flip-flopper," someone who voted for a bill before voting against it.

This perceived trait did not arise in a vacuum. It had "Iraq war" written all over it, even though Kerry may have had problems with adopting consistent positions before. The war put most Democrats in high positions in a quandary. Taking a decisive position on it was a problem for

TABLE 3.15. Favorable References to Gore, Kerry

	2000 Gore	2004 Kerry
Generally good man, capable, experienced	91	34
Record and experience		
Military service, war record	10	91
Government experience	179	50
Close to Bill Clinton	65	—
Qualifications and abilities		
A leader, has vision, inspires people	16	18
Unites country	7	31
Strong, decisive	23	44
A good politician	14	1
Good people around him	0	3
Intelligent, understands nation's problems	82	80
I like his ideas, stands (unspecified)	62	57
Good speaker, communicates well	30	41
Good in debates	8	15
Good campaign	29	13
Lesser evil, I dislike opponent	61	157
Personal qualities		
Honest, has integrity, ideals	93	74
Sense of duty, patriotism, dedicated	28	49
Religious	10	0
Kind, warm	5	2
Likable, nice personality, I like him	54	39
A family man, good family, I like spouse	86	8
Humble	3	1

Note: — = not applicable.

the party, not just a personal one for Kerry. So the battle over personal attributes of the candidates in some way is a replay of the battle over the issue of war and peace, though with a different outcome. What one candidate appears to be losing in the arena of policy he may be able to make up in the arena of character, and vice versa. Bush gained in personal evaluation ("decisive") for a decision that cost him dearly in policy evaluation ("Iraq war"). And Kerry lost his advantage on the Iraq war as a policy issue in personal evaluations of his handling that issue (flip-flopper). In a similar vein, Gore's terrible reputation for honesty is hard to fathom without the background of Clinton's problems in that domain. With Clinton not on the ballot, his vice president bore the brunt. Questioning Gore's character was another way of voicing displeasure with the

TABLE 3.16. Unfavorable References to Gore, Kerry

	2000 Gore	2004 Kerry
Generally not a good man, not qualified	42	52
Record and experience		
Bad war record, his service in Vietnam	3	97
Not done much, voting record in Congress	43	90
Too close to Bill Clinton	175	—
Qualifications and abilities		
Not a leader, lacks charisma, uninspiring	23	34
Divides country	1	3
Weak, indecisive, wishy-washy	63	302
Too much of a politician, part of Washington crowd	74	54
Bad people around him	1	0
Unintelligent, unrealistic	13	23
I don't like his ideas, stands (unspecified)	38	52
Poor at explaining himself	34	43
Not good in debates	17	21
Campaign tactics, soliciting campaign funds	92	85
Personal qualities		
Dishonest, taking undeserved credit	305	170
Unpatriotic (after coming home from Vietnam)	—	67
Not religious	3	12
Cold, aloof	7	2
Too negative	1	56
Not likable, I don't like him	57	59
I don't like his spouse	18	29
Too cocky	18	10

Note: — = not applicable.

Clinton scandals. Attributions of personal traits to a presidential candidate are not clinical diagnoses of his psyche but largely speak to performance and policy decisions.

THE DYNAMICS OF IMAGE FORMATION

We have presented a portrait of presidential politics during the Bush
years, not as a record of history, but as seen through the affective lens of
the general public. Our summary of unprompted responses to questions
about the good and bad points of parties and candidates lets us glimpse
the "sense" ordinary Americans made of the political world in the elections of 2000 and 2004. What is more, the foregoing analysis points to
some general ideas about the dynamics of political image formation in
the American electorate.

Objects and Images

Some images are more enduring than others, and for good reasons. The
Democratic and Republican parties are long-term fixtures of the American political universe, while presidential candidates pass by like shooting stars, rarely visible for more than two presidential cycles. The images
of the parties are steeped in the lore of the past, while novelty is at a premium for candidates, although the load of the recent past, for better or
worse, also weighs on them. No image seems as impervious to change as
the one linking the parties with social groups: on one side, the Democratic Party as the champion of the less well-to-do, and on the opposite
side, the Republican Party as the protector of the rich. More than half a
century past the Great Depression, which gave rise to them, these twin
images may seem quaint, but they register with as much vitality in the
2000 elections as they did in the 1950s. These images are firmly woven
into the social fabric of the American electorate and are constantly reinforced by an individual's social ties.

In contrast, images related to matters of policy prove more changeable. The most dramatic example in our study is the question of war and
peace. In the interval between the two elections studied here, feelings
about this issue turned markedly unfavorable for Republicans. Much of
the change, as we have seen, centered on the Iraq war and registered in
perceptions of President Bush far more than it did in perceptions of the
parties. Foreign policy is a domain where the political parties have
found it hard to establish durable reputations with the electorate. They

have had comparatively greater success (or misfortune) in doing so in domestic politics, where the social implications of policy are more visible than is the case in foreign policy.

Level of Awareness

Most people do not pay a lot of attention to politics most of the time. The limited salience of national politics implies that the public is unfamiliar with new presidential candidates. Aside from their party affiliation, much of the content that individuals can supply to their evaluations of such candidates derives from past or present administrations. In a rare twist, both candidates in 2000 were defined in the public eye as successors of that sort (Weisberg and Hill 2004). For better or worse, Al Gore bore the brunt of Clinton's legacy, while George W. Bush bore his father's. Oddly enough, in the public ledger of these legacies a defeated president was worth more than a current president with impressive approval ratings. In the appraisal of the challenger in the 2004 election, strikingly, John Kerry's strongest personal (i.e., individual, as distinguished from party) asset was not a quality of his own, be it his war record, Senate career, or intelligence, but a visceral animosity among respondents toward the incumbent president. At the same time, Kerry's major liability in the public's estimate was that he lacked the major asset attributed to George W. Bush—being strong and decisive. In both the positive and the negative realm the challenger was defined in terms of the incumbent.

Another implication of limited attention to politics is that deeds in office make a stronger impression on the public than words out of office. As an example, consider one of the key qualities claimed by presidential candidates in election campaigns: leadership. The contest over who is the better leader is fought almost entirely on the incumbent president's turf. Through his performance in office a president running for reelection has either earned that mantle or lost it. Without the test of the office, the challenger finds it nearly impossible to impress the public in this domain. All he can do is deny the incumbent's claim or change the subject. When he ran for president in 2000, few respondents in our surveys thought of George W. Bush as a strong, decisive leader. In 2004, that was his most dominant asset, propelling him to victory. Performance in office, as judged by the public, had earned him that capital. Failure in office would have tarred him as a poor and ineffective leader, jeopardizing his electoral prospects.

And finally, the limited salience of politics leads to disproportionately large effects of rare catastrophic events. Short of an acute threat to national security from abroad or an ongoing U.S. military intervention, foreign policy is a dormant concern for the American public. Whatever the pronouncements by Al Gore or George W. Bush in the 2000 campaign, the American public took little note of their views on the U.S. role in the post–Cold War era. How different the response in the 2004 campaign! After barely registering a pulse four years earlier, feelings on war and peace had risen to a fever pitch. The 9/11 attacks, coupled with the response by the Bush administration, are a stark, albeit rare example of what it takes to change the public's image of politics, at least for one election cycle. The long-term consequences of change emanating from war and peace, however, must remain in doubt.

Generalization of Images

While individual voters hold distinct images of parties and candidates, the current images of the parties are heavily influenced by specific presidents in the past. The most obvious example of this process of image transfer and generalization is the continuing advantage of the Democratic Party in the domain of group linkages. It is a legacy that bears the imprint of Franklin D. Roosevelt's New Deal, following the Depression under a Republican administration. Relatively few respondents these days have personal experience of the administrations of FDR and his Republican predecessor, but the groups that respondents associate with the parties today speak to these presidents long ago. In a similar vein, the Republican edge on war and peace in the interviews in 2000, however minimal the volume of references, owes much to the success of Eisenhower and Nixon in extricating the country from the unpopular wars in Korea and Vietnam, followed by the end of the Cold War under Reagan and the elder Bush. It remains to be seen whether the Iraq war under the current Bush reverses the parties' images on war and peace.

We must also note that the imprint of the Iraq war in our responses is clouded by the tendency of some individuals to use the war to comment on the candidates' personal qualifications, rather than assess it as policy. As noted before, George W. Bush in 2004 was widely praised as a strong, decisive leader, whereas Kerry was stigmatized as a flip-flopper. We have no doubt about what inspired these contrasting images—the candidates' handling of war and peace, especially the Iraq war. Respondents apparently engaged in a common psychological process of transferring an impression from one element (policy) to another (personal qualifications). That, of course, is unremarkable. What is remarkable is that while the policy responses on war and peace were mostly unfavorable for Bush, the personal responses were mostly favorable. So perhaps rather than transferring impressions from one domain to another, individuals engaged in a selection process of choosing a particular domain for voicing their views. Those unhappy with Bush over war and peace picked the policy domain to register their disapproval, whereas those supporting the war picked the personal domain to register their approval. Why individuals frame their views on essentially the same subject matter in such contrasting ways is an intriguing question, to which we have no confident answer. One thing is clear, however. Many who disapproved of Bush's handling of the Iraq war expressed that sentiment in response to the open-ended questions (about two in three), whereas few who approved of Bush's handling of the war did so (one in five). Opponents were more vocal than supporters. Perhaps this is a special feature of the issue of war, which in the past has pitted noisy protesters against "silent majorities" (Rosenberg, Verba, and Converse 1970; Mueller 1973). Yet whatever the issue, responses to parties and candidates in these elections often clashed in affect. In subsequent chapters we delve into the roots from which this affective energy springs.

COMMENTARY AND CONTROVERSY

For all the insights they offer into the public's sense of the political world, the open-ended questions of the National Election Studies have rarely been exploited in the fashion of this chapter. A widely used textbook on voting behavior, for example, neither devotes a chapter to images of parties and candidates nor treats personal attributes of the candidates as a factor in electoral choice (Abramson, Aldrich, and Rohde 2006). Some students of this subject have doubts about the wisdom of using open-ended instruments altogether. But others have extended and refined the scheme of categories used to capture the public's image of the political world. Of special interest to students of election campaigns has been the influence of party images on the perceptions of candidates in a given election.

Open-Ended Questions and Political Images

The use of open-ended questions to elicit the public's image of parties and candidates has not gone without criticism. A major problem is a person's ability to recall elements stored in memory (Lodge, Steenbergen, and Brau 1995). Just like students taking an examination, voters asked an open-ended question may be unable to remember what they have learned about parties and candidates. Yet they once recorded that information and, with a little prompting, could supply it. Thus an instrument that relies on a respondent's memory may fail to reveal information that individuals possess and that affects their electoral choices, or so critics claim. Without doubt, many respondents are unable to cite anything good or bad about parties and candidates, and few are able to provide more than two pieces of information on a given party or candidate. What is more, some researchers question the value of the material that does emerge in the responses to questions on likes and dislikes, suggesting that the responses are subject to a rationalization effect (Rahn, Krosnick, and Bruening 1994). That is, at the time the questions are asked, many respondents have decided how they will vote and may be inclined to construct images of parties and candidates that justify their choices.

Whatever the merits of these objections, tests so far have not been conducted with the National Election Studies data. Instead, the evidence comes from experimental studies or survey settings that do not replicate the conditions of a presidential election. Though the public's attention to politics even during a presidential campaign may be low by some ideal standard, it is greater than at other times. Election campaigns are exercises in simplification and repetition, sounding a few themes to the point of surfeit for most attentive voters. Reinforcement, the main effect of campaigning, is designed to counteract the tendency of the audience to forget (Lazarsfeld, Berelson, and Gaudet 1948). Hence, we believe that in such a setting relevant information is at the tip of the tongue rather than buried in memory. What is more, we are only interested in information that is affectively encoded, which is a central feature of the "online" model proposed by critics of memory-based models (Steenbergen and Lodge 2003, 149). A person may easily forget factual information about the political world. But once it is affectively loaded and connected to a political party or candidate who is cast in a favorable or unfavorable light, that information becomes very sticky.

Dimensions of Political Images

Aside from theoretical concerns, practical obstacles impede the researcher who grapples with the bewildering array of responses to open-ended questions about parties and candidates. It helps that responses have been coded by the National Election Studies staff according to a master coding scheme, which is publicly available; but the analyst must still organize the material in categories that have theoretical meaning and high reliability. The most comprehensive effort to track party and candidate images with the open-ended questions on likes and dislikes is Kessel's work (2004). His research covers all presidential elections in the NES series from 1952 onward. Kessel's scheme consists of three broad components (parties, candidates, and issues), with more specific domains within each component. Some of the major issues identified by Kessel closely correspond to those considered in this chapter:

- International involvement
- Economic management
- Social benefits

Kessel's typology of candidates' qualities lists the following categories.

- General
- Record-incumbency
- Experience, management
- Intelligence
- Trust
- Personality

Some of these overlap with qualities featured in this chapter, while others are more encompassing (e.g., personality).

The main advantage of fixed categories is that they allow comparisons across elections. For example, the analyst can determine whether in 2004 international issues favored the Republican candidate more or less than in past elections. On the other hand, a scheme of fixed categories cannot cope with newly salient issues and is burdened with vanishing concerns. What is more, some categories may be too broad to register what is truly remarkable, such as Kerry's reputation for indecisiveness. For example, "management" (presumably the applicable category) would not be very revealing about this image.

Traits of Candidates

Researchers have attempted to identify core dimensions of evaluations of candidates' personal qualities (as opposed to their role as representatives of parties and issues). There is broad agreement on two such core traits:

one, ability to do the job well, based on performance in office (incumbency) or a previous record of accomplishment; and two, a reputation for honesty. However, there is considerable dispute on which other traits merit attention.

One of the most rigorous attempts to map the structure of candidates' images revealed by responses to questions on likes and dislikes (and excluding issue- and party-related references) relied on factor analysis (Miller, Wattenberg, and Malanchuk 1986). The result was a five-dimensional configuration that proved quite robust over time (1952–84). It consists of the following dimensions:

- Competence
- Integrity
- Reliability
- Charisma
- (Purely) personal qualities

Individuals want more than competence and integrity in candidates for office. The charisma dimension recognizes the importance of leadership in evaluations, but it also includes items that could be considered purely personal (humble, humorous, kind, warm). The reliability dimension aims to carve out a niche for proven ability rather than qualifications such as previous experience and intelligence, which largely define competence. But in doing so, reliability bleeds into charisma. The quality of being strong and decisive, which seems related to leadership, winds up in the category of reliability, not charisma. There are limits to factor analysis in constructing a neat theoretical structure of the dimensions of candidate evaluations from open-ended responses.

Leaving aside open-ended questions, Kinder (1986) proposed a set of four traits (dimensions) that were tested with a battery of fixed-response questions:

- Competence
- Integrity
- Leadership
- Empathy

The scheme adds leadership and empathy to the core dimensions of competence and integrity. While the first three dimensions figured prominently in the open-ended responses examined in this chapter, empathy did not; nor did it in the Miller, Wattenberg, and Malanchuk (1986) analysis. Given the strong partisan loading of empathy, with Democratic candidates doing well and Republicans doing poorly, this "personal" quality most likely is grounded in the group associations of the parties, and is not specific to the candidates. Overall, the test of the four-dimensional structure showed that the candidate traits were highly correlated with one another. A replication of this analysis using subsequent election studies (1984–92) confirmed the high degree of correlations among those four traits (Funk 1996, 106).

The NES surveys continue to probe candidate evaluations with closed-ended questions about these traits. Miller and Shanks (1996, chap. 15) have shown that this type of question produces different results for the effects of candidate traits than do open-ended questions on likes and dislikes. Miller and Shanks claim that the closed-ended question is "better suited to describing the role of such evaluations in shaping vote choice than 'mentions' of such qualities in response to open-ended questions" (437). Yet what the closed-ended questions do not capture is the salience of the traits in a given election. Curiously enough, the NES questionnaires have modified the attribute list from election to election. For 2004, a newly added question concerned each candidate's ability to "make up his own mind." The salience of this quality, which was evident in the responses to the open-ended questions, would not have emerged with the standard repertoire of closed-ended questions.

The Media and Image Formation

How does the public get the impression that a candidate lacks the ability "to make up his own mind"? That is an assessment hard to make without knowing a person very well, and citizens do not often observe candidates closely enough to make informed judgments. Instead, they depend on the mass media for information, through news coverage or campaign advertisements, or through talking with others who pay attention to the media. Since the earliest campaign studies we have known that this information comes through affective layers and selective filters (Lazarsfeld, Berelson, and Gaudet 1948).

Media coverage conveys images of the candidates through "frames" and "narratives" (Jamieson and Waldman 2003). In the 2000 election, the media seized on honesty as the key frame for Al Gore (the "lying panderer") and reported numerous stories about alleged missteps; for

Bush the key frame was lack of intellect and preparation (the "inexperienced dolt"). As the election year unfolded, each candidate saw his reputation on his key trait dwindle (Jamieson and Waldman 2003, 59, 67), although Gore suffered worse damage. This may be related to Bush's strategy of wooing the media. The "rules of engagement" between candidate and press were such that the latter got access and the former got good coverage.

> He [Bush] was obviously using—and relishing—this opportunity to try to charm us, to get us to see him as flesh and blood, to personalize the situation to the point where we might think longer and harder about reporting anything derogatory. (Bruni 2002, 113)

Quite aside from coverage by the news media, the candidates' own organizations do their utmost to supply the electorate with the right frames and narratives through advertising (Diamond and Bates 1988; Hacker 2004, Jamieson 1984; West 2005). Proving that these ads shape or alter the public's assessments of candidates, however, is no easy task, requiring careful designs that typically go beyond a single survey. Tracking respondents over time, Patterson and McClure (1976) found that television ads helped the public gain a more accurate assessment of where the competing presidential candidates stood on policy. But these ads appeared to have little effect on the public's views of presidential traits. Subsequent studies, however, have reported evidence of a link between the media and perceived traits. Exposure to television news or ads improves the public's views of a candidate's electability (West 2005, 97). Perhaps the strongest evidence comes from studies using experimental controls. Iyengar and Kinder (1987, chap. 8) have demonstrated a priming effect of the media for evaluations of candidates. The public's assessments of presidential character—such as competence and integrity—derives to a significant extent from whatever aspects the national media emphasize in their coverage.

Issue Ownership and Campaigns

When it comes to candidates as representatives of policy, the public's perceptions are guided by established associations between the parties and certain policies. The link between parties and issues is so strong that some observers have called the relationship "issue ownership" (Petrocik 1996). If the public consistently believes that one party can better handle an issue, it might be said that this party "owns" that issue. Much evidence shows that the Democratic Party has the advantage on social welfare, while the GOP generally has the edge in foreign policy and social (moral) issues, which is consistent with the patterns shown in this chapter, at least for the 2000 election. The two parties' differing advantages are important for the public's appraisal of candidates, especially those not yet well defined in the public eye. Jimmy Carter, little known when he pursued the Democratic nomination in 1976, was seen as taking typical Democratic stands on most issues (Conover and Feldman 1989). Such partisan inference is an example of generalization from one object (party) to another (candidate) and is a good bargain for voters who seek to buy information at low cost—so long as candidates live up to the party's images (stereotypes). Indeed, a common strategy is for candidates to focus on issues owned by their party and avoid issues owned by the other party (Petrocik 1996).

When candidates deviate from this practice and instead pursue a strategy of ambiguity (Downs 1957), trespassing on the other party's issues, the results may prove counterproductive. Images of the parties may be so deeply etched that voters may fail to recognize when a candidate takes up an issue owned by the opposite party. In the end, trespassing on issues may boost the candidate of the other party by raising the salience of its trademark issues (Norpoth and Buchanan 1992). It is also possible that issue ownership by the party may spill over into "trait ownership" by the candidate (Hayes 2005). So long as the Democrats are favored on issues of social welfare, their candidates will be seen as empathetic, whereas Republicans will be seen as strong leaders because of their advantage in foreign policy. This is another example of personal evaluations of candidates deriving from the public's judgment on their policies.

CHAPTER 4

Partisan Choice

The attitudes and reactions that constitute public perceptions of the parties and candidates are important because of their effect on elections and voting. These attitudes affect the public's choice in presidential elections. The images of parties and their candidates fluctuate with daily news events, but the images prevalent on Election Day will inevitably affect the electoral outcome.

The previous chapter examined the *public's* images of the parties and candidates, but *individual* votes are determined by *individuals'* own perceptions. Therefore, this chapter will focus on individual voters and the effects of images of parties and candidates on the votes of individuals. We view an individual's images of these political objects as a system of "partisan attitudes," and we consider how this system affects voting.

The scholarly literature understates the role that perceptions of the parties and candidates play in determining voting. The literature instead assumes that long-term party ties and demographics determine these perceptions, with images of party and candidate being no more than rationalizations that people give for their votes. Even if that assumption were reasonable, we would still want to map the individual's perception of the parties and candidates. After all, such a map would give us greater understanding of how party ties and demographics such as race, religion, and social-economic status affect people's views of politics.

In fact, perceptions of the parties and candidates are not totally determined by long-term party ties and demographics, since these perceptions can and do change with political events in the real world. Indeed, some events move public opinion among all partisan groups and all demographic groups, though more in some groups than others. As will be stressed in later chapters, individuals' ties to a party are often stable over time, as, obviously, are social demographics such as race and gender. For that reason, fluctuations in each party's proportion of the vote in different elections can only be accounted for by changes in partisan attitudes over time. Using survey data for the 1952–64 period, Stokes (1966a) has shown that the vote shift from the Eisenhower Republican landslide in 1956 to the Johnson Democratic landslide in 1964 can only be explained by changes in the partisan attitudes of individual voters.

A more recent example is provided by the changes in the partisan vote division between 1996 and 2000. The electorate changed minimally over those four years in terms of gender, race, ethnicity, religion, education, and other demographic characteristics, so the larger Republican vote in 2000 cannot be explained by more people being in Republican-leaning social groups. Instead, nearly all social groups became more Republican in their party identification in 2000 (Stanley and Niemi 2004). Furthermore, if we look at self-proclaimed partisanship (to be discussed at greater length in chapter 6), people in every category of partisanship voted more Republican in 2000 than in 1996. Thus, neither long-term social groupings nor partisanship can explain the changes over this period. Instead, the change must be due to differences in evaluation of political objects between 2000 and 1996.[1] Specifically, the Republican candidate in 2000 was viewed more positively than in 1996, and the Democratic candidate was viewed more negatively. We explain this change through different political objects—the nomination of George W. Bush instead of Bob Dole by the Republicans and the attempt by Al Gore to succeed Bill Clinton for the Democrats. Attitudes toward these candidates, and also toward issues, were affected by party ties and demographics, but a change in the objects—and subsequent change in party images—explains the shift in the vote over this four-year period.

---

1. For example, there was not a greater proportion of men in 2000 than in 1996, but a greater proportion of men voted Republican in 2000 than four years earlier. The same was also true for women, so gender does not explain the voting difference between these two elections—it is instead that both men and women evaluated contemporary political objects in a more pro-Republican manner in 2000 than they did in 1996.

A SOCIAL-PSYCHOLOGICAL MODEL OF VOTING BEHAVIOR

Our basic model of voting behavior is social-psychological, emphasizing the role of attitudes in determining the vote. Demographic characteristics correlate with the vote, but a solely demographic model cannot adequately capture the determinants of voting in a particular election. Instead, we focus on the individual's attitudes toward political objects, specifically the Republican presidential nominee, the Democratic presidential nominee, foreign policy issues, domestic policy issues, social group interests, and the performance of the parties as managers of the government. Members of the electorate perceive and evaluate these six objects; each factor can tilt in favor of one party or the other across the electorate, along with an intensity as to how much the public considers that object as leaning in a particular partisan direction that year. At the individual level, each of these six components is evaluated by the voter in a positive or negative direction, and that is what primarily affects his or her vote.

This is not to say that these are the only factors affecting the vote. We will argue that they are the main factors overall, but for some individuals other factors are of greater importance. For example, if a man defers to his wife's political choice without himself evaluating these political objects, then they do not come into direct play. However, more typically people would obtain information about political objects—both candidates and issues—from their spouse, friends, and acquaintances, rather than simply deferring to another person's political choice without themselves evaluating the objects.

We measure these six partisan factors by looking again at the open-ended questions about the parties and candidates that were first analyzed in chapter 3. Recall that these questions are asked in the preelection interview, so this measurement occurs prior to the person's vote. We classify each comment by a respondent according to the six attitudinal components listed above: the personal characteristics of George W. Bush; the personal characteristics of the Democratic nominee (Gore in 2000 and Kerry in 2004), foreign policy issues, domestic policy issues, social groups, and the parties as managers of government.[2] For example, a person who says that she likes the Democrats because they are good for working people is coded as giving a favorable response to Democrats on

---

2. The full classification scheme is available from the authors.

social groups, while a person who says he dislikes the Democrats because of waste in government during the Clinton administration is coded as giving an unfavorable response to Democrats as mangers of government. While it is possible to distribute these comments into a smaller or a larger number of categories (see especially Kessel 2004), these six components encapsulate the main dimensions of partisan evaluation. This is not to say that most respondents expressed comments on all six; indeed, many commented on just one or two.

The measures that we construct have two basic characteristics. First, their sign shows whether the person evaluated the partisan object in a Republican, neutral, or Democratic direction. Second, their magnitude shows how intense the partisan attitude is. For example, a person who made one negative and three positive comments about Bush across the eight open-ended questions is scored as a net +2 in the Republican direction, that is, more intense than a person who made one positive and no negative comments about Bush.

We hypothesize two important effects of these partisan attitudes. First, we expect that a person's vote will be affected by them, both by the attitude in any one category and by all six taken together. The next section of this chapter details how these six partisan components affected the vote in 2004. Second, many voters may favor different parties on different components. That is, there can be conflict between the different partisan attitudes, and the existence and extent of conflict can also have political effects. After examining the effects of the six components on the vote, we will look at effects of conflicting evaluations on other important political matters.

THE PARTISAN COMPONENTS OF THE VOTE DECISION

Partisan components substantially affect voting decisions. Consider, for example, the effect of attitudes toward Bush's personal attributes on the 2004 vote. Both the direction and intensity of this component are related to the vote. Table 4.1 shows how widely the vote varies from one end of the dimension to the other. Those with very negative attitudes toward Bush all voted Democratic. As one moves toward the positive attitudes on the right side of the table, the proportion voting for Bush increases nearly monotonically, and nearly everyone with an extremely favorable view of Bush voted for him. The direction and the intensity of the attitude both matter. People with negative views of Bush strongly tended to vote against him, while those with positive views strongly tended to vote for him. And people with more intense views tended to vote more solidly than those with less intense views. Though the relationships are not always perfectly monotonic, each of the six components has this type of relationship to the vote decision both in 2000 and 2004.

While the relationship between attitude toward Bush and the vote shown in table 4.1 is very strong, it is not perfect. People at either extreme of the scale do vote nearly unanimously one way or the other. Actually, people with negative views of Bush vote against him in large proportions virtually regardless of how intense their attitude, while people with positive views of him vote for him in large proportions again virtually regardless of how intense their attitude is. Note also that the frequencies, indicated at the bottom of table 4.1, show that most people had moderate views toward Bush. In particular, many people made the same number of positive and negative comments about Bush, and so are scored as neutral on the scale. The table shows voters who were neutral toward Bush split their votes fairly evenly between the two nominees, with only a slight preference for Kerry. This fairly even split limits our ability to account for individual votes in 2004 by attitude toward Bush alone.

The points made in the previous paragraph can perhaps be better

TABLE 4.1. Relation of Attitude toward Bush to Party Division of the Vote, 2004 (in percentages)

	Attitude toward Bush							
	Unfavorable				Favorable			
								+
	−					+	+	+
	−	−			+	+	+	+
	−	−	−	0	+	+	+	+
Voted Democratic	100	96	92	55	13	5	0	4
Voted Republican	0	4	8	45	87	95	100	96
Total	100	100	100	100	100	100	100	100
Number of cases	41	56	133	269	149	82	30	28

Note: Due to the small number of respondents who gave large numbers of comments about Bush, the extreme categories are combined, and so the left column includes all respondents who made at least three more negative comments about him than positive ones, and the right column includes all respondents who made at least four more positive comments about him than negative ones.

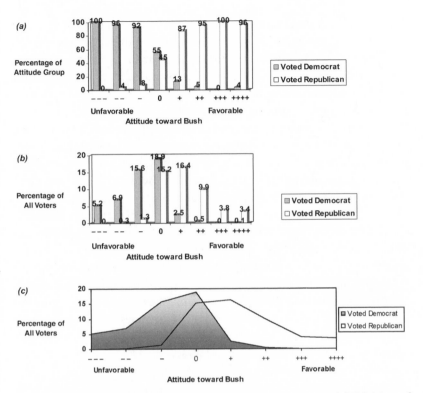

Fig. 4.1. Relation of Attitude toward Bush to Party Vote, 2004. (*a*) Division of the party vote across the scale of attitude toward Bush. (*b*) Party vote within each scale category as a percentage of the total vote. (*c*) Distribution of actual Democratic and Republican voters by attitude toward Bush.

perceived graphically. Figure 4.1 provides several perspectives on the values in table 4.1. Figure 4.1a shows the two-party vote division according to the person's attitude toward Bush. The heights of the bars represent the percentages of table 4.1, illustrating the extreme differences in voting as one transverses the scale. Figure 4.1b shows the vote within each category as a percentage of the total 2004 vote, reflecting the distribution of voters across the dimension. This display emphasizes how few voters were at the extremes, compared to those holding more moderate positions. In particular, one sees that a full third of the electorate was neutral toward Bush on this measure, which contradicts claims at the time of the election that everybody either loved or hated him. Figure 4.1c focuses our attention on the degree of overlap between the distributions of the Democratic and Republican vote. This area under both the curves in figure 4.1c can be considered to be the error that would occur if we predicted 2004 vote solely from attitude toward Bush. There is certainly overlap here, though it is limited.

The two-party vote can be better predicted by considering more than one partisan component at a time. For example, instead of looking only at views of Bush, we can simultaneously include respondents' comments on domestic issues. Table 4.2 shows the Republican proportion of the two-party vote according to position on these two attitudinal components. Attitudes toward Bush are now shown on the vertical dimension, attitudes toward domestic issues on the horizontal dimension. If one follows a row across the table, one sees how people who share the same attitude toward Bush vary in their vote according to their position on domestic issues. For example, looking across the zero row (which represents neutral attitudes toward Bush), one sees that the vote becomes markedly more Republican the more the respondent is on the Republican end of the domestic issues scale. The values in this row actually

TABLE 4.2. Relation of Attitude toward Bush and Attitude on Domestic Issues to Percentage Voting Republican, 2004

Attitude toward Bush[a]		Attitude on Domestic Issues[b] (extent to which attitude favors Republicans)							
		—	—	—	—	0	+	+	+
Favorable	++++	—	—	—	—	92	100	—	—
	+++	—	—	—	—	100	100	—	—
	++	—	—	—	93	86	100	100	100
	+	—	—	—	69	84	95	87	100
	0	6	7	33	28	53	65	91	—
	—	0	0	6	0	6	54	—	—
Unfavorable	— —	—	—	—	4	4	0	—	—
	— — —	—	—	0	0	0	0	—	—

[a]Entries give the percentage voting Republican for each combination of attitudes toward Bush and attitudes on domestic issues.

[b]Both the scale of the attitude toward Bush and the scale of attitude on domestic issues assumed more values than are shown in the table. Due to the low frequencies (less than eight respondents) of some categories, some of the extreme values have been combined in rows. Thus, the percentages in the first and last cells in each row include cases falling in more extreme cells.

increase much more slowly than those in table 4.1.[3] Thus, looking at two partisan components together provides greater explanatory power than looking at just one.

Our full model entails including the effects of all six partisan components at once, since we view the vote as dependent on the individual's attitudes toward all six partisan objects. A cross-tabulation along the six partisan attitudes together in a generalized version of table 4.2 is not feasible because the percentages in most cells would be based on very small numbers of respondents. Instead, we use multiple regression analysis to analyze the effects of the six components on the vote simultaneously. Such an analysis finds that voting decisions can be predicted with a very high degree of accuracy from individuals' positions on the six scales together in both 2000 and 2004. One measure of this is the multiple correlation of the six attitudinal components with the vote. This multiple correlation was .789 in 2004, which is remarkably high given that measurement error and other influences push the value down.

Once again, the success of this model can perhaps best be gauged graphically by looking at the degree of overlap between the distributions of Republican and Democratic voters. Figure 4.2 provides the appropriate graphs. Figure 4.2a shows the distribution of voters by their probability of voting Republican as estimated from the six-component model. The horizontal axis represents how pro-Republican a person's probability of voting is. As one moves from left to right, people become less likely to vote Democratic and more likely to vote Republican. A reasonable prediction is that people with a probability greater than .5 will vote Republican, while those with a probability below .5 will vote Democratic.[4]

Figure 4.2b shows the distributions of probability scores for Democratic and Republican voters separately. Note the small overlap between the Democratic and Republican curves. The prediction error, as represented by this overlap, is much less than in figure 4.1c, showing that the six components together predict the vote much better than does attitude

---

3. Occasional irregularities in the table are generally due to small numbers of cases in extreme categories; for example, very few people have strongly anti-Republican positions on domestic issues while having positive views of Bush.

4. The probabilities are based on the multiple regression analysis used as a linear probability model. The dependent variable is two-party vote with Republican voters scored 1 and Democratic voters scored 0, with the six partisan attitudes being the predictors of the vote.

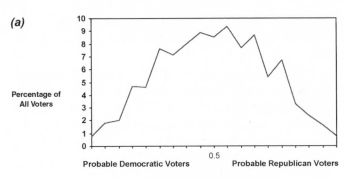

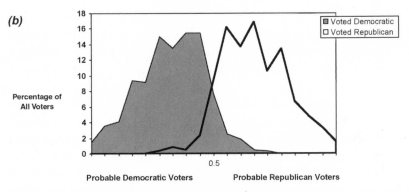

Fig. 4.2. The prediction of voting choice from all partisan attitudes, 2004. (*a*) Distribution of all voters by probability of voting Republican. (Included in all voters are only those who reported voting for one of the two major-party candidates.) (*b*) Distribution of actual Democratic and Republican voters by probability of voting Republican.

toward Bush alone. The amount of error has actually been cut by more than half. In fact, the votes of 92 percent of the electorate are consistent with this model.[5] One way to see the power of this model is to recognize

5. The increase in predictive power for 2004 with the full model as compared to the earlier models is as follows:

When prediction is based on	Correlation of Predictors with Voting Choice	Percentage Correctly Predicted
Attitude toward Bush only	.62	80
Attitudes toward Bush and domestic issues	.69	84
All six partisan components	.79	92

that this percentage is on a par with the percentage of voters whose votes in November corresponded to their statement in the preelection interview as to how they planned to vote. Thus, in a sense, this model actually predicts votes as well as the respondents themselves could (though we should not overemphasize that point, since the prediction in our model is based on a statistical analysis of how they did vote). Conventional social demographic predictors of vote choice have much weaker predictive power. The social-psychological predictors that we employ are so successful because they are much more proximate psychologically to the behavior itself.

The Sources of Error

The partisan component model is so successful that attention naturally turns to the sources of error. What factors help us understand the 8 percent of respondents whose votes do not follow the model's predictions? Several hints are available from the election survey.

There are measurement errors in every research endeavor. For example, some people may not accurately report their votes. Even more important, measurement of the six partisan components is based on a preelection survey that is taken over a period of several weeks before the election. People's partisan attitudes can change over this period in response to events, such as the presidential debates. Tracking polls often find last-minute shifts in public opinion due to events very close to the election, and the NES preelection survey occurs too early for most respondents for these shifts to be detected. Thus, some prediction errors are likely due to changes in respondents' partisan attitudes between the preelection survey and their voting.

Another relevant matter is the statistical method employed here. Regression analysis determines the weights to be given to each of the predictor scales. Attitude toward Bush, for example, may be found to have a large weight, while domestic policy attitudes may be found to have a small weight for the electorate as a whole. However, some voters may care much more about a single issue, such as gay marriage in 2004, even if attitudes toward the incumbent are more important for the electorate as a whole. The regression prediction will use the same weights for all voters, without detecting that those voters are single-issue voters. That will result in some prediction errors in our regression model, since the regression results cannot compensate for individual differences in the weighting of the six components.

The overall model of the vote postulated in chapter 2 brings in an important additional factor: interpersonal influence. As people talk to one another, they receive information, influence, and pressure that can guide their vote decision beyond the partisan components considered here. Table 4.3 suggests the effects of this factor, showing how people voted according to the vote choice of their spouse, family, work associates, church associates, and neighbors. Respondents were asked to name up to four people with whom they discuss politics and were asked questions about their relationship with them. Spouses vote for the same candidate at a remarkably high rate, but consistency is fairly high for all sets of discussants. Bear in mind that these figures derive from reports by respondents on how they believe the other person voted, so error is inevitable—probably in the direction of wrongly believing the person voted as the respondent did, and possibly in assuming that the person voted for the winner. Yet, we would interpret this table as showing that there was a meaningful opportunity for discussion and interpersonal influence to limit the impact of the partisan attitude components on people's voting. A person whose attitudes all line up in a Republican direction is very likely to vote Republican, but a person whose predicted probability of voting Republican is just a little above .5 might well be persuaded in the end by spouse, family, or other close associates to vote for the Democrat. Interpersonal influence is a factor in the funnel of causality of chapter 2 that is very close to the ultimate voting decision, and may cause people to give less emphasis to their own attitudes than they otherwise might.

TABLE 4.3. Relation of Reported Partisan Preference of Primary Groups to Respondent Own Partisan Choice, 2000 (in percentages)

Respondent Voted	Spouse Voted		Family Voted[a]		Work Associates Voted		Church Associates Voted		Neighbor Voted	
	Dem	Rep	Dem	Rep	Dem	Rep	Dem	Rep	Dem	Re
Democratic	92	9	84	24	82	36	73	18	79	2
Republican	8	91	16	76	18	64	27	82	21	7
Total	100	100	100	100	100	100	100	100	100	1(
Number of cases	145	159	171	181	95	192	37	76	90	1

Note: These tabulations are limited to those who reported voting for a major-party candidate for president.
[a]Includes persons that respondents identified as being (nonspousal) relatives.

ATTITUDE CONFLICT

While the preceding section looked at the combined effect of the six components of the vote decision, it is also important to consider conflict among these attitudes. This section will examine conflict among the six partisan attitudes and some of its effects.

Time of Vote Decision

The partisan attitudes discussed in this chapter are often formed well before the presidential election year begins. However, politics becomes more salient to the public during the actual election campaign, and attitudes toward a new candidate are inevitably formed largely during the campaign period. We have only one preelection measurement for each respondent, so we cannot directly trace change in attitude at the individual level. Instead, we can make use of a question included in the NES asking when the person decided to vote the way they did. We should not expect respondents to recall perfectly when they first decided how to vote, but they are likely to have some recollection.

Table 4.4 shows the distribution of reported times of vote decisions for 2000 and 2004. Few voters wait until Election Day to decide how to vote, and more than three-quarters of the electorate know how they will vote before the last two weeks of the campaign. As one would expect, in 2000, when both major party nominees were new presidential candidates, fewer voters knew how they were going to vote all along than in 2004, when an incumbent was running.

Furthermore, the time of decision is related to the predictability of an individual's vote. As shown in figure 4.3, the multiple correlation of

TABLE 4.4. Reported Time of Vote Decision (in percentages)

	2000	2004
Knew all along how they would vote	12	33
Decided before or during the conventions	42	37
Decided after the conventions, during the campaign	24	15
Decided within two weeks of election	18	13
Decided on Election Day	5	2
Not ascertained	<1	<1
Total	101	100
Number of cases	1,095	800

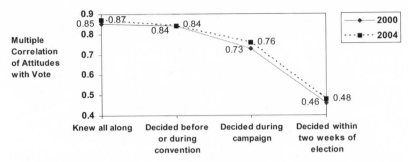

Fig. 4.3. Relation of reported time of vote decision to ability of partisan attitudes to explain the vote

the six components with the vote is very high for people who knew all along how they were going to vote, and lowest for those who decided within the last two weeks of the election. The curves for 2000 and 2004 are virtually identical. Over 70 percent of the variance in voting choice of those who knew all along how they would vote can be explained by the partisan components, compared to less than 25 percent of the variance for those who waited until the last two weeks to decide.

An implication of figure 4.3 is that people whose votes can easily be predicted from their partisan attitudes make up their minds earlier than those who votes are less predictable. This predictability is probably related to the extent of conflict among people's partisan attitudes, leading us to consider in detail the problem of attitude conflict.

Attitudinal Conflict and Demographic Cross-Pressures

The early Columbia voting studies (see chap. 1) initiated a focus on "cross-pressures" in voting. For example, they examined conflict between a person's religion and class. Catholics were more likely to vote Democratic, while middle-class people were more likely to vote Republican, so middle-class Catholics were cross-pressured, as were working-class Protestants. While these are examples of demographic cross-pressures, the term *cross-pressure* implies that the individual experiences psychological conflict. Our study will focus on the effects of cross-pressures, without examining whether their source is social demographic or something else.

Our measures of partisan attitudes permit us to look for conflict among the six components of the vote decision. For example, in table 4.2, those whose attitudes toward Bush and domestic issues place them in the top right portion are consistently pro-Republican, while those placed in the bottom left have attitudes toward Bush and domestic issues that are consistently pro-Democratic. By contrast, people in the top left and bottom right cells of the table have conflicted attitudes.

Of course, many respondents do not give reactions to the parties and candidates that involve all six partisan attitudes. In fact, most respondents either give no reaction to at least one topic or give balanced reactions to at least one topic. Since the meaning of conflict can differ according to how many partisan factors affect the individual, we will graph results separately for people with two, three, four, or five partisan dimensions. (Because of their rarity, we omit those who respond in all six categories. Those who give responses corresponding to just one category or none of them are also excluded since, by definition, they cannot experience conflict.) We term the number of partisan attitudes that a person expresses his or her *attitude level*. For levels 2, 3, 4, and 5, we can compare the effects of conflict in partisan direction with those of consistency.[6]

The Effects of Attitude Conflict

We now will test the effect of conflict among people's partisan attitudes and their time of vote decision. We would expect people with attitudinal conflict to decide later than people without such conflict. The results of our test are shown in figure 4.4. Each line represents a particular level of partisan attitudes, based on how many of the six partisan attitudes the person voiced in the survey. The height of the curve at a particular point portrays the corresponding proportion of voters deciding late in the campaign. The greater the attitude conflict, the greater is the likelihood a person will decide how to vote during the last two weeks of the campaign—and this is generally true at each attitude level. The two ends of each line show that few people who have consistent partisan attitudes wait until the last two weeks of the campaign to decide. In general, the

---

6. We measure conflict by the difference between how many comments the person makes in the Republican and Democratic directions. Scores near 0 show maximum conflict. For example, for people at level 2 (i.e., they make comments about two of the six partisan attitudes), a person who gives one pro-Republican (or anti-Democratic) comment and one pro-Democratic (or anti-Republican) comment is scored $1 - 1 = 0$. Higher scores show less conflict, but the meaning of a $+2$ score, for example, depends on the person's level. For example, a person at level 2 who gives two pro-Republican comments would be scored $2 - 0 = +2$, which would reflect minimal conflict, and a person at level 4 who gives three pro-Republican comments and one pro-Democratic comment would be scored $3 - 1 = +2$, which would reflect moderate conflict.

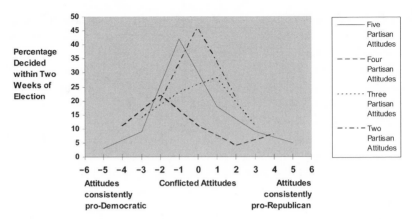

Fig. 4.4. Relation of extent of attitude consistency to reported time of vote decision, 2004

more attitudinal conflict, the greater the proportion who wait until the last two weeks to make their decision. Those with five partisan attitudes have the greatest potential for intense conflict or consistency; nearly all among them with fully consistent attitudes decided before the last two weeks of the campaign, while more than a quarter of those with conflicted attitudes did not decide until the last two weeks.

The results in figure 4.4 help explain the differences in the ability of partisan attitudes to account for voting choice that was evident in figure 4.3. People who decided late in the campaign were generally those whose attitudes were in conflict. This conflict makes their vote less predictable than votes by people whose attitudes were consistent. However, it is important to recognize that the differences in figure 4.3 are not totally due to attitudinal consistency. Politics is of limited interest for some people. Their partisan attitudes may be inconsistent because of that lack of interest, rather than because of active conflict among their views. Some of these people may decide early in the campaign rather than bother to take in more information, while others may wait until late to decide because of lack of attention, not because of the difficulty in resolving inconsistent attitudes.

We expect attitudinal conflict to have additional effects on political behavior. For example, we expect people who experience it to be more likely to vote for different parties for different electoral offices than people whose views line up in the same direction. Figure 4.5 shows the results of testing this expectation by looking at the proportion of people

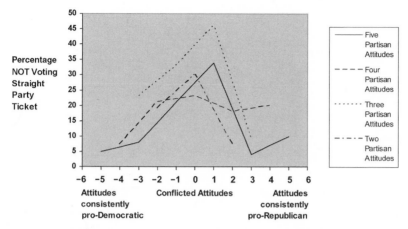

Fig. 4.5. Relation of extent of attitude consistency to degree of straight-ticket voting, 2004

who vote for different parties for president and member of Congress. The NES survey does not include a general question about split-ticket voting, and in any case there would be considerable differences between states as to which other offices are on the ballot in presidential election years. Most states elect governors and other state officials for four-year terms in midterm election years, so the only other statewide position consistently on state ballots in 2004 was U.S. senator, but even that was true for only two-thirds of the states.[7] Even using the vote for U.S. representative poses some difficulty in that some seats are uncontested, and few seats are really competitive. These difficulties notwithstanding, the results shown in figure 4.5 indicate that the greatest split ticket-voting occurred when partisan attitudes were conflicted.

Attitude conflict also affects people's involvement in the election. Our survey data over the years show that people with partisan conflict are less likely to be highly politically involved, less likely to be interested in the election, and less likely to care who wins. In part this is because people with a strong, long-term psychological involvement in politics are likely to be engaged in the specific election and to be partisans. We expect the effect of long-term psychological involvement will be captured through the person's level of attitude—that people who are more

7. Only one-third of the 100 senators are up for reelection every two years, but they represent two-thirds of the states.

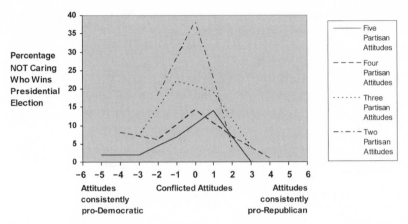

Fig. 4.6. Relation of extent of attitude consistency to degree of indifference to election outcome, 2004

psychologically involved with politics will have attitudes on more of the six partisan attitudes. This is seen in table 4.5, which shows that the proportion of people who do not care who wins the election is related to the number of political attitudes they have. Most people who make no comments on the eight questions about likes and dislikes about the major parties and their presidential nominees do not care who wins the election, while almost everyone with a large number of political attitudes cares who wins.

Finally, we expect people with more conflicted attitudes to care less how the election turns out. Figure 4.6 provides support for this hypothesis. The greatest level of not caring who wins occurs for people with conflicted attitudes, and this is true for every attitude level. The proportion of people with conflicted attitudes who do not care about the outcome is higher than that proportion for people with consistent views.

Overall, our six partisan attitudes, taken together, are powerful pre-

TABLE 4.5. Relation of Attitude Level to Proportion Not Caring How Election Turns Out, 2004

	Level of Attitude						
	None	One	Two	Three	Four	Five	Six
Proportion *not* caring	68%	29%	22%	12%	7%	5%	4%
Number of cases	60	63	129	192	264	233	121

dictors of a person's vote. At the same time, conflict among these attitudes also has effects on people's behavior and on their involvement. We turn more directly to political involvement in the next chapter.

COMMENTARY AND CONTROVERSY

Comparisons with Earlier Elections

The 2000 and 2004 elections were much more polarized than the elections in the 1950s that *The American Voter* studied. This is evident in several of the analyses in this chapter. For example, the relationship of attitudes toward Bush to the vote is much more polarized than was shown in the comparable table for the 1950s, where the gradient in a row was much more gentle (Campbell et al. 1960, 69). Similarly, the overlap in figure 4.1c of the distributions of Democratic and Republican voters by attitude toward the Republican candidate is much more limited than the amount of overlap in a similar analysis for 1956 (Campbell et al. 1960, 70).

The greater polarization in 2000 and 2004 led to greater predictability for these two elections than for the elections of the 1950s regardless of when the person decided how to vote (Campbell et al. 1960, 79). Among those people who knew all along how they would vote, the multiple correlations between the vote and the partisan attitudes are .85–.87 for the 2000 and 2004 elections (see fig. 4.3) versus .79–.80 for 1952 and 1956. For people who decided within the last two weeks of the election, the multiple correlations are .46–.48 for 2000 and 2004 versus .21–.29 for 1952 and 1956. The greater partisan polarization of the electorate in the 2000–2004 era led to greater predictability of the vote across the entire election year.

The polarization also leads to greater concern with the election outcome. Regardless of their level of political attitude, fewer people did not care how the election turned out in 2000 and 2004 than did not care in the 1950s. A typical comparison is that 57 percent of the 1956 respondents with just one political attitude did not care how the election came out, versus only 29 percent in 2004. The pattern in table 4.5 is the same as it would have been in the 1950s, but with a much higher level of people caring about the election outcome in the polarized campaign of 2004.

Alternative Estimation Procedures

There are now more modern statistical methods for analyzing the determinants of the vote decision than were used in the corresponding chapter in *The American Voter*. It employed multiple regression analysis to determine the extent to which the six partisan attitudes affected the vote decision. A person's vote is a dichotomous variable since the choice is between Republican and Democrat.[8] Technically, dichotomous dependent variables are inappropriate for regression analysis, but related techniques such as logit analysis are appropriate in this instance. The basic problem is that regression analysis assumes a linear relationship between a predictor variable and the dependent variable, but it is not possible to have a straight-line relationship between two variables when one is dichotomous and the other is not. Logit analysis instead posits a curvilinear relationship between the variables, with a low probability of voting Republican at one end of the independent variable and a high probability of voting Republican at the opposite end, with a sharp nonlinear increase in probability through the midrange of the predictor variable. In practice, most analyses obtain fairly similar results whether they use regression analysis or logit, but there is no doubt that logit analysis is more appropriate.

Using logit analysis instead of multiple regression affects the results in this chapter only minimally. The only analysis potentially affected is the calculation of predicted probabilities of voting Republican, which in turn affects the calculation of the proportion of votes correctly classified by the analysis. Still, the predictive success with a logit analysis is identical to that given above, 92 percent in 2004. We conclude that the basic analysis in *The American Voter* was on target, even if a more modern data analysis technique would be used today. We return to this issue in chapter 14, where we find that it would be awkward to use logit analysis for some of the purposes that *The American Voter* used regression analysis.

Using Likes and Dislikes as Predictors of the Vote

The analysis in this chapter treats the open-ended like-and-dislike questions as independent variables that can help predict the vote. What if instead they are rationalizations of people's vote decisions? What if people who decided to vote for Bush's reelection in 2004 recognized that they had to say good things about his foreign policy, and people who decided to vote against Bush looked for negative things to say about him and his policies so that they appeared consistent to the interviewer? If this were the case, the regression model in this chapter would still be highly suc-

---

8. We disregard third parties and candidates in this discussion. Rosenstone, Behr, and Lazarus (1996) and Abramson et al. (2000) provide good treatments of voting for third parties.

cessful, but that success would be misleading because the partisan attitudes were caused by the person's vote rather than causing it.

The general concern being raised here is whether survey responses about the parties and candidates are independent of the person's vote or are caused by his or her vote intention. The open-ended questions appear early in the preelection questionnaire, before people are asked about their vote intention and before they actually vote. However, this sequence does not guarantee that the attitudes given in response are causally prior to the vote decision. A person may have decided how to vote months earlier and now feels he or she must give consistent answers to questions about likes and dislikes.

Furthermore, responses to the like-and-dislike questions may be "top-of-the-head" reactions, based on whatever the respondent has heard most recently about politics, rather than on deeply held views. Respondents planning to vote against Bush who have just read a news story about problems in Iraq may say they dislike Bush because of his Iraq policy; those who have read an article about taxes may say they dislike his tax policy. This point reflects a general concern about surveys—that respondents want to answer questions, even if they elicit transitory ideas rather than deeply held beliefs.

An additional problem with open-ended questions is that people give answers of different lengths. One person may say he or she likes George Bush because of his positions on social issues, while another may say he or she likes Bush because of his general conservatism, his position on abortion, his position on gay marriage, and his faith-based agenda. Both respondents would be scored as pro-Republican on domestic issues, but the first person would be scored +1, while the second would be scored +4, even though the main difference between them may be that the first is more terse and the second more garrulous. How many comments a respondent gives on open-ended questions may have as much to do with personality and rapport with the interviewer as with the intensity of attitudes.

Surveys could instead ask respondents directly why they are voting as they are. Social psychologists have found, however, that people cannot accurately report the reasons for their behavior (Nisbett and Wilson 1977; Rahn, Krosnick, and Bruening 1994). Thus, open-ended questions may not be as meaningful as desired. Fortunately, other research finds that people can report the content of their thoughts (Fiske and Taylor 1991, 270, 399–402), which justifies the NES approach of asking people about their attitudes instead of asking them for the reasons for their vote.

Finally, the exclusive use of the open-ended materials as predictors of the vote has been debated over the years. The NES surveys include many closed-ended questions that could be used to measure the impact of issues and the candidates on the vote. The relative advantages of using open- versus closed-ended questions to model the vote have been debated by Kessel and Weisberg (1999). Closed-ended questions allow researchers to ask about topics that respondents may not have thought consciously about, permitting a broader assessment of what affects the vote. On the other hand, closed-ended questions are so easy to answer that people may answer them even if they have not thought about the topic. Furthermore, the open-ended questions are valuable since they allow the respondents to state what they consider important, are fully comparable across years, and allow responsiveness to late-breaking campaign developments on which the researchers had not written closed-ended questions.

Modeling the Vote

The use of the six partisan attitudes as coequal determinants of the vote makes several assumptions. First, it treats attitudes on candidates and positions on issues as independent of one another instead of recognizing that one can affect the other. Brody and Page (1972) distinguished two processes by which such attitudes and positions can interrelate. There can be *persuasion effects* if a candidate's stands help determine voters' positions on issues. Or there can be *projection effects* if people assume that their preferred candidate agrees with them on the issues. Empirical tests suggest that projection effects are greater than persuasion effects (Page and Jones 1979; cf. Converse and Markus 1979), but this still shows that attitudes toward candidates and positions on issues are not independent of one another. To the extent that they are not, including comments both about the candidates and about the issues in the same voting model may be redundant.

Another major assumption is that all of the components have the same logical position in affecting the vote. For example, social groups and issues generally persist over a long period of time and therefore may have more long-term effects on the vote than attitudes toward candidates, who generally change between elections. *The New American Voter* (Miller and Shanks 1996) is an excellent example of parsing out the temporal order of different influences on the vote decision in a comprehensive vote model, though its assumptions about temporal order are themselves debatable. At the end of chapter 14 we discuss these modeling issues in greater detail.

The American Voter also assumes that a single multivariate equation can be used to represent the votes of the whole population. The regression approach recognizes that the six predictors need not deserve equal weights, but it is naive in assuming equal weights for all segments of the population. It would be more realistic to look for different weighting equations for different demographic groups or at least for groups with different levels of political sophistication. The one-equation-fits-all precedent of *The American Voter* quickly became the standard for the field, with very few analysts thinking through whether that makes substantive sense.

Another assumption is that positive comments about one party or candidate are equivalent to negative comments about the opposite party or candidate. Yet an anti-Republican comment is not necessarily equivalent to a pro-Democratic comment. Some research shows that negative reactions can affect behavior more than positive reactions (Lau 1985), so one could weight negative comments more than positive ones. However, partisans are sometimes harsher on their own candidate than on the opponent, even when they are planning to vote for their party's candidate. For example, Republicans may voice quibbles about George W. Bush or his administration, but that does not mean they believe Democrats would do better. Thus, weighting negative comments more than positive comments could weaken the model's predictive success.

The American Voter separated responses to the open-ended, likes-and-dislikes questions on parties and candidates into six partisan attitudes. Kelley and Mirer (1974) instead advocated a "simple model" in which the positive and negative comments about each party and candidate are added up (with proper signs), and which they show is a powerful predictor of the vote. Since their model does not differentiate between different partisan attitudes, it cannot indicate which factors are more important in affecting the vote. However, since it incorporates short-term views, it is a more powerful predictor than party identification alone would be.

CHAPTER 5

Voting Turnout

When citizens cast a vote in an election they do a lot more than ponder the pros and cons of the rival candidates. They must also resolve that the election is important enough to travel to the polling station or send in their ballot by mail. Preference for a particular candidate can matter only if it is expressed on a ballot, and the decision by some citizens to stay home on Election Day may matter as much for the outcome of an election as the choices made by those who turn out. Changes in turnout greatly affect the fortunes of candidates and parties. This is especially noteworthy for turning points in American electoral history, which are marked by sharp fluctuations in turnout. Even in the 2004 election, which confirmed a sitting president in office, turnout increased more than did the winner's share of the vote, in comparison to the election four years earlier.

As in any democracy, participation of the citizenry in elections is valued in American society, leading to exhortations during the election campaign to go out and make your vote count. The democratic ideal is synonymous with universal participation. It looks bad for a democratic country if many of its people stay home on Election Day. It suggests that people are disenchanted with the democratic process and see no point in participating. Indeed, much of the popular discussion of turnout has to do with why so many fail to vote. Turnout in American elections is unimpressive in comparison to other countries; the United States ranks closer to the bottom than the top (Franklin 1996; Powell 1986). And the trend in American elections is, if anything, not encouraging. Even big-draw events like presidential elections bring out no more than two of every three citizens to the polls. For a long time, observers blamed burdensome registration requirements for the low turnout, but this line of reasoning is less persuasive now that registration procedures have become much easier. A great many American adults still fail to ensure that they are eligible to vote on Election Day.

Identifying the motives for nonvoting is important in coming to grips with electoral participation. At the same time, we miss the bigger picture if we deal only with *failure* to vote. What may be remarkable about American presidential elections is the fact that millions make the effort to show up at the polls and cast their vote (or do so by absentee ballot). What are the motivations that lead these people to do so? And does lack of these motivations keep others from voting? What best distinguishes the voter from the nonvoter? As our analysis will show, it is difficult to explain why certain individuals turn out who are not "expected" to (the "deviant voter")—much harder than explaining why someone fails to vote who is expected to (the "deviant nonvoter").

As with the choice between candidates, the decision to vote or stay home derives in the most immediate sense from psychological forces. But nonpsychological factors play a more significant role in turnout than they do for candidate choice. There are barriers to turnout that do not impede the choice among candidates. In this chapter we present evidence for motivational forces that affect the likelihood an individual will vote. At the same time, we are mindful that these causes of turnout, like the attitudinal components of candidate choice, are intervening variables in a more extended process in which a wide array of antecedent factors play a part. Turnout, like candidate choice, is simply the end point of a long and wide causal funnel where motivational forces occupy the place most proximate to the decision itself.

TYPES OF POLITICAL ENGAGEMENT

While many Americans turn out to vote in presidential elections, for most this is their only participation in politics. Few profess to engage in any one of several more taxing political activities, as table 5.1 makes clear. If it is distressing that a bare majority of the electorate shows up at the polls in our presidential elections, the fact that in 2000 only one person in 10 engaged in the most common type of act in the table—showing one's political colors—must be downright depressing. And that was a rather modest act of sporting a campaign button or a bumper sticker or a sign. Even fewer reported giving money to a candidate, political party or campaign-related group. And barely one in 30 engaged in other, presumably more demanding, work for a candidate or party. What is more, it is largely the same people who reported different acts of participation. Someone who gave money was also very likely to go to a rally or sport a bumper sticker. The circle of the politically active was much smaller than the sum of the parts in table 5.1.

Though unimpressive by the standard of the democratic ideal, the degree of overt engagement does increase between the two Bush elections. Nearly every indicator in table 5.1 moved up between 2000 and 2004, yielding a bumper crop for bumper stickers and other displays of political affection. There is no question that the circumstances of the 2004 contest energized Americans to a far greater extent than did the 2000 contest. The proportion of individuals who gave money— most likely, by clicking a credit-card authorization on the Internet in 2004—nearly doubled. Whether the spark of politicization in 2004 so evident in the active segment of the public covered in table 5.1 also ignited the broader electorate will be seen shortly, when we compare voting turnout in those two elections. For now, it is worth keeping in mind that the extent of active participation beyond voting evidenced in 2004 is not written in stone. It would be foolish to expect the surge in 2004 to have launched a trend. It is far more likely that 2004 set a record

TABLE 5.1. Acts of Political Participation, 2000 and 2004 (in percentages)

	2000	2004
Did you go to any political meetings, rallies, speeches, dinners, or things like that in support of a particular candidate?	5	7
Did you wear a campaign button, put a campaign sticker on your car, or place a sign in your window or in front of your house?	10	21
Did you do any other work for one of the parties or candidates?	3	3
During an election year people are often asked to make a contribution to support campaigns. Did you give money to an individual candidate running for public office?	6	9
Did you give money to a political party during this election year?	6	9
Did you give any money to any other group that supported or opposed candidates?	3	6

Note: Entries are percentages of total sample (N = 1,566 in 2000 and 1,066 in 2004) answering affirmatively.

for overt political engagement, which typically settles closer to the 2000 mark.

Of course, many people find ways to become "engaged," if you will, in a presidential contest through other, less demanding, modes. A very common one is informal political discussion. In the 2004 election almost half of the respondents said they talked to other people and tried to persuade them to vote a certain way; in 2000, about one-third said so.[1] This indicates that the general public, not just the active minority, got more caught up in the 2004 campaign than it did four years earlier. Though casual and not connected to organized campaign activity, this activity reveals a psychological involvement that is bound to have an impact on turnout and the division of the vote. By far the most common mode of informal participation is following the campaign in the mass media. Sizable majorities of respondents in 2000 and 2004 reported paying at least some attention to the presidential campaign through the mass media.[2] For some individuals, this means taking a close look at the coverage of the campaign in newspapers and magazines or paying attention to programs on radio and television. For the vast majority, however, the media, television in particular, offer a more passive mode of political engagement. Yet whichever way the mass media enter the world of individual citizens, any consumer of media offerings is apt to screen out vast amounts of content, tuning into some and ignoring other material. The public should not be regarded as a "captive audience" of the mass media, but as one that decides what it will and will not attend. In that sense, using the mass media to get information about an election campaign may count as a mode of participation.

Important as the study of political participation may be, the focus of this book is on the act of voting itself, not other types of participation. Yet some of the determinants of the voting act may also underlie other modes of political participation. A common feature of turnout and other acts of participation is their habitual nature. This pattern probably originates in early socialization, which may foster a general orientation toward politics. We may not be natural-born voters or nonvoters, but

---

1. The question was, "During the campaign, did you talk to any people and try to show them why they should vote for one of the parties or candidates?" In the 2004 NES survey, 48 percent of all respondents answered affirmatively; in 2000, 34 percent did so.

2. The question was, "How much attention did you pay to news on national news shows about the campaign for President?" In the 2004 NES survey, 68 percent of all respondents answered at least "some"; in 2000, 60 percent did.

political socialization establishes quite early a predisposition for either voting or nonvoting as normal behavior. Whether one voted in past elections closely predicts whether one will vote in the current election. Table 5.2 shows the relationship in 2004 between voting in the past and voting in the current election. Nearly all of the respondents who reported taking part in the 2000 election also reported voting in 2004. But fewer than half of the 2000 nonvoters showed up in 2004. If past behavior is such a strong guide to current decisions, our inquiry into the reasons why people turn out to vote is less about a decision made anew in each campaign than about a "standing decision," to borrow V. O. Key's language from another context. As the analysis will show, the most helpful determinants of voting turnout are those that bear on enduring orientations toward politics rather than on fleeting elements of a given presidential campaign.

MEASURING VOTING TURNOUT

Our measure of voting turnout, like that of candidate choice, relies on the report supplied by survey respondents. Days after the election they were asked whether they voted and, if so, for whom. It should be noted that these are the same survey respondents who were already queried before the election about a wide array of attitudes and opinions that form the material from which we draw explanations of their behavior. Verbal self-report, to be sure, is not a totally reliable way of capturing actual behavior. Any inference from such reports to behavior may be flawed if individuals severely distort their choices in the interview. We must be especially alert to this problem if the behavior studied is of the socially desirable variety, as voting is, given the high value placed on it in a dem-

TABLE 5.2. The Relation of Past Voting to Current Voting Turnout (in percentages)

	Voted in 2000	Did Not Vote in 2000
Voted in 2004	92	45
Did not vote in 2004	8	55
Total	100	100
Number of cases	707	297

Note: Voting turnout in the 2000 election was obtained in response to this question in the 2004 election survey: "Do you remember for sure whether or not you voted in that [2000] election?" The tabulation includes only those 2004 respondents who were old enough to vote in 2000.

TABLE 5.3. Estimates of Voting Turnout in 2004 (in percentages)

As a proportion of the voting-age population	56.2
As a proportion of the population of U.S. citizens of voting age	62.1
Current Population Survey	63.8
National Election Study (NES)	76.3

Source: Clerk of the House (for total number of votes cast); Census Bureau, March 2004 report (for estimates of voting age and citizen populations); Census Bureau, May 2005 report (for Current Population Survey estimate); NES survey, 2004.

ocratic society. Many nonvoters may be too embarrassed to admit their failure to vote.

Without much doubt, self-reported turnout rates in NES surveys (76.3 percent in 2004, and 72.1 percent in 2000) overstate actual turnout.[3] How wide the gap is, however, depends on the choice of an "official" turnout statistic. Recording the voting turnout in American elections, it turns out, is not a very exact science. Popular claims in the media and textbooks notwithstanding, no "official" turnout figure is issued by any government agency for presidential elections. What often passes as such a turnout rate is a conventional estimate that divides the number of votes cast for president (122.3 million in 2004, as reported by the Clerk of the House) by the size of the voting-age population (217.8 million in 2004, as provided by the Census Bureau, May 2004 report). As shown in table 5.3, this yields a voting turnout of 56.2 percent for 2004, which the NES survey figure exceeds by 20 points.

But the lower "official" figure is a dubious one for two plain reasons. One, the population includes many residents ineligible to vote, and two, the vote count excludes many who went to the polls but whose vote was not properly recorded or who did not cast a vote for president. If the voting-age population is adjusted to include only *U.S. citizens* of voting age (197 million, as estimated by the Census Bureau, May 2005 report), the turnout rate comes to 62.1 percent. It will rise even higher once we adjust the population estimate for several millions who are imprisoned or deprived of their voting right because of felony convictions. At the same time, a portion of citizens who make it to the polls end up casting a vote that is not properly recorded. The Florida debacle in 2000 taught all of us a lesson in ballot malfunctioning, from confusion over butterfly ballots

---

3. The NES turnout figures are calculated using the postelection weights and may differ slightly from the ones posted on the NES Web site (http://www.electionstudies.org/nesguide/toptable/tab6a_2.htm), which are not weighted.

to hanging chads, to overvotes, rejected absentee ballots, and more. A common estimate puts the percentage of invalid votes in the United States at 2 percent in national elections (Knack and Kropf 2003, 890). In view of all these factors calling for adjustment, the 2004 turnout estimate (63.8) produced by the Current Population Survey (conducted by the U.S. Census Bureau) may come closest to the reality of voting turnout.

Yet even by this standard, the NES estimate overstates turnout. So do some respondents fib when they say they voted? Voting, after all, is proper citizen conduct, and staying home is not. So making up the right response in an interview, saying what is socially acceptable, would be quite understandable. Yet before accepting this conclusion, let us consider several alternatives. One is that the universe of the sample is quite different from the eligible population, even after the exclusion of noncitizens and felons. The design of the survey excludes portions of the population with a low propensity to vote—people residing in institutions (even aside from prisons), those in transit or without fixed addresses (the homeless, in particular). What is more, a sizable portion of the sample eludes repeated attempts to interview them. Many of them, we suspect, are not very much involved in politics. As the analysis in this chapter will show, nonvoters are concentrated among the less involved. Hence the NES samples are bound to contain a disproportionate number of voters. Furthermore, the panel nature of the NES surveys inadvertently, creates a mobilization effect. The interview before the election acts like a visit from a campaign that energizes some respondents to pay attention to the campaign and go out and vote (Clausen 1968; Traugott and Katosh 1979).

All these factors nonetheless are unable to close the gap between survey reports and official turnout statistics. Vote validation studies have shown that roughly one in 10 respondents typically report having voted when in fact they did not (Bernstein, Chadha, and Montjoy 2001; Clausen 1968; Silver, Anderson, and Abramson 1986; Traugott 1989; Traugott and Katosh 1979).[4] In many instances, however, misreporting of voting is a case of faulty memory, not of false reporting. Respondents may honestly believe they voted when in fact they did not. These are individuals who normally vote or thought about voting this time. The

---

4. NES conducted validation checks of reported voting in the election studies of 1964, 1976, 1980, 1980, and 1988, but not in presidential elections since then. Oddly enough, the validation checks revealed that a few respondents reported *not* to have voted when the records showed that they actually did.

ᴧBLE 5.4. Self-Report of Voting Turnout in Surveys: Two Question Versions percentages)

ndard Version of Turnout Question: spondent's Report		Experimental Version of Turnout Question: Respondent's Report	
s, voted in 2004	80	Sure I voted in 2004	73
		Thought about voting this time, but didn't vote in 2004	10
		Usually vote, but didn't vote in 2004	4
, did not vote in 2004	20	Did not vote in 2004	13
Total	100	Total	100
Number of cases	537	Number of cases	529

Note: The standard version, after listing several reasons why people might not vote, asks: "Did you vote in the election November?" The experimental version, using the same preface, asked: "Which of the following statements best cribes you: One, I did not vote (in the election this November); Two, I thought about voting this time, but didn't; ee, I usually vote, but didn't this time; or Four, I am sure I voted?"

evidence in table 5.4 makes clear that such memory lapses inflate turnout reports in surveys. In the half sample in 2004 where respondents were asked straight up whether or not they voted, 80 percent said they did so. In the other half where respondents were given two additional options to tweak their memory, only 73 percent reported voting. What expanded the pool of nonvoters in this half were respondents who either thought about voting or usually voted, but failed to do so this time (Belli et al. 1999). Yet whatever the gap between self-reported and actual turnout, or the explanation for it, the partisan division of the vote in the NES surveys does not greatly depart from the overall result.[5] This does not rule out the possibility that some errors in one direction cancel out errors in the other one, but there seems to be little tendency in respondents to distort their choices to place themselves on the winning side, as the bandwagon effect might predict.

VOTE PREFERENCE AND TURNOUT

As for theoretical approaches to the turnout decision, we begin with the vote preference itself. An individual without a preferred candidate, we submit, is not likely to vote. Who would that person vote for anyway in the polling booth? So why should such a person make the effort? It

---

5. The 2004 NES survey gave Bush 50.2 percent of the major-party vote, the 2000 NES 47.8 percent. These sample percentages are less than two points off the actual results and clearly within the margin of sampling error.

should not matter whether the preference is lacking because the various alternatives are all equally appealing or unappealing, or because none of the alternatives inspires any affect, positive or negative. Either way, such individuals do not have a dog in the fight. In contrast, it is natural to suppose that someone with a strong preference among the candidates turns out to vote because such a person has someone to vote for. Intensity of voting preference catches an important motivational factor that varies in the short run from one electoral contest to the next one. That may be both a strength and a weakness—a strength because it captures the short-term elements of a given election, a weakness because it lacks a long-term dimension.

We have measured the intensity of preference with the help of open-ended questions about presidential candidates and parties, the detailed responses to which were examined in a previous chapter. The more someone made favorable references about one side compared to unfavorable references about the other side, the greater was the intensity of the preference. Our first stab at explaining why some individuals voted and others did not vote relies on the intensity of preference, combining data from the 2000 and 2004 surveys.

The relationship between intensity of preference and voting turnout, as shown in figure 5.1, is quite impressive. The percentage of respondents who reported voting in those two elections rises relentlessly with every step up on the scale of preference intensity, reaching a near-perfect 100 at the top rung (where about 1 in 20 are located). In other words, the more strongly someone preferred the Democratic side over the Republican side (or vice versa), the more likely was that person to cast a vote. Nonvoting practically vanished at the highest level of intensity. At the same time, we have to admit that voting was not extinct at the bottom of the intensity scale. The lowest level of intensity consists of respondents who were either torn between the candidates and parties, or who felt little or no affect for them. Yet nearly every other person in this group still cast a vote for president. And at the next level, where intensity of preference barely registers a pulse, two-thirds went to the polls nonetheless. In other words, at the low end of the intensity scale we encounter "deviant voters." They should be staying home, but they turn up in fairly large numbers anyway.

If strength of preference matters for turnout in a given election, it makes sense to suppose that shifts in aggregate turnout from one election to the next one are prompted, in part, by changes in that strength.

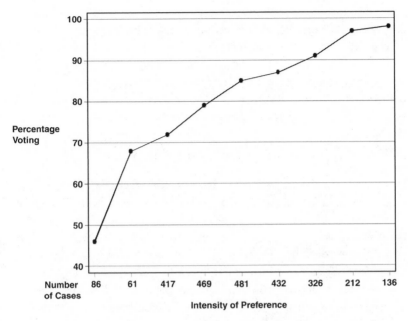

Fig. 5.1. The intensity of voting preference and voting turnout, 2000 and 2004.

The intensity scale is based on responses to the likes/dislikes questions about candidates and parties in 2000 and 2004. Scale values represent the absolute difference between the number of favorable references about one side and the number of unfavorable references about the other side.

Voter turnout, as noted already, rose markedly between 2000 and 2004. Was this the result of stronger feelings aroused by the candidates and issues in 2004? The data indicate that this was so. Our measure of preference intensity registers an uptick between 2000 and 2004. Respondents grew more sharply polarized in their affect toward the candidates and parties. The Bush-Kerry matchup generated more heat in the electorate than the Bush-Gore contest.

The preference for one partisan side in an election nonetheless is not entirely shaped by the circumstances of the given campaign. Current preference is also a carryover from previous ones, and the trail may reach quite a way back. Recall, for example, the nearly unshakable goodwill enjoyed by the Democratic Party as the champion of ordinary Americans. Such affect may persuade some individuals to vote Democrat even if the current standard-bearer does not inspire much confidence. The influence of voting preference on turnout thus reaches a lot further than our measure for a single election is able to show. Yet whatever explanatory power we may be able to extract from the intensity of preference leaves the turnout account incomplete. This is especially glaring at the lower end of the intensity scale. Too many Americans show up at the polls that should not be expected to do so, given their lack or near-lack of any voting preference in the election. What makes these "deviant voters" take the trouble to cast votes for candidates they do not care much about?

POLITICAL INVOLVEMENT AND TURNOUT

Our search for a more exhaustive explanation of voting turnout is not limited to making sense of deviant cases, but concerns the full spectrum of the public. While the decision to vote may derive, in part, from a comparative assessment of the alternatives, we also believe that the act of voting is but one manifestation of a broader "psychological involvement" in politics. Each individual develops a characteristic pattern of involvement in politics. The pattern remains quite stable through successive elections, turning some of us into habitual voters and others into habitual nonvoters. Turnout behavior is guided by the following rule: The stronger a person's psychological involvement in politics, the higher the propensity to participate in politics by way of voting. We have identified specific indicators of the individual's psychological involvement in politics, two of which are election-specific, and two of which refer to politics and elections more generally.[6]

Interest in the Campaign

The first indicator of involvement to be considered is interest in the campaign. Some people are captivated by a particular presidential contest, while others pay no attention. The importance of this attitude for voting turnout can be seen in table 5.5 with data from the election of 2004. Turnout among those very much interested in the campaign exceeded that among persons not much interested by more than 40 per-

---

6. The four measures of involvement, as shown by a principal-component analysis of responses in 2000, form a component, which accounts for close to half of the variance of the measures. The loadings on that component are as follows:

Interest in the campaign	.59
Concern over the election outcome	.56
Sense of political efficacy	.47
Sense of citizen duty	.36

cent. Yet it is surprising to see respondents at the low end of the interest measure turn out in fairly strong numbers, with almost half doing so. Taking campaign interest into account does not give us much added grasp of the "deviant voter," the type who is not expected to vote but does so nonetheless.

Concern over the Election Outcome

Perhaps the answer lies in a person's concern over the outcome of the given election. Some people care deeply about the electoral result, whereas others care little. Though intuitively distinct from political interest, concern over the election result is quite strongly correlated with interest. The association of the two points to the existence of a more general involvement factor. Concern over the outcome makes a sharp difference for voting turnout in 2004, as shown in table 5.6. Still, not

TABLE 5.5. Interest in the Campaign and Voting Turnout, 2004 (in percentages)

	Interest in the Campaign[a]		
	Not Much Interested	Somewhat Interested	Very Much Interested
Voted	47	74	90
Did not vote	53	26	10
Total	100	100	100
Number of cases	169	468	429

[a]Respondents were asked: "Some people don't pay much attention to political campaigns. How about you? Would you say that you have been very much interested, somewhat interested, or not much interested in the political campaigns so far this year?"

TABLE 5.6. Concern about Election Outcome and Voting Turnout, 2004 (in percentages)

	Concern over Election Outcome[a]	
	Don't Care Very Much	Care a Good Deal
Voted	39	82
Did not vote	61	18
Total	100	100
Number of cases	143	918

[a]Respondents were asked: "Generally speaking, would you say that you personally care a good deal who wins the presidential election this fall, or that you don't care very much who wins?"

everyone who did not care very much about the outcome stayed home. About 4 in 10 turned out anyway.

Sense of Political Efficacy

Like interest in the campaign, concern over the election outcome is an indicator of involvement that refers explicitly to the election at hand. As such, these measures capture the ebb and flow of short-term forces. But they most likely tap more enduring attitudes toward politics as well. No election campaign is utterly unique, and most people react to the latest one with a set of predispositions already in place. They vary from person to person, but they have acquired a characteristic pattern of involvement for each person. Only a small fraction of the American electorate follows politics with an intense devotion at all times. And while few on the other side of the involvement dimension lack any connection to the political world, between these extremes the extent of emotional involvement in political affairs varies greatly.

One key indicator of an individual's involvement in politics generally is the "sense of political efficacy" (Campbell, Gurin, and Miller 1954, appendix A). There are people who see politics as something beyond their reach to understand or control. Others believe that the business of government can be understood and influenced by individual citizens. To gauge the effectiveness that an individual feels in relation to politics, we rely on an index of political efficacy, based on a series of questions probing attitudes of this sort. The relation of this index to voting turnout can be seen in table 5.7 for the election of 2004. The rate of voting turnout does rise with the individual's sense of political efficacy, but fewer than 20 percentage points separate the top from the bottom of the index. The

TABLE 5.7. Sense of Political Efficacy and Voting Turnout, 2004 (in percentages)

| | Sense of Political Efficacy[a] | | |
	Low	Intermediate	High
Voted	69	80	87
Did not vote	31	20	13
Total	100	100	100
Number of cases	499	284	279

[a]Respondents were classified according to an index formed from responses (disagree) to two statements: (1) "Public officials don't care much what people like me think" and (2) "People like me don't have any say in what the government does."

TABLE 5.8. Sense of Civic Duty and Voting Turnout, 2000 (in percentages)

	Sense of Civic Duty[a]	
	Rather Not Serve on a Jury	Happy to Serve on a Jury
Voted	61	80
Did not vote	39	20
Total	100	100
Number of cases	621	922

[a]Respondents were asked: "If you were selected to serve on a jury, would you be happy to do it or would you rather not serve?"

bottom category of the efficacy index, unfortunately, contains nearly half of the electorate—too large a portion to offer much discrimination for turnout.

Sense of Citizen Duty

The final indicator of involvement considered in our analysis of turnout also captures a long-term attitude. As noted several times already, voting participation is not just a right, but a duty that society expects its members to perform. To be a good citizen, you have to show up and vote. In those who accept it, this social norm becomes a powerful motive for individual behavior, in this case voting on Election Day (Campbell, Gurin, and Miller 1954, app. B). For those who did not absorb the norm, a key motivation for turnout will be missing. Our measure of citizen duty is based on a simple question outside of the electoral arena, the willingness to serve on a jury.[7] We assume that someone who accepts this duty of citizenship would also endorse it for electoral participation. Indeed, as can be seen in table 5.8 for 2000, this sense of citizen duty makes a pronounced difference for voting turnout, but by no means an overwhelming one.

So far, we have examined the effects of various motivations on voting turnout one at a time. Each of them provides a very close account of the voting side of the turnout problem. We can say with great certainty what kind of Americans go to the polls—the ones at the top of preference intensity, interest in the campaign, concern over the outcome, sense of political efficacy, and sense of citizen duty. Few inhabiting those lofty

7. This is the only item pertaining to the concept of citizen duty that was asked in the NES surveys as recently as 2000.

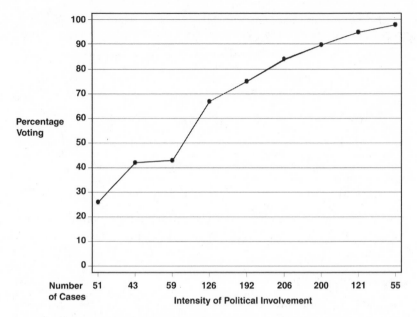

Fig. 5.2. The intensity of political involvement and voting turnout, 2004.

The intensity of political involvement is scaled by an additive combination of the various measures of involvement (interest in campaign, concern over the election outcome, and sense of political efficacy) along with intensity of voting preference.

floors fail to show up on Election Day. But not one of these indicators has pointed out unambiguously what kinds of people do not vote. Our only hope to come to grips with these "deviant voters" is through combining the various motivations considered thus far. This is, of course, how any scientific explanation works. However simple the act may be, the process of getting to the voting decision is highly complex. There is no magic bullet. Hence we have combined various measures in a psychological involvement scale, including the strength of preference, to see how this dimension accounts for the turnout decision.

As is seen in figure 5.2, the rate of turnout increases steadily with political involvement and differs by about 75 percent between top and bottom. At the top level of involvement nearly everyone votes, while at the bottom roughly three in four stay home. The combination of motivations has helped us make much progress in coming to grips with the phenomenon of the "deviant voter," although we have not been able to banish this type altogether. The quest for explanation is not over yet.

Divergent Cases

Our index of political involvement is not adept at distinguishing voters from nonvoters in the middle categories of figure 5.2. At moderate levels of involvement individuals are neither so weakly motivated that they are sure to stay home nor so strongly motivated that they are sure to turn out. For these kinds of citizens the decision to turn out or stay home may derive from factors exogenous to our theoretical concerns. Most challenging for our concerns, however, is "error" in figure 5.2 that is found at the extremes of political involvement. Here we would expect to be quite confident in predicting whether someone votes or does not. Error of prediction for these types of individuals compels us to examine divergent cases so we can understand better the turnout decision.

The popular lore about voting points out ready explanations for error at the high end of involvement. Who has not heard of someone with strong motivation who is kept from making the trip to the polls by circumstances beyond one's control, such as a personal emergency or a registration mix-up? The list of such no-shows even includes presidential candidates (John Edwards), governors (Jesse Ventura), and show-business celebrities (Ben Affleck) who campaigned for presidential candidates and urged others to turn out (Morton 2006, 24–25). Popular lore has less to say about the opposite type of deviant case—the politically unmotivated person who nonetheless turns out. But here group theory may offer a persuasive explanation. Interpersonal influence, especially within the family, exerts strong pressures of conformity, as demonstrated long ago by one of the classic voting studies (Lazarsfeld, Berelson, and Gaudet 1948, chap. 15). In many instances a person with a low degree of political involvement who votes does so to avoid friction with a spouse or a friend. Turning out to vote is the price of peace with one's family or peers.

THE "VOTE" OF NONVOTERS

In the final analysis it is only the preferences of those who turn out that decide who gets elected to political office. Yet the preferences of nonvoters elicit considerable attention nevertheless. The losing side in an electoral contest finds it impossible to resist the temptation to speculate. What if enough of the nonvoters had participated? As one slogan exhorting people to vote says, "Bad people are elected because good people don't vote." Since the early days of polling in the 1930s it has become an unshakable article of faith that nonvoters are mostly Democrats. Given the relationship between social class and voting, Republicans were thought to be more likely to turn out in elections than were Democrats. And hence the nonvoting part of the electorate would favor Democratic candidates more than would actual voters.

Indeed, the vote preferences reported after some elections confirm this hypothesis. After the 1996 election, for example, nonvoters said they would have voted for Bill Clinton over Bob Dole by nearly a five-to-one ratio, far greater than was true for voters. As can be seen in table 5.9, however, other elections fail to support the contention that nonvoters tend to favor Democratic candidates for president. In 2000 and 2004 only about half of the nonvoters said they would have voted for Gore or Kerry, respectively, which closely matches the support among voters. The shift in Democratic support among nonvoters documented in table 5.9 is of an extreme magnitude. Few changes over time in opinion or behavior in the National Election Studies are as striking as this one.

What caused nonvoters to alter their vote preferences so sharply? Whereas the two-party vote division changed by little more than 6 percent among voters, it changed by more than 30 percent among nonvoters during the 1996–2004 period. What accounts for this difference? While several factors may have been at work, we believe that one idea holds the key. Our research thus far has established the most important distinction between nonvoters and voters: psychological involvement in politics. The nonvoter is a person with little emotional investment in politics, including a voting preference of little or no intensity. Such a person will be highly susceptible to massive political stimuli that are nearly impossible to elude even for people with minimal involvement. The stimulus in question here is simply the fact of who won the elec-

TABLE 5.9. Presidential Vote Preference of Nonvoters, Postelection Surveys (in percentages)

	1996	2000	2004
Would have voted for Democratic candidate	83	54	50
Would have voted for Republican candidate	17	46	50
Total	100	100	100
Number of cases	253	295	171

Note: For major-party candidates only.

TABLE 5.10. Change in Candidate Preferences of Nonvoters by Political Interest, 2004 (in percentages)

	Preference for Bush		
	Before Election	After Election	Change
Very much interested	54	48	−6
Somewhat interested	49	49	0
Not much interested	49	52	+3

Note: Entries are percentages favoring Bush, the winning candidate, among those giving a preference for a major-party candidate.

tion, and perhaps how decisively.[8] Nonvoters, we contend, are riding a psychological bandwagon.

We would expect the less involved to exhibit this effect to a greater extent than the more involved. In table 5.10 we have divided nonvoters according to a measure of involvement, interest in the campaign, and compared their voting preferences before and after the 2004 election. It is clear that the nonvoters lowest in campaign interest shifted in the winning direction (Republican) direction, while those who were more involved did not. The swing in the Republican direction debunks the claim that nonvoters are pro-Democratic in their vote preference while making a strong case for psychological involvement as a key to political behavior. Low involvement is the defining quality of the nonvoter, which has far-reaching consequences for behavior.

COMMENTARY AND CONTROVERSY

The Paradox of Voting

While many observers find it troubling that so many Americans fail to show up at the polls, others are vexed by the oddity that so many do take the trouble. The "rational choice" approach to voting, as popularized in our field by Anthony Downs's economic theory, seems to suggest that the act of voting is irrational, and hence a paradox (Downs 1957). The way rational-choice theory sees it, voting is a cost-benefit decision. The benefit (B) is derived from the preferred party winning office

8. The lengthy dispute over the outcome of the 2000 election and the fact that Al Gore won the popular vote may undercut this stimulus for 2000 and account for the close division among nonvoters that year.

to make policy.[9] The costs (C) are the time, effort, information, and so on, required to make a rational voting decision, including going to the polls. Yet however large the benefit of having one's preferred party in office may be to an individual voter, one single vote does little to make it happen. An election, after all, is a collective choice in which the probability (P) of one's own vote deciding the outcome is extremely small, indeed infinitesimal in an American presidential election. Any voter eager to cast a vote on Election Day, but kept from going to the polls by circumstances beyond his or her control, would realize the next day that adding that vote to the tally reported in the news would change absolutely nothing. Sad to admit, but in an election with 120 million voters, any single vote falls under rounding error.

So whatever benefit (B) a voter accrues from one party winning over the other in an election must be discounted by the probability of deciding the outcome (P). The adjusted benefit is negligible compared to the costs (C) of voting, in time, effort, information, and so on, which must be borne by the voter personally. Hence the decision whether or not to vote is faced with the following cost-benefit relationship:

$$C > PB.$$

With costs (C) outweighing discounted benefits (PB), it is irrational to vote. Rational-choice proponents have struggled mightily to resolve the paradox that many citizens, a majority in most presidential elections, do make what must seem like an "irrational" choice to vote (Aldrich 1993; Ferejohn and Fiorina 1974). Perhaps the most compelling solution is adding another term (D) to the benefit side of the calculus of voting, be it the value of democracy as such or the value of doing one's duty as a citizen (Downs 1957, chap. 14; Riker and Ordeshook 1968). On closer inspection, the components of the D term turn out to overlap with the motivations relating to psychological involvement that we have examined above and found to have a powerful influence on the decision to vote. If there is anything paradoxical about voting, the influence of personal considerations should be able to resolve this apparent paradox. Without much doubt there are personal benefits to voting, such as feeling good about showing one's political colors, being a good citizen, or

---

9. This concept bears a striking resemblance to the "intensity of preference" used in the analysis above.

TABLE 5.11. Closeness of Election, Intensity of Preference, and Voting
Turnout, 2004 (in percentages)

	Election Seen As					
	One-Sided			Close		
	Intensity of Preference			Intensity of Preference		
	Weak	Medium	Strong	Weak	Medium	Strong
Voted	51	86	95	67	81	93
Did not vote	49	14	5	33	19	7
Total	100	100	100	100	100	100
Number of cases	68	74	40	325	322	176

keeping peace with one's family and peers. So long as these benefits out-
weigh whatever costs the voting act exacts, it is perfectly rational to vote.
Rational choice does not dictate what we should want, only how to get
what we want. The fact that no single vote makes any discernible difference for the outcome need not diminish the thrill any voter gets from
the act of voting.

Closeness of Election

One consideration that appears quite rational is the common belief that
voting turnout depends on whether the outcome of the election is a
foregone conclusion or a close race: the closer the race, the stronger the
incentive for citizens to go to the polls and make their vote count. This
is a consideration that might affect some persons more than others.
Those with a strong preference for one of the candidates (or a high
B-value, in rational-choice terms) may not need the added incentive of
a close race to find the way to the polls, but someone else with a weak
preference (a low B-value) may require that extra push. Yet the opposite
may be plausible as well. Having a weak preference may discourage participation to such an extent that even closeness does not matter, while
those with a strong preference in a close race want to make sure their
vote counts. As shown in table 5.11, closeness only matters for individuals with a weak vote preference.[10] They turn out more heavily when they
see the race as close than when they see it as foregone conclusion—at

---

10. The outcome in question is the presidential contest in the nation as a whole, not in the respondent's state. It might be argued that the latter race should be more important since the
final choice rests with presidential electors chosen by states and since all of a state's electors are
usually awarded to the candidate with the most votes in a given state.

least they did in the 2004 election. Perception of closeness appears to serve as an additional incentive for persons with a weak vote preference to turn out and make their vote "count."[11]

Education and Age

The examination of voting turnout in this chapter so far has focused on the immediate considerations pertaining to the act of voting. Though immediate, some of these considerations, particularly those of a psychological nature, may reach back far in a person's life history. Early family socialization is probably the most remote antecedent of any adult citizen's inclination to turn out to vote. By the example of our parents alone, many of us are steered on the path of participation or the path of apathy. But the development of political citizenship does not end there.

Formal education is widely recognized as a critical factor in a person's background that influences the propensity to vote.[12] Aside from providing cognitive skills that help the voter find out what's going on in politics, education is largely responsible for fostering several motivations bundled together in the examination above under the heading of "psychological involvement in politics." Hence interest in the campaign, concern over the outcome, sense of political efficacy, and sense of civic duty are all strongly related to level of education. With more formal education comes a stronger interest in politics, a greater concern with elections, greater confidence in playing one's role as a citizen, and a deeper commitment to the norm of being a good citizen. What is more, formal education helps acquire skills and resources important for participation, be it interpersonal skills in dealing with fellow citizens in groups, or skills in dealing with organizations, including such mundane steps as knowing how to obtain a voter registration form and fill it out properly (Wolfinger and Rosenstone 1980; Verba, Schlozman, and Brady 1995). In more ways than one, effective citizen participation depends on the operation of a nation's educational system. Moreover, education is the key ingredient of any relationship between socioeconomic status and voting turnout.

---

11. This is at odds with *The American Voter*. The findings of table 5.3 (Campbell et al. 1960, 99) suggested that closeness affected the turnout of individuals with a strong, but not weak, preference. It must be noted that in both sets of findings the percentage differences are not very big.

12. The Current Population Survey reported for 2004 that in the lowest educational category (less than ninth grade) 38.8 percent voted, compared to 84.2 percent for the highest category (advanced degree). These estimates use the citizen population as a base (U.S. Census Bureau 2005).

Quite independent of education, age has a pronounced effect on voting turnout. Older individuals are more inclined to participate than younger ones.[13] For a variety of reasons, many young citizens eligible for the first time to cast a vote miss their opportunity to do so (Highton and Wolfinger 2001). Voting, for many citizens, is an acquired taste, and the appetite grows with eating. The process at work appears to be quite simple: the more elections one has participated in, the higher the propensity to vote in the next one. In fact, the accumulation of voting participation may feed back on key motivational forces conducive to voting. The act of voting enhances a person's sense of political efficacy (Finkel 1985). Voting also tends to strengthen a voter's partisan attachment (an influence to be examined more fully in a subsequent chapter). The failure of young adults to turn out in large numbers may be largely due to a deficiency of such factors. As these factors develop, so will the propensity to vote, which in turn will boost those factors as well, until participation in elections is all but automatic for individuals of established age.

Mobilization

For all the individual predispositions conducive to voting, what may ultimately account for a person's participation in an election is that someone asked, encouraged, inspired, perhaps even pressured the person to vote. "The essential feature of electoral politics . . . is electoral mobilization," as Rosenstone and Hansen (2003, 161) claim. Indeed, the participation of voters bereft of any sense of political awareness cannot be explained any other way. But the efforts of mobilizing the public to participate are not restricted to that segment of the public, nor are they aimed primarily at them. Though often selective in their targets, campaigns try to mobilize fairly large and quite involved segments of the public. Voting turnout, along with other forms of political participation, is higher among individuals contacted by a political party during a campaign than among those who are not contacted (Rosenstone and Hansen 2003, chap. 6). The side in an election campaign that wins the mobilization battle should expect to win the vote battle as well. The Bush victory in the 2004 election, for example, is widely attributed to the success of Republican mobilization efforts, especially among the religious Right (Balz and Allen 2004;

---

13. The Current Population Survey reported that in 2004, 46.7 percent of the 18- to 24-year-olds voted, compared to 73.3 percent for those 65–74 years old; as usual, turnout dipped somewhat in the oldest cohort, to 66.7 percent in 2004. These estimates use the citizen population as a base (U.S. Census Bureau 2005).

Morton 2006, chap. 3). Such claims, however, must take into account general attitudes as well as specific reactions to issues and candidates that affect turnout even without some external efforts. A study of turnout in 2000, controlling for all those factors, did find a sizable effect for party or campaign contact on turnout (Finkel and Freedman 2004).

Studies of the effect of campaign mobilization on turnout have sparked several controversies. One has to do with negative campaigning. Some say that "going negative" discourages voter turnout by breeding cynicism about politics in the general public (Ansolabahere and Iyengar 1995; Ansolabahere, Iyengar, and Simon 1999). But others have shown that some forms of negative campaigning actually enhance turnout (Finkel and Geer 1998; Kahn and Kenny 1999); do so in some elections (Wattenberg and Brians 1999); are more helpful to challengers than incumbents (Lau and Pomper 2002); or across a wide range of campaigns are no more effective than positive ads (Lau et al. 1999). Another controversy has to do with techniques in a nuts-and-bolts sense of getting out the vote (GOTV). An experimental study showed that personal contact helped boost turnout, while mailings and telephone calls did not (Gerber and Green 2000, 2005), but a replication found telephone calls to be quite effective (Imai 2005). A resolution of this dispute hinges on many highly technical issues of methodology.

Registration

Perhaps the major cost of voting for Americans consists of the requirement to register. Its effect on voting turnout inspired one of the pioneering studies of electoral behavior (Merriam and Gosnell 1924). The findings showed that the reasons for failure to register to vote were very different from the reasons for failure to vote by those who were registered, which is confirmed by reports of the Current Population Survey (U.S. Census Bureau 2006). Registration and voting are two different decisions that make different demands of the citizen and offer different gratifications. It appears that common explanations of turnout—education and age—prove far more compelling for registration than for turnout (Timpone 1998). The registration requirement offers an obvious clue for the relatively low turnout in U.S. elections compared to other countries, which do not have such requirements (Powell 1986).

In a technical sense, there is no better predictor of turnout in American elections than registration. In 2004, voting turnout among registered citizens was 89 percent (U.S. Census Bureau 2005), and 0 percent for the nonregistered. So would overall turnout rise to the astounding level of nearly 90 percent if one could get all the nonregistered onto the rolls? Advocates of election reform tend to think so. It has been estimated that making registration laws more lenient would boost turnout by substantial amounts (Wolfinger and Rosenstone 1980, 73), with eliminating the closing date for registration being the most effective step.[14] But it is highly doubtful that eliminating the need to register would bring the previously unregistered up to par in turnout with the registered. A large number of those who fail to register lack the necessary motivation to participate in elections. In the Current Population Survey, 47 percent of them cited lack of interest or involvement as the reason for being unregistered in 2004 (U.S. Census Bureau 2006, 11). They are as oblivious to registration as to the election. Getting them on the rolls is hardly enough to instill that motivation. Indeed, while not a single respondent at the high end of the involvement scale in 2004 (fig. 5.2) was prevented by the registration requirement barrier from voting, more than half of those at the low end were.[15]

Decline of Turnout

The decline-of-turnout study has become a growth industry, with doomsday titles like the "disappearing voter" and the "vanishing voter" (Teixeira 1992; Patterson 2002). Already low by comparative standards, turnout in presidential elections has edged even lower during the past 50 years, prompting much hand-wringing over the vitality of democracy in the United States. From a theoretical perspective, any decline of turnout during a period of sharply rising educational levels poses a knotty puzzle (Brody 1978). Since formal education is a proven factor, we should have seen an increase, not a decrease, in turnout as the ranks of college graduates began to swell in the 1960s. The same logic goes for the easing of registration requirements. Voting participation, to be sure, has risen among some voting groups affected by legal barriers that were lifted

---

14. The most recent national reforms are the National Voter Registration Act of 1993 (the "motor-voter" law) and the Help America Vote Act (HAVA) of 2002. These efforts notwithstanding, the overall percentage of citizens who were registered to vote in presidential elections did not rise. The Current Population Survey reported about the same rate for 2004 (72.1 percent) as for 1980 (72.3 percent). See U.S. Census Bureau 2007.

15. It is also worth noting that the only state in the nation that has no voting registration, North Dakota, is by no means ahead of the rest of the nation in voting turnout. In fact, North Dakota's turnout is quite similar to that of South Dakota, which does have registration, and to other states in the region.

during the 1960s: black citizens in southern states (Rosenstone and Hansen 2003, chap. 3). And one voting reform was bound to diminish the overall turnout rate: the lowering of the minimum voting age to 18 in 1971. But that effect should have been more than offset by all the other forces putting upward pressure on voting participation in the long run.

The list of culprits for declining turnout in American elections is long and varied, including a decline in "mobilization" of voters by parties and candidates (Rosenstone and Hansen 2003); demobilization through negative campaigning (Ansolabahere and Iyengar 1995; Patterson 2002); and a decline in "social capital" (Putnam 2000), among others. From our perspective the key to changing turnout rates across elections comes from the motivational factors. If the intensity of preference of the average citizen were to drop in one election compared to the previous one, we would expect turnout to suffer, too. This is largely a short-term phenomenon, which would help account for variability of turnout in the short run (Finkel and Freedman 2004). The same goes for interest in the campaign and concern over the outcome. If, however, motivations such as civic duty and political efficacy were to diminish, we would have a handle for any long-term change in turnout. Why these attitudes would decline as educational levels, which should boost them, are rising poses another puzzle. Changes in two motivational factors have made a dent in voting participation: partisan intensity and political efficacy (Abramson, Aldrich, and Rohde 2006). These changes have a strong generational flavor, being concentrated in the post–New Deal cohorts (Miller and Shanks 1996, chaps. 3–5).

Other students of voting, however, claim that the demise of turnout is exaggerated (McDonald and Popkin 2001; and for the 2004 election, United States Election Project 2006). The main argument has to do with the measure of "official" turnout that is used to document the decline. As noted above, that measure has serious flaws that have grown worse over time, especially the use of the voting-age population as a base. Once this base is corrected to exclude noneligible Americans (noncitizens, felons, etc.), whose share of the overall population has been rising sharply in recent years, the signs of change largely vanish. In other words, there is no marked turnout decline in the "citizen population" since 1972. This is consistent with the turnout rates reported by the NES surveys over the past 50 years. Though consistently higher than the "official" rate, they point to no steady erosion after the 1972 election. To the contrary, several presidential elections posted a higher turnout

(1984, 1992, and 2004). And the 76 percent turnout in 2004 did not fall short by much of the all-time high reached in the 1960 NES survey (79 percent).[16] An aggregate view of this sort no doubt overlooks some developments that have boosted turnout in certain segments of the country, most notably the South, and hence masks some slippage in other segments, but that hardly warrants apocalyptic warnings that the American voter is vanishing.

---

16. The Current Population Survey also shows no steady erosion in turnout for the citizen population since 1980, the first election that CPS reported a national estimate for the citizen population (U.S. Census Bureau 2007).

SECTION III

The Political Context

CHAPTER 6

The Impact of Party Identification

Voting can be seen at one level as due to psychological factors. People's attitudes toward the several elements of political conflict comprise a "field of forces" that helps determine their behavior. As seen in chapter 5, the intensity of these attitudes to a good measure explain voting turnout. Similarly, the consistency of these attitudes helps explain why some people cast straight-ticket votes and others split their votes between the two parties. Furthermore, the partisan direction of these attitudes determines the choices that voters make between the presidential contenders.

An important second-order question is what explains the variability of these attitude factors: why some people like the Democratic candidate and others dislike him, why some people tend to the Republican side on foreign issues and others to the Democratic side, and so on. The partisan attitudes can be seen as intervening variables, linking antecedent factors with behavior. We focus in this chapter on one antecedent psychological factor that is political in nature.

It has long been observed that people are stable in their partisan choices between elections. V. O. Key (1959) describes this stability as a voter's "standing decision" to support a particular party. This stability is evident at the aggregate level, where the correlation of the vote proportion received by the parties between successive elections is usually very high, both at the local and the state levels. This stability at the aggregate level in the face of changes in the candidates and issues from election to election implies that many voters must themselves have stable party attachments.

Survey data directly demonstrates the existence of these party attachments. When asked, most people can readily classify themselves as Republicans or Democrats, and panel surveys show that these ties are fairly stable over time. These party ties are important to understanding American elections. They set the playing field within which a particular campaign occurs, and they are an important factor in maintaining the stability of the American two-party system.

THE CONCEPT AND MEASUREMENT OF PARTY IDENTIFICATION

Party identification in the United States does not involve being politically active in the party or holding formal membership. Nor does it imply voting solely for that party, though attachments to a party strongly influence voting. Instead, party identification is a psychological identification with the party. Most Americans form such an identification with either the Republican or the Democratic Party, and that identification strongly affects their attitudes and voting behavior.

In treating partisanship as a psychological identification, we view identification as the person's affective orientation to the group. We use reference group theory, viewing the group as attracting or repelling the individual. The citizen may develop a stronger or weaker identification with the political party, and that identification can be either positive or negative.

Note that we do not define partisan orientation in terms of voting behavior, since such a definition would miss the essential distinction between an attitude and the behavior it causes. Thus, we do not define a Republican as someone who has always voted Republican, or an Independent as someone who does not consistently vote for the same party. Defining partisan orientation in terms of psychological identification allows us to study when people defect from their usual partisanship by voting for the opposite party.

We measure party identification by asking citizens to classify themselves. Respondents in the National Election Studies have been asked the same sequence of questions since 1952 to determine the direction and strength of their partisanship.[1] Except for a few respondents who lack

---

1. The question sequence begins by asking everyone, "Generally speaking, do you usually think of yourself as a Republican, a Democrat, an Independent, or what?" Those who answer Republican or Democrat are then asked "Would you call yourself a strong (Republican/Democrat) or a not very strong (Republican/Democrat)?" Those who declare themselves Independent or decline to answer are instead asked, "Do you think of yourself as closer to the Republican or Democratic Party?"

any involvement in politics, these questions allow us to place people on a partisan continuum from strong Republican to strong Democrat. This continuum allows us to distinguish intensity of partisan attachment, separating strong Republicans and Democrats from weak ones. It also provides a distinction between Independents who lean toward the Republican Party, pure Independents, and Independents who lean toward the Democratic Party.

The resultant party identification scale can be treated in several ways. We can look at the direction and intensity of partisanship together in a seven-point scale, as in table 6.1, where the distribution of party identification from 1952 to 2004 is summarized. We can combine Independents into a single group, leading to five categories, and we can combine strong and weak partisans to obtain a three-point scale that shows only the person's partisan direction. Alternatively, we can fold the seven-point scale at its center, leaving a four-point scale of partisan intensity: strong partisan, weak partisan, leaner, and pure Independent.

The Independent category should be seen as a composite. Some Independents lack positive attachment to either party. Some are repelled by both parties, instead viewing the idea of being Independent as attractive in its own right. After all, many people have absorbed the norm that one should vote "for the person, not the party," and therefore consider it important to be politically independent.

On the other hand, some people who choose the Independent label have a partisan commitment to one of the parties but feel that a good citizen should be independent. Certainly there are "closet partisans" who always vote for the same party even though they claim independent status. We handle this problem by asking Independents which party they are closer to. In any case, we consider closet partisans to be a methodological problem less severe than the problems that would occur if we measured partisanship by voting behavior.

It is useful to look at the consistency of partisan voting among people having different intensities of partisanship. Table 6.2 shows the proportion of respondents who voted for the same party in 2000 and 2004 in a small panel survey taken across those years. The proportion of people voting for the same party in these two elections differs by 20 percentage points between strong partisans and pure Independents. The three-quarters of pure Independents who voted for the same party in both years may seem to be strong evidence that Independents are really closet partisans, but it is important to remember that the Republican

TABLE 6.1. Party Identification by Year, 1952–2004 (in percentages)

	1952	1956	1960	1964	1968	1972	1976	1980	1984	1988	1992	1996	2000	2004
Strong Democrat	22	21	20	27	20	15	15	18	17	17	18	18	19	17
Weak Democrat	25	23	25	25	25	26	25	23	20	18	18	19	15	16
Independent Democrat	10	6	6	9	10	11	12	11	11	12	14	14	15	17
Pure Independent	6	9	10	8	11	13	15	13	11	11	12	9	12	10
Independent Republican	7	8	7	6	9	10	10	10	12	13	12	12	13	12
Weak Republican	14	14	14	14	15	13	14	14	15	14	14	15	12	12
Strong Republican	14	15	16	11	10	10	9	9	12	14	11	12	12	16
Apolitical	3	4	2	1	1	1	1	2	2	2	1	1	1	0
Total	101	100	100	101	101	99	101	100	100	101	100	100	99	100
Number of cases	1,784	1,757	1,911	1,550	1,553	2,694	2,850	1,612	2,236	2,032	2,474	1,710	1,797	1,197

Source: Data from American National Election Studies Web site.

candidate was the same in the two elections so this consistency among pure Independents may simply reflect having a consistent attitude toward George W. Bush.

The party identification figures give a very different picture of partisanship than voting statistics provide. The elections of the last two decades show considerable variance in results, from a moderate Democratic victory in 1992 in an election with a very large third-party vote, a large Democratic victory in 1996, a slight Democratic lead in the popular vote in 2000, and a clear Republican vote victory in 2004. By contrast, table 6.1 shows that the Democratic Party had a fairly steady lead in party identification (strong plus weak categories combined) throughout this period, though with some decline in 2004. (Democratic identifiers have somewhat lower turnout rates than Republican identifiers, so the Democratic lead in partisanship among actual voters was smaller throughout than shown in table 6.1, with the Republicans having a slight edge in partisanship among actual voters in 2004.)

As table 6.1 shows over a broader time frame, the Democrats had a substantial lead in partisanship in the 1950s (though a Republican president was easily being elected and reelected). That Democratic lead was little changed from the 1950s through 1980, at which point it eroded; it changed little from then until 2004. Technically, the similarity of the distribution of partisanship between different years does not necessarily prove that individual party identification was stable. There could instead be a considerable amount of compensating change, but it would be unlikely to have such large stability at the aggregate level if a large portion of the electorate was changing its party ties. It is also important to recognize

TABLE 6.2. Relation of Strength of Party Identification to Partisan Regularity in Voting for President (2000 and 2004) (in percentages)

	Strong Party Identifiers	Weak Party Identifiers	Independents Leaning to a Party	Independents
Voted for same party	95	85	84	75
Voted for different parties	5	15	16	25
Total	100	100	100	100
Number of cases	254	135	116	24

Source: NES 2000-2002-2004 Full Panel File (Inter-University Consortium for Political and Social Research [ICPSR] Study 4293).

Note: Compares 2000 and 2004 presidential votes of those who voted for a major-party candidate only.

that there was a substantial amount of generational turnover between the first and last elections in table 6.1. Only the youngest cohorts of voters in the 1950s were still voting in the early 2000s. Thus, the stability evident in table 6.1 is actually cross-generational stability.

The most basic point is that nearly all of our survey respondents could answer the party identification questions and can be located on the resultant party identification scale. Political parties in the United States are very loose and decentralized, which suggests that, in principle, people might not link themselves so clearly to the parties. Furthermore, there is always considerable sentiment against political parties, so that the high proportion of respondents who consider themselves closer to one party or the other can be seen as surprising. Regardless of these considerations, party identification is nearly universal among the American electorate.

PARTY IDENTIFICATION AND POLITICAL ATTITUDE

Party identification can serve as a source of cues for individuals as they interpret politics. After all, national politics occurs at a level that is remote from most citizens, so people learn about it indirectly, through the media and other sources. Politics can be very complex, so it is important for citizens to be able to use simple cues to interpret what they cannot experience directly.

The political party is a crucial mediating force. It does not have to be invoked directly in order to be effective. For example, the act of a party nominating a candidate for office affects how people will view that candidate. Identifiers with the candidate's party will tend to evaluate that candidate favorably, in political terms and usually in personal characteristics too. At the same time, identifiers with the other party will tend to evaluate that candidate unfavorably, again with respect to both political positions and personal attributes. Many people will learn much about the nominee and use that information in developing an image of the candidate, but even those who are not attentive to politics will usually develop an image based on party identification.

In this way party affects the full set of political attitudes discussed in chapter 4. Figures 6.1 and 6.2 show for 2000 and 2004 the means of each political attitude according to the citizen's party identification. The horizontal axis shows the party identification category, and the vertical height shows how strongly each mean attitude went in the Republican

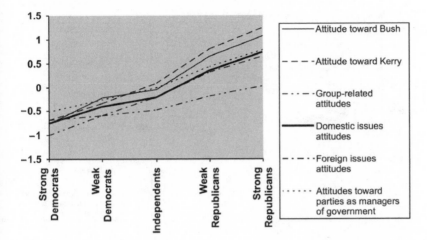

Fig. 6.1. Relation of party identification to partisan evaluations of elements of national politics, 2004

direction. (A positive mean attitude score is pro-Republican, a negative mean attitude score pro-Democratic.[2]) The pattern is clear and strong: strong Democrats have the least pro-Republican attitude on each partisan factor, and attitudes become more pro-Republican as one moves toward the strong Republican end of the party identification dimension. In both elections, the gradient is less sharp for attitudes on foreign issues than for the other partisan attitudes. This suggests that the public was more uniform in evaluating which party or candidate would better handle foreign and defense affairs, so partisanship did not affect this category as much as it did others. Still, party identification had some effect even on attitudes toward foreign issues, showing how pervasive the effects of partisanship are.

This is not to say that party identification completely determines these political attitudes. The gradients in these figures are not as sharp as

2. The mean of each attitude for each party identification category has been divided by the standard deviation of that attitude for that partisanship category, so that the mean is stated in standardized units. For example, the mean attitude of strong Republicans on Bush in 2004 was 1.50, with a standard deviation of 1.40, so the standardized value is 1.50 ÷ 1.40 = 1.07, which is the value graphed in figure 6.1 for strong Republicans as regards the Republican candidate component. This adjustment removes differences in the means that are due to differences in how many references the partisan group makes to the partisan object. (All the partisan attitudes in figures 6.1 and 6.2 have been consistently scored in a pro-Republican direction, so that a positive score on attitude toward the Democratic candidate actually reflects the dislike of that candidate.)

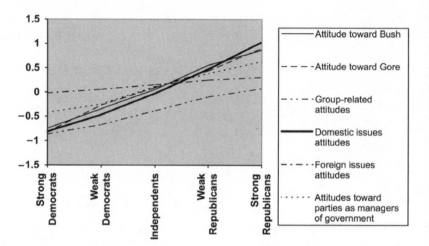

Fig. 6.2. Relation of party identification to partisan evaluations of elements of national politics, 2000

they would be if party identification were the only determinant of these attitudes. Note also that attitudes on some factors can be more favorable to one party throughout the party identification dimension. In particular, people of every partisan persuasion are more pro-Democratic in reference to social groups than the other party attitudes, at least in 2000. (Observe in fig. 6.2 that the mean attitude on the vertical axis, for group-related scores, is always below 0.) Differences such as these must be explained in terms of antecedent factors that operate separately from party identification.

It is also important to emphasize that figures 6.1 and 6.2 do not show the considerable variability of individual respondents within each partisan category. The means cannot convey the variability at the individual level, and this variability cannot be explained by party identification. Other antecedent factors must account for why some strong Democrats, for example, differ from other strong Democrats in evaluating the Democratic presidential nominee.

Partisanship unifies several different attitudes. The six political attitudes are all affected by party identification, giving them a considerable common core. We can examine the strength of a common partisan factor by looking at the intercorrelations among the six attitudes. A single underlying component underlies the six attitudes, accounting for more than a third of the total variance of these attitudes in both election years.[3] Further, each attitude is strongly related to this common partisan component, though foreign affairs was not much affected by it in 2000 (as should be evident from figure 6.1). Overall, the extent to which a common partisan component underlies these different partisan attitudes is quite striking.

Party identification also leads to internal consistency in the person's field of partisan attitudes. After all, partisanship serves as a "perceptual screen" that affects how the citizen perceives political objects. The stronger the people's partisan ties, the more they selectively perceive political events and therefore the more likely they are to have consistent partisan attitudes. Correspondingly, we expect Independents to be less likely to have consistent partisan attitudes. This expectation is tested in table 6.3, which examines the consistency of partisan attitudes among strong party identifiers, weak identifiers, Independent leaners, and pure Independents. We counted the number of respondents with consistent attitudes in each of these categories. We also calculated the number of people who would be expected to have consistent attitudes by chance.[4] We then computed the increase of observed over expected number of people with consistent attitudes. As anticipated, the increase in consistent attitudes is greatest among strong party identifiers. Even

---

3. The correlations among voters between each attitude and the partisan factor (principal component analysis) are as follows:

	2000	2004
Attitude toward Democratic candidate	.733	.773
Attitude toward Republican candidate	.766	.757
Group-related attitude	.511	.509
Attitude on domestic issues	.659	.591
Attitude on foreign issues	.278	.640
Attitude toward parties as managers of government	.542	.579
Total variance accounted for by the partisan factor	36.5%	42.1%

4. The computation of the expected number of people with consistent attitudes takes several steps. For example, we would see how many strong identifiers had three partisan attitudes, and compute how many of them would be expected to have consistent attitudes. If each attitude were pro-Republican or pro-Democratic by chance, there would be a .50 probability of it favoring the Republicans and .50 probability of it favoring the Democrats. The probability of all three of those identifiers' partisan attitudes being pro-Republican would then be $.5 \times .5 \times .5 = .125$. The probability of all three being pro-Democratic would also be $.5 \times .5 \times .5 = .125$. So the probability that a person with three partisan attitudes would have consistent attitudes would be $.125 + .125 = .25$. If there were 20 strong identifiers with three partisan attitudes, the expected number with consistent attitudes would then be $.25 \times 20 = 5$. For each strength-of-identification category, we used this method to obtain the expected number of people with consistent attitudes among people with two, three, four, five, or six partisan attitudes, and summed those values to obtain the first row of the table.

Independents are seen to have more consistent attitudes than would be expected by chance. Looking across categories, there is negligible difference in the percentage increase in consistent attitudes from independent leaners to weak identifiers, showing that weak party identification, by itself, adds very little to attitude consistency.

This analysis is not intended to suggest a unidirectional relationship between party identification and the several political attitudes. After all, our consideration is based on surveys taken during brief election campaigns, and so we cannot reflect the full process of opinion formation and change, a process that can extend over many years. We would expect the causal relations of party identification and the political attitudes to be bidirectional, even in an election campaign. People whose attitudes are consistent with their partisanship will have their party identification reinforced by those attitudes. Indeed, these attitudes will help people maintain their partisan attachment as they discuss politics with others during the election season. However, if people have partisan attitudes that are inconsistent with their partisanship, the party identification may help change those partisan attitudes—or the partisan attitudes may weaken their party identification, possibly enough that their partisanship itself changes. Large-scale changes in party identification across the electorate occur infrequently, but, when they do, the result is electoral realignment that involves long-term change in election results.

Thus, partisan attitudes generally lead to stability in party identification, but may lead to change in partisanship when they conflict with the person's party identification. While both of these possibilities exist, we

TABLE 6.3. Party Identification as an Influence on Partisan Consistency of Attitude, 2004

	Strong Party Identifiers	Weak Party Identifiers	Independents Leaning to a Party	Pure Independents
Number expected to have consistent attitudes	54	56	52	18
Number observed to have consistent attitudes	238	138	123	36
Increase of observed over expected number	440%	246%	237%	195%
Number of cases	339	248	262	65

believe that during the elections studied here, the main influence is of party identification on the partisan attitudes, rather than vice versa. The data show that party identification has been stable for most respondents, probably through most of the time that they have been of voting age. This is the case even though the 2000 and 2004 elections involved new candidates and new issues. Reactions to George W. Bush, Al Gore, John Kerry, foreign issues in the wake of the terrorism attack of 9/11, and other matters differ considerably according to people's partisanship (figs. 6.1 and 6.2), even if these men and issues were new to the presidential campaign. People's general partisan orientation, as encapsulated in their party identification, affects how they view political objects, even (and perhaps especially) new political objects.

The limited political involvement of many Americans means that they may not respond to issues or candidates until they become salient during an election campaign. A campaign focuses public attention on politics, so that citizens may react to topics that had been present for years but had not previously affected public attitudes. Party identification can be expected to affect public evaluations of these lasting topics as well as evaluations of those that come up for the first time during the current campaign.

In chapter 4 we found that voting in a presidential election could be explained by several partisan attitudes. In this section we have demonstrated that stable party identification accounts for much of the variance in these partisan attitudes. We make, however, one qualification to this argument. While partisan attitudes matter for people who pay attention to politics, constituting an intervening causal force between party identification and vote, we expect party identification to have a more direct influence on the vote for people who do not pay attention to politics. The latter group may just consider themselves Republicans (or Democrats) and vote accordingly, without the intervening effects of partisan attitudes.

PARTY IDENTIFICATION AND ELECTORAL CHOICE

Our theory is that party identification is one of several antecedent factors that affect people's attitudes toward such objects as the candidates and the issues of the campaign. In turn, the field of partisan attitudes is what influences vote choice and other behaviors, with the extent of influence being related to the strength, direction, and consistency of the different partisan attitudes. While we hypothesize that the effect of party

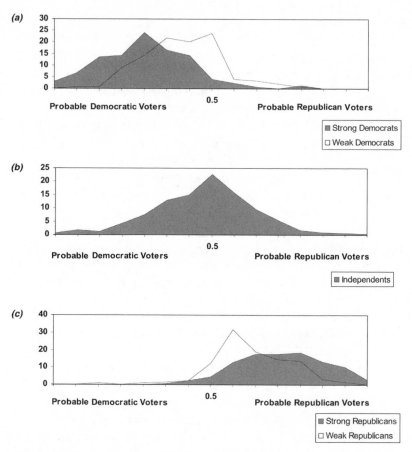

Fig. 6.3. Probable direction of vote by party identification groups, 2004: (*a*) Democrats, (*b*) Independents, (*c*) Republicans.

identification is indirect for most citizens, we expect it to have a substantial effect on behavior.

One way to see the impact of party identification on voting is to return to the multiple regression model introduced in chapter 4. That analysis predicted a person's vote based on his or her values on the six partisan attitudes. Each person's probability of voting Republican can then be determined, ranging from being very unlikely to being nearly certain. To demonstrate the power of party identification in this system, we display in figure 6.3 the predicted probabilities of voting Republican for individuals for different groups of partisans. These are similar to the probability curves shown in chapter 4, but examined within categories of party identification. As shown in the top graph, virtually all strong Democrats had less than a .5 chance of voting Republican in 2004, as did the great bulk of weak Democrats. Independents were about as likely to vote Republican as Democrat. Most weak Republicans had more than a .5 chance of voting Republican, as did nearly all strong Republicans. The shifts of the curves across the five partisanship categories show the impact of party identification in this model.

Figure 6.3 also serves as a reminder that party identification is not the sole determinant of partisan attitudes. After all, there is considerable dispersion to the probabilities for each of the curves, with some partisans being nearly certain to vote for their party and others having a reasonable chance of defecting to the other party. Party identification cannot explain the spread of these curves around their centers.

This discussion of figure 6.3 suggests that there will be considerable differences in the vote division across partisanship categories, without either party having much of an advantage over the other in defections. Table 6.4 shows that this was the case. In 2004, the Democratic presidential vote percentage ranged from 97 percent among strong Democrats to just 3 percent among strong Republicans. The proportion of weak Democrats who defected to Bush was just slightly higher than the proportion of weak Republicans who defected to Kerry in 2004—and the proportion of defections among weak Democrats in 2000 is indistinguishable from the proportion of defections among weak Republicans that year. Note too that Independents tended to vote Democratic in 2004, while they tended to vote Republican in 2000. However, the other shift that occurred was

TABLE 6.4. Vote by Party Identification, 2000 and 2004 (in percentages)

	Strong Dem.	Weak Dem.	Independent	Weak Rep.	Strong Rep.
2000					
Republican	3	15	54	84	98
Democratic	97	85	46	16	2
Total	100	100	100	100	100
Number of cases	233	164	346	128	179
2004					
Republican	3	15	42	90	97
Democratic	97	85	58	10	3
Total	100	100	100	100	100
Number of cases	140	112	244	116	169

that there were more strong Republicans than strong Democrats among 2004 voters, whereas strong Democrats outnumbered strong Republicans among 2000 voters. The higher Democratic presidential vote among Independents in 2004 was not enough to offset this shift in the partisan composition of the actual voters. The 2000 and 2004 elections were both fairly close. The contrast is with the presidential elections of the 1950s, when the Republican nominee won handily, with the votes of 15 percent of strong Democrats and helped by the vote of more than two-thirds of Independents. These are the types of swings that make the difference between close elections and one-sided victories.

An important question is whether party identification has effects on voting behavior beyond its effects on the partisan attitudes. We saw in chapter 4 that the vote could be well predicted from the six partisan attitudes, so the question is whether adding partisanship improves predictability. We find that adding party identification to the multiple regression equation produces real improvement in the statistical estimation, for it fits the data better. However, the predictive accuracy does not change.[5] The partisan polarization of the electorate was considerable enough in the 2000 and 2004 elections that the partisan attitudes can themselves predict the vote with a high level of accuracy; adding party identification to the mix only leads to higher predicted probabilities of partisans voting for their party, which increases the precision of the statistical estimation.

We further expect party identification to have a direct effect on the voting behavior of people who do not have a well-developed set of partisan attitudes. Figure 6.4 shows the distribution of vote probabilities combined for 2000 and 2004. People on the two sides of the distribution have well-developed partisan attitudes that are likely to have a strong motivational effect on their behavior. The people in the center have either relatively undeveloped partisan attitudes or ones without a clear direction. For people with well-developed partisan attitudes, we expect the partisan attitudes to predominate in the rare cases where there is a

---

5. The multiple correlation with the voting choice increases from .74 to .80 in 2000 and from .79 to .84 in 2004 with the addition of party identification to the vote equation, but the proportion of voters correctly classified does not change at all: 89 percent in both equations in 2000 and 92 percent in both in 2004. For comparison, the multiple correlation went from .71 to .73 in 1956 when party identification was put in the vote equation and the proportion of voters correctly predicted went from 86 percent to 88 percent. Thus, the partisan attitudes by themselves were stronger predictors in 2000 and 2004 than were the partisan attitudes and party identification together in 1956. It is important to keep in mind that it is difficult to improve on predictive accuracy this high because of ceiling effects.

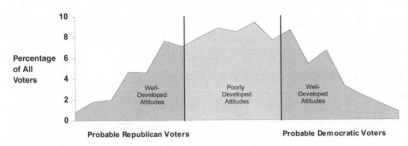

Fig. 6.4. Location of individuals with well-developed attitudes and poorly-developed attitudes within distribution of all respondents, 2004. Included are only those who reported voting for one of the two major-party candidates.

conflict between those attitudes and party identification. For example, Democratic identifiers who favor the Republicans on issues and candidates in a particular election are expected to defect and vote Republican on the basis of their partisan attitudes. However, we expect party identification to have a greater effect for people with poorly developed attitudes. Democratic identifiers whose partisan attitudes are unclear are thus expected to vote Democratic.

It is difficult to test this hypothesis since conflict between voters' partisan attitudes and party identification is rare. Table 6.5 shows that most people with well-developed partisan attitudes vote along with those attitudes when they conflict with their party identification, but we are speaking of only 14 people in 2004. Still, the overwhelming proportion of the partisans voted with their partisanship (table 6.4), as did 92 percent of the few voters (12) who had no partisan attitudes. Thus, the data do give some support for the hypothesis that partisan attitudes predominate when

TABLE 6.5. Relation of Degree of Attitude Development to Direction in Which Conflict of Party Identification and Partisan Evaluations Is Resolved in Voting, 2004 (in percentages)

	Those Who Have Well-Developed Evaluations	Those Who Have Formed No Evaluations at All
Vote agrees with party identification	7	92
Vote fails to agree with party identification	93	8
Total	100	100
Number of cases	14	12

Note: Respondents with poorly developed evaluations are omitted as there are too few (three) to show.

those attitudes are in conflict with party identification, though the rarity of such conflict in 2004 limits our ability to confirm the hypothesis.

PARTY IDENTIFICATION AND POLITICAL INVOLVEMENT

A person's party identification is the most important piece of information that we can obtain to help us understand their political attitudes and vote choice. At this point, it is important to examine the relationship between party identification and political involvement, as discussed in chapter 5. The stronger a person's partisan attachment, the greater the person's involvement in politics.

The popular view of political independents is that they are interested in government and politics, pay attention to both sides in a campaign, and then make an informed judgment. This may describe an ideal Independent, but it does not fit the data very well. Independents are instead less interested and involved in politics than are partisans. They have less information about elections and care less about election outcomes. Consider tables 6.6 and 6.7. Independents were less interested in the 2004 election campaign than were strong partisans, and they cared less who

TABLE 6.6. Relation of Strength of Party Identification to Interest in Campaign, 2004 (in percentages)

	Strong Party Identifiers	Weak Party Identifiers	Independents
Very much interested	57	28	36
Somewhat interested	34	53	46
Not much interested	9	19	18
Total	100	100	100
Number of cases	348	296	406

TABLE 6.7. Relation of Strength of Party Identification to Concern over Outcome, 2004 (in percentages)

	Strong Party Identifiers	Weak Party Identifiers	Independents
Care who wins presidential election	98	86	78
Does not care who wins	2	14	22
Total	100	100	100
Number of cases	348	295	401

won the election. Some Independents were interested in the campaign, and many cared about the outcome, but the results overall show that Independents differ from their popular image. These data cannot tell us which direction the causation flows: whether people who are involved in politics are more likely to develop strong partisanship, or if strong partisans are more likely to become interested in politics, but they do show us that the two go hand in hand, with strong partisans being more politically involved while Independents are less involved. The question of which comes first, though, does turn our attention to the development of political partisanship, which is the focus of the next chapter.

COMMENTARY AND CONTROVERSY

Comparisons with Earlier Elections

There are two important differences between these distributions of voting probabilities and those from the 1950s. First, the probability of partisans defecting to the other party is much lower than it was in the 1950s. This fits with claims that voters are more polarized between the parties than they used to be. Back in 1956, there was some chance of strong partisans voting for the other party and a substantial chance of weak partisans doing so (especially weak Democrats), but figure 6.3 shows that was no longer the case in 2004. Second, there is little sign of partisan bias in these figures for 2004. Democrats were more likely to vote Republican in 1956 than Republicans were to vote Democratic, which indicates that there were powerful short-term factors that year working in the Republican direction. By contrast, in 2004 the likelihood of Democrats voting Republican is fairly similar to that of Republicans voting Democrat, showing that short-term partisan factors were in much greater balance in 2004 than in 1956.

Bartels (2000) developed a model to measure the changing importance of party identification in voting from the 1950s through the 1990s. His methodology takes into account both changes in the distribution of partisanship and in its electoral relevance. He finds a declining impact of party identification on the presidential vote in 1964 and 1972 followed by resurgence since then, to the point that partisan voting was 15–20 percent higher in 1996 than in the 1950s. Thus the finding of high importance of party identification in presidential voting is not limited to the 2000 and 2004 elections. As to partisan bias, Bartels's analysis finds Republicans more loyal to their party than Democrats of the same partisan strength up through 1988 (with the sole exception of the desertion by Republicans from Barry Goldwater in 1964), but with Democrats being more loyal to their party than Republicans in the 1990s.

Alternative Measures of Partisanship

The question series developed by the University of Michigan researchers in the 1950s has been used to measure party identification by the National Election Studies (NES) ever since then. While some other survey organizations use fully comparable questions (especially the *New York Times*/CBS Poll, which also asks Independents which party they are closer to), many political polling operations use other versions. The most important alternative wording is that in the Gallup Poll: "In politics, as of today, do you consider yourself a Republican, a Democratic, or an Independent?" The "as of today" wording obtains a shorter-term version of party identification than the "generally speaking" phrase in the NES question (Borrelli, Lockerbie, and Niemi 1987), with a greater tendency for people to answer in terms of how they are voting currently or how they are planning to vote in the next election rather than giving their identification over the years.

Another variant is to ask people how favorable they are to each party separately, having them locate each party on a "feeling thermometer," answering 100 for groups they like a lot and 0 for groups they dislike a lot. The thermometer difference (how much the person likes the Republican Party minus how much that person likes the Democrats) measures the person's partisanship. Since the question series does not ask respondents to think of the long term, this measure is also likely to be more short-term than the NES question series.[6]

Partisanship is sometimes thought of as behavioral instead of attitudinal. A person who registers as a Republican may be considered a Republican. However, many states do not have registration by party. Also, people often do not bother to change their party registration, unless they want to vote in the primary of the other party, so registration may not reflect their current party. Furthermore, voters sometimes register strategically, for example, registering in the other party so as to be able to vote in a close primary election.

Another behavioral measure is a person's voting history: a person who always votes for the same party is classified as a partisan of that

---

6. See Weisberg 1999 for a comprehensive treatment of alternative measures of partisanship.

party, while a person who sometimes votes for one party and sometimes for the other is an Independent. Political parties often employ this definition of independents, since targeting vote switchers is probably a more successful strategy than targeting people who have always voted for the other party. A variant of this approach is to classify split-ticket voters as independents since they vote for some Republicans and some Democrats at the same election. Most political scientists use an attitudinal measure of partisanship because it allows one to test the effects of attitudes on behavior.

The Nature of Political Independence

One of the most surprising findings of *The American Voter* was that political Independents in the 1950s were uninformed and uninvolved, rather than being the ideal citizens that democratic theory had assumed. Surveys in the late 1960s and early 1970s found a substantial increase in political independence, and this increase was among people who were more informed and involved. That change led to discussion of two types of Independents, with recognition that some are closer to the ideal in democratic theory.

The new Independents of the late 1960s and early 1970s were concentrated among particular demographic groups. One set of new Independents involved southern whites who left the Democratic Party during the civil rights revolution, but were not yet ready to call themselves Republicans. Another set consisted of young people who were dissatisfied with both parties' positions on the Vietnam War. The Watergate scandal of the early 1970s led to further disenchantment with the parties and therefore more Independents. The effects of the civil rights revolution, the Vietnam War, and Watergate were manifest among people who were informed about politics and cared about real political issues. Hence, they could not be considered Independents of *The American Voter* type.

While the developments that led to an increase in Independents are now more than a generation old, the proportion of Independents has remained high. The proportion of the public that calls themselves Independents has stabilized, not growing appreciably since 1972. Since 1988, more people say they are Independents than Democrats, with Republicans coming in third. Many current-day Independents are informed and involved, though there are still many uniformed and uninvolved Independents.

This increase in Independents occurs when one includes "leaners" as

Independents. Leaners are the people who answer "Independent" to the initial party identification question and then answer the follow-up question by saying that they consider themselves closer to one party or the other. However, leaners sometimes vote in a more partisan manner than weak partisans. The resultant lack of monotonicity in the relationship between the seven-point party identification scale and voting behavior is referred to in the literature as an "intransitivity" (Petrocik 1974).

This intransitivity led some researchers to suggest that the "leaners" should be seen as partisans rather than as Independents. After all, if leaners sometimes vote in a more partisan manner than weak partisans, it may be best to combine the two groups (Keith et al. 1992). When leaners are combined with weak partisans, the proportion of real Independents in the American electorate is quite small. The contrary position is that the leaners should be seen as Independents (W. Miller 1991), which makes it look like a substantial portion of the American electorate is Independents. This is how they are treated in political polls that ask people if they are Republicans, Democrats, or Independents without a follow-up question asking Independents if they are closer to one party or the other. One argument supporting this position is that leaners do not turn out to vote at elections at the same high rate that strong and weak partisans vote. Leaners may vote like partisans, but that may be because they answer the follow-up question with the party they are planning to vote for at the next election.

The anomalous nature of Independents also led some scholars to question whether party identification should be considered unidimensional, ranging from strong Democrats at one end to strong Republicans at the opposite end, with Independents in the middle, or whether multiple dimensions underlie partisanship. For one thing, whether or not a person is an Independent could be separate from their position between Democrats and Republicans. For another, people may not see Democrat and Republican partisanship as opposites, but may treat them as just separate entities. Multidimensional partisanship occurs in many multiparty countries, with a left-right dimension to the parties as well as a separate dimension that is religious-secular in some countries. The idea of multidimensional partisanship in the United States was explored in the early 1980s (Weisberg 1980), but the scholarly consensus remains that the unidimensional version fits current politics adequately (Fiorina 1981).

A small detail in *The American Voter*'s presentation of party identification was that there are a few respondents who do not relate enough to the political parties to be able to answer the party identification questions meaningfully. *The American Voter* calls such people "apoliticals." About 3–4 percent of the National Election Studies samples in the 1950s were apoliticals, mainly blacks who were not permitted to vote in the segregated South. With the passage of voting rights reforms in the early 1960s, the proportion of apoliticals was halved, and now only about 1 percent of the public does not have enough interest in political matters to respond to the party identification questions. Not surprisingly, apoliticals rarely vote, so less than 1 percent of voters were apolitical even in the 1950s.[7]

The Normal Vote

While the party identification distribution among the total National Election Studies sample still favors the Democrats, this advantage is considerably offset by the lower voting rates of Democratic identifiers. People with less education and income vote in lower proportions than people with college education and high income, and people with less education and income tend to be Democratic identifiers rather than Republicans. As a result, the Democratic lead in partisanship is not as large as the party identification percentages in table 6.1 suggest. There is also a difference in defection rates between Democratic and Republican identifiers, with Democrats being slightly more likely to defect and vote for the candidate of the other major party.

Converse (1966a) developed the concept of the "normal vote" to adjust the party identification figures for these differences in turnout and defection rates. He estimated the voting patterns in the 1952–60 period for an election in which short-term forces did not favor either party. For example, he found that strong Democrats living outside the South were turning out to vote at a 79 percent rate, compared to 86 percent for strong Republicans; the difference was even starker in the South. Furthermore, 18 percent of weak Democrats were expected to defect to the Republican candidate in such an election, whereas only 16 percent of weak Republicans were expected to defect to the Democratic candidate. Putting these factors together, Converse came up with an estimate that the normal two-party vote in the United States during the 1952–60 period

---

7. These figures probably understate the true proportion of apoliticals, in that many homeless people and some people who are not interested enough in politics to agree to participate in an election survey most likely belong in this category. Indeed, the decrease in apoliticals since the 1950s could be partly due to the lower participation rate in the NES surveys.

was approximately 54 percent Democratic. Replication of the normal vote analysis for the 1960s (Miller 1979) still found Democrats turning out to vote at a lower rate and defecting at a higher rate than Republicans, so that the normal two-party vote estimate remained at 54 percent Democratic.

Several researchers have used the normal vote to estimate the effects of particular issues in an election. They take the partisanship distribution of people on either side of an issue and compute the "expected vote" for each side. They then compare the expected vote of people on each side of the issue with their actual vote to gauge the effect of that issue. For example, the normal vote of abortion supporters and opponents can be estimated on the basis of the partisan distribution among each group. The actual vote of supporters and opponents may then be compared with their respective normal votes to determine the effect of abortion on the vote, with abortion having no independent effect on the vote if supporters and opponents voted just as predicted by their partisanship distribution. However, Achen (1979) demonstrated that such estimates are biased since they do not take into account other relevant variables; in technical terms, the prediction equation is not fully "specified." While that problem invalidates the use of the normal vote to estimate the effects of specific issues, it is still a useful concept for considering the partisan balance in the nation.

Minimally, this discussion emphasizes the importance of discounting the apparent Democratic lead in party identification by the tendency of Democrats to vote in lower proportions than Republicans. Table 6.8 shows how the Democratic lead in the actual electorate has diminished since 1952. Regardless of whether Independents who lean toward a party are included, the Democrats had a double-digit lead in partisanship from the first Eisenhower victory in 1952 through the first Reagan victory in 1980, and since that year their lead has been reduced to a single digit. Exit polls confirm that the difference in the proportions of actual voters who say they are Democrats and Republicans has been trivial since 1984.

Theoretical Understanding of Partisanship

The American Voter developed the concept of party identification out of the reference group theory that was popular in social psychology during the 1950s. People identify psychologically with all sorts of groups, and identification with parties was proposed as an example. The Michigan

TABLE 6.8. Democratic Lead in Partisanship among Actual Voters for President, 1952–2004 (in percentages)

	1952	1956	1960	1964	1968	1972	1976	1980	1984	1988	1992	1996	2000	2004
NES partisans only	14	12	15	25	18	12	11	14	8	3	9	8	7	−3
NES including leaners	17	10	14	27	18	12	12	14	4	2	11	9	7	2
Exit polls	—	—	—	—	—	—	—	—	3	2	3	4	4	0

Note: — = not applicable.

school treated party identification as a short-cut that helps people decide how to vote, especially in low-information contests such as state treasurer or auditor. Modern social psychology would refer to this as a "heuristic," a problem-solving technique.

This psychological foundation for party identification was considered wanting by rational choice theorists in that it seemed to view party identification as based on early (often childhood) associations with the parties instead of seeing it as being affected by contemporary politics. Fiorina (1981) proposed an important alternative view of party identification from the rational choice perspective, calling it a "running tally" of the person's reactions to the parties. Persons come to think of themselves as a Republican from events of childhood and early adolescence, but each subsequent political event can move that tally one way or the other. They may think of themselves as a bit less Republican if there is a major scandal under a Republican president, or a bit more Republican if they benefits from tax cuts initiated under a Republican administration. Statisticians would consider this model as an instance of "Bayesian updating," with the person having a "prior" view that can be modified on the basis of new "data." It also fits with the "online processing" model in contemporary social psychology, which believes that people keep "online tallies" for their attitudes on some matters rather than retaining in their memory each individual incident that contributes to those attitudes.

Reference group theory is not used much in contemporary social psychology. A more modern version is called "social identity" theory. That theory differentiates between a person's "in-group" and "out-group," and it emphasizes that people can easily build up an association with the in-group. Several recent studies of party identification employ this approach (Greene 1999; Weisberg and Hasecke 1999; Green, Palmquist, and Schickler 2002), arguing that partisan identity is indeed a psychological attachment akin to religious, ethnic, or class identity rather than based in rational considerations. That is, party identification is based on affect rather than cognition and is part of a person's self-concept.

Is Party Identification Exogenous?

In presenting the concept of party identification, *The American Voter* portrayed it as highly stable over long periods of time, at both the individual level and the aggregate level. It was depicted as the long-term variable that affected short-term attitudes toward issues and candidates. In this view it was an "unmoved mover"—leading other variables to change while itself remaining unchanged. In more technical parlance, this view of party identification makes it "exogenous"—it is not affected by the political variables that it is used to explain. This assessment overstates what *The American Voter* actually said. It clearly allowed that party identification could change as the result of political forces. However, it viewed that change as largely occurring only as part of a major party realignment, not as part of the normal ebb and flow of politics.

Later work has questioned whether party identification is truly an unmoved mover. Analysis by Jackson (1975), Page and Jones (1979), Markus and Converse (1979), and Franklin and Jackson (1983) treated party identification as endogenous. In some of these models it is affected by a person's positions on issues as well as affecting those positions, and in some models it is affected by a person's vote. Consider a female Republican, moderate on social issues, who votes Democrat for president one year because of her party's stand on abortion and then votes Democrat for president the next election because of her party's stand on gay and lesbian rights. At some point she may begin to consider herself an Independent or even a Democrat because of her position on issues or because she realizes that she is voting Democrat more often than Republican.

Some empirical data also shows that party identification can be variable. In an analysis of tracking polls in the 1984 election, Allsop and Weisberg (1988) found that partisanship varied systematically with political events during the campaign. Brody and Rothenberg (1988) found that change in party identification in the 1980 NES panel survey could be accounted for by short-term factors. The most important research along this line was the MacKuen, Erikson, and Stimson (1989) work on "macropartisanship," which demonstrates that aggregate partisanship varies and is responsive to views of the national economy as well as to presidential popularity (see also Weisberg and Smith 1991; cf. Abramson and Ostrom 1991). Box-Steffensmeier and Smith's (1996) sophisticated time-series analysis shows that changes in party identification last several years, not just the several months that MacKuen, Erikson, and Stimson's work implies, but not the several decades that *The American Voter* claimed.

Some other research finds that party identification is indeed stable. Warren Miller, one of the authors of *The American Voter*, argued in 1991 that one should only look at people's answers to the first party identification question—whether they consider themselves Republicans, Democrats, or Independents. He found answers to that question were very stable during a lengthy period, except for instances of realignment, such as by white male southerners and by blacks from the 1950s through 1980. *The New American Voter* (Miller and Shanks 1996) similarly views party identification as basically stable. Green and Palmquist (1994) show that change in party identification in several panel surveys was mainly due to random measurement error rather than to real change. The effects of short-term variables on party identification largely disappear when that random measurement error is taken into account (Green and Palmquist 1990). Green, Palmquist, and Schickler (2002, chap. 5) suggest that party identification is highly stable so long as images of Republicans and Democrats remain intact.

Data clearly show that party identification does shift, but the question is whether those shifts have real meaning or are just short-term blips. Any claim that party identification is an "unmoved mover" is an overstatement, but it would also be a mistake to overstate the magnitude of changes that occur in party identification other than during realigning periods. Political parties need not view party identification as totally stable—they can attempt to move partisanship even during the course of a campaign. However, the parties must recognize that such changes may be reversed by the subsequent flow of political events. Tremendous forces of stability underlie party identification.

Social Demographics of Partisanship

What is the partisanship of social groups, and to what extent have they changed their partisanship over the years? Which groups have realigned and which have not, and is the amount of change enough to make us reconsider the stability of partisanship?

The popular press often discusses changes in voting by particular social groups, but this chapter implies that what really matters is whether their party identification changes. The best work on this is Stanley and Niemi's (2006) multivariate analysis of the demographics of party identification. Table 6.9 summarizes some of their results relating mainly to groups that are associated with the Democratic New Deal Coalition. Some change is evident here, especially a growth in Democratic partisanship among blacks and lessening of Democratic partisanship among native southern whites and to a lesser degree among Catholics and arguably Jews. Those changes hold up under statistical controls (see bottom half of table 6.9). Additionally, the development of Democratic partisanship by women is visible when one controls for other demographics.

Yet the overwhelming lesson from table 6.9 is that group partisan-

TABLE 6.9. Net Group Partisanship, 1952–2004 (Democratic minus Republican Identification)

	1952	1964	1976	1988	2000	2004
Dem. − Rep. identification						
African Americans	.40	.66	.67	.57	.59	.60
Catholics	.38	.42	.34	.10	.12	.04
Jewish	.73	.51	.50	.24	.57	.43
Female	.19	.28	.15	.12	.17	.12
Native southern whites	.68	.63	.36	.18	−.07	−.17
Dem. − Rep. identification, controlled						
African Americans	.44	.57	.71	.73	.58	.70
Catholics	.45	.40	.40	.17	.09	.11
Jewish	.80	−.11	.64	.48	.38	.56
Female	−.04	.01	−.02	.09	.14	.36
Native southern whites	.80	.63	.39	.26	−.10	−.08

Source: This table is based on Stanley and Niemi 2004, with 2004 data added from Stanley and Niemi (2006). Results are shown for every 12 years up to the 2000 election and for the 2004 election. Their analysis also controls for union household, regular churchgoer, income, white Protestant fundamentalist, Hispanic, and generation.

ship is highly stable. Blacks have been strongly Democratic since the 1960s. Catholics were strongly Democratic through the 1970s, and have been split more evenly between the parties since. Jews remain predominantly Democrat, though the values for Jews are highly variable because they are based on small numbers of respondents. The largest partisanship changes in the table are for native southern whites, who are no longer strongly Democrat. But even they have not completely reversed their partisanship—they are now only mildly Republican in their net party identification. The role of social groups and the vote will be discussed more fully in chapter 11.

CHAPTER 7

The Development of Party Identification

Political parties, like sports teams, evoke strong loyalty and affection in the general public, but also animosity, rejection, or indifference. Most Americans, as the previous chapter showed, feel attached to either the Democratic Party or the Republican Party in a way that shapes their political attitudes, perceptions, and choices. With party identification occupying such a central place, one naturally wonders where this broad attachment comes from, how it develops, and how stable or changeable it proves to be. The discussion of these questions compels us to consider both a person's life experience and key events of the nation's political history.

ORIGINS OF PARTY IDENTIFICATION

The political world penetrates the awareness of many people long before they reach voting age or cast their first vote. Studies of political socialization have shown that partisan attachments, in particular, begin to form in childhood and early adolescence (Jennings and Niemi 1974). Even without being able to express this sentiment at the ballot box, the typical American teenager has no problem expressing a partisan loyalty. And in most cases that loyalty bears a parental imprint. A young person's party identification is an inheritance from one's parents.

By the time an election survey encounters respondents, they have long outgrown that phase of their lives. Such a survey relies on respondents' recall to ascertain information about the preadult experience: What party *did* your parents identify with when you *were* growing up?

TABLE 7.1. Intergenerational Resemblance in Partisan Orientation, 1992 (in percentages)

Party Identification of Offspring	Both Parents Were Democrats	Both Parents Were Republicans	Parents Had No Consistent Partisanship
Strong Democrat	31	6	10
Weak Democrat	27	6	14
Independent Democrat	14	6	18
Pure Independent	7	7	17
Independent Republican	7	16	16
Weak Republican	8	32	14
Strong Republican	6	27	9
Apolitical	0	0	2
Total	100	100	100
Number of cases	885	436	882

Source: NES survey, 1992 (ICPSR Study 6067).

The correspondence between parental identification, as recalled that way, and a respondent's reported identification when interviewed as an adult may then be taken as a rough measure of the extent to which partisanship is passed on to the next generation.

The evidence for an intergenerational correspondence in partisan identification, shown in table 7.1, is very persuasive.[1] In families where both parents conveyed a consistent partisanship, close to three in four offspring adopted the parental party (including Independent leaners). Only about one in 10 offspring rebelled politically against their parents by crossing party lines (and becoming a strong or weak identifier of the opposition). Most of those who failed to follow in the partisan footsteps of their parents opted for an Independent stance. Whenever the parents offered mixed partisan cues or none whatsoever, as far as the respondent is able to recall, an Independent attitude in the respondent is most common, though not universal. In many households of that kind one of the parents may have impressed his or her partisan allegiance upon the offspring.[2]

---

1. The 1992 NES survey is the most recent one that used the recall question for parental party identification.

2. Conventional wisdom would accord the father the dominant role in cases where parents diverge, especially on something as political as party identification. Yet studies have shown that mothers manage to hold their own, and may even come out ahead, in the battle over the offspring's partisanship. They are the dominant voice for daughters: "when the chips are down, the child more often than not goes with the same-sex parent" (Jennings and Niemi 1974, 176).

Hence most Americans grew up in families where party identification could be transmitted across generations. This is very much the pattern that was first reported nearly half a century ago (Campbell et al. 1960, 147). Parents continue to offer partisan guidance to their offspring.[3]

The recall measure, of course, has weaknesses as an instrument for examining parental influence. The recollection may be flawed, and some respondents may have abandoned a party attachment acquired from their parents by the time they are asked about their own identification. A more reliable measure, which is not available in election studies, probes the party identifications of Americans when they are at a young age and the attachments of their parents at that very time. Such a survey of parents and offspring was conducted in 1965 (Jennings and Niemi 1974), with follow-up interviews of both cohorts in 1973 and 1982 (Jennings and Niemi 1981; Jennings and Markus 1984). What is more, in 1997, the by then middle-aged youth cohort of 1965 was interviewed one more time along with their offspring (Jennings and Stoker 2005). This research puts us in a fortunate position to observe not only the intergenerational transmission of partisanship at two distinct junctures, but also to track the persistence of partisanship over (much of) the life cycle. For now, we are interested in the most recent instance of transmission. How well did the parental cohort in the 1997 study transmit its partisanship to its offspring?

The data in table 7.2 do make a strong case for parental influence, confirming the pattern established with recall data in the previous table. Very few children deserted the parental party for the opposite one. If they deviated from the parental norm, they tended to embrace an Independent stance. The parent-offspring survey also allows us to capture the importance of family politicization. The transmission of party identification is far more successful in politically active homes than in inactive homes. When parents talk about politics at home often, as reported by the offspring, children are far more likely to adopt their parents' partisanship. In politically talkative homes, as can be seen in table 7.2, eight of 10 parents with a Democratic attachment imparted that partisanship to

---

3. The rise of single-parent households raises questions about the intergenerational process of partisan transmission. Unfortunately, the 1992 NES survey does not permit us to isolate respondents with only one parent. We suspect that a "don't know" response to the question about a parent's partisanship, in some instances covers for the absence of a parent. Even so, whatever the change in family structure, very few respondents probably grew up with just a single parent throughout their entire preadult stage of life.

BLE 7.2. Intergenerational Transmission of Party Identification, Politically Active and active Homes, 1997 (in percentages)

ty Identification Offspring	Talk about Politics at Home Often			Do Not Talk about Politics at Home Often		
	Parents' Party Identification			Parents' Party Identification		
	Democrat	Independent	Republican	Democrat	Independent	Republican
ong Democrat	35	9	5	13	6	5
ak Democrat	23	14	7	20	20	14
dependent Democrat	22	12	8	19	15	10
re Independent	4	20	9	26	26	20
dependent Republican	4	11	9	10	9	14
ak Republican	5	18	25	10	16	18
ong Republican	7	16	37	2	8	19
Total	100	100	100	100	100	100
Number of cases	75	99	95	123	179	153

ource: Study of Political Socialization: Parent-Child Pairs Based on Survey of Youth Panel and Their Offspring, 1997 PSR Study 4024).

their offspring (including leaners); the rate was seven in 10 for Republican parents. In not so active homes, the corresponding rate for partisan families was only five in 10. Adolescents from inactive homes, especially where the parents profess no identification with a major party, find themselves largely adrift in partisan terms. As with everything else, the adoption of partisan attachments requires parental nurturing.

PERSISTENCE OF PARTISANSHIP

It is one thing to be raised a Democrat or a Republican by one's parents and quite another to maintain such an attachment after leaving the parental nest and facing the thunder and lightning of the political world as an adult. It is also quite a challenge for social science to measure the fidelity with which adults stick to the norms and orientations acquired during their socialization.[4] Studies that monitor a cross-section of the general public through the life cycle are extremely rare. We are fortunate to track

---

4. Estimates of stability have often relied on recall of the kind that asks whether a person ever changed party identification, or what that orientation was when the individual was growing up. These measures often report a high incidence of stability for party identification, confirming a key theoretical claim for this concept as a long-term predisposition. But we cannot be sure whether such recall can be trusted. In any event, no such questions are available in recent election studies.

TABLE 7.3. Stability and Change in Party Identification, 2000–2004 (in percentages)

	Party Identification, 2004						
	Strong Dem.	Weak Dem.	Ind. Dem.	Pure Ind.	Ind. Rep.	Weak Rep.	Strong Rep.
Same party as in 2000	81	70	80	89	74	54	77
Change between 2000 and 2004							
Rep. → Dem.	3	3	—	—	—	—	—
Rep. → Ind.	—	—	4	6	21	—	—
Dem. → Ind.	—	—	16	5	5	—	—
Dem. → Rep.	—	—	—	—	—	8	3
Ind. → Dem.	16	27	—	—	—	—	—
Ind. → Rep.	—	—	—	—	—	38	20
Total	100	100	100	100	100	100	100
Number of cases	178	98	99	43	99	112	190

Source: NES 2000-2002-2004 Full Panel File (ICPSR Study 4293).

the persistence of partisanship with panel surveys, where the same respondents were interviewed multiple times, with years elapsed between interviews. One such panel, which comprised the full electorate, was conducted between 2000 and 2004. Given the unusually turbulent events of that period, we may expect to find less stability in partisan attachments than in more normal times. The entries of table 7.3 nonetheless depict a pattern that can be described as "firm but not immovable" (Campbell et al. 1960, 148). On the average, roughly three in four respondents cling to the same broad allegiance in 2004 as they held four years earlier. Weak partisans, predictably enough, show more movement than do strong ones. What is quite rare is movement from one party to the other. The most common transition involves Independents, moving in and out of the parties.[5]

A four-year panel, of course, only offers a small glimpse of the life

5. The correlation between party identification (as measured by the seven-point scale) in 2000 and 2004 is . 80. High as such a value is for an expression of public opinion over a four-year time period, it understates the true stability of party identification because of measurement error. It is worth noting that the correlations over two-year periods (.84 for 2000–2002, and .85 for 2002–4) are not much higher than the four-year correlation. That is a sign that a good portion of observed instability is due to unreliability of measurement rather than true change. This pattern is very similar to the one found in other four-year panels (Converse and Markus 1979, 37–39) as well as a 1980 panel (Green and Palmquist 1990). The two-year continuity coefficients for party identification in the current panel compare favorably to those reported for the 1950s, 1960s, and 1970s (Converse and Markus 1979, 38).

cycle. To gauge persistence over a longer time period, we return to a most unique data set, described above. To recapitulate, that survey monitored two cohorts over a long, if not full, span of their lives. The younger cohort aged from about 17 years to 50 during those interviews (between 1965 and 1997), while the older (parental) cohort was followed only until 1982. Tables 7.4 and 7.5 have condensed the possible permutations of partisan transitions into a few basic ones. These tables are organized in such a way that they show the breakdown for each of the seven groups of the party identification scale in the final interview. To take an example from table 7.4, which covers the parental cohort, the share of Strong Democrats that maintained an identification with that same party at all time points was 83 percent in 1982. Another 6 percent of Strong Democrats started out as Democrats in 1965, abandoned this attachment later, and then returned to it. The initial socialization imprint may still be credited for this type of constancy. Among Strong Republicans, the persistence of partisanship also proves quite strong in the parental cohort. The rate, predictably, is lower for weak partisans and Independents with partisan leanings, but the degree of persistence over a nearly 20-year span of life is impressive for this cohort.

In contrast, the youth cohort proves less stable in its partisanship.

TABLE 7.4. Stability and Change in Party Identification, 1965–82: Adult Panel (in percentages)

Since 1965	Party Identification, 1982						
	Strong Dem.	Weak Dem.	Ind. Dem.	Pure Ind.	Ind. Rep.	Weak Rep.	Strong Rep.
Same party in three waves	83	69	40	56	40	65	77
Change and return	6	10	14	7	16	9	3
Total same party in 1965 and 1982	89	79	54	63	56	74	80
Change between 1965 and 1982							
Rep. → Dem.	3	4	—	—	—	—	—
Rep. → Ind.	—	—	6	14	30	—	—
Dem. → Ind.	—	—	40	23	14	—	—
Dem. → Rep.	—	—	—	—	—	9	10
Ind. → Dem.	8	17	—	—	—	—	—
Ind. → Rep.	—	—	—	—	—	17	10
Total	100	100	100	100	100	100	100
Number of cases	174	199	86	57	83	126	120

Source: Youth-Parent Socialization Panel Study, 1965–1982: Three Waves Combined (ICPSR Study 9553).

Barely one-quarter of Strong Republicans in table 7.5 maintained their loyalty throughout the full period; another 10 percent returned after straying. Nearly as many contemporary Republicans in this cohort started out with a Democratic as with a Republican identification, or with none at all. Change is also rampant in the Independent groups. Many Independents with a partisan leaning originated as straight partisans, and may find it easy to migrate back to that orientation. Hence, identification with political parties as established in preadult years may not always be an immovable attachment. It is clearly vulnerable to forces of change in one's adult life. Many members of the particular youth cohort examined in table 7.5 ended up with a partisan attachment other than the one of their youth. Such a degree of instability, however, may not be typical of what happens during the adult life cycle. If it were typical, it would be hard to sustain a key claim for the concept of party identification, namely its long-term stability.

The 1965 youth cohort experienced a barrage of turbulent events during its transition to adulthood (the war in Vietnam, antiwar protests, the counterculture, civil rights demonstrations, urban riots, etc.). These were historic circumstances of rare potency that young cohorts growing up in normal times are not exposed to. What is more, the partisanship of

TABLE 7.5. Stability and Change in Party Identification, 1965–97: Youth Panel (in percentages)

Since 1965	Party Identification, 1997						
	Strong Dem.	Weak Dem.	Ind. Dem.	Pure Ind.	Ind. Rep.	Weak Rep.	Strong Rep.
Same party in four waves	51	31	32	46	32	14	26
Change and return	18	24	8	16	12	21	10
Total same party in 1965 and 1997	69	55	40	62	44	35	36
Change between 1965 and 1997							
Rep. → Dem.	10	12	—	—	—	—	—
Rep. → Ind.	—	—	22	16	29	—	—
Dem. → Ind.	—	—	38	22	27	—	—
Dem. → Rep.	—	—	—	—	—	32	34
Ind. → Dem.	21	33	—	—	—	—	—
Ind. → Rep.	—	—	—	—	—	33	30
Total	100	100	100	100	100	100	100
Number of cases	114	170	142	45	132	168	112

Source: Youth-Parent Socialization Panel Study, 1965–1997: Four Waves Combined (ICPSR Study 4037).

middle-age adults (table 7.4) proved far more resistant to such forces of change that affected a young cohort just coming of age with an untested sense of partisanship. Of the two cohorts, the parental one is clearly more representative of the overall American electorate than is the youth cohort. Two other long-term longitudinal projects confirm the strong persistence of partisanship across decades: Newcomb's Bennington study, spanning from the 1930s to the 1980s (Alwin, Cohen, and Newcomb 1991) and the Terman study, which reported an impressive correlation (.50) for party identification between 1940 and 1977 (Sears and Funk 1999, 10–12).

THE PARTISAN LIFE CYCLE

The stronger partisan commitments of older cohorts suggests there may be gradual and commonplace experiences associated with successive phases of the life cycle. In particular, we expect the intensity of partisanship to increase with age: The older the voter, the stronger the partisan attachment and the lower the tendency to stay aloof from partisan commitments. The expectation of age-related changes in partisan intensity is firmly supported by evidence accumulated from election surveys covering a dozen years (1992–2004) and comprising several thousands of cases.

There is a steady increase in strong identification with either party as we move from the youngest to the oldest age cohort in table 7.6. The change is clearly systematic, not random. Few young adults (18–20), eligible for the first time to cast a vote, express a strong party attachment, whereas close to half of the oldest cohort (over 75), with a lifetime of political experiences behind it, does so. An intense attachment to a political party must be regarded as an acquired taste. By the same token, there is a steady decline of independence from parties as we move through the age cohorts in table 7.6. Many of the newly eligible voters enter active lives as citizens without a partisan attachment. Only few in the oldest cohort, in contrast, manage to stay aloof from the political parties. So for some portion of the American electorate, even party attachment itself is a taste acquired in adulthood.

A tabulation by age of the sort shown in table 7.6, however, does not prove that aging explains the change in partisan intensity. Age differences always allow for two competing interpretations. One focuses on age as a moment in history that shaped a person's attitudes in a lasting

TABLE 7.6. Relation of Age to Party Identification (in percentages)

Party Identification	Age													
	18–20	21–24	25–29	30–34	35–39	40–44	45–49	50–54	55–59	60–64	65–69	70–75	>75
Strong Democrat	10	12	12	11	14	15	18	20	22	23	25	29	30
Weak Democrat	18	18	19	20	18	19	18	14	17	19	17	14	17
Independent	49	48	42	40	34	39	36	38	33	30	28	30	26
Weak Republican	16	14	16	17	18	14	14	13	14	12	13	13	12
Strong Republican	7	8	11	12	16	13	14	15	14	16	17	14	15
Total	100	100	100	100	100	100	100	100	100	100	100	100	100
Proportion of strong identifiers	17	20	23	23	30	28	32	35	36	39	42	43	45
Number of cases	457	824	1,085	1,278	1,418	1,303	1,057	846	761	629	582	620	723

Note: These data are combined from seven National Election Studies conducted between 1992 and 2004. They are included in the 1948–2004 NES Cumulative Data File (ICPSR Study 8475).

fashion. The alternative treats age as shorthand for length of experience relevant for an attitude or behavior of interest. Turning to the intensity of partisan attachments, the historical interpretation of age attributes the strong feelings of the older cohorts to the kind of politics prevailing in America decades ago. If this interpretation is correct, we would not expect older cohorts always to be the most partisan. Results would depend on when we observe the age-partisanship relationship. At some other point in time, the youngest or some cohort in between might prove to be most intense in its partisanship.

The alternate interpretation maintains that older adults are invariably more intensely attached to a political party than are younger ones, because age-related experiences strengthen the partisan bond. What favors this explanation is the smooth shape of the age-party relationship shown in table 7.6. The intensity of partisanship rises inexorably and, as might be expected, at a diminishing rate. It does not change abruptly from one historical period to another. It should also be noted that the pattern displayed in table 7.6 for the present period is a faithful replica of the pattern found in another period, half a century ago.[6]

The evidence for age gains in partisan intensity, admittedly, is more ragged in the panel of young adults, who were tracked from 1965 to 1997. In fact, the proportion of strong identifiers in that cohort dropped during their first 10 years or so of early adulthood (table 7.7). Why? Because the life-cycle hypothesis is mistaken? We do not believe so. Instead, abnormal forces of the period (1965–73) overrode the tendency to grow more attached to one's party with increasing exposure. It was a fairly rare instance, where the trajectory of the age-partisanship relationship was thrown off course and distorted beyond recognition (Converse 1976). A heavy dose of bad news for a major party can easily discourage young adults with a budding attachment to that party from growing closer to it. This could lead to a temporary weakening of party attachments overall, especially if the party in question is dominant and the other party is unattractive. But partisan attachments of the youth cohort

---

6. See table 7.5 of *The American Voter* (Campbell et al. 1960, 162). Then as now, nearly 50 years later, the proportion of strong partisans rises steadily from the youngest to the oldest cohort (from 24 percent to 51 percent then, compared to a rise from 17 percent to 45 percent nowadays). And the proportion of Independents steadily falls to half the size (from 31 percent to 16 percent then, compared to a drop from 49 percent to 26 percent now). While the intercept of the age-partisanship relationship may have changed (more Independents and fewer strong partisans now), the slope of the relationship (the change per year of age) is practically the same.

did not evaporate or get stuck at this low point. Partisan strength rebounded and resumed its upward move in later years. It should be noted that while the parental cohort follows a parallel path, its gyrations are far more restrained. Whatever forces affected partisanship in that period swayed the youngest cohort far more than the older ones (Jennings and Markus 1984).

While supporting the hypothesis that age makes individuals more firm in their partisan attachments, our analysis fails to lend any support to another age-related hypothesis that enjoys wide currency. Political lore has it that with age Americans become more Republican. Whatever the theoretical basis of this expectation—most likely that age makes us more conservative and hence more fond of the more conservative party—the entries of table 7.6 refute it. The percentage of Republicans (strong and weak) from the youngest to the oldest forms a flat line. The Republican hold on the 25–29-year-old cohort is exactly the same as its hold on the over-75-year-old cohort (27 percent), and it barely budges in the cohorts between. If anything, it is the support for the Democratic Party that appears to rise with age, proving perhaps that it is the more conservative party. But the pattern of growth is more abrupt than smooth, suggesting that something other than the life cycle may be at work. We shall probe for explanation of the Democratic edge among some older cohorts in the next section of this chapter.

The age-partisanship pattern established thus far accords well with a more general notion of group theory, which holds that identification with any group depends on the length of one's affiliation with it. As for

TABLE 7.7. The Strength of Party Identification in the Youth Panel, 1965–97 (in percentages)

Strength of Party Identification	Year of Panel Wave			
	1965	1973	1982	1997
Strong	25	14	15	25
Weak	39	39	41	38
Independent	36	47	44	37
Total	100	100	100	100
Number of cases	925	929	907	922

Source: Youth-Parent Socialization Panel Study, 1965–1997: Four Waves Combined (ICPSR Study 4037).

Note: The entries in this table are based on the same respondents of the youth panel interviewed at four time points. Over that time span they aged, on average, from 17 years (1965), to 25 (1973), 34 (1982), and 49 (1997).

political parties, the longer individuals think of themselves as either Democrats or Republicans, the stronger the attachment to that party becomes. It is not biological age that is important so much as the time elapsed since the attachment was formed. For many Americans the attachment goes back to preadult experiences, but for some portion of the electorate, as we have seen, the bond is forged later in adult years. For this group the learning clock starts only then, as it would for others who switch over to a new party later in life. The clock must also be adjusted for some "forgetting" of partisan attachments if, as happened in Germany, the democratic process is interrupted (Converse 1969). Whatever the complications, as a person settles into a partisan attachment, increasingly strong pressures are needed to prompt a shift in the attachment, or a vote for a candidate of the opposite party.

We may be able now to outline a general pattern by which party identification develops through the life cycle. Most Americans become familiar with political parties in some form while growing up at home. But even as they enter adulthood few are greatly interested in politics, or feel a strong attachment to a party. One clear manifestation of this aloofness among young adults, as we have seen already, is a widespread failure to turn out to vote in elections. It takes some time for the salience of politics to increase for young adults. Perhaps they are drawn into groups and associations that have a political connection, or become integrated in a community through holding a steady job, buying a home, raising a family, and getting involved in local issues. All these steps would make young adults more aware of their own political interests, the impact of political decisions on these interests, and the central role of political parties in processes of governance.

Once an individual has formed a party attachment, however embryonic, and at whatever stage in life it happened, a self-reinforcing process of momentum takes over. A partisan finds it easy to construe ambiguous events to the advantage of the adopted party and to the disadvantage of the opposite party. The more a person engages in this selective perception, the more likely it is that the bond to the group providing this guidance also strengthens. It is a compelling learning experience to say, if my party is right in most instances of everyday politics, then I must be right in sticking with that party in the long run. What is more, the act of voting for candidates of one's party tends to reinforce the attachment as well. An unbroken string of voting for the same party in successive elections is bound to leave individuals with a more fervent partisan commitment than frequent defections to the other party in the voting booth. Yet no matter how strong the attachments, few Americans are utterly blinded by their partisanship. Some short-term events, be it an economic downturn or a scandal, may defy the ability of partisans to interpret them to the credit of the favored party and invite crossing party lines in an election. And on rare occasions, cataclysmic events or profound social changes operating more gradually have the power to produce a long-term change in partisan loyalties.

HISTORICAL CHANGE IN PARTISANSHIP

While the intensity of party identification waxes quite predictably with the life cycle, the partisanship of the identification is subject to less predictable patterns of change. We subscribe to the view that an attachment with a party, for the most part, is highly resistant to change. To be sure, reports of party identification in survey interviews are not rock solid over time and may be prone to sway, especially among voters in their early years. But many of these moves, few as they are, occur for purely *personal* reasons, which operate idiosyncratically and do not relate to broader characteristics of voters. These forces should be distinguished from *social* forces, which affect groups of voters based on some politically relevant characteristic. Personal forces, such as marriage, a new job, or a new location, may exert pressure on a person to adopt views at odds with his or her own. Even though many citizens find themselves in these situations at various times of their lives and may adapt their party attachments accordingly, the resulting changes in partisanship are uncorrelated with larger social categories. Nor do they affect the prevailing balance of partisanship in the overall electorate or among politically relevant segments of the electorate.

In contrast, an economic crisis or a divisive issue tearing the country apart leaves a similar imprint on groups of voters with political consequences. If the stimulus moves one segment of the electorate in one partisan direction while moving another and equally large one in the opposite direction, the electoral makeup of the parties will undergo a profound change, but the overall partisan balance is not disturbed. If these movements do not offset each other, the comparative strength of the parties in the total electorate will shift substantially, perhaps ending the rule of one party and ushering in a new majority party. It is widely accepted that two national crises in American history have shaken party loyalties so violently as to reverse the prevailing balance of partisanship in the nation as a whole: the Civil War and the Great Depression.

The upheaval associated with the Civil War realigned party attachments along regional lines while putting the newly formed Republican Party in a dominant position in the Union. The South, which had been quite competitive in the antebellum period, turned into the Solid South for the Democrats. It stayed that way for a hundred years or so, occasional defections to Republicans in presidential elections notwithstanding. The Northeast and Midwest, in contrast, with their strong abolitionist sentiments, became strongholds of the Republican Party. The Great Depression, which struck the American economy under a Republican administration and control of Congress, ousted the GOP from the White House for 20 years and, with rare breaks, from control of Congress for over half a century.

This sweeping change is not only evident in election returns, but can also be gauged from reports of party identification as early as 1936 in Gallup polls (Erikson and Tedin 1981). The National Election Studies (NES) conducted in the 1950s demonstrate a massive swing in partisan attachments attributed to the impact of the Great Depression and the New Deal. The partisan balance in the American electorate shifted sharply in favor of the Democrats. As far as distinctive groups are concerned, the Democratic Party drew its new strength mostly from the economically disadvantaged, minorities, especially black and Jewish Americans, and the young generation. The South remained solidly in the Democratic fold, while Catholics, whose association with the Democratic Party predated the 1930s, may have become more strongly attached to it under the impact of the Depression. Though overwhelming in size, this new Democratic alignment was a volatile mix of constituent groups that, sooner or later, would prove hard for political leaders to keep in line. Yet as captured by our measure of party identification, the Democratic Party managed to hold on to a lead over the Republican Party for about half a century following the Depression. It is an impressive testimony to the persistence and resilience of partisan attachments in the face of stressful circumstances.

While no single national crisis has occurred since then that would rival the Depression or the Civil War in their sheer power to shake up prevailing partisan loyalties so violently, the turmoil of the 1960s weakened the Democratic hold on the electorate. The upheavals over the Vietnam War, race, and law and order precipitated an irreversible drop in

Democratic identification, though without awarding the Republicans a commensurate gain. It was not until the Reagan presidency that Republicans scored substantial gains in party identification. The "peace and prosperity" failures of the 1970s led to the election of a president who combined ideological zeal with partisanship in an unprecedented effort to overturn the New Deal agenda. The growing Republican strength in party identification helped break the Democratic control of the House in 1994. And in 2004, with Republicans retaining control of both the White House and Congress, the National Election Studies survey, for the first time ever, gave this party the lead in partisan attachments among voters.

In locating the major groups from which a newly ascendant party draws its strength, we invariably turn to one that feels the events of a period most sharply—youth. With survey data at hand as events likely to shake an attitude such as party identification unfold, we can observe immediately how a certain group responds, not how it remembers its behavior years later. When we compare in table 7.8 the partisanship of young adults in the elections of the Reagan years with elections before and after, we see a sharp turn toward the Republican Party between 1980 and 1988, from barely 30 to almost 50 percent. By comparison, no such movement stirred during Nixon's landslide victory in 1972 among young adults, when most of them embraced an Independent stance. And the upward trend halted and ebbed back once Reagan had departed from the White House. There is no inherent proclivity of the young to the GOP, or the Democratic Party, for that matter. For the most part, the

TABLE 7.8. The Partisanship of Young Adults (under 30 years of age)

Year	Percentage Republican of Two-Party Total	
	Party Identifiers	Presidential Vote
1972	30	62
1976	31	49
1980	37	55
1984	43	59
1988	48	54
1992	47	47
1996	42	45
2000	36	50

Source: The 1948–2004 NES Cumulative Data File (ICPSR Study 8475).

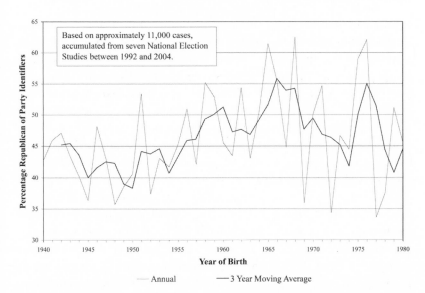

Fig. 7.1. Party identification of party identifiers born between 1940 and 1980

young follow in the partisan footsteps of the adult world represented by their parents. But when, at a given moment in history, the winds of change suddenly blow from one partisan direction, the younger cohorts will follow the political drift more sharply than the rest of the electorate.

Further evidence of how the events of the Reagan years affected those coming of age at that time comes from an accumulation of surveys conducted during the last 10 years or so. In figure 7.1, we can see a visible surge of Republican identification in the cohort born roughly between 1960 and 1970. Many of them cast their first vote in an election that featured Ronald Reagan as a candidate or sitting president. The Republicans have retained the upper hand in this cohort, unlike in older cohorts where Democrats have a decided edge. The Republican surge appears to abate in cohorts born after 1970, when events of the times, especially under a Democratic president, were not as favorable to the Republican Party any more.

All by itself, the embrace of a party by a new generation is not likely to overturn the domination by the other party in the full electorate, even if all the offspring of that generation were to follow suit and so on; it certainly would take a long time. Another group we would expect to be highly susceptible to the winds of change is Independents, whose ranks began to swell in the 1960s. This expectation is confirmed by the behavior of the high school class of 1965 as it passed through the events of the 1970s and 1980s. Just like the American electorate overall, the partisan complexion of this group changed from heavily Democratic in 1965 to parity between Democrats and Republicans more than 30 years later. Only one of three latter-day Republicans in this group started out that way, as was shown in table 7.5. Most of them came of age as Democrats or Independents. Yet few of the Democrats who had become Republicans by 1997 did so through a straight conversion. Most of them navigated this change through a two-step process, first by abandoning the Democratic allegiance for independence, and then adopting a Republican identification. Hence the roots of the new partisan alignment may reach as far back as the upheavals of the 1960s that tore Democrats from their partisan moorings.

A new partisan alignment typically comes with a distinctive group appeal and ideological coloration. Like the New Deal, Reaganomics was heavily ideological in nature, if in another direction (with less government involvement in the economy and on issues like racial equality, holding a tough line in battling communism, and a push for traditional values). This may have had a special resonance for an old constituency of the Democratic Party that had grown estranged from it for some time over these issues, especially on matters of race. Presidential victories in southern states had become commonplace for Republicans since 1972, when Nixon carried every state of the former Confederacy, although many Democrats managed to hang on to their seats in the House and Senate as well as to state-level offices. Republicans had cracked the Solid South, and the loyalties of white southerners to the Democratic Party were ebbing.

During the Reagan years, as shown in figure 7.2, Republicans made significant gains in the party attachments of white southerners, enough to cross the 40 percent mark and shed their image as a party with a chip on its shoulder in that region. Yet when seen over the long haul of half a century, the Republican growth in the American South during the 1980s was undramatic. It was more a continuation of an ongoing trend than a surge. Most surprisingly, the upheavals over civil rights in the 1960s appeared to have slowed rather than sparked any rush toward the GOP in the white South. Perhaps race had less to do with the partisan transformation of the white South than is commonly assumed.

There is no question, though, that this issue left its imprint on the partisanship of black Americans. Whatever residual affection the Re-

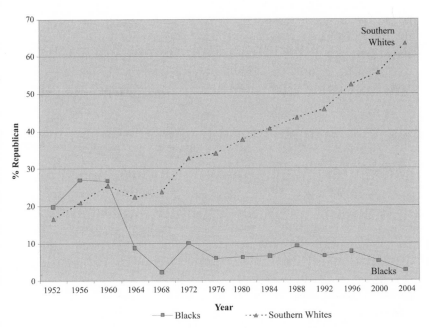

Fig. 7.2. Percentage Republican of party identifiers among blacks and southern whites, 1952–2004. (Data from 1948–2004 NES Cumulative Data File ICPSR Study #8475.)

publican Party still enjoyed in this segment of the electorate vanished in the wake of the civil rights legislation sponsored by a Democratic president in the 1960s. It is worth remembering nonetheless that up until that moment the Republican Party was held in higher esteem by black Americans than by white southerners.

The realignment of the white South, however, does not appear to be primarily the story of specific historic events or the legacy of a particular administration. Instead the pattern so evident in figure 7.2 appears to confirm the hypothesis of a slow, but inexorable "convergence" of the South with the rest of the country (Converse 1966b). Still, the pace of southern change did not halt once convergence was reached in the 1980s. What is striking is that the Republican growth in partisan attachments kept on going among white southerners. Even the White House tenure of a southern Democrat (Bill Clinton), who left office with impressive approval ratings, was unable to stem, let alone reverse, this partisan tide toward the other party. Republicans kept making further strides during George W. Bush's first term; by 2004 they outnumbered Democrats by about two to one among southern whites. This group, which was a solid pillar of Democratic strength for about a century, has now become one of the most distinctive and dependable constituencies of the Republican Party. Were it not for the consolidation of the black vote in the Democratic fold, the region of the former Confederacy might be on the verge of reverting to a "Solid South" again, but this time under the banner of, yes, Lincoln's old party.

COMMENTARY AND CONTROVERSY

Partisan Genes

The close match between the party identification of parents and offspring has long tantalized observers with the possibility of a genetic transmission, though others find the prospect deeply disturbing. Are we born as Democrats, Republicans, or Independents? It is not unreasonable to ask. How else could something that in many families is treated so casually leave such an enduring imprint on children? How else could it correlate across generations as strongly as a trait with a definite genetic component, a person's height?[7] Yet until very recently, a claim made by an early voting study still held true: "Virtually nothing is known about the genetic development of personal identification with political parties" (Campbell, Gurin, and Miller 1954, 97).

Now the study of genetics is finally venturing into political behavior. Research using twins has begun to estimate the genetic component, as separate from the environmental one, of political attitudes about a wide range of concerns (Alford, Funk, and Hibbing 2005). The findings are intriguing and somewhat ambiguous, as the authors themselves concede. While party identification, in the sense that it has been treated in this chapter, is not primarily genetically formed, affect toward each of the major parties is (2005, 161). In other words, we largely become Democrats or Republicans through parental nurturing, but our devotion to a party may be genetically primed. This conclusion, however, runs starkly against some major findings reported in the chapter. The adoption of a particular party seems to come fairly early in one's life, when the political world is but a dim outline, while the intensity of one's partisan attachment grows with exposure to the political world as an adult, and the act of voting, in particular.

---

7. The intergenerational correlation for party identification (.59) in the 1965 socialization study (Jennings and Niemi 1974, 38) actually surpasses the one reported for height (.50) in Pearson's classic study on the laws of inheritance (Pearson and Lee 1903, 378).

Dealignment

For quite some time, much of the discussion of party identification has been preoccupied with decline. Observers have noted the weakening of partisan ties, the growth of the ranks of Independents, and more frequent defections from the party line, all of which seems to be well embodied by the concept of partisan dealignment (Beck 1984; Wattenberg 1998). Most students of elections, however, do not view this as a continuing process that will unravel partisan ties and spell the demise of the major political parties. Rather it is a historic episode, however traumatic, essentially a closed chapter of American electoral history, bracketed by the elections of 1964 and 1976. Studies by Nie, Verba, and Petrocik (1976) and by Jennings and Niemi (1981) made a strong case for the generational hypothesis, with dealignment concentrated among younger cohorts. Yet the contribution of the younger cohorts was not enough to account for the partisan decline in the overall electorate. Converse (1976) emphasized the effect of period forces, working on all cohorts of the electorate, though with a lessening impact for older cohorts with more established partisan attachments. Support for such a period-aging model also came from Norpoth and Rusk (1982). There are strong signs that the process of dealignment was halted and even reversed after 1976 (Miller and Shanks 1996), with the electorate even growing more polarized along party lines (Hetherington 2001). Yet a dissenting voice argues for dealignment as an ongoing process that is bound to alter the meaning and function of party identification as we know it (Dalton 2007).

One manifest consequence of partisan dealignment, to be sure, has been a greater incidence of split-ticket voting. Between the 1950s and 1980s, ticket splitting in voting for president and House members increased sharply (Fiorina 1992, 12–14). In terms of governance, this has meant prolonged periods of divided government, with Republicans controlling the White House and Democrats the House of Representatives being the most common pattern. Balancing theories have been applied to explain the kind of electoral choices that lead to divided government (Fiorina 1992; Jacobson 1990), but the statistical evidence is mixed. Some studies show voters lacking the necessary information and sophistication for such strategic behavior (Sigelman, Wahlbeck, and Buell 1997); or else their choices may be driven by incumbent support (Burden and Kimball 2002). Others have found support for "cognitive Madisonianism," with a portion of American voters consciously exercising a preference for divided government in the way they split their tickets (Lewis-Beck and Nadeau 2004b).

Partisan dealignment also appears to be related to the stronger showing of third-party candidates. It makes sense to expect that "third-party voting should be easier for citizens who have weaker attachments, or who never developed . . . party loyalties in the first place" (Rosenstone, Behr, and Lazarus 1996, 144). Partisan dealignment has greatly enlarged the pool of potential voters for other than Democratic and Republican candidates. The success of George Wallace in getting 13 percent of the presidential vote in 1968 fed on strong discontent of white southern Democrats with their party (Converse et al. 1969). Both John Anderson and Ross Perot drew heavily on voters lacking party allegiance, although dealignment is not able to explain why Perot did so much better than Anderson (Rosenstone, Behr, and Lazarus 1996, 245–48; also Burden and Lacy 1999).

Realignment

Historic change in party identification, where the partisan balance undergoes a dramatic transformation, is closely tied to the concept of electoral realignment.[8] As one of the major proponents of this concept put it, realignments help "divide much of American political history into clearly demarcated 'party-systems eras,' bounded by realigning upheavals from preceding and succeeding eras" (Burnham 1991, 101). By nature, realignments are rare events that are thought to require "the presence of a great national crisis, leading to a conflict regarding governmental policies and the association of the major parties with relatively clearly contrasting programs for its solution" (Campbell 1966, 76). Some voices of dissent (Mayhew 2002) notwithstanding, there is compelling evidence for the realigning status of a few historic elections (Norpoth and Rusk 2007). Realignments are often concentrated in specific regions of the country (Nardulli 1995) or electoral groups (Petrocik 1981; Stanley and Niemi 1995). Central to a realignment as an *electoral* phenomenon is a condition embodied in V. O. Key's definition of a "critical election": a "profound readjustment" in the electorate's "standing decision" that proves "durable" (Key 1955). What is being adjusted is a voter's long-standing attachment

---

8. The literature is too voluminous to be reviewed here in any detail. For a reader's guide and bibliography listing over 600 publications, see Bass 1991. For a current overview of the realignment literature, see Rosenof 2003.

to a political party that is hard to change in normal times. It is in electoral realignments where the distribution of party identification undergoes lasting change.

To accommodate some changes that do not proceed in the manner of "critical" realignments, Key (1959) introduced the notion of a "secular" realignment. This is a gradual type of change that may help capture the realignment associated with the South, especially white voters in that region in recent years (Black and Black 1992). In such a process partisan loyalties decay over time and are replaced by those for another party. Such change may also conform to the "issue evolution" model, where polarization of elites on issues of great importance such as civil rights triggers a large-scale sorting out along party lines in the mass public (Carmines and Stimson 1989). The unabated pace of the southern white realignment, however, suggests that the "evolution" of issues goes beyond race and involves moral-cultural issues (Carmines and Layman 1997).

One realignment theory that requires no movement in individual party identification is based on a process of generational replacement. According to this view, the partisan balance shifts when a new generation of young voters enters the electorate with a partisan imprint that distinguishes it from the rest of the electorate, which stays put. Campbell et al. (1960) make a strong case for this process of change to account for the New Deal realignment. Another theory that does not require the conversion of partisans focuses on the mobilization of the nonpartisan segment of the electorate that had largely stayed aloof from the electoral politics and then turned out heavily for the Democratic side in the 1930s (Andersen 1979). Others, however, find it impossible to account for large-scale shifts in the partisan balance without conversion. Erikson and Tedin (1981) offer evidence from Gallup polls that by 1936 both established and young voters had swung toward the Democratic side in party attachments.

Whatever the explanation for the partisan change during the New Deal era, critics of the realignment concept have noted the failure of a certifiable realignment to materialize since then (Shafer 1991; Mayhew 2002). The Reagan years, however, have proved quite compelling for realignment claims (Aldrich 1995; Hurley 1991; Miller and Shanks 1996; Norpoth 1987). Miller and Shanks (1996, 166) concluded that "between 1980 and 1988, at least a limited version of the long-heralded partisan realignment took place." The Reagan years sparked a "growth in Republican identification that shrank the overwhelming Democratic lead dating from the New Deal realignment" (Meffert, Norpoth, and Ruhil 2001, 961). While there were strong signs of generational change, large-scale mobilization of Independents into Republican ranks among established cohorts was also required to account for the overall shift toward that party, though there was very little in the way of straight conversion (Norpoth 1987). Still, the tenuous lead of Republicans leaves many observers skeptical of realignment claims.

CHAPTER 8

Public Policy and Political Preference

It is a basic principle of democratic theory that citizens influence public policy within their political system. Even as citizen preferences shape policies in a democratic system, those policies are likely to affect the thoughts and actions of the very same citizens. As a result of these complementary processes, substantive issues are likely to enter the field of forces that affect electoral decision making. To state it simply, voters are more likely to support parties and candidates that take positions close to their own.

Our analysis has already considered issues as one of the attitudinal factors most proximal to individual voter choices. But at that point the issues are already imbued with partisan content; in other words, the controversy over policy is relevant to the voter's decision precisely because the person perceives its substantive implications work in favor of one candidate, work against the other, or do both. But how are these connections made in the first place?

In this chapter, we look more closely at the process through which partisan valence is attached to an issue. In so doing, we move further backward along the chain of influences that ultimately determine the vote. Our analysis shows that citizens experience various difficulties as they work out the partisan implications of their own issue preferences. These problematic elements of the translation process, in turn, limit the potential for policy issues to exert a direct influence on voting behavior within the American electorate.

NECESSARY CONDITIONS FOR ISSUE INFLUENCE ON VOTING CHOICE

For several reasons, the impact of a given issue on the vote is usually very limited. First, any single issue is just one in a field of several policy controversies that exist with the electoral environment. Even during periods when one policy concern seems to dominate public attention (e.g., Iraq and the war on terror in 2004, the economy in 1992, and so on), candidates for public office routinely express a broader slate of issue positions that they seek to operationalize if they win office.

Second, there is the simple fact that, in the vast majority of American elections, voters make their choices among candidates and not policy positions. Candidates possess a variety of characteristics that are indirectly linked to specific issues (i.e., their partisan affiliation) or largely unrelated to policies (i.e., their personal traits, such as honesty, intelligence, and the like). Such characteristics are often more salient and immediately discernible than are the details of a candidate's stands on policy. Hence, they also serve as criteria for guiding the voting choices of some citizens. In so doing, these alternative guideposts further limit the impact of issues.

These limitations on the influence of issues are reinforced by the nature of the act of voting, which does not require voters to explain the reasons they vote as they do. Therefore, it is very difficult to say what determines any given electoral outcome. Did one side make a superior effort at mobilization? Did voters respond favorably to one candidate's personality, or unfavorably to the other's? Were they happy with the incumbent's performance in office, or unhappy with the way things have been going since the preceding election? Have specific policies driven voters' decisions—and if so, which ones? Such thorny questions cannot be resolved by observing election results alone—even if media commentators and pundits try to do exactly that.

Even as the effects of issues on American elections are circumscribed by features of the external environment, so too are they limited by characteristics of the individual voters. It is to the latter that we now turn. Let us begin by acknowledging that willingness to express an opinion on an issue in response to a survey interviewer is not, in itself, sufficient evidence that the issue will affect the person's vote. In fact, several criteria must be fulfilled in order for a given issue to have an impact on an individual's electoral decision:

1. The issue must be recognized by the voter.
2. The issue must evoke some degree of preference for one policy solution over another.
3. The voter must believe that one candidate is more likely to work for the voter's preferred policy solution.

The three criteria are simple, but they cannot be taken for granted. In order for issues to affect voters' actions, those issues must be recognized as a legitimate basis for political debate. This assertion may seem so obvious as to be trivial. Nevertheless, issues and conflicts over policy are not prominent elements in most Americans' everyday lives, thoughts, and opinions. This simple fact is recognized by political activists of all stripes: When they engage in public relations efforts (as opposed to lobbying public officials), their activities are usually aimed at maximizing public awareness of the problems that they believe to be the major ones confronting society. From the environmentalist who articulates the dangers of air and water pollution, to the antiabortion protestor decrying the murder of unborn children, to the union official who warns of the social burdens that will arise from cuts in retirement benefits, the main task is to get the public to acknowledge the problem. For the social scientists studying the impact of issues on political behavior, the coincident objective is to determine the success of those efforts at generating recognition: Just how familiar is the public with the issues confronting American society?

The second criterion is that the voter maintain a nonneutral position on an issue. From a logical perspective, a controversy cannot affect a person's electoral choice unless that individual really prefers one policy over another to address the underlying problem. Such preferences are more likely when the issue arouses some intensity in the person's beliefs about the relative merits of alternative issue positions. Given the "distance" of many policy disputes from the everyday lives of citizens, this condition often goes unmet. For example, people may understand that there is ethnic conflict in Bosnia or that the poor require welfare services. But without direct exposure to, or experience with, the problem, they may lack motivation to develop a preference for a particular response to it. In contrast, a person with family ties to the region or one who is the low-income head of a single-parent family would have immediate substantive motivations to prefer certain kinds of governmental action. Furthermore, the degree to which the respective issues impinge on everyday life could well affect the strength of feelings about those policy activities. Of course, it stands to reason that the subsequent impact of the Bosnia and welfare issues on voting decisions will be greater in the latter case than in the former. And that, in turn, suggests the importance of understanding the variations in the intensity of issue attitudes throughout the mass electorate.

The preceding two criteria determine whether an individual has a personal preference regarding a policy. But in order to affect the vote the individual's attitude must be imbued with a partisan motivation. After all, even an intensely felt issue cannot guide a voting choice if the candidates have ignored it in their campaigns. And even if the issue has been mentioned, the candidates must espouse different positions. Analogous to the situation of a voter who takes a completely neutral stand on an issue, undifferentiated stands on an issue by candidates provide no basis for voters to choose between them. Perhaps more subtly, different positions by the candidates are still not enough to enable an issue-based vote: The voter must believe that one candidate is more aligned with his or her preferred policy solution than the other candidate. Otherwise, the voter would face a choice between two differing, but equally beneficial (or onerous), alternatives; in effect, they would cancel each other out as an influence on their decision. For these reasons, it is important to move beyond individual attitudes to examine perceptions of the candidates with respect to the same set of issues.

The three criteria proposed here should not be impenetrable barriers to issue-based voting. Indeed, it is relatively easy to fulfill each of them. Nevertheless, these criteria might be viewed quite reasonably as a set of successive hurdles that must be overcome, in a cumulative manner. Only after passing over all of them is it possible for an issue to affect a person's voting decision. Readers may find it a bit surprising to see how few members of the American electorate actually achieve this end. And it is probably worth pointing out that these criteria only comprise necessary rather than sufficient conditions for issue voting. They only identify the pool of potential issue voters. It is certainly possible that some of these people still base their electoral decisions on other, nonissue, foundations.

ISSUE FAMILIARITY

In assessing the public's recognition of issues, it is critical that we focus on the individual citizens and their beliefs, rather than on the issues and their "objective" prominence within the external political environment. There are several reasons for doing so. For one thing, the contents of the environment are subject to overt attempts at manipulation by partisan political actors. It is a fundamental principle of campaign strategy for candidates to emphasize the issues that provide them with an advantageous position, while simultaneously avoiding those that evince weakness. For example, in 2004, Republicans referred repeatedly to their prosecution of the war on terror (an issue that they believed worked to their electoral benefit) but said very little about the corporate corruption scandals that had emerged over the preceding years (which might have been blamed on Republican officials). Of course, their hope was that this varied salience of the respective issues would affect the policy factors that people had in mind as they entered the voting booth.

Similarly, the coverage of issues in the mass media provides only an imperfect gauge of the public's response to those issues. The content of televised news broadcasts is subject to the decisions of news directors, just as the space devoted to issues in newspaper and magazine stories is affected by editorial judgments. Being commercial, profit-oriented enterprises, the mass media try to play to their respective audiences by dealing with the kinds of concerns that people are already thinking about. At the same time, however, it is important to remember that "news" is effectively defined as what is different in the world today from that which existed yesterday. Hence, the media are also engaged in an ongoing quest to find new, exciting, and different stories that will seize the attention of their audience and, hopefully, bring new people into that audience. However, this causes serious complications in the present context because many political issues arise from long-standing social problems that do not change much over short time spans. The appropriate strategies for dealing with poverty, environmental pollution, and the trade-off between national security and civil liberties—these are ongoing questions. They can enter into voters' thinking even if they have not been prominent recently in the evening news or in newspapers.

The general problem is that the presence and overt salience of social problems and policy controversies is quite different from the public's propensity to receive information about the resultant political issues and think about the implications of the conflicting positions. Citizens are confronted with an array of information sources, the scope of which would have been unimaginable a few years ago. Nobody can pay attention to everything; even the person who feels a civic responsibility to become informed about important issues must select among sources of information. If media coverage varies from one outlet to the next, then these individual choices will have an impact on the set of issues that eventually enters into each person's consciousness.

For many people, dealing with political issues is too much of a bother. Conflict over policy, by definition, involves weighing difficult trade-offs and making choices among costly alternatives. The benefits to be gained from taking the effort to wade through the competing claims and thinking about the implications in order to formulate a personal stand are distant and murky, at best. Undoubtedly, some segment of the public simply avoids the whole thing by screening issues out of their personal perceptual fields. For such individuals, the substantive issue coverage in the media becomes formless "noise" that is either ignored or endured until other, more interesting material becomes available. The general point, of course, is that the widespread availability of information does not, in itself, guarantee that issues will become part of a voter's conscious reasons for supporting one candidate over another.

Some telling evidence about public familiarity with issues can be gained by considering a controversy that played a prominent role in the campaign rhetoric of the 2004 election. During his first term in office, George W. Bush signed a series of bills that dramatically reduced federal taxes. The resultant changes involve more than one trillion dollars in annual revenues and, regardless of any long-term consequences, the immediate beneficiaries were drawn from the wealthier strata of American society. The tax cuts were controversial when they were passed and they remain so at the present time. The stakes involved in this issue were only sharpened by the rapid increases in federal spending that accompanied the onset of the war on terror and the invasion of Iraq. Disagreements over the status of the tax cuts were one of the most vehement domestic issues of the 2004 campaign. Yet when asked a very broad question about tax cuts, one-third of the respondents to the 2004 National Election Study reported that they hadn't thought very much about the issue, or didn't know about it. Mass attention to an issue is not a simple reflection of elite attention.

Components of Issue Familiarity

The task of measuring public familiarity with specific issues is rendered more difficult precisely because people generally try to cooperate with the survey interviewers who ask them about those issues. Whether it is an attempt to appear well informed or a simple desire to help, most individuals provide answers to survey questions. The question, of course, is whether the overt responses express crystallized attitudes or merely reflect random "noise."

In order to avoid misleading impressions that might be caused by the latter, we must take care to insure that those who respond to a question have given thought to the issue it addresses. This involves both attention to detail in the construction of the survey questions and a willingness to employ indirect evidence drawn from the combination of responses that an individual gives to different, but related, items. Given the constraints in any survey interview, these requirements restrict the issues we can employ for the analysis.

The 2004 National Election Study includes six issues for which sufficient information was collected to make them useful for present purposes: Two of the issues involve foreign policy questions (increasing or decreasing defense spending; solving international problems through diplomacy or through military action). A third issue focuses on a "lifestyle" question (the role of women in society). One additional issue taps concerns over civil rights by asking whether the federal government should provide assistance to blacks. The two final issues evoke broad views about the government's role in society (increasing or decreasing federal spending and services; government-guaranteed jobs and standard of living versus leaving individuals to get ahead on their own).

Thus, our analysis is limited to a fairly small number of issues. But they do cover a broad array of varied, substantive concerns. We believe this breadth to be particularly important for our present objectives— even if we had suitable information on a larger set of issues, our strong suspicion is that the substantive interpretations and conclusions would be no different from those we report here.

As the first step of our analysis, we exploit one of the details in the wording of the survey questions. For each issue, respondents were read a brief statement introducing two contrasting positions on that issue, along with a seven-point scale representing degrees of adherence to one or the other position; in other words, the two positions on each issue were depicted as polar opposites along a unidimensional continuum. Then the question was posed: "Where would you place yourself on this scale, or haven't you thought much about this?" The latter clause in this question is particularly important for our purposes because it provides an easy way for people to opt out of professing an opinion on an issue that is unfamiliar to them. Anyone who said that they had not thought about an issue was not placed along the continuum of positions for that issue.[1]

If we use this standard, the public does think about issues on a fairly widespread basis. The vast majority of the survey respondents were willing to place themselves on most of the issues. Fully two-thirds (about 68 percent) offered personal stands on all six issues, with about one-fifth more (20 percent) taking positions on five of the six issues. At the other extreme, nobody refused to offer an opinion on all of the issues and less than 1 percent declined on five or more issues.

An immediate interpretation of the preceding evidence might be that American public opinion is attentive to policy issues. But we must warn again that so far we have employed a simple and permissive standard. According to the cliché, talk is cheap, and that may well be the case here. The simple willingness to place oneself along a seven-point scale provides no information about the reliability of that placement or the degree to which it reflects an actual consideration of the competing positions. Social psychologists argue that attitudes—affective reactions to stimuli—must be constructed on a foundation of cognitions—beliefs about those stimuli. The problem, at least so far, is that we have no indication whether any cognitive reasoning exists to bolster the scale self-placements.

In order to address this point, we will make use of information

---

1. For defense spending, the two issue positions are presented to the respondents as follows: "Some people believe that we should spend much less money for defense. Suppose these people are at one end of a scale, at point 1. Others feel that defense spending should be greatly increased. Suppose these people are at the other end, at point 7. Of course, some other people have opinions somewhere in between, at points 2, 3, 4, 5 or 6." On diplomacy versus military action, the statements are these: "Some people believe the United States should solve international problems by using diplomacy and other forms of international pressure and use military force only if absolutely necessary. . . . Others believe diplomacy and pressure often fail and the U.S. must be ready to use military force." For women's rights, the statements are these: "Recently there has been a lot of talk about women's rights. Some people feel that women should have an equal role with men in running business, industry, and government. . . . Others feel that a woman's place is in the home." For civil rights, the statements are worded, "Some people feel that the government in Washington should make every effort to improve the social and economic position of blacks. . . . Others feel that the government should not make any special effort to help blacks because they should help themselves." On government spending or services, the wording is this: "Some people think the government should provide fewer services even in areas such as health and education in order to reduce spending. . . . Other people feel it is important for the government to provide many more services even if it means an increase in spending." Finally, the wording of the statements on guaranteed jobs is this: "Some people feel the government in Washington should see to it that every person has a job and a good standard of living. . . . Others think the government should just let each person get ahead on their own."

gleaned from additional survey items. After placing themselves along each issue scale, the NES respondents were asked to do the same for the two major presidential candidates and parties.[2] As an indirect indicator of issue-related cognition, we will take each person's willingness to specify a position for both the Democratic and Republican parties. All of the issues under consideration have been features of the American political landscape for many years. In each case, the issue has evolved to the point that the general policy objectives associated with the respective parties are well known. And we feel safe in asserting that at least minimal familiarity with the partisan stands should be a component of a truly formed opinion on that issue. To borrow the language of social psychology, articulation of the parties' stands on issues signals that the positions on issues have been associated with other prominent belief elements (i.e., the parties) in the individual's field of vision.

The requirement that people also specify the parties' stands produces a more limited estimate of issue awareness than we obtained from personal positions on issues alone. But even this more stringent standard does not lead to conclusions markedly different from those reported earlier. Just over half of the respondents (54 percent) identified both parties' positions on all six issues, with one-fifth more (20 percent) placing the parties on five of the six issues. At the opposite extreme, only about 3 percent could not place the parties on any of the issues. So, while this more stringent standard produces a slightly lower estimate of mass familiarity with issues, it still appears that most people are at least minimally aware of the issues that confront the electorate.

Table 8.1 summarizes the results so far, by giving the evidence regarding familiarity with each of the six issues. As we can see in the leftmost column, the size of the segment that refuses to profess an opinion varies somewhat from one issue to the next. At one extreme, nearly everyone has a personal preference on the lifestyle issue of women's role in society. Only 5 percent of the respondents said they hadn't thought much about this issue. The question of diplomacy versus military action also exhibits a fairly high level of opinion, with only about 6 percent refusing to place themselves relative to the alternatives. On the remaining four issues, the subsets that refuse an opinion hover at about one-tenth of the total sample.

---

2. After placing themselves along each seven-point scale, respondents were asked, "Where would you place George W. Bush (John Kerry/the Democratic Party/the Republican Party) on this issue?"

The second column of table 8.1 shows the percentages who profess a personal opinion, but refuse to place the two parties on each issue. The figures in this column are all quite small, suggesting that personal issue stands are usually accompanied by beliefs about the party positions. But there are interesting differences across the issues. The two smallest values occur for defense spending and diplomacy versus military action; the parties' stands on these foreign policy issues are widely recognized. The two socioeconomic issues of government services and guaranteed jobs also coincide with widely recognized partisan positions. In each case only about 7 percent of the electorate professed a personal opinion, but refused to place the parties. The situation is different with civil rights, where almost 13 percent of those holding opinions could not identify the party positions. The lifestyle issue carries this a bit further: Almost 15 percent did not know the parties' stands regarding women's roles.

To summarize the analysis so far, we have suggested a combination of two conditions that, when met simultaneously, signal enough familiarity with an issue for us to assert that an individual actually possesses an opinion on that issue. The existence of a "real" opinion might still be questioned, because our conditions are not particularly difficult. So we added the requirement of party positions in order to cancel out the effects of people who believe it desirable that they profess opinions to the survey interviewer, even if they have given no real thought to the policy conflicts about which they are being questioned. However, note that we regard the statements of party issue stands as a relatively subjective mat-

TABLE 8.1. Familiarity with Issues (in percentages)

Issue	Haven't Thought Much about Issue or Refuse to Place Self on Issue	Place Self but Not Willing to Place Both Parties on the Issue	Place Self and Both Parties the Issue
Government spending versus services	12.5	6.8	80.7
Defense spending	12.5	5.7	81.8
Government guaranteed jobs and living standard	9.0	8.4	82.6
Government assistance to blacks	11.5	12.9	75.6
Equal role for women	4.5	14.5	81.0
Diplomacy versus military action	6.3	4.4	89.3

Note: Percentages sum to 100 percent within each row. Number of observations for the first five issues is 1,212. For diplomacy versus military action issue, the number of observations is 1,066. Data source is the 2004 National Elec Study.

ter—we impose no requirement of accuracy in the individual placements of the parties. So it is at least possible that many people are simply
making up their beliefs about the party stands as they go along. Nevertheless, despite the leniency of the criterion, the fact remains that nontrivial segments of the electorate fail to clear the first "hurdle" mitigating
against the ability to cast a vote on the basis of an issue.

The Development of Issue Familiarity

Why does familiarity with issues vary across the electorate? We believe
that two sets of factors are relevant to this question. First, there is the
overall salience of each issue within the external environment. The
widespread recognition of party stands on foreign policy issues suggests
that the immediacy of the wartime environment in 2004 enhanced the
salience of those policy questions for the electorate. The results for the
other four issues in table 8.1 suggest the very reasonable conclusion that
a controversy's longevity on the public agenda is a relevant factor for its
degree of familiarity within the electorate. Questions about government
services and its role in promoting employment can be traced back over
70 years, into the New Deal period. Accordingly, many people are willing
to place the parties on these issues. On the other hand, civil rights issues
only evolved into their modern form in the 1960s, and public debate
over the proper role for women began very shortly thereafter. It would
probably be an exaggeration to say that the latter two are "young" issues
in any absolute sense. But, relatively speaking, they have not provided a
focus of partisan disagreement for as long a time span as foreign policy,
along with the more general social welfare issues. This does seem to have
an immediate impact on public recognition of where the parties stand.

Differences across policy controversies are relevant for the public's familiarity with the resultant issues. But they are likely to have relatively uniform effects across the electorate. We still need to determine why familiarity with a single issue or a common set of issues varies from one citizen to
the next. Here we believe that the existence of cognition is the critical factor. People must recognize that varying courses of action on a social problem can lead to differing outcomes, and they must also understand that
competing political actors are associated with particular policy objectives.

The existence of these cognitions is dependent upon individuals'
possession of contextual knowledge about the problems, policies, and
partisan causes relevant to particular issues and also the reasoning ability required to make the appropriate connections between them. This

combination of knowledge and ability is, presumably, one of the most visible outcomes of the educational process. Therefore, we can hypothesize a positive relationship between individual education levels and issue familiarity.

The evidence for testing this hypothesis is presented in table 8.2, and the empirical results are clear-cut. As educational attainment moves from lower to higher levels, so too does familiarity with the set of issues that we include in our analysis. Among people who have not completed high school, 28 percent were familiar with two issues or fewer; for respondents with at least a college degree, the comparable figure is only about 2 percent. At the opposite end of the spectrum, about 48 percent of the people in the lowest educational category are familiar with at least five of the issues, while 91 percent of the college graduates report this same high level of familiarity. Thus it appears that a combination of systemic and individual-level factors acts to confine the very existence of meaningful opinions on policy issues to a large, but still limited, subset of the more general public.

THE INTENSITY OF ISSUE OPINION

Devoting some thought to a policy controversy, along with a willingness to state the positions taken by the two major parties with respect to that controversy, is not enough in itself to signal the presence of an opinion that could guide an individual's vote on the basis of that issue. Recall our

TABLE 8.2. Issue Familiarity and Level of Education (in percentages)

	Educational Attainment		
Familiarity with Issues	Did Not Complete High School	High School Graduate	College Graduate
Low	28.1	10.1	2.2
Medium	24.0	18.7	7.1
High	47.9	71.2	90.7
Total	100.0	100.0	100.0
Number of cases	96	647	323

Note: High issue familiarity means that respondents placed themselves and both parties on five or six issues. Medium issue familiarity means that respondents placed themselves and both parties on two, three, or four issues. Low issue familiarity means that respondents placed themselves and the parties on none of the issues or on only one issue. The six issues are the same ones used in table 8.1, and the data source is the 2004 National Election Study.

second criterion for issue voting, which states that the person must prefer one policy solution over another. There are undoubtedly some people who are familiar with an issue but, for one reason or another, have not determined their own personal stand. In some cases, the individual may be withholding an opinion until more information is available. In other cases, the merits of the competing positions might seem to be equally balanced. And we must admit a third possibility—that some people claim familiarity with an issue and then profess a centrist stand in order to mask the fact that they do not really know anything about the underlying policy conflict.

Regardless of its precise source, a neutral position on an issue is equivalent to no opinion, at least with respect to issue-based voting. In order to serve as the basis for a choice between partisan alternatives, the individual must prefer one of the policy stands that are placed into conflict with each other by the issue itself. A position midway between the competing policies—operationally, this is a respondent who selects position 4 on an issue response scale that ranges from 1 to 7—simply cancels them out within the field of influences on an individual's vote. For this reason, we must move beyond issue familiarity and assess the extent to which people profess actual opinions. Again, the latter are defined here simply as a willingness to support one policy over an alternative.

Using the more stringent criterion of a nonneutral policy preference, opinionation is still widespread in the American electorate. Very few people (less than 1 percent) in the NES sample refused to state a preference on all six issues. More than half of the respondents (55 percent) adopted nonneutral positions on four or five of the issues. About one-fifth of the sample professed stands on all six issues.

Table 8.3 presents the results separately for each issue. While the precise figures vary somewhat, there appears to be a regular pattern across most of the issues: In five of the six cases, about one-fifth of the respondents are familiar with the issue (by our two-component definition of familiarity) but place themselves at a neutral position between the two policy alternatives. The one exception is women's rights, where only about 8 percent meet the familiarity standard but refuse to state a preference.

It is useful to pause for a moment in order to consider the implications of the evidence presented in table 8.3, because the figures can be interpreted in two quite different ways. From one perspective, it is safe to say that most people take positions on most of the issues we are investigating. This could lead to an optimistic interpretation of the evidence, as signaling a relatively high level of policy awareness among the electorate. But it is also possible to state a contrasting perspective, by recalling that the existence of nonneutral issue positions constitutes the second in a series of successive criteria for issue voting. The proportion of respondents who clear this hurdle never exceeds three-fourths on any of the issues, and it is usually a good deal less than that; the average across the six issues is about 64 percent. Thus, the pool of potential issue voters is whittled down significantly beyond the set of those who meet a minimal criterion of familiarity with issues.

Variation in Intensity

When we focus on the direction of an individual's opinion about an issue, it is natural to consider the degree of intensity associated with that preference. For some people, one policy seems only a slight improvement over its alternative. Others may have a much stronger sense that the relative merits of the competing positions are pronounced and important. Such differences in intensity of opinion are relevant to our investigation because strong preferences are likely to count more heavily in choices than weak preferences. A passionate preference for one policy stand over another will be salient among the factors that feed into the vote. More casual opinions are likely to "become lost" among the other elements of belief that are competing for the voter's attention.

In our data it is a straightforward task to measure the intensity of issue opinions. Recall that the respondents located themselves along a graduated continuum ranging from one issue stand, through a neutral mid-

TABLE 8.3. Opinion Holding on Issues (in percentages)

Issue	Unfamiliar with Issue	Familiar with Issue but Place Self at Neutral Position	Familiar with Issue and Place Self a Nonneutral Positi
Government spending versus services	19.3	21.0	59.7
Defense spending	18.2	21.6	60.2
Government guaranteed jobs and living standard	17.4	17.0	65.6
Government assistance to blacks	24.4	18.6	57.0
Equal role for women	19.0	7.9	73.1
Diplomacy versus military action	10.7	20.1	69.2

Note: Percentages sum to 100 percent within each row. Number of observations for the first five issues is 1,212. For diplomacy versus military action issue, the number of observations is 1,066. Data source is the 2004 National Elect Study.

point, to the other, competing issue stand. Individuals who place themselves at either of the end points of the continuum are expressing stronger stands than are those who locate themselves closer to the neutral center.

Before proceeding, we should establish that intensity of opinion is, in fact, different from familiarity with an issue. On intuitive grounds one could argue that the issues most familiar to the electorate are precisely those that arouse the greatest feeling. But that is not the case in our data. Consider the question of diplomacy versus military action in American foreign policy. This issue has a very high level of recognition (fully 89 percent have thought about it and know the positions of the two parties). However, the proportion of the respondents taking extreme positions is quite low, at only 17 percent. In contrast, familiarity with the question of government's role in helping African Americans is relatively low, at only 76 percent. But the number of citizens taking extreme positions (about 22 percent) equals or exceeds those who feel strongly about the more familiar social welfare issues of government-guaranteed jobs and government spending versus provision of services (with 23 percent and 16 percent taking extreme positions on the respective issues). Finally, women's rights was not an issue distinctive in its degree of familiarity to the public, but it certainly evoked strong reactions, with 61 percent of the respondents placing themselves at either of the most extreme positions on this issue. Thus, issue familiarity and intensity of opinion vary independently from one issue to the next; they are not different manifestations of a single characteristic.

There is yet another way that intensity differs from the other elements of issue opinions that we have examined so far. Recall that, at the individual level, familiarity and basic opinionation frequently extended across issues. In other words, those who have thought about, and taken a nonneutral position on, one issue are likely to array themselves similarly on other issues. That is not generally the case when it comes to intensity of opinion. Nearly one-fourth of the sample (24 percent) does not express an extreme position on any issue. Just over one-third of the respondents (35 percent) take an intense position on only one issue, while a segment of similar size (31 percent) reports extreme stands on two or three issues. This leaves only about one-tenth of the sample who report strong feelings about more than half of the issues in our study. Thus, even though familiarity and opinionation are widespread, citizens are much more narrowly focused with respect to the policy questions that arouse strong feelings. There is an informal "division of labor" wherein some people focus their emotions on one issue while others feel strongly about another. General extremism on issues is a rarity in the American electorate.

Our observation of pronounced variability in the intensity of issue opinions raises an obvious question: Why do some people feel passionately about a given issue while others do not? We can suggest at least two answers. First, an issue is likely to arouse intense feelings when it bears on an individual's personal circumstances. The person who perceives an immediate, tangible reward (or cost) from some form of governmental activity will be more likely to support (or oppose) that activity than an individual who does not feel any immediate consequences from that particular policy initiative. Second, issues produce relatively intense reactions when they engage an individual's core values. If a policy appears consistent (or inconsistent) with a value that a person holds dear, they are likely to feel more strongly about it than would be the case if it did not engage a basic sense of what is good or bad in the world.

Both of the preceding hypotheses are easily tested with our data. In the first case, we would expect African Americans to feel more strongly about governmental efforts to help blacks than whites and members of other racial groups. That is precisely what occurs: Altogether, about 25 percent of the NES respondents expressed strong opinions either in favor of, or opposing, governmental action in this area. But the percentage of African Americans expressing strong feelings (either for or against) is much larger (at 39 percent). The immediacy of the policy controversy affects the intensity of reactions to it.

Of course, there is still quite a bit of variation in support for civil rights initiatives among the white respondents. This leads us to the test of our second hypothesis. The 2004 NES included a battery of six questions intended to tap individual support for equal opportunity in American society.[3] Restricting our attention to whites only, we can distinguish

---

3. The question battery begins as follows: "I am going to read several more statements. After each one, I would like you to tell me how strongly you agree or disagree. The first statement is 'Our society should do whatever is necessary to make sure that everyone has an equal opportunity to succeed.' Do you agree strongly, agree somewhat, neither agree nor disagree, disagree somewhat, or disagree strongly with this statement?" The remaining five statements are these: "We have gone too far in pushing equal rights in this country." "One of the big problems in this country is that we don't give everyone an equal chance." "This country would be better off if we worried less about how equal people are." "It is not really that big a problem if some people have more of a chance in life than others." "If people were treated more equally in this country we would have many fewer problems." On the first, third, and sixth statements, agreement is considered an egalitarian response. On the second, fourth, and fifth statements, disagreement is the egalitarian response.

those who gave a majority of responses in favor of equality, those whose responses signaled a net opposition to equal opportunity for all, and those whose answers were equally balanced between the two. Among those who support government activity to help blacks, 10 percent of the egalitarian white respondents placed themselves at the most extreme position, compared to only 3 percent of those who are neutral or opposed to equal rights. On the opposite side of the issue, 23 percent of those opposed to egalitarianism also took the most extreme position against government assistance to blacks. Only about 17 percent of the whites who felt neutral or favorable about equal opportunity took the same position.

Taken together, the analyses in this section support the conclusion that people feel most strongly about the issues that affect the things they believe to be important. While perhaps not very surprising, this interpretation confirms systematic factors are at work that help to pinpoint the locations within the electorate where issues are likely to have the strongest impact on the vote. After all, a nonneutral opinion merely places an individual among the pool of potential issue voters. We feel confident in asserting that a stronger opinion will increase the likelihood that this potential is actually realized in the person's electoral decision.

PERCEPTION OF CANDIDATES' DIFFERENCES ON ISSUES

Our final precondition for issue voting is that the individual perceive the candidates to espouse different positions with respect to the issue. Our reasoning here is based upon the simple observation that an issue-based choice is only possible when the voter is presented with meaningful alternatives from which to choose. As was the case with our earlier consideration of the parties' issue stands, we believe that individual perceptions of the candidates are more important for present purposes than objective reality, however that is defined. Regardless of the clarity with which the candidates have differentiated themselves from each other, the resultant polarization is irrelevant unless it is recognized by the voters. If they fail to see different stands by the candidates, they cannot use that issue as a basis for an electoral decision. It makes no difference whether the lack of differentiation is due to the candidates, the media, or the voters themselves. Only when voters recognize differences in the candidates' stands will it be possible for them to say that one of the candidates comes closer to their own position than does the other. That is the essence of issue voting—selecting the candidate that represents the clearest reflection of one's own policy preferences.

Even among the relatively informed segment of the population—that is, those who fulfill our first two preconditions—there are sizable sets of people who do not see differences between the candidates. The exact numbers vary from one issue to the next. On the four issues covering social welfare and foreign policy, three-fourths or more of the informed citizens also recognized that the candidates took different positions on the issue. It was harder for people to see the same kinds of differences on the two newer issues. About 69 percent indicated that they saw differences between the candidates on civil rights, while only about 55 percent saw differences with respect to women's roles in society. Thus, the need to supply a candidate-based motivation for a policy-oriented vote winnows the potential pool of issue voters even further than the previously discussed factors of personal familiarity and opinionation.

A number of factors limit the mass public's perception of differences on policy between the candidates. For one thing, on some issues the contenders for office take similar positions. In 2004, women's rights may well have been such a nonpolarizing question. Neither George W. Bush nor John Kerry advocated anything less than full equality for women. In so doing, they effectively removed this issue as a potential basis for a voter's choice between them.

Another limitation stems from the fact that American political parties are large and heterogeneous. Even during periods of relatively high partisan polarization, like the early years of the twenty-first century, there is intraparty variability in preferred policies. An obvious example from 2004 lies in the varying support that Democratic officials gave to the Iraq invasion. Perhaps less salient, several Republicans expressed doubts about the high levels of defense spending, out of concern over the budget deficits. So in some instances a single policy position finds supporters within both parties. If certain voters rely upon sources of information that are attentive to such bipartisan issue appeals, then it is only reasonable that their beliefs about the parties' candidates reflect the the candidates' common ground

Still another reason for undifferentiated perceptions arises from the mixed messages that candidates sometimes deliver. The candidates' stands on policy may change over time—John Kerry's successive Senate votes for and against the Iraq war stand as a case in point that played a prominent role in the 2004 campaign. In other instances, political actors

find it advantageous to be ambiguous. For example, rare is the contender for public office who would advocate increased government
spending, despite the need for resources to support the candidates' own
policies. In any such instances where the candidates themselves do not
provide overt signals about their own stands, public perceptions reflect
the same lack of clarity.

Undoubtedly, the realities of the electoral campaign can limit the degree to which the public distinguishes the candidates' issue stands. At the
same time, however, we suspect that many undifferentiated perceptions
of candidates in our data stem from characteristics of the citizens themselves. After all, knowledge of the candidates' positions represents information, which is costly for some people to acquire. In certain situations,
people may be unwilling to exert the energy or devote the resources necessary to gain that knowledge.

Just as with issue familiarity, education plays a critical role in perceptions of candidates. Once again, formal schooling not only conveys factual material, but also provides training in skills that are useful for gathering information. Table 8.4 confirms that differentiated perceptions of
candidates do covary with educational attainment. Among people who
have not completed high school, nearly half (45 percent) failed to place
the candidates at different positions on at least five of the six issues;
among college graduates, only about one-tenth showed the same lack of
differentiation. In contrast, only about 10 percent of those in the lowest

TABLE 8.4. Perceptions of Differing Candidate Issue Positions by Education
(in percentages)

	Educational Attainment		
Differentiation of Candidate Issue Positions	Did Not Complete High School	High School Graduate	College Graduate
Low	44.8	24.3	10.2
Medium	44.8	57.1	57.6
High	10.4	18.6	32.2
Total	100.0	100.0	100.0
Number of cases	96	647	323

Note: High issue familiarity means that respondents placed themselves and both parties on five or six
issues. Medium issue familiarity means that respondents placed themselves and both parties on two,
three, or four issues. Low issue familiarity means that respondents placed themselves and the parties on
none of the issues or on only one issue. The six issues are the same ones used in table 8.1, and the data
source is the 2004 National Election Study.

education category reported perceptions of differing stands by candidates on at least five of the six issues, while nearly one-third (32 percent) of the most highly educated stratum were able to do so. The same clear pattern occurs on each of the separate issues. In every case, increasing education corresponds to a greater probability that an individual places the two candidates at different positions with respect to that issue.

Another telling feature of our data can be gleaned from a closer look at those who clear the first two hurdles for issue voting, but fail to meet the third criterion. To clarify, these are people who are familiar with an issue and express a nonneutral opinion of their own, but do not perceive differences between the candidates on that issue. This situation can arise in two different ways: First, the individual may perceive that the candidates occupy identical positions on the issue; as we have seen, campaign practices may encourage this kind of undifferentiated perception.

Second, a person may simply profess ignorance (either directly or indirectly) and refuse to place one or both of the candidates on the issue, at any position. If we look only at those who are familiar with, and opinionated on, an issue, the exact numbers that take the latter route vary from one issue to the next, from a low of 18 percent on the role of women in society to a high of 45 percent on government spending and services; for the remaining four issues, the figures are always 30 percent or higher. Although this evidence is indirect, we believe it adds important weight to our argument. It is well known that survey respondents do not like to profess ignorance; indeed, the opposite problem (expressing beliefs and opinions when none really exist) probably arises more frequently. The fact that so many people are willing to admit that they do not possess relatively basic information about the most prominent stimuli from a presidential campaign indicates that, for a substantial segment of the electorate, the messages from elite actors are not getting through to their intended audience.

Overall, the analysis in this chapter reveals the limited capacity for issue voting that exists within the American electorate. We have proceeded in a step-by-step manner, considering a set of criteria that must be met in order for citizens to choose between candidates on the basis of one or more policy issues. Each of these steps has been small and, perhaps to many readers, obvious. But as we have seen, they have nontrivial and cumulative effects that work in concert to restrict the size of the issue-oriented segment within the general population.

Table 8.5 shows the percentages who meet all three of the preconditions on each of the issues we have examined. For five of the six issues, less than half of the general public displays the combination of familiarity, opinionation, and differentiated perceptions of candidates we believe to be necessary for casting a vote based upon that issue. These percentages are shocking because the issues under consideration have long been present on the public agenda. Even on the single issue where a majority meets all three criteria—the question of diplomacy versus military action—less then two-thirds of the population maintains meaningful opinions and places the candidates at different positions. Thus, even pressing issues of war and peace leave more than a third of American citizens without the foundation for a policy-oriented vote.

It is also important to reiterate that the analysis in this chapter has addressed only individual capacities for issue voting. That is, we have identified the people who are able to link different policy positions with sufficient partisan content to select one candidate or the other on that basis. But this is no guarantee that these considerations are the most salient criteria voters bring to bear on their decision-making. This conclusion, combined with the findings laid out in the preceding pages, can only leave us with some nagging doubts about the degree to which electoral decisions indicate the policy preferences of the American mass public.

CONSENSUS ON CANDIDATE ISSUE POSITIONS

The questions we have raised about the potential for issue voting within the electorate also suggest additional concerns about the policy consequences of American elections. How can an election signal the public's

TABLE 8.5. Potential Issue Voters, by Issue (in percentages)

Issue	Percentage Who Meet All Three Conditions for Issue Voting
Government spending versus services	47.8
Defense spending	48.8
Government guaranteed jobs and living standard	49.0
Government assistance to blacks	37.8
Equal role for women	39.0
Diplomacy versus military action	62.1

Note: Number of observations for the first five issues is 1,212. For the diplomacy versus military action issue, the number of observations is 1,066. Data source is the 2004 National Election Study.

desired allocation of governmental resources if many of the citizens voting experience difficulties when attempting to transform their own preferences into a choice between the candidates? Thus, the personal characteristics of voters guarantee that the general policy significance of a specific electoral outcome—that is, one candidate or party's victory over another—will be muted. At best, the election reflects the preferences of that population subset which has cleared all three of the hurdles we discussed earlier.

But additional problems arise whenever one tries to impute issue significance to an election result. Even if most citizens are familiar with an issue, maintain opinions on it, perceive differences between the candidates on it, and provide majority support for one of the candidates on it, this outcome can only provide direction on policy if beliefs about the winning candidate's stands on policy are relatively homogeneous throughout the electorate. That is the only way the election provides unambiguous guidance for governmental policy.

Consider the situation when the public's beliefs about a candidate are not very uniform: Say, for example, that voters are motivated by policies for government aid to minorities, and that the Republican candidate is elected on that basis. If some of the voters believed this hypothetical Republican would reduce public assistance while others thought the same candidate intended to increase it, then the Republican victory provides no direction on policy. Instead, it would be possible to find some mass support from the supporters of the winning candidate for either increasing or decreasing public assistance for minorities; in effect, officeholders could move in any direction they believed appropriate. But this is not popular influence on governmental policy—at least, not in any meaningful sense.

The problem is that there is, in fact, heterogeneity in the public's perceptions of the candidate issue stands. Note that this heterogeneity does not impede the ability of any individual citizen to cast an issue-based vote. Our basic assumption is that subjective perceptions of the candidates can provide a motivation for voting choice, whether or not the component beliefs hold up to some external, objective confirmation. But varying perceptions do become problematic as we move away from questions about the determinants of individual electoral decisions and move toward an attempt to understand the substantive policy implications of an overall electoral outcome.

For this part of the analysis, we will focus on qualitative differences in the candidates' issue stands (i.e., whether they are perceived to take a liberal, moderate, or conservative position on each issue), rather than quantitative distinctions in perceptions about the extremity of the candidates' positions. Accordingly, we can define a perfect consensus to exist when 100 percent of the public places a candidate at a single position. In contrast, maximal dissensus occurs when equal proportions locate a candidate at every possible position (i.e., one-third liberal, one-third moderate, and one-third conservative).

Table 8.6 shows, for each of the six issues we have considered here, the proportion that placed the two 2004 presidential candidates at their modally perceived position on that issue. As an example, consider government services and spending. Here, the mode for Bush is the conservative position (i.e., reduce spending, even if it means a reduction in services) because the largest subset of respondents (about 54 percent) located him on the conservative side of the scale (positions 1 through 3), compared to 21 percent who placed him at the neutral midpoint, and 25 percent who placed him on the liberal side (i.e., increase spending to provide more services, positions 5 through 7 on the scale). The mode for Kerry on this issue is the liberal position, because 69 percent placed him on that side of the scale, compared to 17 percent at the midpoint, and 14 percent on the conservative side.

In almost every case, this mode occurred at the expected position—with more people locating Bush at the conservative position than any other, and more people placing Kerry at the liberal position than any other. But the clarity of these modes varies considerably from one issue to the next. For example, there was nearly a consensus in public perceptions

TABLE 8.6. Degrees of Consensus on Candidate Issue Positions (in percentages)

Issue	Percentage Placing Bush at Modal Position	Percentage Placing Kerry at Modal Position
Government spending versus services	54.4	69.4
Defense spending	87.2	47.4
Government guaranteed jobs and living standard	73.5	62.8
Government assistance to blacks	61.9	57.2
Equal role for women	47.2	70.4
Diplomacy versus military action	89.3	67.4

Note: Table percentages are based only on those respondents who placed the candidates at different positions on the respective issues. Numbers of observations used to calculate the table percentages range from 829 to 1,040. Data source is the 2004 National Election Study.

about George W. Bush's position on foreign policy. Just under 90 percent believed that he would increase defense spending and rely on military action rather than diplomacy. In contrast, less than half the survey respondents (47 percent) indicated that Kerry would reduce defense spending. The same proportion believed that Bush favored an equal role for women in American society. The other percentages in the table fall between these extremes. But the general thrust of the empirical results is that there is quite a bit of disagreement within the electorate about where the candidates stand on the issues. This perceptual variability limits the significance of any electoral outcome as a guide to policy.

We suspect that a great deal of the heterogeneity in perceptions of the candidates stems from the same factors that lead to undifferentiated perceptions of candidates. The major American political parties speak with a variety of voices, and the content of their messages is often ambiguous. Hence, it is only natural that different members of the audience hear different things about the parties' and candidates' policy stands.

Once again, however, it seems likely that the characteristics of citizens within the electorate play a large role in generating the perceptual variance in our data. Here we believe that party identification is the operant factor. Specifically, individuals are most comfortable when they find themselves in agreement with the positions articulated by "their own" candidates—that is, the representatives from the party to which they feel a personal sense of attachment. This agreement can occur in at least three ways. First, political parties can fulfill their traditional role as the purveyors of meaningful policies. Citizens examine and compare the platforms of the respective parties and align themselves with the party that comes closest to their own personal issue preferences. Undoubtedly, the process does work this way for some people. But it requires a level of societal awareness and political sophistication that is quite rare within the general population.

Second, political parties can be a central component in opinion formation for some citizens. One understanding of party identification is precisely that parties serve as reference groups for their adherents. In this capacity, the stands adopted by partisan leaders provide an easy standard for orienting one's own attitude toward an issue. This is an easier route to correspondence between individual and party than the "comparison shopping" that occurs in the first process. Nevertheless, it still requires an attentiveness to elite cues that exceeds the motivation (or, perhaps, the ability) of many citizens.

The third process is simple rationalization: An individual maintains a personal stand on an issue, and merely assumes that his or her party takes the same position. Virtually no information costs are associated with this process, and it enables people to avoid the potentially uncomfortable situation of disagreeing with their own partisan leaders and candidates. Given the ease with which this rationalization can be used, it is probably fairly widespread in the electorate. But it militates against coherent, consistent public beliefs about the parties and, therefore, makes it far more difficult to understand the policy implications of any election result.

In conclusion, it appears that most citizens are capable of providing reactions to policy issues. But this does not mean that they actually vote on the basis of those issues. Nontrivial difficulties restrict the process of instilling opinions with the partisan valence required to vote with such motivation. Two serious consequences flow from this fact: First, the potential for issue-based voting is confined to a portion, usually less than one-half, of the electorate. As increasing numbers of citizens fail to meet the necessary and sufficient conditions on a given issue, the potential pool of issue-based voters becomes even smaller. Second, it is extremely difficult to discern any mandate on policy in the outcome of an American presidential election. Parties, as well as voters, are often linked to issues in ambiguous ways.

COMMENTARY AND CONTROVERSY

The analysis reported in this chapter differs from the original work in *The American Voter* in several respects. For one thing, its authors examined sixteen issues, far more than the six that we included. At the same time, they defined the preconditions for issue voting a bit differently than we do. For Campbell et al., a person had to (1) hold an opinion on an issue; (2) know what the government was doing with respect to that issue; and (3) perceive that the parties held different positions on it.

The reason for these differences is simple and obvious: We had to adjust for the differing survey questions that were included in the 1956 Survey Research Center and 2004 National Election Study interview schedules. The 1956 instrument contained a unique battery of items that elicited respondents' own positions on each of sixteen issues, their beliefs about whether the government was doing too little or too much on each of them, and their beliefs about which party better represented their own position on the issue (as opposed to seeing no difference between what the parties would do). In contrast, the 2004 survey asked respondents' opinions on a large number of issues. But it did not include questions about the government's current policy on those issues, and only the six issues discussed in this chapter were targeted in questions about perceived positions of parties and candidates.

Despite differences in the specific details, we believe that our criteria for issue voting are conceptually identical to those employed in *The American Voter*. In each case, issue voting involves a combination of three components: First, the person must express a meaningful attitude on the issue. In both 1956 and 2004, this is measured by having the survey respondent explicitly describe his or her adherence to a policy position (the positions themselves were presented singly in 1956, and as part of an opposing pair of positions in 2004). Second, the person must understand (at least subjectively) the current status quo with respect to the issue. In 1956, this was assessed through a question about what the government was doing on the issue. In 2004, we measured this through respondents' willingness to place both major political parties on the issue. Third, the person must believe that the electoral contenders offer a meaningful choice on the issue. In 1956, the respondents were asked about the parties' positions, while in 2004 we used differential candidate issue placements to measure this criterion.

Given the conceptual congruence in the respective measures of issue voting, it is probably not too surprising that our empirical results parallel those reported in *The American Voter*. Just as in this chapter, Campbell et al. showed that the successive conditions winnow the number of citizens who could cast a ballot on the basis of any particular policy consideration. They also find that familiarity with issues is correlated with education, and that the interpretation of elections as policy mandates is problematic because of varying public perceptions of the parties' issue positions.

Their estimates of the numbers of issue voters are quite a bit smaller than ours, ranging from a high of 36 percent (for "acting tough toward Russia and China) down to only 18 percent (for "giving aid to neutral countries"). Recall that the corresponding figures from our analysis are about 62 percent (for "diplomacy versus military action") and about 38 percent (for "government assistance to blacks"). This apparent increase in the public's level of issue awareness is probably due to a combination of increasing levels of education within the population (e.g., only 28.5 percent of the 1956 SRC sample had graduated from high school, compared to 90.8 percent of the 2004 NES sample), the growth of the mass media (e.g., 73.7 percent of the 1956 sample reported following the presidential campaign on television, compared to 86.1 percent in 2004), and the evolution of new issues (e.g., the "spike" in potential issue voting on the question of diplomacy versus military force is undoubtedly due to the overall salience of the Iraq war and the war on terrorism). Again, the most prominent finding in both analyses is that only a subset of the overall electorate meets a set of reasonable preconditions for making vote decisions on the basis of an issue of public policy.

Attitudes, Opinions, and the Survey Response

Before we trace some of the lines of research into the nature and prevalence of issue voting, it is useful to consider briefly some of the social-psychological concepts that underlie the empirical data employed in the analyses. As discussed in previous chapters, our model of voting choice depends heavily on the idea that individuals possess attitudes toward the stimuli that are relevant to any given electoral contest. According to psychological theory, an attitude is a predisposition to respond favorably or unfavorably toward a stimulus object (Fishbein 1963).

From a functionalist perspective, attitudes represent external manifestations of inner psychological states (e.g., Smith, Bruner, and White 1956; Katz 1960). However, that particular understanding of the attitude concept is not particularly amenable to survey research. Therefore, it has had little direct impact on the study of mass political behavior (e.g., Oskamp and Schultz 2005). Instead, the predominant theoretical perspective (e.g., Fishbein and Ajzen 1975; Eagly and Chaiken 1993) stresses that attitudes toward an object represent a combination of cognition (i.e., what does the person know about the stimulus object?) and affective feelings (i.e., how does the individual feel about the various characteristics that he or she associates—through cognitions—with the stimulus object?). Models of voting behavior based explicitly upon this theoretical view have been developed by social psychologists (Fishbein and Coombs 1974) and political scientists (Shapiro 1969; Reynolds 1974).

More recent analyses in political science have also stressed "online" cognitive processing (Lodge, McGraw, and Stroh 1989; Rahn, Krosnick, and Breuning 1994; Lodge, Steenbergen, and Brau 1995). In this model, people essentially maintain a running mental tally of the positive and negative information they have received about a given stimulus object.

While the proponents of the online processing model emphasize their differences from memory-based psychological models, the net result still appears to be an affective reaction that is quite similar to an attitude.

Attitudes, like many other psychological states, are unobservable phenomena. This simple fact can cause enormous problems for researchers, because overt survey responses may be affected by factors apart from the attitude that is the intended object of measurement. These factors include a desire to avoid professing ignorance and the desire to cooperate with the interviewer (e.g., Schuman and Presser 1981); ambivalence about the attitude object in question (e.g., Alvarez and Brehm 2002); the race of the interviewer (e.g., Davis 1997); and social desirability pressures (Kuklinski, Cobb, and Gilens 1997; Berinsky 2004). Analysts now recognize that a survey interview involves social interaction, not just a veridical reading of the things on a respondent's mind (e.g., Tourangeau, Rips, and Rasinski 2000), and the predominant view in political science stresses that survey questions elicit the "considerations" that are currently most salient in a respondent's short-term memory, rather than specific, crystallized attitudes (Zaller and Feldman 1992). As we will see, many of these seemingly technical considerations have been directly involved in controversies about issue voting within the American electorate.

The Spatial Model of Voting

The spatial model of voting is another idea that has had an enormous impact on the study of issues in mass political behavior. In its simplest form, this model represents voters and candidates (or parties) as two sets of points that exist together in a space. The dimensions of the space (i.e., the axes used to locate the voter and candidate points) correspond to the policy issues that exist in a given electoral context (i.e., during a particular presidential campaign). Voting choices are easily determined in this model: Each person evaluates the distances from his or her own point to the points for the various candidates, and selects (i.e., votes for) the candidate whose point is closest.

Building upon work in economics (Hotelling 1929), the spatial voting model was developed initially by Downs (1957) and refined by subsequent researchers (e.g., Davis, Hinich, and Ordeshook 1970; Enelow and Hinich 1984, 1990). Much of the work on the spatial model has been formal (i.e., abstract) in nature, and aimed at assessing rationality in the behavior of voters (i.e., how does a voter maximize his or her return from a voting choice?) and parties or candidates (i.e., can parties or candidates find a stable position that maximizes their support relative to their competitors?). Indeed, the rational-choice perspective underlying much of this work is often touted as a theoretical "competitor" to the primarily psychological orientation of the so-called Michigan model epitomized by *The American Voter* (e.g., Green and Shapiro 1994).

However, the differences between these theoretical perspectives may have been exaggerated or, at least, overemphasized. A number of researchers have made important contributions by operationalizing the spatial model in an attempt to understand the evaluative dimensions underlying voters' choices (e.g., Weisberg and Rusk 1970; Rabinowitz 1978; Enelow and Hinich 1984; Poole and Rosenthal 1984b; Poole 1998; Hinich and Munger 1994).Thus, the spatial model of voting has provided valuable empirical, as well as formal, insights. For present purposes, the spatial model is important because it has influenced the way political scientists think about issues and public opinion.

The Literature on Issue Voting after The American Voter

The American Voter has often been interpreted as a pessimistic assessment of the public's issue capacities and the policy content of overall election outcomes. Analyses of subsequent presidential contests by researchers from the University of Michigan (including various authors from *The American Voter*) seemed to confirm this view. For example, Converse, Clausen, and Miller (1965) suggested that the Republican Party leadership overestimated the ideological fervor of the rank-and-file party followers in nominating a strong conservative as its candidate in the 1964 election. In a similar vein, Converse et al. (1969) showed that the opinions of Democratic primary voters on the Vietnam war may have been drastically misinterpreted, in ways that affected Lyndon Johnson's refusal to stand for reelection in that year.

To be sure, there were dissenting voices during this time period. The most prominent of them was V. O. Key, whose posthumously published book, *The Responsible Electorate* (1966), argued that "voters are not fools." But the central evidence in Key's analysis involved what would now be called retrospective judgments (e.g., Fiorina 1981), rather than explicit attitudes on issues. Therefore, his book did not challenge directly the evidence regarding issue voting in the sense described by the authors of *The American Voter*.

The prevailing scholarly view changed markedly in the 1970s. Influential articles in the *American Political Science Review* provided evidence that citizens' issue preferences came more closely into line with their party affiliations during the 1960s, the parties' policy stands became more widely recognized within the mass public, and individual attitudes on issues had effects on vote choice that were discernible and separable from the baseline factor of party identification (Boyd 1972; Pomper 1972). Thus, issue voting became far more widespread during the middle to late 1960s and on into the 1972 presidential election (Schulman and Pomper 1975; Nie, Verba, Petrocik 1979). In fact, the effect of issues seemed to be so pronounced during the latter election that intraparty disagreements over policies contributed to the defeat of the Democratic Party, despite its majority status within the electorate (Miller et al. 1976).

A number of scholars did express different reservations regarding some or all of the conclusions about the rise of issue voting (e.g., Brody and Page 1972; Kessel 1972; Popkin et al. 1976; Steeper and Teeter 1976; RePass 1976; Margolis 1977). The separate impact of issues (relative to partisanship and other factors) receded somewhat in the 1976 election (Nie, Verba, and Petrocik 1979; Miller and Levitin 1976; Miller 1978). But the political environment never reverted to the "issueless" state that supposedly characterized the mass public of the 1950s. Instead, empirical analyses of elections from the 1970s (e.g., Markus and Converse 1979; Page and Jones 1979), through the 1980s (e.g., Miller and Shanks 1982; Shanks and Miller 1990), the 1990s (Alvarez and Nagler 1995, 1998; Miller and Shanks 1996), and on into the twenty-first century (Jacoby 2004; Wagner and Carmines 2006) have all shown that issue attitudes continue to affect individual voting choices. The remainder of this commentary will discuss various refinements that have occurred and controversies that have arisen about the extent, nature, and consequences of issue voting within the American electorate.

Measurement

Relatively few political scientists have followed *The American Voter*'s lead in specifying a set of preconditions that citizens must meet in order to vote on the basis of issues (e.g., Meier and Campbell 1979). However, the predominant strategies used to measure issue attitudes and perceptions have changed over the years. Many of these changes seem to incorporate the substantive intent of the conditions established by Campbell, Converse, Miller, and Stokes. The type of survey item used in *The American Voter* asked respondents whether, and how strongly, they agreed or disagreed with a statement about an issue. For example, the interviewer would read a statement like "The government ought to cut taxes even if it means putting off some important things that need to be done." The respondent would then express her feelings about the statement, on a five-point scale, ranging from "agree strongly" to "disagree strongly." A neutral midpoint was included among the alternative responses, but respondents had to volunteer, on their own, if they had no opinion on the issue in question.

The first serious modification to the format of the issue questions came in 1964, when respondents were allowed to opt out of answering an item if they were not interested in that issue. A typical question read as follows: "Some people are afraid the government in Washington is getting too powerful for the good of the country and the individual person. Others feel that the government has not gotten too strong for the good of the country. Have you been interested enough in this to favor one side over the other?" Only those respondents who expressed interest would be asked their own position on the issue. This may appear a very subtle change from the previously used format. However, it has major consequences, because it serves as a "filter" to identify and set aside at least some of those people who do not possess meaningful attitudes on the issue in question.

This filter is advantageous because it addresses the problem of issue familiarity among the survey respondents. However, it also problematic because it may render the response distributions incomparable over time (e.g., Bishop 2005). Some of the apparent increases in issue voting may be due simply to the fact that the survey questions are now more effective at eliminating respondents who do not have real opinions.

The second modification was measuring respondents' perceptions of the parties' and candidates' positions on issues, as well as the respondents' own positions. Drawing upon the spatial theory of voting, analysts defined "issue proximity" as the difference (or, using the spatial metaphor, the "distance") between the respondent's own position on the issue and his or her perception of a candidate's (or party's) stand on it (Beardsley 1973). A rational voter acting on the basis of issues would support the candidate who is most proximal (i.e., closest) to his or her own position, across an entire set of salient campaign issues.

Issue proximities were first used in 1968. The basic idea behind this approach is that citizens' subjective assessments of the candidates' and parties' policy stands are more important than any "objective" reality (e.g., Shapiro 1969; Prothro 1973). The candidate or party placements allow analysts to address the question of whether citizens perceive meaningful choices between parties and candidates on the issues (Page and Brody 1972). This latter point is important, not only because it is one of *The American Voter*'s preconditions for issue voting, but also because candidates' issue stands are not always presented very clearly to the public (Page 1978).

At the same time, issue proximity measures also open up the potential for rationalization on the part of the survey respondents (Brody and Page 1972). Particularly troublesome is the possibility of projection effects, in which people assume that their already preferred candidates share their own issue stands. Grounded in psychological processes called "assimilation and contrast" effects (Granberg and Brent 1974), projection could cause overestimates of the extent of issue voting, since the correspondence between the respondent's and the candidate's position is a consequence, rather than a source, of the choice of a candidate. Empirical analyses of projection and other forms of rationalization in political perception are difficult for methodological reasons (particularly the potential for reciprocal influence between perceptions and choices). Overall, the evidence suggests that projection effects do occur, but their impact is relatively limited (e.g., Markus and Converse 1979; Conover and Feldman 1982; Feldman and Conover 1983; Martinez 1988).

A third, and closely related, change in the measurement of mass issue orientations is the use of seven-point scales. Recall that the original issue questions had respondents agree or disagree with a single statement. The new format presents the respondent with two opposing issue positions, and has the person locate himself or herself along a scale running between them, at numbered positions ranging from 1 to 7. A typical question in this format reads as follows:

> Some people think the government should provide fewer services, even in areas such as health and education, in order to reduce spending. Suppose these people are at one end of the scale, at point 1. Other people feel it is important for the government to provide many more services even if it means an increase in spending. Suppose these people are at the other end, at point 7. And of course, some other people have opinions somewhere in between at points 2, 3, 4, 5, or 6. Where would you place yourself on this scale, or haven't you thought much about this?

While reading the question, the interviewer hands the respondent a card showing the numerical scale, with the contrasting statements on government services at the two ends. This question format was first used on a limited basis (i.e., for only two issues) in 1968. Since then, it has become a standard feature of the American National Election Studies, employed for a wide variety of issues.

The seven-point scales appear to operationalize the locations of the various actors in the spatial model of voting very effectively. They facilitate the calculation of the issue proximities. Despite their general acceptance in the research community, critics have suggested that problems exist in different interpretations of the numerical scales (Aldrich and McKelvey 1977), variable psychological differences between scale intervals that are equal in terms of the numerical scores (Lodge and Tursky 1979), and the reliability of the seven-point scales relative to other possible question formats (Krosnick 1991). However, analyses of the seven-point scales' measurement properties suggest that most of these problems are relatively minor (Aldrich et al. 1982; Jacoby 1996). Therefore, their prevalence in political behavior research over the past four decades is quite reasonable.

Issue Importance

The authors of *The American Voter* believed that citizens are motivated only by issues they consider important and that attitudes about the importance of an issue could vary from one individual to the next. However, direct measures of personal issue importance were not incorporated in the early empirical analyses. Some critics argued that the extent of issue voting was underestimated because public opinion surveys confronted people with issues that simply were not important to them. But when asked about issues that were salient to them, respondents seemed to exhibit much higher levels of awareness. People were also able to translate their policy preferences on salient issues into voting choices very effectively (RePass 1971).

Despite early theoretical (Dahl 1956) and empirical (Shapiro 1969) support for the concept of personal issue importance, subsequent research has produced mixed results. On the positive side, Krosnick and his colleagues find that attitude importance does serve as an important mediator for the impact of issues on subsequent political behavior (Krosnick 1988; Miller, Krosnick, and Fabrigar 2003; also see Rivers 1988). In fact, some analysts argue that the variability in personal salience effectively divides the electorate into relatively discrete "issue publics," each of which is interested in, and divided over, a single issue, while largely unconcerned about other issues (Maggiotto and Piereson 1978; Krosnick 1990; Glasgow 1999).

On the negative side, several studies have found that incorporating personal salience adds nothing to models of voting behavior (e.g., Hinckley, Hoffstetter, and Kessel 1974; Markus and Converse 1979; Niemi and Bartels 1985). Such results are not surprising when one recognizes that individual citizens do not control the issue agenda during an election campaign (Verba and Nie 1972). Consistent with this latter observation, still other research suggests that personal salience has a significant, but not overwhelming effect (Rabinowitz, Prothro, and Jacoby 1982). Because of this heterogeneity in findings, the topic is likely to remain a frequent target of scholarly investigation.

Different Types of Issues

Political scientists have often distinguished between different kinds of issues, with varying categories based upon the substantive content of the policy disagreement or the general nature of the controversy that is involved. For example, the rise in issue voting during the 1960s was generally attributed to the onset of new issues with greater relevance to the American public than had existed during the 1950s time period covered by *The American Voter* (Pomper 1972; Nie, Verba, and Petrocik 1979). Relatively esoteric and distant questions about governmental support for rural electrification or American involvement in dimly recognized foreign countries were replaced by immediate, visible, and hard-hitting controversies like desegregation, poverty in America, urban unrest, changing lifestyles, and the Vietnam War.

Some analysts also suggested that a general backlash against these new issues emerged in the late 1960s. Scammon and Wattenberg (1970) argue that responses to the new activism in American society could be grouped under a single heading that they called the "Social Issue," which could be used strategically by conservatives to challenge the control of the seemingly unassailable Democratic majority in American government. While the Social Issue may have been a reasonable description of elite political discourse during this period, the evidence suggests that it actually divided the public along the same lines as the more traditional socioeconomic issues that have existed since the New Deal of the 1930s (Nie, Verba, and Petrocik 1979).

Attempts to differentiate these kinds of substantive concerns actually predate *The American Voter* (e.g., Berelson, Lazarsfeld, and McPhee 1954, chap. 9). Similar arguments have been made more recently about the emergence of "culture wars" in the United States, pitting social conservatives against advocates of "new" lifestyles (Hunter 1991, 1995; Layman and Carmines 1997). Again, however, concerns about a realignment of American politics along these lines seem premature (Fiorina, Abrams, and Pope 2006). Issues centering around the United States' status and responsibilities as a modern welfare state still seem to dominate the American political scene (Geer 1992; Carmines and Shanks 2006).

Several political scientists have developed classifications of issues based upon the generic nature of the conflict, rather than the specific substantive content of the policies. For example, Stokes (1963) distinguished between "position" issues and "valence" issues. With position issues, the controversy involves different policy objectives (e.g., should taxes be reduced for large corporations or for middle- and lower-income families?), with each one advocated and supported by different partisan groups. With valence issues, there is a societal consensus on the objective (e.g., winning the war against terrorism), and the major questions focus on which party or candidate is most likely to achieve it. Valence issues arise frequently in American politics, although they generally spawn position issues focusing on the specific initiatives required to achieve the consensual objective (e.g., should covert government surveillance of American citizens be permitted in order to combat terrorism?). From a theoretical perspective, valence issues are problematic, because it is difficult to incorporate them into the spatial model of voting (Stokes 1963; Enelow and Hinich 1984; Green and Shapiro 1994).

Carmines and Stimson (1980) offer a different dichotomous categorization, between "easy" and "hard" issues. Their easy issues fit three criteria: (1) they involve symbolic rather than technical and substantive questions; (2) they deal with ends rather than the means of reaching those ends; and (3) they have been the focus of public attention for a long time. Carmines and Stimson use desegregation as an example of an easy issue, and American involvement in Vietnam as a hard issue. They suggest that the distinction between these two broad types of issues is important because it modifies the relationship between political information and issue voting. To recast their argument in terms of *The American Voter,* citizens can more readily fulfill the preconditions for voting on the basis of easy issues than they can for voting on the basis of hard issues. That, in turn, accounts for the existence of fairly widespread issue voting within the electorate, despite relatively low levels of political information or involvement on the part of many citizens.

The Sources of Political Issues

How do issues arise? Do issues follow a discernible "path" throughout their existence? Until recently, such questions received relatively little attention from political scientists, despite recognition that the ability to "create" issues, or to block the emergence of certain controversies, is a powerful political resource (e.g., Bachrach and Baratz 1962, 1963; Elder and Cobb 1983). A great deal of attention has focused on the media's role in setting the governmental policy agenda—that is, determining the set of issues that receives attention from political elites and the mass public at any given time (McCombs and Shaw 1972; Iyengar and Kinder 1987). The media exert further influence by "priming" citizens to evaluate political stimuli (e.g., candidates and officeholders) in terms of particular issues (Iyengar and Kinder 1987; Krosnick and Kinder 1990). Finally, the general phenomenon of issue framing effectively sets the terms of debate on any particular issue, through selective descriptions of the controversy over policy (e.g., Iyengar 1991; Gamson 1992).

Despite the common dynamic patterns seemingly followed by all issues (Downs 1972), and the apparent primacy of the mass media as a set of institutions linking individual citizens with the distant elements of policy controversies (e.g., Jerit, Barabas, and Bolsen 2006), it is increasingly clear that the dynamics underlying issues comprise an inherently political process, in which the ability to control the governmental agenda is an effective, powerful tool (e.g., Baumgartner and Jones 1993; Jones and Baumgartner 2005). Issues do evolve according to a fairly predictable process, but one in which the crucial steps are polarization across the major parties, followed by partisan patterns of mass response (Carmines and Stimson 1989). Similarly, the articulation of specific issue frames is now widely recognized as a regular component of elite political strategy (e.g., Jacoby 2000; Druckman 2001; Nelson 2004). The recent proliferation of research on these topics shows that any complete consideration of issue voting must consider where the issues come from, as well as the ways citizens react to issues once they come into existence.

The Sources of Issue Attitudes

In this chapter, we followed the lead of *The American Voter* by examining personal characteristics and values as the likely sources of individual preferences on issues. In so doing, our approach is consistent with rational-actor models, which stress that people adopt policy stands that maximize their material returns (Downs 1957; Riker and Ordeshook 1973). It also coincides with psychological theories of value choice, which hold that fundamental beliefs about right and wrong (i.e., values) provide general guidance for all aspects of human behavior, including politics (e.g., Rokeach 1973). However, subsequent political science research has generated results that only provide partial support for these theoretical perspectives.

The current scholarly consensus holds that self-interest is not a major determinant of issue attitudes or voting choices (e.g., Sears and Funk 1990). Such a conclusion is, admittedly, counterintuitive. But it is based upon an enormous amount of empirical research that has produced almost uniformly consistent results: A personal stake in the outcome of a controversy over policy has little, if any, impact on a person's issue preferences (e.g., Sears et al. 1980). This basic finding holds for both domestic and foreign policy issues, covering a very wide variety of substantive areas, including energy conservation (Sears et al. 1978), American involvement in Vietnam (Lau, Brown, and Sears 1978), racial desegregation (Sears, Hensler, and Speer 1979), and multiculturalism (Citrin et al. 2001).

In some situations self-interest shows an effect, but they involve relatively rare circumstances in which personal lives are juxtaposed with public policies. Examples include public employees during an era of tax rollbacks (Sears and Citrin 1985), gun owners and attempts at firearms regulation (Wolpert and Gimpel 1998), and welfare recipients' support of governmental services (Schneider and Jacoby 2003). Furthermore, many of the apparent linkages between self-interest and policy preferences may simply be methodological artifacts, due to problematic elements in the design of public opinion surveys (Sears and Lau 1983). This "technical" explanation for self-interest effects has been the focus of some disagreement (e.g., Lewis-Beck 1985), but the evidence does seem to be fairly uniform that, even when such effects do exist, they are relatively weak determinants of issue attitudes (e.g., Lau, Sears, and Jessor 1990).

What accounts for the apparent lack of self-interest effects among individual attitudes? Sniderman and Brody (1977) suggest that there is a general ethic of self-reliance in America that leads to a psychological disjunction between personal life circumstances and opinions about governmental affairs. Alternatively, Mutz (1992) argues that the mass media cover political issues in ways that systematically downplay the relevance of personal experiences for political issues. David Sears (e.g., 2001) argues that symbolic predispositions trump self-interest in forming individual political attitudes. This latter perspective will be covered in greater detail in the "Commentary and Controversy" section in chapter 9. For the moment, we will merely note that symbolic predispositions are stable affective orientations like party identification and ideological self-placement, which provide citizens with ongoing guidance for reacting to specific issues as they arise.

From a somewhat different perspective, there is a voluminous literature on core values and their implications for political behavior (e.g., Feldman 2003). The empirical results generally suggest that individual value preferences do affect issue attitudes (Feldman 1988; Grant and Rudolph 2003). But important caveats need to be considered. For example, it is not entirely clear which values are relevant for understanding American public opinion (Kuklinski 2001). Value conflict can generate ambivalence, which complicates the translation from core feelings to policy preferences (e.g., Feldman and Zaller 1992; Alvarez and Brehm 2002). It also appears that values may be themselves products of more fundamental political loyalties (Goren 2005). So the net impact of values on issue attitudes is comparable to, but not appreciably greater than, that of the symbolic predispositions discussed above (Jacoby 2006).

The Directional Theory of Issue Voting

Until the late 1980s, all of the formal models and most of the empirical analyses of issue voting relied on proximity-based processes to represent the ways that citizens translated their issue orientations into a vote. Once again, the predominant assumption in this proximity model is that citizens evaluate the distances from their own policy positions to those articulated by the candidates and parties. A person's utility (i.e., degree of positive or negative feeling) is assumed to be inversely related to distance in the policy space. Therefore, a rational individual votes for the candidate located closest to his or her own position.

Despite its intuitive appeal, the empirical support for the proximity model is surprisingly weak. Specifically, parties and candidates typically adopt relatively extreme positions rather than the moderate stands that would bring them closer to the majority of voters in their constituencies (e.g., Budge, Crewe, and Farlie 1976), while voters' preferences fail to conform to the curvilinear patterns that would be expected under strict spatial logic (Rabinowitz 1978). Accordingly, Rabinowitz and Macdonald (1989) formulated an alternative theory to account for these inconsistencies.

Their directional theory of issue voting holds that most citizens do not maintain the clear positions that are assumed to exist under proximity-based spatial models. Instead, they argue that people have more diffuse preferences, corresponding to a preferred direction of policy activity. Voters support those candidates who articulate the clearest stands in the direction that they prefer. For this reason, directional theory predicts that centrist candidates and parties will lose electoral support, compared to more extreme alternatives. Rabinowitz, Macdonald, and their colleagues report a great deal of empirical support for the directional model, under a wide variety of electoral circumstances and settings (e.g., Listhaug, Macdonald, and Rabinowitz 1990, 1994; Macdonald, Listhaug, and Rabinowitz 1991; Rabinowitz, Macdonald, and Listhaug 1991).

A number of scholars have criticized the directional theory, arguing that the empirical investigations have not directly addressed the model's components (e.g., Westholm 1997), that the competing models are indistinguishable in statistical tests (Lewis and King 2000), and that directional theory makes unrealistic assumptions about variability in voters' perceptions (e.g., Gilljam 1997; Pierce 1997; Merrill and Grofman 1999). The proponents of directional theory have responded to all of these criticisms (e.g., Macdonald and Rabinowitz 1997; Macdonald, Rabinowitz, and Listhaug 1997, 1998, 2001). It is difficult to say at this point whether one or the other model holds the upper hand in the scholarly consensus. It is probably sufficient to follow Macdonald, Rabinowitz, and Listhaug in saying that "if the concern is simply to use issues in predicting the vote, then either the proximity or the directional model will suffice" (1998, 681). However, in the same passage, they also point out that the directional model seems to be superior for understanding the interaction between voters and parties (or candidates) within democratic political systems.

The Macro-Level Consequences of Issue Voting

In concluding this commentary, it is useful to follow the authors of *The American Voter,* by stepping back to consider the political consequences of issue voting. A number of scholars have pointed out the difficulties involved when trying to understand the implications for policy of a given electoral result (e.g., Verba and Nie 1972; Kelley 1983; Grossback,

Peterson, and Stimson 2006). But attempts to do so are facilitated by two findings from recent research: First, a substantial proportion of citizens do cast votes "correctly," in terms of their personal policy interests (Lau and Redlawsk 1997). Second, much of the variability in political perceptions and preferences that exists within the mass public can be viewed as random "noise" and measurement error, which is canceled out in the process of aggregating individual-level opinions to form an overall measure of public opinion (Stimson 1999, 2004); the result is an accurate summary of the general policy preferences that exist within the electorate. Governmental policy-making activities do seem to be closely consistent with, and seemingly responsive to, this macro-level expression of citizen preferences (Stimson, MacKuen, and Erikson 1995). The net result is a democratically responsive macro-polity (Erikson, MacKuen, and Stimson 2002) in which a rational public constitutes an essential element (Page and Shapiro 1992).

CHAPTER 9

Attitude Structure and the Problem of Ideology

As we have just seen, only a fraction of the general public shows the potential to cast a vote on the basis of a given issue. At the same time, there is disagreement within the electorate regarding the issue stands of the major parties' presidential candidates. Based upon findings like these, it is natural to question the degree to which questions about public policy are "translated" into mass voting decisions and electoral outcomes. It appears that the salience and vehemence of partisan debate on a substantive issue cannot be used to predict the degree to which the public will react to that issue in the next election.

The apparent nonresponsiveness to policy issues is particularly striking when juxtaposed against the temporal stability of party identification. Presumably, one of the major functions of political parties in a democratic system is to articulate alternative, competing stands on controversies regarding the course of public policy. Since new social problems regularly emerge, party leaders must adjust their platforms accordingly. This could be a major source of partisan change. Traditional democratic theory holds that citizens respond to such change in the policy environment by "updating" their partisan choices from one election to the next, moving when necessary to provide support for the party that best represents their own preferences on newly emergent issues. However, if the political implications of social issues are not clearly understood or the parties' positions on the resultant policy controversies are not recognized, then the apparent inertia of party identification is more understandable. Individual partisan attachments are unlikely to be shunted aside if the issues that have the potential to do so never become crystallized elements of citizens' perspectives on the political world.

Of course, we should not be hasty in drawing pessimistic conclusions about the public's capacity for issue-based electoral behavior. Other interpretations are consistent with the evidence presented so far. For example, there may be a "division of labor" in mass issue orientations. One subset of the electorate may be interested in, knowledgeable about, and divided over one issue—say, foreign policy—but largely inattentive to domestic controversies. A second stratum may be intensely concerned about environmental issues, with little regard for other policy areas. A third set of individuals may be motivated solely by matters of health care, with little time left over for other concerns in contemporary American society. Suppose that the overall electorate were, in fact, divided into a series of "issue publics" like this. In that case, the aggregate-level evidence would probably show widespread ignorance and apathy on most issues, even though relatively small subsets of the public were making informed electoral choices on the basis of the single issue of most concern to themselves.

However, such a view of a divided mass public does not seem to square with our empirical evidence. The conditions for issue voting are not distributed widely and evenly throughout the electorate, across different issues. Instead, the potential for issue-based electoral choice is fairly concentrated. People who are familiar with the political alternatives on one issue are likely to exhibit a similar grasp of other issues, even though they involve different substantive elements. But this fact in itself suggests that there may be theoretical utility in examining patterns of individual attitudes across issues, rather than confining our attention to the ways that people react to a single issue in isolation from others.

It is also possible for citizens to possess a well-formed general sense of the broad differences between the parties, even though they retain very little knowledge about specific partisan issue stands. If that is the case, then people could connect these macro-level considerations to their own personal values and political orientations. Such a view suggests that individuals are capable of making rational and issue-consistent electoral choices, without having to invoke explicitly the minutiae associated with specific policy initiatives.

This latter hypothesis also provides another theoretical foundation for the empirical stability of party identification. The reasoning is straightforward: As already suggested, partisan elites constantly jockey for advantageous positions on currently salient issues. But the overall magnitude of these ongoing movements is generally quite small because party leaders are constrained by such factors as the preferences of rank-and-file party officeholders, past policy commitments, and the need to maintain credibility in the future. Therefore, the shape of the overall party system tends to remain quite stable over time. Parties with long-standing reputations for liberal or conservative solutions to social problems simply do not "move past each other" along the underlying dimensions of political conflict despite the adjustments to positions that are a regular element of the give-and-take that constitutes politics. If citizens are more attentive to these broad contours of the party system than they are to specific issues, it is perfectly reasonable that their partisan preferences remain fairly stable across long time periods, as well.

If people do think about political actors in broad terms, the effect should be to provide guidance on individuals' reactions to the array of policy conflicts that have defined the general partisan alignment. This, in turn, suggests once again that it is important to examine "clusters" or structures of attitudes toward political issues. We will do so in this chapter by determining whether discernible patterns exist in the opinions expressed on different issues. Then we will consider the kinds of generalized orientations that might give rise to these patterns in the first place. Before doing so, however, let us explicate the concept of an "attitude structure."

ATTITUDE STRUCTURES

For our purposes, an attitude structure exists when a common element underlies the ways that an individual reacts to different political issues. In other words, the person's opinions on two or more issues are functionally related to each other. As a simple example, consider someone who states that he or she believes the government has a responsibility to provide health care for everyone. This person might go on to say that government policies should guarantee a minimal living standard to poor citizens and also that government should take the lead in cleaning up the environment. Here the substantive nature of the social problem varies markedly from one policy to the next. But a single idea, governmental responsibility for dealing with social issues, runs through this person's opinions on all of them. If the source of the functional dependence changes—that is, the person decides that government is not responsible for ameliorating social problems—then we would expect all of the specific opinions to change accordingly.

The exact nature of the functional relationship is open to question. One possibility is that citizens' attitudes are rooted in their personal conceptions about the overall objectives of American society. In that case, we would expect people to support policies they believe are likely to achieve their social goals and to oppose policies that are not. Another possibility is that issue attitudes are interrelated because they reflect a fundamental personal orientation toward society. For example, an individual who distrusts strangers and unfamiliar groups may on that basis rationalize attitudes favoring punitive measures against criminals and aggressive maneuvers in foreign policy.

Regardless of its specific organizational principles, we expect a fully articulated attitude structure to span idea elements that vary widely in specificity. In fact, one of the central psychological functions of such a structure is to link specific opinions and general value orientations. For this reason, it is convenient to think of attitude structures as hierarchically organized mental constructs. Thus, we may trace out the levels of this structure by starting at the most specific component, such as an opinion toward a state law establishing the eligibility criteria for the receipt of welfare benefits. The person's response to this legislation may be based upon a more general belief about the good or bad points of the American welfare system that is, in turn, drawn from ideas about the sources of poverty and the need for welfare services. Finally, the latter beliefs may reflect the individual's basic value orientations (e.g., feelings about the importance of equality and social equity relative to individual freedom, etc.), which themselves comprise a fundamental aspect of personality.

Of course, an attitude structure can only go so far in determining the specific opinions a person expresses. Most of the stimuli that arise in the social and political world are complex; therefore, responses to them may be viewed as manifestations of several general belief classes, some of which may conflict with each other. For example, an individual who supports aid to the poor (and, therefore, may be expected to support generous eligibility criteria for the receipt of benefits) may simultaneously believe that the current welfare system creates a culture of dependence among its recipients and, on that basis, prefer more stringent criteria that limit the distribution of welfare services. Furthermore, opinions may be deflected from their "natural" course by considerations that fall outside the attitude structure itself. A person sympathetic to the plight of the poor still could oppose specific welfare legislation if it was likely to harm his or her own economic well-being. Thus, idiosyncratic circumstances peculiar to specific issues can "dilute" the empirical manifestation of an underlying attitude structure.

On the other hand, attitude structures are never directly observable. Any judgment about their presence or absence involves an inferential leap on the part of the investigator. Functional connections between distinct attitudes are presumed to exist when an individual's answer to one question about an issue can be predicted from his or her answers to questions on other, substantively distinct policy issues. However, it is important to recognize that seemingly consistent responses could also arise from separate lines of reasoning that coexist without a common framework of belief elements to link them.

For example, a person might oppose welfare programs to help the poor because they are expensive and lead to a higher tax burden. This same individual might oppose civil rights legislation out of personal hostility toward other racial minorities. Despite the psychological separation between this individual's ideas, the pattern of responses to the survey questions on these issues would be identical to those provided by another individual who opposes welfare and civil rights policies on the basis of a more general opposition to governmental activity. The difference is that a common thread links the separate attitudes in the latter case; the former individual reaches his or her seemingly consistent attitude more or less "by accident."

Such issue-specific foundations for attitudes undoubtedly exist within the American electorate. However, their idiosyncratic nature would probably lead individuals to widely varying configurations of responses across policy areas. As a result, their effects should cancel each other out in any overall assessment of mass attitude structure. In contrast, we believe that relatively robust correlations across survey responses on different issues signal the presence of underlying psychological dimensions that provide unifying structure across attitudes toward distinct areas of public policy.

A number of methodologies could be employed to evaluate the dimensional structure of correlated survey responses. We will employ a straightforward strategy based upon the degree to which the data conform to cumulative or "Guttman" scale patterns. The basic idea is that attitudes that lie along a common dimension vary in their extremity in systematic ways. To provide a simple example, consider two issues:

(1) government control of major industries; and (2) government assistance to the poor. In each case the issue arrays supporters of government activity against those who oppose it. But in contemporary American society, support for government control of industries is considered a much more extreme position than government assistance to the poor. We would expect anyone who supports the more radical pro-government position to favor governmental activity under less extreme circumstances (i.e., to help the poor). In contrast, anyone who is so hostile toward government action that he or she opposes assistance for the poor would also be expected to reject more extreme policies (i.e., government control of industry). This reasoning can be used to establish criteria for determining when the empirical data conform to a pattern that signals the existence of a common dimension underlying the responses to the separate issues. When these scaling criteria are met, the individuals providing the responses can be assigned scores that locate their relative positions along the resultant continuum.

While the techniques for establishing the existence of structured attitudes are relatively clear-cut, the procedures for determining the meaning of the dimensions that provide the structure remain subjective and open to interpretation on the part of the researcher. Hopefully, the issues that match the criteria for a scale will exhibit substantive content that is similar enough to allow us to discern a common thread running through them. If so, we will conclude that this more general theme provides insight regarding the psychological criteria that organize the attitude structure.

But we must admit some uncertainty in our interpretations. Suppose we find that a single dimension accounts for individual reactions to issues like public employment programs, assistance to the poor, civil rights, and environmental protection. An obvious thread seems to connect these areas, involving the extent of governmental activity. But this apparent connection could be due to individual feelings about the government itself, to economic self-interest, class-based considerations, or a broad ideological stance. Again, all of these organizational foundations could produce the same configuration of attitudes, even though they have widely varying theoretical implications.

As an objective check on our interpretations, we will compare the issue scales to relevant external criteria. Completely separate survey questions will be employed to obtain direct empirical measures of the "master" psychological orientations that seem to organize attitude structures. Admittedly, this process is not infallible since these general orientations are themselves difficult to measure. Nevertheless, if we can demonstrate that these master attitudes are related to the positions individuals occupy along the issue continua recovered from the scaling procedures, that supports the validity of our interpretations of the underlying dimensions. Alternatively, if we find no relationship between the general orientations and the scaled issue positions, then we must call into question our initial hypotheses regarding the nature of individual attitude structures.

Ideology

Although all attitude structures have potential utility in guiding electoral choices, we are particularly interested in those that may be characterized as ideologies. The latter entail a set of beliefs and evaluations that are crystallized, interlocked, and broad in scope. An ideological attitude structure probably would be grounded in broad assumptions about the nature of society and appropriate social objectives. These fundamental principles imply the institutional arrangements appropriate for governance, along with values to guide political action. In this manner, an ideology summarizes a person's overall stance toward the political world.

But it does far more than this. An ideology can also give political meaning to an enormous variety of observations, events, and experiences that fall outside the immediate realm of politics. Ideological principles may underlie a person's ideas about appropriate family structures, the specific content of educational curricula, the role of religion in society, and the sources of economic stress. It is useful to conceive of ideology as a subjective lens through which the ideologue observes the rest of the world. As such, ideology facilitates the translation process through which new phenomena are made relevant to political decisions.

Two features of ideology are immediately relevant to our analysis. First, a well-developed ideology is almost certainly organized according to broad, abstract principles. An ideology functions as a taxonomy, in the sense that incoming information is classified according to its relationship with the central concepts that define the ideological system. In order to deal with the diverse perceptual experiences to which an individual might be exposed, the organizational concepts of the classification system must themselves be broadly defined. So we can surmise that a true ideology is characterized by abstractions that transcend the specific content of the policy controversies in American society at any point.

Second, the existence of ideology reduces the potential cacophony of issue considerations in the mass public to more manageable proportions. Every policy controversy involves unique features, such as the historical circumstances behind the social problem that generated the issue, the demographics of the opposing sides on the issue, the particular governmental institutions that have attempted to address the issue, and so on. A central function of an ideology is to cut through the idiosyncrasies and highlight the common ground across different issues. In so doing, it provides general evaluative dimensions that can stand in for the specific issues.

Note that the preceding two aspects of ideology simultaneously complicate and facilitate systematic empirical analysis. On the one hand, the nature of the organizational principles underlying ideology makes it difficult to determine their existence. Broad abstractions are difficult to encapsulate in the succinct questions that are usually posed to survey respondents. Unfortunately, it is not feasible to ask people directly how they organize their own political attitudes.

On the other hand, the existence of a common evaluative dimension stemming from ideology assists empirical analysis because we are able to combine each individual's separate issue responses to estimate his or her location along the general continuum presumed to supply the common structure across those responses. Once we have reliable measurement of the ideological dimension, the distinct issues subsumed by that dimension lose much of their separate importance—at least for analytic purposes. If this process works out as we anticipate, fewer variables need be tracked over the course of the analysis.

Many abstract value systems may provide the basis for ideology. But we anticipate that one, in particular, will dominate the ideological content of American opinion: The liberal-conservative continuum. This general dimension can be employed readily to locate virtually all of the positions on issues that arise in contemporary political discourse. The substantive details of specific issues can vary enormously, from fairness in employment practices among private businesses, to domestic surveillance for curbing terrorism, to the standards of health care that should be available to all (among many other issues). But in each case, a liberal or conservative stance helps an individual define a personal position, grounded in common ideas that pertain to most social, economic, and political processes and interactions.

This ideological dimension is currently defined largely in terms focused on the scope of governmental activity and the degree to which governmental resources should be mobilized to ameliorate social problems. Liberals tend to favor governmental action (particularly at the federal level) in order to insure equitable economic arrangements and guarantee that no subgroup within American society is unduly constrained by institutional or societal limitations. In contrast, conservatives hold that economic productivity and efficiency, along with optimal social interactions, will obtain when government takes a more limited stance toward the rest of society.

But liberal-conservative differences go beyond the relatively simple question of more or less government activity. In the realms of law enforcement and the standards for personal expression, for example, the conservative position generally places government and its representatives in a relatively favored position compared to private citizens. Here, conservatives favor government action to promote public safety and adherence to societal norms. Conversely, the liberal preference usually calls for less governmental "intrusion" into such areas of everyday life. Thus, the appropriate ideological response toward questions of governmental intervention depends upon the specific nature of the intervention being called into question.

There are no absolute criteria that define the belief systems associated with particular ideological terms. For example, the classical liberalism of John Locke involves an understanding of socioeconomic systems that comes remarkably close to the kind of position espoused by modern conservative political commentators. More recently, the activist foreign policy favored by American liberals in the mid-twentieth century has been supplanted by a more cautious view that is skeptical of aggressive confrontation with potential enemies. During the first decade of the twenty-first century, conservatives (who were previously opposed to sending excessive amounts of American resources overseas) were quite vocal in their advocacy of regime change within nations that are hostile to American interests. Stated simply, an issue stand that is considered liberal (or conservative) in one era could easily become a conservative (or liberal) position under different circumstances.

The liberal-conservative distinction is ubiquitous in American politics. Ideological terminology is used routinely by journalists, government officials, and candidates for public office. Therefore, it is likely to figure prominently as citizens bring their feelings about public policy to bear on their own electoral choices. In this chapter, we will begin with fundamental questions about attitude structures and the degree to which individual issue preferences are consistent with a more general liberal-conservative dimension. In the next chapter, we will continue our inquiry by trying to determine whether the empirical attitude structures truly constitute "ideology."

ATTITUDE STRUCTURES IN PUBLIC POLICY ISSUES

The preelection component of the 2004 National Election Study survey contains four items that ask respondents' opinions on foreign policy, and twelve items on domestic policy.[1] Analysis of these sixteen items reveals three distinct sets of opinions that conform to the Guttman scale criteria.[2] This, in turn, suggests that three distinct attitude structures regarding political issues exist within the American electorate.

One scale combines the individual responses to all four foreign policy items.[3] It includes judgments about whether the Iraq war is worth the cost, whether the Iraq war has reduced the threat of terrorism, whether the Afghanistan war is worth the cost, and whether defense

---

1. Prior to the scaling analysis, all of the issue items are dichotomized, so that each one contrasts respondents who agreed with the liberal position on that issue to those who took either the conservative or the neutral stance. Although collapsing categories in this manner discards some information about the response distributions, Guttman (1944) argued that such dichotomization has little effect on the scaling results. That appears to be the case here: Replications of the analysis using a polychotomous version of the scaling procedure, and also using factor analysis, produce virtually identical scales to those discussed here.

2. The Guttman scaling analysis begins with a pool of potentially scalable items—in this case, the 16 questions on issues from the 2004 National Election Study. The objective is to find one or more subsets of the items with response distributions that conform to the cumulative pattern described earlier. Here, three item subsets form mutually cumulative, or scalable, response patterns. The degree to which a set of items conforms to a scalable pattern is determined by a goodness-of-fit measure. With Guttman-type scales, at least three such measures may be used: The coefficient of reproducibility gives the proportion of total responses that are consistent with the cumulative response pattern. The coefficient of scalability measures the proportional "improvement" in predicting responses to individual items that the scale provides, relative to simply guessing responses, based upon the item marginal frequencies. The H coefficient measures the proportional improvement in predicting responses using the scale, compared to the predictions obtained from a statistically independent set of items. The coefficients of reproducibility and scalability are discussed by Dawes (1972) and McIver and Carmines (1981), while the H statistic is explained in Sijstma and Molenaar 2002.

3. The coefficient of reproducibility for this scale is .90, the coefficient of scalability is .69, and the H statistic is .48. By the usual standards employed in the research literature (e.g., Sijstma and Molenaar 2002), these values indicate that the data for these four items show moderately strong conformity with the cumulative response pattern.

spending should be increased or decreased.[4] The implied continuum ranges from those at one extreme who question the effectiveness of, and need for, American military action, to those at the other extreme who believe not only that the wars in Iraq and Afghanistan are worthwhile endeavors but also that further resources should be devoted to national defense.[5] The common theme of the four items suggests that this scale measures individual attitudes toward military action in American foreign policy. Unfortunately, however, the lack of additional survey questions precludes any investigation of whether this attitude structure extends to additional, nonmilitary, aspects of American foreign policy.

The second attitude structure is formed from responses to three of the twelve items on domestic issues.[6] The common content in this case centers around questions about lifestyles. At one extreme are located people who believe that a woman's place is in the home, that government should not provide funding for abortion, and that gay marriage should be banned.[7] The other extreme is occupied by those who believe women should have an equal role, that government should fund abortions, and that gay couples should be permitted to marry.[8]

---

4. The defense spending question is the same one introduced in chapter 8. The remaining three questions are worded as follows: "Taking everything into account, do you think the U.S. war against the Taliban government in Afghanistan was worth the cost or not?"; "Taking everything into account, do you think the war in Iraq has been worth the cost or not?"; and, "As a result of the United States military action in Iraq, do you think the threat of terrorism against the United States has increased, decreased, or stayed about the same?"

5. Note that the ordering of the items in this scale is meaningful in substantive terms, and can be interpreted as the "degree of liberalism" associated with each of the policy positions. So agreeing that the Iraq war is not worth the cost is the least liberal stand, followed by agreement that the Iraq war has not reduced the threat of terrorism, and agreement that the Afghanistan war is not worth the cost. Stating that defense spending should be reduced is left as the most extreme liberal position among these four stands on issues.

6. The coefficient of reproducibility for this scale is .93, the coefficient of scalability is .78, and the H statistic is .44. Once again, these values indicate that the data for these three items conform quite closely to the cumulative pattern that characterizes a Guttman scale.

7. Two of the three questions are worded as follows: "Would you favor or oppose a law in your state that would allow the use of government funds to help pay for the costs of abortion for women who cannot afford them?" and "Should same-sex couples be allowed to marry, or do you think they should not be allowed to marry?" The third question uses the seven-point scale format to have respondents place themselves along a continuum from "Women should have an equal role with men in running business, industry, and government" to "A woman's place is in the home."

8. Here, the positions on issues are ordered as they are mentioned in the text. That is, believing that women should have an equal role is the least liberal issue stand, while supporting gay marriage is the most liberal stand.

A separate, third, "cluster" of opinions is revealed in the responses to four more of the questions on domestic issues.[9] These involve individual reactions to government spending and services, government versus private health insurance, government-guaranteed jobs, and government assistance to African Americans.[10] All of these items deal with the use of government resources to help meet citizens' basic needs. Therefore, this scale can be interpreted as an empirical measure of a social welfare attitude structure.[11]

We do not claim that the items employed in this analysis comprise a comprehensive list of the issues that were salient during the 2004 presidential campaign. Instead, we prefer to interpret them as a sample, drawn from the "population" of policy questions confronting the 2004 electorate. We do believe that these items constitute a fairly representative microcosm of the "issue universe"; it is likely that alternative samples (i.e., different sets of survey questions) would produce evidence of attitude structures quite similar to those we find here.

THE CLARITY OF ATTITUDE STRUCTURES

We interpret the three separate structures into which our issues fall as reflections of the policy agendas confronting the electorate. But we are seeing these agendas from the perspective of the mass public, and not from that of the political elites (i.e., candidates, officeholders, journalists, etc.) who are primarily responsible for creating these agendas. Therefore, it is useful to consider the degree to which coherent information about public policies is actually "getting through" to individual citizens. In other words, are individual perceptions consistent with the predominant structures of variability across separate policy issues?

---

9. The coefficient of reproducibility for this scale is .85, the coefficient of scalability is .57, and the *H* statistic is .40. Here, the data exhibit a moderate (but still perfectly acceptable) fit to the cumulative pattern of responses across items.

10. The questions about government spending and services, government-guaranteed jobs, and government assistance to African Americans are the same ones used in chapter 8. The fourth item uses the seven-point scale format to have respondents place themselves along a continuum ranging from "A government insurance plan which would cover all medical and hospital expenses for everyone" to "All medical expenses should be paid by individuals through private insurance plans like Blue Cross or other company paid plans."

11. Once again, the scale order of the issue stands corresponds to the order that they are mentioned in the text: From least to most liberal, the positions are support for government spending, public health insurance, guaranteed jobs, and assistance to African Americans.

The clarity of the attitude structures can be gauged by the proportions of individuals whose responses to the questions on issues conform perfectly to the cumulative patterns that characterize the Guttman scaling criterion. The figures are 56.3 percent for the foreign policy scale; 80.5 percent for lifestyle issues; and 47.4 percent for social welfare. These percentages show that, within each domain, a substantial subset of people endorses a relatively extreme liberal position while simultaneously rejecting at least one liberal stand that is less extreme. There appears to be a consensus on the relative ordering of the lifestyle items, where slightly more than four-fifths of the respondents conform to error-free scalar response patterns. Apparently, societal norms about the variability across women's rights, abortion, and gay marriage are crystallized. But deviations from the dominant cumulative patterns are much more pronounced for the foreign policy scale and, especially, the social welfare scale. In each of the domains, about half of the respondents (slightly less than that in the foreign policy scale, slightly more on social welfare) provide nonscalar sets of responses.

These results are somewhat surprising, given the specific salience of foreign policy issues in the 2004 campaign and the long-standing presence of social welfare questions on the American issue agenda. Given the overall prominence of these kinds of issues, it would be reasonable to hypothesize a high degree of clarity in citizens' responses to them. However, the evidence shows that is not what occurs. Apparently, there is some "slippage" in the transmission of issue-related messages and information from elites to the mass public.

The "Boundaries" of Attitude Structures

Do individuals' structured responses to issues actually encompass the full range of controversies over policy that confront the electorate (at least, insofar as we have measured that full range with the NES data)? Or, are there discernible "boundaries" that not only separate the different issue domains, but also exclude certain issues entirely from these common structures? In fact, the empirical evidence points to the latter. Let us consider briefly the nature of these boundaries and their implications for understanding citizens' orientations toward the policy agendas that confront the American electorate.

The bounded nature of the attitude structures is indicated by the fact that several additional issues were excluded from the two scales of domestic policy responses. The five items that failed to meet the Guttman scalability criteria are federal restrictions on purchasing firearms; the trade-off between jobs and environmental protection; reactions to the Bush tax cuts; a possible ban on late-term abortions; and the death penalty.[12] On the one hand, the fact that these items do not cluster with the others narrows the substantive content of each scale; and, that facilitates our attempts to interpret the nature of the underlying attitude structures. Questions about topics like gun control and the death penalty apparently activate different considerations than those that lead to coherent sets of responses in the realms of lifestyles and social welfare.

On the other hand, there seem to be fine distinctions between items that are included in the scales, and some of those that are not. For example, opinions on federal funding for abortion exist within a more general "lifestyles" attitude structure, while reactions to late-term abortions remain separate. Similarly, the economic ramifications of environmental protection could easily raise questions about the relative importance of social welfare goals (i.e., employment) compared to other desirable social objectives (i.e., reducing pollution); nevertheless, responses to the jobs-environment trade-off remain distinct from the social welfare attitude structure.

These separations between opinions on apparently similar topics may suggest that attitude structures within the mass public actually have limited scope. Certainly, they do not appear to be consistent with the broad coherence that should be evidence of a well-developed ideology. Thus, we might expect that one's general orientation toward programs intended to help the needy would extend to opinions regarding the sources of revenue to support those policies. However, feelings about the Bush tax cuts are largely independent from the social welfare attitude structure.

Before proceeding to a closer investigation of the attitude structures themselves, it is important to emphasize that the nonscalable nature of

---

12. The wordings for four of these questions is as follows: "As you may recall, President Bush signed a big tax cut a few years ago. Did you favor or oppose the tax cut, or is this something you haven't thought about?"; "There has been discussion recently about a law to ban certain types of late-term abortions, sometimes called partial birth abortions. Do you favor or oppose a law that makes these types of abortions illegal?"; "Do you think the federal government should make it more difficult for people to buy a gun than it is now, make it easier for people to buy a gun, or keep these rules about the same as they are now?"; and "Do you favor or oppose the death penalty for persons convicted of murder?" The fifth item uses the seven-point scale format to place respondents along a continuum ranging from "Protect the environment even if it costs some jobs or otherwise reduces our standard of living" to "Protecting the environment is not as important as maintaining jobs and our standard of living."

certain issues does not say anything about the quality of the opinions about them. Individual responses on the items excluded from the three scales are no more haphazard or muddled than are those on the items that meet the scalability criteria. To the contrary, narrowly defined economic self-interest seems to be guiding opinions on two of the issues: Lower-income individuals are less supportive of the Bush tax cuts and less interested in environmental protection at the expense of employment opportunities than are higher-income respondents.

Furthermore, all of the nonscalable issues are related to party identification. Individuals who profess an attachment to the Democratic Party are more likely to oppose the Bush tax cuts, the death penalty, a ban on late-term abortions, economically motivated cutbacks in environmental protection, and loosening controls on firearm purchases than are Republicans, who tend to take the opposite positions on these same issues. Such clear patterns would not exist unless the responses to the issue questions were based, in some measure, on underlying evaluative feelings about the various policies. It is just that each of the latter issues seem to be considered separately on their respective merits; they are not subsumed within a broader framework of functionally related beliefs and evaluations.

The Interrelationship of Attitude Structures

The three attitude structures cover different areas of public policy. It is certainly the case that foreign policy, lifestyle choices, and social welfare each involve distinct substantive problems and considerations. Nevertheless, there are relationships of moderate strength between the positions that individuals occupy on the three scales employed to measure these attitude domains. For example, a person who supports military action in American foreign policy is more likely to favor traditional lifestyles and oppose programs that provide benefits to needy citizens than to take the opposite positions in the latter areas. Similarly, an individual who is willing to permit innovative lifestyle arrangements is more likely to support social welfare policies than to oppose them.

The connections between the different attitude structures are quite reasonable, given the issue environment of American politics. An aggressive foreign policy, based upon military strength, was a central component of the Bush presidential campaign in 2004. The Republican Party actively sought support from fundamentalist Christians, the sociodemographic group that is strongest in its vocal support of traditional lifestyles and family arrangements. Of course, Republican opposition toward (or, at least, uneasy tolerance of) many elements of the modern welfare state has been an ongoing component of the predominant partisan alignment since the 1930s.

On the other side, the Democratic Party was the only serious rallying point for those who opposed the wars in Afghanistan and Iraq and those who are tolerant of alternative lifestyle arrangements, even though some of its rhetoric on these kinds of issues was ambiguous. Welfare programs were not a particularly salient topic of debate during the 2004 campaign, but Democratic candidates did not try to evade their traditional reputation as advocates for underprivileged elements of society. Given the relative clarity of the two parties' positions, the interrelated configurations of attitudes that we find within the electorate may simply be straightforward responses to the respective sets of issue stands that are espoused by national partisan elites.

One potential problem with this interpretation is that it appears to be at odds with the conclusions reported in the previous chapter. Recall that our analysis of the preconditions for issue voting revealed a sizable amount of confusion and outright ignorance regarding the candidates' positions on specific issues. If that is the case, then it seems improbable that reactions to those same candidates are producing orderly arrangements of issue responses like those in the attitude structures we have found here. Instead, it seems likely that the sources of attitudinal consistency lie elsewhere, rather than in the immediate campaign environment of the 2004 election. The possibilities include long-standing partisan loyalties that transcend specific electoral contests, socioeconomic self-interest, and generalized belief orientations that may, at least for some citizens, approach the scope and complexity that would define a personal ideology. We will examine all of these factors in an effort to explicate the fundamental nature of citizens' attitude structures, as well as the political significance of those structures for voting choices.

THE SIGNIFICANCE OF ATTITUDE STRUCTURES ON POLICY ISSUES

Despite the substantive differences between the three attitude structures, the remainder of our analysis will consider them simultaneously. As we will see, the nature and degree of the interrelationships between opinions on foreign policy, lifestyle issues, and social welfare on the one hand, and other political orientations on the other, are quite similar. For this reason, our general conclusion will be that all three kinds of issues are making important contributions to voters' choices.

We begin by presenting some descriptive evidence. The three panels of figure 9.1 graph the frequency distributions for the respective Guttman scale scores assigned to the survey respondents. To reiterate, we believe these scores to be empirical manifestations of individual policy preferences within the respective attitude structures. In each case, larger scores correspond to more liberal positions: on the foreign policy scale, they signify greater opposition to military action; on the lifestyles scale, they show greater tolerance for alternative family arrangements; and, on the social welfare scale, they represent support for governmental programs that help needy segments of American society.

The graphs in figure 9.1 reveal that the American electorate leaned in a decidedly conservative direction on the major clusters of issues in 2004. This pattern is clearest with respect to foreign policy and social welfare (figs. 9.1a and 9.1b). In each case, slightly more than 50 percent of the respondents fall within the two most conservative categories, and the remaining category percentages decrease steadily as we move toward the liberal pole of the respective continuum. There is more division with respect to lifestyle issues. Here, a small majority of the respondents (53 percent) still falls on the relatively conservative side of the continuum. And just under half the public (about 47 percent of the sample) support the more liberal alternatives on most of the relevant issues. This relatively mild imbalance favoring conservative lifestyles provides a contrast to the skewed distributions in the other two issue areas. But the general thrust of the evidence still shows that conservative positions on issues held majority support across all three substantive domains.

Partisanship and Attitude Structures

It is, perhaps, natural to assume that conservative opinions on the issues contributed to George W. Bush's electoral victory in 2004. After all, he was the candidate of the more conservative party, so a simple matching process could have led voters from their policy preferences to an electoral decision. But the findings from the previous chapter indicate the need for caution before jumping to such a conclusion. We have already seen that many citizens did not meet the necessary preconditions for casting a vote that was based explicitly on policy motivations. At the same time, however, it is possible for people to cast votes that are consistent with their own orientations on issues, even if those attitudes were not a part of an individual's conscious decision-making process. To the extent that this occurs, an electoral outcome could have significance for policy, even in the absence of actual policy-based voting.

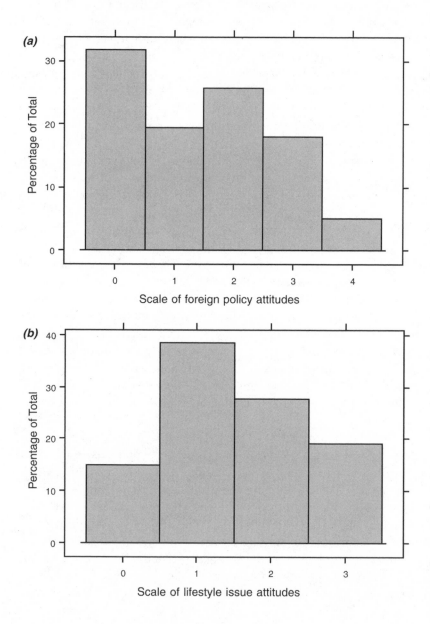

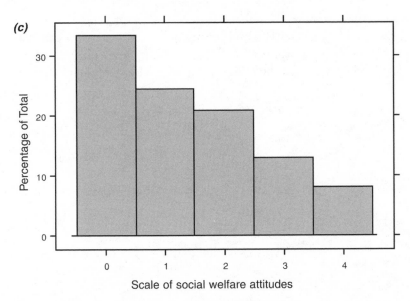

Fig. 9.1. Histograms for Guttman scales measuring attitude structures. (*a*) Foreign policy attitudes; (*b*) lifestyle issue attitudes; (*c*) social welfare attitudes. On each scale, the score represents the number of issues within that scale on which a respondent articulated a liberal position. The number of observations is 1,130. (Data from 2004 National Election Study.)

The evidence in figure 9.2 suggests that there may be some merit in this line of reasoning. The figure shows the mean scores on each of the three issue scales, calculated separately within categories of party identification. The scale scores measure positions along the dimensions corresponding to the different attitude structures. In operational terms, the specific scale value for an individual gives the number of issues within that domain on which that person has expressed a liberal attitude. Therefore, the minimum possible score on each scale is 0 (for a person who does not articulate a liberal preference on any of the issues). The maximum possible scores are 4 for the foreign policy and social welfare scales and 3 for the lifestyle issues scale; in each case, these maximum values would be assigned to a person who adopted liberal stands on all issues within the respective substantive areas.

The three panels of figure 9.2 show a consistent pattern: As we move across the partisan continuum from the strongly Democratic pole to the strongly Republican pole, the mean scale score shifts in a monotonic pattern toward smaller—that is, more conservative—values. Republicans are uniformly more likely than Democrats to favor American military action, traditional lifestyles, and constrained social welfare programs.

Along with the clear partisan "tilt" in these findings, two other details in figure 9.2 are worth mentioning. First, the clarity of the relationship

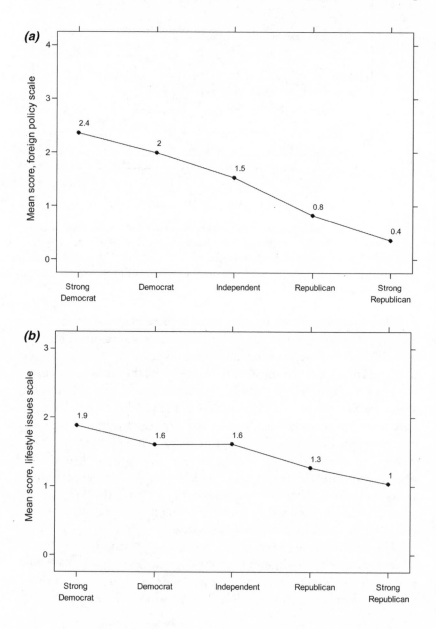

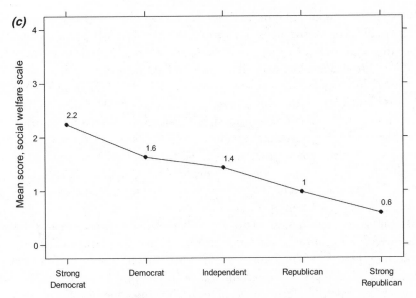

Fig. 9.2. The relationship between issue attitudes and party identification. (*a*) Foreign policy attitudes; (*b*) lifestyle issue attitudes; (*c*) social welfare attitudes. The number of observations is 1,114. (Data from 2004 National Election Study.)

between issue attitudes and party identification is a bit muted (although it still exists) in the lifestyles domain. Here, even the most extreme partisans exhibit attitudes that fall within the middle region of the scale's overall range. Apparently, strong Democrats do not uniformly support women's rights, government funding for abortions, and gay marriage, while strong Republicans are not uniformly opposed to these social arrangements.

Second, there is some asymmetry to the impact of party identification in the foreign policy and social welfare domains. In both cases, Republicans fall very close to the conservative end of the scale. For example, individuals who identify themselves as strong Republicans tend to express conservative opinions on at least three out of four foreign policy and social welfare items. However, Democrats do not exhibit similar clarity in their preferences for liberal issue stands. Instead, they occupy relatively centrist positions along the two scales. Strong Democrats choose liberal alternatives on just over two out of the four issues within both the foreign policy and social welfare areas.

The results so far show that partisan considerations do coincide with particular issue orientations. However, the degree of structuring varies markedly across issue areas and also across the two major parties. These findings are not at all unreasonable. Again, current American military efforts are closely identified with the incumbent Republican administration, while social welfare issues have divided Republicans from Democrats for at least 70 years. In contrast, serious public debates about equality for women, abortion, and gay rights have only occurred much more recently; and they have occasionally led to almost as much intraparty divisiveness as interparty disagreement. So the varying amounts of crystallization in partisan orientations toward issues is understandable.

At the same time, the Democratic Party has long represented a much more diverse coalition of interests than has the Republican Party. Furthermore, certain liberal stands on policy could, at least arguably, be viewed as contrary to some central tenets of American political culture. Both of these points probably contribute to some restraint in the degree to which Democrats embrace liberal positions on issues. Republican identifiers are less affected by such limitations, and the result is greater uniformity in their support for conservative positions on issues.

Ideological Self-Placement in the Mass Public

As we have just seen, the attitude structures that exist within the American public divide citizens in ways that may well have electoral significance. But it is still necessary to investigate further in order to determine the organizational foundations of these attitude structures. Are personal attachments to partisan labels the "glue" that holds together the separate attitudes within each issue domain? Or are issue preferences aligned according to more abstract and general considerations— that is, the broad principles that could reasonably be considered to characterize an ideology?

Earlier in this chapter, we argued that the most prominent capping abstractions in American political discourse stem from a general continuum organized along liberal-conservative lines. Therefore, a reasonable starting point in our analysis is to examine the relationship between citizens' own positions along this ideological dimension and their orientations toward issues. The data include survey respondents' self-placements among seven ordered categories, with labeled positions ranging from "extremely liberal" to "extremely conservative." In order to be consistent with our earlier treatment of party identification, we will use a five-category variant of this ideological identification scale, in which the two most extreme categories at either end are combined (i.e., extreme liberals are grouped together with liberals, and extreme conservatives are grouped with conservatives).

Before proceeding, it is imperative that we point out caveats to the analysis that follows. First, our use of the liberal-conservative continuum immediately restricts our attention to a subset of the overall electorate, because a sizable segment of the public simply do not place themselves along such an ideological dimension. In the 2004 NES data employed here, fully 24.0 percent either said that they "haven't thought much about this" or refused to answer the survey question. Second, of those who do place themselves along the liberal-conservative scale, nearly one-third (32.3 percent) select the neutral category, calling themselves "moderate; middle of the road." Thus, only a bare majority of our respondents (51.4 percent) consider themselves to be either liberal or conservative at any degree of extremity. Furthermore, this is a selective group of people: Nonneutral positions along the liberal-conservative continuum are much more prevalent among highly educated individuals, as well as those who are more interested in, and attentive to, the political world.[13] This is a pattern we will consider in much greater detail in chapter 10. But for now, we must emphasize that the empirical relationships between liberal-conservative self-placements and individual positions within the respective attitude structures probably do not reflect patterns within the entire electorate. Instead, they are confined to the stratum of citizens who are sufficiently adept in their political thinking to be willing to attach ideological labels to themselves.

Ideological Self-Placement and Attitude Structure

Figure 9.3 shows the mean scale scores that occur at each of the five positions we differentiate across the liberal-conservative continuum. Just as was the case with party identification, a clear pattern emerges: The means decrease monotonically as we move from left to right across the ideological dimension. People who call themselves liberals tend to prefer

---

13. Among people who have a college degree, 65 percent place themselves at a nonneutral position along the liberal-conservative continuum, compared to only 42 percent among people who do not report any education beyond high school. Similarly, 65 percent of those who say they are "very much" interested in following political campaigns place themselves at a nonneutral ideological position, compared to 42 percent who say that they are only "somewhat" or "not much" interested. Fifty-eight percent of those who say they pay a "great deal" or "quite a bit" of attention to presidential campaigns place themselves at nonneutral positions along the ideological dimension, compared to 44 percent of those who say they pay "some," "very little," or no attention.

liberal positions on a larger number of specific issues than those who call themselves conservatives. The issue stands of self-identified moderates fall between those of the opposing subgroups that are willing to attach ideological labels to themselves.

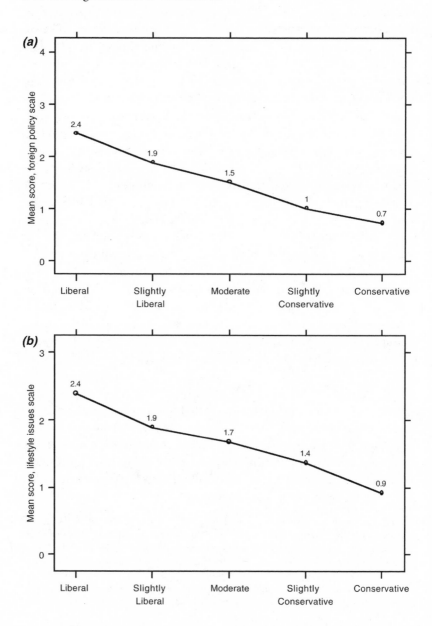

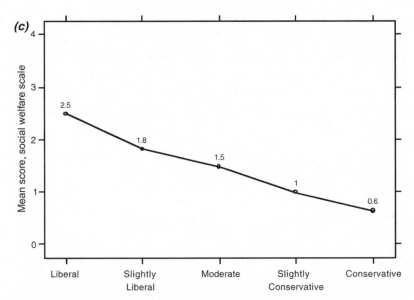

Fig. 9.3. The relationship between issue attitudes and liberal-conservative iden-tification. (*a*) Foreign policy attitudes; (*b*) lifestyle issue attitudes; (*c*) social wel-fare attitudes. The number of observations is 869. (Data from 2004 National Election Study.)

Once again, a comparison across the separate issue domains is inter-esting. In the areas of foreign policy and social welfare, the relationships between liberal-conservative identification and issue orientations looks nearly identical to the corresponding relationships between party iden-tification and those same attitude structures. In these cases, the differ-ences in preferences between self-identified liberals and conservatives parallel closely those between Democratic and Republican identifiers. The situation is a bit different with respect to lifestyle issues. Here, the contrast between liberals and conservatives is greater than that between Democrats and Republicans. For example, the difference in the mean scale scores of liberals and conservatives is nearly 1.5, while the differ-ence for strong Democrats and strong Republicans is only about 0.9.

The evidence shows that liberal-conservative structure in issue atti-tude structures is at least as clear as is partisan structure. But this, in itself, does not provide sufficient evidence that citizens are actively organizing their orientations along ideological lines. Part of the hesitation in draw-ing such a conclusion stems from the fact that party identification and ideological self-placement are themselves related fairly strongly. This is definitely the case with political elites, but it is also true within the mass public (even though the contrasts might not be quite as stark). Among Republicans, self-identified conservatives abound, while liberals are virtually nonexistent. On the other side of the partisan spectrum, a scant majority of Democrats consider themselves to be liberals, while less than

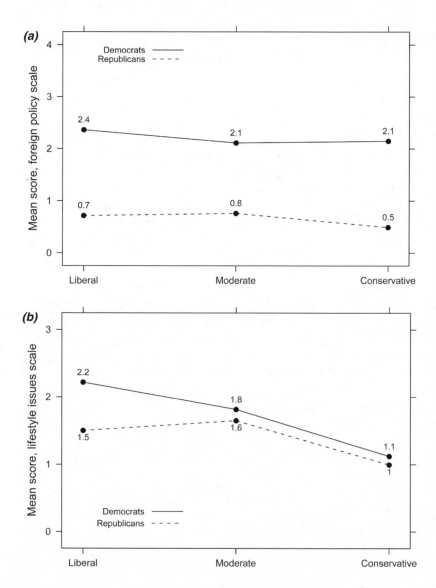

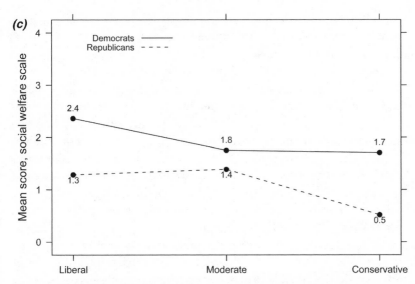

Fig. 9.4. The relationship between issue attitudes and party identification, controlling for liberal-conservative identification. (*a*) Foreign policy attitudes; (*b*) lifestyle issue attitudes; (*c*) social welfare attitudes. The number of observations is 869. (Data from 2004 National Election Study.)

one-fifth call themselves conservatives. Hence, an empirical correlation between partisanship and issue attitudes might be spurious and actually due to the fact that self-identified liberals (who tend to be Democrats) favor liberal issue stands, while self-identified conservatives (who tend to be Republicans) prefer conservative policy solutions. Of course, the possibility also exists that the correlation between ideology and issues is spurious, and really due to the underlying impact of party identification.

The only way to sort out the effects of partisanship and ideology is to examine the simultaneous relationship between those two variables on the one hand, and issue attitude structures on the other. Figure 9.4 does this by plotting the mean issue scale scores for Democratic and Republican identifiers within ideological categories. Note that small numbers of observations (especially among Republican liberals) force us to abandon our relatively detailed measures of partisanship and personal ideology.[14]

---

14. Even with partisanship and ideology each collapsed to three categories, the numbers of observations within each combination of categories remains rather small. For example, there are only 14 Republicans who call themselves liberals, 54 who call themselves moderates, and 222 who call themselves conservatives. Among Democrats, 133 call themselves liberals, 81 call themselves moderates, and 41 call themselves conservatives.

Instead, the graphs in the figure are constructed from three-category versions of these variables that differentiate partisan and ideological directions, but not intensities.

The evidence in figure 9.4 indicates that the organizational bases of mass attitude structures vary across the issue domains. The first panel of the figure shows foreign policy orientations. Here, the differences between Republicans and Democrats are clear-cut, while those between liberals and conservatives are muted. Specifically, the mean scale scores for Republicans are always less than 1.0, while the means for Democrats are always greater than 2.0, across all three ideological categories. But within partisan categories, there is little variability along liberal-conservative lines. Among Democrats, the means only range from about 2.4 (for liberals) to 2.1 (for both moderates and conservatives). Among Republicans, the mean scale scores are confined to the interval from about 0.8 (for moderates) to 0.5 (for conservatives. Thus, foreign policy attitudes within the 2004 electorate were structured along partisan, rather than ideological, lines.

The second panel of figure 9.4 shows that the opposite situation occurs in the area of lifestyle issues. Here, there is quite a bit of variability across ideological categories, while the differences between the two partisan groups are very small. For example, among conservatives and moderates, the Democratic-Republican differences in the mean scores are only 0.1 and 0.2, respectively. A larger partisan difference (0.7) occurs among liberals, but this is almost certainly due to the fact that there are only 14 liberal Republicans in the data. Within partisan categories, the differences across liberal-conservative lines are more prominent: The mean scores range across 1.1 units among Democrats and 0.5 units among Republicans. These results indicate that, not only are lifestyle attitudes structured more closely along ideological rather than partisan lines, but also that the overall degree of structuring is less than that which exists for attitudes on foreign policy.

Finally, the third panel of figure 9.4 shows sizable differences on social welfare attitudes across both ideological and partisan categories. Within both Democratic and Republican ranks, self-identified liberals are more supportive of social welfare programs than are conservatives; the margins of difference are 0.7 scale units among Democrats and 0.8 units among Republicans. At the same time, Democrats and Republicans differ quite clearly in their attitudes on social welfare, even within the ideological categories. For example, the mean scale score for Democrats exceeds that for

Republicans by 1.1 units among liberals and by 1.2 units among conservatives. Thus, it appears that party identification and ideology make reinforcing, but separate, contributions to the overall degree of structure in citizens' attitudes on social welfare issues. Self-identified Democrats or liberals favor more programs to help needy segments of American society than do self-identified Republicans or conservatives.

Value Choices and Attitude Structure

The analysis to this point has shown that attitude structures with respect to public policy are organized in ways that are, to varying degrees, consistent with partisanship and ideology. But does this really indicate that people are actively formulating their policy orientations along these lines? Or, are we merely seeing the electorate respond to the messages emanating from partisan and ideological leaders prominent within the current political environment?

These two possibilities have differing implications for understanding the nature of mass opinion. In the first case, the stability of partisan loyalties and the relatively long-standing divisions that exist across ideological camps imply that attitude structures effectively "anchor" citizens in their general policy positions. This should, in turn, provide a degree of inertia that would dampen mass responses to political appeals and, perhaps, insulate the public from elite attempts at manipulation. In the second case, any empirical structure that spans a person's responses to separate policy questions would not be due to that individual explicitly linking attitudes together, based upon functional connections within his or her own belief systems. Instead, it would stem from a simpler stimulus-response process wherein people adopt the "bundle" of policy positions espoused by the partisan and ideological leaders they admire, and reject the policies advocated by those they perceive to be political opponents.

The difference between these two possibilities involves the depth of organization that underlies individual attitude structures. Recall from the definitions laid out at the beginning of this chapter that a fully developed attitude structure should be arranged in a hierarchical manner, with elements ranging from very narrow and specific at one extreme to the most general and abstract at the other. Thus, opinions about particular policies are derived from partisan and ideological orientations that are themselves the products of the individual's feelings about certain core values, and so on. On the other hand, if people are merely responding to elite appeals, then the organization of individual attitude structures should not extend beyond the partisan and ideological lines that divide those elites and differentiate their messages.

Fortuitously, our data include some measures of the broad value configurations that we believe underlie the three dominant issue attitude structures. In the case of foreign policy attitudes, we have a survey item that asks respondents their general preference for diplomatic or military steps in American foreign policy.[15] For lifestyle issues, there is a measure of "moral traditionalism" that differentiates respondents according to their feelings about morality, traditional family ties, and "newer lifestyles."[16] Social welfare issues can be compared against respondents' feelings about the overall role of modern government, ranging from the belief that less government is better to the idea that a large, powerful government is necessary for dealing with modern problems.[17] It is important to emphasize that the survey questions used to measure these three value orientations are all framed in very general terms, with no mention of specific societal issues or governmental policies. For that reason, we argue that they tap the kinds of organizational principles that should provide the foundations for the respective policy attitude structures.

---

15. The item used for this purpose is a seven-point scale, with end points corresponding to the statements, "Some people believe the United States should solve international problems by using diplomacy and other forms of international pressure and use military force only if absolutely necessary" and "Others believe diplomacy and pressure often fail and the U.S. must be ready to use military force." The original version is collapsed down to three categories, indicating support for diplomacy, military force, or a stance midway between the two.

16. Respondents were asked whether they agreed with each of four statements: "The newer lifestyles are contributing to the breakdown of our society"; "The world is always changing and we should adjust our view of moral behavior to those changes"; "This country would have many fewer problems if there were more emphasis on traditional family ties"; and "We should be more tolerant of people who choose to live according to their own moral standards, even if they are very different from our own." Moral traditionalism is indicated by agreement with the first and third statements, and disagreement with the second and fourth statements. Our measure is created by counting up the number of moral traditionalist responses a person gives, and then collapsing the total score into three categories indicating low, medium, and high levels of moral traditionalism, respectively.

17. Our measure of the respondents' beliefs about the role of government is created from responses to three survey questions. The first asked whether they believed "the main reason government has become bigger over the years is because it has gotten involved in things that people should do for themselves" or that "government has become bigger because the problems we face have become bigger." The second asked whether "we need a strong government to handle today's complex economic problems" or "the free market can handle these problems without government being involved." The third asked whether the respondent believed "the less government, the better" or "there are more things that government should be doing." Our variable is created by counting up the number of times each respondent gave the pro-government response out of the pair.

It is definitely the case that these value orientations are related to their corresponding attitude structures. People who prefer military over diplomatic foreign policy are more favorable toward defense spending and the wars in Afghanistan and Iraq. Those who prefer traditional moral values are opposed to policies that support newer lifestyles such as funding for abortions or legalizing marriage for gay couples. Advocates of smaller government are more willing to place limits on the kinds of public benefits that are available to needy segments of the population. These connections are all to be expected; indeed, it would be more surprising if they did not exist.

But it is not the bivariate relationships between values and policy preferences that are important for present purposes. Instead, we want to determine whether these value orientations actually constitute more fundamental sources of the partisan and ideological patterns that we identified above. Again, if general value choices (say, the preference for diplomacy or military actions) affect both political loyalties (say, personal identification with a political party) and specific policies (say, support for the Iraq war), then controlling for the value should cause the relationship between the loyalties and the policy attitude to vanish.

Figures 9.5, 9.6, and 9.7 present the relevant evidence. Each figure graphs the relationship between one of the attitude structures and its related general value, controlling for the most relevant political correlate. For example, we saw earlier that foreign policy attitudes are structured mainly along partisan lines. Therefore, figure 9.5 plots mean foreign policy scale scores against general feelings about diplomacy versus military action, separately for Democrats and Republicans. On the other hand, lifestyle issues seem to be more a matter of ideological self-placement. Therefore, figure 9.6 plots mean lifestyle scale scores across categories on the measure of moral traditionalism, separately for liberals and conservatives. Finally, socioeconomic attitudes are structured according to both partisan and ideological considerations. Accordingly, the two panels of figure 9.7 plot mean social welfare scale scores against feelings about the size of government, separately for Democrats and Republicans (in fig. 9.7a), and for liberals and conservatives (in fig. 9.7b).

The three figures all tell the same story. General value orientations and more immediate political loyalties both make separate contributions to the empirical structure in citizens' attitudes on issues. In figure 9.5, Democrats still exhibit more liberal policy preferences than Republicans, just as they did in figures 9.2 and 9.4. But within partisan categories,

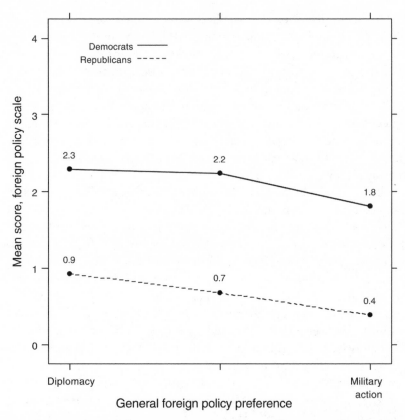

Fig. 9.5. The relationship between foreign policy attitudes and general feelings about diplomacy versus military action, controlling for party identification. The number of observations is 928. (Data from 2004 National Election Study.)

support for the wars and for defense spending increases as we move from a preference for diplomacy to general support for military action. A similar pattern occurs for the relationship between ideology and opinion on policies affecting lifestyles, while controlling for moral traditionalism (fig. 9.6). Here, liberal identifiers continue to espouse policies that support nontraditional living arrangements, while conservatives oppose them. But within ideological strata, opposition to gender equality, abortion funding, and gay marriage increases along with adherence to moral traditionalism. Finally, figure 9.7 shows that, even though Democrats and liberals are always more supportive of social welfare policies than Republicans and conservatives, the level of support that exists within the respec-

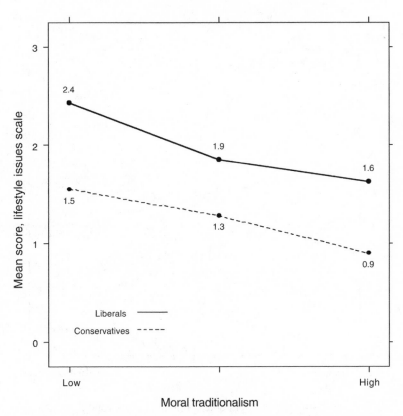

Fig. 9.6. The relationship between lifestyle issue attitudes and moral tradition-alism, controlling for liberal-conservative identification. The number of observations is 869. (Data from 2004 National election Study.)

tive partisan and ideological categories still erodes as we move away from a generalized belief in the need for large, strong government and toward a preference for small, limited government.

To conclude, our analysis shows that coherent, but limited, attitude structures regarding political issues do exist within the mass electorate. These configurations of individual policy preferences are organized in ways that are consistent with the realities of conflict over issues in American politics. In other words, citizens seem to differentiate between foreign policy, lifestyle, and socioeconomic issues. Their responses to the respective areas seem to be connected to more fundamental value orientations. An optimistic interpretation of these findings would be that citizens actually display a capacity for fairly sophisticated political reasoning.

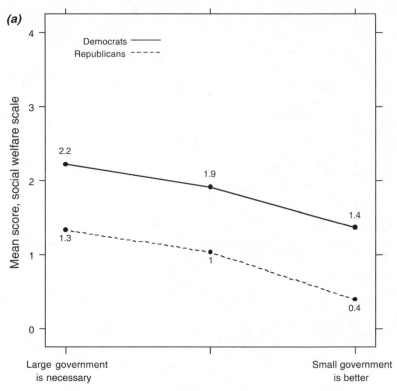

(a)

General beliefs about size & power of government

A more cautious perspective on these results might introduce some caveats: We have seen that separate attitude structures exist for different areas of public policy. The three clusters of attitudes are aligned with partisan loyalties, personal ideological labels, and choices on relevant values. However, there is little evidence for the widespread existence of truly comprehensive belief systems organized according to broad, abstract principles that span the substantive content of specific policy areas and issues. In short, there seems to be little in the way of broad ideology, of a type that would join together an individual's responses to disparate issues. This is true despite the willingness of many people to describe themselves in liberal-conservative terms. At this point, we believe that such an interpretation must be viewed as tentative, contingent upon a more direct analysis of the organizational principles that individuals employ to structure their personal framework of political beliefs

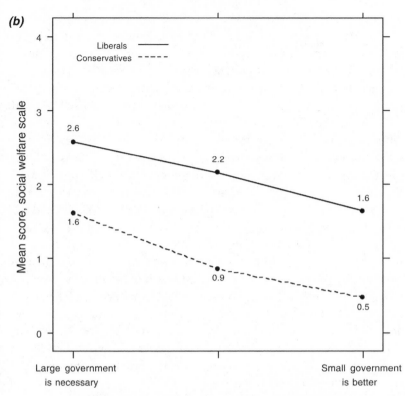

Fig. 9.7. The relationship between social welfare attitudes and feelings about the size and power of government, controlling for party identification and for liberal-conservative identification. (*a*) Controlling for party identification; the number of observations is 951. (*b*) Controlling for ideological self-placement; the number of observations is 757. (Data from 2004 National Election Study.)

and evaluations. That is the precise task that we will take up in the next chapter.

COMMENTARY AND CONTROVERSY

To those first reading this chapter, the results might appear to differ from those reported in *The American Voter*. First, Campbell, Converse, Miller, and Stokes found only two distinct attitude structures—one for foreign policy and the other for domestic socioeconomic issues. Our analysis does produce two attitudinal dimensions that are quite similar to those. But we also find another distinct structure that encompasses lifestyle issues. This may indicate that the substantive scope of mass attitudes is broader in the twenty-first century than it was during the 1950s.

Second, *The American Voter* states, "Not only do the differences in . . . [foreign policy attitudes] fail to correlate with placement on the . . . [domestic policy] dimension; they fail as well to show a correlation with political partisanship in 1956" (198). We find exactly the opposite: The tau-c correlation between individual positions on the foreign policy scale and on the lifestyles scale is a respectable .23, while the correlation (tau-b) between foreign policy attitudes and social welfare attitudes is slightly stronger, at .29.[18] Thus, citizens who prefer an aggressive foreign policy also tend to support more conservative domestic policy, and vice versa.

Our analysis of figures 9.2a and 9.4a established that, unlike the results for 1956, modern foreign policy attitudes are related to individual partisanship. As a reflection of this, the tau-b correlation between the foreign policy scale and the party identification index is .44. The empirical evidence shows that, for the 2004 electorate, opinions on foreign policy are not isolated, unconnected ideas; instead, they are closely consistent with orientations toward domestic issues and partisan loyalties.

Third, the authors of *The American Voter* state unambiguously that citizens' issue attitudes are neither derived from, nor particularly consistent with, ideological principles: "the pattern of responses to our domestic issues is best understood if we discard our notions of ideology and think rather in terms of primitive self-interest" (205), and "conservatism shows a patchwork of negative, positive, and indeterminate relationships with various of the social welfare and domestic items" (211). Again, our empirical results reveal that this is just not the case in the 2004 data. Summarizing the relationships illustrated in figure 9.3, the tau-c correlation between the lifestyles dimension and the ideological self-placement scale is .71, while the tau-b correlation for the social welfare scale and ideological self-placement is .58. The patterns revealed in figures 9.6 and 9.7 further demonstrate that citizens' reactions to the respective sets of public policy issues are rooted in more general value orientations. In other

---

18. In reporting these correlations, and the others to follow, we employ Kendall's tau-b for a bivariate relationship in which each variable has the same number of ordinal categories. If the two variables have different numbers of ordered categories, we use Stuart's tau-c. Also note that we employ the five-category versions of the party identification and ideology variables in the correlations.

words, the evidence from 2004 is not at all inconsistent with the existence of constrained issue attitude structures within the American electorate.

Fourth, *The American Voter* reports that "there is no significant correlation between conservatism and party identification" (211). In contrast, the correlation (tau-b) between ideological self-placement and partisanship in our 2004 data is quite strong, at .62. Admittedly, Campbell et al. used a very different measure of ideology than the one we employ. Theirs was adapted from the work of Herbert McClosky (1958) and focused on individual reactions to change and innovation. Unfortunately, the items necessary for replicating this measure are not available in the 2004 National Election Study. But our scale of moral traditionalism (used in fig. 9.6) is somewhat similar, and its correlation with party identification is also of moderate strength (tau-b = .30). Therefore, we are confident that our different interpretation of the connection between partisanship and ideology is not due merely to changes in the measurement strategies employed for these variables.

The preceding list of apparent differences might lead to the conclusion that nearly every aspect of the findings reported in this chapter stands in contrast to the results obtained by Campbell, Converse, Miller, and Stokes. However, while not wanting to cast doubt about the veracity of our analysis, we do want to point out some reasons for circumspection before accepting any such broad conclusions. For example, as already pointed out, self-identified liberals and conservatives comprise only a bare majority of our respondents. They also represent a subset of the electorate that seems to be particularly attuned to the political world. Therefore, we hesitate to suggest that any of our analyses that employ the ideological self-placement variable (in either an explanatory or control capacity) truly represent the public at large. Individuals who place themselves at nonneutral positions along the liberal-conservative dimension are already displaying an unusual degree of political acumen in doing so. Therefore, the clear empirical connections to issue attitude structures, while very reasonable for this group of citizens, do not say anything about the broad stratum of the electorate that does not view the world through a liberal-conservative lens.

At the same time, it is instructive to consider differences in the kinds of survey questions used to elicit issue attitudes. The analyses in *The American Voter* employed items from the 1956 SRC interview schedule that referred to relatively specific steps that the government should or should not take, such as providing foreign aid to neutral countries; getting tough with Russia (*sic*) and China; providing electrical power; promoting school integration; and so on. In contrast, the issue questions from the 2004 NES interview schedule tend to be phrased in broader terms, referring to government aid to blacks, government spending and services, guaranteed jobs, and defense spending.

The differences in the kinds of issue questions employed in 1956 and in 2004 are potentially important because they may affect the degrees of attitudinal structure that appear to exist within the responses. The earlier SRC questions employed language that often appeared in actual speeches by candidates and in partisan rhetoric. In order to produce consistent responses across issues, survey respondents really had to consider the substantive merits of the respective policies. The more recent NES questions are phrased in ways that transcend particular electoral contexts, in order to facilitate comparisons over time. As a result, they invoke broader political orientations that may "go together" more easily, since respondents do not have to think about detailed policy steps. This may well contribute to our findings of relatively coherent attitude structures. Furthermore, broad policy orientations like these might be psychologically "closer" to more fundamental political loyalties like party identification than are specific policy details; that could help explain our findings on the apparent relationships between issue attitudes and personal partisanship, ideology, and value orientations.

For the preceding reasons, we believe that at least some of the apparent contrasts between our findings and those reported in *The American Voter* are due to differences in the questions that were asked of the respective survey respondents in 1956 and 2004 rather than to fundamental changes in the basic nature of mass political thinking. As was the case with the preconditions for policy voting (back in chap. 8), it does appear that the electorate's degree of attitude structuring on issues has increased somewhat since the 1950s; however, we would argue that our general conclusions remain fairly similar. While Campbell et al. described an electoral environment characterized by a nearly total absence of integrated and consistent attitude structures, we find that the latter do exist, but only within relatively circumscribed subsets of the overall public.

Strategies for Measuring Individual Attitude Structures

The approach used to measure issue attitude structures in *The American Voter* and in most subsequent political science research involves applying a scaling technique to a battery of survey items pertaining to respondents' attitudes on a range of specific issues. Although there is a wide variety of specific scaling procedures that operate in many different ways, they all share a common objective: Scaling methods attempt to combine information from separate variables in order to produce a new variable (or set of variables) that "captures," in some specified way, any common characteristics that the original variables share.

In the present context, our substantive question is whether citizens employ broad evaluative criteria to organize their issue attitudes. In order to answer this question, a scaling technique is applied to survey responses to issue questions. If the analysis does reveal patterned consistency underlying the separate items, we conclude that this empirical structure reflects the underlying sources of attitudinal constraint. The substantive nature of this constraint is inferred from the content of the items that are combined in the scale. Classic treatments of scaling methodology include Torgerson 1958 and Coombs 1964. Maranell (1974) provides a sourcebook covering a number of methods, while Jacoby (1991a), and Dunn-Rankin et al. (2004) provide more recent discussions of scaling strategies.

In this chapter, we use a specific methodology, called "Guttman scaling," to assess constraint in issue attitudes. Our main reason for doing so is that the authors of *The American Voter* used this technique in their own analysis. As explained earlier, Guttman scaling assesses the degree to which a cumulative structure exists among responses to items. This, in turn, enables us to estimate an ordering of both the items and the respondents along a common dimension, if such a dimension actually exists. This technique is named after the mathematical psychologist Louis Guttman, who discovered that cumulative structure can be revealed by the existence of a particular pattern of entries in a data matrix, which he called a "scalogram" (Guttman 1944). Useful discussions of Guttman scaling can be found in Dawes 1972 and McIver and Carmines 1981.

The Guttman scaling approach has two distinct advantages in the present context: First, a Guttman scale is based upon a fairly stringent criterion of unidimensionality. Therefore, it is a relatively cautious approach for deciding whether a common trait or continuum underlies the separate responses. Stated differently, we are less likely to make a type I error and conclude that a common dimension exists when there is no real common structure within the data.

Second, the Guttman scale scores assigned to the individual respondents can be interpreted directly in terms of their responses to the individual survey questions: Specifically, each person's score gives the number of items on which that individual gave a liberal response. Furthermore, the cumulative structure implies that, once we know the number of liberal responses for a given respondent, we should also know exactly which items received those liberal responses (since the scaling method orders the items along the dimension, as well as the respondents). In this sense, we can interpret the Guttman scale scores as succinct summaries of the empirical data. Again, this is a relatively cautious interpretation strategy that does not require tenuous assumptions about the scale being an empirical manifestation of some latent trait.

Despite these two advantages, the methodology behind a Guttman scale is now considered a bit primitive, and the approach is seldom used in the modern research literature. Indeed, it was seldom applied to individual issue attitudes after *The American Voter* (Jacoby 1990), although it has been used occasionally to measure other characteristics, such as political participation (Milbrath 1965) and political trust (Miller 1974). However, even though the specific Guttman scaling technique has fallen into disuse, the cumulative response model remains vitally important and relevant for political research. The latter provides the foundation for an important new area of psychological measurement called item response theory (e.g., Sijtsma and Molenaar 2002; Baker and Kim 2004). Various item response theory methods have been applied to public opinion questions, including individual feelings about abortion (e.g., Andrich 1985), attitudes toward government spending (Jacoby 1994), and citizen ideologies (Treier and Hillygus 2006). More generally, the methods developed by Keith Poole (e.g., 2005) for analyzing legislative roll-call data are fully consistent with a cumulative model, and there is a great deal of work in progress aimed at developing new estimation methods for this model that are applicable to the study of mass political behavior (Jackman 2004). Thus, it seems to be the case that technical aspects of measurement evolve, but basic scholarly conceptions of organization among issue attitudes have remained fairly stable.

While modern item response theory models may represent the cutting-edge methodologies for assessing attitude structure, they have not appeared very frequently in the research literature so far. Instead, the most common approach for measuring attitude structure relies upon one or both of two related methods: Principal components analysis (PCA) and factor analysis (FA). Both of these strategies begin with a relatively large set of issue attitude variables. PCA seeks to find a smaller number of composite variables (i.e., weighted sums of the original variables)—called "components"—that encompass as much of the variance in the original set of items as possible. FA tries to find a small set of latent (i.e., unobserved) variables—called "factors"—whose common impact on the observed variables data generates intercorrelations among them.

There are enormous literatures on both of these methodological strategies; Bartholomew et al. (2002) provide an accessible introduction to both principal components and factor analysis that highlights the similarities and differences among the techniques, as well as their relationships to the IRT models discussed above. Although they really are different from each other in a number of ways, the empirical results produced by PCA and FA usually appear to be quite similar when they are applied to the same data. Speaking informally, if the original issue attitude variables are highly correlated with each other, then it will be possible to summarize the data very effectively, using a small number of components (in PCA) or factors (in FA). This, in turn, is usually interpreted as evidence regarding the degree of attitudinal constraint manifested by the survey respondents. Again, the nature of that constraint is determined by looking for interpretable patterns in the ways that the empirical variables are related to the components or factors.

Principal components and factor analysis have been used very frequently to study the structure of issue attitudes over the past four decades. Some representative examples of these analyses, spanning the time period, include Luttbeg 1968; Stimson 1975; Nie, Verba, and Petrocik 1979; Gopoian 1982; Peffley and Hurwitz 1985; Abramowitz 1994; Davis, Dowley, and Silver 1999; Layman and Carsey 2002; and Goren 2004. It is interesting to note that, although they produce very different kinds of output, the attitude structures revealed by PCA and FA are often very similar to the results generated by Guttman scaling and related procedures. For example, factor analysis of the 2004 NES issue items reveals almost exactly the same three-dimensional configuration of attitudes as those encompassed in the Guttman scales discussed earlier in this chapter. Such similarities in the results are important and reassuring, because they suggest that the empirical findings are fairly robust, and not merely methodological artifacts due to the use of particular analytic or statistical techniques.

Attitude Constraint at the Aggregate Level

Four years after the *The American Voter,* Philip Converse (1964) published an enormously influential essay titled "The Nature of Belief Systems in Mass Publics." This work will be discussed, in greater detail, in the "Commentary and Controversy" section in chapter 10. For now, however, it is relevant because the analysis contained therein altered the dominant approach that political scientists used for measuring attitudinal constraint. Whereas *The American Voter* focused on the extent to which individual responses on a battery of issue questions conform to common structures, Converse examined tables of pairwise intercorrelations among the separate attitude items. While this is a different way to operationalize constraint, the logic behind it is identical to the arguments laid out earlier in this chapter: If people really do rely upon broad judgmental principles for structuring their issue attitudes, then we should find that they take similar positions across issues. If an abstract evaluative standard—presumably of an ideological nature—leads an individual to take a liberal stand on one policy controversy, then he or she should also be guided to similar positions on other policy questions as well. The net result would be reasonably consistent—in a word, correlated—positions across the full set of issues. Conversely (pun intended!), lack of consistency—that is, low correlations—across survey items would signal that people are not using a consistent criterion to select their positions on different issues.

Converse's analysis (1964) produced stark results. By any standards, the empirical intercorrelations of citizens' issue responses were very low. For example, the mean absolute value of the coefficients was .16. Compared to a maximum possible correlation of 1.00, this average seems to suggest that citizens' attitudes approximate a state of random variation, rather than consistency. Converse also provided a more concrete standard for evaluating mass-level attitude constraint by comparing the preceding intercorrelations with those obtained from a sample of political elites (defined as candidates in congressional elections). For the latter, the mean absolute correlation coefficient (calculated across all pairs from the same set of issues) was .34. While still not very large by absolute standards, this average correlation suggests that political elites are much more consistent than "ordinary" citizens in their professed policy stands.

The rather pessimistic conclusion of unconstrained issue attitudes within the mass public remained the dominant scholarly view throughout the 1960s. However, this changed in the 1970s, when Nie and Andersen (1974) replicated Converse's strategy of examining pairwise correlations among issue attitudes, using Survey Research Center data from a sequence of presidential election years. Their results showed that the intercorrelations were very low in 1956 and 1960 (i.e., the same general period of time covered by Converse's analysis). However, they shot upward in 1964, and remained quite high through 1972. Nie, Verba, and Petrocik (1979) carried out a more detailed analysis of the same data, and confirmed that the higher correlations continued on into 1976.

Nie and his colleagues also went further, by demonstrating that these apparent heightened levels of constraint were not due to changes in the American electorate itself (e.g., increasing education levels, generational replacement, the influx of new social groups like African Americans and 18- to 21-year-olds). Instead, they conclude that the higher levels of consistency across issue positions is due to clearer "packages" of issues in the public agenda. That is, citizens simply found it easier to make connections between the various issues that were salient during the 1960s and 1970s (e.g., civil rights, antipoverty programs, urban strife, Vietnam, changing lifestyles, etc.) than with the more distant and abstract policy concerns of the 1950s (e.g., domestic communism, nuclear weapons, the threat of war, etc.). Of course, this is entirely consistent with the theoretical explanations for the rise of issue voting, which were discussed in "Commentary and Controversy" in chapter 8. While there were some skeptics at the time (e.g., Margolis 1977; Bishop and Frankovic 1981), the scholarly consensus did seem to accept that a rise in attitudinal constraint genuinely did occur within the mass public.

Despite the long-standing prominence and continuing importance of the constraint concept in the scholarly debates on ideological thinking (e.g., Kinder 2006), empirical analyses based upon intercorrelations of survey questions on issues have now largely disappeared from the research literature. The reasons for this shift in focus (which occurred quite suddenly in the late 1970s) are primarily methodological in nature. Perhaps most important, several teams of researchers argued that the apparent increase in ideological constraint that occurred in the mid-1960s was due almost entirely to changes in the survey items that were used to elicit attitudes from respondents (e.g., Bishop, Tuchfarber, and Oldendick 1978; Brunk 1978; Sullivan, Piereson, and Marcus 1978). Experimental evidence, using several versions of a common interview schedule in a public opinion survey, shows that seemingly innocuous variations in question wording have major effects on the consistency in responses across separate issues. As might be expected, the proponents of the "revisionist" view (i.e., that mass-level issue constraint did increase during the 1960s) disagreed with their critics, and the result was a series of fairly sharp exchanges on the topic within the pages of some leading professional journals (Nie and Rabjohn 1979; Sullivan et al. 1979; Bishop et al. 1979; Judd and Milburn 1980; Converse 1980). The most recent consensus seems to be that it is hazardous to attempt comparisons of attitude structures between the kinds of items employed in the early SRC surveys and those included in the more recent National Election Studies instruments (Bishop 2005).

A second methodological critique focuses on the use of correlation coefficients to measure attitudinal constraint. Barton and Parsons (1977) and Wyckoff (1980) both point out that doing so involves a sort of ecological inference problem. Correlation is inherently a characteristic of an aggregate body (e.g., the electorate, or some stratum within it). But attitudinal constraint is a characteristic of an individual's belief system. These researchers argue that high levels of individual-level constraint could easily be accompanied by only modest correlations between issue variables. Once again, the earlier evidence (i.e., intercorrelations) used to demonstrate the absence or presence of attitude structure within the electorate is suspect, for technical reasons.

A third problem is that the use of attitudinal consistency—regardless how it is measured—may not be a particularly valid measure of attitudinal structure in the first place. Several researchers have shown that attitude consistency levels are not very strongly related to other measures of ideological awareness or political sophistication (e.g., Converse 1975; Wray 1979; Wyckoff 1987). The latter are widely regarded as manifestations of structured attitudes (e.g., Luskin 1987). Hence, attitude consistency fails to achieve acceptable standards of criterion or convergent validity.

Finally, there is a conceptual issue: Recent scholars have recognized that "constraint" involves the dependence of specific issue attitudes on more general underlying principles; for example, the degree to which attitudes are consistent with the liberal-conservative continuum (e.g., Peffley and Hurwitz 1985; Jacoby 1991b; Miller and Shanks 1996). Of course, this is not a new idea; Converse articulated precisely this position in "The Nature of Belief Systems in Mass Publics." Nevertheless, such an interpretation implies that the empirical intercorrelations among responses are actually spurious and due to their common dependence on the same organizational dimension. As such, these correlations are not particularly interesting in themselves.

Attitude Stability

"The Nature of Belief Systems in Mass Publics" also introduced another standard for assessing structure within citizens' issue attitudes. Converse argued that a tightly constrained belief system provides a relatively stable perspective from which an individual can think about major questions of public policy. In turn, this should produce responses to issue questions that are relatively stable over time (Converse 1964, 1970, 1975).

The empirical evidence seems to demand a very different conclusion. Continuity correlations (mostly calculated from panel study data collected in 1956–60 and 1972–76) for most issues are uniformly very low, except on those few matters that arouse particularly strident, emotional responses (e.g., race in the 1950s and moral issues in the 1970s). The coefficient values are not only very weak in absolute terms. They are also dwarfed by the much greater stability that seems to exist in other political orientations, such as party identification and candidate evaluations (Converse 1970; Converse and Markus 1979).

Of course, the low correlations could be a manifestation of reasoned individual responses to external changes in the political environment. But that does not seem to be the case: The patterns of movement across issue positions appear to be haphazard, rather than systematic, with a great deal of "flip-flopping" from liberal to conservative positions, and back again. Converse concluded that no single process could be operating uniformly throughout the mass public to produce such unpredictable patterns. Instead, he proposed a "black and white model" in which the general public is composed of two distinct segments of people: (1) a set of individuals with perfectly stable issue attitudes; and (2) a set of individuals whose positions change randomly over time. The size of the first subset varies from one issue to the next (generally getting larger as the substantive content of the issue becomes more laden with emotional symbolism, and less focused on socioeconomic conflict); but regardless of the policy question, there always appears to be a significant number of people who have no meaningful personal preferences about alternative courses of governmental action—in short, they possess "nonattitudes" on the issue.

The empirical evidence is sufficiently unambiguous that the existence of widespread, random turnover in mass opinion has never been questioned very seriously. Instead, critics of the black-and-white model have focused on exactly how the low continuity correlations should be interpreted. A number of researchers argue that the survey items used by the SRC/NES to elicit issue attitudes are extremely unreliable. Accordingly, the answers provided by the respondents to these surveys contain a sizable amount of random "noise" variability. The latter will, in turn, mask any underlying stability that actually may exist in issue attitudes (e.g., Pierce and Rose 1974; Achen 1975; Judd and Milburn 1980; Krosnick 1991). From this perspective, the sources of temporal instability lie with the survey questions rather than with the survey respondents.

The low reliability levels that are central to the latter interpretation surely do exist. But Converse has responded that they could just as easily be due to noncrystallized attitudes among the survey respondents as to vague issue statements and response alternatives in the survey questions (e.g., Converse 1974, 1980; Converse and Markus 1979). The data employed in the analyses cited above provide no way to disentangle these two distinctly different possibilities.

The overall problem of "allocating" response instability to respondents or to questions was addressed by Norpoth and Lodge (1985). Their empirical results (based upon observations of panel survey data, with respondents stratified by levels of political sophistication) indicate that both sources contribute to low levels of temporal stability: Survey questions on political issues invariably contain nonnegligible amounts of random measurement error. Still, sophisticated respondents exhibit more stable issue attitudes than do nonsophisticated respondents.

Scholarly analyses continue to be carried out on stability and reliability in survey questions on issues (e.g., Krosnick 1991; Krosnick and Berent 1993). Much of the recent work raises additional challenges to the basic black-and-white model originally proposed by Converse. For example, Hill and Kriesi (2001) suggest that an accurate model of temporal change in mass issue attitudes must allow for "durable changers" as well as perfectly stable and perfectly random subsets of the overall public. Working from a quite different perspective, Lacy (2001) argues that empirical assessments of stability are affected by the existence of nonseparable preferences, which lead survey respondents to give varying answers to questions about a single issue, depending upon their responses to questions about a different issue. According to this theory, the very notion of temporally stable attitudes on issues must be called into question. Taber and Lodge (2006) also show that prior beliefs cause asymmetries in the ways people process new incoming information, leading to further changes that would decrease the correlations over time, even as they lead to greater polarization in attitude distributions. Finally, the prevalence of weakly held opinions on public policy—basically, the nonattitudes that produce the random component of the black-and-white model—comprises a central component in an influential current theory about the general dynamics of public opinion (Zaller 1992). To summarize, the current research literature does not really question the existence of seemingly unstable issue attitudes. However, it has provided a number of potential explanations for the changes that occur over time, apart from the widespread existence of nonattitudes within the mass public.

Ideological Self-Placements and Issue Attitudes

The analysis presented in this chapter follows the lead of *The American Voter* in suggesting that ideology—particularly, an individual's stance along a liberal-conservative continuum—should function as a particularly effective source of attitudinal constraint. Given this emphasis, it is somewhat ironic that the SRC data used by Campbell et al. did not include a direct measure of respondents' personal ideological positions! In fact, ideological self-placements were not included in the SRC/NES interview schedules until 1972. But starting in that year, they have employed a "graphical scale" for this purpose. That is, respondents are handed a card showing a line segment with seven labeled and numbered points (from 1 for "extremely liberal" to 7 for "extremely conservative"). Then they are asked to place themselves and several other political figures (usually, the major party presidential candidates and the two parties) along the scale.

Such liberal-conservative identification questions seem to provide fairly detailed information about survey respondents' positions along a single summary dimension of political conflict. But it is important to recognize some potential limitations with this item. For example, many of the NES respondents (typically, about one-fourth) fail to locate themselves along the liberal-conservative continuum, stating that they "haven't thought much about this." Furthermore, a sizable proportion of those who are willing to place themselves select the neutral midpoint (typically, one-third).

More generally, respondents' placements along the seven-point ideology scale are completely subjective; there is absolutely no attempt to specify the "correct" political views associated with the liberal or conservative positions. Of course, this separation between ideological labels and their substantive implications is intentional. But it does raise questions about the quality and exact meaning of the responses to the ideology question.

Despite any such reservations, the current scholarly consensus holds that ideological orientations do serve as an important influence on issue attitudes (Jacoby 1991b, 1995, 2002). As mentioned in "Commentary and Controversy" in chapter 8, this basic finding has been replicated across a broad variety of substantive policy controversies, and it seems to exist regardless of the immediate content of the current issue agenda confronting American society (Fleishman 1986). In fact, newly emerging policy conflicts like race or civil rights, lifestyle concerns, nuclear power, and religious influence in social life have conformed to, rather than supplanted, traditional ideological distinctions (e.g., Nie, Verba, and Petrocik 1979; Kuklinski, Metlay, and Kay 1982; Carmines and Stimson 1989; Gamson and Modigliani 1989; Layman and Carsey 2002).

A general explanation for ideology's pervasive impact on issue attitudes can be found in symbolic politics theory (e.g., Sears 1993, 2001). This holds that liberal-conservative identifications constitute a broad and largely nontangible predisposition for most citizens—that is, a stable, affective outlook that originates in childhood socialization and persists, largely unchanged, into adult political life (Sears 1983). The connection between general ideological positions and specific issue attitudes depends upon the fact that virtually all political issues are defined in highly symbolic terms (e.g., Edelman 1964). The predominant symbols of American political culture (e.g., freedom, liberty, equal opportunity, etc.) comprise a highly salient element of the political environment confronting the mass public (Bennett 1980) and they have been remarkably stable over time (Devine 1972; McClosky and Zaller 1984). So it is easy for people to adopt those issue positions on which the symbolic content matches their own liberal-conservative predispositions.

In this manner, ideology operates on a nearly emotional level, triggering habitual responses to stimuli in the political environment. Symbolic politics theory thus provides a parsimonious explanation for the existence of an ideological bias within American public opinion. It does so without requiring that individual citizens' belief systems be tightly organized or structured along detailed liberal-conservative lines.

Other Sources of Structure in Issue Attitudes

Of course, ideology is not the only possible way for citizens to organize their issue attitudes. In fact, *The American Voter* itself identified a second potential structuring mechanism—personal attachments to political parties. The general arguments about the impact of party identification on attitudes are quite similar to those given above for ideological self-placements. Partisanship provides individuals with a stable reference point for evaluating the political world. In effect, incoming information is passed through a "perceptual screen" that enables each person to interpret issues according to their own partisan proclivities; policy stands associated with prominent leaders from an individual's own party constitute powerful influences on that person's own attitude with respect to those same policy issues (e.g., Miller 1976).

Admittedly, a number of scholars have questioned both the strength of the connection between party identification and issue attitudes (Searing, Schwartz, and Lind 1973) and the direction of that relationship (e.g., Jackson 1975; Page and Jones 1979; Macdonald, Rabinowitz, and Brasher 2003). But researchers have identified a number of theoretical perspectives that specify a causal linkage moving from partisanship to issues (e.g., Goren 2005). These include schema theory (Lodge and Hamill 1986), reference group theory (Jacoby 1988a), and social identity theory (Green, Palmquist, and Schickler 2002; Weisberg and Greene 2003). Note also that Sears and his colleagues consider party identification to be one of the symbolic predispositions that influence issue attitudes, along with ideology. More recently, Tomz and Sniderman (2005) argue that partisanship supplies a "brand name" through which citizens can easily make connections (and, thereby, establish constraint) across various separate policy domains. Thus, there are several specific mechanisms and processes through which party identification could affect the structure of issue attitudes.

Individual choices among core values provide another set of general orientations that may influence the structure of attitudes on specific issues. In this context, values can be defined as each individual's abstract, general conceptions about the desirable and undesirable end states of human life. Presumably, values guide an individual's reactions to the world, by helping to define what is "good" and what is "bad" in the external environment (e.g., Rokeach 1973). In this capacity, values provide a potential structuring mechanism for citizens' political orientations. Values are within everyone's mental grasp, so they could be employed as a general evaluative standard for reactions to issues (Schwartz 1992). This process is facilitated by the fact that the rhetoric on issues confronting the public is, itself, almost always phrased in terms of values

(Stone 1997). Thus, individual citizens do not even need to make the connection between issues and values on their own; instead, it is often done for them by issue entrepreneurs and opinion leaders.

Given the obvious connections between values and politics, it is perhaps a bit surprising that researchers have only recently given serious attention to the possible connections between value preferences and issue attitudes (e.g., Kinder 1983). For example, Peffley and Hurwitz (1985) suggested that the influence of ideology actually works indirectly, by shaping value orientations that then impinge on individual reactions to specific issues. Feldman (1988) goes a bit further, arguing that feelings about core values may take the place of ideological principles in organizing political attitudes for many citizens within the mass public. Research by Goren (2001, 2004) is consistent with the latter interpretation because it shows that the influence of values is fairly uniform throughout the electorate (unlike ideological principles, which generally show stronger effects among more sophisticated strata of the public). The apparent effects of values are also quite broad, encompassing attitudes on a wide variety of substantive issues, including foreign policy (Hurwitz and Peffley 1987), race relations (Kinder and Sanders 1996), welfare (Gilens 1999; Feldman and Steenbergen 2001a), campaign finance (Rudolph and Grant 2003), and government spending (Jacoby 2006).

Despite the preceding positive evidence, scholars have also raised questions about the relevance of personal values to public opinion. For example, both psychologists and political scientists have noticed that relationships between values and attitudes are sometimes contradictory, weak, or even nonexistent (e.g., Kristiansen and Hotte 1996; McCarty and Shrum 2000; Kinder and Mendelberg 2000; Sears, Henry, and Kosterman 2000). There is also a great deal of ambiguity about which values need to be taken into account (Kuklinski 2001). Many analysts rely on principles drawn from the classical liberalism of John Locke, such as liberty, freedom, individualism, and equality (e.g., McClosky and Zaller 1984; Markus 2001). Others stress the importance of additional ideas drawn from contemporary American political culture, such as moral traditionalism (McCann 1997) and humanitarianism (Feldman and Steenbergen 2001b). Finally, there has been some doubt expressed about the basic conceptual status of values, raising the possibility that they might be relatively shallow "truisms" rather than fundamental building blocks of human behavior (Maio and Olson 1998). Recognizing this troublesome lack of clear theoretical underpinnings, Feldman (2003) concludes that "political psychologists . . . incorporate values into their research in a piecemeal fashion" (503).

Factors That Work against Coherence in Attitude Structures

So far, the discussion in this chapter has focused on the possible sources of organization and structure in issue attitudes. But it is important to emphasize that the predominant view, from the earliest modern considerations of public opinion (Lippmann 1925) up to the relatively recent scholarship (e.g., Smith 1989), has stressed the general lack of coherence in citizens' reactions to policy issues. For the most part, the research literature has simply attributed haphazard patterns in public opinion to low levels of political sophistication within the electorate (e.g., Luskin 1987, 1990). More recently, however, analysts have identified systematic factors operating apart from (and, sometimes, in opposition to) sophistication that may lead to combinations of attitudes that appear to be mutually contradictory or disorganized.

For example, feelings of ambivalence seem to be widespread in Americans' political opinions (e.g., Martinez, Craig, and Kane 2005). Attitudinal ambivalence is usually defined as holding strong, but contradictory, beliefs about some stimulus object (Thompson, Zanna, and Griffin 1995). With respect to issue attitudes, ambivalence exists when an individual recognizes that both positive and negative consequences are associated with a particular policy stand. Since ambivalent feelings, by definition, "pull" a person in two directions simultaneously, they will almost certainly reduce the overall degree of consistency across attitudes on different issues.

Political scientists and psychologists have shown that ambivalence can result in several empirical manifestations that have been associated traditionally with poorly structured attitudes. For example, ambivalent attitudes exhibit lower levels of temporal stability than nonambivalent attitudes (Craig, Martinez, and Kane 2005). This may occur, at least in part, because ambivalent attitudes are more open to persuasion (Armitage and Conner 2000). At the same time, ambivalence inhibits the effects of the various structuring mechanisms discussed above; that is, ambivalence makes it more difficult to predict attitudes on the basis of party identification, ideological self-placement, and value choices (Alvarez and Brehm 2002).

The impact of ambivalence is not uniform throughout the mass public. In fact, its effects may well be strongest among relatively sophisticated strata. The reasoning here is that one must, in the first place, recognize that two competing considerations are both relevant to a single attitude before it is possible to feel conflict because of those considerations. Thus, a person must understand that abortion pits the sanctity of human life against freedom of choice, in order to feel ambivalent about that issue, or that welfare requires a balance of egalitarian feelings against individual self-determination (e.g., Alvarez and Brehm 1995; Gainous and Martinez 2005).

There may also be a political bias in the distribution of ambivalence throughout the electorate: Feldman and Zaller (1992) argue that liberals' attitudes toward the modern American welfare state are affected by mixed feelings to a much greater extent than are conservatives' attitudes. The net result is that liberals' policy preferences seem to be more weakly held. Thus, recent research demonstrates that ambivalence reduces the clarity of attitude structures in ways that are quite separate from factors like education, knowledge, political involvement, and so on.

Finally, it appears that the inconsistencies that do exist between ideological loyalties and specific attitudes in American public opinion are themselves unevenly distributed. By modern standards, ideological consistency exists when self-identified liberals prefer active governmental activity to ameliorate social problems and self-identified conservatives prefer solutions that remain in the private sector. As the discussion so far has emphasized, only a subset of the mass public typically shows this kind of consistency. But among those exhibiting ideologically inconsistent opinions, self-labeled conservatives who prefer activist governmental policies far outnumber self-identified liberals who want private-sector solutions.

This asymmetry in ideological inconsistencies has been noticed as a fairly regular feature of American public opinion, at least since the 1960s (Free and Cantril 1967; Bennett and Bennett 1990; Cantril and Cantril 1999). Stimson (2004) calls those citizens who exhibit this combination of ideological labels and policy preferences "conflicted conservatives." At this point, the sources of this conflicted conservatism are not clear, and research continues on this general topic (Stimson and Ellis 2005).

Conflicted conservatives are particularly interesting because their electoral responses are likely to vary depending upon the kinds of campaign rhetoric articulated by parties and candidates. Stimson (2004) argues that Republican elites can gain their support through symbolic appeals (where their conservative self-labels come to the forefront), while

Democratic leaders can mobilize them by references to specific policies (where their preferences for government action dominate). Thus, it seems likely that conflicted conservatives make a disproportionate contribution to electoral change over time. More generally, this phenomenon is comparable to the previously discussed ambivalence, in that an empirical pattern (i.e., inconsistency between ideological identification and issue attitudes) that is often attributed to a lack of sophistication within the electorate actually turns out to have systematic consequences for understanding the dynamics of American politics.

In conclusion, the findings from this chapter are distinctive compared to those in other chapters of the book, in that they differ from the results reported in *The American Voter*. Where the latter emphasized unconstrained issue attitudes, we find several sources of structure underlying citizens' policy preferences. As the discussion in this "Commentary and Controversy" section should make clear, our data are quite consistent with the general thrust of the research literature over the past few decades. While our analysis has not really tried to explain why our findings differ from those obtained by Campbell et al., it seems reasonable to assume that differences in the external political environment play a major role. Specifically, it is sometimes asserted that *The American Voter* was based upon data obtained during a quiescent era in American politics (e.g., Nie, Verba, and Petrocik 1979). It may well be that our own analysis is rooted in a time when conflict over issues and polarization over policies are especially pronounced (e.g., Layman and Carsey 2002; McCarty, Poole, and Rosenthal 2006).

CHAPTER 10

The Formation of Issue Concepts and Partisan Change

Commentaries on American electoral politics routinely invoke ideological terminology in order to account for election outcomes and patterns of voting behavior. For example, strong performances by Republican candidates, such as those in the elections of 1994 and 2002, are often viewed as evidence that the public favors conservative approaches and solutions to the policy issues facing society. In contrast, Democratic victories (such as those in the 1992 or 1996 presidential elections, and the 2006 midterm elections) are heralded as manifestations of popular preferences for more vigorous governmental action to address salient problems. The discussion often becomes quite complex, with analysts looking in detail at the fortunes of, and friction between, the more extreme and relatively moderate factions within each of the major parties.

Of course, widespread attention to ideology does not necessarily imply a consensus regarding explanations for election results. A strong Democratic showing at the polls may indicate that the public has become more liberal in its preferences. Or it may reflect increased extremism within the Republican Party. Or it may suggest that Democrats have moderated their own traditionally liberal stands. To state the problem in more general terms, an electoral outcome may be generated by movements within the electorate, by one party, by both parties, or by any combination of these actors. To further complicate matters, there may be additional factors that trump ideological considerations: When confronted by poor governmental performance (manifested by lack of progress in addressing domestic or foreign issues), voters may consciously ignore their liberal-conservative proclivities and simply "vote the rascals out."

Despite the different conclusions implied by the preceding accounts, the latter all reflect the fundamental assumption that an ideological continuum provides a reasonable baseline for evaluating American elections. This, in turn, presupposes that the electorate is (1) aware of its own position along a dimension that ranges from liberal policy alternatives on the left to conservative policy alternatives on the right; (2) reasonably cognizant of the parties' locations along the same continuum; and (3) sensitive to significant movements by any of the major actors—significant groups of voters, political parties, and candidates—that may occur over time. The notion of a continuum is also important. It is not merely the case that voters, parties, and candidates are simply ordered to the left or right of each other. Instead, there is a clear sense that the actual distance of each party or candidate from its relevant constituency figures into the voting calculus.

But is this idea of an ideological baseline a realistic or useful way to think about the political behavior of the American electorate? The evidence on this point obtained so far from our own analysis is mixed. The discussion in the previous chapter shows that, within one subset of the mass public, attitudes toward domestic issues are structured in a way that is consistent with the liberal-conservative continuum. So it might appear that there is an ideological cast to some citizens' view of political objects. But this occurs in barely half of the electorate. And even this degree of apparent ideological structure could simply reflect the way that political stimuli are presented by partisan actors and transmitted through the mass media, rather than any active liberal-conservative thinking on the part of individual citizens. Recall our earlier consideration of the preconditions for issue voting, which suggested that a sizable element within the electorate experience difficulties in translating their policy preferences into specific choices among the candidates. Those results could indicate that many citizens are not adept in dealing with the relative positioning of political stimuli along policy-related dimensions. So it remains to be seen whether individual voters actually do bring explicit ideological concepts to bear on their own electoral decisions.

Pursuing this line of thinking, we also have to consider alternative viewpoints that people may bring to bear on the political world, apart from ideology. For example, we have already mentioned performance evaluations as a judgmental standard. And it is conceivable that some individuals evaluate parties and candidates in terms of their impact on personal life situations. To generalize this latter perspective a bit: politics is often discussed in group terms, so it is reasonable to expect that some citizens view elections as contests with potential rewards or penalties for the reference or membership groups that are prominent in their own lives. And still other citizens may simply think about voting choices in terms of the candidates' own personal characteristics.

We do not think that the use of alternative judgmental standards will necessarily lead to behaviors that differ systematically from those that would stem from ideological voting. Thus, an ideologue might vote for Republican candidates because of a general preference for private-sector rather than governmental solutions to social problems. At the same time, a business executive might support the same Republican candidates because the party platform promises to roll back regulations on industrial production. And a performance-motivated voter might observe that Democratic incumbents have not had much success at fostering economic growth, thereby prompting another vote for the Republicans. In each case, the immediate, tangible outcome is the same—electoral support for the Republican Party. But the motivations that led to this result differ from one voter to the next.

Aggregating such individual decisions to the level of the entire electorate, we believe that it is necessary to determine the evaluative standards that voters employ in order to accurately interpret any "messages" or mandates that might be conveyed by a given electoral result. For example, George W. Bush has interpreted his victories in the 2000 and 2004 presidential elections as a mandate for sweeping conservative policy initiatives. But such an interpretation would be questionable, at best, if the American electorate acted on the basis of other, nonideological, considerations. Therefore, the analytic objective in this chapter is to determine precisely what judgmental criteria citizens use when thinking about parties and candidates before their voting decisions.

THE FORMATION OF POLITICAL CONCEPTS WITHIN THE MASS PUBLIC

In our attempt to understand the ways that citizens approach the political world, we will rely upon a general idea drawn from the field of social cognition. That is, individuals develop their own information-processing routines, or habitual ways of interpreting new stimuli that confront them in the mass media and through social interactions. A "mental habit" of this sort is sometimes called a "schema," although it is important to point out that this specific term has been the focus of some controversy and has fallen out of general usage in the political science literature. Nevertheless, it remains a useful starting point for our investigation. Psychologist Susan Fiske writes,

> A schema is a cognitive structure that contains a concept's attributes and the links among those attributes. . . . When a person responds schematically, the person draws on organized prior knowledge to aid the understanding of new information. A new person, event, or issue is treated as an instance of an already familiar category or schema. Representative Geraldine Ferraro [the Democratic vice-presidential candidate in 1984] could be viewed as an instance of a northeastern urban Democrat, a typical glad-handing politician, a harebrained female, or a pragmatic feminist. Whichever schema one applies, it enables one to focus on schema-relevant information and to ignore irrelevant information in forming an impression of her. (1986, 42–43)

Fiske's description covers exactly the kind of information that we seek to recover from individual citizens within the electorate. What cognitive structures do they bring to bear on parties and candidates? Into what conceptual categories do they place the candidates, parties, and other stimuli that emerge during an election campaign?

Again, we believe that these are important questions because their answers delimit the kinds of interpretations that can be applied to the outcomes of American elections. If we find, for instance, that a sizable segment of the electorate actively thinks about political stimuli in liberal-conservative terms, then the kinds of ideological prognostications that occur so frequently in journalistic political discourse would be reasonable ways to present American politics and elections. But if most people use other categories to organize their beliefs about parties and candidates, then ideological interpretations would be mere impositions created by the commentators. The important—indeed, critical—point is that the nature of mass-level political thinking is an empirical question.

Unfortunately, we encounter formidable obstacles when we try to uncover the organizational foundations of citizens' political beliefs. For one thing, we cannot simply ask people directly, because most individuals have minimal awareness of their own mental processes. At the same time, we are hesitant to gauge the nature of individuals' cognitive structures from their responses to closed-ended survey questions. A person's willingness or ability to place specified stimuli (e.g., the major political parties and current presidential candidates) within predefined categories (e.g., at ordered positions along a liberal-conservative continuum) while answering an interviewer's queries does not indicate whether they do so when left to their own thoughts.

In order to avoid the preceding problems, we will use survey respondents' own words to provide insights regarding the evaluative standards that they employ in thinking about politics. Specifically, we will go once again to the now-familiar series of open-ended questions asking respondents what they like and dislike about the major parties and their presidential candidates. Previously, in chapters 3, 4, and 6, we used these items to construct measures of partisan attitudes. Here, we will use them differently, to gain insights about the ways people organize their own political thinking. The responses are recorded nearly verbatim. If people really do rely upon particular evaluative standards or judgmental routines for thinking about political stimuli, then their nature should be revealed through the terms and phrases these individuals use to describe their own reactions to prominent elements within the political world—that is, the parties and the candidates.

The immediate analytic task is to develop a taxonomy that differentiates among the survey respondents according to the organizational principles underlying their political cognitive structures. As we will see, this entails a reasonably straightforward coding task, albeit one that is rather tedious in the execution: The transcripts of the open-ended responses are read to determine whether (1) particular terms and themes appear in the comments provided by individual respondents, and (2) the terms and themes can themselves be placed into a reasonably small number of categories, based upon the general ideas the respondents are expressing. The great advantage of this approach is that the basic data for the taxonomy emanates from the respondents themselves. Therefore, so long as the categories accurately differentiate the content of their likes and dislikes, we can be reasonably certain that the taxonomy reflects variation in the ways these citizens really do think about the political world, and not a preconceived organizational scheme imposed by scholarly researchers.

As we will see, there are some clear-cut differences in the structure of political ideas within the mass public. One subset of citizens does think about politics in broad, abstract terms that seem consistent with standard depictions of liberal-conservative ideology. But a second, and somewhat larger, component of the public organizes its thinking according to salient groups within their personal environments. A third subset associates political actors with good and bad conditions in society and the world at large. And, finally, there is a fourth subset—almost a residual category—composed of people who appear to think about politics in terms that are completely separate from any policy considerations at all.

It is important to emphasize that we believe the differences between the preceding four sets of citizens to be qualitative in nature. They represent categorical variations in the basic mental objects that are most salient to the ways people conceptualize the political world and, particularly, electoral competition. Nevertheless, there does seem to be an implicit ordering subsumed within our classification scheme. As we move from the first through the fourth subsets, the organizational principles that define the groupings vary systematically in the scope and generality of their content. For this reason, we believe it is more accurate to depict our scheme as levels of political conceptualization, rather than mere nominal distinctions.

Before proceeding to our definitions and discussion of these conceptual levels, it is important to lay out several of the potential problems and biases that we encountered—but, hopefully, avoided—while constructing our taxonomy. First, our classification is strictly based upon the thinking revealed in the respondents' comments and not the partisan implications or conclusions that they produce. So, for example, a person who likes the Democratic Party because of its liberal policy proposals is placed in the same level as an individual who dislikes the Democratic Party on the same grounds. Both cases manifest a similar use of an ideological continuum even though these specific individuals probably fall at different positions along that dimension.

A second, and closely related, point is that the type of thinking used to define each of our conceptual levels can encompass a wide variety of substantive content. For example, a person who favors the Democratic Party because of its support for minority groups is included in a common category with a person who favors the Republican Party because of its pro-business policies. In each case, the respondents are using a prominent reference group as a benchmark for their political thinking. The fact that they employ completely different kinds of groups is far less important to our objectives than the common group-based nature of the organizational principles employed by these individuals.

Third, our coding rules place little emphasis on the "objective" accuracy of the respondents' comments. So a person who likes the Republican presidential candidate because of that candidate's liberal views is not necessarily placed into a different level from the person who dislikes the same candidate because of his conservative policy stands. For one thing, there is usually enough ambiguity in the political that it is often difficult to specify the "true" nature of things. But, more generally, as long as each person's comments provide reasonable evidence that they are relying on a general ideological standard to produce the respective evaluations, we believe they are conceptualizing politics according to a common type of viewing perspective—even though each person uses that perspective differently in each case. Note, however, that the question of accuracy is largely moot; in carrying out the actual coding, we found virtually no examples of comments that would be regarded as egregious misrepresentations from the perspective of a highly sophisticated observer.

Fourth, we were very careful to remove from consideration the degrees of enthusiasm, loquacity, and verbal ability exhibited by the respondents. Once again, it is the nature of the organizational principle, rather than the elegance with which that principle is articulated, that determines the conceptual level to which each respondent is assigned. At the same time, it seems possible that broad abstract conceptualizations may well be communicated very efficiently, perhaps making additional statements about a given party or candidate largely unnecessary. For these kinds of reasons, neither the overall number of likes and dislikes expressed by each respondent nor the grammatical quality of the specific statements was systematically involved in the classification.

DIFFERENCES IN POLITICAL CONCEPT FORMATION

Two coders worked separately to place the 2000 NES respondents in the various levels of conceptualization. In order to assess the reliability of the placements the coders independently classified 300 of the same respondents. Their classifications agreed in 82 percent of the cases. Most of the discrepancies were separated only by a single category. Let us next consider the definitions of the categories, along with some examples of the kinds of statements that cause a respondent to be placed into each one.

Level A: Ideology and Near-Ideology

This level is reserved for people who exhibit some evidence of ideological thinking. Note, however, that we distinguish two gradations within this broad category. Individuals within the highest level, whom we will call "ideologues" explicitly articulated a sense of an abstract, general, dimension underlying electoral competition. People who showed more limited use of ideological terms or ideas were placed into a second, slightly lower category within this same broad level; we call these individuals "near ideologues."

The ideologues typically display an understanding of the liberal-conservative continuum through their explicit references to party or candidate locations. These same references frequently mention a personal position along that same continuum. Classification as an ideologue also requires evidence that the respondent possesses some understanding regarding the substantive implications of the ideological positions mentioned in the likes and dislikes toward the parties and candidates. While the latter requirement poses a risk of confounding verbal ability with conceptualization, we still believe it is suitable because it differentiates people who may simply be mimicking terms they have heard in the media or through social interactions from those individuals who really do use ideological concepts to organize their political thinking.

We were also open to alternative forms of ideology, apart from the liberal-conservative distinction. However, very few showed up in the open-ended comments. We made explicit allowances for individuals who seemed to be thinking in terms of a general dimension of political differentiation, without using specific summary terms to describe positions along that continuum. The overriding criterion for placing a respondent into the highest category of Level A is the use of a broad abstract judgmental standard to distinguish among the various elements of the electoral environment (i.e., the parties and candidates) along with the ability to relate the abstractions to specific, tangible, stimuli such as issues, policy programs, and forms of governmental activity.

Let us next consider a few examples of the kinds of comments that were provided by the individuals we classified as ideologues. Parenthetically, we must note that privacy regulations prohibit exact quotes from the verbatim transcripts of the interviews. Therefore, the following passages should be regarded as generic illustrations, rather than representations of specific respondents' likes and dislikes.

The first example represents the kind of respondent who conforms almost perfectly to our definition of a full ideologue:

(Anything you like about Al Gore?) Yes, I definitely like his stand on Social Security. He'll keep it and improve it. (Anything else?) His strong protection of the environment and stand against drilling oil in Alaska. (Anything else?) He is trying to work on the health program, which will be slow going. (Anything else?) I love his pro-choice stance and his program for schools.

(Anything you dislike about Al Gore?) His personality bothers me a lot. He does not come across well as a public speaker.

(Anything you like about George W. Bush?) No.

(Anything you dislike about George W. Bush?) His whole platform, gun control, the environment, Social Security, and health care. (Anything else?) Social Security. He is going to try to eliminate the program and have people invest on their own.

(Anything you like about the Democratic Party?) Lots of things. They are trying to help middle-class families. (Anything else?) They want to do some things that will make us a better America. We need government and people together to make it work.

(Anything you dislike about the Democratic Party?) Sometimes they get a little carried away, and need to be reined in. It would help if they were just a little more conservative in their views and programs.

(Anything you like about the Republican Party?) Sometimes I like the fact that they are a little conservative. Still, I don't really agree with them on most issues.

(Anything you dislike about the Republican Party?) They don't have a clue about what America is all about. All they think about is themselves.

Notice that this person mentions an array of issues, and a general stance with respect to governmental activity, as well as an explicit ideological position. This is exactly the kind of mixture of abstract and concrete idea elements that suggests the individual is applying an overall standard relatively consistently to a range of political objects.

The next set of comments reflect the kind of person who seems to be thinking in ideological terms, without explicitly articulating the terminology:

(Anything you like about Al Gore?) He is pro-choice and more experienced than Bush in governing and foreign affairs.

(Anything you dislike about Al Gore?) He is not for limiting government, and I don't understand his stand on Medicare and Medicaid.

(Anything you like about George W. Bush?) He is for limiting government. (Anything else?) He wants to lower government spending and stop government interference. (Anything else) He wants the states to manage education. (Anything else?) He wants to reduce the deficit and provide tax cuts.

(Anything you dislike about George W. Bush?) He's not pro-choice, and he doesn't come across well.

(Anything you like about the Democratic Party?) They seem to be more socially broad-minded and accepting of diversity.

(Anything you dislike about the Democratic Party?) They want more taxes and more government at the federal level.

(Anything you like about the Republican Party?) Limited government.

(Anything you dislike about the Republican Party?) They are not pro-choice.

Clearly, such an individual is using a general criterion for evaluating the parties and candidates. The idea of limited government serves as a broad standard, and it is also accompanied by a preference for state rather than federal activity. The pro-choice stance provides further evidence that the person prefers government to remain in the background of everyday life. All of these comments conform to a highly consistent ideological position. Thus, we have no hesitation in classifying this person as an ideologue despite the fact that the term *conservative* is never mentioned in the open-ended responses.

The previous two examples represent people who have little difficulty in "translating" general standards into specific political preferences. But we want to emphasize that classification as an ideologue does not necessarily imply a highly sophisticated, or even well-stated, perspective on the political system. Consider the following set of comments:

(Anything you like about Al Gore?) No.

(Anything you dislike about Al Gore?) Basically, that he won't uphold the Clinton administration's ideas. I think Bush has the right approach.

(Anything you like about George W. Bush?) Overall, he probably has the experience and knowledge. (Anything else?) He's made positive changes in his state. (Anything else?) He's more of a "we" person.

(Anything you dislike about George W. Bush?) Just the background stuff.

(Anything you like about the Democratic Party?) They are a little more liberal and pro-life. They are more about "How can we help more people?"

(Anything you dislike about the Democratic Party?) Their political issues as to control of the people. (Anything else?) Pro-choice issues. (Anything else?) They put the money where it will help the people.

(Anything you like about the Republican Party?) The only thing is that they tend to be more conservative.

(Anything you dislike about the Republican Party?) They are overly conservative at times, like with gun control and other controlling laws.

This person does not appear to be particularly articulate, and the comments display some confusion about the policy positions associated with the respective parties and candidates. Nevertheless, these statements seem to suggest that broad (if, perhaps, poorly crystallized) perspectives are at work, leading to the specific likes and dislikes expressed to the interviewer.

Generally speaking, we gave respondents the benefit of the doubt when placing them in the levels of conceptualization. The result is that many of our ideologues definitely do not possess a fully articulated personal political philosophy. Again, the hallmark of the ideologue is the simple ability to articulate abstract ideas that serve as a structuring principle with respect to concrete political stimuli. Any fear that such "generosity" in our coding rules will overestimate the ideological content of American public opinion should be put to rest by the empirical results: Only 10.5 percent of the respondents in the 2000 NES are classified as ideologues.

The people who occupy the second category within Level A, the near-ideologues, all show some awareness of ideological terminology. But unlike the "full" ideologues, they do not make an explicit connection to specific policies or issues. For example, a substantial number of these respondents used liberal-conservative terms in disconnected contexts. Consider the following comments:

(Anything you like about Al Gore?) No.
(Anything you dislike about Al Gore?) His ethics; I don't trust him.
(Anything you like about George W. Bush?) I appreciate his strong stand on abortion and that he acts like he is an honest person.
(Anything you dislike about George W. Bush?) No.
(Anything you like about the Democratic Party?) No.
(Anything you dislike about the Democratic Party?) I feel like they're too liberal.
(Anything you like about the Republican Party?) I like their conserva-

tive views. (Anything else?) I just appreciate that they will take stands not to make people feel good, but to do what's right. (Anything you dislike about the Republican Party?) No.

This person places the two parties in the "correct" ideological positions. But there is no attempt to relate the liberal and conservative labels to actual policies. In fact, there are no specific issue stands articulated throughout the comments; even the reference to Bush's abortion position is ambiguous. Therefore, we are unwilling to assume that this person really does use ideology to sort out the complexities of electoral politics. Still, we cannot ignore the fact that the respondent mentioned ideological labels without specific prompting for them. So we cannot merely discard this information, either. The near-ideologue category provides a convenient and reasonable way to handle such problematic cases.

We also assigned near-ideologue status to some people who didn't use ideological terms, but did exhibit very limited reliance on broad substantive standards for evaluating political positions. The following set of comments illustrates this situation:

(Anything you like about Al Gore?) His political party affiliation. (Anything else?) His view on environmental issues. (Anything else?) Gun control and education.

(Anything you dislike about Al Gore?) I can't think of anything.

(Anything you like about George W. Bush?) No.

(Anything you dislike about George W. Bush?) Well, political party affiliation.

(Anything you like about the Democratic Party?) Their views on government aid and social programs. I believe that the government's role should be to assist and encourage different aspects of the economy and the country. (Anything else?) I believe that if the government can assist with social programs, then we can leave people to help themselves.

(Anything you dislike about the Democratic Party?) Their views on certain moral issues. They are moral issues and should not be a part of politics.

(Anything you like about the Republican Party?) No.

(Anything you dislike about the Republican Party?) Certain views that they have, gun control, the death penalty, and social programs.

Now, this individual's comments about the Democratic Party suggest a broad belief about the government's proper role. But it is not laid out in any detail, and the remaining comments about the parties and candidates do not seem to complement the single broad statement. Stated simply, they seem to reflect some relatively disconnected concerns. And it is precisely this "disconnectedness" that precludes placement in the ideologue category. In a similar way, fragmented references to the size of government suggest near-ideologue status, as in the following set of comments:

> (Anything you like about Al Gore?) No.
> (Anything you dislike about Al Gore?) Trustworthy.
> (Anything you like about George W. Bush?) More moral character.
> (Anything else?) Less government. (Anything else?) Lower taxes.
> (Anything you dislike about George W. Bush?) No.
> (Anything you like about the Democratic Party?) No.
> (Anything you dislike about the Democratic Party?) No.
> (Anything you like about the Republican Party?) Less government and government control.
> (Anything you dislike about the Republican Party?) They could make their case a little better.

Once again, there is a general standard mentioned in the array of open-ended responses, but it is not applied very uniformly across the complete set of objects. And for that reason, we cannot say that this person shows clear evidence of broad ideological structuring in his or her political ideas. Still another kind of response configuration involves the use of a potentially broad ideological term in a manner that clearly conveys a fairly limited meaning. Consider the following:

> (Anything you like about Al Gore?) I generally agree with his views on things, especially the environment stand. His plans and view of the country's general direction are similar to mine.
> (Anything you dislike about Al Gore?) I think he sometimes panders to the elderly, but this is not an overriding issue. (Anything else?) Teachers. He goes overboard in not supporting testing of teacher standards.
> (Anything you like about George W. Bush?) No.
> (Anything you dislike about George W. Bush?) He is too general in his statements. He talks about balancing the budget, but his plans don't support that.
> (Anything you like about the Democratic Party?) I generally agree with their viewpoints on social issues.
> (Anything you dislike about the Democratic Party?) I think they have

some vestiges that are pandering to different groups just because of the historically strong power base. They are a little too overly sensitive to labor unions and the elderly. They are too easily politically swayed.
   (Anything you like about the Republican Party?) Those who are willing to work hard. They also support a strong defense.
   (Anything you dislike about the Republican Party?) The religious Right. I used to be a Republican, but the Reagan era changed me and alienated me. I dislike the control they are under by the Far Right such as abortion and prayer in schools.

In this case, the respondent makes a series of comments involving socioeconomic groups (i.e., the elderly, teachers, and labor unions). But the dislikes about the Republican Party bring in "the religious Right" and the "Far Right," conveying a sense of spatial positioning. Taken by itself, this might suggest a broad abstraction. But the specific context indicates a fairly narrow interpretation of this phrase centering on some specific social issues.

To summarize, the near-ideologues constitute respondents who, in one way or another, use words that could imply ideological thinking. But the circumstances in which they occur lead to doubts about the scope of their meaning and their applicability to political objects. The near-ideologue category comprise 9.4 percent of the respondents. Thus, combined with the full ideologues in the previous category, our data suggest that slightly less than one-fifth of the electorate uses ideological abstractions to organize their political thinking.

Level B: Group Benefits

The people that we place into the second-highest level of conceptualization are similar to those in Level A in that they employ a particular evaluative standard when they think about political parties and presidential candidates. In this case, however, that standard is rooted in one or more specific, identifiable stimulus objects, rather than in ideological terms and abstract principles. Our Level B respondents judge political phenomena according to the degree to which they provide rewards and benefits, as opposed to penalties and disadvantages, to particular groups within American society.

Group-based political thinking within the mass public is not at all unreasonable. For example, political candidates often speak in these terms while on the campaign trail. Similarly, journalists often find group labels to be a convenient way of communicating patterns of political support. So it should come as no surprise that many citizens find analogous utility in thinking about the ways that parties and candidates interact with, or affect the fortunes of, social groups.

Furthermore, there are many ways in which group-based thinking is an effective approach for understanding the political world. After all, group affiliations are often associated with socioeconomic strata within American society, along with life circumstances, aspirations, and objectives. In short, group-related concerns permeate the everyday experience of modern society. As a result, their impact on patterns of political thought within the electorate may, at times, be nearly as pervasive as the more abstract ideological concepts that characterize the thinking of citizens within Level A. It is merely that the evaluative criterion is rooted in group interest rather than a liberal-conservative stance. For this reason, conceptualizations of the political world based upon group benefits might be regarded as "ideology by proxy."

Nevertheless, there is a fundamental distinction between ideological and group-based conceptualizations. By definition, ideology is based upon broad abstract principles. The great advantage they provide is inherent in their generality; the logical consequences of an ideological position can be worked out to determine the implications for any new issue or social problem that may arise over time. Presumably, most ideologues are reasonably adept at accomplishing this translation process on their own. Again, it is the ideology itself that provides the "tools" for doing so.

In contrast, group-benefits conceptualizations shift the responsibility for the political translation process over to the group. If group spokespersons or opinion leaders frame an issue in a manner that highlights its implications for the group's membership, then it becomes an element in the belief system of those who think about politics in terms of that group's interests. On the other hand, a given issue may not be juxtaposed against a particular group in political discourse. And in those cases, there is no reason to expect group-benefits thinkers to pay any particular attention to the issue—it is simply not relevant to the concept (i.e., the group) that defines their own belief system. For this reason, we argue that the kind of thinking that defines Level B represents a more narrowly defined way to conceptualize the political world than the kinds of thinking that exist within Level A.

Let us begin to illustrate the kinds of thinking included within Level

B by showing comments expressed by a respondent who comes very close to the "ideology by proxy" notion mentioned earlier:

> (Anything you like about Al Gore?) I think he has better morals and is a family man with more concern for the country. (Anything else?) His health care reforms, so that senior citizens will not have any out-of-pocket expenses; that is the direction we need to head.
> (Anything you dislike about Al Gore?) No.
> (Anything you like about George W. Bush?) No.
> (Anything you dislike about George W. Bush?) His military record; he did not fulfill his commitment and he is living off his father's coattails. (Anything else?) I just don't trust him. (Anything else?) I don't care about his health reform. They want the HMOs to handle it all. Senior citizens will be out of their pocket expenses. The upper income will get the benefit, the lower and middle income will suffer.
> (Anything you like about the Democratic Party?) Their health care, but I am still skeptical about where they are for the senior citizen. (Anything else?) I don't believe they are very strong military-minded.
> (Anything you dislike about the Democratic Party?) When they control the House and the Senate, they rule in kind of a monarch state and they forget that they were voted in by the people. In my opinion, they are controlled too strongly by lobbyists and not the people.
> (Anything you like about the Republican Party?) I like their past record in getting bills passed and keeping control of the country. (Anything else?) Health care is one thing they have pushed, and Social Security—not cuts, they have made progress. (Anything else?) They are heavily into health care.
> (Anything you dislike about the Republican Party?) Too many scandals.

This person regards health care and Social Security as salient issues. But notice how the latter relate directly to the interests of senior citizens. One gets the sense that these issues are important for this person precisely because of their immediate consequences for seniors and not because of their intrinsic characteristics. Thus, it is the social category—senior citizens—that serves as the central focus for the belief system, and political stimuli are evaluated in terms of their stands relative to this reference group.

A wide variety of groups are mentioned by the Level B respondents. Along with the senior citizens that served as the focus for the previous person, we found that women, ethnic categories, African Americans,

Hispanics, "people in my age bracket," single parents, rich people (or "the wealthy"), poor people, the middle class, and the working class all appeared with some regularity within open-ended comments. However, groups based upon socioeconomic strata—whether explicitly defined as "classes" or simply identified in descriptive terms like "rich people"—dominated the category. In fact, many people who started out by mentioning gender, age, or racial groups also brought up economic categories. This is illustrated by the following statements:

> (Anything you like about Al Gore?) I believe in women being allowed to make up their mind about abortion. And the tax cut would be better off put to Social Security.
> (Anything you dislike about Al Gore?) No.
> (Anything you like about George W. Bush?) No.
> (Anything you dislike about George W. Bush?) I think he is more for the wealthy than for the middle- or lower-class people.
> (Anything you like about the Democratic Party?) I think they are more for the everyday common person, the middle and lower class.
> (Anything you dislike about the Democratic Party?) No.
> (Anything you like about the Republican Party?) No.
> (Anything you dislike about the Republican Party?) They tend to push things that are for the upper class. Also, I am for education and the Republicans don't do much there.

In some cases, respondents elaborated upon a group interest by making a link to a specific policy. The preceding respondent illustrates this by linking his or her evaluation of Gore to women and abortion. Similarly, at least one other respondent disliked George Bush because he "does not believe in a woman's right to choose." Another liked the Republican Party due to its "stance on taxes for the middle class." Although such associations between groups and issues do occur in the data, it is far more common for people to mention a group without invoking any issues or positions on policy. The following configuration of comments is quite typical:

> (Anything you like about Al Gore?) Because he is on the right side of the people. (Anything else?) He will need a lot of help.
> (Anything you dislike about Al Gore?) No.
> (Anything you like about George W. Bush?) No.
> (Anything you dislike about George W. Bush?) He sees things straight

ahead, one way; he has a nearsighted attitude. (Anything else?) He has the highest rate of dying with the death penalty.

(Anything you like about the Democratic Party?) They are more regular people.

(Anything you dislike about the Democratic Party?) No.

(Anything you like about the Republican Party?) No.

(Anything you dislike about the Republican Party?) They are for the big rich people.

In this case, the group-based nature of the belief system is inferred from the single reference to "big rich people." Note that we do not consider the earlier references in this set of comments to "the people" and "regular people" to be indicative of group-benefits conceptualizations. These vague allusions simply do not identify a specific subset of the overall population who might receive benefits or penalties from political actors. Hence, they seem to exist more as tautologies or truisms than as evaluative standards.

Finally, we want to emphasize that we regard the connections between social groups and the political world as existing "in the eye of the beholder." This means that we do not pass judgment on statements that have questionable validity, in view of contemporary American politics. Thus, an individual giving the following combination of statements would be placed in the group benefits level of conceptualization, despite any reservations we might have regarding the accuracy of the comments:

(Anything you like about Al Gore?) No.

(Anything you dislike about Al Gore?) The main issue is why he just didn't talk to Clinton. (Anything else?) I just do not like the man. (Anything else?) He does not seem to have a voice of his own.

(Anything you like about George W. Bush?) No.

(Anything you dislike about George W. Bush?) The thing that I would vote against him for are his thoughts on abortion.

(Anything you like about the Democratic Party?) Well, there are times when the Democrats seem to be for the U.S. in general. Then something happens to show that they do not care. It seems that they are not for the middle or lower class. We pay higher taxes than the higher-class people do.

(Anything you dislike about the Democratic Party?) Mainly because of the underlying innuendoes. They leave loopholes for the wealthy.

(Anything you like about the Republican Party?) The Republican

Party seems to be going more for the little people. They seem to be giving the middle- and lower-income people breaks on taxes and medical insurance and so on.

(Anything you dislike about the Republican Party?) I guess mainly because they seem to try, but they don't try hard enough. If something doesn't go through the first time, then they don't try again.

Once again, groups are salient stimuli in everyday social life, and their fortunes can be tied to political actors in a number of ways. For these reasons, it should probably come as no surprise that Level B is the modal category in our levels of conceptualization. Fully 28.2 percent of the respondents provided open-ended comments that resulted in their placements within this category.

Level C: The Nature of the Times

Moving downward one more category in our taxonomy, the next conceptual level encompasses a very heterogeneous mixture of reactions to the parties and candidates. The common characteristic across them is a tendency to judge political actors according to their coincidence with external environmental conditions. Basically, a Level C respondent favors one party and its candidates because good times and favorable conditions ensue when they take office and control the workings of government. The other party is to be avoided because of the problems that seem to be associated with its attempts at governing and policy-making.

We explicitly want to avoid judgmental comparisons of the responses in this level relative to the two "higher" levels already considered. Indeed, one could argue that assessments of past performance—one of the judgments that characterize this kind of thinking—comprise a very rational way to determine voting decisions. However, these people simply are not employing the same kind of broad evaluative standards as are those who rely on ideological abstractions or group-based judgments.

Instead, they are based upon a very specific and relatively inflexible criterion—what the party or its candidates did in the past, or the conditions that they seem to promote (or inhibit) within the rest of society. Furthermore, it is the case that many of the comments that emerge in the empirical data reveal somewhat nebulous, vague, and even fragmented feelings about political stimuli. The content of the judgments may be relatively unsophisticated by scholarly, journalistic, or even practical political standards. Nevertheless, they still suggest at least a minimal awareness that political actors can be judged on the basis of tangible substantive considerations.

In order to illustrate one of the more sophisticated lines of thinking that appear within Level C, consider the following comments:

> (Anything you like about Al Gore?) Only that he's part of the current administration and I believe they have done a good job. Their commitment has been clear for education, health care, and domestic economics. I think they have been good for the country. In the last eight years, my income has almost tripled. I believe that's due to the strength of the American economy.
>
> (Anything you dislike about Al Gore?) Only that he was born into politics and he is another professional politician.
>
> (Anything you like about George W. Bush?) No.
>
> (Anything you dislike about George W. Bush?) First, I am not very impressed with his performance as governor of Texas. I don't think he has made a big difference here, I don't have a good feeling about him as a person, and I have no knowledge of anything noteworthy that he has accomplished in this state. Clinton did a much better job in Arkansas, where he dramatically improved education for kids. When he began, Arkansas did not have good schools. But scoring on standardized tests rose during his term there. His commitment was clear.
>
> (Anything you like about the Democratic Party?) Just that their performance has been better. The national debt has been reduced. It would have been nice if their commitment to health care had shown up. I have my own health care, but I don't know how they've been providing that to others.
>
> (Anything you dislike about the Democratic Party?) I don't believe that they impacted education as much as they wanted to. For all the importance they assigned to education, I don't think there was much action to go with it. I personally wanted to be a teacher, but decided that I could only do that when money is less important to me. I think teachers should be professionals, and I am disappointed that others have not made a big push for this.
>
> (Anything you like about the Republican Party?) Their social positions.
>
> (Anything you dislike about the Republican Party?) No.

There are several interesting elements in the preceding statements. For one thing, this person judges the candidates and parties in terms of their performance in specific issue areas. At the same time, this individual relates national conditions to personal life circumstances. So even though there does not seem to be any broad "mental yardstick" (ideological or otherwise) being brought to bear, this person does use a consistent standard to evaluate political circumstances and actors.

The preceding comments stand out precisely because they are quite unusual for the Level C respondents. Most of the latter had much less to say about the parties and candidates overall, and their judgments were usually expressed in more narrowly phrased terms. The following comments are, perhaps, a bit more typical. Note, however, that they do still mention relatively specific national policies:

> (Anything you like about Al Gore?) He shows more public interest. (Anything else?) He brought about welfare reform. (Anything else?) He is for the people, and he helped to cut the deficit.
> (Anything you dislike about Al Gore?) No.
> (Anything you like about George W. Bush?) No.
> (Anything you dislike about George W. Bush?) No.
> (Anything you like about the Democratic Party?) No.
> (Anything you dislike about the Democratic Party?) No.
> (Anything you like about the Republican Party?) No.
> (Anything you dislike about the Republican Party?) No.

Some of the nature-of-the times responses focused on more general conditions, like the following:

> (Anything you like about Al Gore?) No.
> (Anything you dislike about Al Gore?) No.
> (Anything you like about George W. Bush?) No.
> (Anything you dislike about George W. Bush?) No.
> (Anything you like about the Democratic Party?) Clinton has done a good job with the economy.
> (Anything you dislike about the Democratic Party?) No.
> (Anything you like about the Republican Party?) No.
> (Anything you dislike about the Republican Party?) No.

And many respondents in Level C assessed the parties or candidates in terms of their supposed effect on their own lives:

> (Anything you like about Al Gore?) No.
> (Anything you dislike about Al Gore?) No.
> (Anything you like about George W. Bush?) No.

(Anything you dislike about George W. Bush?) He is a Republican. I have been in construction for the last 33 years and every time there has been a Republican in office, I've been in the unemployment line. When there is a Democrat in there, I have work. I really don't like either candidate very much right now.

(Anything you like about the Democratic Party?) When they are in, my construction work goes better.

(Anything you dislike about the Democratic Party?) They fight with the Republican Party.

(Anything you like about the Republican Party?) No.

(Anything you dislike about the Republican Party?) Every time they are in office, I am unemployed and I cannot feed my family. They are in there to run the country, not to fight among themselves.

Finally, some responses merely indicate a vague sense of dissatisfaction (or satisfaction) with the way the government has been operating:

(Anything you like about Al Gore?)

(Anything you dislike about Al Gore?) I think that after eight years, the country is ready for a change.

(Anything you like about George W. Bush?) I feel he is an honest person and will live up to his word.

(Anything you dislike about George W. Bush?) No.

(Anything you like about the Democratic Party?) No.

(Anything you dislike about the Democratic Party?) They promise too much giveaway at taxpayer expense.

(Anything you like about the Republican Party?) They are willing to help you so you can work out your needs. People should not remain on welfare all of their lives.

(Anything you dislike about the Republican Party?) No.

In summarizing the content of the Level C evaluations, it is probably easier to explain what is not found among the comments of its members than to describe the myriad ways that judgments about external conditions enter into political evaluations. Again, these people do not show evidence of employing abstract or group-based standards. But their comments are not devoid of any sense that political activity affects real-world conditions. This leaves a wide range of nature-of-the-times judgments that combine to produce another heavily populated conceptual level: 27.8 percent of the 2000 NES respondents fall in Level C.

Level D: Absence of Issue Content

Our last and "lowest" level of conceptualization consists of those people who displayed no issue content whatsoever in their open-ended remarks. Originally Level D was devised as a sort of residual category, for those respondents whose comments are so lacking in substantive policy concerns that they cannot be placed in any of the preceding three levels. But perusal of the data reveals that people are generally placed in this category for one of three reasons. First, about one-third of the Level D respondents expressed no likes or dislikes about any of the parties or candidates. Note that these do not represent missing data. Instead, these are people who stated to the interviewer that they had nothing to say. And from this we infer that they did not employ any particular mental routines to organize their political thinking. Second, a subset of the Level D respondents used partisanship as a standard, either as a justification for liking or disliking the candidates or as a general reaction to the one or more of the parties. The third—and, by far, the most frequent—basis for inclusion in Level D involves comments about the candidates' personal characteristics.

As an example of a particularly articulate set of comments that occurs within this conceptual level, consider the following:

> (Anything you like about Al Gore?) He has been there for eight years, his father was tremendous, and I believe he really cares about people. In fact, I feel the same way about Bush. (Anything else?) His wife. Tipper is the one with stronger opinions, about labeling records and all. She stood up for her beliefs and still does.
>
> (Anything you dislike about Al Gore?) His alliance with Clinton. He has been totally in politics, rather than the private sector. When you live in D.C., it's hard to see the rest of the country.
>
> (Anything you like about George W. Bush?) His sincerity. He surrounds himself with good people and he is well connected.
>
> (Anything you dislike about George W. Bush?) During the debates, he was evasive on certain questions. There was some talk that he had taken three million dollars from Social Security. I do not think you should take anything from Social Security and give it to young people. They can't even handle their own credit cards.
>
> (Anything you like about the Democratic Party?) Appreciation of a multitude of opinions.

(Anything you dislike about the Democratic Party?) No.
(Anything you like about the Republican Party?) No.
(Anything you dislike about the Republican Party?) How they are exclusive to people of different opinions.

The preceding respondent clearly had some well-formed ideas about the two candidates. As such, this person stands out within Level D. But notice that there is still some lack of specificity and apparent misinformation in the comments. And the specific reactions vanish almost entirely when the interview moves on to the parties, rather than the candidates.

Unlike the previous respondent, most Level D respondents are far more terse in their reactions. The following is a typical example:

(Anything you like about Al Gore?) He was already vice president, so he knows a lot about the job.
(Anything you dislike about Al Gore?) No.
(Anything you like about George W. Bush?) No.
(Anything you dislike about George W. Bush?) No.
(Anything you like about the Democratic Party?) No.
(Anything you dislike about the Democratic Party?) No.
(Anything you like about the Republican Party?) No.
(Anything you dislike about the Republican Party?) No.

Many people apparently judge the candidates by the company they keep. In this case, the most common references are to Gore's association with Clinton and to Bush's father, former president George H. W. Bush. Note that these associations can be interpreted as either positive or negative characteristics. For example, many people brought in the notion of scandals when they mentioned Clinton, while others expressed admiration for the first President Bush's handling of the 1991 Gulf War. The following set of comments illustrates a number of these themes:

(Anything you like about Al Gore?) No.
(Anything you dislike about Al Gore?) Bill Clinton, his association with him.
(Anything you like about George W. Bush?) Just that he's a Republican and his dad did a good job.
(Anything you dislike about George W. Bush?) No.

(Anything you like about the Democratic Party?) No.
(Anything you dislike about the Democratic Party?) The scandal that went on in the Oval Office. It was a mockery.
(Anything you like about the Republican Party?) They do a good job in general, like the Reagan years, which is why we are doing so good now. Beyond that, nothing specific.
(Anything you dislike about the Republican Party?) No.

The preceding comments also segue into the other major theme that shows up in Level D, references to partisanship. The latter play a much more prominent role in the following set of responses:

(Anything you like about Al Gore?) No.
(Anything you dislike about Al Gore?) No.
(Anything you like about George W. Bush?) No.
(Anything you dislike about George W. Bush?) No.
(Anything you like about the Democratic Party?) No.
(Anything you dislike about the Democratic Party?) The fact that I am not a Democrat. (Anything else) The Clinton presidency has not been agreeable, because of his personal life and behaviors.
(Anything you like about the Republican Party?) Just that I am a Republican and the presidents that they have run, I have agreed with.
(Anything you dislike about the Republican Party?) No.

While there is wide variety in the specific content of the Level D responses, further examples are probably unnecessary, since most of them would simply be variations on the themes that we have seen already. Respondents focused on different elements of the candidates' personalities (e.g., their abilities, their decisiveness, their experience, etc.). And they used partisan labels in several different ways, from a consistent standard for both candidates, to a nearly tautological justification for liking or disliking a party (e.g., "I dislike the Democrats because they are not the Republicans").

As we have stated several times already, we do not want to make judgments about the intrinsic quality of the open-ended responses. But it is difficult to overlook the lack of detail and fragmentary reactions that often appear in these comments. Clearly, matters of public policy are only of peripheral relevance, at most, to the people who are placed in this level of conceptualization. This simple descriptive statement is a finding of potential importance, since the "No issue content" level contains just under one-quarter of the NES respondents (24 percent).

Summary: The Levels of Conceptualization

Table 10.1 summarizes the overall distribution of respondents across the levels of conceptualization. The leftmost column gives the percentages calculated across the entire sample from the 2000 National Election Study. These results suggest that explicit ideological thinking is not particularly widespread within the American public. Even taking the near-ideologues into consideration, barely one-fifth of the respondents show evidence of thinking about politics in terms of an overarching dimension that orders the relevant electoral actors with respect to each other.

This finding, in turn, justifies the caution about interpreting electoral outcomes that we discussed at the outset of this chapter. It is problematic to attribute ideological meaning to aggregate voting patterns when most of the individuals making their decisions about the candidates are not motivated by ideological concepts. Of course, the analyses we reported in earlier chapters do reveal that individual orientations toward issues are structured in ways consistent with liberal-conservative orientations. But the current findings suggest strongly that these patterns do not arise, for the most part, from explicit ideological thinking by the general public. Thus, the data simply do not support the view that American elections constitute a clash of broad perspectives regarding the nature of politics within society. Instead, the four-fifths of the electorate that fall within the lower levels of conceptualization indicate that the results of presidential elections are determined on the basis of

TABLE 10.1. Distribution across the Levels of Conceptualization, Calculated Separately for the Total 2000 NES Sample and for Self-Reported 2000 Voters (in percentages)

Level of Conceptualization	Percentage of Total Sample		Percentage of Voters	
A. Ideology	19.86		24.53	
Ideologues		10.51		13.28
Near-ideologues		9.35		11.25
B. Group benefits	28.17		30.20	
C. Nature of the times	27.84		28.93	
D. No issue content	24.13		16.34	
Total	100.00		100.00	

Note: Data source is the 2000 National Election Study. Numbers of observations are 1,807 (total sample) and 1,182 (voters only).

more concrete, and often more limited, criteria like group interests, assessments about the nature of the times, and reactions to the candidates' personal characteristics.

One possible objection to this interpretation hinges on the observation that the active electorate only comprises a subset of the general public. If ideologues and near-ideologues tend to be more concentrated within the ranks of voters than nonvoters, then their impact on election outcomes would be magnified. However, the rightmost column of table 10.1 shows that there is not a great deal of empirical support for this argument. Level A respondents do occur more frequently, and Level D respondents less frequently, among voters. However, the magnitude of the difference from the general population is quite small. Ideologues and near-ideologues still comprise less than one-fourth of the voters in our sample. And the mode (with about 30 percent of the respondents) remains at Level B, group benefits. So in terms of basic organization of political thinking, the active electorate is just not that different from the population at large.

THE CORRELATES OF CONCEPTUALIZATION

Our finding that people within the mass public think about politics in fundamentally different ways raises an obvious question: What leads to this variability? One could make an argument quite easily for homogeneity in political perceptions, based upon the fact that attention during a presidential campaign is riveted on a small set of actors, whose activities are communicated through a finite number of media channels, which tend to rely upon the same sources and report information in remarkably similar ways. What, then, would lead only a small subset of the electorate to think about things in terms of an ideological "big picture," while others make relatively vague judgments about socioeconomic conditions, and still others focus narrowly on the candidates' personalities?

It will probably come as no surprise that the major factor affecting the capacity for issue-based voting and the clarity of policy attitude structures also exerts a clear impact on political conceptualization. An individual's education has a profound influence on the way that person organizes his or her thinking about the candidates and parties. The empirical relationship is summarized in table 10.2.

The effect of education can be observed most clearly in the two endmost levels of conceptualization. On the upper side, the proportion of ideologues and near-ideologues increases from a minuscule 2.8 percent among those who did not complete high school up to about 31 percent among those with education beyond high school. At the lower end of the continuum, we observe the opposite trend: No-issue-content conceptualizations made up 42 percent of the people who did not graduate from high school, but only about 12 percent of those with at least some college.

There are probably several reasons for the positive relationship between education and conceptualization. One is the simple fact that educational attainment is, itself, determined (at least in part) by intellectual ability. And along with the latter comes a capacity for taking broader perspectives on the various elements of everyday life. This, in turn, fosters the abstract thinking that characterizes the higher levels of conceptualization.

Some supportive evidence for this latter assertion can be found by examining the two "middle" levels in table 10.2. Earlier, we suggested that the group benefits level could be viewed as ideology by proxy, since the individual's relationship to his or her reference group provides an evaluative standard for anything that is relevant to the group. But despite this potential, reliance on a group still comprises a fairly narrow view of the world. And the nature-of-the-times level often represents a fairly incomplete assessment of electoral phenomena; but it is still connected to broad events within the outside world. Returning to table 10.2, we note that the group benefits stratum decreases in size, while the nature-of-the-times level increases, when moving upward among the educational categories. These trends are not very strong. Nevertheless, they are clear enough that we believe they do represent an aspect of

TABLE 10.2. The Relationship between Education and Level of Conceptualization (in percentages)

Level of Conceptualization	Education		
	Less than High School	High School Graduate	At Least Some College
A. Ideology	2.78	14.73	30.66
B. Group benefits	32.78	28.01	27.21
C. Nature of the times	22.22	27.23	30.25
D. No issue content	42.22	30.03	11.88
Total	100.00	100.00	100.00
Number of cases	180	896	724

Note: Data source is the 2000 National Election Study.

systematic, education-based effects on the breadth and scope of political thinking within the electorate.

Another avenue of educational influence occurs because schooling can expose people to contextual information about the political world. It seems reasonable to suppose that the more factual knowledge one can bring to bear on any given subject, the more one will be able to make connections among the various facets of the topic. With respect to politics, an understanding of the substantive policy stands articulated by the parties and candidates, as well as exposure to their past history and records of accomplishment (or lack thereof) should reveal fairly quickly that candidates, officeholders, and political parties are all characterized much more by consistency and continuity in decision- and policy-making than by marked and surprising shifts from one direction to another. That should, in turn, facilitate the broader, more inclusive perspectives that exist at the higher, ideological levels of conceptualization.

We can test the effects of political knowledge, using some additional variables drawn from the 2000 National Election Study. The interview schedule included 10 factual questions about which party controlled each house of Congress, the offices held by several public figures, and the home states of the presidential and vice presidential candidates.[1] We can score each respondent's level of factual knowledge by summing the number of correct responses to these questions. The raw scores are categorized to divide the overall sample into three roughly equally sized knowledge levels.

Table 10.3 shows the breakdown of conceptualization across the three knowledge categories. Our expectations are borne out very nicely by the data. The ideologically oriented respondents (i.e., those classified as ideologues or near-ideologues) make up less than 7 percent of the least knowledgeable respondents. In contrast, about one-third of the

---

1. The first two political knowledge questions are worded as follows: "Do you happen to know which party had the most members in the House of Representatives in Washington (the U.S. Senate) before the election this month?" Shortly afterward in the interview schedule, respondents were asked, "Now we have a set of questions concerning various public figures. We want to see how much information about them gets out to the public from television, newspapers, and the like. The first name is Trent Lott (William Rehnquist/Tony Blair/Janet Reno). What job or political office does he (she) now hold?" Following those four questions, they were asked, "Next, I'd like to ask you about the candidates who ran for President and their running mates. We're interested in some of the things that people may have heard about these candidates. The first candidate I'd like to ask you about is George W. Bush. What U.S. state does George W. Bush (Al Gore/Dick Cheney/Joe Lieberman) live in now?"

most knowledgeable subset fall at this conceptual level. The opposite pattern occurs in the no-issue-content level: Those people comprise fully 41 percent of the least knowledgeable stratum and only 8.5 percent of the respondents who exhibit the highest level of political knowledge. Notice that the proportions in the two middle conceptual levels (group benefits and nature of the times) hardly change across the three knowledge categories. Thus, the impact of political knowledge seems to occur at the two polar extremes of conceptualization. It increases the propensity to view the world according to overarching ideological abstractions, and decreases the frequency of assessments that are devoid of policy-oriented content.

We would warn against making too much of the preceding relationship, since the effects of political knowledge—though clear-cut—seem limited. Again, only one-third of the most knowledgeable respondents exhibit an ideological outlook on the world. And recall that the classification scheme used to create the conceptual levels deliberately downplayed the importance of objective "correctness" in opinions as a criterion for placement.

In fact, we can easily imagine circumstances wherein an individual does not possess a sizable inventory of concrete facts about political actors, but still understands both the ideological underpinnings of a party's or candidate's position and its general implications for the types of policies that would be advocated by each. Here, personal "proximity" to politics is probably the key factor: A person who is involved in the political

TABLE 10.3. The Relationship between Political Knowledge and Level of Conceptualization (in percentages)

Level of Conceptualization	Political Knowledge		
	Low	Medium	High
A. Ideology	6.42	21.66	33.74
B. Group benefits	26.50	29.64	30.10
C. Nature of the times	25.67	29.12	27.68
D. No issue content	41.41	19.58	8.48
Total	100.00	100.00	100.00
Number of cases	483	577	495

Note: Data source is the 2000 National Election Study. The measure of political knowledge is obtained by summing the number of answers to 10 factual questions and categorizing the resultant scores to produce roughly equally populated categories. The "low" knowledge level contains respondents who gave 0–2 correct answers, the "medium" knowledge level contains those who gave 3–5 correct answers, and the "high" knowledge level contains respondents who gave 6–10 correct answers.

TABLE 10.4. The Relationship between Personal Political Involvement and
Level of Conceptualization (in percentages)

Level of	Political Involvement		
Conceptualization	Low	Medium	High
A. Ideology	8.07	16.94	31.67
B. Group benefits	16.59	29.89	29.88
C. Nature of the times	13.45	29.80	29.68
D. No issue content	61.88	23.37	8.76
Total	100.00	100.00	100.00
Number of cases	223	1,074	502

Note: Data source is the 2000 National Election Study. The measure of political involvement is created from questions about the respondent's interest in the campaign and concern over the outcome. Those who say they are both "very much interested" and "care a good deal" are placed in the "high" involvement category. Those who say they are "not much interested" and "don't care very much" are placed in the "low" involvement category. Individuals in the "medium" involvement category gave mixed or intermediate responses to the two survey questions.

world will simultaneously be exposed to greater quantities of politically relevant information and be motivated to seek out additional information to facilitate his or her effectiveness as a political actor. Note, too, that we regard involvement as a psychological characteristic rather than an organizational membership. A person may feel emotionally engaged in an electoral contest without exhibiting overt activity.

Table 10.4 shows the relationship between an index of personal political involvement and the levels of conceptualization. The former variable is created from the responses to two survey questions about attention to the 2000 campaign and concern over the outcome of the presidential election.[2] The entries in the table show the now-familiar pattern of increasingly frequent ideological conceptualizations, and fewer non-issue-oriented viewpoints, when moving from the lowest to highest involvement category. The contrasts are fairly stark: Level A (ideologues and near-ideologues) respondents up only about 8 percent of the least-involved respondents, and almost one-third of the most involved. Level D respondents (no issue content) are almost 62 percent of the least in-

---

2. The wording of the first question is, "Some people don't pay much attention to political campaigns. How about you? Would you say that you have been very much interested, somewhat interested, or not much interested in the political campaigns so far this year?" The second question (asked immediately after the first in the interview schedule) is, "Generally speaking, would you say that you personally care a good deal who wins the presidential election this fall, or that you don't care very much who wins?"

volved, and only 9 percent of the most involved. Thus, a personal pattern of attentiveness to electoral politics "pays off" in the form of a broad, inclusive viewing perspective on the political world.

So far, we have identified three separate correlates of the conceptual levels, education, political knowledge, and political involvement. Of course, we expect that these three factors are themselves closely connected. We have already noted that education should increase knowledge. But it should also affect involvement, by providing individuals with the cognitive tools useful for relating the elements of politics to one's own life.

Despite the obvious interrelationship among them, we still think that education, knowledge, and involvement are separately related to conceptualization. Empirical tests of this assertion are provided in table 10.5. The first panel, table 10.5a, shows the relationship between knowledge and conceptualization separately, within the three levels of educational attainment. The second panel, table 10.5b, shows the relationship between involvement and conceptualization, again controlling for education. We must exercise some caution in assessing these results, because some of the cells are quite sparse; for example, very few people in the lowest education category show high levels of knowledge or involvement. Despite this caveat, we can see that the previously described positive empirical relationships still hold. Both political knowledge and psychological involvement in electoral politics correspond to increased probability that an individual will be placed in the highest levels of conceptualization, and outside the lowest level. These patterns operate independently of education, and the latter continues to show effects beyond these other two explanatory variables.

In the case of education, we feel reasonably comfortable in asserting that the causal sequence runs unidirectionally from schooling to conceptualization. On the other hand, we do not think the underlying structure is quite so simple with respect to knowledge and involvement. For one thing, the latter are "intermediaries" that funnel part of education's total impact on conceptualization. At the same time, we suspect that knowledge and involvement may themselves be enhanced when a person maintains a broader conceptualization of the political world and the various elements within it. So there are likely to be reciprocal causal influences working among these factors. For that reason, we are more comfortable concluding that we have uncovered some of the primary correlates of conceptualization, rather than its determinants.

TABLE 10.5. The Relationship between Level of Conceptualization and Knowledge, and Level of Conceptualization and Involvement, Controlling for Respondent's Education (in percentages)

A. Level of conceptualization and political knowledge, controlling for education

	Respondent's Education								
	Less than High School			High School Graduate			At Least Some College		
	Political Knowledge			Political Knowledge			Political Knowledge		
Level of Conceptualization	Low	Medium	High	Low	Medium	High	Low	Medium	High
A. Ideology	0.00	5.00	30.00	5.49	17.16	27.21	16.67	30.35	37.46
B. Group benefits	29.29	42.50	30.00	26.12	30.03	31.36	24.44	26.92	29.21
C. Nature of the times	20.20	25.00	20.00	27.15	27.72	27.81	27.78	31.62	27.94
D. No issue content	50.51	27.50	20.00	41.24	25.08	13.61	31.11	11.11	5.40
Total	100.00	100.00	100.00	100.00	99.99	99.99	100.00	100.00	100.01
Number of cases	99	40	10	291	303	169	90	234	315

B. Level of conceptualization and political involvement, controlling for education

	Respondent's Education								
	Less than High School			High School Graduate			At Least Some College		
	Political Involvement			Political Involvement			Political Involvement		
Level of Conceptualization	Low	Medium	High	Low	Medium	High	Low	Medium	High
A. Ideology	0.00	2.58	7.70	5.43	12.12	28.02	21.15	27.72	37.08
B. Group benefits	28.95	31.90	42.31	11.63	30.74	31.40	21.15	28.22	26.97
C. Nature of the times	0.00	28.45	26.92	18.60	28.39	28.99	11.54	32.18	30.71
D. No issue content	71.05	37.07	23.08	64.34	28.75	11.59	46.15	11.88	5.24
Total	100.00	100.00	100.01	100.00	100.00	100.00	99.99	100.00	100.00
Number of cases	38	116	26	129	553	207	52	404	267

Note: Data source is the 2000 National Election Study.

CONCEPTUALIZATION AND PARTISAN CHANGE

We have examined political conceptualization in the mass public in order to test one of the major assumptions underlying many accounts of partisan change in American elections. Most of these commentaries are built upon the idea that differences in voting patterns, both over time and across subsections of the electorate, reflect varied locations or movement along a general continuum ranging from liberal positions on the left, to more conservative positions on the right. But our empirical results show that such a view of politics is only maintained by a relatively small minority of the American electorate. This fact, alone, may raise serious questions about the traditional assumptions.

However, some additional investigation is necessary before we reject the conventional wisdom. For example, the ideological level of conceptualization is small, but not exactly minuscule: It comprises nearly one-fifth of our total sample. This represents a sizable enough segment to produce significant electoral change. After all, many lopsided Electoral College outcomes are based on only single-digit percentage point differences in the popular vote support for the winning and losing parties.

At the same time, ideologues and near-ideologues are far more likely to turn out to vote than are the individuals that fall within the other levels of conceptualization. Table 10.6 shows the relevant figures. Among the former group, nearly nine out of 10 (89.8 percent) actually vote. But this figure decreases to only a little more than half (54.5 percent) at the no-issue-content level. Thus, our Level A respondents occupy a position that could have a major impact on election outcomes, despite their small "absolute" numbers within the population.

Nevertheless, we consider it unlikely that ideologues are actually the driving forces behind the recent sizable swings in voting support across

TABLE 10.6. Percentage Turning Out to Vote, by Level of Conceptualization

Level of Conceptualization	Did Not Vote	Voted	Row Total
A. Ideology	10.22	89.78	100.00 (323)
B. Group benefits	20.31	79.69	100.00 (448)
C. Nature of the times	20.28	79.72	100.00 (429)
D. No issue content	45.48	54.52	100.00 (354)

Note: Data source is the 2000 National Election Study. Figures in parentheses are the numbers of observations within each row.

the two parties. The problem is that broader conceptualizations of the political world appear to be more closely associated with stability than with intra-individual variability in political orientations and preferences. To state it simply, individuals in the higher levels of conceptualization exhibit stronger partisan attachments. Apart from that, they are also more likely to be consistent in voting for their respective parties.

The evidence to support the preceding assertions is summarized in table 10.7. The leftmost column of the table shows the percentage within each level who identify strongly with one of the major parties. This figure ranges from about 42 percent in Level A down to only about 18 percent in Level D. Conversely, the second column shows the percentage who refuse any partisan attachment—the so-called nonleaning independents—within each level. Here, the percentages increase from less than 5 percent to almost 23 percent as we move downward through the levels.

These complementary trends are important because, as our earlier analyses have documented, partisanship provides citizens with a perceptual screen for developing reactions to the candidates in each new election. Stronger attachments to a party signal a greater propensity to rely on the implied "standing decision" to support its candidates and oppose those from the other party. If we extrapolate from these ideas, it seems that the ideologically oriented levels are more likely to contribute to electoral inertia than to change.

The rightmost column of table 10.7 confirms the latter interpretation. The figures represent the percentage at each conceptual level who reported voting for the same party's presidential candidate in both 1996 and 2000 (i.e., either voting for Clinton and Gore, or for Dole and Bush). Again a clear pattern emerges, wherein vote consistency decreases monotonically while moving downward through the levels. At one end

TABLE 10.7. Partisan Strength and Presidential Vote Consistency, by Level of Conceptualization (in percentages)

Level of Conceptualization	Strong Party Identifiers	Nonleaning Independents	Consistent in Presidential Vote, 1996–2000
A. Ideology	42.02	4.48	55.43
B. Group benefits	42.29	7.11	49.31
C. Nature of the times	28.63	11.90	43.34
D. No issue content	18.23	22.78	22.48

Note: Data source is the 2000 National Election Study.

of the continuum, a bit more than half of Level A respondents report consistent voting choices. The comparable figure is only about 22 percent among the Level D respondents.

Three major conclusions may be drawn from the analyses presented in this chapter. First, we have determined that the electorate's attentiveness to ideological themes is relatively scant. Second, broad and abstract conceptualizations of politics are most likely to be found among those who are educated, knowledgeable, and already integrated into the political world. And third, ideologically based perspectives on the political world correspond to higher levels of temporal stability in electoral preferences. Taken together, these conclusions indicate that the questions we raised at the beginning of this chapter are reasonable in light of the empirical evidence. From the viewpoint of the mass public, at least, American elections cannot be accurately characterized as contests among opposing ideologies. Instead, electoral outcomes vary on the basis of more limited factors, like evaluations of governmental performance and assessments of the candidates' personalities. Of course, there is nothing whatsoever inherently wrong with this state of affairs. However, it does lead to skepticism about the degree to which elections can really serve as policy mandates, or even provide broad, coherent direction for future governmental activity.

COMMENTARY AND CONTROVERSY

The empirical results in this chapter are highly consistent with those reported in *The American Voter*. First, let us consider the public's distribution across the levels of conceptualization: In 1956, only about 11 percent were placed into the "ideology" level, compared to about 20 percent in 2000. In 1956, 42 percent of the respondents were classified at the "group benefits" level, compared to only 28 percent in 2000. Thus, currently more people think about politics in ideological terms, and fewer organize their perceptions along group-based lines, than was the case during the 1950s. This is reasonable given increases in aggregate education levels, the growth of the mass media, the increasing polarization of American politics, and the ongoing breakdowns of traditional partisan coalitions. But these changing percentages among the higher levels are offset by what appears to be remarkable stability in the sizes of the lower conceptual strata: We found about 28 percent at the "nature of the times" level, and 24 percent at the "no issue content" level. The comparable figures for 1956 are 24 percent and 23 percent, respectively. Apparently, about half of the elec-torate continues to think about politics in very limited ways, with only tenuous connections to general ideologies or specific policy controversies.

Perhaps more important than the public's distribution across the levels of conceptualization, the relationships between the latter and other theoretically relevant variables remain virtually identical to those reported by Campbell, Converse, Miller, and Stokes. Just as in 1956, indi-vidual placements among the levels of conceptualization remain posi-tively correlated with educational attainment, political sophistication, and political involvement. Furthermore, the broader psychological per-spectives implied by relatively comprehensive views of the political world (including the "ideology by proxy" that occurs at the "group ben-efits" level) correspond to higher voter turnout rates, stronger partisan ties, and increased temporal consistency in voting choices. It remains the case that ideological thinking promotes stability, rather than change, in political preferences.

The Impact of "The Nature of Belief Systems in Mass Publics"

The analysis in this chapter can be viewed as in investigation into the na-ture and consequences of individual differences in the ways that people organize their thinking about the political world. It is a ironic that the au-thors of *The American Voter* conducted this exercise in order to under-stand the nature of partisan change, because that has not been the focus of subsequent research. Instead, more recent work has aimed at eliciting the nature and extent of ideological reasoning within the mass public, along with the overall quality or sophistication of citizens' political orien-tations. This shift in emphasis is probably due to the influence of Philip Converse's seminal essay "The Nature of Belief Systems in Mass Publics," which was mentioned in "Commentary and Controversy" in chapter 9.

"The Nature of Belief Systems" makes the general argument that it is inappropriate to characterize public opinion in ideological terms be-cause people simply do not exhibit the organized, broad, and stable views of politics and society that are implied by the term *ideology*. In a tightly reasoned and comprehensive analysis, Converse uses the levels of conceptualization as evidence against the widespread existence of ideo-logically constrained belief systems. But he also allows for the possibility that people may recognize and understand ideological terms, even if they do not use them spontaneously in their own discourse. Here, about half the public seems capable of meeting this less stringent criterion. But they, too, tend to fall within the more educated and sophisticated strata. As we might expect, there is a moderately strong correlation between recognition and understanding of ideological terms and placement among the higher levels of conceptualization.

The "Commentary and Controversy" for chapter 9 discusses Converse's use of correlations between responses to survey questions about policy issues as a measure of attitudinal constraint. In the present context, it is important to note that the constraint was observed to be highest among those segments of the population where the use of ideological reasoning is also most widespread—political elites along with the most sophisticated, active strata of the mass public. The low intercorrelations that characterized the broadest elements of the electorate are used to forestall any counterargument that citizens may, in fact, be thinking in broad terms that simply do not correspond to a liberal-conservative dimension. Taking this line of reasoning further, Converse argues that even idiosyncratic ideologies should contribute a degree of stability to personal attitudes. But the empirical evidence shows high levels of temporal variability—indeed, seemingly random patterns of change—in survey responses to issue questions over time (i.e., when the same respondents are asked the same questions at two or more time points).

Thus, the evidence seems to be irrefutable: Most citizens do not organize their political orientations according to broad, abstract, judgmental standards. Ideological thinking (explicit or implicit) is largely confined to the most sophisticated strata within the population. Converse finishes the essay by considering the implications of his analysis for the interpretation of political change: He applies the lessons learned from the direct observation of public opinion in the 1950s to the abolitionist movement in the United States during the first half of the nineteenth century, and to the rise of the Nazi Party in Germany during the 1920s and 1930s. In so doing, Converse clearly establishes the political importance of belief system structure, apart from the obvious relevance of his findings for the social-psychological foundations of public opinion.

The scholarly impact of "The Nature of Belief Systems in Mass Publics" has been enormous. It clearly set the path of all subsequent research into citizen competence, political reasoning, ideological thinking, and the structure of political attitudes. It is no exaggeration to say that the essay is required reading for all who profess expertise in the fields of public opinion and political behavior. From the various complementary ideas developed in "The Nature of Belief Systems," the remainder of this

"Commentary and Controversy" section will focus on the levels of conceptualization and other research aimed at understanding differences in the ways people organize their political thinking.

Replicating the Levels of Conceptualization

The importance of any scientific concept lies in its degree of general applicability: In other words, how far-reaching is the class of phenomena for which that concept provides theoretical insight? In this respect, the levels of conceptualization variable has been hampered by the fact that it is extremely difficult to replicate. The current authors can attest, from personal experience, that the content analysis of the open-ended survey responses is a difficult and time-consuming task, prone to errors and misclassifications. For that matter, the verbatim transcripts of the survey interviews, which provide the "raw data" for placing individuals among the levels, are not generally available to the research community.

Despite the difficulties in creating the variable, there were two different replications of the conceptual levels carried out with the open-ended data from the 1964 National Election Study (Klingemann 1973, 1979; Pierce 1970). But these analyses were exceptions to a more general trend: All of the other early replication studies relied on "surrogate" versions of the levels of conceptualization. The latter are created from the precoded content categories for open-ended responses that are included in the codebooks for the National Election Studies during presidential election years. These "Master Codes" indicate whether respondents' expressed likes or dislikes about the candidates and parties fall within particular categories, such as (likes candidate X because he is) "more conservative than other Republicans," (dislikes party Y because) "they are more likely to get us into a war," or (likes candidate Z because) "he is an honest man."

While the Master Codes do not enable the researcher to determine exactly what the respondent said, or how he or she organized his or her comments, they do provide information about the kinds of ideas that each person expressed in response to the series of open-ended questions. The codes are very detailed, in that they typically allow for over 300 different kinds of comments. Therefore, the Master Codes seem to provide a very reasonable foundation for reconstructing the levels of conceptualization.

Two surrogate versions of the levels of conceptualization emerged during the 1960s and 1970s: First, Field and Anderson (1969) used a three-category version that divides the public into explicit ideologues (people who use explicit liberal-conservative terminology in their responses), implicit ideologues (people who give relatively coherent, structured, policy-based responses without explicit ideological language), and nonideologues (those who show no awareness of ideology). Second, Nie, Verba, and Petrocik (1979) developed a more detailed levels of conceptualization variable with six ordered categories, defined as follows: ideologues (responses contain liberal-conservative themes as well as references to issues and social groups); near ideologues (references to ideological themes, without elaboration); issue reference (responses mention specific social problems or political issues); group reference (focus on benefits or disadvantages to particular social groups); party reference (vague statements about political parties); and apolitical (various nonpolitical responses).

The surrogate levels of conceptualization were used occasionally during the late 1970s (Coveyou and Piereson 1977) and the 1980s (Jacoby 1986). But they are now largely unnecessary, due to the efforts of Hagner, Pierce, and Knight (1989), who replicated the levels of conceptualization from the actual, open-ended responses for every presidential election year from 1952 through 1988. This is a major contribution to the field, because these researchers followed exactly the same steps employed by the authors of *The American Voter* to produce the original variable. Along with the coding used in this chapter, efforts are currently under way to extend the open-ended response versions of the levels from 2004 back through 1992 (Jacoby and Moore 2006; Jacoby, Duff, and Pyle 2008).

If we compare the different measures, the surrogate, Master Code–based levels of conceptualization always place more people in the ideologically oriented levels than do the versions based upon the open-ended responses. But apart from this difference, all versions of the conceptual levels behave in very similar ways. They all show that ideological thinking became much more prevalent during the 1964 election, remained at heightened levels until the mid-1970s, declined a bit in 1976, and have remained largely stable since then with yearly distributions very similar to that which we found for 2000. Thus, the general conclusion seems to be that ideological awareness within the mass public is noticeably higher than during the 1950s, but still confined to a fairly small segment (i.e., about one-fifth) of the overall electorate.

Criticism of the Levels

Over the years, several criticisms of the levels of conceptualization have appeared in the research literature. Some of these are relatively minor, involving questions about the ordinal nature of categories (e.g., Lau 1986; Luskin 1987), or the amount of substantive differentiation between adjacent levels (e.g., Converse 1975; Miller and Levitin 1976; Jacoby 1991b). But the most vocal critic has been Eric R. A. N. Smith (1980, 1981, 1989), who has questioned the fundamental validity of the levels of conceptualization, on methodological and conceptual grounds.

Smith's arguments are straightforward: From a methodological perspective, an individual's belief system structure should be a stable characteristic; that is, the judgmental criteria that people employ to evaluate the political world should not change very much over time. But Smith shows there is, in fact, quite a bit of temporal variability in the Master Code–based levels. He argues that the turnover that occurs across two- and four-year periods is so large that the levels possess an unacceptably low degree of reliability. This, in turn, compromises their utility as an analytic variable.

Smith's conceptual objection stems from his assertion that open-ended answers to the questions about the candidates and parties are not empirical manifestations of the judgmental criteria that survey respondents bring to bear on those political stimuli. Instead, he argues that the open-ended responses result from a brief memory search wherein people recall the political information to which they have been recently exposed. Accordingly, any taxonomy constructed from those responses (such as the levels of conceptualization) merely reflects the content of recent political discourse and rhetoric, rather than the fundamental structural abstractions underlying individual-level political thinking. If this is the case, then the levels of conceptualization are not measuring the phenomenon they claim to measure—in other words, they are invalid. Smith's stark conclusion is this: "The principal uses of the levels indexes have been to assess the number of ideologues in the population and to assess the change in that number over time. Neither use is justified. . . . [F]or virtually everything that we judge important, the levels indexes do not work" (1989, 104).

Responses to Criticism

Several researchers responded to the criticisms made by Smith. For example, Cassel (1984) demonstrated that the reliability of the levels of conceptualization is fully comparable to the reliabilities of variables that are commonly employed to measure many other prominent political attitudes. Cassel also joined Abramson (1981) in pointing out that, contrary to Smith's conclusions, the levels are almost perfectly stable once measurement error is taken into account. Thus, the levels of conceptualization's measurement characteristics do stand up to close scrutiny, based upon the same standards that are routinely applied to other variables in the field of mass political behavior.

The validity issues have been addressed in a number of different ways. Hagner and Pierce (1982) immediately established the criterion validity of the open-ended response variable (i.e., the version of the levels used most frequently since they were made available in the early 1980s) by showing that the levels covary in theoretically predictable ways with many different measures of political involvement and participation. Jacoby (1988b, 1995) has also shown that the conceptual levels account for significant variations in the degree of mass-level ideological thinking, even after other indices of political awareness (e.g., education, interest, overt participation, etc.) are taken into account. Knight (1990) and Hagner and Pierce (1991) both show that the proportion of ideologues (i.e., people in the "highest" level of conceptualization) does not covary directly with the ideological content of presidential campaign rhetoric. Therefore, Smith's charge that the levels only tap superficial responses is not supported empirically. In summary, the validity of the levels of conceptualization seems to be established quite firmly.

Changing Focus in Research on Mass-Level Ideology

Into the early 1980s, most of the research on mass-level ideology focused on questions about what proportion of the overall electorate was able and willing to think about politics along liberal-conservative lines (Luttbeg and Gant 1985). But it was never really clear why this was an important question in itself. A number of scholars expressed frustration at the seeming lack of theoretical progress in the study of mass belief systems (e.g., Bennett 1977; Kinder 1982, 1983; Hamill and Lodge 1986). As if in response to such frustrations, the focus of research shifted around this time, to examine the consequences of ideological conceptualizations for mass political behavior. In this new (and still ongoing) line of work, the levels of conceptualization and other similar variables (mainly, measures of political sophistication) are generally viewed as "moderators" that determine the degree to which individuals' personal liberal-conservative feelings impinge on their other political orientations, choices, and behavior.

As discussed in chapter 9, an ideological dimension provides a convenient mechanism for citizens to structure their beliefs about political parties, candidates, and issues. But the analysis presented in chapter 10 suggests that this might only be the case for those people who explicitly think about the political world in liberal-conservative terms. A great deal of empirical research confirms this general hypothesis. For example, people who are attentive to ideological concepts are more likely to identify candidate and party positions on issues than those who do not view the world in liberal-conservative terms (e.g. Wright and Niemi 1983; Hamill, Lodge, and Blake 1985; Granberg and Brown 1992). Reliance on the liberal-conservative dimension also promotes relatively accurate perceptions of candidate and party issue stands; that is, ideological thinkers tend to place Democratic stimuli (i.e., the party and its candidates) to the left of Republican stimuli on specific issues (e.g., Levitin and Miller 1979; Sharp and Lodge 1985; Jacoby 1988b).

The "Commentary and Controversy" for chapter 9 discussed the work that uses liberal-conservative self-placements as a determinant of issue attitudes. But there is also a sizable body of research that shows that the magnitude of this ideological influence varies across levels of conceptualization and sophistication (e.g., Kuklinski, Metlay, and Kay 1982; Sniderman, Brody, and Kuklinski 1984; Jacoby 1991b; Sniderman et al. 1991). Still other work has shown that the internal consistency of a person's issue attitudes is enhanced by an ideological outlook on the world (Hamill, Lodge, and Blake 1985; Sharp and Lodge 1985; Jacoby 1991b).

Finally, the level of ideological awareness often affects the degree to which, and manner in which, liberal-conservative ideas impinge on candidate evaluations, political participation, and electoral decisions (e.g., Jacoby 1986; Finkel 1989; Rahn et al. 1990; Macdonald and Rabinowitz 1993). For individual citizens, consistency between liberal-conservative identification and vote choice increases markedly, along with degrees of cognitive sophistication and levels of conceptualization. The same general pattern has occurred in presidential elections from the 1970s (Stimson 1975) through the 1980s (Knight 1985; Lyons and Scheb 1992), and into the 1990s (Knight and Lewis 1996; Knight and Erikson 1997). Interestingly, this pattern seems to be broken with the presidential elections of 2000 and 2004; in those years, liberal-conservative self-placements appear to have no direct effect on voting (once other factors are taken into account), regardless of an individual's political sophistication (Jacoby 2004, 2005). However, the indirect effects of ideology (i.e., through their impact on issue attitudes, on the candidates' personalities, etc.) remain both clear-cut and prone to sophistication-based individual differences. Finally, the reciprocal relationship between conceptualization and political activity is confirmed by Leighley (1991), who shows that sophisticated ideological thinking promotes individual political participation, while certain kinds of participation (particularly campaign work and activities aimed at solving national problems) encourage a more ideological view of parties and candidates.

Alternative Approaches

The discussion so far has focused explicitly on the levels of conceptualization and variability in liberal-conservative thinking within the electorate. This emphasis has been deliberate, for two main reasons: First, the levels of conceptualization are an influential theoretical construct, taken directly from *The American Voter*. Second, there is enormous evidence that political elites view the world in liberal-conservative terms (e.g., Jennings 1992; Poole and Rosenthal 1984a; Fiorina, Abrams, and Pope 2005). For both of these reasons, it is important to trace the voluminous research that has addressed the relationships between conceptualization, ideology, and political behavior. Still, a number of other approaches have also been employed to examine individual differences in the ways that people think about political phenomena.

Some research has focused on ideas that seem to be functionally equivalent to the levels of conceptualization, even though grounded in different aspects of psychological theory (Jacoby 2002). In the 1980s, for example, a great deal of attention was devoted to schema theory as a general approach for understanding the structure of political attitudes and behavior (e.g., Lau and Sears 1986). A typical definition of a "schema" was provided at the beginning of this chapter and that should suffice to demonstrate that the nature and functions of schemas are remarkably similar to those attributed to the levels of conceptualization. While much of the political cognition research focused on "consensual" schemas (i.e., those existing more or less uniformly throughout the population), there was also some important work devoted to individual differences in schema usage throughout the general public (Fiske and Kinder 1981; Lodge and Wahlke 1982; Conover and Feldman 1984; Lodge, Hamill, and Blake 1985).

In fact, many of the conclusions generated by this line of work were, basically, interchangeable with those derived from more traditional approaches to belief system structure and ideological thinking. As a result, serious questions were raised about the degree to which the schema concept itself facilitated serious theoretical advances (Kuklinski, Luskin, and Bolland 1991). While defenders of the schema concept had immediate answers to those questions (Conover and Feldman 1991; Lodge and McGraw 1991; A. Miller 1991), this general approach has largely disappeared from the research literature.

A somewhat different, but largely equivalent, approach to political reasoning relies on "heuristics," or cognitive short-cuts. This concept has a long history in the psychological literature (e.g., Simon 1985), and it seems to have been first explicitly invoked in political science as a means of accounting for seemingly rational voting choices, made in the face of limited information-processing capacities (Herstein 1981). The basic idea is that people rely upon fairly simple and easily accessible criteria (e.g., their feelings about prominent social groups) to guide decision-making in a variety of contexts (Popkin 1994). Sniderman and his colleagues have gone farthest in developing this general approach (Brady and Sniderman 1985; Sniderman, Brody, and Kuklinski 1984; Sniderman et al. 1986). They also stress individual differences within the general public, with less-educated people relying on affect-driven heuristics, while more sophisticated citizens base their decisions on cognitive criteria (Sniderman, Brody, and Tetlock 1991). Other authors have demonstrated that reliance on heuristics varies with both external conditions and individual-level characteristics (Kuklinski et al. 2001) and also that heuristic-based reasoning increases the quality of voting decisions for well-informed citizens, but reduces it among the less-informed strata of the electorate (Lau and Redlawsk 2001). Thus, the nature of the heuristics tend to covary systematically with political sophistication in a manner that is analogous, if not exactly identical, to differences that occur across the levels of conceptualization.

In contrast to the preceding approaches, other researchers have examined individual differences in political thinking from perspectives that are quite different from the tradition started by *The American Voter*. Some analysts have investigated sources of belief system structure that exist largely within the heads of the citizens themselves—that is, the "psychological" rather than "social" foundations of attitudinal constraint (Converse 1964). A few scholars have used in-depth interviews to probe the details of individual belief systems (e.g., Lane 1962; Lamb 1974; Rosenberg 1988; Gamson 1992). This investigative strategy reveals that people often maintain detailed, but personalized, views about the nature of government and the political system. The quality of the reasoning and the scope of the thinking can often be questioned; however, the content of these idiosyncratic belief systems does seem to be quite functional for the individuals who possess them.

Another approach focuses on the dimensionality of political thinking, suggesting for various reasons that the research derived from *The American Voter* is wrong in assuming that sophistication should lead to the largely unidimensional views of the world that are implied by the general liberal-conservative continuum. Some authors have argued that the evaluative dimensions underlying political judgments are domain-specific (e.g., Peffley and Hurwitz 1985; Feldman 1988). Others suggest that there are not only multiple evaluative dimensions underlying mass political orientations; there is also a great deal of variability from one person to the next in the degree to which individuals rely upon the respective dimensions to structure their own beliefs and attitudes (Marcus, Tabb, and Sullivan 1974). Still another line of work indicates that political sophistication leads to greater cognitive complexity and, therefore, multidimensionality in political thinking (Luttbeg 1968; Tetlock 1983, 1984).

The various approaches that stress complexity in mass political orientations are noteworthy precisely because they show that even relatively unsophisticated citizens can, and do, maintain views of government and political phenomena that make sense, at least from their own personal viewpoints. However, this work does not really address the degree to which mass political orientations are congruent with those of political elites. Hence, it is difficult to work out its implications for understanding the quality and external rationality of individual voting decisions.

The Increasing Theoretical Importance of Political Sophistication

Despite the contributions that the levels of conceptualization have made to theories of political behavior, they have not appeared in many recent empirical analyses. Instead, the primary source of individual differences in political thinking is now believed to lie in variations in individual degrees of political sophistication. Luskin (1987) defines sophistication as a combination of three belief system characteristics: (1) Size, or the number of beliefs an individual maintains; (2) range, or the scope of the substantive concerns encompassed by the person's beliefs; and (3) constraint, or the degree of consistency across different beliefs. Thus, a sophisticated individual is a person who possesses many political beliefs, spanning a wide variety of policy areas, whose beliefs in one substantive domain are predictable from the beliefs held in any other domain.

Political sophistication has been measured in a variety of different ways. These include composite indices, based upon the an individual's ability to recognize and differentiate among ideological stimuli (Luskin 1987); ratings of survey respondents based upon the judgments of trained interviewers (Luskin 1990); and individual educational attainment (e.g., Sniderman et al. 1991). However, a consensus has emerged recently that sophistication is measured most effectively by a person's general factual knowledge regarding the elements of American politics (Zaller 1992). Some conceptual and measurement issues do still remain: For example, Kuklinski et al. (2000) raise the problem of widespread misinformation within the mass public, as a countervailing force, working against effective use of political knowledge by the public. Mondak (2001) argues that survey respondents' varying willingness to guess at the answers to factual questions leads to systematic biases in political knowledge as an empirical indicator of political sophistication. Gilens (2001) also demonstrates that domain-specific political knowledge is much less closely related to sophistication than is general knowledge. Despite these potential shortcomings, political sophistication is now typically operationalized through the use of political knowledge.

The empirical relationships between political knowledge and other phenomena are not particularly surprising, in light of the previous voluminous literature on sophistication: Aggregate levels of knowledge are quite low within the mass public (e.g., Bennett 1995, 1996). Political knowledge is closely related to citizens' abilities to translate their personal political orientations into effective choices among policy positions and candidates for public office (Delli Carpini and Keeter 1996; Nie, Junn, and Stehlik-Barry 1996; Althaus 2004).

These recent analyses have been particularly attentive to the normative implications stemming from skewed distributions of political knowledge. They argue, quite convincingly, that poor factual understandings of the political system inhibit the lines of communication between the mass public and political elites, thereby compromising the quality of representation in modern democratic societies. But this seems to be largely a change in emphasis (albeit an important one) from the earlier work: Again, the findings based upon political knowledge generally mirror those obtained with other measures of political sophistication and ideological awareness.

On the other hand, there are dissenting views regarding the impact of citizens' knowledge on political behavior. In a carefully crafted set of experimental analyses, Lau and Redlawsk (e.g., 1997, 2006) build upon the heuristics literature and trace out the ways that individuals cope with the sizable amount of information that streams in during an election campaign. They argue that it is nearly impossible to process and assimilate all of the stimuli that emanate from the candidates, parties, and mass media. Therefore, people make decisions based upon limited subsets of the available information. Nevertheless, sizable majorities still "vote correctly," in the sense that they reach the same decision that they would have made if they had, in fact, taken all of the information into account. Such findings suggest that detailed policy information need not be widely held within the electorate, in order to achieve a reasonable degree of democratic popular control over government. They also demonstrate that scholars continue to disagree about the normative implications of citizens' knowledge, sophistication, and competence within the American electorate.

In conclusion, the analyses presented initially in chapter 10 of *The American Voter* and replicated in the current chapter involve issues that continue to play a central role in the study of public opinion and political behavior. Some supporting evidence on this point lies in the fact that the journal *Critical Review* recently published a symposium in which a number of leading scholars (including Philip E. Converse) debated the normative and empirical concerns raised by Converse's essay "The Nature of Belief Systems in Mass Publics" (Friedman 2006). Again, those concerns were first anticipated in *The American Voter*. While the specific concepts and operational versions of the variables have changed somewhat over the years, the general thrust of the findings and conclusions has remained remarkably consistent: It is impossible to understand how citizens deal with the complexities of the political world without taking into account the rather extreme variability in ideological awareness and political sophistication that exists within the mass public.

SECTION IV

The Social and Economic Context

CHAPTER 11

Membership in Social Groupings

The majority of Americans are not formal members of a political party. But they do feel some psychological affiliation to a party, and that strongly shapes their political behavior. Official party activists compose a very small group, but the group that is psychologically attached to a party is large. That group identification helps us greatly in analyzing their individual political choices. Citizens are part of other groups, besides parties, and these groups can also wield political influence. In the course of a campaign, there may be talk of the "Jewish vote," the "black vote," the "union vote," and so forth. Unlike parties, these groups are not obviously political. They did not come into being because of politics, and serve other purposes. Unions exist to secure benefits from business for their workers; Jewish communities seek to practice their religious beliefs. While such groups have a life separate from politics, their members may reason and act differently in the political arena. We suppose these different ways are brought about, in some manner, by influence of the group on its members.

THE PROBLEM OF GROUP INFLUENCE

The idea of a group influencing its members may seem contradictory. Obviously, the group is only the sum of its individual members. When we assert that the group (a collection of individuals) has an impact on the individuals in it, we may be accused of tautological thinking. This apparent flaw in reasoning has bothered some investigators of groups. For a period, the explanation was that there was a "group mind," distinct from the thoughts of the individual members, that had a life of its own. It was this outside collective mental force that somehow moved group members to be different from others. However, this idea fell from favor, and for a time the problem was left unsolved, although the different behavior of group members persisted.

Eventually, what seemed a compelling argument became dominant. The reality of a group can be psychological, and that reality can change our behavior. When we feel close to our union, that gives the union a separate existence, and it affects our actions. If we learn the union opposes certain legislation, such as passage of the North American Free Trade Agreement (NAFTA), we do not think of the individual members and their different tasks at work. Instead, we consider the union as a whole, acting in our name. Individual leaders we hold to be merely agents for the group. These psychological interpretations color our attitudes and acts. If we know that the union opposes NAFTA, we as individuals will tend to oppose it, because of our feelings for the union.

We respond to groups as single entities, and this gives them their power over us. Our response may be unfavorable or favorable. Bill may oppose NAFTA because his union opposes it. Sally may support NAFTA because she knows Bill's union opposes it (and she herself would never join that union). That is, those who are not group members can be swayed by the politics of the group. Put another way, groups in society stand as guideposts in deciding our own politics, serving as positive or negative *reference groups*. Individuals within a group do not all see the group in exactly the same way. Nevertheless, they do hold in common certain beliefs about the purposes of the group. The beliefs generate notions of behavior appropriate to a sincere group member.

They shape responses to such questions as, "What should a loyal unionist do?" These group norms exist for people, and direct their behavior.

Here we explore the political influence of large national groups, such as unions, blacks, or Jews. These are not small "primary" groups, such as friends, neighbors or family. Still, many of the processes of influence are the same in these "secondary" groups. Further, it seems fair to assume that the influence of primary groups on partisan behavior tends to cancel out on balance. After all, membership in groups of family and friends occurs regardless of party attachment, with no perceptible difference from party to party. The same cannot be said for secondary group memberships, however, which are capable of inducing movement in the national vote, especially under certain conditions.

For secondary groups, membership is pretty much a factual manner. The individual is or is not black or Jewish or in a union. All members are equal, in that they are all simply in the group or not. However, they are not equal in their degree of psychological feeling for the group. Some individuals within a group feel highly attached to it, and some do not. This level of group identification, it turns out, is a useful tool for sorting out voting, looking within different blocs, such as the "Jewish vote." The phenomenon of group identification offers a more general model for understanding the political influence of social groupings.

THE ELEMENTS OF THE MODEL

Several purposes should be served by a model of group influence. First, it should show that the group has a distinctive political norm. Second, it should help explain why some members are less likely than others to follow the group norm. Third, it should help explain the level of group distinctiveness over time. For one example, why do the members of one group persist in conforming to the group norm, maintaining its political homogeneity? For another example, why do members of another group decreasingly conform to the group norm, making it less different from the rest of society? The model expresses itself in the relation of three elements: the individual, the group, and the political world. Our special interest in this chapter is the relationship of the individual to the group, and the group to the political world. The group has a reality, exercising varying amounts of influence on the individual's political behavior. The group acts on the individual as a force, pushing with weight and angle. The vote decision occurs in the context of a field of forces, group and nongroup, positive and negative. The influence of group forces is lessened to the extent other forces are strong. For instance, the Democratic tug of a union endorsement will have less weight if the Republican candidate has immense popular appeal. Below, we first look at the strength of the group force, for different social groups. Then, we examine how that varies over individuals and over time.

ESTABLISHING THE FACT OF GROUP INFLUENCE

The first step involves figuring out the weight of group forces. This is tricky, given that other forces are also acting on the individual voter. Indeed, we will never be 100 percent certain that we have discovered the unalloyed contribution of group influences. Nevertheless, we can establish some useful baseline estimates of that group strength, before going on to develop the group identification model further.

At the beginning, it is important to establish that group behavior should be assessed in a relative sense. That is, how different is the group's behavior relative to the behavior of those not in the group? For example, imagine two categories of voters (category A includes those in the group; category B includes those not in the group), and two candidates for president, a Republican running against an incumbent Democrat. Suppose all A voted Democratic for a Democratic percentage score equal to 100, and all B voted Republican for a Democratic percentage score equal to 0. Then group A is quite distinctive relative to B (A Democratic score − B Democratic Score = 100 − 0 = 100). In contrast, if A and B were exactly alike in their Democratic support, say 64 and 64, then they would not be distinct at all (A Democratic score − B Democratic Score = 64 − 64 = 0). And this lack of distinction would hold even though A voted Democratic by a wide margin (64 percent). A key point, then, is how different A is relative to B. To take a real example, look at African Americans in the 2000 presidential election. Of that group, 92 percent said they voted for Gore, while only 47 percent of other races voted for Gore. In this election, blacks appear quite distinctive as a voting group, 92 − 47 = 45.

Table 11.1 looks at other groups, using this measure of distinctiveness. The degree of adherence to the norm of Democratic voting across the 2000 and 2004 presidential elections is examined for six major secondary groups: union members, Catholics, Jews, blacks, Hispanics, and women. Observe that the amount of distinctiveness varies, from group to group, and from election to election. Further, despite the variation, each group tends to maintain its relative rank in terms of distinctiveness. For example, Catholics show the least distinction, with both year's score near 0. Union members are about in the middle in terms of distinction. Blacks demonstrate the most distinctiveness, in both elections, followed by Jews. One implication is that the pattern of group voting does not change greatly from election to election. In other words, there may be a fair amount of stability in a group influence model.

Before accepting such a measure of distinctiveness, however, other sources of this distinctiveness, besides the group itself, must be ruled out. Theoretically, the observed distinctive behavior of group members may come from two sources. One possibility is that those in the group psychologically connect with the group norm and react accordingly. For example, union members may believe that they should vote Democratic because "that is what we do in our shop." This would be an example of the group influence the model postulates. But another possibility is that the distinctive vote of the group members actually has nothing to do with any sort of connection to, or identification with, the group itself. For example, union members may tend to vote Democratic because they are lower-income. Perhaps they believe that the Democrats are more likely to help less well-off people like themselves. Then the fact of the distinctive Democratic vote of union members would have nothing to do with the union per se. Union membership would be an accidental accompaniment to the real source of their Democratic vote—their lower income.

If the first possibility prevails, then group influence is operating. If the second possibility prevails, then something other than group influence, economic hardship in this example, is operating. Of course, in the real world, voters might be influenced by a mix of their group membership, their economic circumstances, and other politically relevant life situations. To assess more carefully the actual impact of the group, we need to separate out its influence from these other forces. That means comparing group members to nongroup members, among voters who

TABLE 11.1. The Distinctiveness of Voting Behavior among Several Social Groupings, 2000–2004

	2000	2004
Union[a]	+11	+18
Catholics[b]	+1	−1
Jewish[b]	+39	+28
Blacks[c]	+45	+50
Hispanics[c]	+12	+18
Women[d]	+9	+7

Note: Each entry indicates the difference in percentage Democratic presidential vote (of the two-party vote) between the group members and the nongroup members. If the number is positive, that indicates the group was more Democratic than the nongroup. If the number is negative, that indicates the group was less Democratic than the nongroup. Sample sizes for each comparison ranged from 711 to 1,054 in 2000 and from 526 to 788 in 2004, depending on the group. Data are from NES postelection surveys, 2000 and 2004.

[a]"Union" refers to respondents living in a household where at least one person belonged to a union.

[b]Religion is determined by a question about what religious services the respondent attended.

[c]Racial group is determined by the respondent's self-description.

[d]Gender is determined by the interviewer's observation.

have the same life circumstance. To achieve this control, one might measure the distinctiveness of union members within subsamples of voters who have an equivalent income. If it were found that, among lower-income voters, union membership still made for the distinctively Democratic voting reported in table 11.1, then belief in the reality of group influence would be increased.

However, before that conclusion was drawn, the group voting pattern would have to be checked for middle- and high-income voters as well. And any firmer assessment would await consideration of other life situation variables, such as education. This could become a very long variable list, and we might never be able to definitively answer the question. Fortunately, we know that certain outstanding variables account for much of the difference in an individual's life situation, namely, education, occupational status, income, and age. The politics flowing from such central life characteristics are studied in more detail in the next chapter. For now we wish to control for their influence, to see if they are distorting the group effects we appear to be observing.

This controlling could be done with a series of tables of subsamples of the data, as described above. But that would take a long time, and be quite inefficient. The number of respondents in each category would dwindle to dangerously low numbers as we divided the data into more and more detailed control categories, for example, elderly employed voters with low income and low education. And that would be only one table among

TABLE 11.2. Distinctiveness of Presidential Vote among Certain Groups, with Life Situation Controlled, 2000 and 2004

	2000	2004
Union	+18	+22
Catholics	+3	−0.3
Jewish	+38	+31
Blacks	+43	+46
Hispanics	+11	+22
Women	+9	+2

Note: Entries are coefficient estimates from a multiple regression (ordinary least squares), treated as a linear probability model (where the dependent variable = 1 if Democratic vote, 0 if Republican). The control variables in each equation are as follows: education (highest grade completed), occupational status (employed or not), income, and age. The groups are defined as in table 11.1. Data are from NES postelection surveys, 2000 and 2004.

many that would need to be analyzed. Thus, instead of this cumbersome tabular method of control, we employ the statistical control that multiple regression affords. Conceptually, it is equivalent to looking at group effects within subsamples of voters of the same socioeconomic characteristics. But it maintains a high sample size, arriving at an instantaneous mathematical separation of group influences from the influences of these life situation variables. We see the results of this analysis in table 11.2.

When the voting distinctiveness scores of tables 11.1 and 11.2 are compared, we observe that little has changed. The new numbers are generally quite close to the old ones. While different life situations may shape the vote in their own right, they essentially operate independently of group membership, which has an effect unique unto itself. For example, Catholics, we see, remain the least distinctive in their voting pattern. Union members still hover near the middle of the pack, even though their Democratic tendency becomes somewhat clearer. Blacks continue to be the most distinctive voting group. Even though this exercise of statistical control does not alter our substantive interpretation, it moves us closer to identifying the true electoral impact of group membership. Moreover, it firms up the notion that some groups wield more influence than others. Why is that? To answer that question, we need to consider further aspects of the model.

THE RELATIONSHIP OF THE INDIVIDUAL TO THE GROUP

It is necessary to measure how much an individual relates to his or her group. Some members are very attached to the group, others less. While everyone may be in the group in name, certain members will be strongly pulled by the group, others will be pulled only weakly, and still others may actually feel nothing for the group. Thus, even though all members carry the same group label, they can differ substantially in their psychological attachment to it. Further, this attachment may have different sources. Members may like the group because of the friendship circle, the tangible benefits, or the status it provides. Our concern is not with these various roots of group identification. Rather, we simply seek a general measure of its strength. To measure party identification, we have used survey items that tap the respondent's feeling of closeness to a political party. Similarly, to measure group identification, we employ items to assess the respondent's feeling of personal belonging to the group.

Different questions, which vary appropriately according to the group, are available for this purpose. Consider the following type of item:

Please tell me if X is a group you feel particularly close to. Yes or no.

Items of this form were used to measure group identification in the 2000 NES, for those respondents who were classified as union members, blacks, Hispanics, or women. Those who responded "yes" were coded as high identifiers. (Unfortunately, this question was not available in the 2004 NES.) To measure group identification with the different religious groups, the following type of item was posed in the two surveys, to those first classified as Catholic or Jewish; those who responded "yes" were considered high identifiers.

Do you consider religion to be an important part of your life or not? Yes or no.

Here is the initial hypothesis of the model: the more identified the individual with the group, the closer he or she will adhere to the group norm. Table 11.3 offers clear support for this hypothesis. Within five of the six groups, those who more highly identify are more likely to vote with the Democratic norm. For example, Hispanics who feel close to Hispanics as a group were 12 percent more likely to vote Democratic. The most dramatic example comes from Jewish voters. Those who felt their religion was important were 26 percent more likely to vote Democratic.

TABLE 11.3. Vote Division within Test Groups, According to Strength of Group Identification, 2000

	High Id.	Low Id.	Discrepancy
Union	70	54	+16
Catholics	48	63	−15
Jewish	93	67	+26
Blacks	94	92	+2
Hispanics	69	57	+12
Women	62	50	+12

Note: Entries in columns one and two indicate the percentage of the two-party vote that was Democratic in the 2000 presidential election. Entries in column three are the column two score subtracted from the column one score. Positive discrepancy scores indicate that high identifiers are more likely to vote Democratic, while negative discrepancy scores indicate that high identifiers are more likely to vote Republican. The data are from the NES postelection survey, 2000.

Strength of group identification is a variable that obviously should remain in the model. Establishing this fact is rather an accomplishment, since it is something that people do not like to admit to directly. That is to say, few of us want to believe that we are voting a certain way because we are the member of some group. We prefer to believe that we arrived at our vote choice as a free agent, independent of the influence of such social forces

Further examination of table 11.3 reveals some interesting group differences. High Catholic identifiers are more at odds with low Catholic identifiers than might be guessed from the mild difference reported in table 11.1. Catholics with low identification are more likely to be Democratic, in line with the traditional view of the Catholic voter. But Catholics with high identification are slightly Republican. The implication is that the Catholic group voting norm may be in transition. Another surprise is with blacks. Those who highly identify with their race barely distinguish themselves from low identifiers. That difference, it turns out, is mostly due to ceiling effects. Almost all blacks are Democratic voters, over 90 percent in each category of identification. It is extremely difficult to arrive at high discrepancy scores, given a near consensus. This leads to consideration of relevant group-level characteristics that might explain the table 11.3 results.

Group identification can be examined from the individual and the aggregate levels. Looking at individuals, our results show that those most likely to break away from the group are those that are weakly identified with it. Looking at groups as a whole, we may expect some to have many dedicated members, while others do not. Let us call the former groups highly *cohesive*. To the extent a group is cohesive in this sense, it many exercise more power over its members.

In table 11.4, our groups are labeled for "higher cohesiveness"—over 80 percent of members highly identified, or "lower cohesiveness"— under 80 percent highly identified. Of all these groups, blacks appear the most cohesive, while union members appear the least. Interestingly, knowing the cohesiveness of a group helps little in predicting its electoral distinctiveness. To appreciate this, observe that the rank of the 2000 vote distinction scores of table 11.2 corresponds poorly, for the most part, with the 2000 election cohesiveness scores of table 11.4; respectively, union members (3, 6); Catholics (6, 2); Jews (2, 5); blacks (1, 1), Hispanics (4, 4); women (5, 3). To account for these vote distinction scores, it is necessary to understand other aspects of the group influence model.

TABLE 11.4. Relation of Group Cohesiveness to Group
Identification, 2000

Cohesiveness	Identification Score	Group
Higher	91.4	blacks
	89.7	Catholics
	84.6	women
Lower	79.0	Hispanic
	75.0	Jewish
	54.4	union

Note: For blacks, Hispanics, women, and unions, the entry is the percentage who felt "close" to the group. For Catholics and Jews, the entry is the percentage who believed their religion was "important." The data are from the NES presidential postelection survey, 2000.

THE RELATIONSHIP OF THE GROUP TO THE WORLD OF POLITICS

The individual relates to the group by psychological identification with it. The group relates to politics by *proximity* to it. Secondary groups, such as those studied here, have a life apart from the world of politics. Still, in carrying out their purposes, distance from the political arena may vary. In fact we can order groups along a continuum of closeness to politics. Certain groups in our society are highly political, for example, the Democratic Party, the Republican Party, the American Civil Liberties Union. Other groups appear not political at all, for example, the Numismatic Society, the Elks, the National Tennis Association. Others are in between, for example, the National Rifle Association, the American Medical Association, the Sierra Club. It seems easy enough to place such groups in terms of political proximity. For our secondary groups under study, one might judge "unions" as the closest to politics. If we think about why this placement is made, we realize we are rating groups according to their links with objects that are traditionally viewed as political—issues, candidates, lobbying, courts, elections.

Groups, in trying to further their basic ends, are evaluated here according to their use of political avenues. Of course, we would not expect everyone, even every group member, to agree with all political activities of the group. At the one extreme are those who believe that the group has no business in politics. At the other extreme are those who believe that the group should be fully engaged in political pursuits. In other words, members vary in their belief in the legitimacy of political activity on the part of the group. We hypothesize that *to the extent members think the group should keep its distance from politics, their voting pattern will be less distinctive, even for those fully identified with the group.*

Fortunately, we can test this hypothesis because, in addition to measures of group identification, we have measures of the political legitimacy of the group. In the 2000 NES, respondents were asked the following question:

> Some people think that certain groups have too much influence in American life and politics, while other people feel that certain groups don't have as much influence as they deserve. I am going to read you a list of groups, for each one tell me whether that group has too much influence, just about the right amount of influence, or too little influence.

On the one hand, those who see the group as having "too much" influence grant it little political legitimacy. They want the group to undo some of its ties to politics. On the other, there are those who see the group as having "too little" influence. For them politics is a legitimate group enterprise, and they want the group to be more engaged in that arena.

In table 11.5, we relate feelings of groups' political legitimacy to voting distinctiveness, at the same time controlling for group identification. Not all of our secondary groups could be examined, because of issues of sample size or cell size. And in one case we had to substitute a feeling thermometer measure because the legitimacy measure was absent. Nevertheless, we managed a look at three groups—women, union members, and Catholics. For each of the groups, the distinctiveness of presidential vote varies with belief in legitimacy (see the "Total" column in each part of the table). The association appears greatest among union members, which show a 29-percentage-point difference depending on whether they believe strongly or weakly in group political action. Still, the spread is large for all these groups, as the numbers show.

Moreover, this strong association persists after controlling for group identification, as we hypothesized. (The pattern is clearest reading down the first column, the high identifiers, in each part of the table.) Once this control is imposed, it is actually the Catholics who demonstrate the biggest effects from the political legitimacy variable, again for an absolute 29-point difference ($33 - 62 = 29$). The last finding merits reflection. It shows that, even among self-identified Catholics who all give their religion high priority, attitudes about the proper political role of the church clearly affect their vote. Those who strongly believe in the political legitimacy of the church are decidedly more Republican. Again, the suggestion is that Catholics may be undergoing a change in their group voting norm.

TABLE 11.5. Presidential Voting across Secondary Membership Groups, by Strength of Group Identification and Belief in Legitimacy of Group Political Activity, 2000 (in percentages)

A. Women (N = 577)

Belief in Legitimacy[b]	Group Identification[a]		
	High	Low	Total
Strong	63	62	63
Medium	48	39	46
Weak	50	13	38

B. Union (N = 174)

Belief in Legitimacy[c]	Group Identification[a]		
	High	Low	Total
Strong	77	58	73
Medium	64	67	65
Weak	50	43	44

C. Catholics (N = 235)

Belief in Legitimacy[b]	Group Identification[d]		
	High	Low	Total
Strong	33	x[e]	40
Medium	47	57	48
Weak	62	80	65

Note: An entry indicates the Democratic percentage share of the two-party vote for that particular mix of group identification and belief in legitimacy scores. The column headed "Total" indicates the association between belief in legitimacy and the Democratic vote share, without controlling on group identification. The data are from the NES postpresidential election survey, 2000.

[a]Group identification as measured by whether the respondent feels "close" to the group (high) or not (low).

[b]Belief in group legitimacy as measured from an assessment of group influence variable, where strong = "too little influence," medium = "about the right amount of influence," and weak = "too much influence."

[c]Belief in group legitimacy as measured by feeling thermometer scores toward the group: strong (>75), medium (50–75), and weak (<50).

[d]Group identification as measured by whether they see their religious life as "important" (high) or "not" (low).

[e]The number of cases in this cell is less than five.

To this point, we have gone over different links—the group to politics, the individual to the group. If these elements are added together, we should be able to better estimate the more global impact of group factors on the voting decision. Consider both variables in table 11.5. The effects appear most dramatic for women (table 11.5.a). Study the two extreme cells—high identification and strong belief (= 63) versus low identification and weak belief (= 13). Women who are highly gender-identified and strongly committed to group political action are a great deal more likely to vote Democratic when compared to women who are not highly gender-identified and believe they should "back off" politics (63 − 13, a 50-percentage-point difference). Legitimacy, an expression of the group-politics connection, and identification, an expression of the individual-group connection, take us some way to a fuller understanding of the distinctive vote of social groupings.

SECONDARY GROUPS, THE POLITICAL PARTY, AND THE INFLUENCE PROCESS

The political party can be considered a group, and psychological attachment to it an example of group identification. While the political party fits into a general model of group membership, it is a special case. We have just discussed the components of the relationship between social groups and politics. If we examine the party in terms of these components, we see that it stands for the extreme case. With respect to the variable of proximity, it lies no distance from the political world; instead, it is at the center of it. Political parties, as least the major ones, have high salience, election after election, and always have members who are candidates for office. Their main goal is to achieve victory at the polls, rather than attain some social end for the group via politics. They are recognized as fully legitimate actors in the political world, and they take explicit stands on a range of issues.

Because the party is a sort of "supergroup" with respect to politics, membership in it will usually wield more political influence than membership in any social group. That still does not mean social groups are without political influence, as this chapter has shown. One source of this political influence, which we have thus far neglected, is its persistence over time. The distinct vote of a group is not a simple product of the issues of the current election. For example, the particularly Democratic nature of the union vote in 2000 does not come from the issues debated in that campaign. That is part of it, surely, but perhaps a small part. The political influence of a group, when it manifests itself, tends to operate over time, across elections. With respect to our union example, we observe that its Democratic character continued little changed into the 2004 election; respectively, 2000 = 18 and 2004 = 22 (recall table 11.2).

Political parties exercise a pivotal role in ensuring this transmission of group distinctiveness, from election to election. Sometimes, the group's link to a party is obvious, as when a member of the group is a candidate for office, or the issue of the day bears directly on group interests. A secondary group example might be when a Hispanic is running for office, and the issue is English as the official state language. Given such a situation, the group member has little need to be told directly that the group has political interests at stake. But under more usual electoral circumstances, when the group connection to the campaign is less than clear, group leaders need to explain how the particular contest is relevant for their members. This is where the political party comes in. Candidates, elections, issues come and go, but the party lives on. To the extent psychologically attached group members are convinced that they are better served by a particular party, they come to identify with it. Once that party identification establishes itself in the group context, it acts as a beacon guiding the member through the political thicket. As new candidates and issues arise, they will be judged in terms of how well they conform to the dictates of the party that defends the group standard.

Over time, this pattern tends to be self-reinforcing, as group voters learn from repeated electoral contests that their party does better by them. Their party identification comes to act as a filter, sorting incoming political stimuli positively or negatively, according to their agreement with the group-party connection. Hence, once the distinctiveness of group voting is established, it is highly resistant to change. It is no accident that the patterns of group voting appear as stable as they do from the 2000 to the 2004 presidential election. (Recall tables 11.1 and 11.2.) According to the theory developed here, that is more or less expected. Of course, change in the group vote is not impossible. Extreme events or intense feelings on a particular issue may bring group leaders to recommend a switch in allegiance. While this new direction may face opposition at first in the rank-and-file, that can diminish. An outstanding example is the Catholic vote. Historically, it was distinctively Democratic. However, that pattern began to alter, as early as the 1950s. In these current data, one sees that the Democratic vote of Catholics has essentially been effaced and, taken as a whole, it is no longer a distinctive voting group in American society. Indeed, by 2004 even the residual differences seem to have disappeared. (Recall table 11.2.) Further, our multivariate results point to the possiblity that the Catholic voting group norm may become Republican (recall table 11.5).

POWER AND LIMITATIONS OF THE MODEL

To elaborate the funnel of causality, more remote influences have been explored, in particular the peculiar politics of membership in secondary social groups. The model takes as real examples six of these groups: union members, Catholics, Jews, blacks, Hispanics, and women. These groups do, and have, played a major role in U.S. politics. This enumeration does not cover all possible social groupings that might have been considered. Still they seem a typical selection and offer a broad testing ground for group theory. Further, the framework constructed, and the findings elicited, seem to apply equally well to the political party when it is treated as a group.

The group influence model, then, has wide application. Still, it does not apply everywhere. Some social cleavages are merely arithmetic, allowing for physical separation but no psychological connection. For example, the geographic blocks in a census tract demarcate people, but those people are not expected to have a group consciousness. Of course, that could occur in some areas, where there was a psychological identification with a certain neighborhood. Then group identification, and its potential for political consequences, could exist. But the map divisions themselves promise no such group influence.

In terms of social influences on politics, two pure types can be noted: group behavior and structural behavior. In this chapter, the focus has been on group behavior. The next chapter will eventually consider structural behavior, that is, individuals with the same social characteristic who tend to act in concert politically, even though they have no psychological connection with each other. Of course, in the real world, these two types may be joined in one set of individuals. Social class is an outstanding example of this mix, and is the first topic of consideration in chapter 12.

COMMENTARY AND CONTROVERSY

Group Theories

The fundamental argument of this chapter, from *The American Voter* (Campbell et al. 1960), is that the group shapes the politics of its members because they psychologically identify with it. Recent scholarship supports this argument. Clark and Masters (2001), for example, reveal that greater belief in union goals leads to greater support of union-sponsored candidates. Further, Rapoport, Stone, and Abramowitz (1991) show that union activists give stronger backing to union-endorsed candidates than the rank-and-file. In a recent paper, McDermott (2006) demonstrates that AFL-CIO Democratic candidate endorsements act as electoral information cues. Generally speaking, social groups help voters organize the political world, offering valuable signals in the typical low-information election (Sniderman, Brody, and Tetlock 1991;Wlezien and Miller 1997).

Labor Unions

Leaders of organized labor have generally been committed to the Democratic Party, at least since 1936, when they supported FDR's reelection (see the useful summary in Chang 2001). Truman, who followed Roosevelt in the White House, vetoed the antiunion Taft-Hartley Act, passed in 1946 by a Republican congressional majority. When Congress sustained this right-to-work law over Truman's veto, the labor movement wedded itself still closer to the Democrats. In 1952, the American Federation of Labor (the AFL) formally backed Stevenson for president. In the 1960s, Kennedy curried labor favor by seeking to amend Taft-Hartley. His successor, Johnson, was close to Walter Reuther of the CIO (Congress of Industrial Organizations). While AFL-CIO head George Meany could not back McGovern in 1972, their leadership returned to the Democratic fold in 1976. Reagan's staunch opposition to labor elicited fierce AFL-CIO backing of Mondale in 1984. President Clinton endorsed certain policies that unions opposed, for example, NAFTA and favored trade status for China; however, he managed to garner organized labor support because he put his name to the Family and Medical Leave Act and other legislation unions supported. In 2000, the United Auto Workers and the International Brotherhood of Teamsters, incensed over the issue of trade with China, held off backing Gore and flirted with the third-party Nader candidacy. However, union voters stayed away from Nader, remaining solidly in the Democratic column.

We observe, then, that labor leadership tends to declare for the Democratic presidential contender. In looking across U.S. presidential election results, one expectation is that this Democratic commitment will be generally reflected in the union rank-and-file. It certainly is in the 2000 and 2004 contests analyzed in this chapter. (Recall tables 11.1 and 11.2.) Does this distinctive pro-Democratic voting on the part of union households manifest itself in earlier elections? Different scholars have explored that question, using NES data back to 1948 (Chang 2001; Sousa 1993). These efforts show that, regardless of the presidential election, 1948–96, this pro-Democratic union sentiment manifests itself.

Another expectation is that the union/nonunion Democratic voting distinction would vary, in response to varying commitments by union leaders. This hypothesis seems borne out. For at least two of the contests union bosses were outspokenly in favor of the Democrats. In 1948, they were very pro-Truman because of his stand against Taft-Hartley. In 1984, they were very pro-Mondale, because of Reagan's bitter antiunion stance. For these two elections, we observe the largest differences across the period, respectively, 37 points and 20 points. In contrast, for another two contests, union leadership was either against the Democratic candidate (as in 1972) or ambivalent toward him (as in 1992). For these two elections, we see the vote gap at its narrowest, at about 10 points each time. These seem to be especially clear examples of the role of group leaders in communicating to their membership the stakes of the contest.

These days some argue that unions no longer serve members the way they once did. Others argue that Democrats no longer differ from Republicans in terms of union policies. Either of these notions, if true, could precipitate a decline in the Democratic distinctiveness of the union vote. Is there, indeed, such a decline? The 1948–2004 NES difference scores reveal no such trend. It is true that there are some extreme values, as reported above, that is, 1948, 1972, 1984, 1992. Nevertheless, the decade-by-decade average score since the 1950s is just under 20 points. Thus, our results for 2000 and 2004 are in line with the past trend. Note especially that the differences, respectively, for 2000 and 2004, are 18.3 and 21.5, once relevant life situation variables are controlled (see table 11.2). Our contemporary analyzes fully support the conclusion earlier reached by Sousa (1993, 748): "The conventional wisdom that there has been a steady decline in the union effect on voting in presidential elections is wrong."

What *has* declined is the portion of the workforce in a union household. The Gallup organization over time has asked respondents whether they are a union member. That percentage has dropped from 15 percent in 1955 to 10 percent in 2005. Maybe in response to this diminishing number, contemporary respondents (August 2005) are more likely to say they want labor unions to have more influence (38 percent) rather than less influence (30 percent). However, this attitude is highly partisan, with 60 percent of Democrats wanting them to have more influence, as opposed to only 17 percent of Republicans. Moreover, when asked directly if they approve of labor unions, 77 percent of the Democrats say "yes," in contrast to only 38 percent for Republicans. What these current numbers indicate is that the union remains an important, highly partisan voting group in our society.

Blacks

Of all the major secondary groupings in the United States, blacks voting patterns are the most distinctive. African Americans overwhelmingly vote Democratic in presidential elections, and have done so for some time. Why is that? There are multiple reasons. Here we have noted that they are a very cohesive group, with extremely high levels of identification. Indeed, sometimes so strong that it becomes difficult, using survey research, to track differences in black public opinion. As Kinder, Burns, and Vieregge (2005, 32) observe, in their recent study on liberalism, race, and taxes, "Virtually every black interviewed in 2000 reported that they felt close to their racial group. This is interesting and perhaps even important, but it sabotages our particular purpose here, since we are interested in accounting for variation in black opinion."

The politics of group identity has long-standing theoretical origins. (Besides the *American Voter*, see Smith, Bruner, and White 1956.) When that identification intensifies, so does the political reaction. For blacks, then, the expectation is still greater anti-Republican sentiment, under those conditions. Kinder, Burns, and Vieregge (2005, 21–22), using NES feeling thermometer scores, placed blacks into two categories, those who were "warm" to their group and those who were "relatively cool." They found that black Americans who were "warm" were less likely to support the Bush tax cuts of 2001 and 2003.

The indication is that black Democratic support is issue-based, rather than merely symbolic. Indeed, during the depression, the Democrats began to pursue policies that especially resonated with the economic needs of black Americans (Walton 1985). Under the civil rights banner of the 1960s, and carrying out the War on Poverty, the Democrats became the party better representing racial equality and economic opportunity (Carmines and Stimson 1989). Black citizens have not merely sought out the Democrats; the Democrats have sought them out in turn. A recent study by Wielhouwer (2000), examining data across the 1952–96 period, demonstrates that the Democrats are more likely to contact black voters, through canvassing and other party activities, than are the Republicans.

Of course, African Americans are not exclusively Democratic. There are black Republican voters and candidates. An interesting question is whether black Republican candidates draw more votes from black voters than would be the case if the candidate were white. Kidd et al. (2005) reported a study examining a 2004 congressional race (Third District of Virginia) where there were two black candidates. They discovered that the black electorate basically stayed with the Democratic candidate, resisting the policies advocated by the Republican candidate, despite the racial identity. This suggests the importance of substantive issues for blacks, as opposed to symbolic issues alone.

Will the overwhelming Democratic voting pattern persist among blacks? It is hard to say. Thus far, it has persisted a long time. In the 1952 NES survey, the first available on the question, they registered a +41.2 percentage vote difference in favor of Democrat Adlai Stevenson, comparable to the distinctions reported here for 2000 and 2004. Moreover, this difference in favor of the Democrats held, even among southern blacks by themselves, where a Republican preference might have been imagined (Campbell et al. 1960, 302). White flight from the Democratic Party in the South poses a relatively new and strong barrier to black movement into the Republican camp. Finally, the media can play a role in maintaining African Americans as a Democratic bastion, by refusing to acknowledge that bastion. For example, a current study by Philpot and White (2005) content analyzed TV news transcripts concerning the Trent Lott affair (when the Senate majority leader wished that Strom Thurmond had been elected president in 1948). They found that 22.5 percent of the African American commentators were Republican, a share over twice that in the population of African American voters. Thus, average white American voters may be prompted to believe that black Republicans are much more numerous than they are. Republican political activists, then, have less incentive to recruit them. Such a disincentive helps keep black Americans in the Democratic Party.

Hispanics

Historically, Americans of Hispanic origin have been largely Democratic in their partisanship (Cain, Kiewiet, and Uhlaner 1991; Welch and Sigelman 1993). In the main, this comes from their disadvantaged socioeconomic status. In addition, the Democratic Party has done more on other issues Hispanics care about: civil rights, Spanish language programs in school, immigrant services. Of course, not all Latinos are Democrats. While certain key groups, such as Mexican Americans and Puerto Ricans, largely are, Cuban Americans are not.

These distinct voting patterns among different groups of Hispanics remind us that our focus is on how group identity influences the vote. Mexican Americans' group identity inclines them to the Democrats, while for Cuban Americans the inclination is Republican. This supports our notion that the stronger the group identity, the more likely it is that a member will vote for the group's preferred party (recall table 11.3.) Uhlaner and Garcia (2005, 82) specifically pursue this hypothesis: "Those Latinos most integrated into their national-origin group we expect to be most likely to adopt the group's dominant party preferences." They analyze data from the Latino National Political Survey (LNPS), where respondents were asked questions about their group integration. Specifically, they build an out-group contact measure, which taps the proportion of friends and other social acquaintances who were Anglo as opposed to Latino.

The test idea is that the more out-group contact members have, the less likely they are to support the group's preferred party. This hypothesis is most clearly sustained for Mexican and Cuban Americans. Other group markers, such as Spanish language reliance and Catholic religion, also support this pattern. The authors conclude: "we have established a strong relationship between group social integration and partisanship. Among these Latino groups, where identifiers with one party far outnumber other partisans, those people whose social interactions stay more within the group are more likely to share the dominant partisanship, while those whose social interactions move outside of the group are more likely to identify with the minority party" (Uhlaner and Garcia 2005, 89). These results provide a vivid example of the power of group identity to influence political choice.

Recently, there has been speculation that Latinos are shifting their political allegiance, perhaps because of greater integration into the larger American community. In particular, there has been talk that the Republicans are making a substantial number of converts among them. The notion is growing that they are a "swing" voting group, that might make or break an election (Martin 2002; Mason 2002). In 2000, George Bush hazarded a better party image, attempting to speak Spanish and offering Hispanics other symbolic gestures (Sabato and Scott 2002). One Republican exit poll actually gave Bush 35 percent of the Hispanic vote, up from 21 percent in 1996 (Nicholson and Segura 2005, 52). However, this estimate is contradicted in our table 11.1. The 66 percent Hispanic vote for Gore, calculated from the Tomás Rivera Policy Institute preelection poll, contradicts it as well (Nicholson, Pantojy, and Segura 2006).

It has been argued that for Republicans to change Hispanic voting in a lasting way, they must change Hispanic party identification. Republicans appear not to have managed this, because they are pushing social conservatism and candidate image, issues not especially important to this population. As Nicholson and Segura (2005, 52–53) remark: "On issues that matter to Latinos, including economic opportunity, crime, education, and especially racial issues, Latinos continue to perceive the Democratic Party as more credible and supportive of their preferences and interests." In an analysis of the Tomás Rivera 2000 poll, Nicholson, Pantojy, and Segura (2006) found that Hispanics with low information tended to favor Bush more often than those with high information. Where issues count (which it did for the majority of these voters), they weigh in favor of the Democrats.

In 2004, certain exit poll analyses suggested that the Republicans had turned the corner for the Hispanic voter, gaining something like 45 percent of their vote (Alonso-Zaldivar 2004; Johnson 2004). However, it seems more likely that Hispanics voted something like two to one for Kerry over Bush (Leal et al. 2005). The results in our table 11.1 indicate that Kerry beat Bush by a wide margin in this group, clearly wider than Gore beat Bush in 2000. All in all, the 2004 outcome favors the argument that the Republicans have failed at making inroads into the Hispanic voting block.

The Gender Gap

The "gender gap," the difference in voting preferences of men and women, has existed at least since surveys have tried to measure it. It may even have existed since the start of female suffrage (Mueller 1988). If the early NES studies of presidential vote choice are examined, the gap initially favored the Republicans. Not until the 1960s did it turn Democratic, where it has remained. Across the 1980s, Democratic presidential candidates won about seven percentage points more from female voters. In the 1990s, it peaked at 1996, when Clinton made the lead over 12 points. Some even said that the women's vote was responsible for Clinton's reelection. (An excellent review of trends since 1948 appears in O'Regan, Stambough, and Thorson 2005.) Our data of table 11.1, with gap estimates of +9 and +7, respectively, for the 2000 and 2004 presidential elections, indicate that it has returned to a "normal" level, the 1980s benchmark.

The 1980 election appears to have been pivotal, producing a significant expansion of this gap from prior low levels (Chaney, Alvarez, and Nagler 1998; Kaufmann and Petrocik 1999). Reagan's positions on the Equal Rights Amendment, welfare, and abortion, for example, seemed to move some women into the Democratic camp. A considerable literature has developed that suggests women have a different issue agenda from men, and that this causes them to move away from the Republicans (Sapiro and Conover 1997). Women, Howell and Day (2000) argue, care more about "compassion" issues—abortion, child care, education—while men care more about "force" issues—defense, capital punishment, gun control. As a group, women see compassion issues as of special interest, and tend to vote disproportionately for Democrats, who are usually rated better on their handling of these issues.

According to group theory, women who are highly identified should be more likely to vote for the group majority party. Elizabeth Cook (1993, 230–35), utilizing the NES surveys, created a measure of "feminist consciousness," which combined responses to one item on equal roles for women with another item on feelings toward the women's movement. She found that women who strongly supported role equality and felt positive toward the women's movement were much more likely to vote Democrat, at least after 1980. For instance, in 1988, feminist women gave 74 percent to Dukakis, whereas nonfeminist women gave only 36 percent to him. Interestingly, this difference is similar to that shown in table 11.5 between women who are highly identified and believe they should have more political say, and those less identified who believe the opposite. Those results also differ, however, in that they do not necessarily measure what Cook here calls feminist consciousness.

In the 2004 presidential election, Republicans got a little bit more of the women's vote than they had in 2000. A popular reason given for this in the press was Bush's appeal to the "security moms," alleged to have helped him to victory, just as the "soccer moms" had done for Clinton in 1996. Carroll (2005) studied this question through analysis of media contents and exit poll data. Carroll identified the chief sociological characteristics of security moms as follows: married, white, living in the suburbs, with children. Politically they were defined by her as swing voters very concerned about terrorism and protecting their families. Exit poll data on these "security moms" showed them no more likely than others to vote for Bush. Moreover, white, married men with children were more likely than these "security moms" to worry about terrorism.

Compared to other groups of women, Carroll's security moms did not manifest higher levels of concern over terrorism. Further, there was no evidence that they were swing voters. Instead, most had made up their minds early. Carroll (2005) concludes: "despite considerable media attention, empirical support for the common characterization of security moms was found to be sorely lacking in the national exit poll data from 2004." By her analysis, the top issues for women in 2004 were health care, education, the economy, and jobs.

The Catholic Vote

Our analyses suggest the Catholic vote as a distinctive Democratic bloc is vanishing, if not already vanished (see table 11.1). For perspective on that result, long-term trends are worth consulting. (Here we draw on the excellent paper by Gray, Peri, and Bendyna [2005].) An examination of final Gallup polls and the NES frequencies for 1952–2004 presidential elections shows that in 10 of those 14 contests Catholics declared a majority (50 percent or more) for the Democratic versus the Republican candidate. (For Gallup, it was otherwise in 1972, 1980, 1984, and 1992; for NES it was otherwise in 1956, 1972, 1980, and 1984.)

Historically, then, across the post–World War II period, Catholics have favored the Democrats. However, more subtle measures reveal this support in steady decline. From 1952 to 2004, in the NES, Democratic Party identification among Catholics closely followed a downward linear trend, from about 70 percent to about 50 percent. Gray, Peri, and Bendyna (2005, 32) assess the impact of Catholic religious affiliation on presidential vote choice, in a carefully specified logistic regression model estimated for 1960, when Kennedy was running. They find the impact large (7.37) and highly statistically significant (at .001). For comparison, they estimate the same model for the Kerry contest in 2004. The find the coefficient much reduced in magnitude (1.54), but still statistically significant (at .05).

This multivariate result from the 2004 contests seems to summarize well the current state of things with regard to the Catholic vote. Catholic religious identification produces a statistically significant, but substantively very small, tendency to vote Democratic in presidential elections. One may be surprised that any effect is left, especially in light of our tabular results on identity and legitimacy differences (recall table 11.5). However, Gray, Peri, and Bendyna (2005, 30) provide some interesting evidence for the persistence of this residual Catholic support. They code statements of bishops on moral goals in political life, and conclude that 16 favor the Democrats while only seven favor the Republicans. This recalls the notion that at the base of group identity, and hence group voting, lies a set of preferences on issues. What remains to be seen is whether in the long run the Democrats will be able to use such an advantage on moral issues to reverse their almost extinct Catholic base.

Is There a Protestant Vote?

In this chapter, we have focused on the politics of secondary group membership. With respect to such religions as Catholicism or Judaism, the group idea is easy to grasp. Basically, individuals identify themselves religiously as Catholic or Jewish by virtue of membership in those bodies, which possess a fair amount of doctrinal homogeneity. By way of contrast, it may seem a bit of a stretch to identify with the broad category of Protestant, which hundreds of different churches or sects. The designation appears more sociological than psychological, if you will. Analysis of Protestants as a whole tends to "spin statistical fictions" (Stark and Glock 1968, 6). However, the group identity idea perhaps applies to certain subcategories of Protestants.

In particular, scholars of religion and politics have profitably distinguished between mainline Protestants and evangelical Protestants. The former include members of the following churches: Episcopal, Friends, Lutheran, Methodist, Presbyterian, Reformed. These denominations tend to be theologically moderate. The latter include members of these churches: Assemblies of God, Baptist, Church of Christ, Church of God, Church of the Nazarene, Pentecostal, Wesleyan Methodist. These denominations tend to be theologically conservative. Evangelical Protestant churches have seen great growth in membership, and have come to see presidential election politics as increasingly relevant to their religious mission. This led some commentators to talk of "The Year of the

Evangelical," first denoted as 1976 by George Gallup, but assigned a different year by others (Kellstedt et al. 1994, 309).

Regardless of the year chosen, party preference has changed among evangelicals. In the 1960 presidential contest, an estimated 60 percent of evangelicals voted Democratic, in contrast to only 40 percent in 1988. For mainline Protestants, the comparable estimates held essentially constant, at 37 percent and 36 percent, respectively (Kellstedt et al. 1994, 311). One observes that by 1988 the two types of Protestant had become quite similar in their presidential choice. That changed, however, in 1992, with evangelicals staying with candidate Bush, while a greater number of mainliners departed for the Perot camp. What caused this divergence was essentially a split over issues: Evangelicals were much more concerned than the mainliners over abortion, family values, gay rights, and defense (Kellstedt et al. 1994, 318–21). Of course, these have come to be core issues for religious groups on the political right.

In a pooled analysis of presidential NES surveys, 1980–94, Layman (1997, 296–97) offers an elaborately specified model, accounting for almost 50 percent of the variance in presidential choice over the period. Despite the imposition of strong statistical controls (e.g., party identification, SES characteristics, economic perceptions, various interaction terms), evangelicals register a statistically significant preference for the Republican candidate. This sophisticated treatment suggests that this religious category merits placement along side the more standard religious categories (i.e., Catholic, Jewish), in any multivariate explanation of the presidential vote.

In a recent study, Guth et al. (2005, 2) propose two kinds of religious variables, one for group membership (called the "ethnoreligious perspective") and another based on beliefs and behavior (called the "religious restructuring perspective"). They explore these perspectives to better understand the theological "culture wars" between conservatives and liberals (Hunter 1991). Guth and his colleagues (2005, 7) label these two battling tribes the "traditionalists" and the "modernists." The former are committed to orthodox beliefs, practice their religion frequently, and hold conservative values. The latter reject orthodoxy, participate irregularly, and express modern views.

To investigate the politics of these factions, Guth et al. employ the National Survey of Religion and Politics for the 2004 presidential election. They contend that "Evangelicals have become the religious mainstay of the GOP" (2005, 15). For example, 77.5 percent of evangelicals said they voted for Bush, in contrast to 50.0 percent for mainline Protestants, 53.5 percent for White Catholics, and 26.7 percent for Jews. Furthermore, within the evangelical group, 86.5 percent of traditionalists voted Bush, in contrast to only 48.4 percent of the modernists (Guth et al. 2005, 32). Interestingly, from our perspective, this difference between traditionalists and modernists could be interpreted as the difference between high and low group identifiers. Future research might do well to pose such socio-psychological items to respondents more directly.

These authors do tackle the question of the relative importance of religion for presidential vote choice in 2004 (Guth et al. 2005, table 5). In a model with only religious measures, the pseudo-R^2 is .17, and all the major membership categories are statistically significant (Guth et al. 2005, table 5). This result holds when demographic controls are added. However, when a party identification control is added as well, the evangelical Protestant and white Catholic membership variables are significant, but the mainline Protestant and Jewish ones are not. Nevertheless, Guth et al. conclude that "[b]oth religious tradition and traditionalism-modernism had important effects on vote choice" (2005, 24). Unfortunately, this conclusion rests essentially on the pattern of statistical significance uncovered. For a fuller assessment of the relative effects, it would have been useful also to report comparisons of the direct effects of religious and nonreligious variables, say in terms of change in the vote probability.

In another study of the 2004 contest, Mockabee (2005) examines the impact of religious group membership, plus religious commitment. The commitment is not to any specific religion, but generally to attendance of services, frequency of prayer, and religious guidance in daily life (2005, 6). When this religious commitment variable is included in a fully specified vote model, neither the evangelical nor the mainline Protestant variables manage statistical significance. However, the religious commitment variable does (2005, table 5). Provocatively, this result implies that beliefs and attitudes, rather than religious group identity itself, are what counts.

Looking more carefully at Guth et al. (2005, table 5), their findings show that, in fact, only traditionalist evangelicals are significantly more likely to vote Bush. Evangelicals whose thinking is modernist, or even centrist, demonstrate no significant propensity toward Bush. Issues themselves, rather than group membership per se, seem to motivate these voters. In this scenario, religious affiliation becomes a tool for furthering an ideological agenda. Being a member of the group, in the sense of identifying with it, ceases to be important. What matters is how the group furthers the ends of members. Religious affiliation loses its exogenous, fixed status. Instead, it becomes endogenous, subject to the choice and change of religiously zealous voters.

Groups and the End of the New Deal Coalition?

Group identification carries with it a group vote. Groups that have a highly cohesive, identified, membership may even vote heavily in favor of one party. But that does not mean the group necessarily contributes a major share of the *total* votes for the party. For that to happen, much depends on group size. A highly partisan group that is small in number may have less overall impact in a presidential race than a moderately partisan group that has large numbers. To take an example, blacks add fewer votes to the Democratic column than women, although they are much more pro-Democrat, simply because they compose a smaller proportion of the electorate. This leads to a more general question: in a presidential contest, what are the group sources of the overall Democratic (or Republican) vote? And are there stable patterns suggesting a coalition of certain groups in favor of one party or the other?

In his seminal work, Axelrod (1972, 1986) poses such questions. Through a simple formulation, he measures the aggregate group contribution to the presidential vote, taking into account partisanship, size, and turnout. Measuring these three components with a mix of survey data and election returns, he calculates "the proportion of a party's total votes that is provided by a given group" (1972, 13). For instance, he reports that the black contribution to the Democratic vote rose from 7 percent in 1952 to 25 percent in 1984, while the union contribution fell from 38 percent to 30 percent, respectively (1986, 282). The groups he designates are from the New Deal coalition: "the poor, Blacks, union members, Catholics and Jews, Southerners, and city dwellers" (1972, 13). Over the period 1952–84, the groups more often than not favor the Democrats, in that sense supporting the New Deal coalition idea. However, that loyalty is far from complete, and in some elections is not evident (Axelrod 1972, 17). Clearly, groups are only part, perhaps a small part, of the presidential voting story.

One difficulty with the Axelrod work is its bivariate methodology, which does not allow spurious associations to be ruled out—for example, separating out the relative effects among black union members living in cities. Erikson, Lancaster, and Romero (1989), in a lucid analysis, attempt to remedy this difficulty. Employing the NES data, they carry out a logistic regression analysis of each presidential election, 1952–84. One sees that across the period Democratic group loyalty persists (except for the poor in 1960 and 1968, and southern whites in 1968 and 1972). They observe that "group differences in the vote have not decayed" (1989, 341, 343). Furthermore, any changes in group size, on net, have not reduced the aggregate impact of group voting, aside from a slight drop among southern whites (344). They conclude: "Differences in group voting have survived nicely in the years since the New Deal" (345).

In contrast, after the 1992 election, Stanley and Niemi (1995, 237) decided that "it is time to declare the New Deal [Democratic] coalition dead." Their dependent variable is not vote, but rather party identification, in a logistic regression analysis of each NES presidential election study, 1952–96. They arrive at the percentage of the Democratic coalition from a given group (by taking the mean predicted probability of a Democratic Party identification for that group, multiplied by the group's number of respondents). Thus, the measure takes into account loyalty plus size, much like the original Axelrod measure. One simple way of assessing trends in the New Deal groups is to look at the end points, 1952 and 1996 (Stanley and Niemi 1995, table 22.3). The black contribution has increased, 10 percentage points to 21 percentage points, and the Catholic contribution is stable at, respectively, 27 and 28. However, other members of this coalition have experienced decreases: Jews from 5 points to 3 points, southern whites from 26 to 17, union households from 32 to 20.

Stanley and Niemi (2006) have updated their work on party identification through 2004 and conclude that the New Deal coalition has not risen from the grave. In particular, they claim that Democrats "appear to have the problem that the coalition has lost important group support that has not been replaced by the support of significant new groups" (2005, 10). Let us assess this proposition, by looking at the component parts. Focusing on the traditional New Deal coalition, and inspecting the 25-point time series indicates that the group contributions of blacks and lower-income (below the upper third) Americans are up. (For example, comparing the estimates of 1952 and 2004, respectively, yields 10 points to 29 points, and 63 points to 71 points.) Further, the Jewish and Catholic contributions are stable. (The estimates of 1952 and 2004, respectively, yield 5 points to 5 points, 27 points to 26 points.) This leaves southerners (white) and union households, where the numbers are down. (For example, comparing the estimates of 1952 and 2004, respectively, yields 26 points to 17 points, 32 points to 20 points) (see Stanley and Niemi 2006, tables 1 and 2).

Clearly, the New Deal coalition is not what it was. However, four of its six key contributors—blacks, Jews, Catholics, and lower-income—continue in their importance. Further, among the fifth—union households—it must be emphasized that at the disaggregate level (the probability of the individual union member vote), it is still very much a Democratic group, as we have observed in table 11.1. Essentially, then, the real source of change in the original New Deal coalition lies with the last contributor—southern whites. This group, if such a heterogenous category can be called a group, has left the Democratic Party in droves. Even here it is worth remembering that its share only seriously declined recently, after 1996. (Its 1952 contribution was 26 points, virtually matching its 1996 contribution of 25 points.) One might conclude then, that the Democratic body of the New Deal coalition remains alive, but with a wounded southern arm, a wound that may or may not heal.

Whether the Democrats can revitalize its group coalition depends on its openness to new groups, such as women, Hispanics, and church groups. While not an explicit part of the traditional New Deal coalition, women have been steadily moving into the Democratic column. (In 2004 they contributed 65 percentage points, up from 55 in 1952.) Hispanics, not politically visible until fairly recently, have increasingly contributed to the Democratic margin. (In 2004, their contribution was 11 points, up from five in 1980.) These two groups, the first large, the second growing, could represent serious targets for the Democrats.

The picture for religious groups is decidedly more mixed. A common assumption is that white fundamentalist Protestants have gone full over to the Republican Party. A careful inspection of the numbers suggests otherwise. In the Stanley and Niemi (2006, table 4) data, this group registered a 13-percentage-point Republican contribution in 1972, the first year of its measurement. This percentage began to show increases, and peaked in 1994 at 21 points However, it began a steady decline from then, falling to only 16 points in 2004. Furthermore, among regular churchgoers of whatever denomination or doctrine, there has been no movement to the Republicans (their contribution remaining at 42 points for both years). In sum, Democratic chances for a revived coalition may be greater than supposed.

CHAPTER 12

Class and Other Social Characteristics

In any democracy, the behavior of the voting public may be studied as individuals or as members of groups. Among all possible social groupings, none has received more notice than social class. This is because, first, the concept is exhaustive, excluding no one. Every voter holds a place in the nation's class structure. That place may not be exalted; rather, it may be lowly or "lower," that is, of lower status than someone else in the social hierarchy, who may be "upper" class. All citizens, once located on the class spectrum, compose the country's entire social structure. Second, the class concept can be applied to any society. Scholars of social stratification tell us that all societies are layered from top to bottom, with the different layers receiving different amounts of valued goods.

If we examine different nations at different historical periods, it may appear that these strata are complex and dissimilar. One country is made up of aristocrats, the bourgeoisie, and peasants. Another social structure is defined by captains of industry, merchants, and workers. While these groups appear diverse, each pursues economic interests. Varying success in pursuit of these economic interests puts them at competing rungs of the social ladder. While different in name, some of these groups may in fact form a common class. It is this notion of an underlying shared structural interest that makes the class concept a powerful one for investigating social hierarchies generally.

The idea of class attracts researchers from many disciplines because it intersects with society, economics, and politics. Social classes are generally conceived to be guided by economic goals, to be achieved through the political system. When one social class has fewer valued goods than another, it may engage in political actions to further a redistribution of those goods. The quest for this redistribution may lead to revolution, as in the Marxist scenario where the workers violently overthrow the exploiting capitalist bosses. But one does not have to be a Marxist or a revolutionary to see that a very unequal distribution of goods and services between rulers and ruled could bring about great pressure for political change. Elites, under increasing challenge, grow more defensive. The masses, in response, become more alienated from the system. Conflict ensues, followed by repression, or perhaps reform, as new leaders less distant from the people take power.

A political drama such as this, based on different European theories of social change, does not easily fit the American story. That does not mean that "class politics" has not been a common feature of political life in the United States. From the founding of the Republic, there was concern, expressed in *Federalist* No. 10, over classes as "the most common and durable source of faction." In the era of Andrew Jackson, members of the upper crust worried over the rise of populist rule. Before World War I there was widespread, class-inspired, socialist organizing among the U.S. labor movement. This activity intensified in the 1930s, after the Great Depression, with the labor masses moving to the political left.

Social class we consider separately from other social characteristics partly because it is surrounded by its own controversy, and partly because it is not necessarily a strictly structural factor. While sociologists readily acknowledge that societies are riddled with status differences, they dispute its meaning. Is class an objective category of analysis, where one is a member by virtue of, say, an occupation? Or is class something subjective, requiring the conscious choice of membership? For example, is Jill a member of the working class simply because she works on the assembly line at Ford, or only because she declares herself a member? The latter implies that Jill "identifies" with the working class, much like the member of any group (as discussed in the last chapter). How one conceives of social class, then, depends on whether one treats it as merely another social group. As shall be shown, class is sometimes best treated as a group phenomenon, and sometimes as an analytic construct indicating place in the social structure, much like any other social characteristic.

Unlike membership in a group, the possession of a social characteristic—for example, college education, middle age—normally indicates place in a scheme of sociological categories, rather than psychological identification with the category. Still, the distinction between group and category is sometimes blurred. As with social class, at times a category of people may become conscious of themselves and their uniqueness. For example, a subset of people in the demographic category of those age 65 and over may identify as "senior citizens" and seek special benefits from the government. In that case, they take on the manner of a group, and can be more profitably studied through the model of group influence developed in the last chapter.

However, the broad social attributes examined in this chapter—at least those of years of education and age—seldom produce psychological group attachments. That does not mean those in different categories are similar in their behavior. Instead, they can differ for at least two reasons. First, the same social situation tends to engender some of the same experiences and correspondent political attitudes. For example, college students who rely on student loans may be sensitive to campaign promises of educational aid. Second, a changed social placement can lead to different expectations about one's political role. For example, middle-aged, educated citizens may be expected to participate actively in the political system, whereas just-out-of-high-school teenagers may not.

We begin with a consideration of social class, which may or may not function as a group. Then we move to consideration of other social characteristics, such as education and age, which rarely act as group attributes. We also examine the impact of gender, which, in addition to producing the group identification discussed in the last chapter, can act in purely structural ways. As shall be observed, these four social variables—class, education, age, and gender—all shape the American voter's choices, with respect to partisanship or participation.

SOCIAL CLASS AS A POLITICAL GROUP

While a social class may function as a group, it is not a formal, organized group. There exists no such organization as an Upper-Middle-Class Club, with officers and a political agenda. Of course, organizations do exist that may further the interests of the upper middle class, for example, the National Manufacturers Association. But few people actually belong to such organizations. Even though the social classes lack formal organization or official advocates, most people feel they belong to a social class. When voters say they "favor every-day working folks over big business," they are depicting two conflicting political factions in society, and siding with the former. This identification with "working folks" against "big business" exemplifies class thinking. And it is the identification with the group of workers that makes social class a reality for them.

If individuals understand themselves to be part of a social class, then social class acts to influence political behavior, in the same manner as groups do. Class identification, when it is like group identification, is equivalent to Marx's idea of class consciousness. Marx distinguished between class "in itself," and class "for itself." In terms of the economic system, at an early stage of development a class may objectively exist "in itself"; for example, a factory has a group of workers. At a later stage of development, class exists "for itself," as its members come to be like-minded and pursue a common interest; for example, the factory workers share a bond and engage in collective action.

This old Marxist distinction carries over into modern sociology. Because all societies pass out rewards unequally, each has a population with different layers, or social strata. For example, we could stratify a society by the income individuals receive, categorizing them into low income, middle income, and high income. While these income layers exist, the members probably do not have any sense of unique belonging to such a category. In contrast, belonging to another stratum may carry a feeling of identification with it. Consider, for example, occupational strata. It is very possible that the members of the category "blue-collar worker" share a psychological attachment with each other, in which case they move from being a stratum to being a self-conscious class. In other words, a stratum persists, while its characterization as a class is variable, appearing and disappearing as conditions change.

STATUS POLARIZATION

While it is useful to distinguish between a class and a stratum, the layers of a society should not be described exclusively in terms of one or the other category. Typically, social layers have traits of both. For example, some laborers identify with the working class, while others merely find themselves in that occupational stratum. The level of consciousness, awareness of a sharing of interests, is likely to be scattered at most times. Nevertheless, the intensification of economic struggle may generate more class feeling. When different strata vigorously face off in a political dispute, we have a condition of status polarization. Societies experience status polarization to varying extents. At the one extreme, high polarization, the layers of opposition clearly appear as classes; at the other extreme, of depolarization, these layers are merely strata.

Suppose two social status groups, an upper and a lower, oppose each other. The extent of their opposition reveals the extent of their status polarization. Indeed, the formation of a class out of a stratum depends, as social theorists Karl Marx and Max Weber recognized, on this active opposition from another stratum. That tension is the crucible of polarization. Note that polarization is a group concept, since it cannot emerge from a single element or individual. However, individuals are not irrelevant, for their degree of identification defines the class scope. Hence, differences in status polarization are mirrored in the nature of members' class identification. Under the condition of high polarization, the majority in contrasting strata see sharply differing interests, and have considerable class feeling. In contrast, under the condition of low polarization, class identification is largely absent. Further, because polarization manifests itself in a clash of aims, we expect it to be more vivid in certain policy arenas. Due to its nature, it is likely to be most intense in the realm of economic issues, but can spread to other issues if the class struggle becomes complete. As students of the social background of political action, it is important for us to understand what causes status polarization, and how status polarization intrudes on politics.

DETERMINING SOCIAL CLASS

The fact that a class sometimes acts like a group and sometimes does not creates definitional difficulties. Is each citizen a member of a class? If so, which one? In contrast to the secondary groups analyzed in the last chapter, membership is not always easy to assign. Moreover, unlike the democracies of Western Europe, the notion of class is not part of the common political parlance in America. Indeed, Americans often actively resist the notion that class has any relevance for them as individuals, preferring instead to believe in the openness and opportunities of the American Dream. These uncertainties surrounding the meaning of social class pose two problems. First, given that the class idea lacks clarity for many people, might its potential political effects be blunted? Second, since individuals may be vague about their place, if any, in a class structure, how do we assign them to one? We answer the first question after the second, by establishing more precise measures of social class.

There are two basic approaches to measuring social class, one "objective," the other "subjective." The objective approach uses observable social strata, for example education, or occupation, singly or in combination. The last, occupation, is usually preferred, in part because of the theory, derived from Marx, that class position comes from an individual's relation to the means of production. For example, the owners of the means of production are necessarily of the capitalist class, whereas the workers, who own only their labor, are necessarily of the proletariat. The subjective approach, by way of contrast, assigns to individuals the social class they identify with. This more flexible method allows some individuals to refuse a class assignment, whereas the objective method does not.

Followers of the subjective approach commonly conduct surveys, asking the respondents to name their social class, from a list of alternatives presented to them. For example, "Which of the following social classes would you say you belong in? lower class, working class, middle class, or upper class?" The source of their choice, not surprisingly, is often their occupation, showing the link between the two types of measures. Nevertheless, the link is far from perfect. Many in blue-collar occupations identify themselves with the middle class, while those in white-collar occupations not uncommonly select the working class category for themselves. Another difficulty is that, at least in the United States, very few respondents are willing to label themselves lower class or upper class.

Last but not least, a difficulty with this subjective assessment is that it does not take into account the depth of class feeling. It is merely a simple response to a brief survey item, and what it shows may well be a far cry from the "class consciousness" that Marx envisioned. Indeed, some respondents may be naming a class merely because they are asked to, in much they same way they would respond if asked, "Which of these towns do you live in?" Saying I live in Iowa City, as opposed to Des Moines and other designated Iowa cities, does not mean I identify with Iowa City. Similarly, picking a category when prompted, such as working class, does not mean I feel any solidarity with workers. We need to ask more before we have much confidence in the quality of a person's class commitment.

Concern over the substantive meaning of these closed-ended responses to the above question on class is underlined when we examine the results of asking a prior question, namely, "Do you ever think of yourself as being in one of these classes?" About one out of three respondents say they have not reflected on being a member of a class. Nevertheless, they do not hesitate in going on to select from a list of class choices, when it is presented to them. For this one-third of the respondents, class is not something to psychologically identify with; rather, it is a mere "zip code." It seems reasonable then, that a prerequisite for meaningful class identification be awareness of the class idea. That is, a class identification question should be preceded by a filter question that asks, "Do you ever think of yourself as being in one of these classes?" Among those who respond yes, the choice of a social class label should have some substance.

Speaking practically, we do not have to decide definitively between objective and subjective measures of class. Both, as is now clear, have strengths and weaknesses. Moreover, we have both sorts of measures available in the NES data. Therefore, we will draw on each, in particular the objective indicator of occupation and the subjective indicator of

TABLE 12.1. The Relationship between Subjective Social Class and Presidential Vote, 2000 and 2004 (in percentages)

A. 2000 Election

	Working Class	Middle Class
Gore	59.0	51.9
	(170)	(240)
Bush	40.9	48.0
	(118)	(222)
Total %	100.0	100.0
Total N = 750		

B. 2004 Election

	Working Class	Middle Class
Kerry	60.6	47.3
	(134)	(163)
Bush	39.3	52.6
	(87)	(181)
Total %	100.0	100.0
Total N = 565		

Note: These respondents said "yes" when asked if they "ever thought of themselves as working class or middle class." They were then asked to identify themselves as either middle or working class. They also said "yes" when asked "did you vote for President?" They were then asked for whom they voted, and the answers are coded here as the Republican or Democratic candidate. Column percentages are rounded to 100 percent. Figures in parentheses are cell N. The data are from the pre- and postelection NES surveys, 2000 and 2004.

class self-placement, as filtered by awareness. As it turns out, either measure produces essentially the same empirical results, in examining the simple relationship of social class to political behavior.

In table 12.1, we observe the relationship between social class and presidential vote for the 2000 and 2004 elections. In both elections, a mild association appears. For each contest, workers were somewhat more likely than the middle class to vote for the Democratic candidate, as class theory would predict. That is, workers are more persuaded by the Democratic appeal, presumably because of its more liberal, pro-worker economic policies. For the 2004 contest, in which John Kerry was the candidate, the effect is about twice as large as for Al Gore in 2000. (The percentage difference is +13 and +7, respectively, in favor of the Democrats.) Still, overall, the class effect is not great. We can gain further appreciation of this fact by considering the results in the light of status polarization hypotheses.

In table 12.2, different theoretical scenarios for status polarization are

TABLE 12.2. Theoretical Possibilities for Status
Polarization (in percentages)

A. Depolarization

	Working Class	Middle Class
Democrat	50	50
Republican	50	50
Total	100	100

B. Intermediate Polarization

	Working Class	Middle Class
Democrat	75	25
Republican	25	75
Total	100	100

C. Polarization

	Working Class	Middle Class
Democrat	100	0
Republican	0	100
Total	100	100

given. These provide a way of thinking about possibilities for class conflict in the mass electorate. In table 12.2a, class conflict is absent, for the system is totally depolarized. That is, class membership makes no difference for the vote. At the opposite extreme is table 12.2c, where class conflict is rife in a completely polarized system. That is, class makes all the difference in the voter's choice. If you are a worker, you will only vote Democratic; if you are middle class, you will only vote Republican. The middle scenario, in table 12.2b, is more realistic; workers are much more likely to vote Democratic, but a not inconsequential group of workers (25 percent) defects to the Republicans. Still, the middle scenario offers much stronger effects than we observe in fact in table 12.1. Contrast the percentage difference in worker vote for Democrats in 2004 (+13) to the percentage difference in table 12.2b (+50). Relatively speaking, status polarization appears weak in these contemporary elections. Instead of using percentage differences, we could make the same point more efficiently by examining the summary bivariate measures of association between these two variables. This we do below in an exploration of the variation in status polarization over a long series of elections.

FLUCTUATION IN STATUS POLARIZATION OVER TIME

Political scientists and sociologists have heavily investigated social class and its ties to political behavior. A persistent finding is that voters of higher-class rank (measured objectively or subjectively) lean more to the right and the Republican Party, while voters of lower-class rank lean more to the left and the Democratic Party. The robustness of this finding convinces us the hypothesis of a class-politics nexus is not misguided. However, knowing this is not enough. What happens to class voting, election after election? Does it follow a pattern? Does it change dramatically? Why is it sometimes so weak, at least in the contemporary elections just examined? To answer such questions, we estimate the association (tau-b) between class (working versus middle) and vote (Democratic versus Republican), over a series of presidential elections. While it makes little difference empirically, we here use an objective measure of class—occupation. Theoretically this has the virtue of reducing the measurement error that comes from the "false consciousness" of the subjective measure, for example workers regarding themselves as middle class. In figure 12.1 the time trend in status polarization is reported for the 1960–2004 presidential elections.

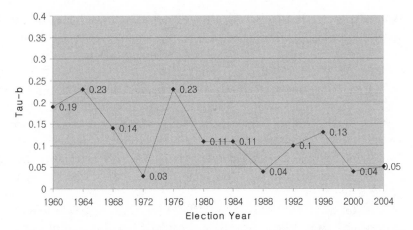

Fig. 12.1. Status polarization of presidential votes, 1960–2004. Each dot shows the correlation (tau-b) between respondent occupation (farmers excluded) and two-party presidential vote choice. (Data from NES surveys, 1960–2004.)

Initially, we observe that, in these twelve elections, the relationship always leans in the expected direction. That is to say, the working class without exception is more likely to favor the Democratic candidate, the middle class the Republican candidate. However, this relationship is by no means consistent in magnitude. Sometimes it is very small, for example, 1972, 1988, and 2000, and other times not small, for example 1960, 1964, and 1976. The most extreme years are 1972 with tau-b equal to .03, and 1964 and 1976 with tau-b equal to .23. (The measure of association, tau-b, has a range of possible values from .00 to 1.00. These limits are illustrated, respectively, in tables 12.2a and 12.2c). Thus, rather than a fixed degree of left or right voting depending on social class, it varies according to the electoral context. The link always exists, but it may be greater or lesser, depending on conditions yet to be identified. To put it another way, status polarization varies. It is this variation that we aim to explain.

THE CONDITIONS OF STATUS POLARIZATION: KEY PSYCHOLOGICAL TERMS

We have already remarked that being aware of the idea of social class gives the concept more "bite." We now state explicitly that this awareness acts in a fashion similar to group identification in the last chapter. That is to say, those who have class awareness, like those who are high group identifiers, more readily manifest the expected political behavior, for they see more clearly their collective interest. It is among the class aware, then, that we can most easily locate the psychological sources of status polarization.

Full examination of the correlations between class and vote in figure 12.1 shows they are usually toward the low end. One reason for this may be that voters, including voters who are aware of their social class, do not see the political connection between their class position and candidate choice. For example, a skilled laborer may self-identify as working class but not see how a Democratic vote might decrease his or her chances of escaping unemployment.

If we follow this line of reasoning, status polarization may be highest among class-aware voters who have considerable political sophistication, and lowest among those who lack such sophistication. There are different ways of measuring political sophistication. In the study of class and politics, two elements seem especially important: interest and ideology. (For now, we set aside the complications of ideology raised in earlier chapters). Our expectation is that among those who actively identify with a class, and have a clear liberal-conservative ideology and high political interest, the class vote will be sharpest. The data from the 2000 presidential election, a very tough test given the low overall correlation reported in figure 12.1, provide unambiguous support for this hypothesis. Figure 12.2 presents these results.

We see that the class vote is at its height among the most politically sophisticated, but steadily diminishes as sophistication decreases. Indeed, among those who have no special interest in the campaign and lack a political ideology, the expected class vote is simply absent. In the 2000 contest, then, the small amount of status polarization that did occur was largely a product of the highly politically sophisticated voters. These individuals could locate themselves on a liberal-to-conservative continuum and were very interested in the campaign. Given that the electoral potency of social class is restricted to this relatively small group of aware people, it becomes difficult to talk of class voting as a broad, mass-based phenomenon. Further, the limited appeal of class to most voters seems to have its psychological roots in their lack of political savvy. If they were more engaged in politics, they might see more clearly their class interest, and act on it. But they are not so engaged.

These patterns come to the fore upon investigation of status voting and real political involvement. One source of political sophistication is

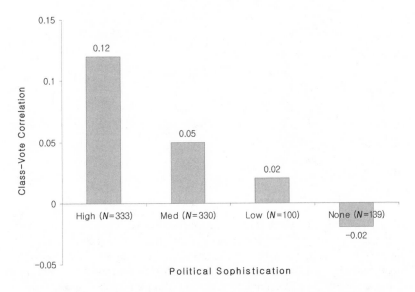

Fig. 12.2. The relationship of political sophistication to status voting, 2000. Correlations on the *Y*-axis are the tau-b, between subjective social class (working or middle) and vote (Democratic or Republican), among respondents who are aware of social class. The correlations between these two variables, within the different levels of political sophistication (PS), are represented by bars the heights of the correlation. high PS = did place self on seven-point liberal-conservative scale + said was "very interested" in political campaigns; medium PS = did place self on seven-point liberal-conservative scale + said only "somewhat" or "not" interested in political campaigns; low PS = did not place self on seven-point liberal-conservative scale + said was "very interested" in political campaigns; no PS = did not place self on seven-point liberal-conservative scale + had only "somewhat" or "no" interest in political campaigns. The figures in parentheses are the number of cases. (Data from NES survey, 2000.)

actual participation in politics. In the American system, there are many opportunities for participation, and several are measured in the NES (as we saw in chap. 5). We built a political involvement index, adding up how many of the following seven participative acts the respondent committed: influence another's vote; display a political statement; go to a rally; work in a campaign; contribute money to a candidate, party, or political group. As is typical in American elections, there is a pyramid of participation, with the very few carrying out a large number of these activities. Over one-half of the sample (50.5 percent) chose to do none of them. Ahead of that group, another 31.6 percent managed to engage in

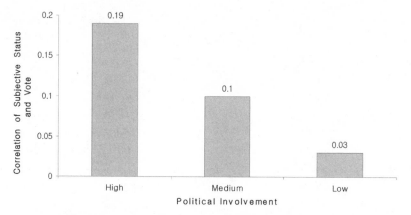

Fig. 12.3. Relation of political involvement to status voting, 2000. Vote is a dichotomy, Gore versus Bush. Social class is subjective, working class versus middle class. Political involvement is an index based on summing seven yes-no political participation items: influence others, display button, go to meetings, campaign, contribute to candidate, give money to party, give to group. Two or more mentions = high involvement (N = 135), one mention = medium (N = 238), no mentions = low (N = 381). (Data from NES survey, 2000.)

one. Leading these two categories were the rest of the voters (17.9 percent), who carried out two or more of these activities.

In figure 12.3 we relate these three categories of political involvement to the degree of class voting. As one climbs the ladder of political participation, the vote choice becomes more and more structured by class. Among the most highly involved, the influence of class even approaches a moderate level of strength, by the conventions of survey research. This group has some sense of its class stake in the political system and acts on it. However, like the political sophisticates, they are relatively small in number. American citizens who do not go beyond voting in their political participation are in the majority, and for them class standing is almost bereft of political content.

POLITICAL MANIFESTATIONS OF
STATUS POLARIZATION

Status polarization may be modified by psychological factors, such as class awareness and political sophistication. In addition, it may be modified by explicitly political objects, namely parties. A first condition for this to occur is that parties offer policies that differ in terms of their class appeal. For many political campaigns in America, class content is not readily apparent. One might charge that, on such issues, the Democrats and the Republicans are too often Tweedledum and Tweedledee. However, in the 2000 election, which we just examined, most voters did not see the Democrats and Republicans as equivalent. Among the "class aware" surveyed in the 2000 NES data, 78 percent declared they perceived "important differences" between the two major parties.

A second condition necessary for parties to influence the level of status polarization is that, once the voters observe differences in the parties, they vote for the party closer to their own class interests. The 2000 NES data show that this condition, too, is met. Again looking at the class aware ($N = 753$), the class-vote correlation (tau-b) is .10 among those who see the parties as different. For example, workers identify with their class, see the Democrats as different from the Republicans, and tend, if only mildly, to favor the Democratic candidate. In contrast, the comparable correlation among those who fail to see party differences is tiny and actually negative, at $-.04$. This indicates, for example, that workers who fail to distinguish between the parties actually are a bit more likely to go against their class interests and vote Republican.

Party differences, to the extent they are perceived, help ensure a modicum of class voting. We can imagine that, as the parties converge or diverge with regard to class-based policies, status polarization decreases or increases accordingly. Political parties manage to structure class voting in another way, by their presence in the hearts and minds of voters. That is, the more strongly voters identify with a party, the more we would expect them to engage in a class vote. For example, a worker who is a strong Democrat is more likely to vote for the Democratic candidate than a worker who is a weak Democrat. Why might this be so? For one reason, the strongly Democratic worker may be staunchly Democrat because they believe that party best represents blue-collar interests. The weak Democratic worker, in contrast, may only vaguely perceive the link between their class and the party politics. In other words, the strong identifiers will tend to have more class consciousness, and exercise that politically. The data in figure 12.4 support this contention.

In both the 2000 and 2004 presidential contests, class voting is clearly higher among the strong partisans. Apparently, a firm commitment to party causes the voter to act more consistently with regard to their class interests. In contrast, among weak identifiers and Independents, the class vote tends to be feeble. One implication is that party identification

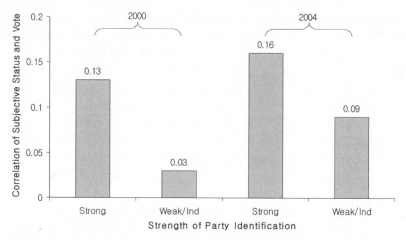

Fig. 12.4. Status voting and strength of party identification, 2000 and 2004. The vote variable is a dichotomy, the Democratic candidate versus the Republican candidate. Social class is measured subjectively and is dichotomous, working class versus middle class. Party identification is dichotomous, strong partisans (Republican or Democrat) versus weak partisans and Independents. For 2000, $N = 538$; for 2004, $N = 710$. (Data from NES surveys, 2000 and 2004.)

generally supports status polarization. To the degree partisanship is strong and widespread in a society, class conflict at the ballot box may be expected to increase. But as party ties begin to loosen, as some argue for more contemporary times, status polarization is likely to decrease. Our data lend support to such a conclusion. Recall figure 12.1. Status polarization in the first half of that election series (1960–80) is about twice as great as in the second half of the election series (1984–2004). Respectively, the average correlation in the first half is .16, and in the second half .08. Overall, it appears that class, except perhaps for highly partisan sophisticates, has ceased to play a vital role in the choices made by the American voter.

EDUCATION

Education is another measure of social status, and at first it may seem redundant once we have taken account of class. After all, it seems a commonplace that more educated individuals have higher social standing. The college-educated, one might say, are all middle class, whereas high school graduates are likely to be blue-collar. Still, years of education dictates neither one's occupation nor perception of that occupation's prestige. Those with many years of formal education may drive taxis or work without pay. Those who are basically self-taught may rise to the heights of industry. Education, for all its overlap with other status indicators, such as class, occupation, and income, does have an independent impact on political behavior. Partly, this is because the educational experience is a main source of political information for most citizens. In school, we learn "political facts" and how to think about them. This happens directly, in courses on history, politics, and society, but also indirectly, in informal discussions with fellow students and teachers. "Well-educated" persons consider themselves able to talk intelligently about the world of politics, absorbing and ordering the daily flow of new information.

Overall, formal education provides citizens with the tools for doing democracy, much as Thomas Jefferson envisioned. Of course, this does not mean that everyone receives equal civic benefit from additional years of schooling. Institutions of learning differ in their quality, and students differ in their abilities and motivation. In the main, however, our expectation is that more formal education facilitates greater participation in politics. It makes participation "easier," by providing citizens with relevant knowledge, analytic skills, and urgent social questions. First evidence of this comes from table 12.3, where level of education is related to the attempt to influence the vote of others. (Here, and elsewhere during this discussion of the effects of education, we focus on the 2004 results, since they closely parallel those from 2000.)

Citizens who attempt to influence other's politics may be thought of as opinion leaders, and the majority of Americans shy away from this role, perhaps because it is intimidating. Nevertheless, increasing formal

TABLE 12.3. Relation of Education to Attempt to Influence the Vote of Others, 2004 (in percentages)

	Junior High	High School	College
Yes	37.9	46.0	54.8
No	62.1	54.0	45.2
Total	100.0	100.0	100.0
Number of cases	153	546	367

Note: Education is coded into three categories: junior high = received at most 11 years of schooling, did not receive high school diploma; high school = received a high school diploma but no higher degree; college = received a community college degree or higher. The attempt to influence variable is a dichotomy: "yes" = the respondent tried to influence the vote of others; "no" = otherwise. The data are from the NES survey, 2004.

education makes adoption of the role more likely. Whereas just over a third of those who had not completed high school made an influence attempt in 2004, over half of those with a college degree did so. The effects of education are still more pronounced in the vote itself, as illustrated in table 12.4. (Recall our introduction to this point in chapter 5, the "Commentary and Controversy" section.) When citizens are asked if they voted, they may say they did even when they did not, because voting is viewed as a highly desirable behavior. Still, not everyone claims to have voted, and the differences across categories can be quite revealing, as here. Among the college-educated, 92 percent declared they had voted, in contrast to only 51 percent among those with no more than a junior high school education. This 41-percentage-point difference suggests, rightly, that years of schooling is a major predictor of vote turnout.

The fact that increasing formal education heightens the likelihood of these individual political actions—influencing the vote, and the vote itself—leads us to ask if the education effect is generalizable to group political actions, and to political involvement generally. Recall figure 12.3, where we built a political involvement index on the 2000 data set. We now do the same for the 2004 data, again looking at seven types of participation: influence others; display a button; go to a meeting; work in a campaign; contribute money to a candidate, party, or group. As in 2000, very few engaged in all, or even most, of these activities. The modal category, once more, was "none." What is remarkable is how education moves voters out of this "do nothing" category. The percentages in table 12.5 tell the story. For the junior high group, over half did nothing. In contrast, only one-third of the college group failed to participate in any of the seven types of activities.

We may ask, what is it about education that gets people politically involved? The increased amount of raw information it makes available to

TABLE 12.4 . Relation of Amount of Formal Education to Presidential Vote Participation, 2004 (in percentages)

	Junior High	High School	College
Voted	51.4	78.4	92.0
Didn't vote	48.6	21.6	8.0
Total	100	100	100
Number of cases	70	269	199

Note: Respondents were asked, "Did you vote in the elections this November?" Valid codes were "yes" or "no." Education is coded as described in table 12.3. The data are from the NES survey, 2004.

them, in conjunction with intellectual tools to organize this information, have already been mentioned. In addition, it instills civic responsibility, the idea of voting as a duty. But it is more than these things. Educational attainment, especially beyond the high school years, imparts a feeling of confidence in one's ability to understand politics, and to do something about it. Politics ceases to be a foreign playing field, becoming a place where citizens believe they can make a difference. In other words, it gives citizens a sense of political efficacy. (Recall our introduction to the concept of efficacy in chapter 5.) The concept has various components, one of which is a belief that ordinary citizens can effect change. In the 2004 NES, for example, respondents were asked to agree or disagree with the statement, "People don't have any say in government." Among college graduates 60 percent disagreed, manifesting their strong sense of efficacy. In contrast, among the junior high group, only 21 percent disagreed.

A more general measure exhibits the same pattern. Besides the foregoing item, respondents were asked to react to two statements: "Public officials don't care" and "Politics is too complicated." Of course, efficacious voters tend to think that public officials listen, at least to them, and that they themselves understand the ins and out of politics. The 2000 NES asks all three of these items (unlike the 2004 NES), permitting us to combine them in a political efficacy index, which we relate to education in table 12.6. We observe that efficacy sharply increases as one ascends the educational ladder, taking an especially large jump from high school to college. (From junior high to high school, the percentage difference in the high-efficacy category is +10, whereas from high school to college, it is +14.) It is the college experience, especially, that contributes to the strong belief that the world of democratic politics is subject to one's own influence.

TABLE 12.5. Relation of Amount of Formal Education to Political Involvement, 2004 (in percentages)

	Junior High	High School	College
Involvement			
High	12.5	20.1	32.8
Medium	33.3	36.0	33.6
Low	54.2	43.9	33.6
Total	100	100	100
Number of cases	153	544	366

Note: The education variable is constructed as in table 12.3. The political involvement variable is constructed as in figure 12.3. The data are from the NES survey, 2004.

TABLE 12.6. Relation of Education to Sense of Political Efficacy, 2000 (in percentages)

	Junior High	High School	College
Efficacy index			
High	23	33	47
Medium	14	9	9
Low	63	58	44
Total	100	100	100
Number of cases	97	480	352

Note: Education is measured as in table 12.3. Efficacy is a summary index based on three items (five-point agree-disagree scales), soliciting responses to the following statements: "public officials don't care"; "people don't have any say in government"; "politics is too complicated." The items were collapsed to three categories and each respondent given a summary score from 3 to 9; then those scores were recoded into high efficacy (7 or more), medium efficacy (5–6), and low efficacy (less than 5). The data are from the NES survey, 2000.

GENDER

The social characteristic of gender, and its politics, was first considered in the last chapter. There, the focus was on women and how their group identification helped shape their partisan choices. Here we have a different focus. Society can be divided into strata—class, education, gender— with no reference to psychological group traits. Indeed, the idea of women as a psychologically distinct, self-identified group is relatively new in voting studies. But the historic legal and political restrictions against female political participation are not new. In the United States, it was not until 1920, after amendment of the Constitution, that women gained the suffrage. A first question, then, is how the vote participation rate of women compares to men. Is it possible that these ancient barriers to a woman's right to vote still manifest trace effects? Or that perhaps other more subtle obstacles still stand in the way of women's full and equal voting participation?

Simple examination of the current evidence marks the beginning of our response. According to our analysis of the 2000 survey, the gender gap was tiny, 4.7 percentage points in the direction of greater male participation. By the 2004 survey, that gap had effaced further, to only 1.4 percentage points. Essentially, then, the gender gap in turnout has disappeared. But this generalization, telling as it is, leaves details of the story unsaid. Within certain social categories, there remain residual pockets of

gender differences in voting. These seem related, in particular, to education. Table 12.7 shows the relationship between gender and turnout for
different levels of schooling.

For both men and women, education has a substantial impact. However, that impact is greater for women. (Compare the percentage differences between the junior high and college categories; women = +36.4,
men = +24.3). Further, there is not gender equity in participation
within each education level. Indeed, ill-educated women vote at a noticeably lower rate (51.4 percent) than ill-educated men (65.4 percent).
Only at the highest educational level do gender differences in voting
effectively disappear. Among college-educated women, 87.8 percent said
they voted, a figure almost equal to the 89.7 percent of the men who said
they voted.

Why does this peculiar pattern exist? One speculation roots it in sex
roles. When someone plays a "social role," they confine their actions to
what is right and proper in the eyes of others. Traditionally, in mid-
twentieth-century America, a husband was head of the household, and
guided the family's politics. The wife tended hearth and home, with politics decidedly a secondary concern. In the twenty-first century, these
gender roles are out-of-date. The change in roles is most apparent among
society's university-educated. From that high stratum, the new role of
women in politics filters down the rungs of the educational ladder. Our
expectation is that soon the ancient vestiges of traditional gender role
effects on voting will evaporate.

TABLE 12.7. Relation of Gender and Education to Presidential Vote Turnout,
2000 (in percentages)

	Men			Women		
	Junior High	High School	College	Junior High	High School	College
Voted	65.4	76.6	89.7	51.4	73.1	87.8
Didn't vote	34.6	23.4	10.3	48.6	26.9	12.2
Total	100.0	100.0	100.0	100.0	100.0	100.0
Number of cases	26	244	156	72	238	197

Note: Gender is based on the interviewer's assessment. Education and presidential vote turnout are
coded as in table 12.4. The data are from the NES survey, 2000. (We selected this data set over the 2004
NES survey because it afforded a larger sample size; however, the patterns that each reveals are not
dissimilar).

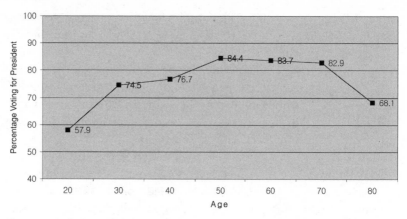

Fig. 12.5. Relation of age to voting participation. (Data from 2000 and 2004 NES samples.)

AGE

In general, the likelihood of voting increases with age, but only to a point, as figure 12.5 shows. When young voters move into their thirties, there is a noteworthy jump in participation. Vote turnout continues at an ever-higher rate, as the cohorts advance in years. Peak participation occurs for those 50–60. After that, vote turnout essentially stabilizes, with a faint decline becoming a pronounced decline after the seventies. This curvilinear relationship between age and vote is not surprising. Young people just eligible to vote, by virtue of passing their eighteenth birthday, become "politically legal." But politics is new to them, with the candidates less familiar, the issues harder to digest, and the parties more vague in image than they are to older citizens. But as the young acquire political experience, they develop knowledge and commitments, and strengthen the voting habit. In middle age, many are stable partisans, and reliably show up at the polls to express their preferences. However, among the very elderly, the cost of the act of voting mounts. It becomes harder to read the fine print in the campaign brochures, the walk to the polling station seems longer on a cold day in November, and driving the car is no longer an option. A elderly voter faced with such obstacles may conclude it is too much trouble to go out and vote.

The strong positive relationship between aging and the vote that exists across most of the life cycle merits special attention, because it appears to defy expected effects of formal education. We have learned in this chapter that more schooling leads to more turnout. But, with aging, we superficially observe the reverse. The younger voters (say under 35) participate less, though they clearly have more education than older voters (say over 35). However, when we control for these cross-cutting generational differences in education, as in table 12.8, we see that the impact of age on vote participation fully maintains itself.

Table 12.8, with its 18 cells, can be complicated to read. Its interpretation can be simplified by explaining how it controls for the effects of education. The modal amount of formal education, regardless of age, is a high school diploma. Let us imagine that everyone has the same educational attainment; for example, everyone has graduated from high school but not college. Among this group of high school graduates, what is the impact of advancing age? It appears rather hefty, if we examine the changes across age categories: under 35 years old, only 59 percent vote; between 35 and 54 years of age that number jumps to 75 percent. And it jumps again for those 55 and over, to 85 percent. Thus, the turnout rate differences attributable to age appear at least as large, taking education into account. What does this mean? It means that advancing years influence vote participation independent of the citizen's educational attainment.

The processes of aging itself, at least through the active years, encourage citizens to vote. This fact has important consequences for the nation's politics, as the age distribution of the electorate changes. Look at the two ends of the age spectrum, young and old. When the pool of young voters (say under 30 years of age) is expanded, the system experiences an influx of citizens with few political attachments. The ensuing

TABLE 12.8. The Relation of Age, Education, and Presidential Vote Turnout, 2000 (in percentages)

	Under 35			35–54			55 and Over		
	Junior High	High School	College	Junior High	High School	College	Junior High	High School	College
Voted	33	59	72	62	75	92	65	85	96
Didn't vote	67	41	28	38	25	8	35	15	4
Total	100	100	100	100	100	100	100	100	100
Number of cases	27	107	74	24	224	185	46	151	92

Note: Age and vote turnout are measured as in figure 12.5. Education is measured as in table 12.3. The data are from the NES survey, 2000.

potential for increased political instability is at least partly offset by their limited interest in voting. In contrast, when the pool of senior voters (say around the age of 60) is expanded, the number of participative, strong partisans definitely increases. The latter appears close to our current situation, as the baby boomer generation moves into retirement. Their strong political participation should serve them well in any struggle to reshape Social Security.

COMMENTARY AND CONTROVERSY

Traditional Measures and the Class Voting Trend

Traditionally, class has been measured as a simple occupational dichotomy, working versus middle. Categorization into one or the other can be "subjective," based on individual self-placement, or "objective," based on placement according to character of the occupation itself. Regardless of which of these methods is used, the trend over time is downward (Abramson, Aldrich, and Rohde 2003, 113–15; Bibby 1996, 274; Flanigan and Zingale 2006, 115–18; Hershey 2005, 125; Lawrence 1997, 40). This decline, observed here in figure 12.1, "may be part of a widespread phenomenon that is occurring in advanced industrial societies" (Abramson, Aldrich, and Rohde 2003, 115). From this perspective, it is tempting to conclude that class voting is over.

Class and Turnout

Social class influences whether someone turns out to vote. Leighley and Nagler (1992), in an examination of NES and Current Population Survey data (1964–88), find that conclusions about class and turnout are affected by whether occupation, education, or income measures of class are used. They argue that income measures are preferred because level of income is a likely basis of government policies, and because the other indices have over-time measurement problems. The highest income group (the top quintile) averages about 70 percent turnout in presidential elections, compared to about 50 percent for the lowest income group (the bottom quintile) (Leighley and Nagler 1992, table 1). Furthermore, according to Gini coefficients, this class bias, or inequality, in turnout is stable over time. In a more elaborate study, looking at NES presidential election surveys, 1948–92, Hout, Brooks, and Manza (1995, 824) discover essentially the same result, although they use an occupation-based measure of class. They remark, "A conclusion of 'little or no change' in the effect of class on voter turnout should not be mistaken for a conclusion of 'no effect.' Class has a substantial effect on turnout. The gap between the turnout for professionals and for semiskilled and unskilled workers . . . corresponds to a range of 77 percent to 40 percent."

Education and Participation

The very strong link between education and political participation is well established (Rosenstone and Hansen 2003; Verba, Schlozman, and Brady 1995; Wolfinger and Rosenstone 1980). Multiple reasons have been offered for this educational benefit (Delli Carpini and Keeter 1996; Nie, Junn, and Stehlik-Barry 1996). Students learn information about the political system, such as facts about the Constitution. Students acquire skills, such as reading and reasoning, that make the world of politics more understandable. Students are taught the importance of being an attentive citizen, of "doing their duty." Students, at least college students, eventually achieve higher social positions, with more opportunities for participation. The central role of education in making democracy work better has been stressed since the days of Thomas Jefferson.

Is the Link between Education and Participation Spurious?

Overwhelmingly, education is seen to be a cause of participation. The learning and socialization experiences of college, especially, are assumed to bring about the large differences in political involvement we observe, for example, in table 12.5. Recently, this orthodoxy has been seriously challenged. Kam and Palmer (2006, abstract) contend that education "is not cause, but proxy . . . [for] pre-adult socialization experiences and predispositions." In support of their contention, they examine the Jennings and Niemi Political Socialization Panel Study. Responses from the 1965 wave compose the independent variables, with the 1973 wave offering the dependent variable of political participation (in an additive index of eight acts). Of course, the time lag in this design gives it considerable inferential power.

The independent variable of principal interest is attending college (yes or no). However, other independent variables must be controlled for in order to get at the true effect of a college education. Kam and Palmer use an innovative technique, propensity score matching, which allows comparison of groups that are practically equivalent, except for the treatment (i.e., going to college). When they test for statistically significant differences between the two groups in terms of participation, they find none, concluding that education itself is not a cause but a proxy.

A proxy for what? That question is answered by considering the propensity score matching technique, which is essentially a means for controlling, or removing, the effects of common prior influences, that is, 1965 student and parent measures on cognitive ability, efficacy, personality, and civic responsibility. Following Kam and Palmer's reasoning, it is a combination of these things, not the educational experience itself, that produces greater participation.

Take a hypothetical example. High school student Betty Brown follows politics in the news, believes the government listens to the people, sees her life in a positive light, and is active in clubs. Her parents have similar attitudes and involvements. Another high school student, Sally Smart, has basically the same personal and parental profile. Sally goes to college but Betty does not. Eight years after high school graduation, both are asked about their political participation. No difference is found. Both are rather active, Betty in spite of the fact that she did not go to college. But as her friends might have said, if you knew Betty in high school, you would not be surprised at her current enthusiasm for politics. Likewise for Sally, college did not really change her; she was already an activist before she attended.

This scenario, or something like it, illustrates the provocative argument Kam and Palmer lay out. In ordinary models, then, the education variable merely serves as a stand-in for these preadult characteristics; once their influence is taken into account, education is left with no independent effect. The impact of education appears spurious.

However, this conclusion receives direct challenge from the work of Hillygus (2005). She tests three hypotheses linking higher education and political engagement—social networks, political meritocracy, and civic education. She finds the "civic education" received in college has a significant effect on political participation. Using data from the Baccalaureate and Beyond Longitudinal Study, she tracks the effect of a social science curriculum after graduation. "B&B graduates who concentrated study in social science were found, six years later, to be among the most politically active citizens compared to those who majored in any other field, even controlling for a multitude of other factors" (2005, 37).

Specifically, controls were imposed on race, ethnicity, gender, parent's education, Scholastic Aptitude Test scores, age at graduation, grade point average, martial status, and political interest. Hillygus's conclusion is that the connection between education and participation is not spurious. At least, it is not when that education is measured for its "civic" content. Of course, as Hillygus (2005, 41) herself admits, this begs the larger question of "the disparate rates of engagement between those with and without a college degree." Undoubtedly, the controversy—to what extent is the link between education and participation spurious?—will vibrate the academic debate for years to come.

Female Candidates and the Electoral Participation of Women

The gender gap in vote turnout has been virtually effaced in presidential contests, as it has at lower levels of political office, with men and women voting at effectively the same rate. Accompanying this change has been the rise in the number of females contending for office, and winning. The larger presence of women in the campaign arena has contributed, almost certainly, to the relative rise in female electoral participation (Mansbridge 1999; Reingold 2000). The 1992 elections were sometimes dubbed the "Year of the Woman," partly because of the unprecedented number of candidates that year (Wilcox 1994).

Recognizing this opportunity, Sapiro and Conover (1997) used the 1992 NES data to examine directly the impact of female candidacy in gubernatorial and congressional races. They found that, in constituencies where all the candidates were male, women respondents reported lower political involvement then men. However, these differences vanished when there was a female candidate in the district. Koch (1997) found a similar result for 1992 Senate races. Looking at data from a Citizen Participation Study, Burns, Schlozman, and Verba (2001) report that, in the context of more female politicians, women's participation tends to rise.

Individuals, Groups, Structures: Age

In these last two chapters, we have considered the influence of social group or social structure membership on a citizen's political behavior. Sometimes, the group character of the membership is clear, as with union members. Other times it is not, as with class, which can take on characteristics of a group (e.g., "I identify with the working class,") or of a structure (e.g., "I am classified a worker but feel no class attachment"). Frequently, however, social structure membership is unambiguous, with placement carrying no group connotations. Education is the outstanding case here. College graduates, for example, partake of the same educational categorization, but do believe they compose a self-aware group. Of course, this does not mean simply being in the same structural category cannot shape political behavior. It can, as we have seen with education.

Still, the political consequences of many social labels remain ambiguous. What are the politics of Generation Xers, Generation Y, soccer moms, yuppies? And the ambiguity may persist even with more enduring labels, like young and old. Rhodebeck (1993) addresses well the difficulties of capturing the political distinctness of the elderly. She argues that "older Americans share common age-related concerns, but they are hardly subject to the solidifying experiences typical of blacks or the disabled," and wonders openly, "Is age less effective than other group attributes in structuring political attitudes and behavior?" (Rhodebeck 1993, 342–43). On the whole, her answer is yes.

In her examination of seven NES surveys, she fails to find consistent age differences on issue or policy positions regarding health insurance or Social Security (Rhodebeck 1993, 344–51) (see also Day 1990). The only qualification is that she finds a mild tendency for the elderly to weigh these issues more in evaluating candidates than do the nonelderly. This leads her to suggest that the elderly are likely to have a distinctive vote in elections "where age-related issues are especially salient" (Rhodebeck 1993, 362). We observe, then, for the elderly, group politics is a sometime thing. Their place in the general age structure holds variable meaning. Their views on most issues differ little from the rest of the population. However, they weigh certain of these issues, for example, Social Security, differently, giving them more importance. Hence, when such issues appear on the agenda, they trigger an elderly vote.

The Political Behavior of Farmers

In the 1950s, farmers were more marginal in terms of their political involvement than any other major occupational group. The most important demonstration of that claim appeared in Campbell et al. (1960, chap. 15), who found farmers were relatively lacking in psychological, organizational, or behavior links to politics. This description was supported by other scholars around the same time (Bone and Ranney 1963, 45; Flanigan 1972, 54; Milbrath 1965, 128–30). However, by the 1970s, the picture had changed. Lewis-Beck (1977), in an investigation of the 1952–72 NES presidential election surveys, found that farmers had become highly participative in politics. After an examination of indicators on voting, letter-writing, campaigning, and organizational activity, he concluded, "Today farm people, especially the younger ones, form one of the most politically attentive groups in our society. Along key participation dimensions, they are more active than all but the thin upper strata of urban professionals" (1977, 561).

Subsequent work, focusing in particular on the 1980 and 1984 elections, generally corroborated this political transformation of the American farmer (Sigelman 1983, 1987). What do things look like now? We attempted to find out, using the 2000 and 2004 NES. Unfortunately, this proved unfruitful, due to perilously small sample sizes. In the replication of table 12.1, for example, only 13 farmers were available. Sample size attrition continues with the 2004 data set. These tiny samples are not the product of a faulty research design. Rather, they reflect the dwindling number of farmers in the national labor force. Clearly, agrarian political behavior, as an object of study in the NES, is a thing of the past, unless the group is systematically oversampled in future surveys.

Is There a Decline in Class Voting?

While traditional measures of social class, based on simple occupational dichotomies, indicate a decline in class voting, alternative measures do not. Some have argued that income, not occupation, is the preferred measure. For example, Stonecash and Mariani (2000, 97–100) find an increase in class voting when income is so used. They divide NES respondents into three family income categories, and calculate the percentage difference in Democratic presidential voting between the low and high groups. (They exclude blacks to reduce bias, since they tend to be more Democratic and have lower income.) Then, they average this low-high spread by decades: 1950s = 4, 1960s = 2, 1970s = 9, 1980s = 15, 1990–92 = 18 (Stonecash and Mariani 2000, table 1). Here we see a steady rise in class voting beginning in the 1970s, with the low-income group about twice as likely to vote Democratic in the 1990s as in the 1970s.

In 1994, class voting actually peaked, according to this analysis, with a low-high difference of 26 percentage points in favor of the Democrats (Stonecash and Mariani 2000, 105). These authors contend that this intensification of class voting was a direct product of policy differences between the Democrats and Republicans—over health care, welfare reform, and the Republican's "Contract with America." This example contributes to our earlier discussion of increasing status polarization through the sharpening of policy differences between the parties. In the 1996 presidential election itself, this low-high difference remained virtually the same, at 25 percentage points. Stonecash and Mariani (2000, 110) conclude: "It does not appear that the class reactions in 1994 were a fluke. The parties have continued to pursue differing agendas that affect classes differently." (In his book on the subject, Stonecash [2000] makes the same point.)

Other authors have reached a similar conclusion, with still other measures. Hout, Brooks, and Manza (1995, 805–9) incorporate advances in stratification theory, to redefine the occupational measure of class in a more complex way. They offer a "total class" index based on six occupational categories: professionals, managers, owners, white-collar workers, skilled blue-collar workers, semi- and unskilled blue-collar workers (1995, 810). An examination of the NES presidential election data, 1948–92, shows that professionals, managers, and white-collar workers have become more Democratic, owners and skilled workers have stayed about the same, while semi- and unskilled workers have become more Republican (table 2, 818). When these changes are taken together in the total class index, there is "no evidence of a decline in the political significance of class. Thus, the gross effect of class on voting outcome fluctuates from election to election without any discernible long-term trend" (816). Manza and Brooks (1999) apply the same approach and come to the same conclusion.

Thus far, class has been treated as a measurable demographic characteristic. But it is possible to think of class as a motivating idea. Certainly, this is the impetus behind Marx's notion of "class consciousness." Simmons (2006) proposes that the "class idea" has as much electoral force as ever. "When class is treated as an interpretation of the political scene, an orienting political idea, or a reason for taking action . . . it becomes possible to see how concerns of a class character might still dominate the intellectual agenda of Democratic presidential politics" (Simmons 2006, 9). He cleverly content-analyzes the candidate likes-dislikes responses in the NES, 1952–2004, coding them in terms of the justifications they employ for voting Democratic (or not).

He finds that the Democratic "signature idea" of reform, where politics is seen as a struggle of the have-nots against the haves, dominates presidential vote choice, when compared to seven other possible justification variables. Simmons concludes, "When class is treated as the general impulse to protect the little people against various species of elites, class politics remains an important, consistent and even dominant effect on individual voting behavior" (2006, 25). On this basis one might expect the presidential campaign of John Edwards, on the "Two Americas," to have more resonance than otherwise supposed.

Class Voting and the "Kansas Hypothesis"

In his recent, popular book *What's the Matter with Kansas?* Thomas Frank (2004) argues that disadvantaged Americans have betrayed their economic interests in favor of a conservative moral agenda and the Republican Party. A specific outcome is that workers have turned away from Democratic candidates, their traditional allies, and joined up with the party of business. Is this charge true? Larry Bartels (2005b, 9), offers a thoughtful answer to Frank's question. Using the NES, 1952–2004, he explores the voting patterns of different income groups (whites only) in a manner similar to Stonecash, discussed above. He uses "the terms 'low-income' and 'working class' interchangeably to refer to people with family incomes in the bottom third of the income distribution" (Bartels 2005b, 11).

Bartels contrasts Democratic presidential voting, plotting low-income and high-income lines across the period (2005b, fig. 1). From 1952 to 1972, little difference in the voting of the two groups appears. However, from 1976 to 2004, there is a clear voting gap between the two, averaging 51 percent Democrat for the low-income group, and only 37 percent for the high-income group. Interestingly, this average result is closely reflected in the 2004 contest, where Kerry got 50 percent of the low-income group compared to 39 percent for the high-income group. (Note this difference of about 11 points is not far from the 13 points separating working- and middle-class voters in our table 12.1.) Bartels (2005b, 14) concludes that "economic status has become more important, not less important, in structuring the presidential voting behavior of white Americans over the course of the past half-century." In sum, Frank's "Kansas hypothesis" does not apply to the nation as a whole. Working-class Americans are, if anything, relatively more committed to the Democratic Party than they have been in the past.

Do Female Candidates Boost the Vote Turnout of Everyone?

It seems clear that, at least in certain contexts, the presence of a female candidate can elevate the women's vote. But what of its effect on the overall, general voting turnout rate? Dolan (2005, 10), in her insightful study, points out that "[p]revious research, while illuminating, does not provide a complete understanding of the mechanism by which the presence of women candidates increases public engagement in politics." She argues that men, as well as women, are capable of being influenced by women candidates. "I suggest that people [men or women] with a particular psychological orientation to women's issues are those who would be most likely to hear and act on the symbols and messages sent by women candidates" (Dolan 2005, 11).

Given this circumstance, it is plausible that women candidates can raise overall turnout. Dolan tests this proposition on 1998–2004 NES House and Senate election data. The dependent variable is a vote dichotomy (yes or no), and the independent variables include a standard set of political and socioeconomic controls. The key independent variable is a dummy, measuring whether the respondent lives in a constituency with a female candidate. Following a cue from Atkeson (2003), before analysis she divides the data into four subgroups: female respondents facing a competitive contest; female respondents facing a noncompetitive contest; male respondents facing a competitive contest; male respondents facing a noncompetitive contest. The coefficients are in the right direction, at least for the House. However, in general the null hypothesis cannot be rejected.

As Dolan (2005, 14) reports, "[T]he analysis indicates that there is little support for the hypothesis that women candidates help to excite or mobilize vote turnout." A series of analyses fails to alter this general result. Dolan (2005, 19) then proposes a persuasive speculation: "the findings here signal not that women candidates don't have an impact on voter turnout so much as they might illuminate a general diminishing of the impact of candidate sex as women candidates become more commonplace and less of a novelty."

CHAPTER 13

Economic Antecedents of Political Behavior

The notion that economics shapes politics is well-worn. Dramatic events, such as the Great Depression, can bring down presidents and put workers in welfare lines. Continued hard times can lead to demands for a change in the two-party system, including calls for a radical third party to bring about more economic justice in the marketplace. Lesser crises, such as recession, can trigger a pocketbook reaction among the voters to "throw the rascals out." In previous chapters, we have hinted at the political role of economic forces. To illustrate, a common sense of economic exploitation may strengthen group or class bonds, and help direct their political choice.

Yet these sociological characteristics do not house the economic interests of every voter. For one thing, class politics these days is relatively weak, and mostly confines itself to the more politically active. In contrast, many citizens, even those who restrict their politics to the routines of voting, care about "good times," about the prosperity of the country generally. It seems useful, then, to focus directly on the political consequences of these economic conditions, as they relate to the behavior of the contemporary American voter. We look first at how general feelings of economic distress color political thinking, and vice versa. Then, we examine how perceptual indicators of overall economic well-being, personal and national, help us explain vote choice in their own right.

ECONOMIC PRESSURE AND ECONOMIC CONCERN

In the years surrounding the elections under study—2000 and 2004—the United States did not experience economic depression. That does not mean the period was free of economic problems. After an extended period of growth, the economy began to slow as 2000 ended. The terrorist attack of September 11, 2001, administered an economic, as well as a political, shock to the nation. Generally, inflation was low, but the trade deficit was large and unemployment persistently at higher than optimal levels. Going into the 2004 presidential election, gross national product (GNP) growth was a moderate 3 percent annually, and job growth itself was quite sluggish, near a historic low. Of course, not all citizens are harmed (or helped) equally by macroeconomic fluctuations. In downturns some are harder hit than others, perhaps because of the region of the country they live in, perhaps because of their occupational sector. We might expect those experiencing more financial pressure to express their concern in a presidential election. After all, the president has come to be viewed as the CEO of the nation's economy. It is not unreasonable to suppose that certain citizens might blame him for bad times and vote against his party.

Economic pressure takes many forms. Unemployment, or its threat, is the most direct. The loss of a job, or the fear of it, galvanizes people's attention, for the situation calls for immediate action. Dental bills must be paid, groceries purchased, the car repaired, new school shoes ordered. Something must be done, someone—individual or institution—must come to the rescue. Moreover, citizens do not actually need to be unemployed themselves to be affected. If friends or neighbors are unemployed, that evokes a concern for the well-being of the community, even if the concerned themselves are financially secure. In table 13.1, we look at perceptions about the job situation, and how it relates to presidential vote choice.

Before the 2000 election, respondents were asked whether it had gotten easier or harder to find work. Only about half (50.9 percent) said it had gotten easier. In 2004, just before that contest, a similar question was asked, about whether unemployment had gotten better or worse. Here, just under one-third (28.8 percent) said it had gotten better. Clearly, job concerns are on many voters' minds. In both elections, we observe that those more worried over unemployment were more likely to vote against the party currently occupying the White House. In 2000, among

TABLE 13.1. Relation of Worries about Unemployment to Presidential Vote, 2000 and 2004 (in percentages)

A. 2000

	Worried	Not Worried
Democrat	43.4	56.1
Republican	52.6	40.1
Others	4.0	3.8
Total	100.0	100.0
Number of cases	504	576

B. 2004

	Worried	Not Worried
Democrat	61.7	15.4
Republican	37.1	84.1
Others	1.2	.5
Total	100.0	100.0
Number of cases	496	201

Note: Presidential vote was coded as Republican candidate, Democratic candidate, others. Worries about unemployment, for the 2000 survey, was coded "worried" = gotten harder to find enough work, somewhat harder, same; "not worried" = easier to find enough work, somewhat easier. For the 2004 survey, "worried" = level of unemployment has gotten worse, or stayed about the same; "not worried" = level of unemployment has gotten better. Data are from, respectively, the 2000 and the 2004 NES surveys.

the worried, vote for Republican challenger Bush was 52.6 percent, in contrast to 43.4 percent for incumbent candidate Gore. In 2004, among the worried, vote for Democratic challenger Kerry was 61.7 percent, in contrast to 37.1 percent for incumbent candidate Bush. An implication is that the perceived job situation, for individuals and communities, is a causal antecedent to vote choice. This possibility of an economic voting connection we pursue below.

ECONOMIC PRESSURES AND POLITICAL RESPONSE

Reporting a connection between an economic stimulus and a political response is helpful as far as it goes. But we still need to answer why this connection exists. What is the political translation? We turn to the role of party identification, which we have found can offer a general explanation for much political behavior. Apparently, a citizen's perception that they are under economic pressure is at least partly attributable to their partisanship. In 2004, voters were asked if they were worried about losing their job. As table 13.2 shows, this attitude is related to their party identification. Republicans were less likely to perceive a job threat than Democrats. For example, comparing strong Republicans to strong Democrats, there is a 16.2-percentage-point difference.

A citizen's personal job perception seems shaped, to a degree, by whether he or she is attached to the party of the president. A similar partisan filter appears to operate on attitudes toward economic policies in general. As table 13.3 illustrates, when voters identify with the president's party, they are very much more likely to approve of that administration's economic policies. Republicans are very much in favor of what the president is doing for the economy, perhaps merely because he is of their party. Democrats are very much against, perhaps again just because he

TABLE 13.2. Relation of Party Identification to Personal Reaction to Job Situation, 200 (in percentages)

| | Party Identification | | | | | |
	Strong Dem.	Weak Dem.	Ind.	Weak Rep.	Strong Rep.	To
Worried	30.5	37.7	33.5	22.1	14.3	2ł
Not worried	69.5	62.3	66.5	77.9	85.7	7
Total	100.0	100.0	100.0	100.0	100.0	10ł
Number of cases	95	106	257	104	112	67ł

Note: Party identification is based on the question, "Generally speaking, do you usually think of yourself a Republican, a Democrat, an Independent, or what?" If the respondent considered himself or herself a partisan, they w then asked whether the identification was "strong" or "not very strong." Personal reaction to job situation was based the question, "How worried are you about losing your job in the near future: a lot, somewhat, or not much at all?" ł category worried = "a lot" + "somewhat"; not worried = "not much at all." The data are from NES survey, 2004.

TABLE 13.3. Relation of Party Identification to Approval of the President's Handling o the Economy, 2004 (in percentages)

| | Party Identification | | | | | |
	Strong Dem.	Weak Dem.	Ind.	Weak Rep.	Strong Rep.	To
Approve	5.4	17.4	33	74.4	90.5	4
Disapprove	94.6	82.6	67	25.6	9.5	5
Total	100.0	100.0	100.0	100.0	100.0	10ł
Number of cases	168	150	342	130	178	96ł

Note: Party identification is measured as in table 13.2. Approval is based on the question, "Do you approve disapprove of the way George W. Bush is handling the economy?" Data are from NES survey, 2004.

TABLE 13.4. Relation of Evaluation of President's Handling of the Economy to Party Identification and Personal Reaction to Job Situation, 2004 (in percentages)

	Worried			Not Worried		
	Dem.	Ind.	Rep.	Dem.	Ind.	Rep.
Approve	13.2	26.5	64.7	16.7	37.0	87.0
Disapprove	86.8	73.5	35.3	83.3	63.0	13.0
Total	100.0	100.0	100.0	100.0	100.0	100.0
Number of cases	68	83	34	132	165	177

Note: Evaluation of the president's handling of the economy is measured as in table 13.3. Party identification is measured with the same item as in table 13.2, but it is collapsed into the three categories of Democrat, Independent, and Republican. Personal reaction to job situation is measured as in table 13.2. The data are from NES survey, 2004.

heads the opposition. This raises the question of whether there is any real economic content to these presidential policy evaluations.

To answer this question, we control for party identification and explore whether unemployment worries still make a difference in the political response (see table 13.4). These percentages indicate, as expected, that partisanship is related to approval of the president's economic policies. However, they also reveal that, beyond partisanship, unemployment worries reduce support for the administration's efforts. Indeed, the effect is fairly sharp. Among Republicans who had personal job concerns, only 64.7 percent approved, in contrast to 87 percent for Republicans with no job concerns (for a 22.3-percentage-point difference). Thus, unemployment worries are more than just a psychological rationalization of partisan attitudes. This conclusion is reinforced when the Independents are examined. Among this group, which lacks any party attachment, those with job worries were over 10 percentage points less likely to support the president's economic policies.

ECONOMIC OUTLOOK AND POLITICAL BEHAVIOR

On the basis of our analysis thus far, it seems clear that unemployment, or its threat, can induce a political response. But what about other economic issues? Is there a general economic attitude that can stand for a summary of the citizen's view, incorporating multiple relevant aspects of the economy? If so, we could move from the testing of specific hypotheses to the exploration of more global theories of economics and political behavior. We believe the concept of *economic outlook* offers such a possibility.

The concept is broad, and suggests that a person evaluates economic matters along a continuum, from rosy to dark. Like other attitudes we have examined, it is formed from what the individual perceives, and the values he or she attaches to the things perceived. Economic outlook is not the same as concern over a particular situation, such as unemployment. Rather, it differs in multiple ways. For one, while it lacks any political substance, direct or indirect, it may bear on any number of political choices—parties, candidates, or policies. For another, it tends not to be related to other important social cleavages, such as group or class. That is to say, its impact does not depend on these conditions, but instead operates the same way across categories, as we shall see below.

An individual's economic outlook can be divided conceptually into views toward two distinct sets of objects: one's personal economic circumstance, and the economic condition of the country. Anyone's economic outlook is to some extent subjective, since it is based on a person's conception of events. Nevertheless, there is evidence that these perceptions are not divorced from real-world economic fluctuations. In other words, economic attitudes tend to track key macroeconomic indicators. That being said, it is important to recognize that the link is not perfect, and that the fortunes of an individual can be quite different from the fortunes of the nation. Given these things, we would expect personal and national economic conditions to relate differently to political behavior.

To measure the personal component of a voter's economic outlook, we use the responses to the following item: "We are interested in how people are getting along financially these days. Would you say that you (and your family) are better off, worse off, or just about the same financially as you were a year ago?" In table 13.5, we see the distribution of opinion of this personal financial situation variable, and how it relates to two-party presidential vote choice. We see, first, that voters varied widely in their personal economic outlook, with a good share offering each of the possible responses. Note especially that, among those who perceive their pocketbooks as worse off, the incumbent presidential candidate fails to receive majority support, in either 2000 or 2004. This is not true, however, among those who feel their own financial situation has bettered.

One question that has been thus far neglected is the role of socioeconomic variables in shaping the relationship of economic outlook and presidential vote. Are variables such as occupation, income, or education behind this apparent connection between economics and the vote? If they were brought into the picture, would the link change, even disappear? Supposing that were the case, then economic attitudes would amount, in the end, to nothing more than rationalizations of a person's position in a status hierarchy. It is difficult to look at all these SES variables at once; but, we can examine the influence of one that is related to them all—social class. As we saw in the last chapter, societies are layered by class, and one's particular rank could influence economic as well as political attitudes.

Working-class voters may be more likely to see themselves as worse off economically, and so support the opposition. Indeed, perhaps the perception of "doing worse" is entirely confined to the working class, in which case the variable of economic perception would have no independent political impact. Another possibility is that an economic effect persists, but varies from class to class. For instance, it may be that workers have a more intense class consciousness, more readily translating their

TABLE 13.5. Relation of Personal Financial Situation to the Presidential Vote, 2000 and 2004 (in percentages)

A. 2000

| | Personal Financial Situation | | |
	Worse	Same	Better
Gore (I)	45	51	56
Bush	55	49	44
Total	100	100	100
Number of cases	56	291	164

B. 2004

| | Personal Financial Situation | | |
	Worse	Same	Better
Bush (I)	28	50	64
Kerry	72	50	36
Total	100	100	100
Number of cases	219	208	354

Note: "I" indicates the candidate of the party in the White House. Data are from NES pre- and postelection survey, NES 2000 and 2004. "Personal financial situation" codes (see italics) responses to the following item: "We are interested in how people are getting along financially these days. Would you say that you (and your family) are *better* off, *worse* off, or just about the *same* financially as you were a year ago?"

economic grievances into a vote. In other words, the political strength of economic perceptions would be conditional on class, changing as it changed.

In table 13.6, one sees the relation between pocketbook and vote within the working class and the middle class. First, note that the working class is subject to somewhat more economic pressure, in that 32 percent (103/318) declare their personal finances have worsened, compared to only 24 percent (105/438) among the middle class. However, this sensitivity does not translate into workers having a bigger economic vote. The percentage difference in blue-collar support for the president is +31, going from "worse" to "better" economic conditions, somewhat less than the comparable white-collar percentage difference (of +40). Thus, pocketbook effects do not really depend on class standing. Moreover, the overall effect is essentially undiminished, regardless of class. In the simple bivariate table 13.5b, we observe that the "worse" minus "better" percentage difference is +36. Once class is controlled for, as in table 13.6, this percentage difference hardly changes. Social class, as important as it may be in its own right, does not diminish the unique impact of personal economic outlook.

How does this compare to the impact of the national economic outlook? An individual's view of the national economy has it source in nu-

TABLE 13.6. Relation of Personal Financial Situation and Presidential Vote, within Categories of Social Class, 2004 (in percentages)

	Working Class		
	Worse	Same	Better
Bush (I)	23.3	47.9	54.2
Kerry	76.7	52.1	45.8
Total	100.0	100.0	100.0
Number of cases	103	71	144

	Middle Class		
	Worse	Same	Better
Bush (I)	31.4	53.1	71.4
Kerry	68.6	46.9	28.6
Total	100.0	100.0	100.0
Number of cases	105	130	203

Note: "I" indicates the candidate of the party in the White House. The variables of personal financial situation and presidential vote are coded as in table 13.5. The social class variable, working versus middle, is based on the respondent's subjective self-placement. The data are from NES survey, 2004.

merous things, some subjective, some objective. On the objective side, the most obvious is the actual functioning of the macroeconomy, as measured by gross domestic product (GDP) and other relevant indicators. On the subjective side, two citizens may see the same macro-economy but evaluate it differently. This could be because, say, one values low inflation more than economic growth, while the other has the opposite priority. As voters look at the varied aspects of a country's economic performance, they distill them into a summary judgment about the direction the nation is going. Not everyone will agree on that direction. Some will believe that the economy is moving vigorously ahead, while others will worry about a slowdown. Regardless, this overall assessment should activate them politically.

To measure the national component of economic outlook, we use this item: "Now thinking about the economy in the country as a whole, would you say that over the past year the nation's economy has gotten better, stayed about the same, or gotten worse?" We observe in table 13.7 that

TABLE 13.7. Relation of National Economic Situation to the Presidential Vote, 2000 and 2004 (in percentages)

A. 2000

	Economic Situation		
	Worse	Same	Better
Gore (I)	31	45	69
Bush	69	55	31
Total	100	100	100
Number of cases	154	487	408

B. 2004

	Economic Situation		
	Worse	Same	Better
Bush (I)	20	58	87
Kerry	80	42	13
Total	100	100	100
Number of cases	319	243	211

Note: "I" indicates the candidate of the party in the White House. The data are from NES surveys, 2000 and 2004. National economic situation codes (see italics) responses to the following item: "Now thinking about the economy as a whole, would you say that over the past year the nation's economy has gotten *better*, stayed about the *same*, or gotten *worse?*"

people vary widely in their opinions about how the economy is going. Furthermore, opinion varies across election years, as well as within an election year. In 2000, only 15 percent of these voters believed the economy had gotten worse, in contrast to 41 percent in 2004. These voters, convinced of economic deterioration, acted overwhelmingly against the incumbent party candidate, irrespective of whether he was Democratic or Republican. President Bush seems especially to have suffered at their hands, for only 20 percent of this large group cast their support for him. This finding goes a long way toward explaining his very narrow victory.

ECONOMIC OUTLOOK AND PARTISAN ATTITUDES

Earlier we showed that evaluations of candidates and parties are tangled up with attention to all sorts of economic questions. A nagging worry is that a citizen's economic outlook may merely be a projection of his or her partisan attitudes. This is implied by economic outlook's strong association with party identification, reported in table 13.8. We observe,

TABLE 13.8. Relation of Party Identification to Economic Outlook, 2004 (in percentages)

A. Personal Financial Situation

	Democrat	Independent	Republican
Worse	43.8	33.6	15.4
Same	24.5	21.8	26.2
Better	31.7	44.6	58.4
Total	100.0	100.0	100.0
Number of cases	322	348	317

B. National Economic Situation

	Democrat	Independent	Republican
Worse	66.9	48.0	14.9
Same	23.3	32.8	36.4
Better	9.8	19.2	48.7
Total	100.0	100.0	100.0
Number of cases	317	348	316

Note: Party identification is measured as in table 13.4. Personal financial situation is measured as in table 13.5. National economic situation is measured as in table 13.7. The data are from NES survey, 2004.

for 2004, that Republicans are more likely than Democrats to possess a positive view of economic matters. The contrast is stark. Most Republicans think they personally are better off, while most Democrats do not. Are these Republicans saying they are better off because, simply put, they are happy to have a president in the White House, while the Democrats are saying the contrary because they are in the political opposition?

For example, if I am a Republican, I may perceive an improvement in business conditions simply because the president, whom I consider CEO of the economy, is a Republican. In that case, a vote for Bush in 2004 would really be determined by my party affiliation. My economic assessment, such as it was, would have no independent effect on my vote; instead, it would just reflect my partisanship. If such a scenario holds, then the positive results on economic outlook and the vote, reported in tables 13.5 and 13.7, are spurious. That is, they show an observed relationship which, at bottom, represents no real causal connection.

Thus, it is extremely important to test this hypothesis of spuriousness. We can do this by controlling for party identification. Once it is held constant, if economic outlook has no voting impact, the link between the two variables will disappear. In table 13.9a, the relation between personal financial situation and presidential vote is reexamined, within categories of party identification. Among Independents, who by definition have no party, the optimists are definitely more likely to vote for the incumbent president (better minus worse is a 34-percentage-point difference). However, active partisanship acts as a brake on this influence from economic perceptions. For Democrats, the relevant percentage difference (better minus worse) drops to +14; for Republicans, it drops to +10. Nevertheless, the financial effect is not totally eliminated.

The persistence of a unique economic impact is seen more vividly in table 13.9b. Among Democrats who see the national economy as worse off, virtually all (97 percent) voted Kerry. In contrast, among Democrats who see the national economy as better off, only about two-thirds (68 percent) voted Kerry. Obviously, being a Democratic identifier was not the whole story, as far as Kerry support was concerned. Beyond that, the voter's own assessment of how the economy was doing tipped some Democrats closer to or away from their party's candidate.

The same picture emerges for the Republicans, if less sharply. That is to say, while Republican partisans were overwhelmingly loyal to President Bush, they were not 100 percent across the board; one thing that made a difference was their economic assessment. Among those who were dissatisfied with the national economic situation, 16 percent defected to Kerry. In sum, what these tables tell us is that a citizen's economic outlook does exert influence over the vote, over and above the influence of partisanship itself. While that influence is not nearly as great as that from party identification per se, it is still not trivial. These economic judgments, subjective as they are, have their own independent political reality.

Where do we place economic outlook in a general theory of voting? Its place in the causal chain might vary from person to person. For citizens who have experienced deep and enduring economic hardships, it may be primary. For those who have learned about economic issues from campaigns and the media, it may follow, rather than drive, political changes. Nevertheless, for the typical contemporary American voter, we hold that more lasting factors, such as socioeconomic status and party identification, are formed first. While these rather entrenched forces can bend economic opinion, individuals' financial situation at home and their

TABLE 13.9. Vote for President, as a Function of Economic Outlook, among Three Categories of Party Identifiers, 2004 (in percentages)

A. Personal Financial Situation

	Democrat			Independent			Republican		
	Worse	Same	Better	Worse	Same	Better	Worse	Same	Bett
Bush (I)	4	3	18	22	41	56	86	95	96
Kerry	96	97	82	78	59	44	14	5	4
Total	100	100	100	100	100	100	100	100	100
Number of cases	100	65	85	67	58	91	43	78	16[illegible]

B. National Economic Situation

	Democrat			Independent			Republican		
	Worse	Same	Better	Worse	Same	Better	Worse	Same	Bett
Bush (I)	3	12	32	20	45	82	84	94	97
Kerry	97	88	68	80	55	18	16	6	3
Total	100	100	100	100	100	100	100	100	100
Number of cases	165	57	22	98	76	44	38	99	14[illegible]

Note: "I" indicates the candidate of the party in the White House. Party identification is measured as in table 13 Personal financial situation is measured as in table 13.5. National economic situation is measured as in table 13.7. T data are from NES survey, 2004.

interpretation of national business conditions have some existence apart. These economic perceptions exercise their own will over political behavior. Thus, economic outlook occupies a midway position in the funnel of causality, as an intervening variable operating after the anchors of partisanship and social structure are sunk, antecedent to the act of voting.

PROSPERITY AND POLITICAL CHANGE

In the 2004 election, the Republican candidate received more support from voters who had a positive economic outlook. Is this because those economic optimists were particularly attracted to Republican policies? Such an explanation does not seem likely, since economic optimists in the 2000 election favored the Democratic candidate, not the Republican (recall tables 13.5 and 13.7). In other words, the same economic attitudes led to increased support for different parties in the two elections. It is improbable that economic optimists suddenly switched their allegiance from a Democratic to a Republican set of policies. Instead, something else is going on. That is, those who see economic good times are, in both elections, voting more in favor of the party in the White House.

When the economy appears prosperous, voters tend to attribute that prosperity to the policies of the incumbent party, and reward it with support. As these two contests suggest, no party has a lock on the positive electoral benefits of good times. On the one hand, if the party in the White House produces economic well-being, it will receive more votes, regardless of its label. On the other hand, its failure to produce economic well-being costs it votes. When these costs are high enough, they can even bring about a change in the governing party, as voters act against the incumbent candidate. Because democracy includes accountability of the government to the people, we are encouraged to report that the people are able to effectively sanction the White House for poor economic performance.

COMMENTARY AND CONTROVERSY
Economic Voting Theory

The notion that economics matters for elections has considerable cachet among the people and politicians, as well as among observers and scholars. The idea that a presidential candidate won or lost an election because of the economy is often bandied about by Monday-morning quarterbacks. Why might vote totals be influenced by such matters? The core model is reward-punishment. The president receives the reward of a vote for good economic times, and the punishment of an opposition vote for bad economic times (see especially Kiewiet 1983). Two rival general theories of this economic vote have emerged: the retrospective and the prospective.

Retrospective economic voting theory derives from V. O. Key's (1968, 61) argument that the elector acts as "appraiser of past events, past performance, and past actions. It judges retrospectively." In other words, voters assess the economic past. Prospective economic voting theory derives from Anthony Downs (1957, 39), who contends an elector "is helping to select the government which will govern him during the coming election period. . . . He makes his decision by comparing future performances he expects." In other words, voters assess the economic future.

Fiorina (1981, 26) has become the chief theoretician of retrospective economic voting in American national elections, viewing them "as referenda on the incumbent administration's handling of the economy." Fiorina (1981, 12–16) also incorporated Downs in his retrospective schema on the ground that, empirically, expectations had to be made up of retrospections (since the future was necessarily unknown). From this vantage point, the classical retrospective-prospective distinction collapses. Some scholars, however, prefer to maintain it. They argue that the prospective dimension of economic voting is unique, resting, among other things, on measurable campaign promises (Clarke and Stewart 1994; Lewis-Beck 1988, 130–31; Lockerbie 1992).

Aggregate Functions: Popularity and Vote

Initial attempts to link economic change to support of the administration examined the dependent variable of presidential popularity, in analyses of national time series. These studies from the 1970s and 1980s generally demonstrated that macroeconomic fluctuations had significant, expected effects (see the review in Lewis-Beck and Stegmaier 2000, 184–88). However, there was not convergence on which indicators were responsible for them, for example, unemployment, inflation, income, or GDP. Perhaps because of this failure, more recent work on popularity has abandoned these objective indicators for subjective ones, namely aggregate attitudinal measures of how the economy *was* (retrospective), or *will be* (prospective). Strong economic effects have been found, but of an opposite kind. For example, Norpoth (1996, 783) reports "a substantial influence of retrospective views of the economy," but not of prospective views. Erikson, MacKuen, and Stimson (2000, 311) report that voters "respond in terms of their expectation of the future level of prosperity."

The electoral effects of economics cannot really be sorted out with popularity as the object of explanation, since the variable of ultimate interest remains the vote itself. Fortunately, a number of equations with a vote measure as the dependent variable have been estimated, mostly on annual time series across the post–World War II period (Abramowitz 1988; Erikson 1989; Fair 1978; Hibbs 1982; Lewis-Beck and Rice 1984; Tufte 1978). Because of the scarcity of observations, the models tend to be parsimonious, and the statistics straightforward. A typical specification reads like this:

Presidential Vote = f(Economics, Politics)

with Presidential Vote measured as the incumbent share of the two-party (Democrat-Republican) popular vote, Economics measured by a macroeconomic indicator such as income, and Politics measured by a macropolitical indicator such as presidential popularity in a Gallup poll.

These models have generally uncovered a strong influence from the economy. For example, Erikson (1989) finds that a percentage change in disposable personal income (weighted over the term) generates an expected change in the two-party presidential popular vote share of 2.77 percentage points. While this result, and others of its kind, provide support for the economic voting hypothesis, they have what some consider a fatal problem—they face the ecological fallacy. Observation of a firm aggregate link between the economy and the electoral outcome does not mean individual voters themselves actually act on the basis of these economic swings. For example, it may be that the link appears simply because with a good economy the incumbent party fields a strong candidate, while with a weak economy it fields a weak candidate. Even if the link is not spurious, its presence does not reveal the mechanics of economic voting, as exercised by the average citizen. For that understanding, we must turn to the analysis of individual electors in scientific surveys.

Election Surveys

If voters are, in fact, responding to the economy, at what conditions are they looking? The popular assumption holds they peer into their pocketbooks. If my personal finances are suffering, I put blame on the president, and vote against him, at least so the reasoning goes. Recall our positive evidence for this hypothesis in the 2000 and 2004 presidential elections (see table 13.5). Does the pocketbook voter hypothesis sustain itself for other presidential elections, and under multivariate controls? A standard pocketbook item (such as that of table 13.5)—personal financial situation is better, worse, same—has been posed regularly in the NES. Sometimes it fails to demonstrate a statistically significant impact, once included in a regression model with the everyday controls on party identification, SES, and perhaps other issues. Even when it does register statistical significance, it does not reach substantive significance (Alvarez and Nagler 1995, 1998; Fiorina 1981, 40; Kiewiet 1983, 98; Lanoue 1994; Markus 1988, 1992).

Overall, the pocketbook voting hypothesis receives faint support. If economics makes an important difference, that difference must come from elsewhere. We find this in what have come to be called "sociotropic" effects (Kinder and Kiewiet 1981). Sociotropic evaluations assess the collectivity, rather than the individual. The leading sociotropic item routinely employed in the NES is that of table 13.7, asking about national economic conditions. The sociotropic effect emerges as consistently statistically significant, and substantively strong, even after the imposition of rigorous controls. See especially the analyses of the 1992 and 1996 elections by Alvarez and Nagler (1995, 1998). When a voter's assessment of the national economy moved from "worse" to "better," the probability of a Clinton vote climbed by .38, making it more powerful than all other issues (Alvarez and Nagler 1998, 1360–62). Even for the troubled 2000 election, the sociotropic coefficient continued relatively strong according to Norpoth (2004, 54).

The foregoing has focused on the testing of the retrospective model. What of the prospective? Partly because of wording inconsistencies and item availability, the evidence here is spottier. However, various prospective measures have come up statistically significant in different studies (Fiorina 1981, 170; Lanoue 1994; Lewis-Beck 1988, chap. 8). In an extensive sequential examination of NES surveys from 1956 to 1988, Lockerbie (1992) finds prospective effects clearly exceed retrospective ones, but admits to difficulties in comparing measurements.

Nadeau and Lewis-Beck (2001) attempt a broad, systematic comparison of retrospective and prospective influences, in their pooled analysis of the 1956–96 NES surveys. They construct the National Business Index (NBI) as a retrospective measure of the country's economic performance, and the Economic Future Index (EFI) as a prospective measure of the country's economic performance. NBI equals the percentage of respondents who see last year's economy as "good" less the percentage who see last year's economy as "bad." Thus, the more positive the number, the better off the public's assessment of the economy. EFI follows a parallel calculation, from respondents' assessment of next year's economy. These aggregates serve as scores for each voter and vary according to the election year. When they are included in a well-specified logistic regression analysis, NBI and EFI both have statistically significant effects (Nadeau and Lewis-Beck 2001, 175). Thus, the presidential vote appears subject to prospective as well as retrospective national economic evaluations. Further, ceteris paribus, these competing variables in general have approximately the same impact.

Responsibility and Divided Government

The reward-punishment model of economic voting rests on a theory of attribution of responsibility. The voter perceives the condition of the economy, attributes that condition to the government, and uses the vote as an instrument of praise or blame. To the extent that the objects of attention are clear, the mechanism is simple. Ideally, the economic indicators, the government actors, and the links between are unambiguous. Of course, the world can be less than ideal. Already, we have seen that uncertainty can arise over what economic measures are relevant. It can also arise concerning government actors.

With respect to making U.S. economic policy, key actors include the president, the Congress, the Federal Reserve Board, the courts, and business itself. If power were concentrated exclusively in the hands of the president, then the economic voter could ignore the other actors in assigning praise or blame. However, in the real world, power is divided among the different actors. How does this dispersion of power influence economic voting? One might expect that, as government becomes more divided, the economic vote in presidential elections will diminish; voters will see that, under these conditions, the president has less responsibility, so they will blame him less.

In the aforementioned study, Nadeau and Lewis-Beck (2001) tested this hypothesis. For each election, governing party unity was measured, on a scale from full unity (e.g., 1980, where the president and the Congress were of the same party for four years) to no unity (e.g., 1992, where the president never controls either house). Their expectation was that the strength of the economic voting coefficient would increase as government showed more unity. Voters would see the president's greater ability to move his economic program through Congress, and reward (or punish) him as necessary. Perhaps surprisingly, the analysis shows no support for this hypothesis (even under various definitions of unified government).

The economic voting coefficient is not significantly altered, as presidential power becomes more divided (Nadeau and Lewis-Beck 2001, 172). This counterintuitive result receives support in an independent study of voters in exit surveys, on the impact of having a president of one party and a House of another : "Divided government, in sum, does not thwart economic voting in American national elections, neither in 1992 nor in 1996" (Norpoth 2001, 426). Further, in an aggregate time-series investigation on national election observations from 1964 to 2000, Lewis-Beck and Nadeau (2004a, 145) again demonstrate strong economic voting effects, unaltered by divided government. These authors conclude that voters perceive the president as the fundamental political leader of the economy, and act on that basis.

Forecasting Equations

Election forecasting, especially American presidential election forecasting, has become a major industry. The first models began to appear around 1980 (see the reviews in Lewis-Beck and Rice 1992; Campbell and Garand 2000). It has become the custom, before each contest, for a host of scholars to unveil their equations and make their predictions. Economic variables invariably play a central role in these efforts. In terms of theory, the equations carry specifications similar to those of the aggregate vote functions discussed earlier. However, they are different, if only because the independent variables must be measured *before* the election, rather than after (as is common with other election research).

The red-letter year for the accuracy of U.S. presidential forecasting models was 1996, with seven of seven forecasting teams correctly predicting an easy win for Clinton (Campbell and Garand 2000). Riding on this wave, in spring 2004 forecasters released their predictions for the fall, through a cover story in the *Washington Post* (Robert Kaiser, May 26, 1). They unanimously foretold a Gore landslide, with 53 to 60 percent of the two-party popular vote. After such a major faux pas, the value of the forecasting enterprise was questioned. This, despite the repeatedly made point that other prediction alternatives, such as the polls, did not offer a better alternative (Lewis-Beck 2001).

Fortunately for the forecasting community, performance in 2004 was decidedly better. Six of seven forecasting teams correctly called Bush the winner (see the review in Campbell 2005). Moreover, the overall quality of the models in terms of accuracy, lead, parsimony, and reproducibility was often very good, comparing well to other approaches (Lewis-Beck 2005, 151–60). The model of Abramowitz (2004), with a forecasting error of 2.5 percentage points (53.7 vote share predicted—51.2 Bush received), is not atypical. Further, it serves to illustrate the strategic place of the economy in such efforts:

$$V = 50.73 + .107P + .818E - 5.14T,$$

where V = incumbent two-party vote share, P = a measure of presidential popularity from the June Gallup poll, E = annualized real GDP growth over the first two quarters of the election year, and T = a measure of incumbent time in office, scored 1 for more than one term, 0 otherwise. The regression coefficient for E indicates that when the economy grows one percentage point (in the first half of the election year), the party in the White House can expect a vote boost of almost the same amount. This underlines the importance of economic conditions in the determination of presidential election outcomes.

Where Was the Economy in 2000? Understanding Institutional Context

In the first half of 2000, economic growth was chugging along at a fast clip, an annual rate of about 5 percent. Conventional wisdom had it that the economy was working strongly for the Democrats in Gore's presidential election bid. Commentators and politicians made this assumption. Statistical modelers, who based their forecasts heavily on economic patterns, seemed to confirm it. But this Democratic economic engine, strong as it was, failed to pull Gore to victory. What happened? Had the economy ceased to matter for voters once other concerns were taken into account? One argument is that economics still mattered, but indicators other than preelection growth needed to be examined. Another argument was that, indeed, economic growth had ceased to matter. Below, we counter both of these arguments.

The pace of the stock market was slackening on the way into the election. In addition, there were worrisome signs on the economic horizon. Further, the long-term trend in economic growth was down; for example, it was lower in 2000 than in years before, and the third quarter of 2000 itself looked weaker. Finally, there was some subjective angst about future business conditions. It may be that it was actually these economic forces that dragged Gore down at the ballot box.

To examine this possibility Lewis-Beck and Tien (2002, 179–82) carried out specification tests on their 2000 forecasting model, selectively including the following economic measures: Dow-Jones index; a subjective survey measure of future problems; objective leading indicators; a subjective survey measure of future business conditions; trends in economic growth; third-quarter economic growth. They found that none of these variables made a statistically significant contribution to the prediction of the presidential vote. In sum, while the "alternative economic indicators" hypothesis has an intuitive appeal, analysis does not support it as an explanation for the Gore defeat.

Did traditional economic growth fail to deliver an electoral punch as well? Lewis-Beck and Tien (2001) contended that its effect remained, but worked differently in 2000. Gore benefited little from preelection economics because he himself was only a candidate. However, presidents who had run for reelection received a big boost from positive retrospective economic performance. These aggregate time-series results built on earlier work by Nadeau and Lewis-Beck (2001) in their pooled survey analysis of the NES 1956–96. They found that national economic voting on incumbents running for reelection was more retrospective, while that for first-time candidates was more prospective. Such findings conform nicely to theory: candidates who are president are mostly judged by performance in office (i.e., retrospectively), while candidates who have not held the office are mostly judged by their promises (i.e., prospectively).

The implication is that if President Clinton had been able to stand for office again, he would have benefited handsomely from the surging preelection economy. However, because of the term limit set by the Constitution, he could not do so. His party candidate, Gore, did run, but little of the glow from that economic growth rubbed off on his vote totals (Norpoth 2004). Further, the prospective economic picture, spotty if not negative, did not allow him to counterbalance his retrospective vote losses. Economic forces seem deeply at work in the 2000 contest, following a clear path, once it is understood.

Homogenous versus Heterogeneous Economic Voters

In the literature, the working assumption is that the economic voter is of a type. The expectation is that the idealized voter responds to the same stimuli in the same way. For purposes of scientific generalization, this assumption has value. Still, it is important to remember that economic voters can be heterogeneous in their attitudes, rather than homogenous (Duch, Palmer, and Anderson 2000). For example, one premise is that they assign responsibility for the economy to the president. But this can vary, with voters placing responsibility elsewhere. Rudolph and Grant (2002, 811), in a unique 2000 election poll, found that about 25 percent of the respondents attributed economic responsibility to the president, but the rest attributed it to Congress, the Fed, or business elites.

Further, economic voters can be heterogenous in their response, according to the sociological or psychological group they find themselves in. In table 13.5, we explored the possibility that the pocketbook response varied by social class, and found that it did not. A study of earlier elections, though, found otherwise (Weatherford 1978). Sophisticated voters, it has been argued, are more sociotropic, while unsophisticated voters are more affected by the pocketbook (Goren 1997). However, Gomez and Wilson (2001) have argued the opposite. Bélanger and Godbout (2005), show, by way of contrast, that unsophisticated American presidential voters depend on sociotropic judgments, while the sophisticated depend on both sociotropic and pocketbook judgments.

Without doubt, certain subgroups of the electorate can be found to deviate from a "typical" economic voter. This can provide useful information for diagnosing the outcomes of particular elections or policies. Nevertheless, it should not be forgotten that the notion of a homogeneous economic voter is extremely useful, not to say indispensible. We want to answer the basic question, How does Jane Q. Elector respond to economic boom or bust? The direct (additive) coefficient of the sociotropic variable, in a properly specified regression equation, tells us that.

Objective versus Subjective Economic Measures

In these studies, the concept "economics" has been measured in many ways. Two broad categories are "objective" and "subjective". The former are associated with macroeconomic indicators, the latter are associated with survey opinions.

The advantages of objective measures are that they are empirically hard—"real"—and are capable of generating strong model fits. Disadvantages are selecting which to use, and determining how the measure chosen links to the actual decision-making process of the voter. These disadvantages appear to find remedy in the use of survey data.

However, with surveys, the problems are multiple. Which economic items should be posed? Given these are perceptual economic responses, they will contain error (Kramer 1983). How much of that error is random? How much systematic? For example, the respondent wrongly attributes some personal financial hardship to government policy. Is it possible to separate the part of the economy the government is responsible for from the part it is not? (Alesina, Londregan, and Rosenthal 1993, 14). Take the typical sociotropic question, "Over the last year, has the economy gotten better, worse, or stayed the same?" In his classic paper, Kramer (1983) argued that in a cross-sectional survey, variance in the responses to such an item would merely represent error, since the electors at that point in time would all be subject to the stimulus of the same (invariant) economy.

The Markus (1988) methodology promised a solution to the "Kramer problem." Pooling each NES cross-sectional survey from 1956 to 1984, he created one common data-set of individual voters, who were subjected to different macroeconomic conditions depending on the election year. For analysis, the actual macroeconomic indicator represents a variable whose score is carried by each respondent. In a regression model containing controls on party identification and SES, he estimated that a one-percentage-point rise in real disposable income (RDI) generated a 2.6-percentage-point rise in incumbent presidential party support. The great advantage of the approach is that it directly links a "real" macroeconomic variable to the behavior of individual voters. One disadvantage is that the selection of this particular variable—RDI—seems incomplete given the possibility of others to choose from. Another disadvantage is that it does not allow for any subjective feelings about the economy to enter into the vote. For example, I might think that a 3.5 percent income growth rate showed a "good" economy, but you might think it showed a so-so economy. In such a case, our economic vote might be different, with me voting for the incumbent and you not.

A way to overcome both these disadvantages has been proposed by Nadeau and Lewis-Beck (2001). They adopt the innovative Markus design, in the analysis of NES from 1956 to 1996, but instead of using an objective retrospective economic measure, such as RDI, they use a subjective one. Specifically, they create a national business index (NBI) for each election year, by subtracting the percentage in the survey who believe business conditions are "worse" from the percentage who believe it is "better." For instance, this difference for 1996 is 28 points, indicating considerable enthusiasm for the economy before President Clinton's reelection. In a carefully specified logistic regression model, NBI has a highly statistically significant effect, whereas RDI does not (Nadeau and Lewis-Beck 2001, 167).

NBI seems a useful retrospective measure of the national economy. First, it captures multiple macroeconomic indicators (e.g., earnings, unemployment, inflation, GDP, and RDI, when regressed on NBI, generate an R^2 of .88). Second, it has a subjective component, representing the value weighting by voters of the different elements of the economy (e.g., suppose Sally weights inflation more heavily than Brenda does). The fact that NBI captures more of the relevant economic stimuli receives support from a comparison of its impact with that of the RDI. That is, a one-standard-deviation change in NBI yields an expected change of 5.5 percentage points in the incumbent vote, whereas the same change for RDI yields an expected change of only 4.9 (Nadeau and Lewis-Beck 2001, 165–66).

The greater power of NBI appears to stem from its incorporation of the objective and the subjective. Smith (2005, 13), in a recent analysis of presidential elections from 1954 to 2004, adds further support to the notion that the two are important: "the analysis to follow shows that public *perceptions* of the parties [their economic management ability] register noticeable impacts on top of those stemming from the objective economy."

Does Economics Not Really Matter? Endogeneity Issues

Economic questions appear to matter greatly to the American presidential voter. In a recent summary of that literature, which is voluminous, Lewis-Beck and Stegmaier (2007) concluded that "of all issues facing the American electorate, economic ones are generally at the top of the list in terms of their impact on voter choice." This seemingly unexceptionable view has recently received a vigorous challenge: "conventional wisdom is likely to considerably overstate the importance of retrospective economic considerations for political preferences" (Evans and Andersen 2006). The essential argument is that the link between economic perception and the reported vote is largely spurious, a product of the distorting influence of party identification. For example, if I am a Republican and the president is Republican, I will tend to say the economy is good (simply because I like a Republican president). Such bias, multiplied across the electorate, would produce a strong correlation between economic perception and reported vote, one having little to do with economic reality.

While Evans and Andersen contend that such spuriousness generally holds across Western democracies, their empirical tests are based on panel analysis of the British survey data. Moreover, their measurement decisions, path models, and different error assumptions have been questioned (see the critique in Lewis-Beck 2006). What is known is that, for the United States as well as the United Kingdom, macroeconomic growth indicators correlate highly with incumbent vote support, and with aggregate subjective economic measures (Lewis-Beck 2006, 210). Further, as has been shown in this chapter, tabular controls on party identification reduce, but by no means eliminate, the apparent influence of economic evaluations on the U.S. presidential vote. This is only preliminary evidence, however. Necessary are dynamic panel analyses of the NES data, with the endogeneity of economic perception *and* party identification corrected. Such work is currently under way, employing the recent U.S. presidential election panels. Results indicate that, once these variables are carefully exogenized and their coefficients estimated within well-specified probit models, economics appears to yield an even greater impact (Lewis-Beck et al. 2008).

Has Rising Income Inequality Reduced the Economic Vote?

In the first decades after World War II, the real income of the typical American worker tended to rise. Moreover, the inequality of income between high- and low-earners, while great, remained steady. Since the 1970s, however, median worker income has shown little growth, especially once inflation is taken into account. Moreover, the inequality between the rich and the poor has begun to increase. Economist Paul Krugman (*New York Times,* July 14, 2006, A19) reported from economic studies that in the year 2004 real median family income fell and the number in poverty increased. Further, income growth for the top 1 percent was 12.5 percent, while for the rest (the remaining 99 percent), income growth was only 1.5 percent.

Recognition of the rich-poor gap is reflected in survey attitudes. In the 2002 NES, respondents were asked if "the difference in incomes between rich people and poor people in the United States today is larger, smaller, or about the same as it was 20 years ago?" An overwhelming 74 percent said larger (either "much" or "somewhat"). These income changes have been accompanied by changes in the job market, where there are rising reports of job insecurity, job inferiority, or job scarcity

Research attempting to express these conditions in an economic vote is remarkably scarce. Lacy and Mughan (2002) explored electoral consequences of job insecurity, finding it did move voters, in particular toward Perot's third-party candidacy. (Mughan, Bean, and McAllister [2003] examine the political reaction to job insecurity in the context of globalization.) Before the 2004 presidential contest, Krugman (*New York Times,* April 9, 2004, 19) severely criticized Bush economic policies for their inability to generate new jobs, declaring, "If the election is driven by economics at all . . . [i]t will reflect the job situation on the ground, which remains grim." This comment was echoed in a similar indictment of his father's policies, when "George Bush senior lost the 1992 election during a lackluster, job-scarce recovery" (*The Economist,* June 12, 2004, 27).

Intrigued by the "jobs" issue, Lewis-Beck and Tien (2004) introduced into their presidential election forecasting model a measure of job creation over each incumbent term. The addition greatly improved the equation's statistical fit, and passed numerous regression diagnostics. Moreover, its inclusion clearly reduced the ex ante forecasting error, generating a very precise forecast, off only 1.3 percentage points (Campbell 2005; Lewis-Beck and Tien 2005). A shortcoming of this "jobs" variable is that it does not fully tap into the more general condition of income inequality.

Can a direct connection be established between income inequality and presidential vote? Recent work by Bartels (2005a, 16), on support for Bush's 2001 and 2003 tax cuts, suggests a healthy skepticism: "The results of my analysis suggest that most Americans supported tax cuts not because they were indifferent to economic inequality, but because they largely failed to connect inequality and public policy." Drawing on economic voting theory, if voters do not hold the president responsible for changes in income inequality, they would not be expected to either reward or punish him for it at the ballot box. This hypothesis begs to be tested.

SECTION V

The Electoral Decision and the Political System

CHAPTER 14

The Electoral Decision

It is common to seek to ascertain the meaning of a national election. Starting on election night itself, pundits attempt to read the tea leaves as to why citizens voted as they did. Many potential explanations are proposed by the media and by interest groups eager to have the election interpreted in their favor. In due course, several understandings enter the conventional wisdom. Political scientists and historians eventually interpret the election in broader terms, particularly once the election can be viewed in historical perspective.

Interpretations of elections used to be basically impressionistic. Little evidence was brought to bear. Different observers would give widely varying interpretations of the same election—that one candidate was strong, that the opponent was weak, that one issue predominated, that one group of voters was crucial, that one community was a bellwether, that one state was pivotal, that one candidate did not respond quickly enough to the opponent's ads, that one candidate made a serious error in the debates, that one candidate's strategy was weak, and so on. These explanations were not only varied, but they also often were incompatible with one another. As a result, they did not serve as a serviceable framework for judging the relative importance of different factors across elections.

The model presented in this book provides a means for making objective generalizations about voting determinants within and across elections. Previous chapters have examined the factors affecting the voting behavior of individual citizens. What remains is to aggregate these results across the citizenry, and then determine the relative importance of the different factors in contributing to the winning majority. Additionally, it is important to compare the partisan effects of the different attitudinal factors in an election with the partisan balance within the country. The attitudinal factors work in the direction of the partisan majority in the country in some elections, but sometimes these forces work in the opposite direction. Indeed, when the attitudinal factors are strong enough, they can lead to changes in the very balance of party identification in the electorate. This chapter will conclude with a classification of presidential elections along this line after first considering the components of the voting decision in the 2000 and 2004 elections.

COMPONENTS OF THE DECISION

The analysis in chapter 4 demonstrated that voting decisions are affected by attitudes toward a variety of partisan objects. We can predict people's vote very effectively from the direction and intensity of their attitudes toward six political objects. Attitudes toward the two candidates, on domestic and foreign issues, on the parties as managers of government, and on the social group basis of politics together provide a powerful explanation of individual votes.

It is useful to illustrate how this works. Say in 2004 that a hypothetical Republican voter was slightly favorable to Kerry and slightly unfavorable to Bush, was slightly favorable to the Democrats on domestic issues but very strongly favorable to the Republicans on foreign and security issues, was neutral on the parties as managers of government, and somewhat pro-Democrat as regards social groups. It only makes sense to ascribe this person's Republican vote to his or her views on foreign issues, as the other attitudes either balanced out or were mildly in the Democratic direction.

Using a similar logic, we can analyze an election result in terms of the aggregate effects of these six attitudinal components. We can sum each factor across our sample of respondents to see which works in a Republican or Democratic direction and how strongly. Statistical analysis then allows us to determine the relative importance of each of these factors in affecting individual vote decisions. For a factor to affect the aggregate vote outcome, it must both have a strong effect on individual decisions and work strongly in the direction of one party.[1] If it has little effect on individual decisions, then it cannot affect the aggregate vote outcome. In addition, it will not affect the aggregate vote outcome if its impact balances out among the electorate between those who see it as favoring the Republicans and those who see it as favoring the Democrats.

Using this approach to analyze the George W. Bush elections provides a fascinating set of results, which are displayed in figure 14.1. Each partisan component is represented with a bar. Bars that extend to the left of the midline show that the factor helped the Democrats, while those that extend to the right show that the factor favored the Republicans. The longer the bar, the more that factor aided the party. The absence of a bar shows that the attitude did not move the vote toward either party.

The 2000 election is unusual in that the popular vote winner did not become president. Al Gore received about a half million more votes than George W. Bush, but Bush prevailed in the Electoral College. Our analysis is necessarily focused on the popular vote, so we are attempting to explain a Gore victory in 2000. However, the popular vote was so close that we are really trying to explain an even election in which neither candidate scored a decisive win. Figure 14.1a displays this even election in an intriguing way. Social group attitudes strongly favored the Democrats, but that was the only attitude working to their advantage. Domestic issues, which have generally favored the Democrats over the years, were neutral. The other four attitudes were in the Republican direction, but none of these other attitudes had a very strong impact.

Let's take these one at a time. Bush as a candidate helped his own cause, not a lot but at least positively. Gore as a candidate did not help his own cause; attitudes toward him actually moved the vote somewhat in the Republican direction—not a lot, but actually more than attitudes toward Bush moved the vote in the Republican direction. Thus, the Republicans were advantaged in 2000 by attitudes toward the presidential candidates. Domestic attitudes did not matter in the end; their impact

---

1. Multiple regression of the vote on the six components is used to determine regression coefficients for each partisan attitude, and these coefficients are multiplied by that attitude's mean to determine the attitude's impact on the aggregate vote. (See Stokes, Campbell, and Miller 1958.) For example, multiple regression analysis shows that a one-unit change in the social groups component has an expected change of .04 in the two-party vote, while the average value on the social groups component for 2004 was −.79, reflecting more pro-Democratic and anti-Republican comments mentioning social groups than pro-Republican or anti-Democratic comments. The product of those two values shows that this component moved the vote about 3.2 percent in the Democratic direction when the other components are controlled.

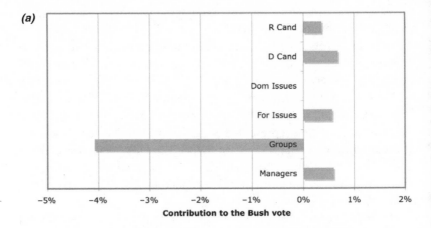

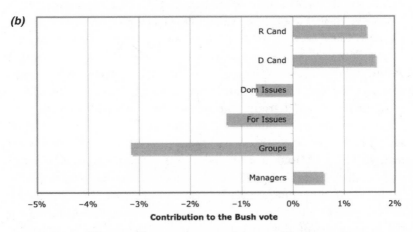

Fig. 14.1. Vote components: (a) 2000; (b) 2004.

averaged out across the electorate. Republican attacks on the foreign and defense policies of the Clinton years did have an effect, with foreign policy slightly helping the GOP. The effect of the Lewinsky affair and other scandals during the Clinton administration was that the country favored the out-party as to managing the government, as has usually been the case after one party has controlled the White House for a period of years. However, public attitudes toward the social group basis of parties have usually aided the Democrats, and that proved to be the case again in 2000. Add together one strongly pro-Democratic factor and several slightly pro-Republican factors and the result is a close election with a very narrow Democratic popular vote victory, so narrow that it could not be translated into an Electoral College win.

It is also worth emphasizing how small the partisan advantages were in 2000 on most of the factors. In an era of partisan polarization, some people like the Republicans on a factor and some like the Democrats on that factor, and the two generally balance out. Neither candidate was so appealing that attitudes toward him would propel him to victory; neither candidate was so poor that attitudes toward him would lead to ignominious defeat. Each party's partisans could prefer their own party on domestic issues. Foreign issues were interpreted through a less partisan screen than were domestic issues, leading to the slight Republican advantage. Nothing could balance out the effects of Monicagate in helping the Republicans, but even that was interpreted through a partisan screen, so that the Republican advantage on managing government was small. Partisan polarization was unable to diminish the impact of only one factor: social groups, which traditionally has worked to the Democrats' advantage since that party is virtually a coalition of social groups.

The 2004 election played out quite differently than did the election of 2000. For one thing, George W. Bush won the popular vote as well as the presidency. He talked after the election about the "political capital" that it gave him, but, in fact, it was a small victory margin, well below the mandate-size margins achieved when Eisenhower, Nixon, Reagan, or Clinton was reelected. Figure 14.1b displays this situation by finding stronger Republican advantages on the candidate factors in 2004 than in 2000, but ones that are counterbalanced by Democratic advantages on the issue factors. Managers of government still helped the Republicans, while social groups helped the Democrats less than in 2000. These sum up to a greater Republican advantage than in 2000, but not a landslide victory.

Again, let's take the six partisan attitudes one at a time. Bush helped his own cause, and more than he did in 2000. The public apparently had become comfortable with him as a wartime leader, leading to an advantage for him. Kerry, however, was unable to help his own cause. The Republicans were better able to define him for the electorate than he was able to define himself. Instead of being able to portray himself as a wartime hero for his exploits in Vietnam, the Swift Boat Veterans ads were able to discredit Kerry's wartime service and emphasize his leading role in the antiwar movement when he returned from Vietnam. The Democratic candidate factor actually aided the Republicans more in 2004 than it had in 2000, and it aided the Republicans a tad more than the Republican candidate factor aided them.

By contrast, the Democrats were advantaged on the issues. Domestic issues have generally worked to the Democrats' advantage over the years, and that situation returned in 2004. Foreign issues have generally worked to the Republicans' advantage, but 2004 proved to be an exception. Bush may have been able to portray himself as a strong wartime leader in his run for reelection, but the foreign situation was complex. The war on terrorism was popular, and polls showed that the public approved of Bush's handling of the war in Afghanistan. The war in Iraq, however, was another matter. As much as the Republicans portrayed it as another front in the war on terrorism, the Democrats were able to claim that Iraq was a diversion from that larger war. The result is that foreign issues helped the Democrats even more than domestic issues did, a very rare configuration over the years. What we cannot tell from this analysis is how much is due to rationalization by voters; that is, whether voters who had decided to vote for Bush chose to support his position on foreign policy, so that vote intention affected attitudes on the war rather than vice versa. In any case, the results here echo those of chapter 3, with the war on terrorism giving Bush a positive image in terms of being a strong and decisive leader, while the Iraq war was unpopular enough to push the foreign issues component against the Republicans (see also Abramson et al. 2007; Norpoth and Sidman 2007; Weisberg and Christenson 2007).

The social group advantage of Democrats remained intact in 2004, though not quite as much as in 2000. Meanwhile, the Republicans retained the lead they had in 2000 in terms of managing government. The first Bush administration was efficient and without notable scandal, and the implicit comparison with the Clinton years still worked to the GOP's advantage.

Putting these factors together, Bush's election victory in 2004 had several similarities to the 2000 election, but with some differences that were important enough to give him a decided victory, albeit not a large one. People were more positive toward him and more negative toward his opponent than in 2000. The Republicans were hurt by the issues, losing the previous Republican foreign policy advantage, but they were able to retain their advantage on managing government while diminishing a bit the impact of the usual Democratic advantage on social groups. Thus, 2004 comes off as a candidate election, with the issues helping the losing party more than the winning one.

ELECTORAL COMPONENTS AND PARTY IDENTIFICATION

Voting behavior is inevitably affected directly by a person's evaluations of the contemporaneous political world. Measuring those attitudes permits us to explain the person's vote as well as decomposing the election outcome into its attitudinal determinants at the aggregate level. However, as seen throughout this book, political evaluations are not all based on contemporaneous matters. People's political orientations are not developed afresh each election year. Some political orientations are of long standing. In particular, a person's party identification is an enduring orientation, and one that has considerable effects on the person's full range of political attitudes.

Party identification is not, however, the only influence on a person's partisan attitudes. If it were, then all six attitudinal factors would agree with the party identification of the majority of citizens, each partisan attitude would favor that majority party, and that party would win the election. There have been some national elections in which party identification predominates in these senses, but party identification is not the only influence on a person's partisan attitudes, and in many elections party identification does not predominate in these senses. Some of the partisan attitudes may not run in the same direction as the majority party identification in these elections, and the minority party may be favored enough on these attitudes to elect its candidate. Thus, an important aspect of election analysis is determining the extent to which the partisan attitudes affect the vote beyond the influence of party identification.

The prototypical example of this deviation is the 1952 election. Party identification ran strongly in the Democratic direction, but the partisan attitudes did not all run in that direction. Instead, Eisenhower was such a popular candidate that attitudes toward the Republican candidate were sufficient to pull the election over to him.

The 2000 and 2004 elections do not provide such strong indications of deviation from long-term partisanship. Figure 14.2 shows the effect of adding party identification to the model, so that the net contributions of each component to the vote can be ascertained with party identification controlled.[2] The biggest change from figure 14.1 involves the social group factor. It is closely aligned to partisanship, so its pro-Democratic impact

---

2. We have added party identification as a predictor in the multiple regression analysis, and then multiplied each of the new regression coefficients by the mean of the corresponding partisan attitude to measure the impact of the attitudinal factor on the vote with partisanship controlled (see the table in the appendix to this chapter).

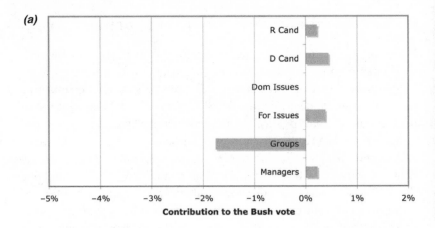

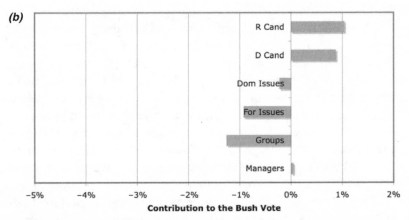

Fig. 14.2. Vote components with party controlled: (*a*) 2000; (*b*) 2004.

is considerably reduced when party identification is controlled. The same is true, to a lesser degree, for domestic issues in 2004. Also, part of the pro-Republican effect of Democratic candidate component is due to partisanship, so its impact is reduced when party is controlled, and the same is true of parties as managers of government, especially in 2004. Figure 14.2 shows that the candidate components helped the Republicans in both 2000 and 2004, with Bush helping himself more in 2004 than in 2000 and with Kerry's candidacy hurting the Democrats more in 2004 than Gore's in 2000. Foreign issues mildly helped the Republicans in 2000, while domestic issues were neutralized; foreign issues more strongly helped the Democrats in 2004 with domestic issues having a muted effect. But the main point made in these two graphs is that party identification is so important to the vote that none of the vote components moved the vote as much as 2 percent in either direction once the voters' party ties are controlled.

The extreme would be if the partisan attitudes affecting the vote differed so much from the usual party identification balance that partisanship would change. While we have depicted party identification as essentially long term, it can change under some circumstances. In particular, national crises have had large effects on the distribution of partisanship. The prelude to the Civil War led to people's partisan attitudes diverging so much from their traditional party identification that the Whig Party entirely lost its base of support, the popular basis of the Democratic Party was entirely changed, and the newly formed Republican Party won control of the federal government. This was indeed a rare situation, but it illustrates how national crises can lead to radical shifts of party identification. Thus, to argue that party identification is essentially long-term does not mean that we consider it immutable.

A CLASSIFICATION OF PRESIDENTIAL ELECTIONS

Looking back at American elections, one finds considerable continuity in presidential contests, even while the candidates and issues change. The long-term partisan balance of the electorate is sufficiently stable across time that much apparent election-specific change turns out to be transient. We have shown how voting in a particular election can be decomposed in terms of the six partisan attitudes, and we have seen how the partisan balance provides a backdrop for how these attitudes play through in any specific election. We now make use of this approach to develop a classification of presidential elections.

The classification that we develop is based in part on whether one party has a clear majority in the normal vote, which is based on the distribution of party identification between the two major parties, discounted by differences between the turnout patterns of supporters of each party. As described in chapter 6, for example, calculations of the normal vote for the 1950s (Converse 1966a) found an expected Democratic proportion of the two-party vote in the range of 54 percent, an estimate that takes into account the large lead of Democrats over Republicans in party identification as well as the tendency of Democrats to turn out to vote in a lower proportion than Republicans.

A basic classification of American presidential elections offers five types: maintaining, deviating, reinstating, realigning, and balancing elections.[3] The first three types are relevant when one party has a clear majority in the normal vote. A maintaining election is one in which stable partisan attachments continue to be a major determinant of election results. The party that has a majority in terms of party loyalties wins the presidency, generally through affecting the partisan attitudes. While we lack survey data, we would expect that most citizens were Republican following the Civil War, for example, and that this Republican majority accounts for the numerous Republican presidential victories from the Civil War through 1928. There may have been occasional weakening of Republican ties during parts of that period, but that majority was soon restored.

A deviating election would then be one in which the short-term partisan attitudes lead to the election of the presidential nominee of the minority party, without a fundamental shift in the party identification balance in the nation. The 1916 election constitutes a case in point. The country had been electing Republican presidents from 1896 through 1908, with Woodrow Wilson winning in 1912 only because the Republican vote was split between incumbent President Taft and his predecessor, Teddy Roosevelt. In 1916, however, Wilson's incumbency combined with public views on foreign policy with the start of World War I in Europe to lead to Wilson's winning in a two-party contest. This was but a short-term deviation, though, with the Republicans demonstrating their majority through their presidential wins in the three elections of the 1920s. This example also serves to call attention to the reinstating election (Converse et al. 1961), which occurs when the majority party wins the White House back after a deviating election, as when William Harding reestablished Republican dominance in the 1920 election.

It is important to emphasize that this definition of a deviating election is based on short-term defection from partisanship due to the six partisan attitudes, not a long-term decline in the strength of partisan ties. Long-term partisan decline could be demonstrated only when the majority party loses election after election, in which case evidence accumulates on behalf of long-term partisan realignment. The concept of party realignment was developed by V. O. Key (1955; see also Key 1959). The realigning election is one in which the partisanship of people changes. Politics becomes so intense that some people change their

---

3. This classification was inspired by Key (1955) and Converse et al. (1961).

party identification. This probably happens to some small extent in every election, but the realigning election is when it happens to a large extent.

While different researchers have sometimes declared several elections as realigning, there is a consensus on only a few. The 1860 election, with the Republican Party gaining ascendancy due to the issue of slavery and maintaining it after the Civil War, constitutes an instance of realignment. The 1896 election, marked by weakening of the Democratic Party and a shift in the regional basis of the parties, is also generally considered a realigning election. The New Deal era of the 1930s became a major realigning period. Under the Republican Hoover administration, the country fell into the Great Depression with the collapse of the stock market and very high unemployment. The Republican majority crumbled. Franklin D. Roosevelt took the presidency for the Democrats in the 1932 election, and the Democrats kept the presidency in each of the following four elections. The Democrats built a majority in party identification during this period. There is some evidence that the realignment actually began along class lines in the 1928 presidential election, in which Democratic New York governor Alfred E. Smith began to pull the working class, Catholics, and New Englanders to the Democratic column. However, that might have just been a short-term deviation had the Depression not occurred.

To be clear, not all partisan change that occurs in a realignment is unidirectional. The South moved to the Democratic column after the Civil War, but that was not enough to overcome the Republican gains in the North (particularly during the Reconstruction Era, when many white southerners were disenfranchised because of their support for the Confederacy). The West moved to the Democratic column starting with the 1896 election, but the population of the West was so small in those days that their shift was overwhelmed by Republican gains in the East. Some middle-class voters became Republicans in the 1930s, but the working-class voters who became Democrats considerably outnumbered them. Thus, it is the net shift that affects the lasting change of a realigning election.

In addition, we emphasize the social group basis of realignment. Individuals may change because of a variety of factors, but that change can be idiosyncratic. Systematic change occurs when issues motivate social groups to move to one party and when change is reinforced through one's social groups. Thus, the movement of Catholics and Jews into the Democratic Party marked the New Deal realignment of the 1930s, and that movement led to stable Democratic ties for these people because of group reinforcement.

The fifth type of election that we differentiate here is a "balancing" election, one in which neither party has a majority in party identification. The partisan balance is so close that either party could win. This is not an election in which short-term forces work against the majority party, but one in which it is not possible to speak of a majority party. One party may have a lead in party identification, but that lead disappears when turnout differences between the parties are taken into account.

We can use this elections typology to discuss electoral history of the past three-quarters of a century. The New Deal realignment is now more than seven decades old, but there is no consensus on realignments since then. Fortunately we have high-quality survey data for all the presidential elections since 1952, the first time the Republicans won the White House back after the New Deal years, so we can use survey results to amplify our discussion of these elections.

The Eisenhower victories in the 1950s are as pure examples of deviating elections as one can imagine. Surveys indicate that the Democrats had a clear advantage in party identification, but the personal popularity of Dwight Eisenhower prevailed. Attitudes toward the Republican candidate strongly advantaged the GOP, so that the Republicans could win the White House regardless of the Democratic lead in party identification.

The 1960 contest was a classic reinstating election. The Democratic Party reasserted its majority, with John Kennedy winning the presidency back (Converse et al. 1961). The Democratic win that year was actually very narrow. That election was marked by religious cleavage in which Catholics went more Democratic and Protestants less Democratic than usual, but that voting pattern proved transient once Kennedy became the first Catholic elected president.

The 1964 election was a maintaining election. There was speculation at the time that Johnson's electoral landslide constituted realignment, with the Republicans no longer being competitive in national politics. As is often the case, events soon made that speculation irrelevant, which usefully reminds us that realignments can be seen only in historical perspective, requiring confirming events over a period of years so that the partisan change becomes long term rather than just short term.

Richard Nixon's victories in 1968 and 1972 can be considered as deviating elections. The Democratic majority in partisanship remained intact, though a series of issues (particularly civil rights, urban unrest, and the Vietnam War) led many people to defect from that partisanship. From this perspective, Jimmy Carter's election in 1976 would be a re-instating election, bringing the majority Democrats back into power.

As discussed in chapter 6, an important change in partisanship was occurring during this period: an increase in political independence. The civil rights revolution led to some southern whites moving away from the Democratic Party. Many young people became independents because of the Vietnam War. The Watergate scandal loosened the ties of some Republicans to their party. The Democratic advantage remained intact, but the increased number of independents led to greater volatility in elections. In addition, the black vote realigned during this period, becoming solidly Democratic.

The Republicans won the three presidential elections in the 1980s. Jimmy Carter ran for reelection in 1980 with American hostages in Iran and with inflation nearing 20 percent, but Ronald Reagan was seen as a strong leader who could handle these problems. Reagan's success in dealing with those issues led to his easy reelection in 1984. George H. W. Bush's victory in 1988 was narrow, but he benefited from being seen as Reagan's political heir (Mattei and Weisberg 1994). The Republican victory margin in the 1980s was partly due to Reagan Democrats—blue-collar, lifelong Democrats who were attracted to Reagan and gradually gave up their Democratic partisanship, so that by the 1988 election there were fairly equal proportions of Republican and Democratic identifiers among actual voters, making 1988 a balancing election with no definitive majority party.

There clearly was some group realignment during the 1980s. The native southern white identification with the Democratic Party was slipping, as was that of Catholics. Meanwhile, a gender gap developed, with men becoming more Republican, and a marriage gap developed, with married people voting more Republican than unmarrieds (Weisberg 1987). Additionally, religious fundamentalists, who had supported Carter in 1976 but were disappointed by his presidency, began to mobilize in support of the Republican Party, through movements such as the Moral Majority. This led to some social group realignment, as well as issue realignment along the abortion issue (Adams 1997). The Democrats still had a small advantage in partisanship during the 1980s, but it was so small that it could be canceled by the usual lower turnout rate of Democrats.

The Democrats easily won back the presidency in 1992, but independent candidate Ross Perot's 19 percent of the popular vote stopped

Clinton from winning a majority of the popular vote. The Perot phenomenon makes it difficult to claim that the Democrats were really the majority party in this period, since the Republicans might have kept the White House had Perot not backed Clinton when Perot temporarily withdrew from the race in mid-July 1992. Clinton won an easy victory in 1996, but only after the Republicans won control of the House of Representatives in 1994 after 40 years of Democratic control.

The 2000 election continued the pattern of evenly balanced elections, so even that the popular vote winner did not carry the Electoral College. Gore won a half-million more votes than George W. Bush, but Bush became president with the aid of a favorable Supreme Court decision. Bush's victory in 2004 was marked by the Republicans having a very slight partisanship advantage among actual voters. The social group changes described above continued during these elections, but with religious traditionalists becoming more Republican and religious modernists becoming more Democrat. There is also some indication of the electorate becoming more Republican in partisanship in 2004, but the Democratic gains in the 2006 midterm election suggest that we are still in an era of equally balanced parties.

Realignment can be judged only in long-term perspective. The 2008 election promises to be the first presidential election since 1952 in which neither candidate was president or vice president. If a Republican wins this open-seat election and wins reelection in 2012, political historians may well judge that realignment did occur in the 2000–2004 elections. So far, we would contend that the political change in the George W. Bush years was not an instance of realignment. Most of the partisan attitudes that helped him get into the White House in 2000—reactions to Bush himself, to his Democratic opponent, to Clinton's handling of foreign policy, and to scandals of the Clinton era—were only transient. The partisan attitudes that helped him win the popular vote in 2004 were candidate-related, and thus again short term in nature. Bush's response to the 9/11 attacks on America led to a perception in 2004 that he was a strong leader, and he was accordingly reelected, even though evaluations of his foreign policy had soured. Indeed, Bush's low popularity levels throughout 2006 and mid-2007 suggest that Republicans may have a difficult time in 2008. But this is a debate on the margin. The real story of the last 50-plus years of American presidential elections is a weakening of the Democratic lead in party identification to the extent that elections are very close and can be swung by any number of short-term matters.

COMMENTARY AND CONTROVERSY

Comparisons with Earlier Elections

The effects of the partisan attitudes on the vote in the 2000 and 2004 election pale by comparison with those in earlier elections. As reported in Miller and Miller (1976, 837), four of the six components moved the vote more than 3 percent each in 1952 and 1972, with the largest single effect through 1972 being a 7.6 percent shift in the vote in 1956 due to attitudes toward Eisenhower. Each of the six components moved the vote more than 2 percent in at least one election between 1952 and 1972. By contrast, the only sizable effect found here for 2000 and 2004 has to do with attitudes toward social groups.

The six-component model of the vote that *The American Voter* originally presented for 1952 and 1956 has occasionally been replicated over the years. Stokes (1966a) updated it for 1960 and 1964, using that analysis to discuss the variability of the different partisan attitudes over time. He demonstrated that the large change in the vote between Eisenhower's reelection landslide in the 1956 election and Johnson's landslide defeat of Barry Goldwater in 1964 was due to the candidate evaluations. The issue components varied little between those years, while there was substantial change in the candidate components. This analysis was extended to some later elections by Pomper (1975, chap. 7), Popkin et al. (1976), Miller and Miller (1976), Kagay and Caldeira (1980), and Miller and Wattenberg (1981).

The only subsequent systematic effort to apply a model like this across a large number of elections has been by John Kessel (2004, 2005). Rather than follow *The American Voter*'s classification of open-ended comments into six components, Kessel developed a 16-category scheme. Candidate-related comments are divided into general comments, plus ones about their record and incumbency, experience, management, intelligence, trust, and personality. Party-related comments are divided into comments about people in the party (beyond the actual presidential candidate) and other comments that reflect attitudes about the party. Issue-related comments are divided into general comments and comments in six specific areas: international involvement, economic management, social benefits, civil liberties (including civil rights), natural resources (including the environment), and agriculture.

Kessel also modernized the analysis procedure, using probit analysis since multiple regression is not appropriate for a dichotomous dependent variable.[4] The equations are set up so that voting Democrat is coded 1 and voting Republican is coded 0. Unfortunately, there is no simple way to summarize the impact of a variable in probit analysis in a manner analogous to the values in the graphs in this chapter.[5] Instead, Kessel derives two values for each year. The first is a valence term, which shows how many more open-ended comments in a category favored the Democrats over the Republicans, averaged over the number of respondents. The second is a maximum likelihood (MLE) coefficient, which is the analogue to a regression coefficient and shows how much a change in the partisan attitude affects the vote, except that the effect is not linear as in regression analysis. While this pair of values yields a less parsimonious interpretation of the election than do the values in the earlier figures, Kessel's results still provide a fascinating portrayal of how the different factors have varied over the years in affecting particular presidential elections. His model is very effective in terms of predicting people's votes: on average, 88 percent of the votes are being correctly predicted.

The patterns Kessel shows across the years are very informative. The Democrats' largest advantage (in the valence columns) has been in the social benefits category followed by economic management, but economic management has consistently affected the vote more than social benefits (the MLE columns). Another way of saying this is that the fact that the public is most favorable to the Democrats on social benefits is partly neutralized by its having less effect on the vote. The Democrats also have benefited on the general "party affect" comments. Comments about civil liberties have not consistently favored one party or the other over these elections, but they have been slightly in favor of the Democrats starting in

---

4. As an example of the problems that ensue from using multiple regression on a dichotomous variable, the resultant regression equation predicts that some people will vote Republican with a probability greater than 1 and that others will vote Republican with a probability below 0—both of which are impossible results that violate the definition of probability. Probit (and logit) analysis instead guarantees that predicted values will be well behaved in the sense of ranging between 0 and 1.

5. While *The American Voter* authors might have used probit analysis if it were easily available when they did their work, they were sufficiently pragmatic in their approach to data analysis that they might have decided to stay with linear regression instead. After all, the percentages of the vote predicted accurately by their multiple regression analysis and by probit analysis are virtually identical, so they might have reasoned that the gain in being able to make assertions about the impact of the components on the vote more than compensated for the methodological niceties that they would be violating. Indeed, Stokes (1966a, 28) explicitly rejected using probit because the "distribution of the electorate along an attitude dimension is much more easily summarized under the linear model."

1992. Comments on natural resources have also strongly favored the Democrats, but that issue area had a significant effect on the vote only in two elections: 1992 and 2000. The Democrats once had an advantage on agriculture, but the last election in which that issue area had a significant impact on the vote was 1988.

As to the Republican side of the ledger, international involvement is the issue that has most consistently been to the Republicans' advantage over the years, except 1964, 1984, and, notably, 2004. General issue comments have also tended to favor the Republicans over the years—and certainly in 2000 and 2004—with a reasonable impact on the vote. Their real advantage has been on the candidate side—except as to comments about the intelligence of candidates. Comments about the candidates (especially management) and, to a lesser extent, about "people in the party" have generally favored the Republicans, but there is naturally considerable variability on these dimensions depending on who the candidates are. With the exception of 1964, the Republicans seem to have been nominating more attractive presidential candidates over these 14 elections, but that is less of an inherent advantage for a particular party than when a party is seen to "own" an issue. From this perspective, the Republicans "losing" the international involvement area in 2004 could be an important loss if they cannot recover their traditional foreign policy advantage by the next presidential election.

Models of the Vote Decision

Several variants of the original *American Voter* model have been developed over the years. Recall that the original Michigan model in *The Voter Decides* (Campbell, Gurin, and Miller 1954) involved party identification, issue attitudes, and candidate orientation, but with all three accorded the same level of priority. The funnel of causality model of *The American Voter* put party identification into a long-term role as compared to the short-term roles of issues and candidates, which is why party identification is not shown per se in the figures in this chapter but is just used as a baseline for figure 14.2.

The New American Voter (Miller and Shanks 1996) and *The European Voter* (Thomassen 2005) further elaborate this model. First, social demographics can be brought back into the model, but as prior to long-term attitudinal factors such as partisanship. Second, the set of long-term attitudinal factors is expanded to include ideology and values as well as party identification, though with some quibbling as to which comes first. Third, short-term factors are divided up into several stages, in the following order: current policy preferences (e.g., on abortion) and perceptions of current conditions (e.g., if the economy has improved or become worse in the last year), retrospective evaluations of the incumbent president's performance, evaluations of the candidates' personal qualities, and prospective evaluations of the candidates and parties (e.g., which would handle the economy better).

On the one hand, this more differentiated model might be more reasonable than the original *American Voter* model. On the other hand, the specific assumptions about causal order are overly heroic—they may make logical sense, but that does not mean that they are necessarily correct. This order may not correspond to the order in which people come to their voting decisions. And assuming homogeneity in causal ordering across the electorate is especially heroic—different groups of people may rely on different factors, and people with different levels of political sophistication may use different orderings (see Sniderman, Glaser, and Griffin 1991). The problem is that the results of any statistical analysis depend on the assumptions that are made, and assuming a different causal order (let alone heterogeneity in the causal order) removes the underpinnings of the analysis.

The model in *The American Voter* looks only at the direct effects of the partisan attitudes on the vote, though it makes allowances for controlling on party identification. Goldberg (1966) switched to a recursive model (i.e., a model in which causation flows in only one direction and errors are uncorrelated) in which partisanship was exogenous and issue positions affected the vote only through candidate evaluations. This model was extended through 1972 by Schulman and Pomper (1975) and then through 1976 by Hartwig, Jenkins, and Temchin (1980). Taking indirect effects into account, these models found that party identification had the greatest total effect and issues the least.

This modeling approach assumes unidirectional causation, whereas issue positions and evaluations of the candidates could affect party identification as well as being affected by it. Jackson (1975) used a simultaneous equation approach to apply this nonrecursive model. Page and Jones (1979) analyzed the 1972 and 1976 NES surveys with a causal model with reciprocal linkages that could be tested through assuming that some demographic variables are linked to some variables but not others (such as that race affects the respondent's relative closeness to the candidates but not partisanship), while Markus and Converse (1979) used the

1972-74-76 NES panel survey with lagged effects so that issue positions in one year could affect candidate evaluations at the next election. While these two models were both improvements over previous recursive models, they produced very different results in several key respects. In particular, Page and Jones found issues predominant, while Markus and Converse found candidate evaluation to be most important. Markus and Converse found a greater role for partisanship than did Page and Jones. These are both very sophisticated models, but, unfortunately, their results are dependent on the numerous assumptions about the causal flow that they must make.

More purchase on the causal order can be obtained by using a rolling cross-section design in which large daily samples are taken over the entire campaign period. There were two major studies of this type during the 2000 election. Hillygus and Jackman (2003) analyze the 2000 Knowledge Networks survey to see what type of respondents change their candidate support at different times of the campaign. They find, of course, a movement of Bush Democrats to support Gore following the conventions and a movement of Gore Republicans to support Bush following the debates. Johnston, Hagen, and Jamieson (2004) similarly analyze the 2000 Annenberg National Election Survey, using the campaign as a natural experiment to look at which campaign events led to large changes in vote intention and potential predictors of vote. This approach leads to less emphasis on the relative impact of parties, candidates, and issues, but more emphasis on how specific matters moved the campaign. For example, Johnston, Hagen, and Jamieson find that changed impressions of Gore's honesty brought down his intended vote during the middle phase of the campaign, whereas the Social Security issue increased his intended vote during the campaign's last phase.

Classifying Elections

Is the realignment concept really useful? At one point, it was popular to describe American electoral history in terms of five "party systems." The first was the Federalist competition against the Democratic-Republican Party that came to an end when the Federalist Party died out. The second was the Whig competition against the Democrats that came to an end when the Whig Party died out on the eve of the Civil War. The Civil War realignment led to the third party system with Republican-Democratic competition, which was fairly evenly balanced after Reconstruction ended in the South. The Panic of 1893 led to a re-alignment in the 1896 election, with Republican Party dominance through most of the fourth party system from 1896 through 1928. The Great Depression then led to realignment in the 1932 election, which marks the beginning of the fifth party system with Democratic Party dominance.

This is a neat story, especially if one notices that each of the first four systems lasted about 24–28 years, suggesting a periodicity to elec-toral change. It looks from these cases as if it takes that long for a new issue to arise that cannot be resolved within the existing party system and therefore lead to realignment. However, some would argue that the realignment concept is passé. Minimally, we have not seen a major re-alignment of the scope of the New Deal Realignment. One theory is that there is a regular cycle of realignment, followed by "normal poli-tics," followed by dealignment in which people move toward political independence. Paul Beck (1974) has described this cycle in terms of one generation experiencing cataclysmic events (like the Great Depression) that cause it to realign, people of the next generation learning about the realigning events from their parents and therefore continuing their par-ents' partisanship in a period of normal politics, but then the following generation being too remote from the realigning events to care about them and therefore dealigning and being "ripe for realignment" if new cataclysmic events occur. One problem with this theory is that we are now several generations past the New Deal realignment without cata-clysmic events leading to another realignment. A variant of this ap-proach is to view the current era as one of "candidate-centered politics," as opposed to the "party-centered politics" of the era in which political party organizations controlled the large cities and the nominating pro-cess for presidential candidates. But we have actually seen several small social group realignments in the past half-century, even if there has not been a major event realigning the country. Furthermore, the original realignment argument may have been based on myth regarding the New Deal period. The usual contention is that many voters were con-verted from Republican to Democratic identification as a result of the Great Depression. However, Andersen (1979) shows that what actually occurred was mobilization of previous nonvoters, both people coming of voting age but also immigrants to the United States who had not been voting up to that stage. According to this view, older people who have been voting are unlikely to change their votes even during a cataclysmic period, so partisan change comes from mobilization of previous nonvoters. It still is useful to talk about changes in the partisanship of social groups, but, as a result of the above consideration, it may not be useful to speak about realignment as a broader concept.

Pomper (1967) suggested differentiating "converting" elections, in which the majority party stays the same but with a changed support coalition. Looking at correlations in votes by states in successive presidential elections, he finds that the 1892 election was converting rather than realigning, and he suggests that 1964 might also be a converting election. A later analysis by Knuckey (1999) confirms that the 1960, 1964, and 1968 elections constituted a critical election period.

We describe presidential elections starting in the 1980s as "balancing" elections, based on the view that there is no clear partisan majority. As explained above, more respondents in national surveys still call themselves Democrats than Republicans, but that Democratic advantage virtually disappears when the lower turnout rate of Democrats is taken into account. Still, some researchers would argue that the Democrats are still the "majority party" in this country because more Americans consider themselves Democrats than Republicans, so that the elections of the 1980s were deviating elections, the 1992 election was reinstating, the 1996 and 2000 elections were maintaining (counting Gore's popular vote lead as a Democratic victory that year), and 2004 was deviating. Other analysts would point to the great preponderance of Republican presidents since 1980 and the Republican control of Congress in 1994–2006 as evidence that the Republicans are the majority party, so that the 1980s presidential elections were realigning, 1992 through 2000 were deviating, and 2004 was reinstating.[6] We prefer to view the difference in party identification between the Democrats and Republicans as so small in recent years that it is no longer meaningful to speak of either party as having a real majority, hence our calling the elections starting in the 1980s "balancing elections." Given these alternative interpretations of electoral history, some readers may conclude that classifications of elections are inappropriate. However, we would still consider such classification a useful exercise when one party has a clear lead in party identification, as was the case up through the 1970s.

---

6. Knuckey (1999) argues that the Republican majority started as early as 1968, so that 1972 was maintaining, 1976 was deviating, and 1980 was reinstating.

APPENDIX: TABLE OF REGRESSIONS UNDERLYING FIGURES 14.1 AND 14.2

	Mean	b	se	t	b * mean	b	se	t	b * me
2004									
Rcandidate	.17	.085	.009	9.892	.014	.061	.008	7.748	.01
Dcandidate	−.29	−.056	.008	−7.077	.016	−.030	.007	−4.109	.00
Groups	−.79	.040	.008	5.313	−.032	.016	.007	2.271	−.01
Domestic	−.25	.029	.004	7.147	−.007	.009	.004	2.415	−.00
Foreign	−.16	.081	.008	10.596	−.013	.058	.007	8.408	−.00
Managers	.23	.026	.007	3.682	.006	.002	.007	0.343	.00
Party id.		—	—	—		.101	.007	14.462	
Constant		.518	.013	36.683		.194	.025	7.715	
R^2		.622				.704			
2000									
Rcandidate	.06	.059	.008	7.539	.004	.036	.007	5.081	.00
Dcandidate	−.09	−.075	.008	−9.996	.007	−.049	.007	−7.214	.00
Groups	−.80	.051	.007	7.419	−.041	.022	.006	3.514	−.01
Domestic	.00	.044	.003	14.106	.000	.021	.003	6.972	.00
Foreign	.13	.043	.015	2.789	.006	.029	.014	2.145	.00
Managers	.14	.042	.007	5.582	.006	.016	.007	2.352	.00
Party id.		—	—	—		.104	.006	16.59	
Constant		.497	.012	41.586		.195	.021	9.241	
R^2		.550				.644			

Note: Figures 14.1 and 14.2 depict the values in the b * mean columns, respectively. b = coefficient. se = standard error. t = t-statistic. — = not included in model.

CHAPTER 15

Electoral Behavior and the Political System

Most voting studies focus on the causes of the electoral decision, rather than on the effects. They want to know, as we have, what explains the vote choice. Why do voters go to the polls? Why do they select one candidate over another? Answering such questions is a valuable enterprise, and one manifest in the bulk of this volume. However, the question about the effects of electoral behavior should not be neglected altogether. Our discoveries with respect to how voters decide can shed great light on the working of key mechanisms in the political system as a whole. The electoral process joins with other governmental processes in predictable ways.

Of special importance are the psychological aspects of the voting act that we have uncovered. The typical American voter, as we have made clear, shows little political involvement, limited grasp of the issues, and not much ability to think in coherent, ideological terms. Further, he or she is likely identified with one of the nation's two major political parties. These characteristics of American political psychology have deep consequences for at least three aspects of the system of governance. First, they define the limits of popular constraint on the political leadership. Second, they dictate party strategies for vote-getting. Third, they determine the number of players in the party competition. Although we can only touch on these connections in this final chapter, we can suggest their profound importance for the American political system.

ELECTORAL BEHAVIOR AND THE PRESSURES ON LEADERSHIP

A democratic election is a way of holding political leaders accountable to the people. Voters do not directly choose the policy followed by government. But they do choose the individuals who themselves make the policy, and, if they do not approve of that policy, they may vote them out of office. Of course, the viability of this democratic connection, between mass and leader, depends on a few suppositions. For one, it assumes that the people have adequate information about the policy. For another, it assumes that the candidates running offer alternative courses of action regarding the policy. Meeting these assumptions helps ensure that government policy reflects the people's will. What does our evidence suggest regarding them? In particular, what have we learned here about public policy thinking in the electorate, and its link to the parties?

According to our analyses (recall chaps. 8–10), the average voter has at best partial acquaintance with the salient issues of the day. To be sure, a tiny elite knows a great deal, and is easily able to converse about what needs to be done, by whom, and why. But the great bulk of the public is far from such nuanced understanding. Many citizens do not have personal preferences with respect to major policy issues. And even among those who do, a sizable subset of people fail to differentiate the parties' and candidates' positions. When considering multiple issues, it appears that opinions are grouped into domain-specific clusters. In other words, a person's feelings about foreign policy are only tangentially related to his or her reactions regarding lifestyle concerns and social welfare controversies. And even within the respective substantive domains, the coherence of attitudes across separate issues remains clouded for many people. Such evidence leads us to question whether terms like liberal and conservative have any policy-relevant meaning within most of the electorate. Our analysis of individual reactions to the parties and candidates confirms that most people simply do not organize their political thinking along ideological lines. For all of these reasons, a substantial number of citizens undoubtedly experience difficulties during the process of "translating" their own feelings about issues and policies into a choice between presidential candidates.

This situation has two major implications. First, the electoral signal from a vote, that is, the policy direction of the balloting, is vague. If the public's issue preferences are clouded for the reasons just described, then it is difficult for the winning party to claim a mandate for any particular policy. And consistent with this concern, chapter 8 showed that there is quite a bit of variability in the public's beliefs about the candidates' positions on the most prominent issues of the day.

The second implication is a flip side of the first. Because the public does not convey a crystallized set of policy preferences and does not have a clear idea about what public officials are doing, government leaders have considerable freedom to carry out the actions they please. This latitude may be dangerous for the democratic ideal of popular control over public policy (e.g., Bachrach 1967). Or it may be an advantage, since elites can engage in the accommodation and compromise that are necessary to make public policy (e.g., Berelson 1952). In either case, public officials can act without much worry of close scrutiny from the mass electorate.

Of course, government cannot act totally without restraint, pursuing any policies it may wish. The electorate, by its persistent set of attitudes and behaviors, manages to set broad limits on the means and ends of any administration. Take the area of economic policy. Before the Great Depression, government management of the economy was viewed as unwise. The long breadlines of the 1930s changed all that. There was widespread economic hardship, and the people demanded government do something, expressing that desire in the landslide victory of Franklin Roosevelt in 1932. Under the New Deal, the consensus changed, to the opinion that government had a responsibility for keeping the economy healthy. The basic value of economic prosperity became a White House charge. Now, incumbents are routinely punished at the ballot box in the face of economic downturn, as we have seen in chapter 13.

Nevertheless, popular images of the role of government are not immutable. Beginning with the Reagan era, the notions of smaller government and fewer taxes gained ground. A positive public view of a limited government continued its ascendancy, from Bill Clinton to George W. Bush. While this view does not spell out the details of policy, it does serve as an electoral constraint on certain types of government activity. For example, the small government ethos prevalent in the public mind helps prevent the expansion of welfare programs, or tax increases. Indeed, the notion that nontrivial taxation, especially progressive taxation, is necessary for "good government" has come under increasing challenge.

The people and their elected officials are linked in yet another way. Politicians often share the values of their public. No major American presidential candidate advocates socialism or nuclear disarmament. As

Americans, they simply do not believe in those doctrines. Even if in their heart of hearts such policies held a certain appeal, the candidates would not endorse them, because they know the American voter finds such policies unacceptable. Further, candidates are sensitive to changes in public values over the years. At one time, in certain congressional districts, it might have been possible to ignore the Hispanic vote. No longer. Popular views on gay rights are changing, and candidates desirous of election are wrestling with constituents' views on that issue. Anticommunism has ceased to be a value that has a mass-elite resonance, but antiterrorism has replaced it. As these values change, politicians change—or do not, at their peril. This is yet another way in which the people guide their elected representatives.

ELECTORAL BEHAVIOR AND PARTY STRATEGY

What is the winning electoral strategy for a party? Taking inspiration from Anthony Downs (1957), one might say that in order to win, a party has to advocate a more acceptable position than its rivals. To illustrate, suppose a system of two political parties, where the competition is entirely in terms of left-right, or liberal-conservative, ideology. Each party has a place on this left-right scale, as does each voter. Now assume each voter supports the party closer to his or her own position. Given that the party positions cannot change, the majority party depends on the distribution of electoral opinion on this scale. Suppose the distribution is that of figure 15.1. In that case, party B would obtain the majority of votes since it is closer to the location of the median voter. In an actual campaign, the parties' positions could change, as each sought more votes. Here, for instance, party A, to avoid losing, could shift to a more conservative stance. Party B might then move toward those voters, in an attempt not to lose them. In situations such as this, with the distribution of opinion known and having one mode, the parties would naturally move ideologically closer to each other. This phenomenon has been used to account for the fact that real parties often have not dissimilar platforms.

The spatial model of party competition, however, has not gone unchallenged. Stokes (1966b) identified several assumptions in the model that are hard to reconcile with evidence on electoral behavior such as has been presented in this volume. For one thing, the spatial model assumes political controversy is defined by just one dimension. In most campaigns, however, voters care about issues in several dimensions, for

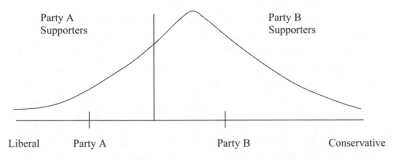

Fig. 15.1. Parties, voters, and the liberal-conservative dimension

example the economy, war and peace, social welfare, and/or moral questions. What is more, the salience of these dimensions is not constant from election to election. In such a circumstance, there may be considerable leadership turnover, as parties jockey for position on favored dimensions.

The situation would seem especially unpredictable if, in addition to multiple dimensions, the anchoring left-right dimension, however meaningful it may be for political candidates, is poorly understood by the mass electorate. This description seems to fit our data from the 2000 and 2004 presidential elections. Unlike the parties, candidates, and political experts, voters themselves are largely neither sophisticated enough to grasp nor motivated enough to follow ideological debate. That is not to say that they have no interest in issues. On the contrary, certain individuals may be issue-oriented. But few meaningfully structure the political universe in terms of liberal versus conservative. Such ideological appeals from candidates, then, would mostly fall on deaf ears.

American politicians, of course, sense this, as they couch their appeals mostly on the basis of other, nonideological dimensions. Instead of taking clear and distinctive positions on policy issues, they often stress widely shared goals that are important to the public. Stokes (1966b) called these concerns "valence issues," as opposed to "position issues." Prosperity and peace are two of the most common valence issues, or to cite negative ones, corruption and crime. The competition is not over where a candidate stands on these issues. There can be no meaningful difference of opinion on such issues. Everyone is for it, if the issue has a positive valence (e.g., prosperity), or against it, if the issue has a negative valence (e.g., corruption). The competition is over which candidate is most able to achieve the commonly desired goal.

The concept of a valence issue also encompasses commonly valued characteristics of candidates such as competence, leadership, integrity, and charisma. It is quite likely that a candidate ahead on such valence characteristics may beat a competitor whose positions are closer to the median voter. In deference to the originator of this concept, Groseclose (2001) calls individuals who make this type of choice "Stokes voters." Concern with the valence aspect of issues and candidates has become quite common in models of party strategy and electoral choice (Enelow and Hinich 1984; Rabinowitz and Macdonald 1989; Merrill and Grofman 1999).

Still another challenge to the traditional spatial model arises from the fact that, contrary to Downsian predictions, parties and candidates in the United States do *not* converge upon each other in the center—despite a largely unimodal distribution of public opinion on the issues over which they are competing. In order to account for this, Rabinowitz and Macdonald (1989) have proposed an alternative spatial model, in which parties differentiate themselves by taking relatively extreme policy positions in order to appeal to relatively inattentive voters. The latter need not make careful evaluations of the distances between themselves and the two parties—instead, they simply need to understand which side of the neutral center each party occupies, especially on issues important to them. This "directional theory" of issue voting might be able to reconcile the various critiques of the traditional spatial model with the limited capacities of the American electorate and the ongoing polarization of the American party system.

ELECTORAL BEHAVIOR AND THE PARTY SYSTEM

In any democracy, the number of parties seriously contending for political power is of tremendous importance. It defines the environment of political competition if the system boasts two parties rather than ten. Throughout this book, a two-party system has been the context in which the electoral behavior takes place. But behavior itself can shape context. We believe that, to some degree, the persistence of the U.S. two-party system is due to how American voters decide.

Our essential focus is on why the system, with two major parties, has endured, not how it came into being. We do not pretend to offer a total explanation. Pivotal historical events, key laws, and institutional arrangements have a good deal to do with it. Obviously, a winner-take-all electoral system favors a two-party arrangement (Duverger 1963; Rae 1971). Yet, compared with these large forces, the individual psychology of the American voter still provides, we believe, a needed part of the explanation. In particular, why is our number of major parties two? Why not three or one instead? A main reason, we contend, is the breadth and depth of party attachment in America. A clear majority of the adult public in our election surveys expresses an outright identification as Democrats or Republicans. In addition, most Independents profess a leaning to one of the major parties. Overall, then, all but a handful of Americans manifest an affinity for one of the two major parties. Clearly, party identification provides a firm foundation for most individual voters. Each presidential election becomes, in its own way, a renewed endorsement of the two-party system. Third parties, even when they emerge, are left with very little political space to themselves, which helps explain why Ross Perot's movement in 1992 and Ralph Nader's in 2000 were more successful than their respective candidacies in 1996 and 2004. Young people and people who have rarely voted in previous elections provide fertile ground for one-time independent candidacies, but do not offer the firm base needed for sustaining new parties.

While limiting competition to two parties, the party identifications of the electorate also give life support to the party that comes in second in a contest. This keeps the vote swing from one election to the next within narrow boundaries. The presidential elections of 2000 and 2004 were especially close, with the national popular voter split nearly evenly between the Democratic and Republican candidates. Even when landslides occur, such as the 1984 victory of Ronald Reagan, the popular vote split (59–41) is not extreme. Further, although a party loses the White House, it still holds on to a number of congressional seats and state houses. In the era of divided government it typically controls the Congress, as Democrats have done for much of the last half century under several Republican presidents. The Democratic edge in party loyalties during that period was a key factor for this success while the presidency went to the other party.

What party identification, however, is unable to explain is the frequent alternation in power, especially in presidential elections. In over 200 years of American national elections no party has managed to become the "permanent majority in office," despite partisan hopes or fears in this respect. However big a victory a party may amass in one election, it tends to lose ground in the next. The flow of the vote behaves in a manner typical of a "regression toward the mean," the mean being the point of equal division of the vote (Stokes and Iversen 1966).

What accounts for the tendency of the national vote to swing from one party to the other? Our analysis of electoral choices in recent elections points to a negativity effect in human behavior: electoral change is instigated primarily by a *negative* reaction to the party in power.[1] As the saying goes, the opposition never wins elections, the government loses them. Consider the Democratic loss of the White House in 2000. However disputed the outcome may have been, the negative reaction of the electorate to incumbent vice president Al Gore was a key factor. It mattered more than favorable views about the domestic record of the Clinton-Gore administration, or reactions to the Republican candidate, George W. Bush.

The failure of the economic boom of the 1990s to guarantee White House control to the incumbent party is not without precedent. Throughout the last 100 years, bad economic conditions have punished the party in office more severely than good times have rewarded it (Bloom and Price 1975). In particular, two major partisan realignments in American politics (1890s and 1930s) were precipitated by economic depressions. The return of prosperity may help the new party in power in the next election, but these electoral gains rarely match the losses suffered in bad times or protect the new party in subsequent elections. FDR in 1936, Ronald Reagan in 1984, and Bill Clinton in 1996 benefited from economic recovery, but they benefited much less than their predecessors suffered from economic distress.

Besides the economy, war is a case in point. The negative reaction to the Iraq war, evident in our survey responses in 2004, threatened the reelection prospects of George W. Bush. Even within the domain of war and peace, ill-feelings about that war trumped any good feelings about the other war (on terrorism). In years past, displeasure over the wars in Korea and Vietnam helped drive Democrats from the White House in the elections of 1952 and 1968. How did Bush in 2004 manage to avoid the fate that afflicted the White House party in those earlier wartime elections? Our analysis suggests an explanation consistent with the negativity hypothesis: the reaction to the challenger. The public assessment

---

1. Evidence for negative voting has accumulated over the years, but so has contrary evidence showing even-handed behavior. For a sampling of the various viewpoints, see Kernell 1977, Lanoue 1988, Lewis-Beck 1988, Lau 1985, and Norpoth 2004.

of John Kerry's qualities in the 2004 survey was very unfavorable. What counted especially against him in a wartime election was that the public saw him as weak and indecisive, whereas Bush received high marks in that area. Compare this with the glowing image enjoyed by Eisenhower as the out-party candidate in 1952. It can be unwise, then, to ignore the public's assessment of the opposition.

To adapt V. O. Key's famous phrase, why are voters more inclined to play god of vengeance than god of reward? The answer, we believe, lies in the fact that bad news is more salient than good news.[2] As the saying goes, good news is no news, only bad news is news. This folk wisdom applies especially well to something like politics, which does not attract a great deal of attention in normal times. But when a calamity strikes, be it economic adversity or foreign catastrophe, the public's attention is aroused and riveted on the incumbent party. The latter is the most visible target to bear the brunt of any public dissatisfaction. But the rule that bad news drives out good news may not be limited to the incumbent party; it may infect the opposition as well. If it becomes clear that the opposition suffers from serious defects in its potential handling of the calamity that is making the president or his party unpopular, the opposition may lose its credibility as an alternative.

Electoral behavior, as we have seen, seriously shapes the political system. Leaders have considerable liberty to make their own decisions, since the public usually pays little attention to the issues. As long as they take care not to go beyond the broad limits of constraint dictated by the basic values of the citizenry, elected officials can decide policy. Parties flexibly pursue vote-getting, along multiple dimensions, since the electorate is by no means wedded to a single, overarching, left-right ideological dimension. Competition between two parties is ensured, given the reach of party identification in the electorate. Moreover, neither party can command an enduring majority because the citizenry, even an inattentive one, eventually throws the rascals out for their conduct in office.

---

2. "Prospect theory" offers a broader explanation for such asymmetrical behavior (Kahneman and Tversky 1979). A key premise of this theory is that in making decisions individuals do not weigh gains and losses equally; rather, "losses loom larger than gains" (Quattrone and Tversky 1988, 724).

AFTERWORD

The American Voter Then and Now

How would we evaluate "the" American voter of the early twenty-first century, and how does he or she compare with "the" American voter of the mid-twentieth century? We can begin to answer these questions by going back through some of the main findings in our earlier chapters.

First, most Americans identify with a political party, or at least consider themselves closer to one major party or the other, just as they did in the 1950s. The proportion of political Independents is larger than it was in the 1950s, but the increase occurred mainly in the late 1960s and early 1970s, with minimal change since then. The characterization of political Independents as largely uninformed and uninvolved is no longer true, if it ever was; that characterization may hold for one set of Independents, but many of the new Independents were informed and involved people. In addition, party identification is still strongly associated with the vote: the relationship may have weakened after the 1950s, but it appears to have rebounded. A person's party identification still bears a strong parental imprint, and for most voters remains quite stable throughout the life cycle.

Second, issue voting does occur, but within bounds. On any given issue, only about half the electorate meets the set of preconditions that are necessary in order to cast ballots on the basis of their preferences with respect to that issue. There is some underlying structure to people's attitudes across different issues. However, substantive content of these structures appears to be limited; it does not generally reflect the broadly based patterns that should occur if substantial segments of the electorate took an ideological stance with respect to major questions of public policy. Pursuing this idea further, we find that about 20 percent of our current respondents can be characterized as "ideologues" or "near-ideologues." This is about twice the size of the corresponding stratum of the electorate from the 1950s. But this still leaves a sizable majority of the mass public that organizes its political thinking and conceptualizes the political world in distinctly nonideological, and often less sophisticated, ways.

The level of education within the American electorate has increased sharply since the 1950s, and this is reflected in more frequent issue voting, greater overall clarity in the structure of mass issue attitudes, and enhanced salience of ideological themes within the public's political thinking. Yet there is a real ceiling to this increase. Politics remains peripheral to the everyday concerns of most voters, and that will almost always be the case. So many people do not vote on the basis of issues, do not have attitudes that fit within common attitude structures, and think of politics along lines that are often quite different from the ways that elites (such as candidates, officeholders, journalists, and academics) view the political world.

Nevertheless, American voters are far from fools. *The American Voter* became known for its evaluation of American voters as minimally involved in politics and not very informed, voting on the basis of their parents' partisanship or candidate characteristics (particularly their "liking Ike" in the 1950s), rather than more rational issue-based voting. This led to "revisionists" who followed V. O. Key's (1966) call to arms when he proclaimed that "voters are not fools."

In truth, *The American Voter* never described voters as fools. (It is worth noting that Key himself was involved in reading and positively commenting on preliminary drafts of *The American Voter*.) Its characterization of voters was actually closer to Anthony Downs's (1957) notion that voters rationally spend only as much on politics as they need to spend. In more modern social-psychological parlance, voters are "cognitive misers," learning only as much as they have to in order to decide how to vote. Our contemporary findings are congruent with this assessment. For example, it need not take much cognitive work for voters to figure out how to vote when the economy is roaring ahead and taking them with it or, for that matter, when the economy is grinding to a halt and pulling them down too.

What about the continued voter reliance on party identification in voting? Is that less than rational? Current social-psychological theory views use of partisanship as a "heuristic"—a short-cut or cue as to how to vote. Again, it may be entirely rational for people to develop short-cuts to working their way through complex decisions. According to this perspective, party identification functions in the voting realm just like brand loyalty in consumer purchases, allowing people to make repeated decisions easily. Just as one can keep buying the same brand of soap until one has a bad experience with it, so one can vote for the same party repeatedly until there is a bad experience causing a reevaluation.

These conclusions seem to imply minimal change from the 1950s to the early 2000s, but there was a fair amount of change among certain groups in the electorate. In the 1950s, African Americans predominantly lived in southern states that disenfranchised them. As a result, they were uninvolved in politics and often apolitical. Their re-enfranchisement in the 1960s resulted in their becoming much more involved in politics, voting at much greater levels, and adopting party identifications in large numbers—and on the Democratic side of the ledger. There was also considerable change among women. With the Nineteenth Amendment giving women the vote adopted as recently as 1920, the analysis of the 1950s election surveys in Campbell, Converse, Miller, and Stokes found that women were still underparticipating and following their husbands in their voting. With the passage of time, the generation of women not used to participating in politics has faded from the scene. Women now participate as much as men with comparable levels of education. Indeed, Census Bureau surveys report women vote more than men. Furthermore, fewer households today include a married couple than in the 1950s, and the women's rights movement made passé the concept of a woman echoing her husband's vote. Women are now fully part of the electorate, being more involved in politics and voting at higher levels. Not only do contemporary women not necessarily echo their husbands' vote, but they have remained Democratic in their voting as men have become more Republican, leading to the now familiar gender gap. As we have seen in chapter 11, Hispanics have become a potentially important voting group that may still be up for grabs between the parties. In addition, fundamentalist Protestants, who were often not voting, have begun voting in larger numbers, and more on the Republican side of the ledger. Thus, there has been considerable change among several groups in the electorate, even if the overall change is limited.

So, overall, how should "the American voter" of the early twenty-first century be characterized? The above changes in the distribution of key variables, comparing the 1950s to 2000s, suggest a significant alteration in patterns of behavior. However, these shifts beg the more fundamental question our colleagues routinely ask: Has the behavior of the individual American voter itself changed in the nearly 50 years since the publication of *The American Voter*? On the one hand, such a question, with its many aspects, seems impossible to answer. Changed how? When? For whom? To what degree? On the other hand, the fundamental question will not go away. We can offer a response, at least if we pose it this way: Does the social-psychological explanation of presidential vote choice, developed in *The American Voter* and symbolized in its famous theory of the "funnel of causality," still hold? The essential answer drawn from our revisit must be yes.

Voter preference for the Republican or Democratic candidate remains largely a function of the same forces. Consider long-term forces. Party identification and social group membership, enduring variables formed at some distance from the vote itself, still operate. Short-term forces, more immediate but nevertheless antecedent to the vote, such as candidate attitudes and economic issues, retain their impact. The funnel of causality model is broad enough to recognize that values and ideology can be additional long-term forces and that campaign debates, the media, and discussion of politics with family and friends can be additional short-term elements leading to voting decisions. Yet the basic ensemble of the variables measured in *The American Voter* offers, then and now, a rather complete accounting of U.S. presidential vote choice. Furthermore, these variables continue to deliver effects of a similar magnitude, in one period compared to another.

To carry home this point—the similarity of effects—the key crosstabulations in the relevant chapters serve as an indispensable baseline. Compare our tables to their original counterparts in *The American Voter*. (The appendix that follows serves as an explicit reference guide for this task.) For example, compare the key cross-tabulations relating the vote to party identification, social group membership, attitudes toward candidates, and economic issues. Although no match is perfect, these straightforward tables suggest that the structure and strength of basic relationships uncovered in *The American Voter* persist.

Of course, continuity across time regarding these simple relationships does not necessarily mean the coefficients of the independent variables in, say, a multiple regression equation have not altered. Much of the literature reviewed in the "Commentary and Controversy" sections deals, directly or indirectly, with such possibilities. While these possible shifts in coefficient magnitude merit attention, they do not alter the overarching conclusion that *The American Voter*'s paradigm for explanation of individual political behavior remains compelling.

APPENDIX A

Counterpart Tables and Figures

The following lists tables and figures in this volume with the counterpart table or figure in the original unabridged version of *The American Voter*. In some cases, when the format could not be exactly replicated, we aimed to preserve the spirit of the original. A few tables and figures are new, although even those are inspired by the original text.

TABLES

Number in This Volume	Counterpart in *The American Voter*	Title in This Volume
3.1	3.4	References to War and Peace
3.2	None	References to the Iraq War and Terrorism in 2004
3.3	3.1	References to Economic Conditions and Policies
3.4	3.2	References to Social Welfare Policies
3.5	None	References to Moral Issues
3.6	3.3	References to Groups
3.7	None	References to Government Management
3.8	3.7	References to Groups by Party and Candidate
3.9	3.8	References to Domestic Issues by Party and Candidate
3.10	3.9	References to Foreign Issues by Party and Candidate
3.11	3.10	References to Candidates in Terms of Party

3.12	3.11	References to Personal Attributes of the Candidates
3.13	3.12	Favorable References to Bush
3.14	3.13	Unfavorable References to Bush
3.15	3.14	Favorable References to Gore, Kerry
3.16	3.15	Unfavorable References to Gore, Kerry
4.1	Same	Relation of Attitude toward Bush to Party Division of the Vote
4.2	Same	Relation of Attitude toward Bush and Attitude on Domestic Issues to Percent Voting Republican
4.3	Same	Relation of Reported Partisan Preference of Primary Groups to Respondent's Own Partisan Choice
4.4	Same	Reported Time of Vote Decision
4.5	Same	Relation of Attitude Level to Proportion Not Caring How Election Turns Out
5.1	Same	Acts of Political Participation, 2000 and 2004
5.2	Same	The Relation of Past Voting to Current Voting Turnout
5.3	None	Estimates of Voting Turnout in 2004
5.4	None	Self-Report of Voting Turnout in Surveys: Two Question Versions
5.5	5.4	Interest in the Campaign and Voting Turnout, 2004
5.6	5.5	Concern about Election Outcome and Voting Turnout, 2004
5.7	5.6	Sense of Political Efficacy and Voting Turnout, 2004
5.8	5.7	Sense of Civic Duty and Voting Turnout, 2004
5.9	5.8	Presidential Vote Preference of Nonvoters, Postelection Surveys
5.10	5.9	Change in Candidate Preferences of Nonvoters by Political Interest
5.11	5.3	Closeness of Election, Intensity of Preference and Voting Turnout, 2004
6.1	Same	Party Identification by Year
6.2	Same	Relation of Strength of Party Identification to Partisan Regularity in Voting for President
6.3	6.4	Party Identification as an Influence on Partisan Consistency of Attitude
6.4	6.5	Vote by Party Identification
6.5	6.6	Relation of Degree of Attitude Development to Direction in Which Conflict of Party Identification and Partisan Evaluations is Resolved in Voting

6.6	6.7	Relation of Strength of Party Identification to Interest in Campaign
6.7	6.8	Relation of Strength of Party Identification to Concern over Outcome
6.8	None	Democratic Lead in Partisanship among Actual Voters for President
6.9	None	Net Group Partisanship
7.1	Same	Intergenerational Resemblance in Partisan Orientation, 1992
7.2	7.1	Intergenerational Transmission of Party Identification, Politically Active and Inactive Homes, 1997
7.3	7.2	Stability and Change in Party Identification, 2000–2004
7.4	7.2	Stability and Change in Party Identification, 1965–82: Adult Panel
7.5	7.2	Stability and Change in Party Identification, 1965–97: Youth Panel
7.6	7.5	Relation of Age to Party Identification
7.7	7.6	The Strength of Party Identification in the Youth Panel, 1965–97
7.8	7.3	Partisanship of Young Adults
8.1	Same	Familiarity with Issues
8.2	Same	Issue Familiarity and Level of Education
8.3	None	Opinion Holding on Issues
8.4	None	Perceptions of Differing Candidate Positions by Education
8.5	8.3	Potential Issue Voters, by Issue
8.6	None	Degrees of Consensus on Candidate Issue Positions
10.1	Same	Distribution across the Levels of Conceptualization, Calculated Separately for Total 2000 NES Sample, and for Self-Reported 2000 Voters
10.2	Same	The Relationship between Education and Level of Conceptualization
10.3	None	Relationship between Political Knowledge and Level of Conceptualization
10.4	None	Relationship between Personal Political Involvement and Level of Conceptualization
10.5	10.3	Relationship between Level of Conceptualization and Knowledge, and Level of Conceptualization and Involvement, Controlling for Respondent's Education
10.6	None	Percentage Turning Out to Vote, by Level of Conceptualization

10.7	10.4	Partisan Strength and Presidential Vote Consistency, by Level of Conceptualization
11.1	12.1	The Distinctiveness of Voting Behavior among Several Social Groupings
11.2	12.2	Distinctiveness of Presidential Vote among Certain Groups, with Life Situation Controlled
11.3	12.3	Vote Division within Test Groups, According to Strength of Group Identification
11.4	12.4	Relation of Group Cohesiveness to Group Identification
11.5	12.8	Presidential Voting across Secondary Membership Groups, by Strength of Group Identification and Belief in Legitimacy of Group Political Activity
12.1	Fig. 13.1	The Relationship between Subjective Social Class and Presidential Vote
12.2	Fig. 13.1	Theoretical Possibilities for Status Polarization
12.3	17.1	Relation of Education to Attempt to Influence the Vote of Others
12.4	17.2	Relation of Amount of Formal Education to Presidential Vote Participation
12.5	17.3	Relation of Amount of Formal Education to Political Involvement
12.6	17.4	Relation of Education to Sense of Political Efficacy
12.7	17.7	Relation of Gender and Education to Presidential Vote Turnout
12.8	17.11	Relation of Age, Education, and Presidential Vote Turnout
13.1	14.2	Relation of Worries about Unemployment to Presidential Vote
13.2	14.3	Relation of Party Identification to Personal Reaction to Job Situation
13.3	Fig. 14.1	Relation of Party Identification to Approval of the President's Handling of the Economy
13.4	14.4	Relation of Evaluation of President's Handling of the Economy to Party Identification and Personal Reaction to Job Situation
13.5	14.2	Relation of Personal Financial Situation to the Presidential Vote
13.6	14.2	Relation of Personal Financial Situation and Presidential Vote, within Categories of Social Class
13.7	14.5	Relation of National Economic Situation to the Presidential Vote

| 13.8 | 14.3 | Relation of Party Identification to Economic Outlook |
| 13.9 | 14.5 | Vote for President, as a Function of Economic Outlook, among Three Categories of Party Identifiers |

FIGURES

Number in This Volume	Counterpart in *The American Voter*	Caption in This Volume
2.1	None	Funnel of Causality
4.1	Same	Relation of Attitude toward Bush to Party Vote
4.2	Same	Prediction of Voting Choice from All Partisan Attitudes
4.3	Same	Relation of Reported Time of Vote Decision to Ability of Partisan Attitudes to Explain the Vote
4.4	Same	Relation of Extent of Attitude Consistency to Reported Time of Vote Decision
4.5	Same	Relation of Extent of Attitude Consistency to Degree of Straight-ticket Voting
4.6	Same	Relation of Extent of Attitude Consistency to Degree of Indifference to Election Outcome
5.1	Same	Intensity of Voting Preference and Voting Turnout, 2000 and 2004
5.2	5.3	Intensity of Political Involvement and Voting Turnout, 2000 and 2004
6.1	Same	Relation of party identification to partisan evaluations of elements of national politics
6.2	Same	Relation of party identification to partisan evaluations of elements of national politics
6.3	Same	Probable Direction of Vote by Party Identification Groups
6.4	Same	Location of Individuals with Well-Developed Attitudes and Poorly Developed Attitudes within Distribution of All Respondents
7.1	Same	Party Identification of Party Identifiers Born between 1940 and 1980
7.2	None	Percentage Republican of Party Identifiers among Blacks and Southern Whites, 1952–2004
9.1	None	Histograms for Guttman Scales Measuring Attitude Structures

9.2	Table 9.2	Relationship between Issue Attitudes and Party Identification
9.3	None	Relationship between Issue Attitudes and Liberal-Conservative Identification
9.4	None	Relationship between Issue Attitudes and Liberal-Conservative Identification, Controlling for Party Identification
9.5	None	Relationship between Foreign Policy Attitudes and General Feelings about Diplomacy versus Military Action, Controlling for Party Identification
9.6	None	Relationship between Lifestyle Issue Attitudes and Moral Traditionalism, Controlling for Liberal-Conservative Identification
9.7	None	Relationship between Social Welfare Attitudes and Feelings about the Size and Power of Government, Controlling for Party Identification and for Liberal-Conservative Identification
12.1	13.2	Status Polarization of Presidential Votes
12.2	13.3	The Relationship of Political Sophistication to Status Voting
12.3	13.4	Relation of Political Involvement to Status Voting
12.4	13.8	Status Voting and Strength of Party Identification
12.5	17.1	Relation of Age to Voting Participation
14.1	19.1	Attitudinal Forces on the Presidential Vote
14.2	19.2	Attitudinal Components on the Vote with Effect of Party Identification Removed
15.1	Figure in chap. 20	Parties, Voters, and the Liberal-Conservative Dimension

APPENDIX B

Replication of *The American Voter*

The American Voter Revisited attempts to replicate the analysis of *The American Voter*. We have tried to do justice to that endeavor, but inevitably obstacles arise. We describe some of them here, partly to document our efforts but more importantly to provide a guide for future researchers who attempt to replicate *The American Voter* in another half-century.

The replication issues vary by chapter and, as we spelled out in the preface, each of our chapters consciously parallels a chapter in the original. Chapter 1 sets the stage, describing the prior course of voting research, and the political context of the 2000 and 2004 presidential elections (as opposed to those of 1952 and 1956). The role and activities of the National Election Studies, barely begun in the 1950s, are documented. Chapter 2 lays out a social-psychological theory of the vote, based on the notion of a funnel of causality. For pedagogical purposes, the funnel is actually diagrammed, unlike in *The American Voter* itself. The case notes from nine voters surveyed are explicitly fictional, since it is not possible to quote directly from the interview protocols because of confidentiality requirements.

The real issues of scientific replication begin with the analytic chapters. Chapter 3, the first of this kind, posed a profound challenge. The analysis of candidate and party perceptions was set in a specific historical context—the depression, the New Deal, the war in Korea, a war hero as presidential candidate, and so on—that could not be replicated, strictly speaking. All we could do was to pick elements of the contemporary historical setting—the Reagan revolution, the rise of moral issues, terrorism, the war in Iraq, and so on—to conduct the kind of analysis of political perceptions done in the original, 50 years ago. In addition, the reliance on open-ended questions in this chapter (the well-known battery of like-or-dislike items), used to probe perception of candidates and parties, posed a technical problem of replication. In particular, the coding categories for those responses have proliferated enormously since the 1950s, requiring numerous decisions to create comparable categories.

Chapter 4 also requires a classification of the open-ended like-and-dislike comments about the parties and candidates, into six partisan attitudes: attitudes toward the Republican and Democratic candidates, attitudes toward foreign and domestic issues, attitudes toward social groups, and attitudes toward the parties as managers of government. Unfortunately, the categorization used by the original authors cannot be located. The closest is a memo written by Art Wolfe of the Center for Political Studies staff that shows the scheme they used for the 1964 study, but it is based on a three-digit coding scheme rather than the four-digit coding scheme now used in the NES surveys. *The American Voter* does not describe the categorization scheme in detail, nor does the earlier *American Political Science Review* article (Stokes, Campbell, and Miller 1958). The most useful delineation of the six categories is one that is provided by Kagay and Caldeira (1980), who would have had the opportunity to discuss the matter with Donald Stokes. In addition, the 1952 codebook itself actually shows a derivation of the six components. With this background, we found that it was in fact easy to categorize most of the "master code" categories used for these questions into the six partisan attitudes. Still, some of the specific categories fall so completely in the intersection of different attitudes that there cannot be a "correct" way of classifying them.

Chapters 3 and 4 offer a contrast to chapter 5, which was one of the simplest to replicate. Most of the measures to explain the decision to turn out at the polls are still being posed in the election surveys, except for the civic duty scale (where we had to substitute a question about willingness to serve on a jury). What is more, the summary indices for partisan intensity and psychological involvement predict turnout in the replication just about as well as they did in the original analysis.

The largest replication problem in chapter 6 involves table 6.3, which compares the observed and expected numbers of respondents with consistent partisan attitudes, with controls on strength of partisanship. It was not only very difficult to determine what exactly *The American Voter* was trying to do in this table, but it was very difficult to generate the results for 2004. Ironically, this was one analysis that was probably easier to conduct in the days when data were punched on physical cards that could be sorted into piles and counted than today, when we try to have the computer generate cross-tabulations. We suspect that the original researchers physically divided their card decks into four piles based on respondents' partisan strength, counted the number in each pile, and then counted how many in each pile had consistent attitudes. On our third try, we generated a cross-tabulation that enabled us to add up various numbers to assemble this table correctly. We have inserted a footnote that explains the calculation of expected values in much greater detail than the original authors provided.

Chapter 7 encounters a different replication problem: key questions used in the original analysis are no longer posed in the National Election Studies, nor are any comparable questions. The particular concern here is over the origins and the persistence of party identification. The National Election Studies no longer query respondents about which parties their parents identified with, nor whether respondents ever changed their party identification, and if so, when and why. The psychological understanding of memory processes now considers answers to such questions to be unreliable. So we decided to venture outside the box of National Election Studies. We turned to socialization studies that ascertain political attitudes of parents and offspring independently. In addition, fortunately for us, these studies have been extended into multi-wave panel surveys that enable us to trace the persistence and change in partisanship over long periods of time. This is a rare instance in which we cannot replicate the original analysis exactly but where our "replication in kind" promises to yield more reliable results than were achieved in the original study. We are confident that the authors of *The American Voter* would have conducted this kind of analysis were they writing their book today.

Our replication of chapter 8 is a "conceptual" replication. That chapter of *The American Voter* created three hurdles that must be passed for a respondent to be able to vote on the basis of an issue. However, the way that questions on issues are asked in the surveys has changed over the years, so we cannot do an exact replication. Here we can do a high-quality substitution to achieve a three-hurdle analysis that is fully consistent with the original, even if the questions are different. Still, a reader might reasonably consider differences between our results and those for the 1950s to be due to the instrumentation changes.

Chapter 9 examines the structure of issue attitudes. Not only are the issues different now than in the 1950s, but the basic question format also has been changed. Instead of being asked how they feel on a particular issue, respondents are usually asked an elaborate question that describes two alternative positions on the issue and then asked to place themselves on a seven-point scale that has those two positions as its extremes. We have conducted an analysis of the current questions on issues in a manner that is parallel to the analysis that was conducted for the 1950s, and we are able to perform sensitivity tests by employing more modern techniques on the current questions.

Chapter 10 requires coding of the original survey protocols as to the respondent's level of conceptualization. Due to confidentiality requirements, access to the original protocols is now severely restricted. We were able to obtain access for the 2000 surveys. However, these data now consist of terse entries in a spreadsheet, rather than the handwritten interview transcripts used by the authors of *The American Voter*. We must admit some concern that the latter contain more detailed and nuanced information than that which is currently available to us. Furthermore, we could not obtain permission to reprint verbatim quotes in order to illustrate the different conceptualization levels; instead, we use "generic" phrases to exemplify the kinds of language and textual themes that characterize the various levels. Despite these potential limitations, we believe our version of the levels of conceptualization faithfully reproduces the same kind of information about belief system structure that was provided by the original classification scheme.

Chapter 11 deals with social groupings, but the relevant social groupings have changed over the years. We have added Hispanics and women to the tables in the main part of the chapter, even though they were not in the original (of union members, Catholics, Jews, and blacks). Our discussion of religion contrasts mainline and evangelical Protestants, a distinction that was not considered relevant in the 1950s. In addition, the earlier distinction between southern and nonsouthern blacks was not maintained. Nevertheless, overall, the replication of this chapter offers a very close parallel to the same tables in *The American Voter*.

Chapter 12, on class and other social characteristics, attempts to replicate the analysis in two original chapters (13 and 17). Except for a few minor tables, reproduction of the class analysis is achieved. However, in the figure on status voting and political sophistication, a some-what different measure of the latter variable had to be employed. The tables relating education to different measures of political activity were satisfactorily replicated, although the distinction between the South and elsewhere was not needed.

In the consideration of the economic voting observed in chapter 13, we were reminded of how ably the original authors brought this subject to the voting behavior literature, anticipating several matters that later researchers would elaborate on. The initial tables in *The American Voter* focus on what is now called "pocketbook" voting, using items that are not routinely posed. However, their key analyses on the influence of "economic outlook" combine two components, personal financial situa-tion and national business conditions. The two standard items on these components, which have been part of the NES since the 1950s, form the core of our replication in this chapter.

We encounter another type of replication problem in this part of the book. While we would have enjoyed revisiting the chapter in *The Ameri-can Voter* on the political behavior of farmers, there are too few farmers in current surveys to do so. As was the case for the original, for certain theoretical questions farmers are the ideal population to examine, but it is impossible to do so without a larger sample. Our suggestion here is that future researchers interested in this population call for "oversampling" farmers in national surveys, or pool comparable national surveys.

One replication issue in chapter 14 is statistical. *The American Voter* used ordinary least-squares regression analysis (OLS) of the vote deci-sion, even though Republican/Democratic vote is a dichotomous vari-able. Nowadays, maximum likelihood methods would be used when the dependent variable is dichotomous, either logit or probit analysis. The authors of *The American Voter* recognized that these methods were tech-nically superior to standard regression analysis, but they used regression because it is easier to understand and gave similar results (Stokes 1966a, 28). In point of fact, the core decomposition of the vote result in chapter 14 depends on multiplying means of independent variables by the corre-sponding regression coefficients, an approach that works only when OLS is used. We replicate *The American Voter* analysis for 2000 and 2004 here because it is illuminating substantively, but we are deeply con-cerned that there is no better methodological solution. Another replica-tion issue in this chapter involves the typology of elections. *The Ameri-can Voter* based its typology on the existence of a majority party. We amplified their typology to handle the case where there is no clear-cut majority party.

Finally, an issue throughout the book is our replication of the original theory of *The American Voter*. It is tempting to redo the book using more modern theories, but we decided instead to show what could be achieved within the original framework. We recognize the limits of the original approach and that replicating it will be controversial, but we believe that there is great value in showing today's readers how *The American Voter* would have analyzed the George W. Bush elections. We hope this gives other authors the impetus to analyze the 2000 and 2004 elections using other theories, so that full-blown comparisons of competing theories can be made.

References

Abramowitz, Alan I. 1988. "An Improved Model for Predicting Presidential Election Outcomes." *PS: Political Science and Politics* 21:843–47.

Abramowitz, Alan I. 1994. "Issue Evolution Reconsidered: Racial Attitudes and Partisanship in the U.S. Electorate." *American Journal of Political Science* 38:1–24.

Abramowitz, Alan I. 2004. "When Good Times Go Bad: The Time-for-Change Model and the 2004 Presidential Election." *PS: Political Science and Politics* 37:743–46.

Abramson, Paul R. 1981. "Comment on Smith." *American Political Science Review* 75:146–49.

Abramson, Paul R., John H. Aldrich, Philip Paolino, and David W. Rohde. 2000. "Challenges to the American Two-Party System: Evidence from the 1968, 1980, 1992, and 1996 Presidential Elections." *Political Research Quarterly* 53:495–522.

Abramson, Paul R., John H. Aldrich, Jill Rickershauser, and David W. Rohde. 2007. "Fear in the Voting Booth." *Political Behavior* 29:197–220.

Abramson, Paul R., John H. Aldrich, and David W. Rohde. 2003. *Change and Continuity in the 2000 and 2002 Elections.* Washington, DC: CQ Press.

Abramson, Paul R., John H. Aldrich, and David W. Rohde. 2006. *Change and Continuity in the 2004 Elections.* Washington, DC: Congressional Quarterly Press.

Abramson, Paul R., and Charles W. Ostrom. 1991. "Macropartisanship: An Empirical Reassessment." *American Political Science Review* 85:181–92.

Achen, Christopher. 1975. "Mass Political Attitudes and the Survey Response." *American Political Science Review* 69:1218–31.

Achen, Christopher. 1979. "The Bias in Normal Vote Estimates." *Political Methodology* 6:343–56.

Adams, Greg D. 1997. "Abortion: Evidence of an Issue Evolution." *American Journal of Political Science* 41:718–37.

Aldrich, John H. 1993. "Rational Choice and Turnout." *American Journal of Political Science* 37:246–78.

Aldrich, John H. 1995. *Why Parties? The Origin and Transformation of Party Politics in America.* Chicago: University of Chicago Press.

Aldrich, John H., and Richard D. McKelvey. 1977. "A Method of Scaling with Applications to the 1968 and 1972 Presidential Elections." *American Political Science Review* 71:111–30.

Aldrich, John H., Richard G. Niemi, George Rabinowitz, and David W. Rohde. 1982. "The Measurement of Public Opinion about Public Policy: A Report on Some New Issue Question Formats." *American Journal of Political Science* 26:391–414.

Alesina, Alberto, John Londregan, and Howard Rosenthal. 1993. "A Model of the Political Economy of the United States." *American Political Science Review* 87:12–33.

Alford, John R., Carolyn L. Funk, and John R. Hibbing. 2005. "Are Political Orientations Genetically Transmitted?" *American Political Science Review* 99: 153–68.

Allsop, Dee, and Herbert F. Weisberg. 1988. "Measuring Change in Party Identifications in an Election Campaign." *American Journal of Political Science* 32:996–1017.

Alonso-Zaldivar, Ricardo. 2004. "Bush Snags Much More of Latino Vote, Exit Polls Show." *Los Angeles Times*, November 7.

Althaus, Scott L. 2004. *Collective Preferences in Democratic Politics: Opinion Surveys and the Will of the People.* Cambridge: Cambridge University Press.

Alvarez, R. Michael, and John Brehm. 1995. "American Ambivalence toward Abortion Policy: Development of a Heteroskedastic Probit Model of Competing Values." *American Journal of Political Science* 39:1055–82.

Alvarez, R. Michael, and John Brehm. 2002. *Hard Choices, Easy Answers: Values, Information, and American Public Opinion.* Princeton: Princeton University Press.

Alvarez, R. Michael, and Jonathan Nagler. 1995. "Economics, Issues, and the Perot Candidacy: Voter Choice in the 1992 Presidential Election." *American Journal of Political Science* 39:714–44.

Alvarez, R. Michael, and Jonathan Nagler. 1998. "Economics, Entitlements, and Social Issues: Voter Choice in the 1992 Presidential Election." *American Journal of Political Science* 42:1349–63.

Alwin, Duane F., Ronald L. Cohen, and Theodore M. Newcomb. 1991. *Political Attitudes over the Life Span: The Bennington Women after Fifty Years.* Madison: University of Wisconsin Press.

Andersen, Kristi. 1979. *The Creation of a Democratic Majority: 1928–1936.* Chicago: University of Chicago Press.

Andrich, David. 1985. "An Elaboration of Guttman Scaling with Rasch Models for Measurement." In *Sociological Methodology, 1985*, ed. N. Brandon-Tuma. San Francisco: Jossey-Bass. 33–80.

Ansolabahere, Stephen, and Shanto Iyengar. 1995. *Going Negative: How Political Advertising Shrinks and Polarizes the Electorate.* New York: Free Press.

Ansolabahere, Stephen, Shanto Iyengar, and Adam Simon. 1999. "Replicating Experiments Using Aggregate and Survey Data: The Case of Negative Advertising and Turnout." *American Political Science Review* 93:901–9.

Armitage, Christopher J., and Mark Conner. 2000. "Attitudinal Ambivalence: A Test of Three Key Hypotheses." *Personality and Social Psychology Bulletin* 26:1421–32.

Atkeson, Lonna Rae. 2003. "Not All Cues Are Created Equal: The Conditional Impact of Female Candidates on Political Engagement." *Journal of Politics* 65:1040–61.

Axelrod, Robert. 1972. "Where the Votes Come From: An Analysis of Electoral Coalitions, 1952–1968." *American Political Science Review* 66:11–20.

Axelrod, Robert. 1986. "Presidential Election Coalitions in 1984." *American Political Science Review* 80:281–84.

Bachrach, Peter. 1967. *The Theory of Democratic Elitism: A Critique.* Boston: Little, Brown.

Bachrach, Peter, and Morton S. Baratz. 1962. "Two Faces of Power." *American Political Science Review* 56:947–52.

Bachrach, Peter, and Morton S. Baratz. 1963. "Decisions and Nondecisions: An Analytical Framework." *American Political Science Review* 57:632–42.

Baker, Frank B., and Seock-Ho Kim. 2004. *Item Response Theory: Parameter Estimation Techniques.* 2nd ed. New York: Marcel Dekker.

Balz, Dan, and Mike Allen. 2004. "Four More Years Attributed to Rove's Strategy: Despite Moments of Doubts, Adviser's Planning Paid Off." *Washington Post,* November 4, A1.

Bartels, Larry M. 2000. "Partisanship and Voting Behavior." *American Journal of Political Science* 44:35–50.

Bartels, Larry M. 2005a. "Homer Gets a Tax Cut: Inequality and Public Policy in the American Mind." *Perspectives on Politics* 3:15–32.

Bartels, Larry M. 2005b. "What's the Matter with *What's the Matter with Kansas?*" Paper presented at the Annual Meeting of the American Political Science Association, Washington, DC.

Bartholomew, David J., Fiona Steele, Irini Moustaki, and Jane I. Galbraith. 2002. *The Analysis and Interpretation of Multivariate Data for Social Scientists.* Boca Rotan, FL: Chapman and Hall/CRC Press.

Barton, Allen H., and R. Wayne Parsons. 1977. "Measuring Belief System Structure." *Public Opinion Quarterly* 41:159–80.

Bass, Harold. 1991. "A Reader's Guide and Bibliography." In *The End of Realignment?* ed. Byron Shafer. Madison: University of Wisconsin Press. 141–78.

Baumgartner, Frank R., and Bryan D. Jones. 1993. *Agendas and Instability in American Politics*. Chicago: University of Chicago Press.

Beardsley, Philip L. 1973. "The Methodology of Electoral Analysis: Models and Measurement." In David M. Kovenock, James W. Prothro, et al., *Explaining the Vote: Presidential Choices in the Nation and the States, 1968 (Part I)*. Chapel Hill: Institute for Research in Social Science, University of North Carolina. 30–92.

Beck, Paul Allen. 1974. "A Socialization Theory of Partisan Realignment." In Richard G. Niemi et al., *The Politics of Future Citizens*. San Francisco: Jossey-Bass. 199–219.

Beck, Paul Allen. 1984. "The Dealignment Era in America." In *Electoral Change and Advanced Industrial Societies*, ed. Russell Dalton, Scott Flanigan, and Paul Allen Beck. Princeton: Princeton University Press. 240–66.

Bélanger, Eric, and Jean-François Godbout. 2005. "Economic Voting and Political Sophistication in the U.S.: A Reassessment." Paper presented at the Annual Meeting of the American Political Science Association, Washington, DC.

Belli, Robert F., Michael W. Traugott, Margaret Young, and Katherine A. McGonagle. 1999. "Reducing Vote Overreporting in Surveys: Social Desirability, Memory Failure, and Source Monitoring." *Public Opinion Quarterly* 63:90–108.

Bennett, Linda L. M., and Stephen Earl Bennett. 1990. *Living with Leviathan: Americans Coming to Terms with Big Government*. Lawrence: University of Kansas Press.

Bennett, Stephen Earl. 1995. "Comparing Americans' Political Information in 1988 and 1992." *Journal of Politics* 57:521–32.

Bennett, Stephen Earl. 1996. "'Know-Nothings' Revisited Again." *Political Behavior* 16:179–201.

Bennett, W. Lance. 1977. "The Growth of Knowledge in Mass Belief Systems: An Epistemological Critique." *American Journal of Political Science* 21:465–500.

Bennett, W. Lance. 1980. *Public Opinion in American Politics*. New York: Harcourt Brace Jovanovich.

Berelson, Bernard. 1952. "Democratic Theory and Public Opinion." *Public Opinion Quarterly* 16:313–30.

Berelson, Bernard R., Paul F. Lazarsfeld, and William N. McPhee. 1954. *Voting: A Study of Opinion Formation in a Presidential Campaign*. Chicago: University of Chicago Press.

Berinsky, Adam J. 2004. *Silent Voices: Public Opinion and Political Participation in America*. Princeton: Princeton University Press.

Bernstein, Robert, Anita Chadha, and Robert Montjoy. 2001. "Overreporting Voting: Why It Happens and Why It Matters." *Public Opinion Quarterly* 65:22–44.

Bibby, John F. 1996. *Politics, Parties, and Elections in America.* 3rd ed. Chicago: Nelson-Hall.

Bishop, George F. 2005. *The Illusion of Public Opinion: Fact and Artifact in American Public Opinion Polls.* Lanham, MD: Rowman and Littlefield.

Bishop, George F., and Kathleen A. Frankovic. 1981. "Ideological Consensus and Constraint among Party Leaders and Followers in the 1978 Election." *Micropolitics* 1:87–111.

Bishop, George F., Alfred J. Tuchfarber, and Robert W. Oldendick. 1978. "Change in the Structure of American Political Attitudes: The Nagging Question of Question Wording." *American Journal of Political Science* 22:250–69.

Bishop, George F., Alfred J. Tuchfarber, Robert W. Oldendick, and Stephen E. Bennett. 1979. "Questions about Question Wording: A Rejoinder to Revisiting Mass Belief Systems Revisited." *American Journal of Political Science* 23: 187–92 .

Black, Earl, and Merle Black. 1992. *The Vital South.* Cambridge: Harvard University Press.

Bloom, Howard S., and H. Douglas Price. 1975. "Voter Response to Short-Run Economic Conditions: The Asymmetric Effect of Prosperity and Recession." *American Political Science Review* 69: 1240–54.

Bone, Hugh A., and Austin Ranney. 1963. *Politics and Voters.* New York: McGraw-Hill.

Borrelli, Stephen, Brad Lockerbie, and Richard G. Niemi. 1987. "Why the Democrat-Republican Partisanship Gap Varies from Poll to Poll." *Public Opinion Quarterly* 51:115–19.

Bowers, Jake, and Michael J. Ensley. 2003. "Issues in Analyzing Data from the Dual-Mode 2000 American National Election Study." ANES Technical Report Series, No. nes010751.

Box-Steffensmeier, Janet M., and Renée M. Smith. 1996. "The Dynamics of Aggregate Partisanship." *American Political Science Review* 90:567–80.

Boyd, Richard W. 1972. "Popular Control of Public Policy: A Normal Vote Analysis of the 1968 Election." *American Political Science Review* 66:429–49.

Brady, Henry E., and Paul M. Sniderman. 1985. "Attitude Attribution: A Group Basis for Political Reasoning." *American Political Science Review* 79:1061–78.

Brody, Richard A. 1978. "The Puzzle of Political Participation in America." In *The New American Political System,* ed. Anthony King. Washington, DC: American Enterprise Institute. 287–324.

Brody, Richard A., and Benjamin I. Page. 1972. "Comment: The Assessment of Policy Voting." *American Political Science Review* 66:450–58.

Brody, Richard A., and Lawrence Rothenberg. 1988. "The Instability of Partisanship: An Analysis of the 1980 Presidential Election." *British Journal of Political Science* 18:445–65.

Bruni, Frank. 2002. *Ambling into History: The Unlikely Odyssey of George W. Bush.* New York: HarperCollins.

Brunk, Gregory G. 1978. "The 1964 Attitude Consistency Leap Reconsidered." *Political Methodology* 5:347–60.

Budge, Ian, Ivor Crewe, and Dennis Farlie, eds. 1976. *Party Identification and Beyond: Representations of Voting and Party Competition.* New York: John Wiley.

Burden, Barry C., and David C. Kimball. 2002. *Why Americans Split Their Tickets.* Ann Arbor: University of Michigan Press.

Burden, Barry C., and Dean Lacy. 1999. "The Vote-Stealing and Turnout Effects of Ross Perot in the 1992 U.S. Presidential Election." *American Journal of Political Science* 43:233–55.

Burnham, Walter Dean. 1991. "Critical Realignment: Dead or Alive?" In *The End of Realignment?* ed. Byron Shafer. Madison: University of Wisconsin Press. 101–39.

Burns, Nancy, Kay Scholzman, and Sidney Verba. 2001. *The Private Roots of Public Action: Gender, Equality, and Political Participation.* Cambridge: Harvard University Press.

Butler, David, and Donald E. Stokes. 1969. *Political Change in Britain.* New York: St. Martin's.

Cain, Bruce E., D. Roderick Kiewiet, and Carole J. Uhlaner. 1991. "The Acquisition of Partisanship by Latinos and Asian Americans." *American Journal of Political Science* 32:390–422.

Campbell, Angus. 1964. "Voters and Elections: Past and Present." *Journal of Politics* 26:745–57.

Campbell, Angus. 1966. "A Classification of the Presidential Elections." In *Elections and the Political Order,* ed. Angus Campbell, Philip E. Converse, Warren E. Miller, and Donald E. Stokes. New York: Wiley. 63–77.

Campbell, Angus, Philip E. Converse, Warren E. Miller, and Donald E. Stokes. 1960. *The American Voter.* New York: John Wiley and Sons.

Campbell, Angus, Gerald Gurin, and Warren E. Miller. 1954. *The Voter Decides.* Evanston, IL: Row, Peterson.

Campbell, Angus, and Robert L. Kahn. 1952. *The People Elect a President.* Ann Arbor: Institute of Social Research, Survey Research Center, University of Michigan.

Campbell, James E., and James Garand, eds. 2000. *Before the Vote: Forecasting American National Elections.* Thousand Oaks, CA: Sage.

Campbell, James E. 2005. "Introduction—Assessments of the 2004 Presidential Vote Forecasts." *PS: Political Science and Politics.* 38:23–24.

Cantril, Albert H., and Susan Davis Cantril. 1999. *Reading Mixed Signals: Ambivalence in American Public Opinion about Government.* Washington, DC: Woodrow Wilson Center Press.

Carmines, Edward G., and Geoffrey C. Layman. 1997. "Issue Evolution in Postwar American Politics: Old Certainties and Fresh Tensions." In *Present Discontents*, ed. Byron Shafer. Chatham, NJ: Chatham House. 89–134.

Carmines, Edward G., and J. Merrill Shanks. 2006. "The Continuing Impact of New Deal Issues on Contemporary Voting Behavior." Paper presented at the Annual Meeting of the American Political Science Association, Philadelphia.

Carmines, Edward G., and James A. Stimson. 1980. "The Two Faces of Issue Voting." *American Political Science Review* 74:78–91.

Carmines, Edward G., and James A. Stimson. 1989. *Issue Evolution: Race and the Transformation of American Politics.* Princeton, NJ: Princeton University Press.

Carroll, Susan J. 2005. "Security Moms and Presidential Politics: Women Voters in the 2004 Election." Paper presented at the Annual Meeting of the American Political Science Association, Washington, DC.

Cassel, Carol A. 1984. "Issues in Measurement: The 'Levels of Conceptualization' Index of Ideological Sophistication." *American Journal of Political Science* 28:418–29.

Chaney, Carole Kennedy, R. Michael Alvarez, and Jonathan Nagler. 1998. "Explaining the Gender Gap in U.S. Presidential Elections, 1980–1992." *Political Research Quarterly* 51:311–39.

Chang, Tracy F. 2001. "The Labour Vote in US National Elections, 1948–2000." *Political Quarterly* 72:375–85.

Citrin, Jack, David O. Sears, Christopher Muste, and Cara Wong. 2001. "Multiculturalism in American Public Opinion." *British Journal of Political Science* 31:247–75.

Clark, Paul, and Marick F. Masters. 2001. "Competing Interest Groups and Union Members' Voting." *Social Science Quarterly* 82:105–17.

Clarke, Harold, and Marianne Stewart. 1994. "Prospections, Retrospections, and Rationality: The 'Bankers' Model of Presidential Approval." *American Journal of Political Science* 38:104–23.

Clausen, Aage R. 1968. "Response Validity: Vote Report." *Public Opinion Quarterly* 32:588–606.

Conover, Pamela Johnston, and Stanley Feldman. 1982. "Projection and Perception of Candidates' Issue Positions." *Western Political Quarterly* 35:228–44.

Conover, Pamela Johnston, and Stanley Feldman. 1984. "How People Organize the Political World: A Schematic Model." *American Journal of Political Science* 28:95–126.

Conover, Pamela Johnston, and Stanley Feldman. 1989. "Candidate Perception in an Ambiguous World." *American Journal of Political Science* 33:912–40.

Conover, Pamela Johnston, and Stanley Feldman. 1991. "Where is the Schema? Critiques." *American Political Science Review* 85:1364–69.

Converse, Philip E. 1964. "The Nature of Belief Systems in Mass Publics." In *Ideology and Discontent*, ed. David E. Apter. New York: Free Press. 212–42.

Converse, Philip E. 1966a. "The Concept of the 'Normal Vote.'" In Angus Campbell, Philip E. Converse, Warren E. Miller, and Donald E. Stokes, *Elections and the Political Order*. New York: Wiley. 9–39.

Converse, Philip E. 1966b. "On the Possibility of a Major Political Realignment in the South." In Angus Campbell, Philip E. Converse, Warren E. Miller, and Donald E. Stokes, *Elections and the Political Order*. New York: Wiley. 212–42.

Converse, Philip E. 1969. "Of Time and Partisan Stability." *Comparative Political Studies* 2:139–71.

Converse, Philip E. 1970. "Attitudes and Nonattitudes: Continuation of a Dialogue." In *The Quantitative Analysis of Social Problems*, ed. Edward R. Tufte. Reading, MA: Addison-Wesley.

Converse, Philip E. 1974. "Nonattitudes and American Public Opinion: The Status of Nonattitudes." *American Political Science Review* 68:650–60.

Converse, Philip E. 1975. "Public Opinion and Voting Behavior." In *Handbook of Political Science*, ed. Fred I. Greenstein and Nelson W. Polsby. Reading, MA: Addison-Wesley. 75–169.

Converse, Philip E. 1976. *The Dynamics of Party Support*. Beverly Hills, CA: Sage.

Converse, Philip E. 1980. "Comment: Rejoinder to Judd and Milburn." *American Sociological Review* 45:644–46.

Converse, Philip E. 2006. "Researching Electoral Politics." *American Political Science Review* 100:605–12.

Converse, Philip E., Angus Campbell, Warren E. Miller, and Donald E. Stokes. 1961. "Stability and Change in 1960: A Reinstating Election." *American Political Science Review* 55:269–80.

Converse, Philip E., Aage R. Clausen, and Warren E. Miller. 1965. "Electoral Myth and Reality: The 1964 Election." *American Political Science Review* 59:321–36.

Converse, Philip E., and Gregory B. Markus. 1979. "Plus ça Change . . . : The New CPS Election Study Panel." *American Political Science Review* 73:2–49.

Converse, Philip E., Warren E. Miller, Jerrold G. Rusk, and Arthur C. Wolfe. 1969. "Continuity and Change in American Politics: Parties and Issues in the 1968 Election." *American Political Science Review* 63:1083–1105.

Converse, Philip E., and Roy Pierce. 1986. *Political Representation in France*. Cambridge: Harvard University Press.

Cook, Elizabeth Adell. 1993. "Feminist Consciousness and Candidate Preference among American Women, 1972–1988." *Political Behavior* 15:227–46.

Coombs, Clyde H. 1964. *A Theory of Data*. New York: John Wiley.

Coveyou, Michael R., and James Piereson. 1977. "Ideological Perceptions and Political Judgment: Some Problems of Concept and Measurement." *Political Methodology* 4:77–102.

Craig, Stephen C., Michael D. Martinez, and James G. Kane. 2005. "Ambivalence and Response Instability: A Panel Study." In *Ambivalence and the Structure of Political Opinion*, ed. Stephen C. Craig and Michael D. Martinez. New York: Palgrave Macmillan. 55–71.

Dahl, Robert A. 1956. *A Preface to Democratic Theory*. Chicago: University of Chicago Press.

Dalton, Russell J. 2007. "Partisan Mobilization, Cognitive Mobilization and the Changing American Electorate." *Electoral Studies* 26:274–86.

Davis, Darren W. 1997. "Nonrandom Measurement Error and Race of Interviewer Effects among African Americans." *Public Opinion Quarterly* 61: 183–207.

Davis, Darren W., Kathleen M. Dowley, and Brian D. Silver. 1999. "Postmaterialism in World Societies: Is It Really a Value Dimension?" *American Journal of Political Science* 43:935–62.

Davis, Otto A., Melvin J. Hinich, and Peter C. Ordeshook. 1970. "An Expository Development of a Mathematical Model of the Electoral Process." *American Political Science Review* 64:426–48.

Dawes, Robyn M. 1972. *Fundamentals of Attitude Measurement*. New York: Wiley.

Day, Christine L. 1990. *What Older Americans Think: Interest Groups and Aging Policy*. Princeton: Princeton University Press.

Delli Carpini, Michael X., and Scott Keeter. 1996. *What Americans Know about Politics and Why It Matters*. New Haven: Yale University Press.

Devine, Donald J. 1972. *The Political Culture of the United States*. Boston: Little, Brown.

Diamond, Edwin, and Stephen Bates. 1988. *The Spot: The Rise of Political Advertising on Television*. Rev. ed. Cambridge: MIT Press.

Dolan, Kathleen. 2005. "Do Women Candidates Exert an Impact on Voter Turnout?" Paper presented at the Annual Meeting of the American Political Science Association, Washington, DC.

Downs, Anthony. 1957. *An Economic Theory of Democracy*. New York: Harper and Row.

Downs, Anthony. 1972. "Up and Down with Ecology—the Issue Attention Cycle." *Public Interest* 28:38–50.

Druckman, James N. 2001. "On the Limits of Framing Effects: Who Can Frame?" *Journal of Politics* 63:1041–66.

Duch, Raymond M., Harvey D. Palmer, and Christopher J. Anderson. 2000. "Heterogeneity in Perceptions of National Economic Conditions." *American Journal of Political Science* 44:635–49.

Dunn-Rankin, Peter, Gerald A. Knezek, Susan R. Wallace, and Shugiang Zhang. 2004. *Scaling Methods*. 2nd ed. Mahwah, NJ: Lawrence Erlbaum.

Duverger, Maurice. 1963. *Political Parties*. New York: John Wiley and Sons.

Eagly, Alice H., and Shelly Chaiken. 1993. *The Psychology of Attitudes*. Fort Worth, TX: Harcourt Brace Jovanovich.

Edelman, Murray. 1964. *The Symbolic Uses of Politics*. Urbana: University of Illinois Press.

Elder, Charles D., and Roger W. Cobb. 1983. *The Political Uses of Symbols*. New York: Longman.

Enelow, James M., and Melvin J. Hinich. 1984. *The Spatial Theory of Voting: An Introduction*. Cambridge: Cambridge University Press.

Enelow, James, and Melvin Hinich, eds. 1990. *Advances in the Spatial Theory of Voting*. Cambridge: Cambridge University Press.

Erikson, Robert S. 1989. "Economic Conditions and the Presidential Vote." *American Political Science Review* 83:568–73.

Erikson, Robert S., Thomas D. Lancaster, and David W. Romero. 1989. "Group Components of the Presidential Vote, 1952–1984." *Journal of Politics* 51:337–46.

Erikson, Robert S., Michael B. MacKuen, and James A. Stimson. 2002. *The Macro Polity*. Cambridge: Cambridge University Press.

Erikson, Robert S., and Kent L. Tedin. 1981. "The 1928–1936 Partisan Realignment: The Case for the Conversion Hypothesis." *American Political Science Review* 75:951–62.

Evans, Geoffrey, and Robert Andersen. 2006. "The Political Conditioning of Economic Perceptions." *Journal of Politics* 68:194–207.

Fair, Ray. 1978. "The Effect of Economic Events on Votes for President." *Review of Economics and Statistics* 60:159–73.

Feldman, Stanley. 1988. "Structure and Consistency in Public Opinion: The Role of Core Beliefs and Values." *American Journal of Political Science* 32:416–40.

Feldman, Stanley. 2003. "Values, Ideology, and the Structure of Political Attitudes." In *Oxford Handbook of Political Psychology*, ed. David O. Sears, Leonie Huddy, and Robert Jervis. New York: Oxford University Press. 477–508.

Feldman, Stanley, and Pamela Johnston Conover. 1983. "Candidates, Issues, and Voters: The Role of Inference in Political Perception." *Journal of Politics* 45:810–39.

Feldman, Stanley, and Marco Steenbergen. 2001a. "The Humanitarian Foundation of Public Support for Social Welfare." *American Journal of Political Science* 45:658–77.

Feldman, Stanley, and Marco Steenbergen. 2001b. "Social Welfare Attitudes and the Humanitarian Sensibility." In *Citizens and Politics: Perspectives from Political Psychology*, ed. James H. Kuklinski. Cambridge: Cambridge University Press. 366–400.

Feldman, Stanley, and John Zaller. 1992. "The Political Culture of Ambivalence: Ideological Responses to the Welfare State." *American Journal of Political Science* 36:268–307.

Ferejohn, John A., and Morris P. Fiorina. 1974. "The Paradox of Not Voting: A Decision Theoretic Analysis." *American Political Science Review* 68:525–36.

Field, John Osgood, and Ronald E. Anderson. 1969. "Ideology in the Public's Conceptualization of the 1964 Election." *Public Opinion Quarterly* 33: 380–98.

Finkel, Steven E. 1985. "Reciprocal Effects of Participation and Political Efficacy: A Panel Analysis." *American Journal of Political Science* 29:891–913.

Finkel, Steven E. 1989. "Effects of the 1980 and 1984 Campaigns on Mass Ideological Orientations: Testing the Salience Hypothesis." *Western Political Quarterly* 42:325–46.

Finkel, Steven E., and Paul Freedman. 2004. "The Half-Hearted Rise: Voter Turnout in the 2000 Election." In *Models of Voting in Presidential Elections: The 2000 Election,* ed. Herbert F. Weisberg and Clyde Wilcox. Stanford, CA: Stanford University Press. 180–205.

Finkel, Steven E., and John G. Geer. 1998. "A Spot-Check: Casting Doubt on the Demobilizing Effect of Attack Advertising." *American Journal of Political Science* 42:573–95.

Fiorina, Morris P. 1981. *Retrospective Voting in American National Elections.* New Haven: Yale University Press.

Fiorina, Morris P. 1992. *Divided Government.* New York: Macmillan.

Fiorina, Morris P., Samuel J. Abrams, and Jeremy C. Pope. 2006. *Culture War? The Myth of a Polarized America.* 2nd ed. New York: Pearson Longman.

Fishbein, Martin. 1963. "An Investigation of the Relationships between Beliefs about an Object and the Attitude toward That Object." *Human Relations* 16:233–40.

Fishbein, Martin, and Icek Ajzen. 1975. *Belief, Attitude, Intention, and Behavior: An Introduction to Theory and Research.* Reading, MA: Addison-Wesley.

Fishbein, Martin, and Fred S. Coombs. 1974. "Basis for Decision: An Attitudinal Analysis of Voting Behavior." *Journal of Applied Social Psychology* 4:95–124.

Fiske, Susan T. 1986. "Schema-Based versus Piecemeal Politics: A Patchwork Quilt, but Not a Blanket, of Evidence." In *Political Cognition,* ed. Richard R. Lau and David O. Sears. Hillsdale, NJ: Lawrence Erlbaum. 41–53.

Fiske, Susan T., and Donald R. Kinder. 1981. "Involvement, Expertise, and Schema Use: Evidence from Political Cognition." In *Personality, Cognition, and Social Interaction,* ed. Nancy Cantor and John F. Kihlstrom. Hillsdale, NJ: Lawrence Erlbaum. 171–92.

Fiske, Susan T., and Shelley E. Taylor. 1991. *Social Cognition.* 2nd ed. New York: McGraw-Hill.

Flanigan, William H. 1972. *Political Behavior of the American Electorate.* 2nd ed. Boston: Allyn and Bacon.

Flanigan, William H., and Nancy H. Zingale. 2006. *Political Behavior of the American Electorate.* Washington, DC: Congressional Quarterly Press.

Fleishman, John A. 1986. "Types of Political Attitude Structure: Results of a Cluster Analysis." *Public Opinion Quarterly* 50:371–86.

Frank, Thomas. 2004. *What's the Matter with Kansas? How Conservatives Won the Heart of America.* New York: Henry Holt.

Franklin, Charles H., and John E. Jackson. 1983. "The Dynamics of Party Identification." *American Political Science Review* 77:957–73.

Franklin, Mark N. 1996. "Electoral Participation." In *Comparing Democracies: Elections and Voting in Global Perspective,* ed. Lawrence LeDuc, Richard G. Niemi, and Pippa Norris. Thousand Oaks, CA: Sage. 216–35.

Free, Lloyd A., and Hadley Cantril. 1967. *The Political Beliefs of Americans.* New Brunswick, NJ: Rutgers University Press.

Friedman, Jeffrey, ed. 2006. "Symposium: Is Democratic Competence Possible?" *Critical Review* 18.

Funk, Carolyn L. 1996. "Understanding Trait Inferences in Candidate Images." In *Research in Micropolitics,* ed. Michael X. Delli Carpini, Lonie Huddy, and Robert Shapiro. Vol. 5. Greenwich, CT: JAI Press. 97–123.

Gainous, Jason, and Michael D. Martinez. 2005. "What Happens When We Simultaneously Want Opposite Things? Ambivalence about Social Welfare." In *Ambivalence, Politics, and Public Policy,* ed. Stephen C. Craig and Michael D. Martinez. New York: Palgrave Macmillan. 47–62.

Gallup Organization. Poll releases, August 30, 2005.

Gamson, William A. 1992. *Talking Politics.* Cambridge: Cambridge University Press.

Gamson, William A., and Andre Modigliani. 1989. "Media Discourse and Public Opinion in Nuclear Power: A Constructionist Approach." *American Journal of Sociology* 95:1–37.

Geer, John G. 1992. "New Deal Issues and the American Electorate, 1952–1988." *Political Behavior* 14:45–65.

Gerber, Alan, and Donald P. Green. 2000. "The Effects of Canvassing, Telephone Calls, and Direct Mail on Voter Turnout: A Field Experiment." *American Political Science Review* 94:653–63.

Gerber, Alan, and Donald P. Green. 2005. "Correction to Gerber and Green (2000), Replication of Disputed Findings and Reply to Imai (2005)." *American Political Science Review* 99:301–13.

Gilens, Martin. 1999. *Why Americans Hate Welfare: Race, Media, and the Politics of Antipoverty Policy.* Chicago: University of Chicago Press.

Gilens, Martin. 2001. "Political Ignorance and Collective Policy Preferences." *American Political Science Review* 95:379–96.

Gilljam, Mikael. 1997. "The Directional Theory under the Magnifying Glass: A Reappraisal." *Journal of Theoretical Politics* 9:5–12.

Glasgow, Garrett. 1999. "Issue Publics in American Politics." Ph.D. diss., California Institute of Technology.

Goldberg, Arthur S. 1966. "Discerning a Causal Pattern among Data on Voting Behavior." *American Political Science Review* 60:913–22.

Gomez, Brad T., and J. Matthew Wilson. 2001. "Political Sophistication and Economic Voting in the American Electorate: A Theory of Heterogeneous Attribution." *American Journal of Political Science* 45:899–914.

Gopoian, J. David. 1982. "Issue Preferences and Candidate Choice in Presidential Primaries." *American Journal of Political Science* 26:523–46.

Goren, Paul. 1997. "Political Expertise and Issue Voting in Presidential Elections." *Political Research Quarterly* 50:387–412.

Goren, Paul. 2001. "Core Principles and Policy Reasoning in Mass Publics: A Test of Two Theories." *British Journal of Political Science* 31:159–77.

Goren, Paul. 2004. "Policy Sophistication and Political Reasoning: A Reconsideration." *American Journal of Political Science* 48:462–78.

Goren, Paul. 2005. "Party Identification and Core Political Values." *American Journal of Political Science* 49:881–96.

Granberg, Donald, and Edward Brent. 1974. "Dove-Hawk Placement in the 1968 Election: Application of Social Judgment and Balance Theories." *Journal of Personality and Social Psychology* 29:687–95.

Granberg, Donald, and Thad A. Brown. 1992. "The Perception of Ideological Distance." *Western Political Quarterly* 45:727–50.

Grant, J. Tobin, and Thomas J. Rudolph. 2003. "Value Conflict, Group Affect, and the Issue of Campaign Finance." *American Journal of Political Science* 47:453–69.

Gray, Mark M., Paul M. Peri, and Mary E. Bendyna. 2005. "Camelot Only Comes but Once? John F. Kerry and the Catholic Vote." Paper presented at the Annual Meeting of the American Political Science Association, Washington, DC.

Green, Donald Philip, and Bradley Palmquist. 1990. "Of Artifacts and Partisan Instability." *American Journal of Political Science* 34:872–902.

Green, Donald Philip, and Bradley Palmquist. 1994. "How Stable Is Party Identification?" *Political Behavior* 16:437–66.

Green, Donald, Bradley Palmquist, and Eric Schickler. 2002. *Partisan Hearts and Minds: Political Parties and the Social Identities of Voters.* New Haven: Yale University Press.

Green, Donald Philip, and Ian Shapiro. 1994. *Pathologies of Rational Choice Theory: A Critique of Applications in Political Science.* New Haven: Yale University Press.

Greene, Steven. 1999. "Understanding Party Identification: A Social Identity Approach." *Political Psychology* 20:393–403.

Groseclose, Tim. 2001. "A Model of Candidate Location When One Candidate Has a Valence Advantage." *American Journal of Political Science* 45:862–86.

Grossback, Lawrence J., David A. M. Peterson, and James A. Stimson. 2006. *Mandate Politics.* New York: Cambridge University Press.

Gunther, Richard, José Ramón Montero, and Hans-Jürgen Puhle, eds. 2007. *Democracy, Intermediation, and Voting on Four Continents.* Oxford: Oxford University Press.

Guth, James L., Lyman A. Kellstedt, Corwin E. Smidt, and John C. Green. 2005. "Religious Mobilization in the 2004 Presidential Election." Paper presented at the Annual Meeting of the American Political Science Association, Washington, DC.

Guttman, Louis. 1944. "A Basis for Scaling Qualitative Data." *American Sociological Review* 9:139–50.

Hacker, Kenneth L., ed. 2004. *Presidential Candidate Images.* Lanham, MD: Rowman and Littlefield.

Hagner, Paul R., and John C. Pierce. 1982. "Correlative Characteristics of the Levels of Conceptualization in the American Public: 1956–1976." *Journal of Politics* 44:779–807.

Hagner, Paul R., and John C. Pierce. 1991. "Liberal Is a Four Letter Word: Campaign Rhetoric and the Measurement of Political Conceptualization." Paper presented at the Annual Meeting of the Midwest Political Science Association.

Hagner, Paul R., John C. Pierce, and Kathleen Knight. 1989. "Content Coding of Level of Political Conceptualization, 1956–1988 (United States)." ICPSR 8151, 4th ed. Inter-university Consortium for Political and Social Research, Ann Arbor, MI.

Hamill, Ruth, and Milton Lodge. 1986. "Cognitive Consequences of Political Sophistication." In *Political Cognition,* ed. Richard R. Lau and David O. Sears. Hillsdale, NJ: Lawrence Erlbaum. 69–93.

Hamill, Ruth, Milton Lodge, and Frederick Blake. 1985. "The Breadth, Depth, and Utility of Class, Partisan, and Ideological Schemata." *American Journal of Political Science* 29:850–70.

Hartwig, Frederick, William R. Jenkins, and Earl M. Temchin. 1980. "Variability in Electoral Behavior: The 1960, 1968, and 1976 Elections." *American Journal of Political Science* 24:553–58.

Hayes, Danny. 2005. "Candidate Qualities through a Partisan Lens: A Theory of Trait Ownership." *American Journal of Political Science* 49:908–23.

Hershey, Marjorie Randon. 2005. *Party Politics in America.* 11th ed. New York: Pearson Longman.

Herstein, John A. 1981. "Keeping the Voter's Limits in Mind: A Cognitive Process Analysis of Decision Making in Voting." *Journal of Personality and Social Psychology* 40:843–61.

Hetherington, Marc J. 2001. "Resurgent Mass Partisanship: The Role of Elite Polarization." *American Political Science Review* 95:619–32.

Hibbs, Douglas A. 1982. "President Reagan's Mandate from the 1980s Elections: A Shift to the Right?" *American Politics Quarterly* 10:387–420.

Highton, Benjamin, and Raymond E. Wolfinger. 2001. "The First Seven Years of the Political Life Cycle." *American Journal of Political Science* 45:202–9.

Hill, Jennifer L., and Hanspeter Kriesi. 2001. "An Extension and Test of Converse's 'Black-and-White' Model of Response Stability." *American Political Science Review* 95:397–413.

Hillygus, D. Sunshine. 2005. "The Missing Link: Exploring the Relationship between Higher Education and Political Behavior." *Political Behavior* 27:25–47.

Hillygus, D. Sunshine, and Simon Jackman. 2003. "Voter Decision Making in Election 2000." *American Journal of Political Science* 47:583–96.

Hinckley, Barbara, Richard Hofstetter, and John Kessel. 1974. "Information and the Vote: A Comparative Electoral Study." *American Politics Quarterly* 2:131–58.

Hinich, Melvin J., and Michael C. Munger. 1994. *Ideology and the Theory of Political Choice*. Ann Arbor: University of Michigan Press.

Hotelling, Harold. 1929. "Stability in Competition." *Economic Journal* 39:41–57.

Hout, Michael, Clem Brooks, and Jeff Manza. 1995. "The Democratic Class Struggle in the United States, 1948–1992." *American Sociological Review* 60: 805–28.

Howell, Susan E., and Christine L. Day. 2000. "Complexities of the Gender Gap." *Journal of Politics* 62:858–74.

Hunter, James Davison. 1991. *Culture Wars: The Struggle to Define America*. New York: Basic Books.

Hunter, James Davison. 1995. *Before the Shooting Begins: Searching for Democracy in America's Culture War*. New York: Free Press.

Hurley, Patricia A. 1991. "Partisan Representation, Realignment, and the Senate in the 1980s." *Journal of Politics* 53:3–33.

Hurwitz, Jon, and Mark Peffley. 1987. "How Are Foreign Policy Attitudes Structured? A Hierarchical Model." *American Political Science Review* 81:1099–1120.

Imai, Kosuke. 2005. "Do Get-Out-the-Vote Calls Reduce Turnout? The Importance of Statistical Methods for Field Experiments." *American Political Science Review* 99:283–300.

Iyengar, Shanto. 1991. *Is Anyone Responsible? How Television Frames Political Issues*. Chicago: University of Chicago Press.

Iyengar, Shanto, and Donald R. Kinder. 1987. *News That Matters: Television and American Opinion*. Chicago: University of Chicago Press.

Jackman, Simon. 2004. "Bayesian Analysis for Political Research." *Annual Review of Political Science* 7:483–505.

Jackson, John E. 1975. "Issues, Party Choice, and Presidential Votes." *American Journal of Political Science* 19:161–85.

Jacobson, Gary C. 1990. *The Electoral Origins of Divided Government*. Boulder: Westview.

Jacoby, William G. 1986. "Levels of Conceptualization and Reliance on the Liberal-Conservative Continuum." *Journal of Politics* 48:423–32.

Jacoby, William G. 1988a. "The Impact of Party Identification on Issue Attitudes." *American Journal of Political Science* 32:643–61.

Jacoby, William G. 1988b. "The Sources of Liberal-Conservative Thinking: Education and Conceptualization." *Political Behavior* 10:316–32.

Jacoby, William G. 1990. "Variability in Issue Alternatives and American Public Opinion." *Journal of Politics* 52:579–606.

Jacoby, William G. 1991a. *Data Theory and Dimensional Analysis.* Newbury Park, CA: Sage.

Jacoby, William G. 1991b. "Ideological Identification and Issue Attitudes." *American Journal of Political Science* 35:178–205.

Jacoby, William G. 1994. "Public Attitudes toward Government Spending." *American Journal of Political Science* 38:336–61.

Jacoby, William G. 1995. "The Structure of Ideological Thinking in the American Electorate." *American Journal of Political Science* 39:314–35.

Jacoby, William G. 1996. "Testing the Effects of Paired Issue Statements on the Seven-Point Issue Scales." *Political Analysis.* Vol. 5, *1993–1994.* Ann Arbor: University of Michigan Press.

Jacoby, William G. 2000. "Issue Framing and Public Opinion on Government Spending." *American Journal of Political Science* 44:750–67.

Jacoby, William G. 2002. "Liberal-Conservative Thinking in the American Electorate." In *Research in Micropolitics: Political Decision Making, Participation, and Deliberation,* ed. Michael X. Delli Carpini, Leonie Huddy, and Robert Y. Shapiro. Vol. 6. Greenwich, CT: JAI Press. 97–147.

Jacoby, William G. 2004. "Ideology in the 2000 Election: A Study in Ambivalence." In *Models of Voting in Presidential Elections: The 2000 Election,* ed. Herbert F. Weisberg and Clyde Wilcox. Stanford, CA: Stanford University Press. 103–19.

Jacoby, William G. 2005. "Ideology in the 2004 Election." Paper presented at the Annual Meeting of the American Political Science Association, Washington, DC.

Jacoby, William G. 2006. "Value Choices and American Public Opinion." 2006. *American Journal of Political Science* 50:706–23.

Jacoby, William G., Jeremy Duff, and Kurt Pyle. 2008. "Levels of Conceptualization Codes, 1992–2004." Center for Political Studies, American National Election Studies, Ann Arbor, MI. Forthcoming.

Jacoby, William G., and Robert Moore. 2006. "Levels of Conceptualization Codes, 2000." Center for Political Studies, American National Election Studies, Ann Arbor, MI.

Jamieson, Kathleen Hall. 1984. *Packaging the Presidency: A History and Criticism of Presidential Campaign Advertisement.* New York: Oxford University Press.

Jamieson, Kathleen Hall, and Paul Waldman. 2003. *The Press Effect: Politicians,*

Journalists, and the Stories That Shape the Political World. New York: Oxford University Press.

Jennings, M. Kent. 1992. "Ideology among Mass Publics and Political Elites." *Public Opinion Quarterly* 56:419–41.

Jennings, M. Kent, and Gregory B. Markus. 1984. "Partisan Orientations over the Long Haul: Results from the Three-Wave Political Socialization Study." *American Political Science Review* 78:1000–1018.

Jennings, M. Kent, and Richard Niemi. 1974. *The Political Character of Adolescence: The Influence of Families and Schools.* Princeton: Princeton University Press.

Jennings, M. Kent, and Richard Niemi, 1981. *Generations and Politics.* Princeton: Princeton University Press.

Jennings, M. Kent, and Laura Stoker. 2005. "Politics across Generations: Family Transmission Reexamined." Working paper.

Jerit, Jennifer, Jason Barabas, and Toby Bolsen. 2006. "Citizens, Knowledge, and the Information Environment." *American Journal of Political Science* 50: 266–82.

Johnson, Kirk. 2004. "Hispanic Voters Declare Their Independence." *New York Times,* November 9.

Johnston, Richard, Michael G. Hagen, and Kathleen Hall Jamieson. 2004. *The 2000 Presidential Election and the Foundations of Party Politics.* Cambridge: Cambridge University Press.

Jones, Bryan D., and Frank R. Baumgartner. 2005. *The Politics of Attention: How Government Prioritizes Problems.* Chicago: University of Chicago Press.

Judd, Charles M., and Michael A. Milburn. 1980. "The Structure of Attitude Systems in the General Public: Comparisons of a Structural Equation Model." *American Sociological Review* 45:627–43.

Kagay, Michael R., and Greg A. Caldeira. 1980. "A Reformed Electorate? Well, at Least a Changed Electorate, 1952–1976." In *Paths to Political Reform,* ed. William J. Crotty. Lexington, MA: Lexington Books. 3–33.

Kahn, Fridkin, and Patrick J. Kenny. 1999. "Do Negative Campaigns Mobilize or Suppress Turnout? Clarifying the Relationship between Negativity and Participation." *American Political Science Review* 93:877–89.

Kahneman, Daniel, and Amos Tversky. 1979. "Prospect Theory: An Analysis of Decision under Risk." *Econometrica* 47:263–91.

Kam, Cindy D., and Carl L. Palmer. 2006. "Education as Cause or Proxy? Unpacking the Effects of Education on Political Participation." Paper presented at the Annual Meeting of the Midwest Political Science Association, Chicago.

Katz, Daniel. 1960. "The Functional Approach to the Study of Attitudes." *Public Opinion Quarterly* 24:163–204.

Katz, Elihu, ed. 2001. *Election Studies: What's Their Use?* Boulder: Westview.

Kaufmann, Karen M., and John R. Petrocik. 1999. "The Changing Politics of American Men: Understanding the Sources of the Gender Gap." *American Journal of Political Science* 43:864–997.

Keith, Bruce E., David B. Magleby, Candice J. Nelson, Elizabeth Orr, Mark C. Westlye, and Raymond E. Wolfinger. 1992. *The Myth of the Independent Voter*. Berkeley and Los Angeles: University of California Press.

Kelley, Stanley, Jr. 1983. *Interpreting Elections*. Princeton: Princeton University Press.

Kelley, Stanley, Jr., and Thad W. Mirer. 1974. "The Simple Act of Voting." *American Political Science Review* 68:572–91.

Kellstedt, Lyman A., John C. Green, James L. Guth, and Corwin E. Smidt. 1994. "Religious Voting Blocs in the 1992 Election: The Year of the Evangelical?" *Sociology of Religion* 55:307–26.

Kernell, Samuel. 1977. "Presidential Popularity and Negative Voting." *American Political Science Review* 71:44–66.

Kessel, John H. 1972. "Comment: The Issues in Issue Voting." *American Political Science Review* 66:459–65.

Kessel, John H. 2004. "Views of the Voters." In *Models of Voting in Presidential Elections,* ed. Herbert F. Weisberg and Clyde Wilcox. Stanford, CA: Stanford University Press. 65–84.

Kessel, John H. 2005. "Structures of Vote Choice: The Larger Context of the 2004 Election." Paper presented at the Annual Meeting of the American Political Science Association, Washington, DC.

Kessel, John H., and Herbert F. Weisberg. 1999. "Comparing Models of the Vote: The Answers Depend on the Questions." In *Reelection 1996,* ed. Herbert F. Weisberg and Janet M. Box-Steffensmeier. New York: Chatham House.

Key, V. O. 1955. "A Theory of Critical Elections." *Journal of Politics* 17:3–18.

Key, V. O. 1959. "Secular Realignment and the Party System." *Journal of Politics* 21:198–210.

Key, V. O. 1966. *The Responsible Electorate.* Cambridge: Harvard University Press.

Key, V. O. 1968. *The Responsible Electorate.* New York: Vintage Books.

Kidd, Quentin, Gus Diggs, Mehreen Farooq, and Megan Murray. 2005. "Social Conservatism in the 2004 Election: Assessing the Pull of Values Issues on African American Voters." Paper presented at the Annual Meeting of the American Political Science Association, Washington, DC.

Kiewiet, D. Roderick. 1983. *Macroeconomics and Micropolitics: The Electoral Effects of Economic Issues.* Chicago: University of Chicago Press.

Kinder, Donald R. 1982. "Enough Already about Ideology! The Many Bases of American Public Opinion." Paper presented at the Annual Meeting of the American Political Science Association, Denver.

Kinder, Donald R. 1983. "Diversity and Complexity in American Public Opinion." In *Political Science: The State of the Discipline,* ed. Ada W. Finifter. Washington, DC: American Political Science Association. 47–68.

Kinder, Donald R. 1986. "Presidential Character Revisited." In *Political Cognition*, ed. Richard R. Lau and David O. Sears. Hillside, NJ: Earlbaum. 233–55.

Kinder, Donald R. 2006. "Belief Systems Today." *Critical Review* 18:197–216.

Kinder, Donald R., Nancy Burns, and Dale B. Vieregge. 2005. "Liberalism, Race, and Exceptionalism: Understanding the American Appetite for Tax Reduction." Paper presented at the Annual Meeting of the American Political Science Association, Washington, DC.

Kinder, Donald R., and D. Roderick Kiewiet. 1981. "Sociotropic Politics: The American Case." *British Journal of Political Science* 11:129–41.

Kinder, Donald R., and Tali Mendelberg. 2000. "Individualism Reconsidered: Principles and Prejudice in Contemporary American Opinion." In *Racialized Politics: The Debate about Racism in America*, ed. David O. Sears, Jim Sidanius, and Lawrence Bobo. Chicago: University of Chicago Press. 44–74.

Kinder, Donald R., and Lynn M. Sanders. 1996. *Divided by Color: Racial Politics and Democratic Ideals.* Chicago: University of Chicago Press.

King, Gary. 1997. *A Solution to the Ecological Inference Problem.* Princeton: Princeton University Press.

Klingemann, Hans-Dieter. 1973. "Dimensions of Political Belief Systems: 'Levels of Conceptualization' as a Variable. Some Results for USA and FRG 1968/69." *Comparative Political Studies* 5:93–106.

Klingemann, Hans-Dieter. 1979. "Measuring Ideological Conceptualizations." In *Political Action: Mass Participation in Five Western Democracies*, ed. Samuel H. Barnes and Max Kaase. Beverly Hills, CA: Sage. 215–54.

Knack, Stephen, and Martha Kropf. 2003. "Voided Ballots in the 1996 Presidential Election: A County-Level Analysis." *Journal of Politics* 65:881–97.

Knight, Kathleen. 1985. "Ideology in the 1980 Election: Ideological Sophistication Does Matter." *Journal of Politics* 47:828–53.

Knight, Kathleen. 1990. "Ideology and Public Opinion." *Micropolitics* 3:59–82.

Knight, Kathleen, and Robert S. Erikson. 1997. "Ideology in the 1990s." In *Understanding Public Opinion*, ed. Barbara Norrander and Clyde Wilcox. Washington, DC: Congressional Quarterly Press. 91–110.

Knight, Kathleen, and Carolyn V. Lewis. 1996. "Does Ideology Matter?" In *Do Elections Matter?* ed. Benjamin Ginsberg and Alan Stone. 3rd ed. Armonk, NY: M. E. Sharpe.

Knuckey, Jonathan. 1999. "Classification of Presidential Elections: An Update." *Polity* 31:639–53.

Koch, Jeffrey. 1997. "Candidate Gender and Women's Psychological Engagement in Politics." *American Politics Quarterly* 25:118–33.

Korchin, Sheldon J. 1946. "Psychological Variables in the Behavior of Voters." Ph.D. diss. Harvard University.

Kramer, Gerald. 1983. "The Ecological Fallacy Revisited: Aggregate- versus

Individual-Level Findings on Economics and Elections and Sociotropic Voting." *American Political Science Review* 77:92–111.

Kristiansen, Connie M., and Alan M. Hotte. 1996. "Morality and the Self: Implications for the When and How of Value-Attitude-Behavior Relations." In *The Psychology of Values: The Ontario Symposium,* ed. Clive Seligman, James M. Olson, and Mark P. Zanna. Vol. 8. Mahwah, NJ: Lawrence Erlbaum. 77–105.

Krosnick, Jon A. 1988. "Attitude Importance and Attitude Change." *Journal of Experimental Social Psychology* 24:240–55.

Krosnick, Jon A. 1990. "Government Policy and Citizen Passion: A Study of Issue Publics in Contemporary America." *Political Behavior* 12:59–92.

Krosnick, Jon A. 1991. "The Stability of Political Preferences: Comparisons of Symbolic and Nonsymbolic Attitudes." *American Journal of Political Science* 35:547–76.

Krosnick, Jon A., and Matthew K. Berent. 1993. "The Stability of Party Identification and Policy Preference: The Impact of Survey Question Format." *American Journal of Political Science* 37:941–64.

Krosnick, Jon A., and Donald R. Kinder. 1990. "Altering the Foundations of Support for the President through Priming." *American Political Science Review* 84:497–512.

Kuklinski, James H. 2001. "Introduction: Political Values." In *Citizens and Politics: Perspectives from Political Psychology,* ed. James H. Kuklinski. Cambridge: Cambridge University Press. 355–65.

Kuklinski, James H., Michael D. Cobb, and Martin Gilens. 1997. "Racial Attitudes and the 'New South.'" *Journal of Politics* 59:323–49.

Kuklinski, James H., Robert C. Luskin, and John Bolland. 1991. "Where is the Schema? Going Beyond the 'S' Word in Political Psychology." *American Political Science Review* 85:1341–56.

Kuklinski, James H., Daniel S. Metlay, and W. D. Kay. 1982. "Citizen Knowledge and Choices on the Complex Issue of Nuclear Energy." *American Journal of Political Science* 26:615–42.

Kuklinski, James H., Paul J. Quirk, Jennifer Jerit, and Robert F. Rich. 2001. "The Political Environment and Citizen Decision Making: Information, Motivation, and Policy Tradeoffs." *American Journal of Political Science* 45:410–24.

Kuklinski, James H., Paul J. Quirk, Jennifer Jerit, David Schweider, and Robert F. Rich. 2000. "Misinformation and the Currency of Democratic Citizenship." *Journal of Politics* 62:790–816.

Lacy, Dean. 2001. "Nonseparable Preferences in Survey Responses." *American Journal of Political Science* 45:239–58.

Lacy, Dean, and Anthony Mughan. 2002. "Economic Performance, Job Insecurity, and Electoral Choice." *British Journal of Political Science* 32:513–33.

Lamb, Karl A. 1974. *As Orange Goes: Twelve California Families and the Future of American Politics.* New York: Norton.

Lane, Robert E. 1962. *Political Ideology.* New York: Free Press.

Lanoue, David J. 1988. *From Camelot to the Teflon President: Economics and Presidential Popularity.* Westport, CT: Greenwood.

Lanoue, David J. 1994. "Retrospective and Prospective Voting in Presidential-Year Elections." *Political Research Quarterly* 47:193–205.

Lau, Richard R. 1985. "Two Explanations for Negativity Effects in Political Behavior." *American Journal of Political Science* 29:119–38.

Lau, Richard R. 1986. "Political Schemata, Candidate Evaluations, and Voting Behavior." In *Political Cognition,* ed. Richard R. Lau and David O. Sears. Hillsdale, NJ: Lawrence Erlbaum. 95–126.

Lau, Richard R., Thad A. Brown, and David O. Sears. 1978. "Self-Interest and Civilians' Attitudes toward the Vietnam War." *Public Opinion Quarterly* 42: 464–83.

Lau, Richard R., and Gerald M. Pomper. 2002. "Effectiveness of Negative Campaigning in U.S. Senate Elections." *American Journal of Political Science* 46: 47–66.

Lau, Richard R., and David P. Redlawsk. 1997. "Voting Correctly." *American Political Science Review* 91:585–98.

Lau, Richard R., and David P. Redlawsk. 2001. "Advantages and Disadvantages of Cognitive Heuristics in Political Decision Making." *American Journal of Political Science* 45:951–71.

Lau, Richard R., and David P. Redlawsk. 2006. *How Voters Decide: Information Processing during an Election Campaign.* New York: Cambridge University Press.

Lau, Richard R., and David O. Sears, eds. 1986. *Political Cognition.* Hillsdale, NJ: Lawrence Erlbaum.

Lau, Richard R., David O. Sears, and Tom Jessor. 1990. "Fact or Artifact Revisited: Survey Instrument Effects and Pocketbook Politics." *Political Behavior* 12:217–42.

Lau, Richard R., Lee Sigelman, Caroline Heldman, and Paul Babbitt. 1999. "The Effects of Negative Political Advertisements" A Meta-analytic Assessment." *American Political Science Review* 93:851–75.

Lawrence, David G. 1997. *The Collapse of the Democratic Presidential Majority.* Boulder: Westview Press.

Layman, Geoffrey C. 1997. "Religion and Political Behavior in the United States: The Impact of Beliefs, Affiliations, and Commitment from 1980 to 1994." *Public Opinion Quarterly* 61:288–316.

Layman, Geoffrey C., and Edward G. Carmines. 1997. "Cultural Conflict in American Politics: Religious Traditionalism, Postmaterialism, and U.S. Political Behavior." *Journal of Politics* 59:751–77.

Layman, Geoffrey C., and Thomas M. Carsey. 2002. "Policy Polarization and 'Conflict Extension' in the American Electorate." *American Journal of Political Science* 46:786–802.

Lazarsfeld, Paul F., Bernard Berelson, and Hazel Gaudet. 1948. *The People's Choice: How the Voter Makes Up His Mind in a Presidential Campaign.* 2nd ed. New York: Columbia University Press.

Leal, David, Matt Barreto, Jongho Lee, and Rodolfo O. de la Garza. 2005. "The Latino Vote in the 2004 Election." *PS: Political Science and Politics* 38:41–50.

Leighley, Jan E. 1991. "Participation as a Stimulus of Political Conceptualization." *Journal of Politics* 53:198–211.

Leighley, Jan E., and Jonathan Nagler. 1992. "Socioeconomic Class Bias in Turnout, 1964–1988: The Voters Remain the Same." *American Political Science Review* 86:725–36.

Levitin, Teresa E., and Warren E. Miller. 1979. "Ideological Interpretations of Presidential Elections." *American Political Science Review* 73:751–71.

Lewis, Jeffrey B., and Gary King. 2000. "No Evidence on Directional vs. Proximity Voting." *Political Analysis* 8:21–33.

Lewis-Beck, Michael S. 1977. "Agrarian Political Behavior in the United States." *American Journal of Political Science* 21:543–65.

Lewis-Beck, Michael S. 1985. "Pocketbook Voting in U. S. National Election Studies: Fact or Artifact?" *American Journal of Political Science* 29:348–56.

Lewis-Beck, Michael S. 1988. *Economics and Elections: The Major Western Democracies.* Ann Arbor: University of Michigan Press.

Lewis-Beck, Michael S. 2001. "Modelers v. Pollsters: The Election Forecasts Debate." *Harvard International Journal of Press and Politics* 6 (2): 10–14.

Lewis-Beck, Michael S. 2005. "Election Forecasting: Principles and Practice." *British Journal of Politics and International Relations* 7:145–64.

Lewis-Beck, Michael S. 2006. "Does Economics Still Matter? Econometrics and the Vote." *Journal of Politics* 68:208–12.

Lewis-Beck, Michael S., and Richard Nadeau. 2004a. "Dual Governance and the Economic Vote: France and the United States." In *The French Voter: Before and after the 2002 Elections,* ed. Michael S. Lewis-Beck. Houndmills, England: Palgrave Macmillan. 136–54.

Lewis-Beck, Michael S., and Richard Nadeau. 2004b. "Split-Ticket Voting: The Effect of Cognitive Madisonianism." *Journal of Politics* 66:97–112.

Lewis-Beck, Michael S., Richard Nadeau, and Angelo Elias. 2008. "Economics, Party, and the Vote: Causality Issues and Panel Data." *American Journal of Political Science* 52:84–95.

Lewis-Beck, Michael S., and Tom W. Rice. 1984. "Forecasting Presidential Elections: A Comparison of Naïve Models." *Political Behavior* 6:9–21.

Lewis-Beck, Michael S., and Tom W. Rice. 1992. *Forecasting Elections.* Washington, DC: Congressional Quarterly Press.

Lewis-Beck, Michael S., and Mary Stegmaier. 2000. "Economic Determinants of Electoral Outcomes." *Annual Review of Political Science* 3:183–219.

Lewis-Beck, Michael S., and Mary Stegmaier. 2007. "Economic Models of the Vote." In *The Oxford Handbook of Political Behavior*, ed. Russell Dalton and Hans-Dieter Klingemann. Oxford: Oxford University Press. 518–37.

Lewis-Beck, Michael S., and Charles Tien. 2001. "Modeling the Future: Lessons from the Gore Forecast." *PS: Political Science and Politics* 34:21–23.

Lewis-Beck, Michael S., and Charles Tien. 2002. "Presidential Election Forecasting: The Bush-Gore Draw." *Research in Political Sociology* 10:173–87.

Lewis-Beck, Michael S., and Charles Tien. 2004. "Jobs and the Job of President: Forecast for 2004." *PS: Political Science and Politics* 37:821–26.

Lewis-Beck, Michael S., and Charles Tien. 2005. "The Jobs Model Forecast: Well Done in 2004." *PS: Political Science and Politics* 38:27–30.

Lippmann, Walter. 1925. *The Phantom Public*. New York: Harcourt, Brace.

Listhaug, Ola, Stuart E. Macdonald, and George Rabinowitz. 1990. "A Comparative Spatial Analysis of European Party Systems." *Scandinavian Political Studies* 13:227–54.

Listhaug, Ola, Stuart E. Macdonald, and George Rabinowitz. 1994. "Ideology and Party Support in Comparative Perspective." *European Journal of Political Research* 25:111–49.

Lockerbie, Bradley. 1992. "Prospective Economic Voting in Presidential Elections, 1956–1988." *American Politics Quarterly* 20:308–25.

Lodge, Milton, and Ruth Hamill. 1986. "A Partisan Schema for Political Information Processing." *American Political Science Review* 80:505–20.

Lodge, Milton, and Kathleen M. McGraw. 1991. "Where Is the Schema? Critiques." *American Political Science Review* 85:1357–64.

Lodge, Milton, Kathleen M. McGraw, and Patrick Stroh. 1989. "An Impression-Driven Model of Candidate Evaluation." *American Political Science Review* 83:399–419.

Lodge, Milton, Marco R. Steenbergen, and Shawn Brau. 1995. "The Responsive Voter: Campaign Information and the Dynamics of Candidate Evaluation." *American Political Science Review* 89:309–26.

Lodge, Milton, and Bernard Tursky. 1979. "Comparisons between Category and Magnitude Scaling of Political Opinion Employing SRC/CPS Items." *American Political Science Review* 73:50–66.

Lodge, Milton, and John C. Wahlke. 1982. "Politicos, Apoliticos, and the Processing of Political Information." *International Political Science Review* 3:131–50.

Luskin, Robert C. 1987. "Measuring Political Sophistication." *American Journal of Political Science* 31:856–99.

Luskin, Robert C. 1990. "Explaining Political Sophistication." *Political Behavior* 12:331–61.

Luttbeg, Norman R. 1968. "The Structure of Beliefs among Leaders and the Public." *Public Opinion Quarterly* 32:398–410.

Luttbeg, Norman R., and Michael M. Gant. 1985. "The Failure of Liberal-Conservative Ideology as a Cognitive Structure." *Public Opinion Quarterly* 49: 80–93.

Lyons, William, and John M. Scheb II. 1992. "Ideology and Candidate Evaluations in the 1984 and 1988 Presidential Elections." *Journal of Politics* 54:573–84.

Macdonald, Stuart E., Ola Listhaug, and George Rabinowitz. 1991. "Issues and Party Support in Multiparty Systems." *American Political Science Review* 85:1107–31.

Macdonald, Stuart E., and George B. Rabinowitz. 1993. "Ideology and Candidate Evaluation." *Public Choice* 76:59–78.

Macdonald, Stuart E., and George Rabinowitz. 1997. "On 'Correcting' for Rationalization." *Journal of Theoretical Politics* 9:49–55.

Macdonald, Stuart E., George Rabinowitz, and Holly Brasher. 2003. "Policy Issues and Electoral Democracy." In *Electoral Democracy,* ed. Michael B. MacKuen and George Rabinowitz. Ann Arbor: University of Michigan Press. 172–99.

Macdonald, Stuart E., George Rabinowitz, and Ola Listhaug. 1997. "Individual Perception and Models of Issue Voting." *Journal of Theoretical Politics* 9:13–21.

Macdonald, Stuart E., George Rabinowitz, and Ola Listhaug. 1998. "On Attempting to Rehabilitate the Proximity Model: Sometimes the Patient Just Can't Be Helped." *Journal of Politics* 60:653–90.

Macdonald, Stuart E., George Rabinowitz, and Ola Listhaug. 2001. "Sophistry versus Science: On Further Efforts to Rehabilitate the Proximity Model." *Journal of Politics* 63:482–500.

MacKuen, Michael B., Robert S. Erikson, and James A. Stimson. 1989. "Macropartisanship." *American Political Science Review* 83:1125–42.

Maggiotto, Michael A., and James E. Piereson. 1978. "Issue Publics and Voter Choice." *American Politics Quarterly* 6:407–29.

Maio, Gregory R., and James M. Olson. 1998. "Values as Truisms: Evidence and Implications." *Journal of Personality and Social Psychology* 74:294–311.

Mansbridge, Jane. 1999. "Should Blacks Represent Blacks and Women Represent Women? A Contingent 'Yes.'" *Journal of Politics* 61:628–57.

Manza, Jeff, and Clem Brooks. 1999. *Social Cleavages and Political Change.* Oxford: Oxford University Press.

Maranell, Gary. 1974. *Scaling: A Sourcebook for Behavioral Scientists.* Chicago: Aldine.

Marcus, George, David Tabb, and John L. Sullivan. 1974. "The Application of Individual Differences Scaling to the Measurement of Political Ideologies." *American Journal of Political Science* 18:405–20.

Margolis, Michael. 1977. "From Confusion to Confusion: Issues and the American Voter 1956–1972." *American Political Science Review* 71:31–43.

Markus, Gregory B. 1988. "The Impact of Personal and National Economic Conditions on the Presidential Vote: A Pooled Cross-Sectional Analysis." *American Journal of Political Science* 32:137–54.

Markus, Gregory B. 1992. "The Impact of Personal and National Economic Conditions on Presidential Voting, 1956–1988." *American Journal of Political Science* 36:829–34.

Markus, Gregory B. 2001. "American Individualism Reconsidered." In *Citizens and Politics: Perspectives from Political Psychology*, ed. James H. Kuklinski. Cambridge: Cambridge University Press. 401–32.

Markus, Gregory B., and Philip E. Converse. 1979. "A Dynamic Simultaneous Equation Model of Electoral Choice." *American Political Science Review* 73:1055–70.

Martin, Gary. 2002. "Latino Vote Bloc Hard to Pin Down." *San Antonio Express-News*, October 2, 18A.

Martinez, Michael D. 1988. "Political Involvement and the Projection Process." *Political Behavior* 10:151–67.

Martinez, Michael D., Stephen C. Craig, and James G. Kane. 2005. "Pros and Cons: Ambivalence and Public Opinion." In *Ambivalence and the Structure of Political Opinion*, ed. Stephen C. Craig and Michael D. Martinez. New York: Palgrave Macmillan. 1–13.

Mason, Julie. 2002. "Hispanics Not Solid for GOP." *Houston Chronicle*, October 4, A1.

Mattei, Franco, and Herbert F. Weisberg. 1994. "Presidential Succession Effects in Voting." *British Journal of Political Science* 88:269–90.

Mayhew, David R. 2002. *Electoral Realignments: A Critique of an American Genre*. New Haven: Yale University Press.

McCann, James A. 1997. "Electoral Choices and Core Value Change: The 1992 Presidential Campaign." *American Journal of Political Science* 41:564–83.

McCarty, John A., and L. J. Shrum. 2000. "Measurement of Personal Values in Research." *Public Opinion Quarterly* 64:271–98.

McCarty, Nolan, Keith T. Poole, and Howard Rosenthal. 2006. *Polarized America: The Dance of Ideology and Unequal Riches*. Cambridge: MIT Press.

McClosky, Herbert. 1958. "Conservatism and Personality." *American Political Science Review* 52:27–45.

McClosky, Herbert, and John Zaller. 1984. *The American Ethos: Political Attitudes toward Capitalism and Democracy*. Cambridge: Harvard University Press.

McCombs, Maxwell E., and Donald L. Shaw. 1972. "The Agenda-Setting Function of the Mass Media." *Public Opinion Quarterly* 36:176–87.

McDermott, Monika L. 2006. "Not for Members Only: Group Endorsements as Electoral Information Cues." *Political Research Quarterly* 59:249–57.

McDonald, Michael P., and Samuel L. Popkin. 2001. "The Myth of the Vanishing Voter." *American Political Science Review* 95:963–73.

McIver, John P., and Edward G. Carmines. 1981. *Unidimensional Scaling.* Beverly Hills, CA: Sage.

Meffert, Michael, Helmut Norpoth, and Anirudh Ruhil. 2001. "Realignment and Macropartisanship." *American Political Science Review* 95:953–62.

Meier, Kenneth J., and James E. Campbell. 1979. "Issue Voting: An Empirical Examination of Individually Necessary and Jointly Sufficient Conditions." *American Politics Quarterly* 7:21–50.

Merriam, Charles E., and Harold F. Gosnell. 1924. *Non-Voting.* Chicago: University of Chicago Press.

Merrill, Samuel, III, and Bernard Grofman. 1999. *A Unified Theory of Voting: Directional and Proximity Spatial Models.* Cambridge: Cambridge University Press.

Milbrath, Lester. 1965. *Political Participation: How and Why Do People Get Involved in Politics?* Chicago: Rand McNally.

Miller, Arthur H. 1974. "Political Issues and Trust in Government: 1964–1970." *American Political Science Review* 68:951–72.

Miller, Arthur H. 1978. "Partisanship Reinstated? A Comparison of the 1972 and 1976 U. S. Presidential Elections." *British Journal of Political Science* 8:129–52.

Miller, Arthur H. 1979. "Normal Vote Analysis: Sensitivity to Change over Time." *American Journal of Political Science* 23:406–25.

Miller, Arthur H. 1991. "Where Is the Schema? Critiques." *American Political Science Review* 85:1369–76.

Miller, Arthur H., and Warren E. Miller. 1976. "Ideology in the 1972 Election: Myth or Reality—a Rejoinder." *American Political Science Review* 70:832–49.

Miller, Arthur H., Warren E. Miller, Alden S. Raine, and Thad A. Brown. 1976. "A Majority Party in Disarray: Policy Polarization in the 1972 Election." *American Political Science Review* 70:753–78.

Miller, Arthur H., and Martin P. Wattenberg. 1981. "Policy and Performance Voting in the 1980 Election." Paper presented at the Annual Meeting of the American Political Science Association, New York.

Miller, Arthur H., Martin P. Wattenberg, and Oksana Malanchuk. 1986. "Schematic Assessments of Presidential Candidates." *American Political Science Review* 80:521–40.

Miller, Joanne M., Jon A. Krosnick, and Leandre R. Fabrigar. 2003. "The Origins of Policy Issue Salience: Sociotropic Importance for the Nation or Personal Importance for the Citizen?" Unpublished manuscript, Ohio State University.

Miller, Warren E. 1976. "The Cross-National Use of Party Identification as a

Stimulus to Political Inquiry." In *Party Identification and Beyond,* ed. Ian Budge, Ivor Crewe, and Dennis Farlie. New York: Wiley.

Miller, Warren E. 1991. "Party Identification, Realignment, and Party Voting: Back to Basics." *American Political Science Review* 85:557–68.

Miller, Warren E., and Teresa E. Levitin. 1976. *Leadership and Change: The New Politics and the American Electorate.* Cambridge, MA: Winthrop.

Miller, Warren E., and J. Merrill Shanks. 1982. "Policy Directions and Presidential Leadership: Alternative Interpretations of the 1980 Presidential Election." *British Journal of Political Science* 12:299–356.

Miller, Warren E., and J. Merrill Shanks. 1996. *The New American Voter.* Cambridge: Harvard University Press.

Mockabee, Stephen T. 2005. "Religion and Cultural Conflict in the 2004 Election." Paper presented at the Annual Meeting of the American Political Science Association, Washington, DC.

Mondak, Jeffery J. 2001. "Developing Valid Knowledge Scales." *American Journal of Political Science* 45:224–38.

Morton, Rebecca B. 2006. *Analyzing Elections.* New York: Norton.

Mueller, Carol M. 1988. "The Empowerment of Women: Polling and the Women's Voting Bloc." In *The Politics of the Gender Gap: The Social Construction of Political Influence,* ed. Carol M. Mueller. Newbury Park: Sage. 16–36.

Mueller, John E. 1973. *War, Presidents and Public Opinion.* New York: Wiley and Sons.

Mughan, Anthony, C. Bean, and Ian McAllister. 2003. "Economic Globalization, Job Insecurity and the Populist Reaction." *Electoral Studies* 22:617–33.

Mutz, Diana C. 1992. "Mass Media and the Depoliticization of Personal Experience." *American Journal of Political Science* 36:483–508.

Nadeau, Richard, and Michael S. Lewis-Beck. 2001. "National Economic Voting in U.S. Presidential Elections." *Journal of Politics* 63:159–81.

Nardulli, Peter F. 1995. "The Concept of a Critical Realignment, Electoral Behavior, and Political Change." *American Political Science Review* 89:10–22.

Nelson, Thomas E. 2004. "Policy Goals, Public Rhetoric, and Political Attitudes." *Journal of Politics* 66:581–605.

Nicholson, Stephen P., Adrian D. Pantojy, and Gary M. Segura. 2006. "Political Knowledge and Issue Voting among the Latino Electorate." *Political Research Quarterly* 59:259–71.

Nicholson, Stephen P., and Gary M. Segura. 2005. "Issue Agendas and the Politics of Latino Partisan Identification." In *Diversity in Democracy: Minority Representation in the United States,* ed. Gary M. Segura and Shawn Bowler. Charlottesville: University Press of Virginia. 51–71.

Nie, Norman H., and Kristi Andersen. 1974. "Mass Belief Systems Revisited: Political Change and Attitude Structure." *Journal of Politics* 36:540–91.

Nie, Norman H., Jane Junn, and Kenneth Stehlik-Barry. 1996. *Education and Democratic Citizenship in America.* Chicago: University of Chicago Press.

Nie, Norman H., and James N. Rabjohn. 1979. "Revisiting Mass Belief Systems Revisited: Or, Doing Research Is Like Watching a Tennis Match." *American Journal of Political Science* 23:139–75.

Nie, Norman H., Sidney Verba, and John R. Petrocik. 1976. *The Changing American Voter.* Cambridge: Harvard University Press.

Nie, Norman H., Sidney Verba, and John R. Petrocik. 1979. *The Changing American Voter.* Enlarged ed. Cambridge: Harvard University Press.

Niemi, Richard G., and Larry M. Bartels. 1985. "New Measures of Issue Salience: An Evaluation." *Journal of Politics* 47:1212–20.

Nisbett, Richard E., and Timothy D. Wilson. 1977. "Telling More than We Can Know: Verbal Reports on Mental Processes." *Psychological Review* 84:231–59.

Norpoth, Helmut. 1987. "Underway and Here to Stay: Party Realignment in the 1980s." *Public Opinion Quarterly* 51:376–91.

Norpoth, Helmut. 1996. "Presidents and the Prospective Voter." *Journal of Politics* 58:776–92.

Norpoth, Helmut. 2001. "Divided Government and Economic Voting." *Journal of Politics* 63:414–35.

Norpoth, Helmut. 2004. "Bush v. Gore: The Recount of Economic Voting." In *Models of Voting in Presidential Elections,* ed. Herbert F. Weisberg and Clyde Wilcox. Stanford, CA: Stanford University Press. 49–64.

Norpoth, Helmut, and Bruce Buchanan. 1992. "Wanted: The Education President: Issue Trespassing by Political Candidates." *Public Opinion Quarterly* 56:87–99.

Norpoth, Helmut, and Milton Lodge. 1985. "The Differences between Attitudes and Nonattitudes in the Mass Public: Just Measurements?" *American Journal of Political Science* 29:291–307.

Norpoth, Helmut, and Jerrold G. Rusk. 1982. "Partisan Dealignment in the American Electorate: Itemizing the Deductions." *American Political Science Review* 76:522–37.

Norpoth, Helmut, and Jerrold G. Rusk. 2007. "Electoral Myth and Reality: Realignments in American Politics." *Electoral Studies* 26:392–403.

Norpoth, Helmut, and Andrew H. Sidman. 2007. "Mission Accomplished: The Wartime Election of 2004." *Political Behavior* 29:175–95.

O'Regan, Valerie R., Stephen J. Stambough, and Gregory R. Thorson. 2005. "Understanding the Changing Dynamics of the Gender Gap in American Presidential Elections, 1948–2004." Paper presented at the Annual Meeting of the American Political Science Association, Washington, DC.

Oskamp, Stuart, and P. Wesley Schultz. 2005. *Attitudes and Opinions.* 3rd ed. Mahwah, NJ: Lawrence Erlbaum.

Page, Benjamin I. 1978. *Choices and Echoes in Presidential Elections.* Chicago: University of Chicago Press.

Page, Benjamin I., and Richard A. Brody. 1972. "Policy Voting and the Electoral Process: The Vietnam War Issue." *American Political Science Review* 66: 979–95.

Page, Benjamin I., and Calvin Jones. 1979. "Reciprocal Effects of Policy Preferences, Party Loyalties, and the Vote." *American Political Science Review* 73: 1071–89.

Page, Benjamin I., and Robert Y. Shapiro. 1992. *The Rational Public: Fifty Years of Trends in Americans' Policy Preferences.* Chicago: University of Chicago Press.

Patterson, Thomas E. 2002. *The Vanishing Voter: Public Involvement in an Age of Uncertainty.* New York: Knopf.

Patterson, Thomas E., and Robert D. McClure. 1976. *The Unseeing Eye: The Myth of Television Power in National Elections.* New York: Putnam.

Pearson, Karl, and Alice Lee. 1903. "On the Laws of Inheritance in Man: I. Inheritance of Physical Characters." *Biometrika* 2:357–462.

Peffley, Mark A., and Jon Hurwitz. 1985. "A Hierarchical Model of Attitude Constraint." *American Journal of Political Science* 29:871–90.

Petrocik, John R. 1974. "An Analysis of the Intransitivities in the Index of Party Identification." *Political Methodology* 1:31–47.

Petrocik, John R. 1981. *Party Coalitions: Realignments and the Decline of the New Deal Party System.* Chicago: Chicago University Press.

Petrocik, John R. 1996. "Issue Ownership in Presidential Elections, with a 1980 Case Study." *American Journal of Political Science* 40:825–50.

Philpot, Tasha S., and Ismail K. White. 2005. "Uncensored: Reducing Social Desirability in the Expression of Racial Attitudes." Paper presented at the Annual Meeting of the American Political Science Association, Washington, DC.

Pierce, John C. 1970. "Party Identification and the Changing Role of Ideology in American Politics." *Midwest Journal of Political Science* 14:25–42.

Pierce, John C., and Douglas D. Rose. 1974. "Nonattitudes and American Public Opinion: The Examination of a Thesis." *American Political Science Review* 68:626–49.

Pierce, Roy. 1997. "Directional versus Proximity Models: Verisimilitude as the Criterion." *Journal of Theoretical Politics* 9:61–74.

Pomper, Gerald M. 1967. "Classification of Presidential Elections." *Journal of Politics* 29:535–66.

Pomper, Gerald M. 1972. "From Confusion to Clarity: Issues and American Voters, 1956–1968." *American Political Science Review* 66:415–28.

Pomper, Gerald M. 1975. *Voters' Choice.* New York: Dodd, Mead.

Poole, Keith T. 1998. "Recovering a Basic Space from a Set of Issue Scales." *American Journal of Political Science* 42:954–93.

Poole, Keith T. 2005. *Spatial Models of Parliamentary Voting.* Cambridge: Cambridge University Press.

Poole, Keith T., and Howard Rosenthal. 1984a. "The Polarization of American Politics." *Journal of Politics* 46:1061–79.

Poole, Keith T., and Howard Rosenthal. 1984b. "U. S. Presidential Elections, 1968–80: A Spatial Analysis." *American Journal of Political Science* 28:282–312.

Popkin, Samuel L. 1994. *The Reasoning Voter*. 2nd ed. Chicago: University of Chicago Press.

Popkin, Samuel L., John W. Gorman, Charles Phillips, and Jeffrey A. Smith. 1976. "Comment: What Have You Done for Me Lately? Toward an Investment Theory of Voting." *American Political Science Review* 70:779–805.

Powell, G. Bingham, Jr. 1986. "American Voter Turnout in Comparative Perspective." *American Political Science Review* 80:17–43.

Prothro, James W. 1973. "Explaining the Vote." In David M. Kovenock, James W. Prothro, and Associates, *Explaining the Vote: Presidential Choices in the Nation and the States, 1968 (Part I)*. Chapel Hill, NC: Institute for Research in Social Science. 1–29.

Putnam, Robert D. 2000. *Bowling Alone: The Collapse and Revival of American Community*. Cambridge: Harvard University Press.

Quattrone, George A., and Amos Tversky. 1988. "Contrasting Rational and Psychological Analyses of Political Choice." *American Political Science Review* 82:719–36.

Rabinowitz, George. 1978. "On the Nature of Political Issues: Insights from a Spatial Analysis." *American Journal of Political Science* 22:793–817.

Rabinowitz, George, and Stuart E. Macdonald. 1989. "A Directional Theory of Issue Voting." *American Political Science Review* 83:93–121.

Rabinowitz, George, Stuart E. Macdonald, and Ola Listhaug. 1991. "New Players in an Old Game: Party Strategy in Multiparty Systems." *Comparative Political Studies* 24:147–85.

Rabinowitz, George, James W. Prothro, and William G. Jacoby. 1982. "Salience as a Factor in the Impact of Issues on Candidate Evaluation." *Journal of Politics* 44:41–63.

Rae, Douglas W. 1971. *The Political Consequences of Electoral Laws*. Rev. ed. New Haven: Yale University Press.

Rahn, Wendy M., John H. Aldrich, Eugene Borgida, and John L. Sullivan. 1990. "A Social-Cognitive Model of Candidate Appraisal." In *Information and Democratic Processes,* ed. John Ferejohn and James Kuklinski. Urbana: University of Illinois Press. 136–59.

Rahn, Wendy M., Jon A. Krosnick, and Marijke Bruening. 1994. "Rationalization and Derivation Processes in Survey Studies of Political Candidate Evaluation." *American Journal of Political Science* 38:582–600.

Rapoport, Ronald B., Walter J. Stone, and Alan I. Abramowitz. 1991. "Do Endorsements Matter? Group Influence in the 1984 Democratic Caucuses." *American Political Science Review* 85:193–203.

Reingold, Beth. 2000. *Representing Women: Sex, Gender, and Legislative Behavior in Arizona and California*. Chapel Hill: University of North Carolina Press.

RePass, David E. 1971. "Issue Salience and Party Choice." *American Political Science Review* 65:389–400.

RePass, David E. 1976. "Comment: Political Methodologies in Disarray: Some Alternative Interpretations of the 1972 Election." *American Political Science Review* 70:814–31.

Reynolds, H. T. 1974. "Rationality and Attitudes toward Political Parties and Candidates." *Journal of Politics* 36:983–1005.

Rhodebeck, Laurie A. 1993. "The Politics of Greed? Political Preferences among the Elderly." *Journal of Politics* 55:342–64.

Riker, William H., and Peter C. Ordeshook. 1968. "A Theory of the Calculus of Voting." *American Political Science Review* 62:25–43.

Riker, William H., and Peter C. Ordeshook. 1973. *An Introduction to Positive Political Theory*. Englewood Cliffs, NJ: Prentice-Hall.

Rivers, Douglas. 1988. "Heterogeneity in Models of Electoral Choice." *American Journal of Political Science* 32:737–57.

Robinson, William S. 1950. "Ecological Correlations and the Behavior of Individuals." *American Sociological Review* 15:351–57.

Rokeach, Milton. 1973. *The Nature of Human Values*. New York: Free Press.

Rosenberg, Milton J., Sidney Verba, and Philip E. Converse. 1970. *Vietnam and the Silent Majority: The Dove's Guide*. New York: Harper and Row.

Rosenberg, Shawn W. 1988. *Reason, Ideology, and Politics*. Princeton: Princeton University Press.

Rosenof, Theodore. 2003. *Realignment: The Theory That Changed the Way We Think about American Politics*. New York: Rowman and Littlefield.

Rosenstone, Steven J., Roy L. Behr, and Edward H. Lazarus. 1996. *Third Parties in America: Citizen Response to Major Party Failure*. 2nd ed. Princeton: Princeton University Press.

Rosenstone, Steven J., and John Mark Hansen. 2003. *Mobilization, Participation, and Democracy in America*. New York: Longman.

Rudolph, Thomas J., and J. Tobin Grant. 2002. "An Attributional Model of Economic Voting: Evidence from the 2000 Presidential Election." *Political Research Quarterly* 55:805–23.

Sabato, Larry J., and Joshua J. Scott. 2002. "The Long Road to a Cliffhanger: Primaries and Conventions." In *Overtime: The Election Thriller*, ed. Larry J. Sabato. New York: Longman. 15–43.

Sapiro, Virginia, and Pamela Johnston Conover. 1997. "The Variable Gender Basis of Electoral Politics: Gender and Context in the 1992 US Election." *British Journal of Political Science* 27:497–523.

Scammon, Richard M., and Ben J. Wattenberg. 1970. *The Real Majority*. New York: Coward-McCann.

Schneider, Saundra K., and William G. Jacoby. 2003. "A Culture of Dependence? The Relationship between Public Assistance and Public Opinion." *British Journal of Political Science* 33:213–31.

Schulman, Mark A., and Gerald M. Pomper. 1975. "Variability in Electoral Behavior: Longitudinal Perspectives from Causal Modeling." *American Journal of Political Science* 19:1–18.

Schuman, Howard, and Stanley Presser. 1981. *Questions and Answers in Attitude Surveys: Experiments on Question Form, Wording, and Context.* New York: Academic Press.

Schwartz, Shalom H. 1992. "Universals in the Content and Structure of Values: Theoretical Advances and Empirical Tests in 20 Countries." In *Advances in Experimental Social Psychology,* ed. Mark P. Zanna. Orlando, FL: Academic Press. 1–65.

Searing, Donald D., Joel J. Schwartz, and Alden E. Lind. 1973. "The Structuring Principle: Political Socialization and Belief Systems." *American Political Science Review* 67:415–32.

Sears, David O. 1983. "The Persistence of Early Political Predispositions." In *Review of Personality and Social Psychology,* ed. L. Wheeler and P. Shaver. Vol. 4. Beverly Hills, CA: Sage. 79–116.

Sears, David O. 1993. "Symbolic Politics: A Socio-Psychological Theory." In *Explorations in Political Psychology,* ed. Shanto Iyengar and William J. McGuire. Durham, NC: Duke University Press. 113–49.

Sears, David O. 2001. "The Role of Affect in Symbolic Politics." In *Citizens and Politics: Perspectives from Political Psychology,* ed. James H. Kuklinski. Cambridge: Cambridge University Press. 14–40.

Sears, David O., and Jack Citrin. 1985. *Tax Revolt: Something for Nothing in California.* Enlarged ed. Cambridge: Harvard University Press.

Sears, David O., and Carolyn L. Funk. 1990. "Self-Interest in Americans' Political Opinions." In *Beyond Self-Interest,* ed. Jane J. Mansbridge. Chicago: University of Chicago Press. 147–70.

Sears, David O., and Carolyn L. Funk. 1999. "Evidence of the Long-Term Persistence of Adults' Political Predispositions." *Journal of Politics* 61:1–28.

Sears, David O., P. J. Henry, and Rick Kosterman. 2000. "Egalitarian Values and Contemporary Racial Politics." In *Racialized Politics: The Debate about Racism in America,* ed. David O. Sears, Jim Sidanius, and Lawrence Bobo. Chicago: University of Chicago Press. 75–117.

Sears, David O., Carl P. Hensler, and Leslie K. Speer. 1979. "Whites' Opposition to 'Busing': Self-Interest or Symbolic Politics?" *American Political Science Review* 73:369–84.

Sears, David O., and Richard R. Lau. 1983. "Inducing Apparently Self-Interested Political Preferences." *American Journal of Political Science* 27:223–52.

Sears, David O., Richard R. Lau, Tom R. Tyler, and Harris M. Allen Jr. 1980. "Self-

Interest vs. Symbolic Politics in Policy Attitudes and Presidential Voting." *American Political Science Review* 74:670–84.

Sears, David O., Tom R. Tyler, Jack Citrin, and Donald R. Kinder. 1978. "Political System Support and Public Response to the Energy Crisis." *American Journal of Political Science* 22:56–82.

Shafer, Byron, ed. 1991. *The End of Realignment?* Madison: University of Wisconsin Press.

Shanks, J. Merrill, and Warren E. Miller. 1990. "Policy Direction and Performance Evaluation: Complementary Explanations of the Reagan Elections." *British Journal of Political Science* 20:143–235.

Shapiro, Martin J. 1969. "Rational Political Man: A Synthesis of Economic and Social Psychological Perspectives." *American Political Science Review* 63:1106–19.

Sharp, Carol, and Milton Lodge. 1985. "Partisan and Ideological Belief Systems: Do They Differ?" *Political Behavior* 7:147–66.

Shaw, Daron R. 2006. *The Race to 270.* Chicago: University of Chicago Press.

Sigelman, Lee. 1983. "Politics, Economics, and the American Farmer: The Case of 1980." *Rural Sociology* 48:367–85.

Sigelman, Lee. 1987. "Economic Pressures and the Farm Vote: The Case of 1984." *Rural Sociology* 52:151–63.

Sigelman, Lee, Paul Wahlbeck, and Emmet Buell Jr. 1997. "Vote Choice and the Preference for Divided Government: Lessons of 1992." *American Journal of Political Science* 41:879–94.

Sijtsma, Klaas, and Ivo W. Molenaar. 2002. *Introduction to Nonparametric Item Response Theory.* Thousand Oaks, CA: Sage.

Silver, Brian D., Barbara A. Anderson, and Paul R. Abramson. 1986. "Who Overreports Voting?" *American Political Science Review* 80:613–24.

Simmons, Solon J. 2006. "The Surprising Life of Class Politics: Salient Justifications in Models of Presidential Voting 1952–2004." Paper presented at the Annual Meeting of the Midwest Political Science Association, Chicago.

Simon, Herbert A. 1985. "Human Nature in Politics: The Dialogue of Psychology with Political Science." *American Political Science Review* 79:293–304.

Smith, Eric R. A. N. 1980. "The Levels of Conceptualization: False Measures of Ideological Sophistication." *American Political Science Review* 74:685–96.

Smith, Eric R. A. N. 1981. "Reply to Abramson and Nie, Verba, and Petrocik." *American Political Science Review* 75:152–55.

Smith, Eric R. A. N. 1989. *The Unchanging American Voter.* Berkeley and Los Angeles: University of California Press.

Smith, M. Brewster, Jerome S. Bruner, and Robert W. White. 1956. *Opinions and Personality.* New York: John Wiley.

Smith, Mark A. 2005. "It's the Economic Reputation, Stupid: Objective Performance, Subjective Perceptions, and Electoral Outcomes." Paper presented at the Annual Meeting of the American Political Science Association, Washington, DC.

Sniderman, Paul M., and Richard A. Brody. 1977. "Coping: The Ethic of Self-Reliance." *American Journal of Political Science* 21:501–21.

Sniderman, Paul M., Richard A. Brody, and James H. Kuklinski. 1984. "Policy Reasoning and Political Values: The Problem of Racial Equality." *American Journal of Political Science* 28:75–94.

Sniderman, Paul M., Richard A. Brody, and Philip E. Tetlock. 1991. *Reasoning and Choice: Explorations in Political Psychology.* New York: Cambridge University Press.

Sniderman, Paul M., James M. Glaser, and Robert Griffin. 1991. "Information and Electoral Choice." In Paul M. Sniderman, Richard Brody, and Philip E. Tetlock, with Henry E. Brady et al., *Reasoning and Choice: Explorations in Political Psychology.* Cambridge: Cambridge University Press. 164–78.

Sniderman, Paul M., Michael Gray Hagen, Philip E. Tetlock, and Henry E. Brady. 1986. "Reasoning Chains: Causal Models of Policy Reasoning in Mass Publics." *British Journal of Political Science* 16:405–30.

Sniderman, Paul M., Michael G. Hagen, Philip E. Tetlock, and Henry E. Brady. 1991. "Reasoning Chains." In Paul M. Sniderman, Richard A. Brody, Philip E. Tetlock, with Henry E. Brady et al., *Reasoning and Choice: Explorations in Political Psychology.* New York: Cambridge University Press. 70–92

Sousa, David J. 1993. "Organized Labor in the Electorate, 1960–1988." *Political Research Quarterly* 46:741–58.

Stanley, Harold W., and Richard G. Niemi. 1995. "The Demise of the New Deal Coalition: Partisanship and Group Support, 1952–1992." In *Democracy's Feast: Elections in America,* ed. Herbert F. Weisberg. Chatham, NJ: Chatham House. 220–40.

Stanley, Harold W., and Richard G. Niemi. 2001. "Party Coalitions in Transition: Partisanship and Group Support, 1952–1996." In *Controversies in Voting Behavior,* ed., Richard G. Niemi and Herbert F. Weisberg. 4th ed. Washington, DC: Congressional Quarterly Press. 387–404.

Stanley, Harold W., and Richard G. Niemi. 2004. "Partisanship, Party Coalitions, and Group Support, 1952–2000." In *Models of Voting in Presidential Elections,* ed. Herbert F. Weisberg and Clyde Wilcox. Stanford, CA: Stanford University Press. 123–40.

Stanley, Harold W., and Richard G. Niemi. 2006. "Partisanship, Party Coalitions, and Group Support, 1952–2004." *Presidential Studies Quarterly* 36:172–89.

Stark, Rodney, and Charles Glock. 1968. *American Piety: The Nature of Religious Commitment.* Berkeley and Los Angeles: University of California Press.

Steenbergen, Marco R., and Milton Lodge. 2003. "Process Matters: Cognitive Models of Candidate Evaluation." In *Electoral Democracy,* ed. Michael B. MacKuen and George Rabinowitz. Ann Arbor: University of Michigan Press. 125–71.

Steeper, Frederick T., and Robert M. Teeter. 1976. "Comment on 'A Majority Party in Disarray.'" *American Political Science Review* 70:806–13.

Stimson, James A. 1975. "Belief Systems: Constraint, Complexity, and the 1972 Election." *American Journal of Political Science* 19:393–418.

Stimson, James A. 1999. *Public Opinion in America: Moods, Cycles, and Swings.* Boulder, CO: Westview.

Stimson, James A. 2004. *Tides of Consent: How Public Opinion Shapes American Politics.* Cambridge: Cambridge University Press.

Stimson, James A., and Christopher R. Ellis. 2005. "Operational and Symbolic Ideology in the American Electorate: The Paradox of 'Conflicted Conservatives.'" Paper presented at the Annual Meeting of the Midwest Political Science Association, Chicago.

Stimson, James A., Michael B. MacKuen, and Robert S. Erikson. 1995. "Dynamic Representation." *American Political Science Review* 89:543–65.

Stokes, Donald E. 1963. "Spatial Models of Party Competition." *American Political Science Review* 57:368–77.

Stokes, Donald E. 1966a. "Some Dynamic Elements of Contests for the Presidency." *American Political Science Review* 60:19–28.

Stokes, Donald E. 1966b. "Spatial Models of Party Competition." In *Elections and the Political Order,* ed. Angus Campbell, Philip E. Converse, Warren E. Miller, and Donald E. Stokes. New York: John Wiley and Sons. 161–79.

Stokes, Donald E., Angus Campbell, and Warren E. Miller. 1958. "Components of Electoral Decision." *American Political Science Review* 52:367–87.

Stokes, Donald E., and Gudmund R. Iversen. 1966. "On the Existence of Forces Restoring Party Competition." In *Elections and the Political Order,* ed. Angus Campbell, Philip E. Converse, Warren E. Miller, and Donald E. Stokes. New York: John Wiley and Sons. 180–93.

Stone, Deborah. 1997. *Policy Paradox: The Art of Political Decision Making.* New York: Norton.

Stonecash, Jeffrey M. 2000. *Class and Party in American Politics.* Boulder, CO: Westview.

Stonecash, Jeffrey M., and Mack D. Mariani. 2000. "Republican Gains in the House in the 1994 Elections: Class Polarization in American Politics." *Political Science Quarterly* 115:93–113.

Sullivan, John L., James E. Pierson, and George E. Marcus. 1978. "Ideological Constraint in the Mass Public: A Methodological Critique and Some New Findings." *American Journal of Political Science* 22:223–49.

Sullivan, John L., James E. Pierson, George E. Marcus, and Stanley Feldman. 1979. "The More Things Change, the More They Stay the Same." *American Journal of Political Science* 23:176–86.

Taber, Charles S., and Milton Lodge. 2006. "Motivated Skepticism in the Evaluation of Political Beliefs." *American Journal of Political Science* 50: 755–69.

Teixeira, Ruy A. 1992. *The Disappearing Voter.* Washington, DC: Brookings Institution.

Tetlock, Philip E. 1983. "Cognitive Style and Political Ideology." *Journal of Personality and Social Psychology* 45:118–26.

Tetlock, Philip E. 1984. "Cognitive Style and Political Belief Systems in the British House of Commons." *Journal of Personality and Social Psychology* 46:365–75.

Thomassen, Jacques, ed. 2005. *The European Voter: A Comparative Study of Modern Democracies.* Oxford: Oxford University Press.

Thompson, Megan, Mark P. Zanna, and Dale W. Griffin. 1995. "Let's Not Be Indifferent about (Attitudinal) Ambivalence." In *Attitude Strength: Antecedents and Consequences,* ed. Richard E. Petty and Jon A. Krosnick. Mahwah, NJ: Lawrence Erlbaum. 361–86.

Timpone, Richard J. 1998. "Structure, Behavior, and Voter Turnout in the United States." *American Political Science Review* 92:145–58.

Tomz, Michael, and Paul M. Sniderman. 2005. "Brand Names and the Organization of Mass Belief Systems." Paper presented at the Annual Meeting of the Midwest Political Science Association, Chicago.

Torgerson, Warren S. 1958. *Theory and Methods of Scaling.* New York: John Wiley.

Tourangeau, Roger, Lance J. Rips, and Kenneth Rasinski. 2000. *The Psychology of Survey Response.* Cambridge: Cambridge University Press.

Traugott, Michael W., and John P. Katosh. 1979. "Response Validity in Surveys of Voting Behavior." *Public Opinion Quarterly* 43:359–77.

Traugott, Santa. 1989. "Validating Self-Reported Vote: 1964–1988." ANES Technical Report Series, No. nes010152. http://www.electionstudies.org/resources/ papers/technical_reports.htm (accessed October 29, 2007).

Treier, Shawn, and Sunshine Hillygus. 2006. "The Contours of Policy Attitudes in the Mass Public." Paper presented at the Annual Meeting of the Midwest Political Science Association, Chicago.

Tufte, Edward R. 1978. *Political Control of the Economy.* Princeton: Princeton University Press.

Uhlaner, Carole J., and F. Chris Garcia. 2005. "Learning Which Party Fits: Experience, Ethnic Identity, and the Demographic Foundations of Latino Party Identification." In *Diversity in Democracy: Minority Representation in the United States,* ed. Gary M. Segura and Shawn Bowler, Charlottesville: University Press of Virginia. 72–101.

United States Election Project. 2006. "2004 Voting-Age and Voting-Eligible Population Estimates and Voter Turnout." Updated June 5, 2006. http://elections .gmu.edu/Voter_Turnout_2004.htm (accessed October 30, 2007).

U.S. Census Bureau. 2004. "Census Bureau Estimates Number of Adults, Older People and School-Age Children in States." March 10. http://www.census

.gov/Press-Release/www/releases/archives/voting/001690.html (accessed October 29, 2007).

U.S. Census Bureau. 2005. "U.S. Voter Turnout Up in 2004, Census Bureau Reports." May 26. http://www.census.gov/Press-Release/www/releases/archives/voting/004986.html (accessed October 29, 2007).

U.S. Census Bureau. 2006. *Voting and Registration in the Election of November 2004.* Current Population Reports P20-556.

U.S. Census Bureau. 2007. Historical Time Series Table A-1. Reported Voting and Registration by Race, Hispanic Origin, Sex, and Age Groups: November 1964–2004. http://www.census.gov/population/www/socdem/voting.html (accessed February 19, 2007).

Verba, Sidney, and Norman H. Nie. 1972. *Participation in America.* New York: Harper and Row.

Verba, Sidney, Kay Lehman Schlozman, and Henry E. Brady. 1995. *Voice and Equality: Civic Voluntarism in American Politics.* Cambridge: Harvard University Press.

Wagner, Michael W., and Edward G. Carmines. 2006. "Issue Preferences and Political Participation in American Politics, 1972–2004." Paper presented at the Annual Meeting of the American Political Science Association, Washington, DC.

Walton, Hanes, Jr. 1985. *Invisible Politics.* Albany: State University of New York Press.

Wattenberg, Martin P. 1998. *The Decline of American Political Parties, 1952–1996.* Cambridge: Harvard University Press.

Wattenberg, Martin P., and Craig Leonard Brians. 1999. "Negative Campaign Advertising: Demobilizer or Mobilizer?" *American Political Science Review* 93:891–99.

Weatherford, M. Stephen. 1978. "Economic Conditions and Electoral Outcomes: Class Differences in the Political Response to Recession." *American Journal of Political Science* 22:917–38.

Weisberg, Herbert F. 1980. "A Multidimensional Conceptualization of Party Identification." *Political Behavior* 2:33–60.

Weisberg, Herbert F. 1987. "The Demographics of a New Voting Gap: Marital Differences in American Voting." *Public Opinion Quarterly* 51:335–43.

Weisberg, Herbert F. 1999. "Political Partisanship." In *Measures of Political Attitudes,* ed. John P. Robinson, Phillip R. Shaver, and Lawrence S. Wrightsman. Rev. ed. San Diego: Academic Press. 681–736.

Weisberg, Herbert F. 2005. *The Total Survey Error Approach: A Guide to the New Science of Survey Research.* Chicago: University of Chicago Press.

Weisberg, Herbert F., and Dino P. Christenson. 2007. "Changing Horses in Wartime?" *Political Behavior* 29:279–304.

Weisberg, Herbert F., and Steven H. Greene. 2003. "The Political Psychology of

Party Identification." In *Electoral Democracy,* ed. Michael B. MacKuen and George Rabinowitz. Ann Arbor: University of Michigan Press. 83–124.

Weisberg, Herbert F., and Edward B. Hasecke. 1999. "What Is Partisan Strength? A Social Identity Theory Approach." Paper presented at the Annual Meeting of the American Political Science Association, Atlanta.

Weisberg, Herbert F., and Timothy G. Hill. 2004. "The Succession Presidential Election of 2000: The Battle of Legacies." In *Models of Voting in Presidential Elections,* ed. Herbert F. Weisberg and Clyde Wilcox. Stanford, CA: Stanford University Press. 27–48.

Weisberg, Herbert F., and Jerrold G. Rusk. 1970. "Dimensions of Candidate Evaluation." *American Political Science Review* 64:1167–85.

Weisberg, Herbert F., and Charles E. Smith. 1991. "The Influence of the Economy on Party Identification in the Reagan Years." *Journal of Politics* 53:1077–92.

Weisberg, Herbert F., and Clyde Wilcox, eds. 2004. *Models of Voting in Presidential Elections: The 2000 U.S. Election.* Stanford, CA: Stanford University Press.

Welch, Susan, and Lee Sigelman. 1993. "The Politics of Hispanic Americans: Insights from National Surveys, 1980–1988." *Social Science Quarterly* 74:76–94.

West, Darrell M. 2005. *Air Wars: Television Advertisements in Election Campaigns, 1952–2004.* 4th ed. Washington, DC: Congressional Quarterly Press.

Westholm, Anders. 1997. "Distance versus Direction: The Illusory Defeat of the Proximity Theory of Electoral Choice." *American Political Science Review* 91:865–83.

Wielhouwer, Peter W. 2000. "Releasing the Fetters: Parties and the Mobilization of the African-American Electorate." *Journal of Politics:* 62:206–22.

Wilcox, Clyde. 1994. "Why Was 1992 the 'Year of the Woman'? Explaining Women's Gains in 1992." In *The Year of the Woman: Myths and Realities,* ed. Elizabeth Adell Cook, Sue Thomas, and Clyde Wilcox. Boulder: Westview. 1–24.

Wlezien, Christopher, and Arthur H. Miller. 1997. "Social Groups and Political Judgments." *Social Science Quarterly* 78:625–40.

Wolfinger, Raymond E., and Steven J. Rosenstone. 1980. *Who Votes?* New Haven: Yale University Press.

Wolpert, Robin M., and James G. Gimpel. 1998. "Self-Interest, Symbolic Politics, and Public Attitudes toward Gun Control." *Political Behavior* 20:241–62.

Wray, J. Harry. 1979. "Comment on Interpretation of Early Research into Mass Belief Systems." *Journal of Politics* 41:1173–81.

Wright, John R., and Richard G. Niemi. 1983. "Perceptions of Candidates' Issue Positions." *Political Behavior* 5:209–24.

Wyckoff, Mikel L. 1980. "Belief System Constraint and Policy Voting: A Test of the Unidimensional Consistency Model." *Political Behavior* 2:115–46.

Wyckoff, Mikel L. 1987. "Issues of Measuring Ideological Sophistication: Level of

Conceptualization, Attitude Consistency, and Attitude Stability." *Political Behavior* 9:193–224.

Zaller, John R. 1992. *The Nature and Origins of Mass Opinion.* New York: Cambridge University Press.

Zaller, John R., and Stanley Feldman. 1992. "A Simple Theory of the Survey Response: Answering Questions versus Revealing Preferences." *American Journal of Political Science* 36:579–616.

Index

Abortion, 211, 214, 231, 326
Affect
  partisan attitudes and, 31–33, 187
  toward political parties, 156
Afghanistan war, 210–11, 216, 231, 398
African Americans
  distinctiveness of vote, 305, 308–13, 322–23
  increase in electorate, 106, 243, 426
  intensity of opinions on civil rights issue,
    176–77
  in New Deal Coalition, 331–33
  party identification of, 151, 154–55, 156,
    322–23, 405
Age, 354–56. See also Young voters
  conservatism and, 148
  dealignment and, 157
  education and, 355
  as a group, 359–60
  party identification and, 144–50, 152–53,
    336, 354
  political participation and, 336, 354–56
  turnout and, 103, 354–56
American National Election Studies. See
  National Election Studies
American Voter, The, 14, 15, 26, 27, 28, 77–78,
  81, 129, 130–31, 132, 134–35, 189, 190, 194,
  195, 196, 248, 290, 297, 298, 299, 301, 320,
  322, 407, 409–10
  challenges in replicating, 435–40
  comparison of results with American Voter
    Revisited, 77, 147n6, 185–87, 235–38,
    247, 253, 289–90, 424–28
Apoliticals, 130–31
Assimilation and contrast effects, 192
Attitude. See also Attitude constraint; Attitude structure; Nonattitude
  ambivalence in, 248, 251–52
  definition of, 168
  measurement of, 187–88, 190–93

self-interest and, 197–98
sources of, 196–98
stability of, 245–47
Attitude constraint, 241–44, 251–53, 290–91.
  See also Attitude structure; Ideology;
  Nonattitude
  among elites, 242, 291
  extent of, 242–43
  liberal-conservative continuum and, 244,
    255, 291, 299
  as measure of attitude structure, 244
  measurement of, 242–44, 291
  psychological nature of, 298–99
  among public, 242–43, 291
  sources of, 216
Attitude structure, 424. See also Attitude
  constraint; Ideology
  alternative sources of, 248–51
  bounded nature of, 213–15
  clarity of, 212–16
  description of, 203–7, 229
  on foreign policy issues, 210–11, 213, 215–
    29, 230–32, 236
  Guttman scale techniques and, 205–7,
    210–12
  as ideology, 207–10, 223–29
  increase in, 238
  interrelationship of foreign, lifestyle, and
    social welfare issues, 215–16, 236
  lack of coherence in, 251–53
  on lifestyle issues, 211, 213, 215–29, 230–32,
    236, 255
  measurement of, 205–7, 238–41, 244
  party identification and, 215, 216, 217–22,
    227–29, 231–34, 236, 249
  on social welfare issues, 212, 213, 215–29,
    230–32, 236, 255
  values and, 204, 229–35, 236–37, 249–51
Awareness of politics, 51–52

Balancing election, 7, 402, 404–6, 413
Bandwagon effect, and turnout, 89, 99
Bayesian updating, 134
Blacks. *See* African Americans
Brady Bill, 8
Bush, George H. W., 52, 277, 389
　Fundamentalist Protestant support for,
　　329
　as Reagan's political heir, 7, 405
Bush, George W., 9, 10, 52, 81, 123, 155, 217,
　　406, 411, 417
　association of, with father, 46, 51, 277
　domestic issues and, 43
　economic issues and, 37, 367, 373–74, 375–
　　76, 389, 422
　evaluations of, and conflict in partisan
　　attitudes, 72–73
　evaluations of, and vote choice, 61–69, 77,
　　78–79, 395–98, 400
　female support for, 326–27
　foreign policy and, 35–37, 43, 52–53, 215,
　　397, 398, 422
　Hispanic support for, 325
　Independents' attitudes toward, 114–15
　management of government and, 41
　moral issues and, 39
　party polarization and, 10
　perceptions of, 33, 44–53, 121, 178, 183–84,
　　406
　social welfare issues and, 38–39
　tax cuts and, 166, 214, 389
　victory of as perceived mandate, 256,
　　397

Campaign finance, 250
Candidate characteristics, 162, 420
　conceptualization and, 276–78
　perceptions of, 44–50, 51–53, 255–56
　personal traits, 55–57, 256
　trait ownership and, 59
Candidate issue positions. *See also*
　　Perceptions of parties and candidates
　consensus on, 181–85, 186, 201
　education and, 179–80
　limitations on perceptions of differences
　　of, 178–81
　party identification and, 184
　perceptions of, 177–85, 186
　political sophistication and, 184
Carter, Jimmy, 37, 59, 405

Catholics
　cross-pressures and, 72
　distinctiveness of vote, 11, 308–13, 315–17,
　　327–28, 330, 404
　Hispanics and, 324
　moral issues and, 328
　in New Deal Coalition, 331–33
　party identification of, 136–37, 151, 313, 316,
　　318–19, 327–28, 403, 405
　support for Catholic candidates, 327, 404
Causality
　funnel of. *See* Funnel of causality
　problems of, 20–22, 409–11
Citizen duty
　education and, 102, 351, 357, 358–59
　turnout and, 95–96, 106
Civic education, and political participation,
　　358–59
Civil Rights Act of 1964, 13
Civil rights issue, 13, 14, 129, 155, 167, 186, 212,
　　250, 323, 404
　African Americans' intensity of opinion
　　on, 176–77
　familiarity with, 169–77
　issue evolution and, 159
　party identification and, 144, 405
　perceptions of candidate positions on,
　　178–81, 183–85
　salience of, to Hispanics, 324
Civil War, 36, 402
　realignment and, 151, 401, 403, 411–12
Class. *See also* Class consciousness; Class
　　identification; Class voting; Status
　　Polarization
　cross-pressures and, 72
　economic outlook and, 370–72
　measurement of, 335–36, 338–42, 356, 361,
　　362
　objective definition of, 335, 338–42, 356
　party identification and, 336, 342–43, 403
　as political group, 335–36
　political participation and, 336, 338
　as social hierarchy, 334
　subjective definition of, 335, 339–41, 356
　turnout and, 98, 356–57
　vote choice and, 6, 341–43, 344
Class consciousness, 337–38, 339, 347, 362, 371
Class identification, 337
　as awareness, 340, 343–44, 346–47
　measurement of, 339–41

Class voting, 346–48
    decline of, 356, 361–62
    Independents and, 347–48
    Kansas hypothesis and, 363
    political involvement and, 346
    political sophistication and, 348
    strength of party identification and,
        347–48
Classical liberalism, 209, 250
Clinton, William J., 10, 46, 61, 155, 397, 417
    economic issues and, 7–8, 38, 380, 384, 386,
        422
    female support for, 326–27
    foreign policy and, 36, 396, 406
    health care and, 8
    labor union support for, 320
    management of government and, 41
    negative effect of on Gore candidacy, 8–9,
        47, 49–50, 51, 277
    nonvoters' support for, 98
    scandals during administration of, 8, 9, 39,
        41, 277, 396, 397, 398, 406
    victory of, in 1992 election, 7–8, 406
Closeness of election, 124
    turnout and, 101–2
    in 2000 and 2004 elections, 421
Cognition
    issues and, 168, 171–72
    partisan attitudes and, 31–33, 187
    schemas and, 257
Cognitive Madisonianism, 157–58
Cold War, 13, 52
Columbia voting studies, 11, 72
Concept formation. *See* Conceptualization
Conceptualization, 256–60, 294
    candidate characteristics and, 276–78
    differences between group-based and ide-
        ological, 268
    education and, 280–82
    external environment conditions and,
        272–75, 287–90
    group benefits and, 267–72, 287–90
    ideology and, 255, 259, 261–67, 287–90
    levels of, 258–59, 260–80, 287, 288–90,
        292–95
    measurement of, 257–58, 259–60, 292–95
    party identification and, 276, 278, 287–89,
        290
    political behavior and, 295–97
    political involvement and, 283–86, 289, 290

    political knowledge and, 282–83, 285–86,
        289
    political sophistication, 290, 295–97, 299
Concern over election outcome
    conflict of partisan attitudes and, 75–77
    correlation with interest in campaign, 93
    education and, 102
    party identification and, 126–27
    party polarization and, 77
    turnout and, 93–94, 106
Conflict of partisan attitudes, 63, 71–77
    concern over election outcome and, 75–77
    demographic cross-pressures and, 72–73
    interest in campaign and, 74, 75
    involvement in politics and, 75–76
    measurement of, 72–73, 119
    party identification and, 119–21, 124–26
    split-ticket voting and, 74–75
    time of vote decision and, 71–72, 73–74
Conservatism. *See also* Liberal-conservative
        continuum
    conflicted conservatives, 252–53
    correlation with party identification, 237
    as dimension of ideology, 208–10
    of electorate in 2004, 217
    issue positions of, 208–9, 252
Converting elections, 413
Corruption, 165, 419
Coveyou, Michael R., 293
Crime, 419
Critical election, 158–59. *See also*
        Realignment
Cross-pressures, and conflict of partisan
        attitudes, 72–73
Culture war, 39, 195, 329–30

Dealignment, 157–58. *See also* Realignment
Death penalty, 214
Defense of Marriage Act, 8
Defense spending issue, 167
    attitude structure and, 210–11
    familiarity with, 169–77
    perceptions of candidate positions on,
        178–81, 183–85
Desegregation, 194, 195, 197
Deviant voter, 83, 90, 92, 95–97. *See also* Vote
        choice: defections in
Deviating election, 7, 402, 404
Diplomacy versus military action issue, 167,
        186

Diplomacy versus military action issue
(*continued*)
attitude structure and, 230–32
familiarity with, 169–77
perceptions of candidate positions on,
178–81, 183–85
as value, 230–32
Directional theory of issue voting, 198–99,
420
Divided government, 157–58, 381–82, 421
Dole, Robert, 8, 10, 61, 98
Domestic policy issues, 197. *See also* Civil
rights issue; Government-guaranteed
jobs issue; Government spending and
services issue; Role of women in society
issue
attitude structure and, 211–12, 255
effects on conflict of partisan attitudes,
72–73
perceptions of parties and candidates and,
37–39, 43
vote choice and, 61–69, 394–98, 399–401

Economic outlook. *See also* Economic
voting; Economy
class and, 370–72
dimensions of, 370
measurement of, 370
occupation and, 370–71
partisan attitudes and, 374
party identification and, 374–77
vote choice and, 369–77, 427
Economic voting, 27, 99–101, 369–74. *See also*
Economic outlook; Economy
divided government and, 381–82
forecasting elections and, 382–83
homogeneity and, 384–85
income inequality and, 388–89
by independents, 375
perception of national economy and, 370,
372–74
pocketbook voting, 370–72, 379–81, 385
prospective, 378–81, 384
retrospective, 378–81, 384, 387
sociotropic evaluations and, 380, 385
theories of, 27, 99–101, 377–78, 387–88
Economy. *See also* Economic outlook;
Economic voting
approval of president's handling of,
368–69

in context of 2000 election, 383–84
as domestic issue, 37–38, 162, 367–69, 417
measurement of, 372–73, 384, 385–87
negativity effect on electoral behavior and,
422–23
public concerns about, 366–67
responsibility for, 366, 377–78, 381–82, 385
Education, 348–52
age and, 355
attitude constraint and, 243, 252, 425
citizen duty and, 102, 351, 357, 358–59
conceptualization and, 280–82, 285–86,
289, 290
correlation with income, 349
correlation with occupation, 348–49
correlation with political involvement,
285
correlation with political knowledge, 285
economic outlook and, 370–71
gender and, 353
heuristics and, 298
ideological self-placement and, 223, 425
importance of to democracy, 349, 351, 357
independent effect of, on political
behavior, 349–52
interest in campaign and, 102
issue awareness and, 186, 425
issue familiarity and, 171–72, 186–87
issue voting and, 425
as measure of social class, 339, 348, 356
opinion leaders and, 349–50
party identification and, 131, 336
perceptions of candidate issue positions
and, 179–80
political efficacy and, 102, 351–52
political involvement and, 102, 350–52
political participation and, 336, 350–52,
357–59
as proxy for pre-adult characteristics,
357–58
turnout and, 102, 131
Edwards, John, 97
Eisenhower, Dwight D., 52, 61, 397, 399, 404,
407
Election of 2000, 8–9, 115, 395–97
as balancing election, 399–400, 406, 413
as Bush mandate, 256
closeness of, 9, 395, 397, 406, 421
economic context of, 383–84
forecasting models of, 380–81

Election of 2004, 9–10, 115, 152, 166, 397–98
    as balancing election, 399–400, 406, 413
    as Bush mandate, 256, 397
    closeness of, 421
    forecasting models of, 380–81
    gay marriage and, 69
    increased participation in, 84–85
    increased voting turnout in, 82, 91
    party polarization in, 77, 124
    party strategies in, 215–16
    as wartime election, 171, 213, 397–98, 398,
        422–23
Elections
    changes in party power and, 421–22
    classification of, 7, 394, 401–6, 411–13
    forecasting outcomes of, 382–83
    importance to democracy, 4–6, 416–18
    party strategy and, 418–20
    as policy mandates, 181–82, 186, 199–200,
        218, 254, 289, 416–17
    political system and, 415
    shift in partisan divisions and, 60–61
Electoral behavior. *See also* Vote choice; Vot-
        ing turnout
    effects of, 415
    negativity effect and, 422–23
    party strategy and, 418–20
    party system and, 420–23
    public constraints on political leadership
        and, 416–18
Electoral College, 5, 15
    popular vote winner and, 9, 395, 397, 406
Electoral decision, 394–98, 415. *See also* Vote
    choice
Elites
    agenda-setting role of, 196, 212
    attitude constraint of, 242–43, 255, 297
    effect of, on mass opinion, 166, 180, 213,
        229–30, 300
    polarization of, 159
    as source of political issues, 196
Environmental issues, 163, 165, 197, 214
Equal Rights Amendment, 326
Ethnoreligious perspective, 329
Evangelical Protestants. *See* Fundamentalist
    Protestants

Factor analysis, 240–41
Family and Medical Leave Act, 8, 320
Farmers, political behavior of, 360–61

Feminist consciousness, 326
Field theory, 25
Foreign policy, 250. *See also* Defense spend-
        ing issue; Diplomacy versus military
        action issue
    attitude structure and, 210–11
    party identification and, 117, 121, 227–29,
        236
    perceptions of parties and candidates and,
        34–37, 43, 50–51, 59, 394–98
    salience of, in 2004 election, 171, 213, 215
    vote choice and, 61–69, 394–98, 399–401
Fundamentalist Protestants
    classification of, 328
    as constituency of Republican Party, 215–
        16, 329–30, 406, 425
    dissatisfaction with Carter presidency and,
        405
    distinctiveness of vote of, 329–31, 333
    increase in membership of, 328
    increase in political activity of, 328, 425
Funnel of causality, 22–28, 319, 409, 427
    alternatives to, 26–28, 409–11
    causal ordering of components in, 409–11
    external factors in, 24
    nonpolitical conditions in, 24
    personal conditions in, 23–24
    political conditions in, 24
    relevant conditions in, 23

Gay marriage, 69, 79, 211, 231, 418
Gender, 352–53. *See also* Gender gap; Women
    party identification and, 136–37, 336
    political participation and, 336, 352–53
    relationship with education, 353
    turnout and, 352–53, 359, 426
    vote choice and, 61, 108–13, 315–17, 325–27,
        333, 352–53, 405, 426
Gender gap. *See also* Gender; Women
    levels of, 325–26
    in political involvement, 359
    in turnout, 352–53, 359, 426
    in vote choice, 325–27, 405, 426
Generational hypothesis of dealignment,
    157
Gore, Al, 52, 61, 320, 341, 367, 422
    association with Clinton and, 8–9, 47, 49–
        50, 51, 277
    domestic policy and, 42–43
    economic issues and, 383–84

Gore, Al (*continued*)
  evaluations of, and vote choice, 61–69, 121,
    394–96, 400
  Hispanic support for, 325
  nonvoters' support for, 98
  and perceptions of personal attributes, 33,
    44, 46–50, 411
  as popular vote winner in 2000 election, 9,
    99n8, 395, 406
  predicted victory of, 382
Government-guaranteed jobs issue, 167
  attitude structure and, 212
  familiarity with, 169–77
  perceptions of candidate positions on,
    178–81, 183–85
Government spending and services issue,
  167, 250
  attitude structure and, 212
  familiarity with, 169–77
  perceptions of candidate positions on,
    178–81, 183–85
Great Depression, 335, 365, 417
  change in party identification and, 151,
    403, 412
  perceptions of parties and candidates and,
    34, 37, 38, 40, 50
Group identification, 307, 320, 331. *See also*
  Group influence model of voting;
  Groups
  cohesiveness of, 313, 331
  development of, 317–18
  distinctiveness of group vote and, 308–9,
    311–13
  measurement of, 311–12
  political legitimacy and, 315–17
  strength of, 311, 313
Group influence model of voting, 305–33. *See
  also* Group identification; Groups
  issues and, 322–23, 326, 328, 329, 330–31
  limitations of, 319
Groups, 305–33. *See also* Group identification; Group influence model of voting
  as basis of realignment, 403–4, 405
  cohesiveness of, 307
  conceptualization and, 259, 267–72, 281,
    287–90
  distinctiveness of vote of, 26, 307–11, 317–18
  economic interest of, 365
  impact of size on elections of, 331
  influence of, on individuals' political

behavior, 305–7, 308–9, 311–14, 320,
    359–60
  influence of leadership of, 320–22
  in New Deal Coalition, 331–33
  party identification and, 60–61, 118, 136–37,
    151, 317–19
  perceptions of parties and candidates and,
    39–40, 60–61
  political legitimacy of, 315–17
  political parties and, 317–19
  proximity to politics of, 314–15
  as reference groups, 184, 256, 305–7
  status polarization and, 338
  vote choice and, 60–61, 394–98, 399–401,
    427–28
Gulf War (1991), 7, 277
Gun control, 197, 214
Guttman scale analysis, 213
  advantages of, 239–40
  attitude structure and, 205–7, 210–12, 213–
    14, 217, 239–40
  interpretation of, 206–7

Harding, William, 402
Health insurance, 212, 360
Heuristics, 116, 134, 298, 426
Hispanics
  distinctiveness of vote, 308–13, 333, 418,
    426
  group integration and, 324–25
  party identification of, 324–25
Hoover, Herbert, 403
Hussein, Saddam, 9, 46

Ideologue, 425. *See also* Conceptualization:
  ideology and; Near-ideologue
  consistency in vote choice and, 287–89
  definition of, 261
  examples of, 261–64
  turnout and, 280, 287
Ideology, 415, 416, 423, 425. *See also* Attitude
  structure; Liberal-conservative
  continuum
  characteristics of, 207–10
  conceptualization and, 259, 261–67, 287–90
  correlation with party identification, 225–
    27, 237
  education and, 223, 425
  issues and, 419
  levels of, 261–64, 292–93

liberal-conservative dimension and, 208–10, 223–29, 295–97, 344
as long-term factor in funnel of causality, 26, 409–10
measurement of, 222–29, 234, 237–38, 247–48, 296, 344
organization of attitude structure and, 207–10, 223–29
party strategies and, 418–20
political socialization and, 248, 251
political sophistication and, 344
by proxy, 268, 269, 281, 290
self-interest and, 236
surrogates for, 254–55
turnout and, 280, 287, 290
vote choice and, 256, 287–89, 296–97
Immigration, 324
Income. *See also* Class
correlation of, with education, 349
economic outlook and, 370–71
inequality in, and economic voting, 388–89
as measure of class, 356, 361
in New Deal Party Coalition, 331–33
party identification and, 131
turnout and, 131
Independents
and approval of president's handling of the economy, 369
characteristics of, 126–27, 129–31
class voting and, 347–48
as closet partisans, 113–15, 421
conflict of partisan attitudes and, 114–15, 119–20
dealignment and, 157, 412
economic voting and, 375
increase of, 405, 424
intransitivity and, 128–29
involvement in politics of, 126–27, 129, 424
measurement of, 112–13, 128–30
parental influence on, 140–41
as split-ticket voters, 129
stability of identification as, 144, 153–54
vote choice and, 123–24
Interest in campaign. *See also* Political involvement
conflict of partisan attitudes and, 74, 75
education and, 102
ideological self-placement and, 223
party identification and, 121, 126–27

political sophistication and, 344
turnout and, 92–93, 99, 106
Interpersonal influence, 306
on political participation, 85, 97
on vote choice, 11, 70
Iraq War, 9, 166, 398
attitude structure and, 210–11, 216, 231
negativity effect of, on electoral behavior, 422–23
perceptions of parties and candidates and, 34–36, 43, 46, 48–49, 50, 52–53
salience of, in 2004 election, 162, 178, 187
Issue awareness, 163, 173–74, 415
education and, 186, 425
increase of, 186–87
issue evolution and, 187
issue salience and, 193
media and, 187, 196
Issue evolution, 159, 187
Issue familiarity, 163, 164–72, 191
challenges to, 166
components of, 166–71
development of, 171–72
and differences with issue intensity, 175
education and, 171–72, 186–87
extent of, 168–71
measurement of, 166–71
Issue ownership, 58–59
Issue proximity, 191–92, 198–99
Issue publics, 193–94, 202
Issues, 162–200
awareness of, 163, 173–74, 186–87, 193, 415
campaign strategy and, 165
and consensus on candidates' positions, 181–85, 201
easy issues, 195
familiarity with, 163, 164–72, 175, 191
group voting and, 322–23, 326, 328, 329, 330–31
hard issues, 195
ideology and, 419
intensity of opinions on, 163, 172–77
media coverage of, 165–66, 197–98, 196
neutral positions on, 173
perceptions of candidate positions on, 177–81, 186
perceptions of party positions on, 168, 169–72, 186
position issues, 195, 419
salience of, 171–72, 193–94, 243, 416

Issues (*continued*)
  sources of, 196
  sources of attitudes on, 196–98
  stability of party identification and,
    201–3
  types of, 194–96
  valence issues, 195, 419–20
  values and, 176
  vote choice and, 162–64, 177–78, 185–87,
    189–90, 193, 194, 195–96
Issue voting, 193, 195–96, 201–2
  challenges to, 189–90
  consequences of, 199–200
  directional theory of, 198, 420
  extent of, 162–64, 186–87, 424–25
  increase in, 190, 194, 243
  political involvement and, 196
  preconditions of, 162–64, 177–78, 185–86,
    190, 195–96, 202, 216, 255, 424
Item response theory, 240–41

Jackson, Andrew, 335
Jefferson, Thomas, 349, 357
Jews
  distinctiveness of vote of, 305, 308–13, 330
  in New Deal Coalition, 331–33
  party identification of, 136–37, 151, 403
Johnson, Lyndon B., 61, 189, 320, 404, 407

Kennedy, John F., 320, 404
Kerry, John, 9, 123, 341
  economic issues and, 363, 367, 375–76
  evaluations of, and vote choice, 61–69, 121,
    397–98, 400
  Hispanic support for, 325
  military record (Vietnam), 9, 35, 397
  nonvoters' support for, 98
  perceptions of, 33, 35, 44, 46–50, 51, 52, 178,
    183–84, 423
Korean War, 36, 52, 422

Labor unions. *See* Union members; Unions
Latinos. *See* Hispanics
Liberal-conservative continuum, 287, 416.
  See also Ideology
  attitude constraint and, 244, 255, 291, 299
  conceptualization and, 255
  definition of ideologue and, 261
  as dimension of ideology, 208–10, 223–29,
    295–97, 344

government activity and, 208–9
  historical changes in, 209
  self-placement on, 222–29, 234, 237–38,
    247–48, 296, 344
Liberalism, 208–10, 252. *See also* Liberal-
  conservative continuum
Life cycle. *See* Age: party identification and
Lincoln, Abraham, 156

Macropartisanship, 135. *See also* Party
  identification
Mainline Protestants, distinctiveness of vote
  of, 328–29, 330
Maintaining election, 7, 402, 404
Management of government
  perceptions of parties and candidates and,
    40–41
  vote choice and, 61–69, 394–98, 399–401
Marx, Karl, 337–38, 339
McGovern, George, 320
Media
  African American party identification
    and, 323
  coverage of political issues by, 165–66,
    197–98
  ideology and, 255, 289
  issue awareness and, 187, 196
  issue framing and, 196
  political image formation and, 57–58
  priming effects and, 196
  use of, as form of political participation,
    85
Memory-based information processing
  models, 188
Michigan model of voting. *See* Social-
  psychological model of voting
Mobilization
  of African Americans, 323
  effect of, on turnout, 103–4, 106
Mondale, Walter, 320, 321
Moral issues, 39, 59, 159, 328
Moral Majority, 405
Moral traditionalism, 230–32, 250

Nader, Ralph, 9, 320, 421
National Election Studies (NES), 13–14
  estimate of turnout by, 87–88, 106–7
  issue questions in, 185–86, 192–93
  open-ended questions in, 33–34, 53–54, 55–
    57, 62, 78–80, 81, 90, 258, 436

party identification questions in, 112–13, 128, 139n1, 437
survey methodology and design of, 15–18
"Nature of Belief Systems in Mass Publics, The," 241–42, 244, 245–47, 290–92
Near-ideologue, 425. *See also* Conceptualization: ideology and; Ideologue
consistency in vote choice and, 287–89
definition of, 261, 264–67
examples of, 264–67
turnout and, 280
New Deal, 152, 154, 171, 195, 417
party identification and, 136–37, 151, 159
perceptions of parties and candidates and, 34, 38, 40, 52
realignment, 159, 403–4, 412
New Deal Coalition, 331–33
News media. *See* Media
Nineteenth Amendment, 352, 426
Nixon, Richard M., 152, 154, 397
elections of, as deviating, 404–5
impeachment and, 41n3
war and, 52
Nonattitude, 245–47. *See also* Attitude
Nonseparable preferences, 246–47
Nonvoters
bandwagon effect and, 98–99
characteristics of, 98
involvement in politics of, 98–99
partisan preferences of, 97–99
North American Free Trade Agreement (NAFTA), 8, 306, 320

Occupation, 348–49, 365, 370–71
as measure of social class, 339–41, 342, 356, 361, 362
Online information processing model, 54, 134, 187–88

Parties. *See also* Perceptions of parties and candidates
affect toward, 156
balance of power between, 421–22
competition of, 418–20, 423
effect of, on group distinctiveness, 318–19
effect of, on status polarization, 346–47
groups and, 60–61, 118, 136–37, 151, 317–19
as heuristics, 116
opinion formation and, 184
perceptions of issue positions of, 169–72,

186, 222, 347, 361, 416–17
polarization of, 10, 77, 124, 127, 196, 253, 289, 397
as reference groups, 184, 305, 317
strategies of, 415, 418–20, 423
Partisan attitudes, 31–81, 394–98. *See also* Conflict of partisan attitudes
affective element of, 31–33
as coequal determinants of vote, 80–81
cognitive element of, 31–33
crystallized, 166–67
dimensions of, 62, 407–8
economic outlook and, 374
error in prediction of vote choice and, 69–70
intervening effect of, 120–21
level of, 73
measurement of, 62, 78–80, 407–8
party identification and, 116–21, 124–26, 399–401
variability of, 407
vote choice and, 60, 61–69, 83, 111, 399–401, 407–9
Party identification, 111–60
age and, 141–50, 152–53, 336, 354
attitude structure and, 215, 216, 217–22, 227–29, 231–34, 236, 249
as attitudinal or behavioral, 112, 128–29
changes in, 141–60, 394, 401–6
Civil War and, 151, 401, 403, 411–12
conceptualization and, 287–89
Great Depression and, 151, 403, 412
ideology and, 254–55
1960s and, 144–45, 147–48, 151–52
periodicity of, 412
personal forces and, 150
Reagan administration and, 152–54
short-term defections and, 402
social forces and, 150–56
sources of, 201–2
changing importance of, 127–28
class and, 131, 336, 342–43, 403
classification of election and, 7, 402–6
conceptualization and, 276, 278, 287–89, 290
concern over election outcome and, 126–27
conflict of partisan attitudes and, 119–21, 124–26
consensus on candidates' issue positions and, 184–85

Party identification (*continued*)
correlation with ideology, 225–27, 237
decline of, 157–58
definition of, 112
dimensionality of, 130
distribution of, 113, 115–16
economic outlook and, 367–69, 374–77
as endogenous or exogenous, 134–36
foreign policy attitudes and, 117, 121, 227–29, 236
gender and, 136–37, 336
genetics and, 156
as group identification, 136–37, 317
groups and, 60–61, 118, 136–37, 151
as heuristic, 134, 426
interest in campaign and, 121, 126–27
involvement in politics and, 126–27
life cycle of, 145–50
as long-term factor in funnel of causality, 26, 409–10
measurement of, 112–13, 128–29
in New Deal Coalition, 136–37, 151, 159, 331–33
origins of, 138–41
parental influence on, 138–41, 152–53, 412, 424
partisan attitudes and, 116–21, 124–26, 399–401
partisan regularity of voting and, 113–15
party system and, 421–23
political socialization and, 134, 138–41, 149–50
region and, 136–37, 151, 403
religion and, 136–37, 151, 215–16, 329–30, 403, 406, 425
stability of, 61, 111–12, 115–16, 120–21, 134–36, 141–60, 201–3, 401, 424
strength of, 113–15, 145–50, 288, 290
theories of, 132–34
turnout and, 131
values and, 231–34
vote choice and, 121–26, 127, 149–50, 305, 399–401, 424, 427–28
Party image, 50–51, 61. *See also* Political images
Party system
as decentralized, 116
number of parties in, 415, 418, 420–23
party identification and, 421–23
Perceptions of parties and candidates, 31–59, 60–61, 394–98, 399–401, 427. *See also* Political images: formation of
endurance of images, 50–51, 58–59
generalization of images, 52–53
measurement of, 33–34, 53–54, 55–57
Period-aging model of dealignment, 157
Perot, H. Ross, 8, 158, 329, 405–6, 421
Persuasion effects, 80
Pocketbook voting. *See under* Economic voting
Political efficacy
education and, 102, 351–52
measurement of, 351
turnout and, 94–95, 103, 106
Political images
dimensions of, 54–55
endurance of, 50–51, 58–59
formation of, 50–54
generalization of, 52–53
issue ownership and, 58–59
media effect on, 57–58
transference of, 52–53
Political involvement, 415. *See also* Concern over election outcome; Interest in campaign; Political participation
attitude constraint and, 252
class voting and, 346
conceptualization and, 283–86, 289, 290
conflict of partisan attitudes and, 75–76
correlation of, with education, 285
correlation of, with political knowledge, 285
durability of, 91–92
education and, 102, 350–52
gender and, 359
of independents, 126–27, 129, 424
issue voting and, 196
measurement of, 92, 345
of nonvoters, 98–99
parental influence on, 140–41
party identification and, 126–27
status polarization and, 344–46
turnout and, 92–97
Political issues. *See* Issues
Political knowledge
attitude constraint and, 252
conceptualization and, 282–83, 285–86, 289
correlation of, with education, 285
correlation of, with political involvement, 285

correlation of, with political sophistication, 300
Political participation, 83–86. *See also* Political involvement; Voting turnout
  class and, 336, 348
  education and, 336, 350–52, 357–59
  gender and, 336, 352–53
  importance to democracy, 82
  increase in, 84–85
  informal discussion as form of, 85, 97
  measurement of, 240, 345
  status polarization and, 344–47
  turnout as form of, 85–86
  use of mass media as form of, 85
Political parties. *See* Parties; Party identification
Political socialization
  and ideology, 248, 251
  political identification and, 134, 138–41, 149–50
  realignment and, 412–13
  turnout and, 85–86, 102
Political sophistication
  attitude constraint and, 291
  conceptualization and, 290, 295–97, 299
  consensus on candidate issue positions and, 184
  correlation of, with political knowledge, 300
  definition of, 299
  divided government and, 157
  ideology and, 344
  interest in campaign and, 344
  measurement of, 299–300, 344
  sources of, 344–45
  stability of attitudes and, 246, 253
  status polarization and, 344, 346, 348
  use of heuristics and, 298
Political translation, 24, 207–8, 268
Political trust, 240
Poverty, 165, 194
Presidential popularity, 378–79, 406
Primary groups. *See* Interpersonal influence
Principal component analysis, 240–41
Projection effects, 80, 192
Prospect theory, 423n2
Prosperity, 377, 417, 419, 422
Protestants, 328. *See also* Fundamentalist Protestants; Mainline Protestants
Public constraint on political leadership, 415, 416–18, 423

Race. *See also* African Americans; Hispanics
  intensity of issue opinions and, 176–77
  party identification and, 136–37, 151–52
  as source of Southern realignment, 154–55
Rational choice approach, 134, 197
  to turnout, 27, 99–101, 425
  to vote choice, 188–89, 425
Reagan, Ronald W., 7, 52, 152, 397, 417, 421
  changes in party identification and, 152–54
  economic issues and, 37–38, 154, 422
  female vote and, 326
  foreign issues and, 305
  labor union support and, 320, 321
  Southern realignment and, 154–56
  young voters and, 152–53
Realigning election, 7, 402–4, 411–12. *See also* Realignment
Realignment, 120, 135–36, 158–60, 401–4, 422. *See also* Dealignment; Realigning election
  Civil War realignment, 151, 401, 403, 411–12
  determination of, 159, 403, 404, 406
  groups and, 403–4
  New Deal realignment, 159, 403–4, 412
  periodicity of, 412
  political socialization and, 412–13
  secular realignment, 159
  skepticism of, 159–60, 411–13
  in South, 151, 154–56, 159
  theories of, 159, 412–13
Recruitment. *See* Mobilization
Reference group theory, 112, 132, 134, 249
Region, 136–37, 151, 366, 403. *See also* South
Registration requirements, 83, 104–5
Reinstating election, 7, 402, 404
Religion. *See also* Catholics; Fundamentalist Protestants; Jews; Mainline Protestants
  party identification and, 136–37
  vote choice and, 329–31
Religious restructuring perspective, 329
Religious Right, 103
Retrospective voting, 189, 272, 378–81, 384, 387
Role of government in society, 208–9, 230–33, 417
Role of women in society issue, 167
  attitude structure and, 211
  familiarity with, 169–77
  perceptions of candidate positions on, 178–81, 183–85

Roosevelt, Franklin D., 37, 52, 320, 403, 417, 422
Roosevelt, Theodore, 402

Schema theory, 249, 257 297–98
Selective perception, 149
September 11 (2001), 9, 34, 39, 43, 52, 121, 366, 406
Social capital, 106
Social class. *See* Class
Social groups. *See* Groups
Social identity theory, 134, 249
Social-psychological model of voting, 6–7, 62–63. *See also* Funnel of causality
    alternatives to, 27–28
    assumptions of, 80–81
    relevance of, 427–28
    statistical methods and, 69–70, 77–78
Social Security, 34, 38, 356, 360, 411
Social welfare issues, perceptions of parties and candidates and, 38–39, 59
South, 151, 333–33
    realignment of, 154–56, 159, 323, 333, 403, 405
Spatial model of voting, 188–89, 191, 198–99, 418–20
Split-ticket voting
    conflict of partisan attitudes and, 74–75, 111
    dealignment and, 157–58
    increase of, 157–58
    independents and, 129
Status polarization, 337–38. *See also* Class
    class awareness and, 343–44, 346
    effect of political parties on, 346–47
    fluctuations in, 342–43
    party identification and, 347–48
    political involvement and, 344–46
    political participation, 344–47
    political sophistication and, 344, 346, 348
    vote choice and, 341–43
Stevenson, Adlai, 320, 323
Straight-ticket voting, 74–75, 111. *See also* split-ticket voting
Symbolic politics theory, 248

Taft, William H., 402
Taft-Hartley Act, 320, 321
Tax cuts, 166, 197, 214, 322, 389
Theory, 6–7, 19–22. *See also* Vote choice: theories of

Third parties, 158, 365, 421
Ticket splitting. *See* split-ticket voting
Time of vote decision, and conflict of partisan attitudes, 71–72, 73–74
Turnout. *See* Voting turnout
Two-party system, 420–23

Unemployment, perceptions of, 366–67
Union members, 305, 322. *See also* Unions
    distinctiveness of vote of, 308–13, 315–18, 320–22
    in New Deal Coalition, 331–33
Unions, 314, 320–22, 335. *See also* Union members

Values
    attitude structure and, 204, 229–35, 236–37, 249–51
    conflict of, 198
    intensity of issue opinions and, 176
    public constraint on political leadership and, 417–18
    as source of issue attitudes, 196–97, 231
    as source of party identification, 231–34
Vietnam War, 14, 36, 52, 129, 189, 194, 195, 197
    Kerry's military record and, 9, 35, 397
    party identification and, 144, 151–52, 404, 422
Vote choice, 60–81, 256, 427–28. *See also* Class voting; Economic voting; Group influence model of voting; Issue voting
    class and, 6, 341–43, 344
    components of, 61–69, 394–98, 399–401
    concerns about unemployment and, 366–67
    consistency in, 287–88, 289
    defections in, 123–24, 125, 127, 131 (*see also* deviant voter)
    economic outlook and, 369–77, 427
    error in predicting, 66, 68–70, 80–81
    gender and, 61, 108–13, 315–17, 325–27, 333, 352–53, 405, 426
    group influence on, 60–61, 394–98, 399–401, 427–28
    ideology and, 287–89, 296–97
    of independents, 123–24
    interpersonal influence and, 11, 70
    issues and, 162–64, 177–78, 185–87, 189–90, 193, 194, 195–96
    marriage gap in, 405

normal vote, 131–32
partisan attitudes and, 60, 61–69, 83, 111,
    399–401, 407–9
party identification and, 121–26, 127, 149–
    50, 305, 399–401, 424, 427–28
predictions of, 72, 74, 77, 382–83
presidential popularity and, 378–79
religion and, 329–31
statistical estimation procedures for, 67,
    69–70, 77–78, 80–81
status polarization and, 341–43
theories of. *See also* funnel of causality; so-
    cial-psychological model of voting
attitudinal approach, 25–26
directional theory of issue voting, 198–
    99, 420
economic, 27, 99–101, 377–88
historical-institutional approach, 27–28
psychological approach, 19, 27–28
rational-choice approach, 188–89, 425
sociological approach, 11–12, 19, 26,
    27–28
spatial model, 188–89, 191, 198–99,
    418–20
Voting research, 7, 10–12, 14–15, 18
Voting turnout. *See also* Political
    participation
age and, 103, 354–56
citizen duty and, 95–96, 106
class and, 98, 356–57
closeness of election and, 101–2
conceptualization levels and, 280, 287, 290
concern over election outcome and, 93–
    94, 106
decline of, 105–7
education and, 102, 131
effect of female candidates on, 359, 363–64
efficacy and, 94–95, 103, 106
as form of political participation, 85–86
gender gap in, 352–53, 359, 426
ideology and, 280, 287, 290
income and, 131
intensity of partisan preference and, 89–
    92, 106

interest in campaign and, 92–93, 99, 106
interpersonal influence and, 97
measurement of, 86–89, 106–7
mobilization and, 103–4, 106
negative campaigning and, 104, 106
partisan preference and, 89–92
party identification and, 131
political involvement and, 92–97
political socialization and, 85–86, 102
rational choice approach to, 27, 99–101,
    425
registration requirements and, 83, 104–5
social capital and, 106
vote validation studies and, 88–89

War
    and negativity effect on electoral behavior,
        422–23
    and perceptions of parties and candidates,
        34–37, 50–51, 52–53
War on terrorism, 9, 13, 166, 195
    and perceptions of parties and candidates,
        34–36
    salience of, in 2004 election, 162, 165, 187,
        398, 422
Welfare, 8, 163–64, 197, 216, 250, 326, 361
Women. *See also* Gender; Gender gap; Role
    of women in society issue
    as candidates, 359
    distinctiveness of vote of, 308–13, 315–17,
        325–27, 333, 352–53
    effect of female candidates on political
        participation of, 359, 363–64
    restrictions on political participation of,
        352
    traditional roles of, 353
    turnout and, 352–53, 426

Young voters, 243
    dealignment and, 157
    effect of Reagan administration on party
        identification of, 152–53
    as independents, 405, 421
    lack of political participation, 354